S0-BRU-608

ENCYCLOPEDIA OF AMERICAN RACE RIOTS

Greenwood Milestones in African American History

Encyclopedia of Antislavery and Abolition
Edited by Peter Hinks and John McKivigan

Encyclopedia of the Great Black Migration
Edited by Steven A. Reich

Encyclopedia of Slave Resistance and Rebellion
Edited by Junius P. Rodriguez

Encyclopedia of the Reconstruction Era
Edited by Richard Zuczek

ENCYCLOPEDIA OF AMERICAN RACE RIOTS

Volume 2, N–Z and Primary Documents

Edited by
Walter Rucker and
James Nathaniel Upton

Foreword by
Dominic J. Capeci, Jr.

Greenwood Milestones in African American History

GREENWOOD PRESS
Westport, Connecticut • London

Library of Congress Cataloging-in-Publication Data

Encyclopedia of American race riots : Greenwood milestones in African American history / edited by Walter Rucker and James Nathaniel Upton ; foreword by Dominic J. Capeci, Jr.

p. cm.

Includes bibliographical references and index.

ISBN 0-313-33300-9 (set : alk. paper)—ISBN 0-313-33301-7 (vol. 1 : alk. paper)—ISBN 0-313-33302-5 (vol. 2 : alk. paper) 1. United States—Race relations—Encyclopedias. 2. Riots—United States—History—Encyclopedias. 3. Ethnic conflict—United States—History—Encyclopedias. I. Rucker, Walter C., 1970- II. Upton, James N.

E184.A1E573 2007

305.8′00973′03—dc22 2006026195

British Library Cataloguing in Publication Data is available.

This book is included in the African American Experience database from Greenwood Electronic Media. For more information, visit www.africanamericanexperience.com.

Library of Congress Catalog Card Number: 2006026195

ISBN-10: 0-313-33300-9 (set) ISBN-13: 978-0-313-33300-2 (set)
0-313-33301-7 (vol. 1) 978-0-313-33301-9 (vol. 1)
0-313-33302-5 (vol. 2) 978-0-313-33302-6 (vol. 2)

First published in 2007

Greenwood Press, 88 Post Road West, Westport, CT 06881
An imprint of Greenwood Publishing Group, Inc.
www.greenwood.com

Printed in the United States of America

The paper used in this book complies with the Permanent Paper Standard issued by the National Information Standards Organization (Z39.48-1984).

10 9 8 7 6 5 4 3 2 1

CONTENTS

N

NAACP. *See* National Association for the Advancement of Colored People

NACW. *See* National Association of Colored Women

Nation of Islam

The Nation of Islam or the Black Muslims is an African American religious movement that was founded in 1930 by W.D. Fard. It is a movement based on an eclectic synthesis of worldly philosophies and religious practices, including traditional Islam adapted to the African American urban landscape. The Nation of Islam had its beginnings in the predominantly African American suburb of Detroit called Paradise Valley, which was the segregated section of Detroit where blacks were forced to congregate by Deed Restrictions that made it illegal for them to rent or own property in other areas. Paradise Valley, eulogized in a series of poems by Robert Hayden called "Elegies for Paradise Valley," was not only the "heart and soul" of black Detroit, it was also the place where the first seeds of the Nation of Islam were sown among the thousands of black people who had come to Detroit in search of a better future but who, instead, became lost and disillusioned. The Nation of Islam offered many of the faithful tangible hope of salvation. This distinctly African American theology blended elements of Christianity with the **Black Nationalism** of **Marcus Garvey** (1887–1940), and his Universal Negro Improvement Association (UNIA), which specifically addressed the plight of working-class African Americans and celebrated the beauty, strength, and endurance of black people. W.D. Fard, for example, taught his followers that human culture began in Africa. He called on people of African descent to renounce the vices of Western culture, including the slave names that had been given them while they were in bondage.

The teachings of the Nation of Islam struck a responsive chord, especially during the great economic crisis of the 1930s. Although social and cultural conditions, **segregation**, and **racism** influenced the spread of Islam in the black community, it was the zealousness of the founders and subsequent leaders of the movement that have helped sustained the Nation of Islam for over three-quarters of a century. At times mysterious and solitary even to their closest adherents, the one thing that all the influential leaders of the Black Muslims have had in common is that they were all insightful, charismatic, and controversial. And they were all "children of freedom," members of the first generation of African Americans born after Emancipation.

Born Timothy Drew on January 8, 1886, in Simpsonbuck County, North Carolina, Noble Drew Ali was the first "prophet" to introduce Islam into the black community in Detroit. He believed that black people in the United States were Moors, a nomadic people of Arab and Berber descent whose civilization flourished in North Africa between the eighth and fifteenth centuries. He founded the Moorish Science Temple of America and published the Holy Qur'an (Koran) of the Moorish Holy Temple of Science. By the mid-1920s, he had established a temple in Detroit. In March 1929, Ali was implicated in a murder and died in jail while awaiting trail.

If Noble Drew Ali was the precursor to the founding of the Nation of Islam, W.D. Fard constructed the final foundation that future leaders were to build on. Another man of mystery, he first appeared in Paradise Valley peddling notions, trinkets, silks, and raincoats. Fard claimed he was from Arabia. He built an organization of 8,000 members, which he called the Lost and Found Nation of Islam in the Wilderness of North America. He also founded the University of Islam, the Muslim Girls Training Corps, and the Fruit of Islam, a group of men trained in the use of firearms and self-defense. In one of his most radical moves, Fard advocated an independent nation of African Americans within the United States. Among these many changes, Fard instructed his followers to renounce their slave names and adopt the last name X to symbolize their independence and rejection of Western values. In 1934, at the height of his popularity as leader of the Nation of Islam, W.D. Fard disappeared, and his disappearance remains a mystery. However, his vision continues to provide a spiritual foundation for the Nation of Islam.

One of Fard's earliest converts was Elijah Poole, a former member of the Moorish Science Temple of America. Under Fard's guidance, Poole changed his name to Elijah Karriem. Once Fard disappeared, Karriem emerged as **Elijah Muhammad**, stating that the Master had anointed him Messenger of Allah and the new leader of the Nation of Islam. His claims did not go uncontested. It took more than a decade and a move to Chicago for him to become firmly established as the leader of the Black Muslims. Elijah Muhammad proclaimed himself Allah's last prophet and his mission was to lead his people out of bondage, to free them from the white man's yoke, because their reign was imminent and blacks must prepare themselves for the day when Allah's chosen people would rule. He urged them to renounce such vices of white society as alcohol, drugs, tobacco, and profanity, and to build a separate black Nation of Islam within the United States. His ultimate goal was separation, not **integration**.

During the 1950s, with the help of **Malcolm X**, the Black Muslim movement gained its greatest popularity. Malcolm X (formerly Malcolm Little) converted to Islam while in prison between 1946 and 1952. After his release, he became a devoted follower of Elijah Muhammad. A mesmerizing, articulate speaker and charismatic leader, Malcolm X rose quickly in the ranks of the Black Muslims. By the early 1960s, he had become chief spokesperson for the Nation of Islam and Muhammad's apparent successor. Malcolm X was an advocate of **black self-defense**. His confrontational style and his demand for black revolution attracted young radicals to the movement. One of his earliest converts was Muhammad Ali.

However, by the 1960s, when Malcolm X had achieved national and international reputation, his influence inside the Nation of Islam was beginning to wane. In 1963, he was publicly reprimanded by Elijah Muhammad because of remarks he made after the assassination of President **John F. Kennedy**. Shortly afterward, Malcolm X resigned from the Nation of Islam. In 1965, he was assassinated. After his death, Elijah Muhammad became less active in the organization. For the next decade, groups inside the Nation of Islam began to challenge Muhammad's authority. After his death in 1975, Muhammad's son Wallace D. Muhammad (later known as Warith Deen Mohammed) was named supreme minister. He renamed the organization the World Community of Islam in the West and later the American Society of Muslims, and opened the group to individuals of all races. This change caused dissension within the Nation and, in 1977, a group of Muslims led by **Louis Farrakhan** split from the main body. However, when Farrakhan announced that whites were no longer viewed as evil and that they were welcome to join the movement, the Nation of Islam split into several groups. In 1995, Farrakhan organized the Million Man March. In 2000, Farrakhan and Mohammed ended their rivalry. Mohammed resigned in 2003. *See also* Civil Rights Movement; Farrakhan, Louis Haleem Abdul; Malcolm X; Muhammad, Elijah.

Further Readings: Clegg, Claude Andrews, III. *An Original Man: The Life and Times of Elijah Muhammad*. New York: St. Martin's Press, 1997; Lincoln, C. Eric. *The Black Muslims in America*. Boston: Beacon Press, 1961; Magida, Arthur J. *Prophet of Rage: A Life of Louis Farrakhan and His Nation*. New York: Basic Books, 1996; Malcolm X, with Alex Haley. *The Autobiography of Malcolm X*. New York: Grove Press, 1965; Muhammad, Elijah. *The Fall of America*. Chicago: Muhammad's Temple No. 2, 1973; Muhammad, Elijah. *Message to the Blackman in America*. Chicago: Muhammad Mosque of Islam No. 2, 1965; Murphy, Larry G., J. Gordon Melton, and Gary L. Ward, eds. *Encyclopedia of African American Religions*. New York: Garland Publishing, 1993.

John G. Hall

National Association for the Advancement of Colored People (NAACP)

The National Association for the Advancement of Colored People (NAACP) is a sociopolitical body dedicated to ensuring social equity and justice for blacks in the United States. Although its current incarnation is a well-respected and influential organization with a widespread membership and board of governors whose members currently represent twenty-nine U.S. states, earlier forms of the NAACP were marginalized by the political mainstream and, in some states, local offices were the site of race hatred and violence.

The beginnings of the NAACP are to be found in a three-day conference held from July 11–13 in Fort Erie, Canada, in 1904. The twenty-nine attendees, all black intellectuals, were gathered together there by activist **W.E.B. Du Bois** to organize what would be known as the "**Niagara movement**." Its purpose was the complete abolition of all forms of racial discrimination and, somewhat ironically, the **segregation** of schools. Race separation was, at that time, desired by some black intelligentsia who felt that **integration** was antithetical to their left-wing social and cultural ambitions. Fearing that integration would result in children who assimilated and thereby valued American capitalism and Judeo-Christian moral dominance, some members of the Niagara movement, Du Bois in particular, argued strongly for educational segregation. This point became too contentious for many more moderate attendees and for any real progress to be made by the movement on a large scale; subsequent efforts by members would thereby forego segregation of education and the long-term wisdom of this decision has been supported by both legislation and the formal mission of what would become the NAACP which "is to ensure the political, educational, social and economic equality of rights of all persons and to eliminate racial hatred and racial discrimination" (NAACP Mission Statement).

In addition to educational segregation, the increased election of blacks into political office and the enforcement of black voting rights in the United States were crucial agenda items of the Niagara movement. Among the notable blacks present at the conference who would become part of its five-year membership as an activist body were John Hope, J. Max Barber, and **William Monroe Trotter**. Although initially a very concentrated and organized effort, the Niagara movement gained little momentum and no popular acceptance, and so its membership and their goals dissolved and revived in the new movement for black rights that would become the NAACP.

The NAACP was founded in New York City on February 12, 1909, heralded by the publication of "The Call." This announcement urged all leaders to abolish racially biased legislation and to take up the black cause in the United States by enforcing the Thirteenth, **Fourteenth**, and **Fifteenth Amendments**. Published in black newspapers across the United States, "The Call" successfully recruited members into the new social and political body whose national office was located in New York City. The initial board of directors for the NAACP was entirely comprised of whites, including the organization's first president, Moorfield Storey, a white attorney. W.E.B. Du Bois, the only black initially named to an important position in the organization, was made publicity director and, by extension, editor of the NAACP's official journal, ***The Crisis***. After the initial call for other progressives to join the racial struggle, the NAACP held its first official conference in New York on May 31, 1909, with more than 300 blacks and whites in attendance. Once the NAACP became relatively established, its board of directors became increasingly comprised of blacks; by 1934, most board members were black, and this trend has continued to the present time.

Among the most notable successes of the new social body was its highly organized protest against Woodrow Wilson's segregation of the federal government (1913) and also against **D.W. Griffith**'s film, ***The Birth of a***

Nation (1915), in which blacks were portrayed as lazy, violent, and ignorant. Many scenes in the film depicted blacks as rapists, thugs, or watermelon-eating field hands, thus portraying a series of horrible stereotypes to a widespread audience. Outraged by these intensely offensive and socially damaging images, the NAACP launched its earliest widespread anti-defamation campaigns. Through the NAACP's rigorous advertising and lobbying, the racist film was banned or no longer shown in many cities around the country. This first use of organized protest against the film and the **Ku Klux Klan (KKK)** it glorified set a precedence of success that inspired the organization to move quickly and loudly against any and all misrepresentations of black people and culture. These two protests forced NAACP organizers to recognize the body's growing power and so, in 1917, they chose to use this power as a lever to force the federal government to allow blacks to be commissioned as officers in World War I. This success led to the commission of 600 black officers and the registration of 700,000 blacks for the draft. Integral to the NAACP's protests of black misrepresentation and segregation was their persistent presentation of blacks as fully enfranchised American citizens whose rights were fundamentally protected in the U.S. Constitution. It would be this Constitutional argument that would finally result in the eradication of widespread **lynching**, arguably one of the early NAACP's most important battles.

Perhaps because of its early emphasis on local organizing practices and rigorous recruitment, the NAACP's membership grew quickly, as did its number of branch offices across the United States. By 1919, the NAACP had more than 300 branch offices and 90,000 members. The year 1919 was also a noteworthy year in the NAACP for its publication of its investigative report, ***Thirty Years of Lynching in the United States: 1889–1918***. Although the organization had spoken out against lynching as early as 1917, with this report, the NAACP took up the anti-lynching cause first emphasized in earnest by journalist **Ida B. Wells-Barnett**. Although the organization never successfully forced anti-lynching legislation to be passed on a federal or state level during this era touted by its chroniclers as the worst period of **racism** in American history, the NAACP's persistent protest against lynching is credited with its decrease and eventual cessation. Equipping all its branches with a flag hung outside each time "A Black Man Was Lynched Today," once again, the NAACP demonstrated the power of collective dissension as President Woodrow Wilson spoke out publicly against lynching. Associated as he was with the Ku Klux Klan prior to his presidency and given his elitist opinions regarding **white supremacy**, Wilson's public anti-lynching statements cannot be underestimated as an important NAACP achievement. Through the body's persistent pressure, Wilson was forced to speak out.

Even as the NAACP was still fighting lynch mobs and mob hostility against blacks on a more general level, they also began to turn their attention to the unequal access to education, housing, health care, and public transportation blacks had historically received. Fighting a series of court cases and legislation involving the unconstitutionality of discrimination in these areas so crucial to civil rights, the NAACP won a string of victories in state and federal court, as well as in Congress. Notable among these victories were *Buchanen v. Worley* (housing districts could not be forced on blacks, 1917), admission of a black student to the University of Maryland (1935), *Morgan v. Virginia* (Supreme Court recognizes that states cannot segregate interstate public transport by bus or train, 1946), discrimination in federal government offices banned (1948), *Brown v. Board of Education* (the doctrine of separate but equal struck down in favor of desegregation, 1954), and the **Civil Rights Act of 1964**.

After a series of race riots and conflicts rocked Arkansas throughout 1919 resulting in sixty-seven blacks being imprisoned and twelve sentenced to death, the NAACP became involved in an ongoing battle on behalf of blacks' receipt of due process under constitutional law (see **Elaine [Arkansas] Riot of 1919**). A nearly five-year engagement in these efforts to ensure fair trial and representation resulted in another landmark case and ultimate win in 1923's ***Moore v. Dempsey***, in which the NAACP made large ground against unfair prosecution of blacks and secured the release of many of those imprisoned in the state of Arkansas and other states.

As the **civil rights movement** gathered momentum in the late 1950s and early 1960s, the NAACP discussed the role it would play in these important times. Resolute in their use of state and federal courtrooms to battle racism and discrimination, the body kept itself as a whole out of the often fractious and dangerous social battles being waged on the streets of the South. This, however, did not prevent individual members from engaging in nonviolent protests. In 1960, the NAACP's Youth Council began a series of lunch-counter sit-ins around the South, resulting in the **desegregation** of more than sixty department store eateries. In addition to these nonviolent protests, NAACP members organized widespread civil rights rallies. Due to the rallies' success, the NAACP named its first field director to oversee the legal and safety concerns of these peaceful protests. Ironically, field director and highly successful organizer **Medgar Evers** was fatally shot outside his home in 1963 (just five months before the assassination of President **John F. Kennedy**).

As the civil rights movement evolved, the NAACP did as well, eventually turning its attention to black participation in self-government through voting. Lobbying for voting sites in high schools, the NAACP persuaded twenty-four states to set up such sites by 1979. Concentration on the black vote would continue through the 1980s, as the NAACP extended the Voting Rights Act (1981) and as they registered record numbers of black voters (500,000 in 1982 alone). In tandem with their persistent efforts in the 1980s to increase political participation among the black community, the NAACP also brought global attention to apartheid in South Africa by rallying in New York City (1989) and by encouraging a boycott of that nation by all people of color. By 1993, the anti-apartheid movement was successful, and in 1994, South Africa held its first all-race elections.

Since then, the NAACP has focused on appointing racially sensitive Supreme Court justices, preventing economic hardship in the black community, promoting higher education among blacks and other people of color, and providing alternatives to gang affiliation and violent behavior for black youths. Still thriving, still with much work to do, the NAACP continues to be a viable social, economic, legal, and political force in, and for, the black community in the United States. Although the organization's earliest and most direct connections to American literature are certainly *Crisis* editor W.E.B. Du Bois (*The Souls of Black Folk*) and poet and lyricist **James Weldon Johnson** ("Lift Every Voice and Sing"), the NAACP is also closely linked to black arts and literature through its nearly forty-year distribution of the Image Awards to black cultural producers such as Nikki Giovanni (*Quilting the Black Eyed Pea*) in 2003.

Further Readings: Cortner, Richard. *A Mob Intent on Death: The NAACP and the Arkansas Race Riots*. Middletown, CT: Wesleyan University Press, 1988; Janken, Kenneth. *White: The Biography of Walter White, Mr. NAACP.* New York: New Press, 2003; Jonas, Gilbert, and Julian Bond. *Freedom's Sword: The NAACP and the Struggle Against Racism in America, 1909–1969*. New York: Routledge, 2004; Kellogg, Clint. *NAACP: A History of the National Association of Colored People*. New York: The Johns Hopkins University Press, 1967; Ovington, Mary White. *Blacks and Whites Sat Down Together: The Reminiscences of an NAACP Founder*. New York: Feminist Press, 1996; Ross, Barbara. *J.E. Springarn and the Rise of the NAACP, 1911–1939*. New York: Scribner, 1972; Smith, John David. *The Ticket to Freedom: The NAACP and the Struggle for Black Political Integration*. Gainesville: University Press of Florida, 2005; Tushnet, Mark. *The NAACP's Legal Strategy against Segregated Education, 1925–1950*. Chapel Hill: University of North Carolina Press, 1987; Wedin, Carolyn. *Inheritors of the Spirit: Mary Ovington and the Founding of the NAACP.* New York: John Wiley and Sons, 1997; Zangrando, Robert. *The NAACP Crusade against Lynching, 1909–1950*. Philadelphia: Temple University Press, 1980.

Deirdre Ray

National Association of Colored Women (NACW)

"Lifting as We Climb" was the motto adopted by the National Association of Colored Women (NACW) formed on July 21, 1896, in Washington, D.C. This organization was led by black activist women who had a long history of working toward equality and social justice for their people. The organization included **Ida B. Wells-Barnett**, Josephine St. Pierre Ruffin, **Mary Church Terrell**, Anna Julia Cooper, Harriett Tubman, and Mary McLeod Bethune. NACW involved the merging of two key black women's organizations—the National Federation of Afro-American Women and the National League of Colored Women. This was a period during which black women's clubs were instrumental in sustaining the spirit and vitality of black communities throughout the United States. NACW published the *National Association Notes* as a tool for disseminating information of interest to black club women.

The black women's club movement evolved out of women joining together to develop mutual aid societies where they could work to ameliorate some of the social problems plaguing their communities. Black women in such cities as Boston, Chicago, Philadelphia, and Washington, D.C., formed intercity clubs to combat particular social ills that they witnessed ravaging their communities. The club women understood that a history of discrimination, oppression, and racial violence was literally crippling thousands of their sisters and they aimed to address these problems through collective social activism. They focused much of their energy on improving the living conditions and status of men, women, and children through educational opportunities, job training, and life skill assessments.

The benevolence of these black women's organizations also inspired them to honor those individuals who were actively engaged in what they deemed important race work on behalf of their people. Club women began to visualize how they might do more to contribute to their various community issues. Thus, the seed was planted for NACW, a coalition of black women's organizations that would build on the history and legacy of the hundreds of black women's charitable organizations.

The formation of NACW grew out of a specific meeting by various representatives of women's clubs who came together on that July day to protest a letter written by James Jacks, the white president of the Missouri Association. Jacks hoped to quell the activities of the anti-lynching campaign organized by Ida B. Wells-Barnett by labeling all black women as prostitutes and thieves in a news publication. In response to this brutal assault of the character and dignity of black women, club women including Terrell and St. Pierre Ruffin held a meeting in Washington, D.C., to discuss how to best respond to Jacks' verbal assault.

At the meeting they rationalized that their response would require a mobilized effort to continue their work for racial and social uplift of their people as a coalition. They elected Mary Church Terrell as their first national president. Terrell, having worked tirelessly to end both racial and gender inequality in the United States, was a founder and natural leader of this organization. Understanding the need for black women's organizations to harness collective energy and individual and/or social activism was essential to her leadership of this organization. Terrell admonished the women in her organization to consider all that they were obligated to do as privileged members of their race who had received education and opportunities for self-improvement. She further acknowledged the dire need for black women to speak out against a heap of injustices across gender and racial lines.

Terrell saw NACW as a vehicle for providing substantive, transformative change in the lives of individuals who were personally affected by the travesty of racial injustice. A gifted orator and leader, Terrell was both convincing and dogmatic in her ability to persuade people to participate in and support her efforts. She regularly gave speeches around the country to increase participation and maximize opportunities to get black women to work together.

Anti-lynching legislation was one of their primary platforms and, more importantly, the NACW women were instrumental in dismantling the oppressive system that allowed lynching to flourish in the United States. During the fifty-year period between 1880 and 1930, there were at least 2,362 black men, women, and children lynched. These startling numbers necessitated action on the part of the NACW. The women of NACW joined forces with the **National Association for the Advancement of**

Colored People (NAACP) and worked within their various clubs to support initiatives to promote black advancement. Specific NACW efforts included fundraising for education, training, and social service care for their people. NACW worked with other organizations to form the **National Urban League**. They also raised funds to restore the home of activist Frederick Douglass. In addition, NACW member Ida B. Wells-Barnett encouraged women to participate in both the suffrage and anti-lynching movements. In 1912, NACW began a national scholarship fund for college-bound black women. In 1913, the Northeastern Federation of Women's Clubs worked with the NAACP to hold anti-lynching rallies. More specifically, women in these organizations worked as members of a group called the Anti-Lynching Crusaders to galvanize one million women to suppress lynching and to pass the Dyer Anti-Lynching Bill. Although the bill was not passed, the efforts of these women were later the model and inspiration for the Association of Southern Women for the Prevention of Lynching in 1930. Black women in clubs were influential in fighting racial and sexual oppression through their active involvement in numerous social service activities and their work was instrumental in countering the hegemonic practices of the nation in which they lived. *See also* Anti-Lynching Legislation; Lynching.

Further Readings: Carson, Emmett, D. *A Hand Up: Black Philanthropy and Self-Help in America*. Washington, D.C.: Joint Center for Political and Economic Studies, 1993; Giddings, Paula. *When and Where I Enter: The Impact of Black Women on Race and Sex in America*. New York: William Morrow, 1984; Salem, Dorothy. "National Association of Colored Women." In Darlene Clark Hine, Elsa Barkley Brown, and Rosalyn Terborg-Penn, eds. *Black Women in America: An Historical Encyclopedia, Vol. II, M–Z*. Bloomington and Indianapolis: Indiana University Press, 1993; White, Deborah Gray. *Too Heavy a Load: Black Women in Defense of Ourselves, 1894–1994*. New York and London: W.W. Norton & Company, 1999.

Kijua Sanders-McMurtry

National Equal Rights League. *See* Equal Rights League

National Urban League

The National Urban League was founded in 1911 to ameliorate the social conditions affecting urban American Negroes. Due to the oppressive forces of **Jim Crow** and **segregation**, many southern blacks began to migrate to the North. On September 29, 1910, in New York City, to address the numerous challenges that these new northerners faced, two important individuals were instrumental in creating an organization called the Committee on Urban Conditions among Negroes. Ruth Standish Baldwin, a widow and social activist, worked with Dr. George Edmund Haynes (the first black person to receive a doctorate from Columbia University) to form this organization.

The evolution of the National Urban League occurred when two organizations (the Committee on Urban Conditions among Negroes and the Committee for the Improvement of Industrial Conditions among Negroes) merged to form the National League on Urban Conditions among Negroes. The name was shortened to the National Urban League in 1920. The National Urban League originally served those Negroes who were migrating from the South to the North in search of jobs and improved social conditions. The primary purpose of the organization in its early days was to address social and economic issues facing Negroes who were in dire need of employment, job training, housing, and health services. The National Urban League worked to provide assistance through community centers, clinics, camps, and affiliated organizations. The league was led by Professor Edwin R.A. Seligman of Columbia University, Mrs. Baldwin, and Dr. Haynes during the early days between 1911 and 1918.

The organization began to strategically attack perceptions of the intellectual inferiority of Negroes during the 1920s and 1930s. Sociologist Charles S. Johnson became the director of research and investigation for the National Urban League in 1921. Johnson founded the League's first publication. Between 1923 and 1949, the organization published a journal, *Opportunity: A Journal of Negro Life*. The motto of the journal was "Not Aims, but Opportunity." As editor of the journal, Charles Johnson also worked hard to dispel myths about Negroes, and the journal published numerous sociological studies with scientific methods for this purpose. Also, under the editorship of Charles Johnson, *Opportunity* was a leading force in publishing the work of Negro literary writers of the time. *Opportunity* published works by Gwendolyn Bennett, Langston Hughes, **James Weldon Johnson**, and Countee Cullen. It was through this vehicle that Charles Johnson became a central figure in the Harlem Renaissance.

Cab Calloway painting a picture for the Urban League Art Exhibit by Famous Amateurs, September 1948. Courtesy of the Library of Congress.

At the helm of the league from 1918 to 1941 was Eugene Kinckle Jones, who was instrumental in organizing boycotts against companies and employers that would not hire blacks. He consistently pushed schools to expand their vocational programs for young people, and pressured Washington, D.C., officials to include blacks in New Deal programs. He also began the work to get blacks included in previously segregated labor unions.

Lester B. Granger was appointed successor to Eugene Jones and continued to work diligently to integrate the racist trade unions that were in existence at that time. Granger's leadership was focused on increasing the number of job opportunities for blacks and he was successful in developing the league's Industrial Relations Laboratory, which worked to integrate the numerous defense plants that were active during this period. Granger was also very supportive of the National Urban League Guild, which was led by Mollie Moon on behalf of the league.

One of the National Urban League's most famous leaders was social worker and civil rights activist Whitney M. Young, Jr., who succeeded Granger as executive director in 1961. Prior to Young's leadership, the National Urban League was considered one of the more conservative civic organizations. Often referred to as the Urban League, the organization was frequently focused on providing direct social services to its target population. Whitney Young worked actively to move the National Urban League forward and align it with other civil rights organizations. Young worked jointly with other civil rights leaders to organize the March on Washington in 1963. The National Urban League also helped to organize the Poor People's Campaign of 1968. During the ten years that Whitney Young was executive director of the National Urban League, there were significant improvements in the Urban League. The number of local chapters of the Urban League increased from sixty to ninety-eight, the staff of the organization increased from 500 to 1,200, and there was an increased amount of monetary support to the league.

Whitney Young died unexpectedly in March 1971. After the death of Whitney Young, Vernon Jordan became president of the organization. Jordan began to lead the organization in the direction of implementing programs that would focus on health, housing, education, and job training. The Urban League began to publish a journal called the *Urban League Review* in 1975. Jordan also promoted Ron Brown to general counsel of the Urban League. Vernon Jordan was shot in the back by a confessed white supremacist on May 29, 1980, in Fort Wayne, Indiana, after delivering an address to the Fort Wayne Urban League. Jordan was hospitalized for months after this attempt on his life. He decided to resign from the Urban League in 1981. Under his leadership, the National Urban League tripled its budget and was able to hire many additional employees due to Jordan's ability to obtain significant corporate funding for the organization.

John E. Jacob succeeded Jordan as the leader of the Urban League in 1982. In 1982, the organization began publishing *The State of Black America*. Jacob established a permanent development fund to secure the financial future of the league and also established awards and programs in honor of former leader, Whitney Young. The Urban League began to highlight important social justice issues affecting the lives of black Americans. The league focused on emphasizing the importance of implementing self-help programs that would address issues of teen pregnancy and single parenthood in the black community.

Hugh B. Price became leader of the National Urban League in 1994. Price established the Institute of Opportunity and Equality in Washington, D.C. This institute conducted a research and public policy analysis of urban issues. Price also focused on implementing scholarship programs and assessing ways to increase academic achievement among black youth. The current president of the National Urban League is Marc H. Morial, a former New Orleans, Louisiana, mayor, who has already contributed greatly to securing millions of dollars in funding for the League's future endeavors.

Further Readings: Estell, Kenneth. *African America: Portrait of a People*. Canton, OH: Visible Ink Press, 1994; Gilpin, Patrick, and Marybeth Gasman. *Charles S.*

Johnson: Leadership Beyond the Veil in the Age of Jim Crow. Albany: State University of New York Press, 2003; Hughes, Langston, and Milton Meltzer. *African American History*. 6th ed. New York: Scholastic, Inc., 1990; "Jordan, Vernon Eulion, Jr." In Kwame Anthony Appiah and Henry Louis Gates, Jr., eds. *Africana Civil Rights: An A-Z Reference of the Movement that Changed America*. Philadelphia: Running Press, 2004; "Jordan, Vernon." In Henry Louis Gates, Jr., and Evelyn Brooks Higginbotham, eds. *African American Lives*. New York: Oxford University Press, 2004. See also http://www.nul.org/history.html; "National Urban League." In Kwame Anthony Appiah and Henry Louis Gates, Jr., eds. *Africana Civil Rights: An A-Z Reference of the Movement that Changed America*. Philadelphia: Running Press, 2004.

Kijua Sanders-McMurtry

Nebraska. *See* Omaha (Nebraska) Riot of 1919

The Negro Family: The Case for National Action (Moynihan, 1965)

Known as the *Moynihan Report* because it was published in March 1965 by U.S. Assistant Secretary of Labor for Policy Planning **Daniel Patrick Moynihan**, the study titled *The Negro Family: The Case for National Action* looked at the potential of contemporary African Americans to move from where they were to where they wanted to be, and where they ought to have been. It found evidence that a weakened and oppressed African American social structure and, in particular, the African American family, was eroding. While many African Americans were advancing socially, many more were falling further behind.

The report acknowledged the effects of chattel slavery and unemployment on African Americans and the inequality that they had experienced throughout the history of the United States. It held that unless this injury was healed, any efforts to end discrimination, poverty, and injustice would result in little change. It did not propose how the injury could be healed, rather it attempted only to define the injury. The report did, however, find that injury to be the most important domestic event of the post–Civil War period in the United States and it recommended that a national effort led by the federal government was required to establish a stable African American social structure.

The findings of the *Moynihan Report* were based on the research of E. Franklin Frazier and other sociologists, who found that the weakened African American family structure served as the basis for many social problems. The findings revealed that almost a quarter of urban African Americans had experienced failed marriages, illegitimate births, and families headed by women. According to the report, these situations meant that the fathers were absent, which caused increased expansion of welfare programs, a predictable outcome on delinquency and crime rates, and the failure of youths to realize the American Dream.

Sociologists, civil rights organizations, and women's organizations viewed the *Moynihan Report* as an instance of blaming the victim. This view persisted because the report was seen as shifting accountability from systematic inequality in the United States to the structural inequality of the African

American family structure. In doing so, it ignored the exclusion of African American men from provider roles and African American families from the commodity culture, consequences that forced African American women into domestic servant roles and prevented African American families from enjoying the benefits of pooling their resources. In essence, the report portrayed the erosion of the American family as a phenomenon unique to African Americans and therefore not as a major problem for other races in the United States.

Further Readings: Ginsburg, Carl. *Race and Media: The Enduring Life of the Moynihan Report*. New York: Institute for Media Analysis, 1989; Moynihan, Daniel Patrick. *The Negro Family: The Case for National Action*. Washington, D.C.: Office of Policy Planning and Research, United States Department of Labor, 1965; Rainwater, Lee, and William L. Yancey. *The Moynihan Report and the Politics of Controversy*. Cambridge, MA: MIT Press, 1967.

Aaron Peron Ogletree

Negroes with Guns (Williams, 1962)

Negroes with Guns is a book written by **Robert F. Williams** in 1962, while he was living in exile in Cuba. The title refers to an armed group called the Black Guard, which was formed to defend the black community of Monroe, North Carolina. The book tells the story of a small black community's harrowing confrontation with the **Ku Klux Klan (KKK)** and a racist Justice Department and law enforcement. It also explores the origins of Williams' controversial philosophy of **black self-defense** and subsequent opposition from the **Federal Bureau of Investigation (FBI)** and civil rights organizations. Although less than 100 pages in length, *Negroes with Guns* inspired a host of black leaders, such as **Stokely Carmichael**, **Huey P. Newton**, **H. Rap Brown**, **Eldridge Cleaver**, and **Malcolm X**, thus helping to usher in the era of **Black Power**.

Black self-defense was not a new concept. After President Abraham Lincoln abolished slavery during the Civil War, anti-black violence ran rampant throughout the South. Free blacks threatened **white supremacy**. As a result, racist whites employed violence, as well as discriminatory laws, to maintain their social, economic, and political dominance. Whites freely threatened, harassed, and murdered individuals and rioted in black communities. In response to these attacks, some blacks fought bravely, though they were rarely successful. During the twentieth century, numerous other black communities were destroyed, such as Greenwood, Oklahoma (see **Greenwood Community**) in 1921 and Rosewood, Florida (see **Rosewood [Florida] Riot of 1923**), and only a few individuals in these communities survived despite attempts at collective self-defense.

In *Negroes with Guns*, Williams explains that he gained his first knowledge of racial violence and black protest through the stories of his grandmother, who had been a slave. Before her death, his grandmother gave him a rifle "that his grandfather had wielded against white terrorists at the turn of the century" (Williams 1998, xvii). After high school, Williams joined the U.S. Marines, where he learned how to handle and use arms.

After being dishonorably discharged from the Marines for challenging its discriminatory practices, Williams returned home to Monroe. Once home, Williams experienced firsthand the violence and threats directed at the small, local chapter of the **National Association for the Advancement of Colored People (NAACP)**. Although many members quit the organization for fear of their lives, Williams stood firm and was elected president of the Monroe chapter of the NAACP in 1956. Over the next few years, Williams transformed the group. In general, the NAACP was comprised of middle-class and professional blacks, and it strictly adhered to the philosophy of **nonviolence**. In contrast, Williams' chapter consisted largely of veterans, laborers, farmers, domestic workers, and the unemployed, and they subscribed to the concept of self-defense.

In *Negroes with Guns*, Williams describes the circumstances that led him to advocate self-defense. In addition to receiving frequent threats, Williams and other activists, while picketing in protest in 1961 for the right of black children to use a public swimming pool, were threatened and harassed by private individuals and police officers. Two black women, one of whom was pregnant, were assaulted by two white men on separate occasions. Both men were acquitted. After the court case involving the beating and attempted rape of the pregnant woman, Williams vowed publicly to meet violence with violence. Consequently, he was suspended from the NAACP for six months. Delegates at an NAACP convention later made a statement in support of self-defense, but **Martin Luther King, Jr**., was the only one to publicly side with Williams.

Williams felt that it was only natural and right for a people to protect themselves against brutality, especially in the absence of support from law enforcement and other authorities established to provide that protection. Williams did not disagree with the concept of nonviolence, and his branch of the NAACP engaged in many nonviolent demonstrations. Williams believed that within the movement, both nonviolence and self-defense were acceptable and essential. But he also argued that his philosophy was more effective than those of other civil rights organizations. Because the members of his group were willing to defend themselves, their demonstrations provoked less violence than activities such as the **Freedom Rides**.

Williams' self-defense group, formed in the 1960s and called the Black Guard, proved to be effective in subduing and averting Ku Klux Klan violence. Members of the Black Guard were trained by Williams and were charter members of the National Rifle Association. They received donations from various organizations, churches, and individuals—whites included—to purchase guns and rifles. On several occasions, they engaged in shoot-outs with **white mobs** and the Klan, without fatalities on either side. The Black Guard was even called on when the freedom riders, an interracial group of activists, arrived in Monroe to help the civil rights cause there. With Williams' support and assistance, the freedom riders found volunteers in Monroe, all of whom took an oath of nonviolence, which meant that they were not allowed to defend themselves if attacked. Williams even "stated that if they could show [him] any gains won from the racists by nonviolent methods, [he] too would become a pacifist" (Williams 1998, 41). However, the freedom riders were attacked, and shortly thereafter, whites drove into the black community and "fired out of their cars and threw objects at people on the streets" (Williams 1998, 47). Blacks armed themselves to defend their community and a riot ensued.

During the riot, Williams helped protect a white couple he believed drove unintentionally into the community. When state troopers arrived to "restore law and order," Williams fled to New York, where he heard that the white couple he had protected had accused him of kidnapping them. Williams was forced to take refuge in Cuba. He moved to China in 1963. He was allowed to return to the United States in exchange for information President Richard Nixon wanted on China. Until his death in 1995, Williams continued to support the struggle for civil rights.

Further Reading: *Negroes with Guns: Rob Williams and Black Power.* Directed by Sandra Dickerson and Churchill Roberts. Gainesville: University of Florida; The Digital Lighthouse, 2004; Williams, Robert F. *Negroes with Guns*. New York: Marzani & Munsell, 1962; Williams, Robert F. *Negroes with Guns*. Detriot, MI: Wayne State University Press, 1998.

Gladys L. Knight

Newark (New Jersey) Riot of 1967

The Newark (New Jersey) Riot of 1967 pitted residents of the city's predominantly black neighborhoods against mostly white police and military forces. After five days of unrest, which ranged from July 12 through July 17, 1967, 23 people were dead, over 700 people were injured, and approximately 1,500 people were arrested. After the **Los Angeles (California) Riot of 1965** (also known as the Watts riot) and **Detroit (Michigan) Riot of 1967**, the 1967 Newark riot was the most severe episode of urban unrest to take place in the United States during the 1960s (see **Long Hot Summer Riots, 1965–1967**). While a majority of white respondents and some African Americans label the Newark event a *riot*, some black and white political activists refer to it as a *rebellion* or *uprising*. Since the majority of victims were killed or injured by the police and military rather than by civilians of the opposite race, it might be a misnomer to call this event a *race riot*.

Underlying Structural Conditions

By July 1967, Newark was "ready to riot" (Wright 1968). After nearly three decades of black migration from the South and the flight of the white population to the surrounding suburbs, by 1967, Newark had become a majority black city. "Between 1960 and 1967, the city lost a net total of more than 70,000 residents. In six years the city switched from 65 percent white to 52 percent Negro and 10 percent Puerto Rican and Cuban" (National Advisory Commission on Civil Disorders, 57). Yet, despite having attained a residential majority in Newark, black people held little formal political power—only two of nine city council seats. Of 1,512 Newark police officers on duty in 1966, only 145 (less than 10 percent) were black. In the schools, black teachers remained a minority, while the student body of several schools became largely black and Latino. In 1967, the local branch of the **National Association for the Advancement of Colored People (NAACP)** urged that Wilbur Parker, the first black certified public accountant (CPA) in the state of New Jersey, be appointed to fill an anticipated vacancy on the Board of Education. Despite such pressure, Mayor Hugh Addonizio appointed an Irish high school graduate named James T. Callaghan to the prestigious post. This fueled resentment among black people in Newark who felt that even with the proper qualifications they could be denied commensurate employment.

For less-educated African Americans, particularly recent migrants from the South, the job situation in Newark was worsening. Drawn by the promise of steady factory employment, southern blacks continued to move to Newark. At the same time, however, large employers like General Electric and Westinghouse were closing their manufacturing plants in Newark. As a result, unskilled and semi-skilled industrial jobs were in short supply. Unemployment rose within the city of Newark. By 1967, unemployment among Newark's black population stood at 11.5 percent, roughly double that of the white population. In Newark's predominantly black neighborhoods, a sense of hopelessness set in.

These structural changes were most strongly felt in Newark's Central Ward, a previously mixed neighborhood of black migrants and Jewish immigrants that, by 1967, had been transformed into an almost exclusively black ghetto. During the 1950s and 1960s, the Central Ward became the site of numerous high-rise public housing projects. By 1967, Newark had the highest proportion of residents living in public housing of any city in the country, earning the nickname *The Brick City*. Then, in 1967, Newark's Central Ward became the target of a massive urban renewal campaign centered around the construction of a new campus for the University Medical and Dental School of New Jersey (UMDNJ), formerly located in Jersey City. Newark city officials believed that the medical school would be an anchor for the redevelopment of the Central Ward and began to draw up plans to declare parts of the Central Ward as dilapidated in preparation to clear land for the medical complex. The city's initial plan was to clear 20 to 30 acres of land, but the medical school asked for 150 acres. As a result, the area targeted for renewal was considerably enlarged, which in turn provoked a wave of protest among homeowners and tenants whose land and homes were slated to be taken by eminent domain. Public meetings regarding the medical school became especially contentious, in part due to the presence of militant activists who sought to disrupt the meetings and derail the construction of the medical complex.

Among these so-called militant activists were members of the Newark Community Union Project, an offshoot of Students for a Democratic Society (SDS), founded by Tom Hayden, as well as members of the **Congress of Racial Equality** (CORE), and representatives of the United Community Corporation (a local anti-poverty organization). Along with the black nationalist poet/playwright Leroi Jones (now Amiri Baraka), these groups gave voice to the anger of the black community at the white political establishment.

A National Conference on Black Power planned for July of that year raised fears among the politicians and police of the potential for racial unrest.

As with the 1967 Detroit riot, a major source of unrest in Newark involved the deterioration in police-community relations. In the years leading up to the riot, Newark police were involved in a series of high-profile incidents. In July 1965, twenty-two-year-old Lester Long was shot and killed by police after a "routine" traffic stop. A few weeks later, Bernard Rich, a twenty-six-year-old African American man, died in police custody under mysterious circumstances while locked in his jail cell. On Christmas Eve that year, Walter Mathis, age seventeen, was fatally wounded by an "accidental" weapons discharge while being searched for illegal contraband. Despite calls for the appointment of a civilian police review board and hiring of more African American policemen, such proposals went unheeded. On July 7, 1967, just five days before the riot began, Newark and East Orange police raided a house inhabited by a group of Black Muslims. In a fruitless search for illegal weapons, they detained and interrogated the occupants of the house, allegedly beating them with their batons. This incident alone had the potential to spark unrest and certainly helped set that stage for the events that followed on July 12.

The Precipitating Incident

The Newark Riot of 1967 began on the evening of July 12 with the arrest of a cab driver named John Smith for an alleged traffic violation. After driving past a double-parked police car, Smith and an unnamed passenger were stopped by Officers John Desimone and Vito Pontrelli and pulled over. As the passenger fled the scene, a scuffle ensued between Smith and the arresting officers. John Smith was reportedly beaten by the police officers en route to the Fourth Precinct's police headquarters on Seventeenth Street and Belmont Avenue (now Irvine Turner Boulevard). According to eyewitness accounts and the officer's testimony, John Smith was dragged into the Fourth Precinct house and placed in a jail cell. A crowd soon began to gather outside, and local civil rights leaders were contacted by residents of a public housing project that stood across the street from the Fourth Precinct building.

A group of civil rights leaders including Robert Curvin, representative of CORE, arrived at the Fourth Precinct at about the same time as Newark Police Inspector Kenneth Melchior. These civil rights leaders entered the building and were allowed to see the prisoner in his cell. Noting that Smith was injured, Curvin persuaded Inspector Melchior to have Smith transported to the hospital. Due to the crowd assembled at the front entrance, John Smith was taken out the back door to a police car and driven to Newark Beth Israel Hospital. Curvin volunteered to speak to the assembled crowd and was provided with a police bullhorn. By this time, rumors had circulated that John Smith had died in police custody. Curvin stood on top of a police car and sought to calm the crowd, but his speech had the opposite effect. He encouraged people to line up for a peaceful protest, but was soon shouted down. A hail of bottles, bricks, and a couple of Molotov cocktails hit the Fourth Precinct. Officers charged out of the building to disperse the crowd, but as the crowd dispersed, people started looting nearby stores. The looting did not spread very far beyond the Fourth Precinct.

Initial Police Response

By the following afternoon, Thursday, July 13, Mayor Addonizio proclaimed that the disturbance was over. However, some police officials worried that that violence might resume at nightfall. A protest rally coordinated by CORE and the Newark Community Union Project (NCUP) was slated to be held at the Fourth Precinct later that evening. Based on his personal premonitions, Deputy Police Chief Redden ordered all of the men under his command to report for twelve-hour shifts. By 7:30 P.M., a crowd of over 300 people stood in front of the Fourth Precinct. Mayor Addonizio sent his personal representative James Threat to inform the crowd that in deference to their demands a well-known African American police lieutenant would be appointed to the rank of captain. This promise failed to ameliorate the anger of the crowd, and soon thereafter, a volley of rocks and bottles was thrown at the police. The event at that time seemed like a replay of the previous evening. Once again, police charged into the crowd and dispersed the protesters, and once again looting spread to the nearby business thoroughfare. But unlike the previous evening, the looting spread in numerous directions, including the downtown. Stores along Springfield Avenue, Prince Street, and downtown on Broad Street were looted and set on fire. By 9:00 P.M., Deputy Chief Redden told the mayor that they needed help, but was overruled by the mayor and Police Director Domenic Spina, who were reluctant to call for assistance from the state police. At 1:30 A.M., Spina called the state police and reminded them of their plan to provide assistance if necessary. At 2:30 A.M., Spina called Mayor Addonizio and said that state police help was needed immediately. Finally, just after 2:30 A.M., Mayor Addonizio called Governor Hughes and asked him to deploy both the New Jersey State Police and the National Guard. By 3:00 A.M., when Colonel Kelly of the New Jersey State Police arrived to meet with Mayor Addonizio, Addonizio proclaimed, "the whole town is gone" (Porambo, 117).

State Police and National Guard Arrive

Around 5:30 A.M., the first detachment of state troopers arrived in Newark, followed by the first National Guard units around 7:00 A.M. The National Guard and state police set up camp at the Roseville Armory in the city's North Ward. Their arrival was cheered by the mostly Italian residents of that community. A loose command structure was put in place with Colonel Kelly of the state police in nominal command of both the state police and National Guard troops. The Newark police remained under the command of Police Director Spina. But due to incompatible radio frequencies and a clash of egos among leaders of the three agencies, there was little actual coordination of police and military units. Indicative of the larger command problems, Colonel Kelly of the state police had to procure his own maps of the city. As troops fanned out across the city, they sought to establish a series of checkpoints, with three guardsmen manning each of 137 street blockades. Until Thursday night, there had been only twenty-six arrests and no reported deaths. By the end of the day on Friday, over 900 people had been arrested, and 10 people had been fatally shot (9 of the 10 by police).

As the Newark police, state police, and National Guard patrolled the city from Friday night through Saturday evening, gunfire erupted. Police and military officials claimed that gunfire was the result of snipers, but in a few well-documented cases, police and guardsmen were in fact firing on one another. On Saturday evening, believing that snipers were firing from the rooftops of public housing projects, national guardsmen and state police unleashed waves of machine-gun fire on those buildings, fatally wounding several apartment dwellers, including Eloise Spellman, a mother of ten children who was shot in the neck while pulling her children away from the window. Also on Friday night, Fire Captain Michael Moran was killed while responding to a false alarm at a building on South Orange Avenue. While climbing a ladder to the second-floor window, he was struck in the back by an alleged sniper's bullet. Moran was one of only two whites to die during the entire five days of rioting. The other was Police Detective Fred Toto, who was also allegedly struck by a sniper's bullet the previous evening.

The Riot Dwindles

By Sunday morning, reports were arriving from residents and merchants who claimed that Newark police and state police officers were shooting into storefronts and looting merchandise. Some shopkeepers, whites included, had painted the words *Soul Brother* on their windows with the hope that their businesses would be left undisturbed, but according to testimony before the Governor's Commission on Civil Disorders, these stories became targets for retribution at the hands of the mostly white police forces. Nonetheless, despite these isolated incidents, the riot was winding down. National guardsmen began distributing food and Governor Hughes offered clemency to any looters who could provide information leading to the arrest and conviction of a sniper (Porambo, 121). During this twenty-four-hour period, from Sunday to Monday morning, three more people were killed: one a suspected looter, another a suspected car thief, and the third, a teenage boy struck by a police bullet while taking out the garbage outside his house. By Monday afternoon, the National Guard barricades had been lifted and the troops had begun their withdrawal from the city.

Aftermath

At the conclusion of five days of rioting, 23 people were dead and over 750 people were injured. Newark firefighters had responded to approximately 250 fires and 64 false alarms. According to an official count, state police and national guardsmen had expended 13,319 rounds of ammunition (Governor's Select Commission on Civil Disorders 1972; Porambo, 122).

Despite the relatively short duration of this episode of unrest, the riot has had a lasting impact on the city of Newark. For some political activists in the black community, the rebellion was empowering, promoting racial solidarity and paving the way for the election of Ken Gibson, the city's first black mayor. Others, both black and white, believe that the riot tore the community apart. After the riot, the pace of white flight accelerated. The last remaining segment of the city's Jewish population, located in the Weequahic section, left the city, as did whites who lived on the city's west side. Those whites who remained were largely from the Italian section in the North Ward and the Portugese population of the East Ward/Ironbound. Both of these communities had been heavily defended during the riots by a combination of armed citizen patrols and National Guard troops. After the riot, racial polarization increased, manifested by clashes over schooling and housing between Italians and African Americans. Several large insurance companies decided to move their corporate headquarters out of Newark (Prudential Insurance Company was a notable exception). Heavy and light industry continued to decline and unemployment continued to increase. The municipal tax base eroded and city services were cut. The 1970s and 1980s were characterized by poverty, crime, and fiscal crisis. As with Detroit, it is quite possible that this situation would have existed anyway, independent of the riots. Yet, Newark, like Detroit, has struggled with the stigma of being a riot city.

In recent years, beginning in the mid-1990s, Newark has made somewhat of a comeback, constructing a world-class performing arts center, renovating its downtown office buildings, and attracting capital investment from New York-based real estate entrepreneurs. With federal HOPE VI funds, the city has demolished much of its high-rise public housing and replaced it with low-rise townhouses available for low-income residents. Yet Newark continues to struggle with a high percentage of its residents on public assistance, an underperforming school system operating under state receivership, and a recent spate of gang-related homicides. Although the central business district has experienced a renaissance, it is unclear how long it will take for this renaissance to bear fruit in the city's more impoverished and neglected neighborhoods. The future of Newark, almost forty years after the riots of July 1967, remains an open question.

Further Readings: Governor's Select Commission on Civil Disorders in the State of New Jersey. *Report for Action: An Investigation into the Causes and Events of the 1967 Newark Race Riots*. New York: Lemma Publishing Corporation, 1972; Hayden, Tom. *Rebellion in Newark: Official Violence and Ghetto Response*. New York: Vintage Books, 1967; Herman, Max. *The Newark and Detroit "Riots" of 1967*. See www.67riots.rutgers.edu; National Advisory Commission on Civil Disorders. *Report of the National Advisory Commission on Civil Disorders*. New York: Bantam Books, 1968; Porambo, Ron. *No Cause for Indictment: An Autopsy of Newark*. New York: Holt, Rinehart, and Winston, 1971; Winters, Stanley B., ed. *From Riot to Recovery: Newark after Ten Years*. Washington, D.C.: University Press of America, 1979; Wright, Nathan, Jr. *Ready to Riot*. New York: Holt, Rinehart and Winston, 1968.

Max Herman

New Bedford (Massachusetts) Riot of 1970

The New Bedford civil disorders of July 1970—sometimes called *the rebellion* by participants, sometimes simply called *the riots* by local residents—occurred during a summer of ghetto rioting in small cities, with upheavals in nearly a dozen communities in nine states, including **Asbury Park**, New Jersey; Fort Lauderdale, Florida; Lima, Ohio; and Mathis, Texas. By the definitions used in the **Kerner Commission Report (1968)**, the New Bedford violence constituted a serious, even major civil disturbance. During the month, this city of just over 100,000 people, sixty miles south of Boston, witnessed extensive arson, intensive looting, dozens of sniper incidents, and sizeable street crowds confronting local, area, and state police. Although the use of National Guard forces was urged repeatedly by the city government, and a unit at the nearby Fall River armory was placed on alert several days into the events, those forces were never used.

The complaints among the aggrieved in New Bedford, heard from the pulpit, dais, and street corner for years, were similar to those that animated rioting in hundreds of communities between 1963 and 1968: high unemployment, inadequate educational facilities, poor housing, and a shortage of recreation space. The trigger was also familiar: the arrest of a young African American man in the early evening hours of July 8 in the predominantly black West End of town, near the main avenue in that section, Kempton Street. An increasing occurrence in the late 1960s that had generated a ritual inundation of the central police station by family and friends, activists, and community leaders, this time the lid seemed to come off a city long perceived as a backwater in an age of civil rights struggles. The city did have a long tradition of dissent. Religiously tolerant, racially diverse, and socially progressive from its earliest days, it was home to Quakers and Baptists, free people of color (including an especially large fugitive slave community), and a significant abolitionist presence. There were warm-weather youthful skirmishes with police in the sixties, but only with **Martin Luther King, Jr.'s** assassination in April 1968, and the violence paled in comparison to what occurred elsewhere in the country. Generally, New Bedford lived in the shadow of big cities like Boston to the north.

July 8 changed that, at least for the moment. Although spontaneous and initially unorganized, by 1:00 A.M. on July 9, the city witnessed clashes between scores of youth and police and firefighters. There were injuries on both sides, the first of many that month. The young people in the West End built homemade barricades from overturned and burning cars, threw rocks and other debris, started numerous fires, and even began sniping at vehicles moving through the neighborhood, including police vehicles, though no one was shot. On more than one occasion, police drew their guns, though they did not discharge them. Most alarming to some was the common chant from the crowds: *Off the pig!* and *Pigs out of the community.*

This was not merely a reflection of what had become common radical parlance; it indicated the presence of the group that had popularized such language, the **Black Panther Party** (BPP), which everywhere sought to organize and direct such rebellions. Begun in Oakland, California, in the fall of 1966 as the Black Panther Party for Self-Defense, by 1968 it had cropped the title to denote a political party and simultaneously went national. That summer, a chapter was established in Boston. Two years later, there was no organized Panther presence in New Bedford, but there was organizing activity, spearheaded by ex–gang member and radicalized Vietnam veteran Frank "Parky" Grace. For six months, he had been bringing from Boston newspapers, buttons, posters—and sometimes Panthers, who spoke to gatherings of young people at a teen hangout on Kempton Street they called The Club. Some in the audience would come to identify as Panthers and form the core of the future New Bedford National Committee to Combat Fascism (1970–1971), a Panther front organization, and the New Bedford branch of the BPP (1971–1972).

But, that part of July 1970 was in the future on the night of July 8. By the time things had calmed in the wee hours of July 9, police had arrested three men in their early twenties, just the initial crop of hundreds arrested during the month. First was Warren Houtman, a militant black, perhaps for driving with a defective car light, perhaps for demonstrating the sound and speed of his souped-up car—eyewitness, police, and press reports conflict, as do memories. Next was Charlie Perry, known for his street-fighting abilities and a good friend of Parky Grace; he would soon become a Panther, too. That night, he was taken in for helping a black girl escape the police in the troubled aftermath of Houtman's arrest. And, finally, there was Jimmy Magnett, arrested, apparently, just for being there. Well known as a fiery voice at local meetings and in the letters-to-the-editor column of the local paper, the *Standard Times*, Magnett was identified in press reports as the Defense Minister of a veterans group called the Black Brothers Political Party, a group to which Grace also belonged.

The next night, July 9, the violence escalated and spread to the South End of the city, which meant significant involvement of Puerto Ricans and the key element in New Bedford's ethnic and racial mix, the Cape Verdeans. The only substantial African migration to America that was not a forced migration of slaves, the Cape Verdeans came from an island archipelago off Senegal that had been colonized in the fifteenth century by the Portuguese as an outpost of the Atlantic slave trade. The islands soon became an entrepot for trade and labor, attracting people from all over the world. Because of extensive intermixing, the islanders ranged in color from dark-skinned to fair-skinned, some with blue eyes and straight hair. The Cape Verdeans, then, were neither white nor black, Portuguese nor African. They came to New Bedford as early as the late eighteenth century—initially, as part of the whaling industry, later to work in the cranberry bogs and textile mills—and found themselves shunned by so-called white Portuguese as "colored," just as they sought to distance themselves from what they derisively called "Americans de couer" (Americans of color). But, in the context of the mid-1960s emergence of black consciousness in America's Negro communities, a younger generation of Cape Verdeans would become "black." And, in New Bedford, the Cape Verdean capital of the United States, the Cape Verdeans outnumbered Negroes by two to one. They would be a significant constituency for those who sought to widen and deepen the rebellion, but especially for those local Cape Verdeans who identified as Panthers.

Parky Grace and Charlie Perry were both Cape Verdean, although they lived in the West End, which was predominantly West Indian, southern black, and Afro-Indian. Another Cape Verdean and Black Panther, Dickie Duarte, would use a megaphone taken in the looting to proselytize young Cape Verdeans at Monte's Park in the South End. Meanwhile, all sought to build ties to the shrewd organizer who emerged among the Latino population farther south, Ramon "Tito" Morales. With a white man arrested carrying a loaded shotgun near the West End, union construction workers threatening to march on it, and three white radicals from Fall River nabbed for attempted arson in support of the rioters—all in the first couple of days—the mayor, city council, police, and press worried about maintaining control.

By Friday, July 10, a crew from Boston's public broadcasting station was in town filming interviews for the July 16 airing of, *Say, Brother!*, the first TV show in the country produced for and by black people. On tape, black men in the West End, where the anger on the screen seemed to rise like the steam from the city's sweltering streets, called the events "the awakening of a sleeping giant"; the mayor called the events a "revolt"; a young black called it a "revolution!" And all this before the incident of Saturday, July 11, which turned street violence into a true conflagration. Early that evening, as scores of mostly young people milled about in front of The Club where the Panthers had proselytized local youth earlier in the year, a gray-and-white 1957 Chevy containing three young whites from adjacent towns breached the barricades set up on the first night of trouble, and stopped in the middle of the street. The driver emerged from the car, laid a shotgun across the roof, and fired point-blank into the crowd. Dozens of shotgun pellets sprayed across the torso of seventeen-year-old Lester Lima, from his neck to his navel, riddling both arms and piercing his heart, liver, and intestines. A Cape Verdean from the South End, he was identified in the press as a black teenager. Whisked from the scene in a car by Magnett and others, Lima died shortly after arrival at the local hospital. Three others were seriously wounded by the scattered pellets.

By the first of the following week, in the wake of a dramatic escalation of violence after the shooting, two outside forces intervened. One, whose effect was largely ephemeral, came from the Massachusetts congressional delegation, most importantly in the person of Edward Brooke, the first black Republican U.S. senator since Reconstruction. After touring the riot areas, he appointed an ad hoc committee of local activists to negotiate with the mayor, city council, and police department. More significant for the course of events was the simultaneous arrival of several Boston Panthers, who set up shop—as a branch of the NCCF—in the partially burned and looted remains of a local institution called Pieraccini's Variety on Kempton Street. For the mayor, the council, and the police, they were the quintessential outside agitators, the cause of the trouble.

During the month of July, this headquarters, as Parky Grace and others called it, became a kind of cross-generational community center; the Panthers ran it, but people of varying degrees of politicization came to talk, debate, discover. It also functioned as a kind of on-the-spot liberation school with outdoor classes; the text was usually *Quotations from Chairman Mao*. Pieraccini's was also a distribution center for Panther literature—leaflets, pamphlets, newspapers, posters. Most crucially, though, for the political and business establishment in New Bedford, the storefront was a fortress, complete with sandbags, gun slots, and a cache of weapons—thanks largely to the expertise of local radicalized Vietnam veterans.

When renewed rioting began in the South End during the week of July 27, after weeks of skirmishing, and especially when the violent winds blew back into the West End, rumors were rife that the city had had enough and intended to raid Pieraccini's to search for illegal weapons. At a press conference on July 30, the Panthers offered to open their doors, as long as their lawyers could be present. The officers came too late. At about 6:00 A.M. on the morning of July 31, a local resident named Stephen Botelho drove to police headquarters to report that he had been shot. While driving home from work on Kempton Street just after passing Pieraccini's, he claimed, a sniper had shot at his car, wounding him in the right ankle. Botelho's report would provide the catalyst for a massive raid by local police, with state police standing by and hovering overhead in helicopters.

Twenty-one people were arrested emerging from or standing outside Pieraccini's that morning, giving birth to what would be known, briefly, as the New Bedford 21. From the beginning and throughout, the group was associated with the Panthers, for Pieraccini's was essentially a Panther building, occupied by several people known to be members of the Boston Panther chapter. Still, some were merely community supporters, some unaffiliated activists, and some complete innocents. In any case, the charges against those arrested were serious: they included conspiracy to commit murder and anarchy, and to incite riot. Moreover, the original total bail was set at well over $1 million. The prisoners were questioned by the **Federal Bureau of Investigation (FBI)**, which immediately opened a file on the NCCF and all associated with it.

Although the civil disorder itself was not the doing of the Panthers, Boston or local, it was clearly affected by them; moreover, the city establishment, especially the mayor, would see the entire affair as a product of outside agitators. And, although there were skirmishes in August and even, on occasion, the following fall, the July 31 raid did deflate the revolt. Organizing on behalf of the New Bedford 21 was the focus of local Panther activity that fall and winter; just before the trial was to begin in late March, all of the serious charges were dropped. As for the three whites charged in the July 11 killing of Lima and the wounding of the others, an all-white jury, after deliberating for forty-five minutes, voted to acquit on all charges. A few fires were set, but New Bedford did not erupt at the verdict. And it never did again. *See also* Martin Luther King, Jr., Assassination of (1968); Black Self-Defense; Civil Rights Movement; Police Brutality; Returning Soldiers (World War I).

Further Readings: Feagin, Joe R., and Harlan Hahn. *Ghetto Revolts*. New York: Macmillan Publishing Company, 1973; Fogelson, Robert M. *Violence as Protest: A Study of Riots and Ghettos*. Garden City, NY: Doubleday & Company, 1971; Gilje, Paul A. *Rioting in America*. Bloomington and Indianapolis: Indiana University Press, 1996; Kerner, Otto, et al., *Report of the National Advisory Commission on Civil*

Disorders. New York: Bantam Books, 1968; Lazerow, Jama. "The Black Panthers at the Water's Edge: Oakland, Boston, and the New Bedford 'Riots' of 1970." In Jama Lazerow and Yohuru Williams, eds. *The Black Panther Party in Historical Perspective*. Durham, NC: Duke University Press, forthcoming.

Jama Lazerow

New Jersey. *See* Asbury Park (New Jersey) Riot of 1970; Jersey City (New Jersey) Riot of 1964; Newark (New Jersey) Riot of 1967

New Orleans (Louisiana) Riot of 1866

The New Orleans Riot of 1866 was one of the largest and most brutal events that occurred during the city's history. Although unique in its severity, the New Orleans riot was hardly a rare event. Race riots occurred in other cities that summer (**Memphis** in May and Charleston in June), and these related incidents are characteristic of the social, cultural, and racial unrest haunting this time period.

Many attribute the origin of the riot to the controversy surrounding the movement to reconvene the 1864 convention and implement the Civil Rights Act of 1866. This act attempted to grant citizenship to all native-born Americans regardless of race thus giving blacks equal rights and protection under the law. By 1866, some members, Republicans in particular, of the 1864 convention lost their power to conservative Democrats in the election of 1865. As a result, some Republicans deemed this situation as an opportunity to regain power in the state of Louisiana. The 1864 constitution provided two avenues for ratification. The conference could either make a request for the new state legislature to assemble a new convention, or they could ask the legislature to amend the constitution themselves and have it ratified by the people in the next state election. But many of the old members, also known as conventionalists, knew that they would have no power in making changes to the constitution because the Democrats would control a majority of the votes; and the second option would not be suitable to the conventionalists because the legislature would attempt to oppose their amendments to the Constitution. As a result, the conventionalists decided to reconvene without any of the newly elected members of the legislature.

The conventionalists' primary obstacle was getting the support they needed to reconvene the convention. The only person who had the power to reconvene the convention was its president, Judge E.H. Durell. Although he refused to assist the conventionalists and left the city, they issued a call to all of the former members of the convention and met on June 26, 1864. During this meeting, thirty-nine of the original ninety-six members were in attendance. The conventionalists ousted Judge Durell as president and elected Judge R.K. Howell as president pro tem. Their second action was to assign June 30 as the date to reconvene the convention. This political maneuver set in motion the social and political basis for the riot a few days later.

The conventionalists' actions created a recipe for civil unrest in the city. The conventionalists' unlawful attempt to amend the Constitution unilaterally, without regard for their position, angered the legislative members who

A nineteenth-century wood engraving of scenes from the New Orleans riot of 1866. Courtesy of the Library of Congress.

controlled the majority of the state's population. Additionally, members of the old planter and merchant aristocracy disliked the conventionalists because they were a threat to the social and political power base they initially established after the war. The larger white population was primarily angered that whites would lose their rights to vote, some former Confederate soldiers would lose jobs in government and, most importantly, that people of African descent might gain the right to vote. The days leading up to the riots were tense and filled with inflammatory speeches made by both supporters of the conventionalists and those who opposed them, which also created tension between the conventionalists and conservatives and blacks and whites.

On the morning of June 30, the city of New Orleans was tense. The first incident of racial violence occurred during a procession of 100 to 150 blacks marching to the Mechanics' Institute, the meeting hall for the convention. Violence erupted when a white boy made insulting remarks to a black participant and kicked him in the back. As the white crowd applauded and laughed, the black man knocked the young man down. A scuffle ensued, which ended in the black man's arrest. Additionally, a black man began to wave his flag in response to jeers from the white crowd. A policeman responded to this action by firing a shot at the flag bearer.

The riot broke out when another young white boy threw a rock into the black processional crowd of around 1,500 people in front of the Mechanics' Institute at about 1:00 P.M. As the blacks began to rush the boy, violence ensued as gunfire started. Initially, the blacks were able to repel the officers and the white crowd; however, the mob was better armed and eventually overtook them. As a result, many blacks dispersed throughout the city while others took refuge in the institute. Whites chased and harassed blacks within a one- to two-mile radius of the Mechanics' Institute, which led to the brutalization of many blacks who had not participated in the processional. Other members of the mob entered the Mechanics' Institute to take on conventionalists and the remaining blacks. Although some attempted to surrender to the mob, there was no sympathy for the trapped members. Anticipating the federal army would come to their rescue, they barricaded themselves in the hall. Due to either miscommunication or ambivalence on the part of the U.S. government, troops did not arrive until 4:00 P.M. By the end of the riot, over 130 blacks were injured and about 34 were killed; 3 whites associated with the conventionalists were killed and about 17 were wounded; 20 members of the police force were slightly wounded, and 1 person from the **white mob** was killed.

The New Orleans riot placed the social and political attitudes of southerners after the Civil War in perspective for northerners. The brutality of this riot gave the Republicans the ammunition they needed to make their campaign for **Reconstruction** a primary issue in the congressional elections of 1866. After gaining the majority in Congress, they were able to bring about radical Reconstruction and the passage of the Reconstruction Act of 1867.

Further Readings: Fogelson, Robert M., and Richard Rubenstein, eds. *Mass Violence in America: New Orleans Riots of July 30, 1866*. New York: Arno Press & New York Times, 1969; Hollandsworth, James G. *An Absolute Massacre: The New Orleans Riot of July 30th, 1866*. Baton Rouge: Louisiana State University Press, 2001; Vandal, Giles. *The New Orleans Riot of 1866: Anatomy of a Tragedy*. Lafayette: The Center for Louisiana Studies, University of Southwestern Louisiana, 1983; Vandal, Giles. "The Origins of the New Orleans Riot of 1866, Revised." In Donald G. Nieman, ed. *African American Life in the Post–Emancipation South, 1861–1900*. New York: Garland Publishing, 1994.

Christina S. Haynes

New Orleans (Louisiana) Riot of 1900

One of the bloodiest race riots in the United States began in New Orleans, Louisiana, on July 23, 1900, after a clash between the police and Robert Charles, a black Mississippian. The riot ended on July 28, as **white mobs** slowly dispersed after a police wagon carried Charles' bullet-riddled body to the city morgue. In the four days of violence, Charles shot twenty-seven whites, killing seven of them, including four policemen. Sparked by Charles' actions, white mobs attacked African Americans, murdering at least twelve and seriously wounding some sixty-nine others.

Blacks made up more than a quarter of New Orleans' 300,000 residents in 1900. Historically, the city held a special appeal for African Americans because of employment opportunities and relative racial tolerance. Below the surface, however, tensions brewed. A lack of jobs and declining wages pitted black and white laborers against each other by the turn of the century. Moreover, the city's largest employers often hired black workers at lower pay than whites. The New Orleans press contributed to deteriorating race relations. Henry J. Hearsey, editor and publisher of the *States*, the city's foremost afternoon daily, proved especially vitriolic. A former Confederate officer, Hearsey suggested that extermination might settle "the Negro problem."

Robert Charles moved to New Orleans in 1894. At twenty-eight, he had already exchanged gunfire with a white train flagman and pled guilty to selling alcohol illegally in Mississippi. During his six years in New Orleans, Charles worked numerous jobs, supplementing his income by distributing literature for two back-to-Africa causes. Several incidents affected him profoundly while in the city. The illegitimate 1896 state elections ushered in a Democratic administration that disenfranchised blacks through new laws and the 1898 Constitution. Also, in 1896, Louisiana recorded twenty-one **lynchings**, marking a new state record. Finally, Charles' acquaintances maintained that the grisly April 1899 lynching of Sam Hose in Palmetto, Georgia, infuriated him. Against this backdrop, Charles and his roommate, Lenard Pierce, encountered three New Orleans police officers shortly after 11:00 P.M. on July 23, 1900.

As the two black men waited on a street for some female friends, Sergeant Jules C. Aucoin called for Patrolmen August Mora and Joseph Cantrelle to help him investigate two suspicious men. According to Mora, when the police approached Charles and Pierce and asked them questions, Charles gave a vague response and stood up threateningly. Mora grabbed him. Patrolman Aucoin leveled his pistol at Pierce's face. Mora and Charles eventually pulled their guns on each other. Both Mora and Cantrelle shot at Charles, who fell to the ground but got up and ran. Mora took a bullet in the right thigh. Captain John Day of the Sixth Precinct soon learned from Pierce where to look for Charles—a rundown cottage on Fourth Street. Day and four others made their way to Charles' room by 3:00 A.M. on July 24 and demanded entry. As the door opened, Charles shot the captain through the heart. He then shot another patrolman through the head. Two lawmen fired back, but Charles retreated and the officers ran to a neighbor's room. At 4:30 A.M., Charles fired at a corporal on the street, grazing his cap. As the corporal and a colleague fled, Charles escaped to an acquaintance's house fourteen blocks away.

Soon, most of the New Orleans police force gathered at Charles' cottage. Unable to find him, a massive manhunt began. By the morning of July 24, white crowds gathered at Charles' house, the Sixth Precinct stationhouse (where Lenard Pierce remained), and outside the city morgue, where the two dead policemen had been taken. During the day, New Orleans' four major newspapers incited a mob mentality with racist rhetoric. Angry whites met on the streets to discuss revenge, and confrontations with blacks occurred. The city finally exploded around 8:30 P.M. on July 25, as 2,000 men and teenagers began their rampage.

Heading downtown, the crowd focused their attention on streetcars, where they shot and beat black passengers. By 9:30 P.M., the mob grew to over 3,000 and moved toward the Parish Prison to lynch Lenard Pierce. Rebuffed by police, the group proceeded to the red-light district, concentrating on mostly deserted businesses that featured black or mixed-blood prostitutes. After midnight, the crowd began to diminish, but sporadic beatings and shootings continued throughout the night. The shorthanded and poorly trained New Orleans police force proved incapable—and in some cases, had little desire—to stop the riot. Mayor Paul Capdevielle requested 1,500 citizens to act as special police. In addition, Louisiana's Gov. William Heard sent all area state militia units to the city. Unfortunately, twelve hours passed before troops arrived, allowing more violence against New Orleans' black community. Finally, by sundown on July 26, these forces surrounded the city's most unstable areas.

Meanwhile, Robert Charles remained hidden. Just before noon on July 27, the police learned his whereabouts from a black informer. When a patrol wagon arrived at the residence, Charles hid in a closet. As two officers entered the house, Charles killed one instantly, and the other died slowly of a gunshot wound to the abdomen. As news spread of his discovery, masses of white men and teens swarmed the scene. Charles retreated to the second floor and indiscriminately shot at the gathering crowd. By 5:00 P.M., between 10,000 and 20,000 people congregated on or near the scene. The mayor ordered the state militia units to the site with their two Gatling guns.

Finally, a fire patrol captain set fire to an old mattress near the stairs of the residence. Five minutes later, Charles escaped the inferno. One of the mayor's special police shot and killed him as he fled. A shooting free-for-all then commenced, but before the mob could completely annihilate Charles' body, a patrol wagon retrieved it. Still hungry for vengeance, a crowd gathered outside the morgue, while other bands of whites went in search of more African Americans. Around midnight, another crowd of whites burned down the renowned Lafon Institute, considered the best black school in Louisiana. The next morning, Saturday, July 28, the riot finally subsided. Of the two dozen whites and blacks indicted in the New Orleans race riot, all but one eventually walked free. Charles was buried in an unmarked grave. *See also* Charles, Robert; New Orleans (Louisiana) Riots of 1866.

Further Reading: Hair, William Ivy. *Carnival of Fury: Robert Charles and the New Orleans Race Riot of 1900*. Baton Rouge: Louisiana State University Press, 1976.

Ann V. Collins

Newton, Huey P. (1942–1989)

Dr. Huey Percy Newton is best known for his cofounding, on October 15, 1966, of the **Black Panther Party (BPP)** for Self-Defense. He was an avid activist, intellectual, and political candidate, emphasizing the right to African American self-determinism and the primacy of critical thought.

Newton was born in Monroe, Louisiana, on February 17, 1942, the seventh and youngest child in his family, from Armelia and Walter Newton, a sharecropper and Baptist minister. He was named after Louisiana's Gov. Huey Long. When he was one year old, his family moved to Oakland, California, where he would grow up in poverty and later graduate from Oakland Technical High School functionally illiterate. He later learned how to read using a combination of audio records of Vincent Price narrating poetry and the corresponding written poems to correlate how the words appeared. Soon, Newton found himself attending Merritt College intermittently, ultimately earning an Associate of Arts degree, as well as studying law at Oakland City College and San Francisco Law School. He eventually earned his Ph.D. in 1980 in the History of Consciousness from the University of California at Santa Cruz.

It was largely due to **police brutality** that the Black Panther Party (BPP) was formed. In response to events like the August 11, 1965, harassment of motorist Marquette Frye, his mother, and brother by the LAPD, which sparked what is now known as the Watts riots (see **Los Angeles (California) Riot of 1965**), Newton's philosophy of race and democracy solidified. As race riots spread across the United States in the summers of 1965, 1966, and 1967 (see **Long Hot Summer Riots, 1965–1967**), the BPP mobilized local chapters to politicize the actions as urban rebellions. Grassroots responses included the development of "legal first aid" by Newton—small books that included statutes and constitutional rights that informed readers of their rights when confronted by police. Additionally, Newton developed Panther Patrols—carloads of BPP members that would follow and monitor police behavior, often informing black citizens of their rights. Because of police discrimination and brutality, coupled with the BPP decision to counter this repression, Newton and other BPP members were involved in an October 28, 1967 shootout with the Oakland police whereby he was wounded and subsequently accused of murdering Officer John Frey. While in jail, several of Newton's BPP members were charged with inciting riots during the **Democratic National Convention of 1968**.

A poster sponsored by the Black Panther Party features Huey P. Newton. Courtesy of the Library of Congress.

Few can deny that Newton's life was strewn with incidents of violence. Critics such as Tom Orloff of the *San Francisco Chronicle*, Stanley Crouch, and author Hugh Pearson have labeled Newton a "thug," "criminal," and "hoodlum," respectively (Jeffries 2002). Several tried to frame Newton in such a reductionist manner.

First, his association with both the black nationalist tradition of **Malcolm X** and the Leninist tradition of Marxism reduced him, in the eyes of many, to that of a radical extremist. Second, Newton's affiliation with communism and socialism coded him as a central figure in the McCarthy-era culture of fear. Third, Newton is often perceived as simply an outlaw and criminal due to his committed or provisional support of the civil disobedience and race riots of the 1960s and 1970s.

While the aforementioned vilification of Newton arrests the perception of his complexity, so does an overly simplistic heroification. During a rally for Newton on February 17, 1968, a reporter present at the rally remarked, "It was almost as though Huey P. Newton were already dead....We usually require of those among us who would be immortal that they first cease to breathe and be buried before claiming the exalted status" (Moore, 113). The fervor resulted in a cult-like worship of Newton, on which 1960s activist Donald Cox wrote as follows:

> For some of us, Huey represented the equivalent of the Messiah. Since we didn't want to see any more of our leaders eliminated, we launched a massive campaign to assure that Huey would not be condemned to the death penalty. A cult of his personality was created. Huey was elevated to the status of the gods, and his every word became gospel. (Cox, 121)

Like many activists, Newton was a complex figure. His radical activism prompted both conservatives and liberals alike to paint Newton as either savior or devil, concentrating on his misdeeds or romanticizing his revolutionary rhetoric. Tragically, in the last years of his life, he developed an addiction to crack cocaine and was fatally shot on August 22, 1989, by Tyrone Robinson, a local drug dealer who, ironically, as a child was fed by the Newton-led BPP breakfast program. *See also* Black Nationalism; Black Panther Party (BPP); Cleaver, Eldridge.

Further Readings: Cox, Donald. "A Split in the Party." In Kathleen Cleaver and George Katsiaficas, eds. *Liberation, Imagination, and the Black Panther Party: A New Look at the Panthers and Their Legacy*. New York: Routledge Press, 2001; Jeffries, Judson L. *Huey P. Newton: The Radical Theorist*. Jackson: University Press of Mississippi, 2002; Moore, Gilbert S. *A Special Rage*. New York: Harper and Row, 1971; Newton, Huey P. *Revolutionary Suicide*. New York: Writers and Readers Publishing, 1973 [1995]; Newton, Huey P. *War against the Panthers: A Study of Repression in America*. New York: Harlem River Press, 1996. (Published version of Newton's Ph.D. dissertation, University of California at Santa Cruz, 1980, History of Consciousness.) Newton, Huey P. *To Die for the People*. Edited by Toni Morrison. New York: Writers and Readers Publishing, Inc., 1973 [1999]; Newton, Huey P., and Erik H. Erikson. *In Search of Common Ground*. New York: W.W. Norton & Company, 1973; Newton, Huey P., and Ericka Huggins. *Insights and Poems*. San Francisco: City Lights Books, 1975.

Matthew W. Hughey

New York. *See* Bensonhurst (New York) Incident (1989); Brooklyn (New York) Riot of 1964; Buffalo (New York) Riot of 1967; Harlem (New York) Riot of 1935; Howard Beach (New York) Incident (1986); New York City

Draft Riot of 1863; New York City Riot of 1900; New York City Riot of 1943; New York City Riot of 1964; New York City Silent March of 1917; Peekskill (New York) Riots of 1949; Rochester (New York) Riot of 1964

New York City Draft Riot of 1863

On Monday, July 13, 1863, the city of New York exploded into racial violence. For five days, the black community was ravaged by mob attacks as disgruntled white rioters expressed their outrage about black emancipation, the Civil War, and the mandatory proscription law President Abraham Lincoln had passed several months earlier. Although the first acts of violence were directed toward government agencies, within hours, the rioters focused on black people, neighborhoods, and symbols of black equality. Before the reign of terror subsided, eleven black men had been lynched, countless men, women, and children had been beaten and maimed, black homes and institutions had been torched, thousands of black people had been driven from the city, and the final death toll still remains unknown. Even after federal troops arrived to restore order, attacks persisted and were not fully quelled until the following Friday. In the months that followed, the devastated black community struggled to reclaim their lives and reassert their right to exist in American society as free and equal citizens.

The prelude to the New York City Draft Riot was deeply rooted in the larger context of American politics during the antebellum era. Not only was

Rioters sacking the brownstone houses in New York. Courtesy of the Library of Congress.

riot behavior a common form of political protest in the United States, but these outbursts routinely expressed distinctly anti-black consciousness. There was a particularly disturbing legacy of racial hostility in New York City, which peaked in 1834 with one of the most violent race riots in antebellum America. Racial tensions increased in 1861, when the United States dissolved into civil war over the issue of slavery, and tensions were exacerbated by the passage of the Emancipation Proclamation two years later. As a result, by early 1863, the specter of black emancipation created growing resentment in the North as the war seemingly dragged on interminably. In fact, the Union Army appeared to be in crisis, for lagging support caused soldiers to flee the battlefields (there were an estimated 100,000 deserters), and new recruits were not volunteering to replace them. In the face of such setbacks, the U.S. War Department and President Abraham Lincoln resolved to take drastic action to ensure a successful and rapid Union victory. In March 1863, Congress passed the stringent Conscription Act, which subjected eligible men between the ages of twenty to thirty-five, and all unmarried men aged thirty-five to forty-five, to possible military service. According to the new law, the names of these men would be placed into a lottery and randomly selected to determine who would fight on behalf of the Union. Essentially, the government had effectively imposed a mandatory draft (Bernstein, 7–8).

Although the federal government's actions may have appeared to be a necessary measure to bolster the war effort, there were powerful objections emanating from New York City that posed major challenges to Republican policies. City leaders had expressed consistent opposition to the war; most notably, beginning in 1860, Mayor Fernando Wood established himself as a "Peace Democrat," which meant that he was adamantly opposed to the possibility of war, and fought to make any and all concessions to the South to keep the Union intact. When it became apparent that compromise between the North and South was hopeless, Wood appeared before the common council in 1861. There he argued that the city should secede from the Union and become an entirely independent entity in order to protect its financial interests in the southern economy. Although New York City obviously remained in the Union, Wood did not temper his views during the war; in fact, he adamantly increased his criticism and blasted the Republican Party for waging a war against slavery. As Wood's antiwar rhetoric increased, he rekindled latent frustrations about black emancipation by directing his anger toward the black community, which he blamed for the sectional conflict. In particular, he denounced Radical Republicans for promising "lazy, unfit blacks immediate suffrage, high pay, and social superiority" (Mushkat, 164, 170, 161).

Wood's attitude atoward black inequality, the necessity of southern slavery, and his extreme opposition to the Civil War revealed deep-seated notions in New York City that became ideological specters that inspired and haunted the draft riots. Although Wood was voted out of office in 1862 and replaced by Republican George Opdyke, Democrats in New York City formed a new organization in early 1863—the Society for the Diffusion of Political Knowledge (SDPK)—that was designed to articulate their frustrations and fears about black emancipation. Soon after its establishment, the SDPK blanketed New York City with pamphlets prophesying the horrors that would befall the United States if a Union victory destroyed southern slavery; these noted, in particular, that full emancipation would destroy the social and economic fabric of the nation. More specifically, they argued that free black people would flood into northern cities, take all the jobs, and demand social and political equality (Bernstein, 146–147; Harris, 279–280).

It was into this firestorm of anti-black thought and political agitation against the Civil War that the Conscription Act was thrust in March 1863. Unfortunately, the imposition of the new law served to exacerbate brewing tensions in the city over the war and over black emancipation, since, in light of the draft law's stipulations, the rhetoric of the Democratic Party articulated the concerns of many working-class white New Yorkers. The mandate more severely impacted poor whites and their families who were dependent on them for economic survival, particularly because it was only possible to escape military service if one could afford to hire a replacement or pay $300 to the government. Even worse, it seemed that the law privileged black men, all of whom were exempt from the draft because they were not considered citizens. As a result, the Democratic Party's insistence that Republican politicians spoiled free blacks and ignored the needs of poor whites appeared to be painfully displayed in the conscription law (Bernstein, 8, 11). Of course, what they failed to recognize is that, to the black community, being relegated to the position of not being citizens was hardly a privilege. But such details mattered little to most white New Yorkers. All they knew was that they were being forced to fight in a war to free the black population, a community they already deeply feared and resented.

Ironically, there was no immediate outcry against the draft law from the white working class in New York City, largely because they believed that the Democratic Party would effectively agitate against the mandate and protect them from military service. Initially, it seemed that they were right. The governor, Democrat Horatio Seymour, vowed that he would fulfill the required quota with volunteers, and if enough people did not appear, he would declare the draft to be unconstitutional. In addition, New Yorkers knew that the local democratic-dominated common council was opposed to the legislation, on the grounds that the Republican federal government was overstepping its bounds. Throughout the month of June, Peace Democrats pacified fears in the city by predicting that a Democrat would be elected as president in 1864, a development that might bring an end to the war, and certainly terminate the Conscription Act. Still, city Democrats apparently felt compelled to renew their public objections to the law the following month at a celebration held in honor of Independence Day. During a rally, they denounced Republican policies, which they described as assaults on rights and liberties. In fact, their protest was so vehement that Governor Seymour predicted that if the draft commenced, the city would be plagued by mob violence. Perhaps recognizing that Seymour might be correct about potential hostility, the city's police superintendent urged

Secretary of War Henry Stanton to cancel a parade of the black 55th Regiment through the city streets. Sadly, however, this attempt to prevent an outbreak of racial violence was not sufficient to stem the tide; shortly thereafter, perhaps to the shock of most New Yorkers, President Lincoln authorized Republican officials to conduct the first draft lottery in New York City, and Governor Seymour's prophesy was fulfilled (Bernstein, 11–12).

Indeed, on Saturday, July 11, the first lottery for the mandatory draft was held in New York City. Although violence was not manifest at the draft headquarters during the day, there were definite rumblings of discontent in the city by that evening. Throughout the night, the streets and taverns were bustling with outraged white workers, expressing their discontent with the draft, the Civil War, the free black population, and plotting an appropriate response. As the editor of the *New York Herald* recalled, "Those who heard the scattered groups of laborers and mechanics who congregated in different quarters on Saturday evening ... might have reasonably argued that a tumult was at hand" (Bernstein, 13). Frustration mounted the following day, although city officials obviously remained unconcerned—Mayor Opdyke spent a quiet Sunday evening attending the theater with friends. Yet, while Opdyke enjoyed the luxury of highbrow entertainment, the streets of New York were beginning to show signs of the coming violence. That night, reports began to pour into police stations of dangerous and threatening activity. The first revealed the actions of a man named John Andrews, who was roaming the Tenth Ward delivering inflammatory speeches to large crowds denouncing the draft and defaming the black community. Soon, news arrived that several black men had been attacked and severely beaten, and an anonymous man declared that there would be a black man hanging from every lamppost in the city by the following day. As the night progressed, there were also numerous arson attacks in the heart of a black community on Carmine Street. City officials did little in response, evidently concluding that some mild disorder was to be expected and, with the coming workday, there would be no more substantial violence. They could not have been any more wrong (McCague, 54–56).

The morning of Monday, July 13, 1863 dawned in the city of New York, largely devoid of usual signs of a typical workday. Perhaps to the surprise of city officials, the grumbling among angry workers that had commenced over the weekend developed into an organized work stoppage, as white male citizens made it clear that they would no longer tolerate the imposition of the draft law or the Civil War and its threat of black emancipation. By 8:00 A.M., the streets were flooded with protesters marching through the city carrying signs emblazoned with the words "No Draft!" This, however, would not be a peaceful protest. Men immediately set to work destroying telegraph lines, and women angrily pried up the railway tracks with crowbars. The message was clear and strong—there would be no labor performed until politicians responded to their appeal. As the morning progressed, the mob began randomly attacking police officers, severely beating them in order to ensure that the campaign would not be silenced. Support for the movement increased as the hours passed, growing to over 12,000 people in the crowd (Bernstein, 18; McCague, 62–63).

Despite these early signs of discontent, the draft lottery proceeded at 10:30 A.M. at the Ninth District office. A crowd had already gathered there, prepared to bring the activities to a standstill. Soon, the protest swung into full action, as a pistol shot rang out and the mob descended on the draft headquarters. Rioters smashed the selection wheel, which was designed to draw the names of potential soldiers, and set the building ablaze. For the next several hours, the city was in chaos. Most economic endeavors had been brought to a screeching halt, and the streets were overwhelmed with angry mobs expressing their anger about the war, attacking various government agencies, and looting the buildings they destroyed. By the middle of that day, Republican officials had to admit that the lottery could not persist, and they called for a temporary cessation of their duties (Bernstein, 19–20).

This decision was obviously not enough to quell the mob. By that afternoon, what had begun as a political protest was clearly becoming a full-fledged riot, intent not just on ending the draft, but also intimidating and eliminating the free black population. Although some of the original protesters denounced the growing violence in the streets, the movement continued to escalate, and could no longer be controlled. Among the first black victims that day were a young boy innocently making his way through the city and a male fruit vendor who was beaten and robbed. In acts reminiscent of the protest against efforts to desegregate streetcars in the 1850s, black people were randomly snatched from the conveyances and savagely beaten. In addition, arson attacks reemerged that afternoon as the mob turned their attention to black homes on the West Side, which they looted and torched. One of the most well-remembered and egregious acts that day was the destruction of the Colored Orphan Asylum, which had been erected to house 200 unfortunate, parentless black children. Punctuated by cries of "Burn the niggers!" several thousand white rioters stormed the building and chased the young people out into the streets. The orphanage was methodically robbed, pillaged, and subsequently burned to the ground. Although the mob refrained from harming most of the children, one small girl who had taken refuge under a bed during the melee was dragged out and executed. The remaining children escaped and were taken to the Twentieth Precinct police station (Bernstein, 20–21, 36; Harris, 280; McCague, 77–78; Cook, 77–78).

By Monday evening, the violence directed toward the black population accelerated. Indeed, it was clear by then that the purpose of the riot was "not merely to destroy but to wipe clean the tangible evidence of a black presence" (Bernstein, 27). Innocent men and women trying to make their way home were subject to violent beatings and were chased through the streets of the city. As one scholar described the events, "Black folk in neighborhoods throughout the lower East and West Sides were being hunted like animals" (McCague, 93). Black workers were particularly in danger of assault, as mobs began patrolling the docks, determined to drive black economic competition out of the area. These actions were motivated, in particular, by the fact that black laborers had been brought onto the docks to work as strikebreakers a few months prior (Harris, 280; Bernstein, 27–28).

The rioters burning and sacking the colored orphan asylum. Courtesy of the Library of Congress.

In addition, boardinghouses that catered to the black population were uniquely targeted, as the inhabitants were driven from their homes, stripped of their belongings, and tortured. As a result, when the first full day of rioting came to close, black New Yorkers began to flee the city in large numbers, yet even this effort did not preclude them from attack. Jeremiah Robinson, for example, disguised himself as a woman and tried to take a ferry to Brooklyn with his wife. However, when his true identity was revealed, Robinson was beaten to death, and his lifeless body was thrown into the river. Those who could not manage to escape sought refuge at local police stations, but soon these sites were so overcrowded that many were turned away and sent back into the streets to fight for their lives (Bernstein, 28; Cook, 83). By Monday night, the city's police force was obviously overwhelmed by the size of the mob and had been rendered powerless to terminate the violence. Yet Mayor Opdyke refused to declare martial law and stood by as the carnage increased (Bernstein, 49).

By Tuesday morning, July 14, it was clear that some sort of extreme action would be required to bring an end to the riot, but politicians were slow to enact an appropriate response. Governor Seymour arrived on the scene and toured many wards in the city, but he did not immediately resort to the use of force to end the violence. Instead, he delivered a speech, hoping to appease the crowd with reassurances that he would do all in his power to declare the draft law unconstitutional and protect his citizens from enlistment (Bernstein, 50). However, what he perhaps did not realize is that the riot was no longer just about the issue of the draft; it had become a ferocious, frenzied effort to eliminate the black community.

As a result, as the second day of the riot began, attacks on individual black people and institutions persisted. William Jones, a brave man who had elected not to abandon the city and attempted to sneak out of his home to obtain some food, was the first slain on that day. However, his boldness was severely punished by the mob; they seized him, put a rope around his neck, lynched him, and then set his body ablaze, all the while pelting him with sticks and rocks. The next attack on a black man occurred shortly thereafter as the mob encountered William Williams, a black sailor, who had made the unfortunate mistake of leaving his ship in search of a grocery store. When the mob found him, he was greeted with cries declaring vengeance on every black person in New York, and he was beaten and stabbed. As the day wore on, the crowd turned its attention to symbols of black success in the city, most notably a black church, which they set on fire and cheered as it burned to the ground. Even the elderly were not above attack; a crowd formed at a home for black seniors and tried to break down the fences and raid the building before a group of benevolent whites intervened. Finally, the angry mob headed into the heart of the black community, where they ravaged dance halls, taverns, and tenements that housed and served the black population. Apparently, they even began to develop a sophisticated strategy for identifying the homes belonging to black people; young boys served as scouts and broke the windows in black houses, which allowed the mob to burn, loot, and plunder those residences that were exclusively black property. As the events on Tuesday made it clear that assistance was desperately needed to end the riot, Mayor Opdyke finally asked Secretary of War Henry Stanton to send troops to the city. Stanton complied and ordered five regiments from the Pennsylvania and Maryland battle lines to regain control of New York City (Bernstein, 27–29, 54; McCague, 103, 120–121; Cook, 98).

Despite the impending threat of military force, violence persisted on Wednesday, as rioters unleashed their rage on black men who had the courage to remain and defend their rights. At 6:30 A.M., James Costello became the first black man to fall. Brandishing a weapon, Costello ventured into the streets, an action for which he would pay a heavy price. He was pursued by an angry group of attackers who dodged a retaliatory pistol shot and viciously beat him. They nearly left him for dead, but when Costello stirred and showed signs of life, the men returned, attempted to drown him in a puddle of water, then dragged him to a tree and lynched him. This was not the only **lynching** that would occur that day. Later in the afternoon, a mob broke into the home of a crippled black coachman named Abraham Franklin. After beating his sister in the streets, they dragged Franklin to a lamppost and hanged him. A similar fate nearly befell Charles Jackson who, in light of the day's events, was finally attempting to escape the city. Before he could succeed, however, a mob pounced on him, beat him, stole his possessions, and threw him into the river, hopeful that he would drown from his injuries. Fortunately for Jackson, he managed to cling to a rock and hide under the wharf until police found him (Cook, 140–141, 143; Bernstein, 28).

What is perhaps the most well-documented assault took place on Wednesday. This attack revealed the mob's twisted obsession with the

An angry mob, many carrying clubs, watches as the body of a lynched African American man burns. Courtesy of the Library of Congress.

threat of black equality in the form of racial amalgamation. Rioters descended on the home of William Derrickson, who had married a white woman, Ann, and had a son, Alfred. Led by Democratic politician William Cruise, a crowd raided Derrickson's residence while shouting their intentions to hang him from a lamppost. When they attempted to break down the door, Derrickson dove out the back window and made an escape, confident that the mob would not harm a defenseless woman and child. However, this assumption turned out to be a serious miscalculation, because their mere existence as a biracial family enraged the ravenous horde. Cruise hit young Alfred over the head with an ax, and another in the crowd beat him with a heavy, iron-bound stick of wood. Derrickson's wife tried to save her son by throwing herself over his body, but the mob simply began pummeling her instead. Alfred, who by this time was unconscious, was stripped naked and dragged into the street where his attackers first planned to lynch him, and then decided to burn him alive. Fortunately, a white man intervened and saved his life, although Alfred was left in the gutter covered in blood. Ann never recovered from her injuries and died in the hospital. William Derrickson apparently survived, but one of the rioters reportedly tried to return for him the following day, threatening that if Derrickson was not dead yet, he would come back that night and finish the job (Bernstein, 31, 35; Cook, 135).

Thursday, July 16, brought new hope that the violence against black New Yorkers would eventually cease. Although rioters remained active, most black people had fled the city and there was little else to do beyond looting. More importantly, by the end of the day, the city was occupied by 4,000 federal soldiers who resolved that they would bring an end to the horrific pogrom that had devastated New York. Their efforts were quite effective. Soon, the city began to demonstrate the signs of resuming normal life: businesses opened and white people returned to their jobs. Yet all indications sent a clear message that black people would still not be safe if they showed their faces in the streets. The children from the Colored Orphan Asylum, who had been hiding out with the police, were evacuated and relocated to Blackwell Island. In addition, city officials made it plain that black people should not yet return; in one case, when four black women asked if their families could go home, the response from the police was unequivocally, "No." Fortunately, by Saturday, July 18, there were 10,000 troops stationed in New York City, determined to impose order and maintain the peace (Cook, 157, 166; McCague, 163). The New York City Draft Riot of 1863 was finally over, but the work of rebuilding the black community had only just begun.

In some ways, the immediate aftermath was almost as distressing for black New Yorkers as the actual events. Although some people trickled back into the city, many refused; in fact, the census of 1865 revealed that the black population had plummeted to its lowest point since 1820—less than 10,000. Indeed, nearly 20 percent of black people who had lived in New York City in 1860 absconded, never to return (Bernstein, 267; Harris, 285). Among the most famous refugees was black activist Albro Lyons, who was well known in his community for diligent work on behalf of fugitives from southern slavery. In fact, during most of the 1850s, the Lyons family operated in defiance of the Fugitive Slave Law and, due to their diligent labor, saved numerous fugitives from the horrors of slavery. However, in the midst of the draft riots, Lyons took his family across the river into Brooklyn and vowed never to return. As one scholar explained, "From the moment they put foot on the boat, that was the last time they ever resided in New York City, leaving it forever" (Harris, 238, 286).

Sadly, however, the decline in population was the least of the black community's problems, because those who returned were faced with the tireless and agonizing work of re-creating their lives. In the months that followed, as black New Yorkers tried to resume their lives, they found that the racial hostility that had prompted the riot persisted. Most black men struggled to find employers who were willing to hire them, and streetcar operators regularly refused admittance to black passengers. Even worse was the painful fact that city and state officials stubbornly refused to offer any substantial public assistance to ease their plight. Although the city had formed a Riots Claim Committee, most applications were dismissed. Since black people had voluntarily abandoned their homes, the city argued that it was not obligated to provide restitution for damage or destruction of property. Even those claims that were entertained offered little compensation because payment was for what the belongings were worth at the time of loss, not the price it would cost to replace them. Since most black people were extremely impoverished at the outset of the riot, most of their possessions were deemed to have little or no value. Adding insult to injury were the committee's nasty retorts that asserted that many black people were simply trying to "cheat the county" by submitting false claims (Cook, 174–176).

Perhaps the most disturbing symbolic demonstration of city officials' indifference came when the black community realized that most rioters, even those arrested, would escape tangible punishment. Of the estimated 12,000 people who engaged in the riot, only 443 were arrested, and more than half of these had their cases dismissed before charges were even leveled against them. Only eighty-one men had a day in court, and most pled guilty to lesser charges and escaped with minor penalties. Ironically, the most severe punishments were enacted on those who had been caught looting; in the end, the men responsible for the beatings, tortures, and lynching of black people essentially emerged with no meaningful repercussions. All of these events nearly caused black New Yorkers to lose all hope, as evidenced by a black clergyman who stated that his only hope for the future of his race was in "the next world" (Cook, 177–178).

There was, however, one redeeming movement among white New Yorkers following the draft riots, which gave black New Yorkers renewed faith that their passion for justice and equality would one day be realized. Days after the conclusion of the riot, a benevolent organization, the Union League Club (ULC), devoted its energies to providing assistance to black survivors. Members of this association had been staunchly opposed to the riot and had pleaded with Mayor Opdyke to bring in federal troops to end the violence. Conscious that city officials were failing to make proper restitution, the ULC raised funds, eventually over $40,000, and employed a well-respected black leader, Rev. Henry Highland Garnet, to help blacks process claims (Bernstein, 56, 157, 159). It was later reported that, under Garnet's careful guidance, financial aid was doled out to more than 6,300 people. Members of the black leadership, including Garnet and Rev. Charles B. Ray, praised the ULC for its unceasing labor on behalf of the black population, stating, "Gentleman, this generation of our people cannot forget the scenes to which we allude, nor will they forget the noble and spontaneous exhibition of charity which they excited. The former will be referred to as one of the dark chapters of our history in the Empire State, and the latter will be remembered as a bright and glorious page in the records of the past" (Garnet, 60).

Perhaps most poignantly, black New Yorkers' resolve was revealed in December 1863, just five months after American citizens had ravaged their people. At the urging of the ULC, War Secretary Henry Stanton gave permission for a black regiment to be raised among New Yorkers to fight against southern slavery. Even after the frightening outbreak of violence, the black community still flaunted its support for the United States and the war they prayed would free their people, and commenced a movement to take up arms on behalf of the Union. The crowning glory of their efforts came on March 5, 1864, when an estimated 100,000 New Yorkers of all races poured into the streets to watch the 20th U.S. Colored Infantry march into battle on a mission to bring the Confederacy to its knees. The irony of this occasion was not lost on black New Yorkers; indeed, less than a year after the destructive pogrom, black activist James McCune Smith noted with pride that black Union soldiers were celebrated in the same streets where some of their people had been ravenously hunted by angry hordes:

> To have been mobbed, hunted down, beaten to death, hung to the lamp-posts or trees, burned, their dwellings sacked and destroyed, their orphan children turned homeless from their comfortable shelter which was destroyed by fire, and then, within a few months to be cheered along the same streets, are occurrences whose happening put ordinary miracles in the shade; the first, more hideous than hell, the last one which might be, and was, smiled on by heaven. (Garnet, 56–58)

For Smith, and likely other black New Yorkers, such triumphant moments signaled that all hope was not lost, that victory could still follow devastating assaults, and perhaps someday black people might be extended the rights of equality and citizenship. In August 1863, the draft quietly, and unceremoniously recommenced, but the black community was forever altered.

Further Readings: Bernstein, Iver. *The New York City Draft Riots: Their Significance for American Society and Politics in the Age of the Civil War*. New York: Oxford University Press, 1990; Cook, Adrian. *The Armies of the Streets: The New York City Draft Riots of 1863*. Lexington: University Press of Kentucky, 1974; Garnet, Henry Highland. *A Memorial Discourse Delivered in the Hall of the House of Representatives, Washington City, D.C., on Sabbath, February 12, 1865. With an Introduction by James McCune Smith, M.D.* Philadelphia: J.M. Wilson, 1865; Harris, Leslie Maria. *In the Shadow of Slavery: African Americans in New York City, 1626–1863*. Chicago and London: University of Chicago Press, 2003; McCague, James. *The Second Rebellion: The Story of the New York City Draft Riots of 1863*. New York: Dial Press, 1968; Mushkat, Jerome. *Fernando Wood: A Political Biography*. Kent, OH: Kent State University Press, 1990.

Leslie M. Alexander

New York City Riot of 1900

The Tenderloin section of Manhattan experienced a short but intense race riot on August 15–16, 1900. The violence began two days after Arthur Harris, an African American laborer, stabbed Robert Thorpe, a white policeman who died shortly afterward from his wounds. Although accounts regarding who precipitated the subsequent episode differ, an interracial scuffle broke out near Thorpe's home on the evening of August 15, causing a gathering white crowd to rampage the nearby black district for several hours. Widespread reports of police negligence of, or outright participation in, the riot filled newspaper accounts in the following days. African Americans bore the brunt of the punishment in the wake of the violence.

The New York City Riot of 1900 featured many of the characteristics that other riots during this time period displayed. The city witnessed a sharp increase of African Americans from 1890 to 1910, swelling its black population almost four times. **Segregation** and discrimination, already existent to a certain degree, had solidified by the turn of the century. With the influx of newcomers, whites thwarted African American efforts to frequent the same churches, theaters, restaurants, saloons, and hotels. Moreover, the Tenderloin region on the west side of the city, where the riot occurred, not only accommodated New York's red-light district and Black Bohemia, but also harbored especially harsh animosities between its black residents and their Irish neighbors. Finally, at the time of the riot, New York City was suffering through one of the worst heat waves in its history.

Like many of his southern counterparts, Arthur Harris migrated north to the New York area from Virginia at the turn of the century to look for work. He held a variety of jobs and met May Enoch, who became his live-in girlfriend and whom he commonly called his wife. On the evening of August 12, 1900, Harris went out to a nearby saloon. Around 2:00 A.M., Enoch went to get him. After Harris left the establishment, he saw a white man grabbing his girlfriend. Not realizing that the man, Robert Thorpe, was a plainclothes policeman charging Enoch with soliciting, Harris fought with him and stabbed him twice with his knife. Enoch fled home and Harris escaped to his mother's house in Washington, D.C. Thorpe died the next day.

In the Tenderloin's racial milieu at the turn of the century, the death of a white policeman at the hands of an African American soon triggered violence. Crowds began to rally outside Thorpe's house, which led to an altercation between a black man and a white police officer. This incident spurred the ensuing riot. News reports the next day depicted the exploding violence as hundreds of white men and women surging from nearby tenements in search of black victims. Throughout the district, in and out of businesses, and on streetcars, the **white mob** attacked unsuspecting African Americans. One person strung a clothesline to a lamppost and sought out someone to lynch. Although the exact number of casualties remains uncertain, a number of black citizens suffered severe beatings and had to be treated at three area hospitals.

Some eighty African Americans later submitted affidavits affirming not only citizen attacks against them, but police complicity in the riot as well. Numerous victims and witnesses attested that when the acting police captain called out the reserves to suppress the violence, many of the authorities instead goaded the mob or simply ignored the brutalities occurring in front of them. The riot itself ended around 2:00 A.M. on August 16, when a thunderstorm struck the city, dispersing the crowd. However, the atmosphere remained charged. In the following month, brawls between blacks and whites broke out periodically, and two people died. Black residents began to stock up on arms and ammunition, and numerous concealed weapons charges followed.

In the wake of the riot, both black and white leaders condemned the unrest and cast blame in numerous directions. Republicans and the Good Government Society politicized the racial violence and traced the **police brutality** to Tammany Hall. Black religious leaders focused their attention on both the white hordes and the police. A citizens' protective league formed to bring suits against the city on behalf of the victims beaten by authorities. No policemen were ever indicted, however. Arthur Harris was detained in Washington, D.C., and was found guilty of murder in the second degree at his trial in New York. He died on December 20, 1908, in the State Prison at Sing Sing after serving eight years of hard labor. *See also* New York City Riot of 1943; New York City Riot of 1964;; New York City Silent March of 1917.

Further Reading: Osofsky, Gilbert. "Race Riot, 1900: A Study of Ethnic Violence." *The Journal of Negro Education* 32 (1963): 16–24.

Ann V. Collins

New York City Riot of 1943

On August 1, 1943, a New York City police officer arrested an African American woman for disturbing the peace at the Braddock Hotel in Harlem. Robert Brady, a black soldier in the U.S. military, observed the fracas. He intervened by trying to get the police officer to release the woman. In the ensuing scuffle, the police officer was allegedly hit by the soldier. The police officer retaliated by shooting the soldier in the arm as he attempted to run from the scene. In the process of taking the serviceman away to a nearby hospital, a crowd of nearly 3,000 began to gather. It picked up momentum and fervor as the two, police officer and soldier, moved toward the hospital. Someone in the crowd shouted that a white cop had shot and killed a black soldier. It was not true, but the rumor ignited the crowd. Emotions escalated to mob proportion. The result was a full-fledged riot. The mostly black rioters set fires, broke windows and doors, turned over vehicles, and otherwise wreaked a wave of destruction, mainly against property. This led to looting. Most of the residents of Harlem at the time were black, while most of the businesses were under Jewish or white ownership. Black and white law enforcement officers moved in to restore order, but not before the rioters were beaten and bludgeoned.

Writer James Baldwin provided a firsthand account of the riot in an August 9, 1943, article in *Newsweek*. He wrote, "Windows of pawnshops and liquor stores and grocery stores were smashed and looted. Negroes began wielding knives and the police, their guns. Thousands of police reserves, many of them Negroes, were rushed to the district.... All traffic was rerouted around Harlem. It came down chiefly [to] a battle between the police and the Negro looters." **Walter White**, the head of the **National Association for the Advancement of Colored People (NAACP)**, wrote in the *New York Times* on August 4, 1943, that Harlem boiled over. His article described the extent of the damage and great loss as a consequence of the riot.

The Negro press and especially the New York-based *Amsterdam News* published a detailed description of the riot; the details spread thoughout the country. After all, the Harlem Renaissance had established Harlem as the cultural center of black Americans. It was also perceived by many as the political center of all black Americans. The mayor at the time was Fiorello LaGuardia. He took swift action to end the riot. He appealed over the radio for calm. Afterward, he sent food to the residents of Harlem. This gesture endeared the mayor to many in the African American community.

Depending on the source, 6 African Americans were killed, from 500 to 1,000 were arrested, and 40 law enforcement officers were injured. It took 6,600 city, military, and civil police officers; 8,000 state guardsmen; and 1,500 civilian volunteers to finally end the riot after nearly two days.

After it was all over, there was much speculation about the causes of the riot. Some advanced the notion that the riot occurred because there were no recreational facilities and parks for the residents of Harlem. Others said the reason was the high cost of food and price gouging by the merchants who owned stores, shops, and other businesses in Harlem. Still another reason given was the need for better housing. **Police brutality** and overall discrimination of Harlem's black population were also cited as reasons.

Those who have studied race riots have found that there are certain sociological and psychological commonalities among race riots. A rumor is one and an environment of mob violence is another. Accepting that observation, the New York City Riot of 1943, which is sometimes called the Harlem Riot of 1943, had these two key elements. According to others, it happened not only as a violent spontaneous response to a specific incident and rumor, but it was also a reaction to **racism**, poverty, **segregation**, and other related socioeconomic factors.

By 1920, Harlem had become predominantly black. The residents were blacks from the West Indies and other states in the United States, especially Virginia, North Carolina, South Carolina, and Georgia. As blacks arrived, whites fled. During the 1920s, 118,792 white people left Harlem, while 87,417 blacks replaced them there. Unrest in numerous towns and cities around the country was erupting. Some of these disorders, including the events in **Detroit** in 1943, rose to the level of a race riot. In 1944, the year after the Harlem Riot, there were 250 race riots in 47 cities and towns in the United States. **Lynchings**, mostly in the South, were common. Blacks who served in World War II were stationed around the city, visited the city, or were moving there after returning home from the war. Many of those seeking a better life encountered segregation and other barriers to their successful attainment of the American Dream in Harlem. Although life for some blacks in Harlem at the time was vibrant, colorful, and intellectually stimulating, this was not the case for other blacks who were struggling. Even though it was the home of such luminaries as Langston Hughes, Countee Cullen, Zora Neale Hurston, **Claude McKay**, Congressman Adam Clayton Powell, Jr., **A. Phillip Randolph**, **James Weldon Johnson**, and a host of others, as well as the home of such established institutions as Small's Paradise, the Cotton Club, the Savoy Ballroom, the Apollo Theater, and the Abyssinian Baptist Church, prosperity existed parallel to poverty in Harlem. The residents of Harlem were ready for a change in the social order regardless of their station in life; the riot of 1943 was a sign of pent-up frustration. It only took a single incident to spark the riot.

Perhaps James Baldwin expressed the seething, underlying frustration best when he reflected on the riot years later by writing, "It would have been better to have left the plate glass as it had been and the goods lying in the store. Would have been better, but it would have also . . . been intolerable, for Harlem needed something to smash" (Baldwin 1943).

The Harlem Riot of 1943 has become an important part of history. It was an aftershock of the Harlem Riot of 1935, and a forerunner of the **New York City Riot of 1964**. All pioneered the way for the **civil rights movement** that swept the country in the 1950s and 1960s.

Further Readings: Baldwin, James. "Harlem Hoodlums." *Newsweek*, August 9, 1943; Brandt, Nat. *Harlem at War: The Black Experience in World War II*. Syracuse, NY: Syracuse University Press, 1996; Capeci, Dominic. *Harlem Riot of 1943*. Philadelphia: Temple University Press, 1977; Ellison, Ralph. *Invisible Man*. New York: The Modern Library, 1994. Originally published in 1952; Powell, Richard. *Homecoming: The Art and Life of William H. Johnson*. New York: Rizzoli International Publications, 1991; Tate, Gayle. "The Harlem Riots of 1935 and 1943." In *Encyclopedia of African American Culture and History*. New York: Macmillan Publishing Company, 1996.

Betty Nyangoni

New York City Riot of 1964

The New York City Riot of 1964 began in Harlem on the night of July 18. The unrest would later spread to the Bedford-Stuyvesant community in Brooklyn on July 20. Four thousand people in Harlem and another 4,000 in Brooklyn took part in the six-day protest. During the riot, 1 person was killed, 118 people were injured, and 465 men and women were arrested. The riot inaugurated an era of urban unrest that would continue throughout the decade. More people were arrested during the course of events in Bedford-Stuyvesant, but both the riot's symbolic precursors as well as the event that sparked the unrest in 1964 can be traced to Harlem.

Symbolically, the riots of the 1960s marked a change in the demographics of the rioting mob. Before Harlem, mob scenes involved whites attempting to keep blacks from joining American society; afterward, they became the symbol of blacks fighting for their right to be let in. Even though the majority of the pre-1960s race riots were started by whites, in Harlem there had been echoes of 1960s-style racial unrest before—once in 1935 and again in 1942, both times under allegations of police misconduct.

The 1964 riot began under similar circumstances. On the morning of July 16, Police Lt. Thomas G. Gilligan killed fifteen-year-old James Powell, a summer school student at Robert F. Wagner Junior High School. In a turn toward the poetic, Powell and his friends were engaged in horseplay with a building superintendent named Patrick Lynch outside 215 East Seventy-Sixth Street. Witnesses alleged that Lynch sprayed the boys with his garden hose and they chased him into a building. Powell attempted to follow Lynch, but Gilligan intervened, firing two shots, the second fatal. Gilligan claimed that Powell lunged at him with a knife. Later, a grand jury would conclude that Gilligan was not criminally liable for the homicide.

The northern and southern struggles for civil rights are often seen as taking place on different registers, but the Harlem Riot demonstrates their connections. Members of the activist organization the **Congress of Racial Equality (CORE)** planned a rally at 125th Street and Seventh Avenue on July 18. Initially, the rally was planned to protest the disappearance of three

Mississippi civil rights workers. After Powell was slain, the group shifted the focus of the rally to the issue of **police brutality**, a long-standing issue of concern for CORE. After the rally, at which particularly noteworthy remarks were offered by seventeen-year-old Bronx high school student Judith Howell, the 250 attendees moved to the Twenty-Eighth Police Precinct. There, the Rev. Nelson Dukes of the Fountain Springs Baptist Church, Charles Russell of CORE, as well as Charles Taylor and Newton Sewell (identified by police simply as "black nationalists") entered the building and demanded that Gilligan be suspended. According to accounts, after this group learned that the matter was under investigation, they left the building.

The crowd that had gathered outside, however, was not so easily appeased. On July 19, 1964, the *New York Times* reported that "thousands of rioting Negroes raced through the center of Harlem last night." Members of the crowd pulled fire alarms and broke store windows. Those arrested faced charges of burglary, felonious assault, resisting arrest, and inciting a riot. Police fired shots into the air to contain the crowds. Five hundred policemen, including the tactical patrol force, of which all members were trained in judo, under age thirty, and over six feet tall, were called into Harlem. The police closed off 125th Street between Third and Eighth Avenues, stood shoulder to shoulder at barricades, and still the unrest was not contained.

Chaos at night and order during the day would mark the six days of unrest. As the protests went on, many Harlem and Bedford-Stuyvesant residents who abstained from the protest resented the implication that everyone who lived in these neighborhoods was involved in the fray, a complaint given credence by the fact that Commissioner Michael Murphy pled for restraint from the pulpit of all Harlem churches the Sunday after the riots began. Black New York City residents would suffer further indignities during official pleas for peace. Mayor Robert Wagner, on his return from a European vacation, proclaimed, "Law and order are the colored citizen's best freedom" ("1964"), a galling statement, considering the roots of the disturbance.

After the riot ended, many weighed in on its cause. There was a racial divide among lay explanations for the riot. Whites saw it as a result of outside agitation—agitation that could be linked to individuals. Those who supported this theory were vindicated when Willie Epton, a member of Progressive Labor, an organization formed after the breakup of Communist Party USA, was charged with criminal anarchy, a crime for which he served one year in prison. On the other side of the racial divide, blacks cited social and economic conditions as the cause of the riot.

Racial division was also cited by elite opinion. Then Undersecretary of Labor **Daniel Patrick Moynihan** recommended a strategy of "benign neglect" in avoiding future riots, suggesting that blacks had been promised more than whites could give them. Riots, then, were a symbol of black frustration. **Martin Luther King, Jr.**, would recognize the logic of these rebellions and attribute them to official misconduct and economic conditions affecting black urban dwellers. Analysts have stressed the logic of this kind of black protest, suggesting that people resort to such acts when other political avenues are closed. Efforts have been made to place such rebellions within the context of American history. Violence, it is claimed—particularly violence across ethnic groups—is part of the American political landscape.

Riots would indeed mark the landscape for the next few years. Riots would break out that summer in **Rochester** (July 24–25), New York; nearby **Jersey City** (August 2–4), Patterson, and Elizabeth (both August 11–13), New Jersey; **Philadelphia** (August 28–30), Pennsylvania; and throughout the country in 1965. The New York City riot occurred less than two weeks after the passage of the **Civil Rights Act of 1964** and the infamous Watts riot (see **Los Angeles [California] Riot of 1965**) erupted the day after Congress passed the Voting Rights Act of 1965. These uprisings are often thought to be the cause of the loss of moderate white support for the cause of civil rights. The riots are held as a symbol of the eclipse of King's message and the goals of racial civility in the South. Afterward, the civil rights focus would shift to incorporate economic justice in post-migration urban centers. *See also* Brown, H. Rap.

Further Readings: Feagin, Joe, and W.P. Sheatsley. "Ghetto Resident Appraisals of a Riot." *Public Opinion Quarterly*, 32 (1968): 352–362; Harris, Darryl B. *The Logic of Black Urban Rebellions: Challenging the Dynamics of White Domination in Miami*. Westport, CT: Praeger, 1999; "1964—Brooklyn Erupts as Harlem Lulls." *Washington Afro American*, July 25, 1964; Upton, James N. "The Politics of Urban Violence: Critiques and Proposals." *Journal of Black Studies* 15 (1985): 243–258.

Shatema A. Threadcraft

New York City Silent March of 1917

On July 28, 1917, the **National Association for the Advancement of Colored People (NAACP)** staged a silent march in New York City to protest the **East St. Louis (Illinois) Riot** that took place earlier that month. The march was not only a condemnation of the riot that claimed the lives of thirty-five African Americans, but a statement of black America's frustration with the wave of racial violence that had saturated the nation since the late nineteenth century.

Beginning with the race riots that swept the South in Tennessee, Louisiana, and Mississippi during **Reconstruction** (1865–1877), racial violence characterized the nadir in the African American experience (see **Black Nadir**). Racially motivated **lynching** reached an all-time high in the late 1890s, and many blacks hoped the turn of the century would portend a reversal of fortune for blacks. However, early-twentieth-century black migration to northern and midwestern cities proved agitating to predominantly white populated urban centers.

Perceived as threats to the social, sexual, political, moral, and labor order, African Americans served as convenient scapegoats for white angst. Under the guise of protecting white womanhood and eliminating black criminality, **white mobs** used the arrest of any black male suspect as justification for storming jails, kidnapping and lynching the accused, assaulting innocent blacks, and burning down black neighborhoods and business districts.

Within the first decade of the twentieth century, race riots seized **New York City** (1900); **New Orleans** (1900); **Springfield**, Ohio (1904 and 1906); **Atlanta** (1906); and **Springfield**, Illinois (1908).

Continued black migration northward during the World War I era (known as the **Great Migration**) exacerbated white paranoia about ever-growing black urban populations. The context of that migration was particularly significant, as many blacks moved to industrial towns to take advantage of job opportunities created by the War Industries Board. Additionally, when the United States entered the Great War (World War I) in 1917, industrial jobs left vacant by white doughboys were filled by black laborers. Because the War Industries Board had the power to mobilize the workforce and settle manager-labor disputes, labor unrest underscored the period. The government shunned strikes as a means to redress labor exploitation and low wages, arguing that wartime demanded the full cooperation of citizens in increasing production. Nonetheless, job tensions exacerbated racial tensions resulting in race riots in cities like East St. Louis, Illinois.

After news of the East St. Louis riot reached black communities nationwide, outraged black newspapers condemned the riot as a massacre. In response, the NAACP sent **W.E.B. Du Bois** and Martha Gruening to investigate the riot and compile a report. Their twenty-four-page "Massacre at East St. Louis" implicated not only the police force and white citizenry, but national guardsmen as well, in allowing blacks to fall victim to mob violence. The NAACP decided to take a visible public stand by organizing a march down Fifth Avenue, a major thoroughfare in New York City. Well-dressed black men and women wearing white shirts and long white skirts, suits, and hats marched down the avenue in total silence. Their sentiments were expressed on picket signs that condemned lynching and race riots as un-American. The black onlookers were also silent as the only sound heard came from a drum.

The NAACP had its origins in a meeting convened, in part, to address the 1908 Springfield, Illinois, riot. Predominantly a white organization in terms of leadership and financial patronage, the NAACP declared itself to be a champion of racial justice. High-profile blacks such as Du Bois, **Ida B. Wells-Barnett** (spearhead of the anti-lynching movement), and **Mary Church Terrell** (founder of the **National Association of Colored Women [NACW]**), helped found the organization. Although the NAACP focused on securing political and civil rights for African Americans, its members did not shy away from addressing racial violence perpetrated against blacks. The demonstration on Fifth Avenue continued a tradition of NAACP and black public protest against racial injustice. *See also* Police Brutality; Segregation.

Further Readings: Brown, Cliff. "The Role of Employers in Split Labor Markets: An Event-Structure Analysis of Racial Conflict and AFL Organizing, 1917–1919." *Social Forces* 79 (2000): 653–681; Ellis, Mark. "'Closing Ranks' and 'Seeking Honors': W.E.B. Du Bois in World War I." *Journal of American History* 79 (1992): 96–124; Jordan, William. "'The Damnable Dilemma': African American Accommodation and Protest During World War I." *Journal of American History* 81 (1995): 1562–1583; Marks, Carole. *Farewell—We're Good and Gone: The Great Black Migration*. Bloomington: Indiana University Press, 1989; Meier, August, and John H. Bracey, Jr.

"The NAACP as a Reform Movement, 1909–1966: 'To Reach the Conscience of America.'" *The Journal of Southern History* 59 (1993): 3–30; Rudwick, Elliot M. *Race Riot at East St. Louis, July 2, 1917*. Cleveland: World Publishing, 1966; Trotter, Joe William, and Earl Lewis, eds. *African Americans in the Industrial Age: A Documentary History, 1915–1945*. Boston: Northeastern University Press, 1985.

Jeannette Eileen Jones

Niagara Movement

Founded in 1905, the Niagara movement, forerunner of the **National Association for the Advancement of Colored People (NAACP)**, changed how African Americans responded to racial inequality during the 1900s. Despite attempts by African Americans to assimilate passively into American culture, whites increasingly used intimidation, legal barriers, and **lynching** to reverse gains won by blacks during Reconstruction. Angered by the increase in lynching of blacks, and disgruntled by the accommodation policies of the Atlanta Compromise, **W.E.B. Du Bois** met with newspaperman **Monroe Trotter** and other prominent African Americans to draft resolutions for the Niagara movement in February 1905. The resolutions called for equal suffrage, civil liberty, and access to free education, decent housing, and economic opportunity.

After Reconstruction, the federal government slowly turned from policies promoting equality for African Americans. A series of court cases—*Reese v. the United States* and *Plessy v. Ferguson*—proved detrimental to African American status. In the early 1900s, there were two schools of thought in the African American community. Statesman **Booker T. Washington** urged blacks not to defy whites and to seek equality through hard work and gradual acceptance. On September 18, 1895, Washington gave his famous "Atlanta Compromise" speech at the **Cotton States and International Exposition** in Atlanta, Georgia. In the speech, Washington urged African Americans to refrain from agitation. According to Washington, work, patience, and passivity would lead to economic and social acceptance from white Americans.

Although many African Americans followed Washington's doctrine, many felt that hard work and persistence did little to advance equality. Washington's policies faltered under white-imposed literacy tests, intimidation, and lynching. Ultimately, lynching proved to be the catalyst leading to the downfall of accommodation policies by African Americans. Determined to maintain superiority over blacks, whites used the law and physical violence to deny African Americans social and political equality. In the late 1800s, even law-abiding African Americans became targets of lynch mobs. The failure of whites to acknowledge attempts by blacks to peacefully assimilate into American society caused people to criticize of Washington.

Two of Washington's most vocal critics were Monroe Trotter and W.E.B. Du Bois. Trotter, a newspaperman, attended meetings and openly heckled Washington. Du Bois lauded Washington's efforts to empower blacks, but questioned his passivity. Both Trotter and Du Bois believed that repeated agitation, not **accommodationism**, offered the best route toward equality for African Americans. An accomplished intellectual and scholar, Du Bois communicated extensively through writing. During the ten years between the "Atlanta Compromise" speech and the formation of the Niagara movement, Du Bois became increasingly radical, using his poetry to incite African Americans to fight for equality. Disgusted with lack of political progress and upward social mobility, in 1903, Du Bois openly criticized the accommodation policies of Washington. His *Souls of Black Folk*, a collection of poetry, celebrates African American culture while denouncing lynching and divisive social practices.

Increasing racial unrest, economic disparity, and social inequality caused more African Americans to renounce Washington's passive stance. On July 11, 1905, at the Canadian side of Niagara Falls, the founders of the Niagara movement met to establish the Declaration of Principles for the Niagara movement. The Declaration of Principles set standards for governing the organization and addressing concerns. The introduction congratulates African American attempts to assimilate into American society. Next, the declaration demands certain rights for all men: suffrage, civil liberty, education, and decent housing. In addition to these rights, African Americans acknowledged the duty to vote, obey laws, work, remain clean, educate, and respect themselves and others. The Niagara movement sought equality for all men.

Initially, the movement excluded women. The only woman invited into the 1905 meeting was white social activist Mary White Ovington, a friend of Du Bois. The leading crusader against lynching, **Ida B. Wells-Barnett**, was denied admittance into the founding meeting. At Du Bois' insistence, the Massachusetts Niagara Women's Auxiliary was established until women were formally admitted into the convention the following year.

Sadly, the Niagara movement lasted only a few years. By 1908, the movement was fading. Du Bois' failure to include the masses of African Americans, limited financing, and his lofty intellectual ideals alienated many Americans. Infighting caused further animosity in the organization. Monroe Trotter maintained a distrust of the wealthy Ovington and other whites. Ultimately, Trotter presented the organization with a revised plan for the movement. When Du Bois refused to give in to Trotter's objections over the role of members, Trotter left and the rift never healed. To make matters worse, it is rumored that Booker T. Washington paid newspapers not to report on the movement, tipped off whites to meeting places, and encouraged organizational disruption.

Despite shortcomings, the Niagara movement united blacks in America and established a vehicle for protest. Although there were few legal victories, it was the first twentieth-century movement championing unrest to challenge racial inequality by blacks. The movement encouraged others. Empowered by the writings and actions of Du Bois, Robert Abbott founded the ***Chicago Defender***, a leading newspaper in the African American community. Founded after the collapse of the Niagara movement, the NAACP effectively won several important legal civil rights decisions during the 1900s. *See also* Accommodationism; Lynching; Segregation.

Further Readings: Bloom, Harold. *Modern Critical Views: W.E.B. Du Bois*. Philadelphia: Chelsea House, 2001; Du Bois, W.E.B. *Souls of Black Folk*. New York:

Signet, 1982; Estell, Kenneth. *African-America: Portrait of a People*. Detroit: Visible Ink Press, 1998–1999; Rhym, Darren. *The NAACP: 2002–2003*. Philadelphia: Chelsea House Publishers, 2003.

Janice E. Fowler

Nonviolence

Nonviolence is a set of moral beliefs and practices that rejects the use of force in the fight for social justice and human or political rights. Although some of the ideas behind the concept date back to the time of Jesus, it is largely associated with Mahatma Gandhi, who used it in his struggle to gain India's independence from Great Britain. In the African American struggle for social justice and civil rights in the 1950s and 1960s, **Martin Luther King, Jr.**, is the emblematic figure of nonviolent resistance.

Mohandas Karamchand Gandhi was influenced by the teachings of Jesus Christ, the Hindu principles of *ahimsa* and *satyagraha*, and the writings of Henry David Thoreau, John Ruskin, and Leo Tolstoy, among others. Thoreau's civil disobedience consisted mainly of writing against injustice, notably in his 1849 essay, "Resistance to Civil Government" (posthumously known as "Civil Disobedience"). Thoreau refused to pay the poll tax because the U.S. government sanctioned the holding of African slaves and was involved in other unjust causes, such as the Mexican-American War. Although he did not stage any movement of civil disobedience, his thoughts influenced both Gandhi and Martin Luther King, Jr.

As for Tolstoy's influence, Gandhi embraced his strong belief in pacifism, nonviolent resistance, love, and kindness to humanity. Both Tolstoy and Gandhi incorporated Christian ideals as spelled out in the "Sermon on the Mount," which praises humility, poverty, abnegation, and love. Tolstoy and Gandhi also employed Jesus Christ's teaching of love for one's enemy and rejection of the "eye for an eye" doctrine. In the celebrated film *Gandhi* (1982, dir. Richard Attenborough), Gandhi is heard saying, "an eye for eye only ends up making the whole world blind."

Also admired by Leo Tolstoy, John Ruskin was Gandhi's greatest influence, as the Mahatma (meaning "Great Soul") himself acknowledged. Ruskin's *Unto This Last* (1860), a book of essays on economy, motivated Gandhi to start nonviolent resistance. Gandhi was touched by Ruskin's rejection of luxury; as a result, he used his family's wealth to help liberate the oppressed. Ruskin's ideas particularly shaped Gandhi's economic and social philosophy called *Sarvodaya* or "well-being of all."

Of paramount importance in the shaping of Gandhi's philosophy of nonviolence are *ahimsa* and *satyagraha*. A religious ideal in Hinduism, Jainism, and Buddhism, the Sanskrit word *ahimsa* means refraining from killing or harming (i.e., nonviolence). *Satyagraha*, also a Sanskrit word, means "holding firmly onto truth" or soul force; the practice of nonviolent resistance involves civil disobedience and noncooperation, but also respect and love for the opponent. Gandhi effectively used it to gain rights for Indian workers in South Africa and to end British rule in India. *Satyagraha* entails *satya* (truth), *ahimsa* (nonviolence), and *tapasya* (readiness for self-sacrifice). The practice of *satyagraha* strives for love for all humanity and demands patience, readiness to be humiliated, acceptance of one's suffering as a means of changing the opponent, and fasting. Far from being passive resistance, nonviolent resistance involves active strategies such as sit-ins, marches, boycotts, peaceful demonstration, workplace occupation, vigils, hunger strikes, and petitions.

The **civil rights movement** in the United States largely followed the principles of nonviolence generally associated with Martin Luther King, Jr., in the struggle to end racial discrimination and social injustice against African Americans. As King argued in his "Letter from Birmingham Jail," he and his followers knew that people who oppress others, in this case the white supremacists in the south, never relinquish power of their own volition. Southern violence against African Americans had to be forcefully exposed to the rest of the country and the world if changes were to occur. Against **police brutality**, mass arrests, and **lynching**, King and his followers offered soul force. Aware of the formidable power of nonviolence, King himself acknowledged his debt to Gandhi with his commitment to nonviolence as a means of fighting to end racial injustice in the United States. Like Gandhi, King and his followers used a combination of strategies of civil disobedience and noncooperation, including marches, sit-ins, and boycotts. On February 1, 1965, King led a march that was reminiscent of Gandhi's march to the sea to make salt in protest against the British salt monopoly in India. King led the fifty-mile march between Selma and Montgomery, Alabama, to demand voting rights for African Americans and to protest racial violence, **segregation**, and discrimination.

Even though the civil rights movement largely adopted the principle of nonviolence, some African American groups and individuals believed that it was not effective and opted for a call to arms, or at least did not rule out the use of violence. **Malcolm X** considered it criminal to rule out the use of violence in self-defense. Groups such as the **Black Panther Party (BPP)** declared open war on **vigilante organizations**, policemen, and sheriffs who used violence against African Americans. These groups that rejected the principle of nonviolence believed in self-defense to protect themselves, their families, and properties because the U.S. government had, since the **Reconstruction** era, largely ignored white-on-black violence and crime. It has been argued that, even though nonviolence eventually led to the success of the civil rights movement, groups advocating violence in self-defense also contributed to the awareness of the social injustice against African Americans.

Further Readings: King, Martin Luther, Jr. *The Measure of a Man*. Philadelphia: Fortress Press, 1988; King, Mary. *Mahatma Gandhi and Martin Luther King Jr.: The Power of Nonviolent Action*. Paris: UNESCO, 1999; Murthy, Srinivasa, ed. *Mahatma Gandhi and Leo Tolstoy Letters*. Long Beach, CA: Long Beach Publications, 1987.

Aimable Twagilimana

North Carolina. *See* Wilmington (North Carolina) Riot of 1898

O

Ohio. *See* Cincinnati (Ohio) Riots of 1967 and 1968; Cincinnati (Ohio) Riot of 2001; Cleveland (Ohio) Riot of 1966; Dayton (Ohio) Riot of 1966; Springfield (Ohio) Riot of 1904

Oklahoma. *See* Greenwood Community (Tulsa, Oklahoma); Tulsa Race Riot Commission; Tulsa (Oklahoma) Riot of 1921

Omaha (Nebraska) Riot of 1919

On September 28, 1919, a **white mob** took a black man named Will Brown from jail, tortured, hung, and shot him, then burned his body. Brown had been accused of assaulting a white woman named Agnes Loebeck. When Mayor Ed P. Smith tried to stop the **lynching** of Brown, the mob attempted to hang him as well. After the lynching, the mob burned out the brand new courthouse and then filtered through the city to the black part of town, attacking any black people they found, breaking windows, looting, and setting black-owned property on fire. Federal troops were called in, and when all the damages were tallied, there had been three deaths, more than fifty injuries, and thousands of dollars in property damage.

Economic opportunity in Omaha had long drawn people from a mix of ethnicities, including blacks, whose population doubled between 1910 and 1920, from around 5,000 to more than 10,000. Omaha's social climate during the summer of 1919 was particularly volatile. Several unions had gone on strike, and companies brought in black replacement workers. Sensationalized coverage of the black strikebreaker angle in local newspapers heightened racial tension. Omaha newspapers expressed varying degrees of criticism of the mayor and police department. All summer, the *Bee* and *Daily News* ran inflammatory front-page reports of alleged sexual assaults of white women by black men. The black weekly, the *Monitor*, edited by Rev. John Albert Williams, a local **National Association for the Advancement of Colored People (NAACP)** leader, asserted that the *Bee* and *Daily News* had contributed significantly to racial prejudice and tension in the city with their biased treatment of blacks.

The black monthly news magazine, ***The Crisis***, reported that Agnes Loebeck and Will Brown knew one another from the Omaha underworld, in which there were several houses where black men met white prostitutes. *The Crisis* asserted that Loebeck took revenge on Brown after a quarrel by alleging the attempted assault. The article also asserted that Tom Dennison was behind the riot as part of an attempt to discredit the mayor and regain political control of the city.

Boss Tom Dennison ran the Third Ward downtown, a vice syndicate, and the local Democratic Party from the back of the old Budweiser saloon on Douglas Street. But beginning in 1916, the Dennison machine came on hard times, lost power, and suffered from infighting. In 1918, Ed P. Smith was elected mayor, forcing Dennison's man, James Dahlman, to give up the mayoral office for the first time in five consecutive terms. The race riot did serve to discredit Mayor Ed Smith's administration, and the Dennison machine returned to power after the 1921 elections.

On the night after the rioting, Omaha was calm. The *New York Times* reported that was due in part to a dramatic rainstorm that drove everyone to find cover all over the city. The article also reported that although business and professional men in Omaha did not approve of the riot, the working class seemed to glory in it, and "scores of young girls in stores and offices were bragging about their part in the mob last night."

The rioting generated a refugee effect. E.L. McDowell, an official at the train station, estimated that 2,000 black people left Omaha by train after the riot. Toll collectors at the Douglas St. Bridge reported that a constant stream of black refugees crossed the bridge to Iowa.

At the request of local officials, the Army sent in Maj. Gen. Leonard Wood, who arrived two days after the riot ended and declared martial law. Detachments were stationed in the black neighborhood at Twenty-Fourth and Lake Streets, at the courthouse and city hall buildings, and in South Omaha at Twenty-Fourth and O Streets. To assist in identifying participants, Major General Wood ordered the confiscation of all pictures and plates made by photographers during the riot. Anyone identified was to be arrested by the military at once. The district court ordered a grand jury to convene and investigate the riots.

The grand jury was impaneled on October 8. A month later, 120 indictments were handed down; among them were George and James Sutij, twins, 25; James Shields; Harry Jenkins, 22; Sam Novak, 17; Henry Louis Weaver, 21; William Francis, 16. Most of the 120 people indicted were never successfully prosecuted. Despite all the investigations, confessions, and photographic evidence, all the suspects were eventually released; no one served time. Maj. Gen. Leonard Wood, having first attributed responsibility for the riot to the local political machine, later blamed the International Workers of the World (IWW) and the Bolsheviks. Wood was soon using the public's fear of such groups as a cornerstone in his campaign for president. The remains of Will Brown were buried with no funeral service and no mourners. *See also* Red Summer Race Riots of 1919.

Further Readings: "Another Woman Attacked in Omaha." *New York Times*, October 2, 1919, 1; "General Wood Orders the Arrest of Omaha's Rioters." *New York*

Times, October 1, 1919, 1; Kitchens, John W., ed. *Tuskegee Institute News Clippings File Microfilm*. Sanford, NC: Microfilming Corporation of America, 1981. Reel 10, Frames 893–898, 908–910; Larsen, Lawrence Harold, and Barbara J. Cottrell. *The Gate City: a History of Omaha*. Lincoln: University of Nebraska Press, 1997; Laurie, Clayton D. "The U.S. Army and the Omaha Race Riot of 1919." *Nebraska History* 72, no. 3 (1991): 135–143; Lawson, Michael L. "Omaha, a City of Ferment: Summer of 1919." *Nebraska History* 58, no. 3 (1977): 395–417; McKanna, Clare. "Black Enclaves of Violence: Race and Homicide in Great Plains Cities, 1890–1920." *Great Plains Quarterly* 23 (2003): 147–160; Menard, Orville D. *Political Bossism in Mid-America: Tom Dennison's Omaha, 1900–1933*. Lanham, MD: University Press of America, 1989; Menard, Orville D. "Tom Dennison, The Omaha *Bee*, and the 1919 Omaha Race Riot." *Nebraska History* 68, no. 4 (Winter 1987): 152–165; NebraskaStudies.org. "Racial Tensions in Nebraska in the 1920s." See http://www.nebraskastudies.org/0700/frameset.html; Willborn, Steven. "The Omaha Riot of 1919." *The Nebraska Lawyer* (December 1999/January 2000): 49–53.

Jan Voogd

Orangeburg (South Carolina) Massacre of 1968

The Orangeburg Massacre, an incident in which three African American students were killed and twenty-seven others were wounded in a confrontation with police, occurred in February 1968 on the adjoining campuses of South Carolina State College (now South Carolina State University) and Claflin College (now Claflin University), two historically black colleges in Orangeburg, South Carolina. Although a great deal of violence occurred during antiwar and **civil rights movement** demonstrations of the 1960s, the Orangeburg Massacre was unprecedented because it was the first time in U.S. history that students were killed on an American college campus. Another aspect of the Orangeburg Massacre that makes it an unparalleled event in the annals of American history is that even though the deaths of the students at South Carolina State and Claflin Colleges occurred two years before the Kent State shootings in which four students were killed and nine others were wounded on May 4, 1970, the Orangeburg Massacre received negligible media coverage. In fact, compared to the national and international media coverage that the tragedy at Kent State received, it was almost as if the Orangeburg Massacre did not happen at all, or, at the very least, was not important enough to report. Perhaps the only event of its kind that received even less media attention was the deaths of two students during an incident at Jackson State University in Mississippi on May 14, 1970. Ironically, the 150 African American students at Jackson State were protesting the incident at Kent State when the National Guard fired into the crowd, leaving two students dead.

There are many possible reasons why the Orangeburg Massacre was neglected by the press. Even in death and injury it seemed that the students of South Carolina State and Claflin Colleges had fallen prey to the racial discrimination they spent their lives trying to overcome. However, an equally plausible reason is that less than two months after the Orangeburg Massacre, while the incident was still under investigation, the nation, particularly the individuals in the civil rights movement who had committed their lives to ending discrimination in this country, were shocked and angered by the assassination of Dr. **Martin Luther King, Jr.**, on April 8, 1968.

Whatever the reason for the neglect of the topic, the fact is that on Thursday night, February 8, 1968, members of the South Carolina Sheriff's Office, the South Carolina Police Department, and the South Carolina Army National Guard shot thirty African American college students who had organized what was intended to be a peaceful protest. Approximately 200 students gathered on the adjoining campuses of South Carolina State and Claflin Colleges to protest the continued **segregation** of the All Star Bowling Lane, a bowling alley on Russell Street, within walking distance of the two colleges. The bowling alley was owned by Harry Floyd, a local businessman. Students were frustrated after a week's attempt to persuade the owner of the bowling alley to comply with the **Civil Rights Act of 1964**, which, in part, authorized the national government to abolish segregation and discrimination based on race, color, religion, national origin, and, in the case of employment, sex. The students organized a peaceful demonstration on the college campuses where they attended school. The act was signed into law on July 2, 1964, by President Lyndon Baines Johnson and, even though the law stressed voluntary compliance, it also included a stipulation that encouraged resolution of problems by local and state authorities.

During the days leading up to February 8, several representatives from South Carolina State and Claflin Colleges met with the mayor of Orangeburg, the chief of police, and the city manager. The students requested but were denied a permit to march through the streets of Orangeburg or to demonstrate in front of the All Star Bowling Lane.

On Monday, February 5, 1968, a group of students from Claflin and South Carolina State Colleges attempted to desegregate the only bowling alley in town, but they were denied entrance and the police were summoned by the proprietor. After a brief stand-off, the majority of the students returned to their respective campuses.

This effort to abolish segregation was not something new for students of Claflin and South Carolina State Colleges. They, along with black and white citizens in South Carolina, played an active role in the civil rights movement. In July 1955, fifty-seven African Americans petitioned the school board to desegregate the public schools in Orangeburg. A year later, students from South Carolina State and Claflin Colleges organized a nonviolent protest march through the streets of Orangeburg. During February and March, students from Claflin, Morris, and Friendship Colleges conducted sit-ins to desegregate the lunch counter at S.H. Kress, a novelty store or "five and dime," founded by Samuel Henry Kress (1863–1955). On March 15, 1960, demonstrators were drenched with fire hoses and tear-gassed as they marched to protest the segregated lunch counter. In September 1963, over 1,000 protesters were arrested for picketing local merchants. A review of this brief history suggests that the events that took place in Orangeburg during February 1968 were not an aberration but part of the long struggle to abolish segregation and racial discrimination, which was a fundamental goal of the civil rights movement.

On Tuesday night, the local police were waiting when students arrived. The door of the bowling alley was locked, but the students refused to move. Chief of Police Roger Poston was called. When he arrived, the door was unlocked to allow him entrance. Several students rushed the door. They were asked to leave. When they refused, fifteen were arrested for trespassing.

When rumors of the arrests reached the campuses, over 300 students gathered outside the bowling alley. They were met by the Orangeburg Police Department, state police, state highway patrol, deputies from the sheriff's office, and the state law enforcement division (SLED). A city fire truck arrived. The students chose that moment to rush the bowling alley. Someone smashed a plate glass window. The police beat back the crowd with nightsticks. Eight students and one officer were injured.

On Wednesday morning, student representatives from both colleges attended a meeting with city officials to discuss the events of the past couple of days and prevent any potential escalation. The students were again denied a permit to hold a demonstration but were able to submit a list of grievances; their list included: (a) closing of the All Star Bowling Lane until it changed its policy toward segregation; (b) establishment of a biracial Human Relations Committee; (c) service from the Orangeburg Medical Association for all persons, regardless of race, color, creed, religion, or national origin; and (d) compliance of local and state officials with the Civil Rights Act of 1964.

On Thursday, February 8, 1968, another meeting was convened on campus and was organized by the Black Awareness Coordinating Committee (BACC), a student organizations that included members of the **Student Nonviolent Coordinating Committee (SNCC)**, the **National Association for the Advancement of Colored People (NAACP)**, and the **Southern Christian Leadership Conference (SCLC)**. Some members of BACC felt that they had been defeated by compromise when the group was denied another permit. The meetings lasted until evening without reaching a solution. The students were denied their permit to demonstrate, and the bowling alley remained segregated. The only concession was that Harry Floyd agreed to close his place of business at 5:00 P.M., several hours earlier than usual. But still, the stalemate continued. Exhausted, frustrated, and disappointed about their lack of progress, dozens of students conversed in small groups. Others wandered aimlessly around the campuses. After the meeting, instead of going straight back to their dorms, over 100 students walked around the campuses, talked in small groups, and wondered what tomorrow would bring.

Because it was a cold winter night, someone suggested a bonfire. It was not long before the blaze became a beacon for other students. It also attracted the attention of the police. Once the authorities arrived they built a barricade on Watson Street separating themselves from the students and the bonfire. There was a sudden tension and a sense of foreboding in the air—the sense that something was going to happen that night.

A fire truck arrived followed by an ambulance, which elicited an angry response from the students. As the firemen extinguished the already dying embers of the bonfire someone out of the darkness yelled, "I'm hit." The police immediately opened fire. Students, stunned by the sudden assault, ran, screamed, fell to their knees, or dove for shelter. From start to finish, the terror lasted only seconds, but in that terrifying interval, twenty-seven students were wounded and three young men were killed.

Samuel Ephesians Hammond, Jr. (1949–1968), Henry Ezekial Smith (1948–1968), and Delano Herman Middleton (1950–1968) were killed. Samuel Hammond, a freshman from Fort Lauderdale, Florida, was shot in the upper back. Henry Smith, a sophomore from Marion, South Carolina, was shot in the right and left sides and in the neck. Delano Middleton, a seventeen-year-old high school student from Orangeburg, was shot in the spine, thigh, wrist, and forearm. His mother worked on campus and he was there visiting friends. This was an unexpected culmination of events that began with so much hope and promise.

Even after an investigation, it was difficult to state exactly what triggered the confrontation. The police claimed that they fired in self-defense. Students claimed that the only shots fired were by the police, that they fired without warning into a defenseless crowd with no means of protecting themselves. The controversy over what actually ignited the Orangeburg Massacre has never been resolved. However, during the 112th Session of the South Carolina General Assembly in 1997–1998, the following resolution was passed (Bill 4576):

> To express profound gratitude for the supreme sacrifice made on February 8, 1968, by three young students, Samuel Hammond, Jr., Delano Herman Middleton, and Henry Ezekial Smith, and to recognize their courageous effort by declaring February 8, as Smith-Hammond-Middleton Memorial Day.
>
> Be it further resolved that we pray the governor of our great state immediately issue posthumously to those three brave young men The Order of the Palmetto, and pray also that these awards be presented to South Carolina State University on February 8, 1998, and that South Carolina State University display them in positions of honor and prominence in its Smith-Hammond-Middleton Memorial Center.

Every year, friends, family, and survivors gather on the campuses of Claflin and South Carolina State Universities to commemorate the Orangeburg Massacre. *See also* Sellers, Cleveland.

Further Readings: Bass, Jack, and Jack Nelson. *The Orangeburg Massacre*. Macon, GA: Mercer University Press, 1996; Brown, Linda Meggett. "Remembering the Orangeburg Massacre (South Carolina State University)." *Black Issues in Higher Education*, March 1, 2001; Watters, Pat, and Weldon Rougeau. *Events at Orangeburg: A Report Based on Study and Interviews in Orangeburg, South Carolina, in the Aftermath of Tragedy. Southern regional Council*, South Carolina, February 25, 1968; Williams, Cecil J. "Selected Movement Photographs of Cecil J. Williams." See http://www.crmvet.org/images/pwilliam.htm.

John G. Hall

P

Palestine (Texas) Riot of 1910

Despite the dearth of information available today, the news of the riot near Palestine, Texas, appeared on the front page of many of the major U.S. newspapers at the time. According to these accounts, on the night of July 29, 1910, a **white mob** of at least 200 people drove black residents near the village of Slocum, about fourteen miles south of Palestine, into a heavily wooded area and killed them. The mob cut the phone lines along the way, thus ensuring that news of the violence would be difficult to confirm. Scattered bands clashed and at least eighteen black people were killed. The bodies were left as they fell, in the woods and on the roads. Some of the news accounts reported the number of deaths as thirty or forty.

Texas State Rangers arrived by the next evening, under the command of Capt. Godfrey Rees Fowler, a local son and former Army officer recently returned from Nicaragua. The presence of militia seemed to bring the violence under control after it had spread to the towns of Denson Springs and Elkhart. The state militia guarded the county jail in Palestine, where the first prisoners were placed.

Tension had been building in the weeks prior to the riot. Black farmers had begun to protest the peonage system. A black man had declined to pay a debt sponsored by a white farmer named Redin Alford, and Alford had to pay it. Then, a white man, according to some accounts named James Spurger, refused to work when assigned to a road crew under a black supervisor. There were rumors of secret meetings among black residents, and a black man allegedly confessed to a plan to kill Spurger and his family.

On the night of the riot, a black man, believed to be carrying a shotgun, was declared to be advancing on Spurger. When he refused to surrender, a posse shot him. The rioting followed shortly thereafter. Farmers and other white citizens stocked up on weapons before County Judge B.H. Gardner ordered the sale of firearms to be discontinued and ordered all saloons closed as well.

Sheriff William Black's description of the situation was later quoted widely by many major newspapers, including the *Washington Post, New*

York Times, and *Atlanta Constitution*. "Men were going about and killing Negroes as fast as they could find them ... without any real cause. These Negroes have done no wrong that I could discover.... It will be difficult to find out just how many were killed.... Some will probably never be found."

A grand jury was formed that included District Attorney Harris and District Judge Gardner. The names of fourteen of the dead were established. There were sixteen white men arrested in connection with the riots, including James Spurger, Reagon McKenzie, and S.F. Jenkins. All were held without bail.

A month after the riot, there was a movement afoot to bring justice to the incident. John Siddon, a white man from Volga, Texas, wrote to Cecil Lyon, the chair of the Texas Republican Committee, informing him of the incident and asking for federal intervention. Lyon wrote to President William Howard Taft asking for an investigation. U.S. Attorney General George W. Wickersham replied, promising to look into the matter. In addition, W.H. Ellis, attorney and "concerned citizen" and a group of black ministers wrote to President Taft as well, but the staff attorney who replied to them said that the government would look into the matter only if a federal crime had been committed—one which they had yet to specify. Lawlessness in Palestine had been the object of a congressional investigation in 1886, when violence became part of a labor dispute between the local railroad and its unions. Federal intervention was considered appropriate in matters of interstate commerce.

In Washington, D.C., a meeting of 600 concerned black citizens was addressed by several clergy, including Professor W.H. Hart, Howard University; Rev. J. Anderson Taylor, Trinity Baptist Church; Rev. J. Milton Waldron, Shiloh Baptist Church; and Rev. R.K. Harris, Israel A.M.E. Church. "When so many black men are murdered without indictment, trial, or conviction, as so recently happened in Texas and Florida, we feel it our duty to appeal to the American people to aid us in reenthroning law and order in every community of our country" ("Race War Denounced," 2). In a sermon at the Cosmopolitan Temple Baptist Church in Washington, D.C., the Rev. Simon P.W. Drew declared that the "tale of the wholesale killing of Negroes in Palestine, Texas, must cause every American with any pride of country or hope for its future to hang his head in shame" ("Condemns Texas Slayers," 12).

Further Readings: Berry, Mary Frances. *Black Resistance/White Law: A History of Constitutional Racism in America*. New York: Penguin Group, 1994; "Condemns Texas Slayers." *Washington Post*, August 8, 1910, 12; "Corpses Strewn through Woods." *Atlanta Constitution*, August 1, 1910, 1; "Eighteen Negroes Shot to Death in Race Clash." *The Atlanta Constitution*, July 31, 1910, 1; "Men Shot Like Sheep." *Washington Post*, August 1, 1910, 3; "More Texas Riot Arrests." *New York Times*, August 7, 1910, 3; "Negroes Are Killed in Texas Race Riot." *Los Angeles Times*, July 31, 1910, 1; "Race War Denounced." *Washington Post*, August 9, 1910, 2; "Scores of Negroes Killed by Whites." *New York Times*, July 31, 1910, 1.

Jan Voogd

Parker, Mack Charles (1936–1959), Lynching of

Mack Charles Parker was a young African American man who was lynched in Mississippi in February 1959 for allegedly raping a white woman. Parker, whose life and death are recounted in Howard Smead's *Blood Justice: The Lynching of Mack Charles Parker*, in many ways served as the impetus for the civil rights legislation of the 1960s and helped bring an end to an era of open and publicly sanctioned acts of violence against African Americans.

Parker was a twenty-three-year-old truck driver who lived in Lumberton, Mississippi. Although he married following his service in the Army, he later divorced and became the sole supporter for his mother, younger sister and her child, and four-year-old brother. Although recognized by his neighbors for taking on the responsibility of this mother and siblings at such a young age, Parker also liked to go out and have a good time with his friends. One such night was Monday, February 23, 1959, when Parker and four friends (Tommy Lee Grant, Curt Underwood, Norman "Rainbow" Malachy, and David Alfred), after receiving their paychecks, went out for the night.

During that same night, June Walters was traveling with her husband, Jimmy, and four-year-old daughter along a road between Poplarville and Lumberton in Pearl River County, Mississippi. At about 11:30 P.M. that night, the Walters' family car stalled and June's husband decided to travel to the nearest town, Lumberton, for assistance. June, who was two months pregnant, and her daughter remained behind, locked in the car. While Jimmy was walking along the desolate road toward Lumberton, Parker and his friends drove by and noticed the car. This is where the events of the night of February 23 and the truth diverge.

What is known is that June Walters and her daughter were attacked. June was taken to an isolated field, beaten, and raped. Her daughter was accosted. After Parker dropped his friends at their homes, he returned to his own home briefly and then went out again. A truck driver found June stumbling along the road, in shock, with her daughter. She claimed that she was attacked by a black man. Parker, who had no previous arrest record, was accused of the crime and jailed. The intersection of race, class, politics, ambition, and hate colored the intervening facts of the case and, inevitably, determined the outcome and Parker's death.

Although no direct evidence connected Parker to the rape of June Walters, this fact did not stop the police from targeting Parker as their primary suspect early in the case. One of the friends with him that night, Curt Underwood, claimed that when they drove past the Walters' car, Parker told him he intended to go back. The father of another of Parker's friends, David Alfred, stated that Parker was the person the police were looking for. In addition, Parker's car was seen that night by a Poplarville police officer. When Parker was brought to the Lumberton jail, after sustaining a bloody beating by police, Walters was unable to identify him in a lineup. Yet, when Parker and the other men in the lineup were asked to repeat the words allegedly spoken by the rapist, Walters identified Parker as the person who attacked her.

From his initial questioning by police until his death, Parker proclaimed his innocence and denied that he had raped June Walters. It wasn't long after Parker was arrested and charged with kidnapping and criminal assault that some of the white residents of Pearl River County began to talk about carrying out their own form of justice. The fact that the victim was unable to identify Parker physically, that there was no evidence linking him to the crime, and that the two lie detector tests he took were inconclusive was not enough to deter locals from wanting to go after Parker. These threats were not taken lightly by Parker, his family, or the local African American community.

Those involved in the conspiracy were from every segment of the Poplarville area community—business owners, laborers, law enforcement officers, farmers, and a preacher. Local sentiment was fueled when Parker's mother hired two African American attorneys to defend her son. There was concern that the attorneys would be allowed to cross-examine a white woman—June Walters—if the case ever went to court. In addition, there was talk that Parker might be cleared of the charges or, if convicted, might win on appeal. The belief that a conviction might be overturned on appeal was a real concern. There were no African Americans on the grand jury that indicted Parker, and there were no African Americans eligible to serve as jurors.

The case transcended the need to convict the person who raped and assaulted June Walters. It was transformed into an occasion to uphold a way of life local residents believed was being challenged and derided. African Americans across the country were demanding legal recognition of their civil rights, demanding the right to vote without encumbrance, the right to equal opportunity in the workplace, and equal educational opportunities. Change was on the horizon and small isolated hamlets and towns like Poplarville felt that they were being ignored by the federal government and the rest of the country, and they were ready to fight back. The incident involving Mack Charles Parker provided them with an opportunity to take a stand and to make a statement.

By the time Parker was transferred to a jail in Poplarville, which served as the county seat for Pearl River, plans were well underway to lynch him. Other prisoners were warned that something might happen and they were directed to point Parker out if it did. On the night of April 24, several cars pulled up to the Pearl River County jail and courthouse, and from among that group, three men entered the jail and forcibly took Parker. They were later identified as J.P. Walker, a former deputy sheriff, James Floren Lee, an itinerant preacher, and Jewel Alford, an officer at the jail.

Although it may not have been a surprise that a lynch mob would come after Parker, it appears that no one who observed the events of that night was prepared for what they saw. Parker, young and strong, despite the beatings given to him by police some months earlier, struggled valiantly for his life. The three men bludgeoned and kicked Parker until he was on the brink of unconsciousness and then dragged him down the jailhouse steps, leaving a trail of blood, and placed him into one of the waiting cars. The mob, minus Jewel Alford, traveled from Mississippi to Louisiana and then back again, stopping at the Pearl River. Parker was bound, beaten and kicked, and then shot in the heart. His body was then weighed down with chains and tossed into the river.

Lynch mobs in the past had little to fear in terms of retaliation or of being arrested. Yet, it was apparent almost immediately that this **lynching** would be different. The first evidence of this was Governor Coleman's decision to contact the **Federal Bureau of Investigation (FBI)**. Only hours after Parker's kidnapping, torture, and death, the FBI, the U.S. Department of Justice, and the White House had been informed of the lynching. In addition, the national press descended on the residents of the county with questions and cameras.

The FBI quickly moved into Poplarville and started their formal investigation. Although some of the residents in Pearl River and the surrounding counties, including Jimmy and June Walters, thought Parker should have been able to stand trial, they also resented what they perceived as the federal government's intrusion. It became clear that not everyone agreed with the actions of the mob, but they would, without hesitation, defend their neighbors, county, and state. More than sixty FBI agents, along with the state police, began an investigation into Parker's disappearance and attempted to locate him.

Ten days after Parker was murdered, on May 4, his body, bloated and decomposed, surfaced. While he was being laid to rest, the FBI accelerated its investigation and attempted to gather evidence that the mob had carried Parker across state lines, from Mississippi to Louisiana, in order to make the charges a federal offense. At every turn, the FBI was met with silence out of fear of retaliation and resentment over their presence. Two potential witnesses who did participate in the investigation later attempted suicide.

Although no confessions were forthcoming from any of the participants in the lynching, the FBI believed that it had enough evidence, including Alford's admission that he helped the mob to gain entry to the jail, to bring indictments and convictions. Despite the testimony of key government witnesses, of the two grand juries (in 1959 and 1960) convened to examine the evidence, neither brought an indictment against any of the members of the mob or their accomplices. None of the individuals who participated in Parker's kidnapping and murder were ever jailed or arrested.

Nonetheless, many Pearl River County residents did not view the inaction of the grand juries as a victory. Tired of the press, government intrusion, and embarrassed that the state's judicial process was not allowed to resolve the case, local citizens were disappointed that Mississippi was not able to show the rest of the country, and the world, they were capable of handling their own problems in a fair and legal manner. This shift in thinking later opened the door for social change in Poplarville, Pearl River County, and the state of Mississippi.

No member of Parker's family remained in Pearl River County after the case was closed. Mack Charles Parker was interred in a simple grave that displayed no vestiges of his horrific death. *See also* Rape, as Provocation for Lynching.

Further Readings: FBI Summary Report. *Civil Rights Investigation into the Abduction of Mack Charles Parker from the Pearl River County Jail in Poplarville, Mississippi*. April 1959. See http://foia.fbi.gov/foiaindex/parker.htm; Smead, Howard. *Blood Justice: The Lynching of Mack Charles Parker*. New York: Oxford University Press, 1986.

Robin Dasher-Alston

The Passing of the Great Race (Grant, 1916)

Madison Grant's *The Passing of the Great Race* (1916), was a best-selling book claiming to trace the origins of the United States to the deeds of a heroic Nordic race. Despite the wave of anti-black riots that swept the nation following World War I, many white academics and intellectuals nevertheless believed that the white race was in danger of being overwhelmed by the darker races of the globe. Grant's book argued that only a stringent application of eugenics (forced sterilization and imprisonment of those whose genes were deemed defective) and immigration restriction would preserve what he termed *the Great Race*. Historians have long disagreed about whether Grant's book represents the last gasp of nineteenth-century racial "science," or is best seen as an adaptation of racist ideology to the changing conditions of the twentieth century.

The Passing of the Great Race became a best-seller because it both vastly simplified racist science and applied that science ruthlessly and viciously. In the late nineteenth century, white European and American intellectuals had argued for the existence of literally hundreds of races, based on a conception of race that combined physical appearance, language, history, heredity, behavior, intellectual ability, and so on. European whites, they claimed, were at the apex of a vast racial and developmental hierarchy. Antiracist critics of this science, like pioneering anthropologist Franz Boas, had proved that the physical markers of race were notoriously inaccurate as scientific tools, and argued that the critical elements of perceived race difference—language, history, and culture—were not related at all to biology or heredity. Grant's *Passing of the Great Race* attacked these arguments by inverting them. In place of the myriad white races of Europe, however, Grant insisted that there were three: Nordics, or northern and western Europeans, including the English, Dutch, and German forebears of Grant's own illustrious family; Alpines, most prevalent in southeastern Europe and Russia; and Mediterraneans, who ringed the coast of the Mediterranean Sea. But culture, far from being the essence of race, was instead merely an effect of racial heredity. Grant asserted that qualities such as intellectual ability, cunning, honor, and virtue were inescapably biological characteristics, imprinted in the genes and passed down from parents to children. These most important racial characteristics were merely manifested in physical appearance, history, and individual behavior. Nordics were the Great Race in Grant's title who had wrested America from Native Americans and extended their imperial dominions across the world in an inevitable working-out of their innate superiority. Since, Grant argued, race was first and foremost biological and inherited, only racially pure offspring would retain the characteristics of their exalted forebears. Based on a common, but distorted, version of Gregor Mendel's experiments with hybridization of pea plants, Grant claimed that racially hybrid people reverted to the inferior type. Thus, he famously asserted, "the cross between a white man and a Negro is a Negro" (1916). The United States, he believed, suffered from a tragic lack of race consciousness, that is, an acknowledgement that Americans' Nordic heritage was primarily responsible for the conquest, settlement, and creation of the republic. As a result, "race suicide" threatened the "Great Race" and the nation it created. Degeneration of racial stock through unregulated immigration and cross-breeding had to be met, Grant argued, with a stringent program of immigration restrictions and eugenics—forced sterilization of individuals deemed by Grant and his allies as possessing defective racial characteristics, and breeding of the remaining members of the Great Race (Grant 1916).

As ridiculous as Grant's ideas are, their influence on, for example, the concepts of race found in Nazi party ideology is chilling. In the American context, Grant's arguments can be seen to some extent as an elaboration and extension of the typical arguments used to rationalize racial violence: that **lynching**, for example, was necessary to protect the virtue of white women. But, at the time *The Passing of the Great Race* was published, only the beginnings of the massive migration of African Americans to northern cities could be observed. Grant himself was far more concerned with restricting the immigration and reproduction of Alpines and Mediterraneans in the North. However, Grant's intellectual scheme, which ultimately concluded that class differences in America were merely an effect of racial differences, provided an important transition for concepts of race challenged by black migration and the 1919 race riots that accompanied the **Great Migration**. Scholars have long seen the period around the 1919 riots as one of critical changes in academic and popular racial thought, but have disagreed about what changed and why the changes are important. Some writers have argued that Grant's assertion of race as primarily biological was already out of step with ascendant academic claims of race as primarily cultural. In their view, in 1916 academics were already rejecting the vicious conclusions and policies Grant and his allies advocated, and arguing for a new, tolerant view of racial difference that would ultimately dominate the twentieth century. Other scholars have pointed to Grant's continuing role in both public life and academia as a sign that his beliefs were still important justifications for racial violence, and which continued to influence violent groups like the **Ku Klux Klan (KKK)** well into the twentieth century. *See also* The Great Migration; Racism; Red Summer Race Riots of 1919.

Further Readings: Grant, Madison. *The Passing of the Great Race; or, The Racial Basis of European History.* New York: C. Scribner, 1916; Guterl, Matthew Pratt. *The Color of Race in America, 1900–1940.* Cambridge, MA: Harvard University Press, 2001; Higham, John. *Strangers in the Land: Patterns of American Nativism, 1860–1925.* Rutgers, NJ: Rutgers University Press, 1984.

Jonathan S. Coit

Peekskill (New York) Riots of 1949

For one week in the waning summer days of 1949, Peekskill, New York, became the center of national attention. Peekskill's days in the limelight came when the celebrated but controversial African American singer, actor, and political activist Paul Robeson appeared to perform in a benefit concert. Between August 27 and September 4, 1949, two riots would occur in Peekskill, the New York State Police would be mobilized, Robeson would be hanged in effigy, a burning cross would light up the night sky, and Peekskill would live, however briefly, on the front pages of America's newspapers. While Paul Robeson was the focal point of all these events, the reasons for the conflict go far beyond Robeson to expose the uneasy intersection of race, anti-Semitism, local politics, and anti-communism in early cold war America. What occurred in Peekskill was in part a race riot, but it is more accurately characterized as a political protest spun out of control, fueled by **racism** and anti-Semitism.

Located forty miles north of New York in the Hudson Valley, Peekskill hardly seems a likely place for cold war tensions to give way to open violence. In many ways, however, conflict in Peekskill should hardly be surprising. The local population of Peekskill in 1949 was predominantly white, Protestant, and voted the Republican Party ticket. Surrounding Peekskill were numerous summer camps filled with vacationers from New York City. These summer residents were largely Jewish, and their politics were not merely leftist but often avowedly socialist or communist. Add to these conditions the normal tensions that exist between full-time and summertime residents in almost any vacation resort area, and the conditions for some type of conflict were present in Peekskill long before Paul Robeson came to town.

Robeson was one of the best known and popular of American entertainers in the mid-twentieth century. After finishing at the top of his class at Rutgers University, while also becoming the first African American all-American football player, Robeson graduated from Columbia University's law school. Finding little work for a black lawyer, Robeson dabbled in professional sports before drawing on his other talents, singing and acting. Robeson's singing quickly propelled him to fame and opened other opportunities for him in acting. Robeson became the first black man to play the role of Othello on Broadway and, most famously, he sang "Old Man River" in the musical "Showboat." Robeson was so popular that CBS Radio chose him to sing the national broadcast premier of the song "Ballad for Americans" in 1939. During the late 1930s and through the 1940s, however, Robeson's stature as an entertainer suffered as he embraced controversial political causes and voiced his admiration for the Soviet Union.

The summer of 1949 was an especially tense time around Peekskill. The early stages of the cold war left many Americans wondering about their future. Revelations about American citizens spying for the Soviet Union, and congressional investigation of the movie industry for traces of subversion left many Americans wary of the loyalty of their neighbors. In Peekskill, the neighbors were easily identifiable and not trying very hard to hide their politics.

The events leading to the Peekskill riots began in April 1949 when Robeson attended a conference of the World Partisans of Peace in Paris. Robeson had long advocated unpopular causes such as the decolonization of Africa. He had openly embraced the Soviet Union and even sent his son to be schooled in Moscow. Robeson also sang for the Abraham Lincoln Brigade during the Spanish Civil War when the United States was trying to stay out of that conflict. These were controversial actions, but largely acceptable to the American public before and during World War II. Robeson's behavior crossed the line of acceptability, however, in the tense post-war atmosphere. During the speech he made in Paris, Robeson announced that "our will to fight for peace is strong. We shall not make war on anyone. We shall not make war on the Soviet Union" (Duberman 1988). In 1949, those comments were controversial enough, but they would be overshadowed by what Robeson said next: "It is unthinkable that American Negroes would go to war on behalf of those who oppressed us for generations against a country [the Soviet Union] which in one generation has raised our people to the full dignity of mankind" (Duberman 1988). These words cemented in many people's minds Robeson's reputation as un-American. In the *Peekskill Evening Star* on April 21, 1949, the headline read, "Robeson Says U.S. Negroes Won't Fight Russia." Four months later, when it was announced that Robeson would be singing in Peekskill, the people there would remember that headline.

By 1949, Paul Robeson had little concern for his popularity. He had all but stopped being an entertainer in order to spend his energy promoting political causes. The only time Robeson would sing was when he was asked to perform in benefit concerts. Such was the case when the **Civil Rights Congress** asked Robeson to perform for them in Peekskill. Once this occured, the setting for the riots was complete: social, political, and religious differences between year-round and summertime residents, the rising tensions of the cold war, Robeson's controversial speech in Paris, and finally, the invitation from the Civil Rights Congress, which had just been added to the attorney general's list of subversive organizations.

Robeson had appeared in Peekskill before 1949 without incident. This concert, like the others, was open to the public, but really was intended for the summer residents in the camps outside of town. In previous years, Robeson had appeared in Peekskill and barely made a ripple on the local political waters. After his Paris speech, however, there would be nothing quiet about an appearance by Paul Robeson. In 1949, the local newspaper in Peekskill, the *Evening Star*, and an ad hoc coalition of veterans' organizations mobilized to announce to the world that Robeson might be coming to their town, but that did not mean that he was a welcome guest.

Starting a week before Robeson's scheduled concert on August 29, the *Evening Star* published a series of articles, editorials, and letters to the editor expressing a common theme that Robeson was no longer welcome in Peekskill. "The time for tolerant silence which signifies approval is running out" (*Peekskill Evening Star*, August 23, 1949) read one editorial. "No matter how masterful the décor, nor how sweet the music," Americans should not be duped into following Robeson and his siren's song of communism (*Peekskill Evening Star*, August 23, 1949). A leader of the Joint Veterans Council in Peekskill wrote an impassioned call to stop the concert: "The irony of this meeting is that they intend to appear at Lakeland Acres Picnic Area ... across the street from the Hillside and Assumption cemeteries. Yes, directly across the street from the resting place of those men who paid the supreme sacrifice in order to insure our democratic form of government. Are we, as loyal Americans, going to forget these men and the principles they died for or are we going to follow their beliefs and rid ourselves of subversive organizations?" (*Peekskill Evening Star*, August 23, 1949).

These passionate words were supported by actions as the Joint Veteran's Council of Peekskill (American Legion, Veterans of Foreign Wars, Catholic War Veterans, and Jewish War Veterans) called for a protest march "as a definite stand against the appearance of Paul Robeson" (*Peekskill Evening Star*, August 23, 1949). As the concert approached, the lines were clearly drawn. The *Evening Star* announced the "Russia Loving Negro Baritone" was singing for a "communist front organization" (*Peekskill Evening Star*, August 23, 1949). The protest march had the approval of the veterans' groups, the local newspaper, the Chamber of Commerce, and all the rest of Peekskill. The concert organizers, on the other hand, could count only a small number of like-minded souls as their allies. As the evening of August 27 approached, both protestors and concertgoers made their way to the Lakeland Acres Picnic Area just outside of Peekskill.

There were rising tensions in Peekskill throughout the day of the concert. At one intersection, Robeson was hung in effigy and signs such as "We've got a rope for Robeson" and "Not Wanted—Commies/Wanted—Good Americans," appeared in town. The protest march was scheduled for 7:30 P.M. and the concert for 8:15 P.M. The protest organizers hoped for 5,000 protestors while the concert planners expected a crowd of 2,500. In the end, only 700 marchers turned out, but they were effective in tying up traffic and blocking access to the concert site. On his way to Peekskill, Robeson was stopped and diverted to a friend's house. He would not sing in Peekskill that night.

Back at the Lakeland Acres Picnic Area, however, tensions were reaching the boiling point. At the entrance to the park, protestors and concertgoers were shouting at each other. The concertgoers were treated with variations of "nigger loving, commie, kike bastards" and they responded by calling the protestors "fascists" and "brownshirts." The few concertgoers who made it to Lakeland Acres were outnumbered and clearly got the worst of these exchanges. However unpleasant these events were, nothing that occurred outside Lakeland Acres constituted a riot on the night of August 27. The real problems were inside the picnic grounds.

Of the expected 2,500 concertgoers, only 200 made it inside Lakeland Acres. Once the protest march closed off access to the site, they were effectively trapped inside—afraid to stay, but even more afraid to leave. Despite the obvious potential for trouble, there was minimal police presence at the concert site. Most of the police officers assigned to the event were not there to keep the peace, but rather to collect the license plate numbers from the concertgoers' cars. When trouble started, these officers were of little help.

Emboldened by the small number of concertgoers and minimal police presence, contingents of protestors left the park entrance and walked inside looking for trouble. Camp chairs and sing-along music books were gathered and burned, concertgoers were terrorized by violence and threats of violence as they huddled together in front of the stage fending off the attacks. Frightening as this was, the worst was yet to come. With the night sky darkened, the concertgoers were startled to see a burning cross on the hillside above them. Fearing the worst, the burning cross was actually the least of the concertgoers' problems. As it turns out, the cross was not the work of the **Ku Klux Klan (KKK)**, but rather of a group of thirteen- and fourteen-year-old boys. Of course, discovering later that the burning cross was little more than an adolescent prank does not change the emotional impact that it had on the concertgoers at the time.

Three hundred protestors entered the picnic grounds to fight the concertgoers. The most serious fighting occurred at a bridge where the concertgoers tried to make a stand, but were eventually pushed back to the stage area. When the police finally intervened and ordered the protestors back to the entrance, they instead circled around and attacked from another direction. In the end, the concertgoers could do little more than create a defensive phalanx and hope for the best. While the rioters burned and destroyed everything in sight, the concertgoers responded by singing "We Shall Not Be Moved." Eventually, the police moved in to restore order and managed to arrange safe transport for the concertgoers.

The first Peekskill riot lasted for four hours, but was not marked by any sustained, organized violence or numerous injuries. It would be wrong, however, to measure the significance of the first Peekskill riot based on the number of injuries incurred. For the concertgoers, this was a truly terrifying event. From their perspective, the roadblocks, the burning cross, the fights inside the picnic grounds, and the delayed police intervention seemed like a coordinated and calculated effort to suppress their political viewpoint. To the protestors, the presence of Robeson seemed like a provocation that required a response. Although most did not participate in the rioting, they quickly blamed the violence on the concertgoers. That the protest of Robeson quickly adopted the language of racism and anti-Semitism shows how close to the surface such feelings were. It does not mean, however, that racism and anti-Semitism were the motivating force behind the riots, only that they were contributing factors. The people of Peekskill took issue with Robeson because of his politics; racial factors just made him that much easier to hate.

The events of August 27, 1949, did not remain a local issue. The Peekskill riot became a front-page story across the nation and provoked much editorial commentary. Most editorials deplored the violence while supporting the cause of the protestors. "Those who are opposed to communism cannot destroy it with violence. Force and strong arm tactics are the handmaidens of communist procedures. They love it. They thrive on it," wrote the *Philadelphia Tribune* (September 3, 1949). In Albany, the *Knickerbocker News* wrote, "We deplore any action that might tend to dignify, or perhaps even martyrize the Negro singer" (September 2, 1949). In newspapers across the nation, this was the consistent interpretation of the first Peekskill riot, except among Robeson's political allies. The Communist Party's *Daily Worker* considered the Peekskill riot an effort to bring about police state terrorism in the America. Aside from this difference in interpretation, Robeson's supporters also asked a different set of questions about the riot; most important was why there was so little police presence and why were they so slow to react? Were they, Robeson wanted to know, working together with the protestors? Just as there is no evidence to support the charges that the concertgoers started the fighting, there is no evidence that the police were involved in a conspiracy to allow the riot.

After the August 27 riot, both the concertgoers and the Peekskill veterans considered their next steps. For the concertgoers, it was obvious that they needed another concert and it needed to be in Peekskill. They quickly secured another site near Peekskill and held a series of public events in New York to publicize a concert featuring Robeson for September 4, 1949. Back in Peekskill, the Joint Veterans Council also organized another protest parade. In spite of the possibility of violence, neither group considered moving its event. If the first Peekskill riot took everyone by surprise, both sides took precautions to be prepared for anything on September 4.

Hoping to avoid a repeat of the violence, New York's Gov. Thomas Dewey called for everyone to keep their heads while placing one-quarter of the entire state police force around Peekskill on September 4. From a variety of jurisdictions, 900 police officers were on hand in Peekskill, along with various emergency vehicles and even a helicopter. They were all in place by 9:00 A.M., five hours before the start of the concert.

In New York, concert organizers loaded buses full of Robeson supporters for the short trip to the Hudson Valley. Among these supporters were some 2,000 men who volunteered to create a human fence around the concert site. Of these, there were a few who would stand around Robeson as human shields while he sang.

The day of the concert was long, hot, and tension-filled. The protestors marched holding up signs that read, "Wake up America—Peekskill Did!" The concertgoers passed through a shower of insults as their buses made their way to the concert site, but once inside, they were able to enjoy the show unmolested. In all, 20,000 people made it to Peekskill to hear Paul Robeson sing on September 4, 1949, while approximately 5,000 protested his appearance.

While Robeson was onstage singing "Go Down Moses," and "What America Means to Me," the protest march broke up. It looked as if there would be no second Peekskill riot. But when the concert ended and the buses and cars filed out of the parking lots, they encountered a strange scene. Stationed along the narrow two-lane roads leading away from the concert site were hundreds of police officers, and behind them were angry mobs of people waiting to throw stones and disrupt the exit from the concert. In an effort to maintain some general sense of order, the police officers were under orders to hold their positions rather than vacate their posts in the event of trouble on the road. There would be plenty to keep the police occupied in the hours ahead.

As the first of the cars and buses eased out of the concert site, they were met by an angry mob. As they pulled away, they were hit with a barrage of stones. When the stones shattered the windows, the drivers were forced from their vehicles and were set on by gangs of young men who beat them. When the police realized what was happening, they stopped the exiting traffic and tried to disperse the crowds. Forty-five minutes later, the exodus began again with only slightly better results. The exit was clear, but as the cars and buses drove away from the police protection, they were showered with stones, logs, and other missiles.

Given the circumstances, it is remarkable that no one was killed in either riot in Peekskill. The reaction to the second riot was predictably similar to the earlier commentaries. Robeson's supporters called it the rise of fascism in America; others denounced the violence but wondered if somehow the communists were to blame. The events in Peekskill were not exactly a race riot because the motivating force behind the protestors was anti-communism. The riots were not even about communism in the abstract—they were about the personification of the communist traveler, Paul Robeson, coming to sing in Peekskill. What is most disturbing about the riots is that they expose how close to the surface racial and anti-Semitic feelings were in Peekskill, and how easily the intersection of politics, race, and a unique set of local issues could erupt into violence.

Further Readings: Duberman, Martin. *Paul Robeson*. New York: Knopf, 1988; Walwik, Joseph. *The Peekskill, New York, Anti-Communist Riots of 1949*. New York: The Edwin Mellen Press, 2002.

J.A. Walwik

Pennsylvania. *See* Chester and Philadelphia (Pennsylvania) Riots of 1918; Philadelphia (Pennsylvania) Riot of 1964; York (Pennsylvania) Riots of 1969

Pensacola (Florida) Riot of 1976

A period of intense racial animosity peaked in Pensacola, Florida, during a police-initiated assault of black protestors on February 24, 1976. Hostilities between the races in northwest Florida began in 1973 when a local high school used Confederate imagery as its mascot. The enormous division that characterized race relations grew in 1975, when five black fishermen disappeared in local waters under circumstances that suggested foul play. Area authorities declared that the men drowned accidentally, but blacks believed whites murdered them. The Pensacola chapters of the **National Association for the Advancement of Colored People (NAACP)** and **Southern Christian Leadership Conference (SCLC)** organized public demonstrations and demanded justice in the matter, but another event soon captured local attention.

On December 22, 1975, an Escambia County Sheriff's Deputy named Doug Raines shot black motorist Wendel Blackwell in the head at point-blank range, killing him instantly. Eyewitness reports differed on whether Blackwell possessed a handgun or if Raines planted it near his body.

The Sheriff's Department, however, declared the shooting justifiable and refused to discipline Raines. The leaders of the local NAACP and SCLC, Rev. B.J. Brooks and Rev. H.K. Matthews, respectively, led demonstrations in downtown Pensacola, met with Gov. Reubin Askew to voice their concerns, demanded a federal investigation of the Blackwell shooting, and boycotted local stores. Most importantly, they met nightly at local churches and organized protests.

On the evening of February 24, 1976, nearly 500 blacks gathered at their usual demonstration site on the grounds of the county Sheriff's Department. They followed their familiar routine of singing, praying, and chanting for white leaders to deliver justice. Although Rev. H.K. Matthews led most activity through a bullhorn, Rev. Jimmie Lee Savage led the crowd in a chant that declared, "Two, four, six, eight, who shall we incarcerate? Untreiner, Raines, the whole damn bunch!" The crowd laughed, joked, and reflected a festive mood, but deputies felt threatened by the particular demonstration and later claimed that blacks displayed weapons and repeatedly threatened them. Because he deemed the group threatening, Sheriff Royal Untreiner ordered seventy nightstick-wielding deputies to dissipate the demonstrators ninety seconds after telling them to leave the premises.

Officers moved into the crowd swinging nightclubs and arresting anyone who offered the slightest resistance. Many protesters received injuries during the melee and required hospital treatment. Untreiner justified his officers' actions and explained that the dangerous mob threatened to riot. In addition to breaking up the crowd, deputies demanded that bystanders from the local newspaper, the *Pensacola News-Journal*, help apprehend and arrest protesters. The journalists were also told not to describe the tumultuous scenes in their articles or they risked punishment, so they complied. Deputies ultimately arrested thirty-four adults and thirteen juveniles on misdemeanor unlawful assembly and malicious trespassing charges. In addition, law enforcement officials added felony extortion counts to the Matthews and Brooks charges three days after their arrests. Police witnesses accused the men of leading chants that threatened to "assassinate" rather than "incarcerate" Untreiner and Raines in an attempt to intimidate the sheriff into removing Doug Raines from active duty.

The arrests of Brooks and Matthews initiated the decline of Pensacola's civil rights struggle. National civil rights organizations withdrew their support of the local movement, and the United Klans of America started a chapter in the racially divided panhandle. On June 10, 1975, a county jury found Brooks and Matthews guilty of felony extortion. The judge gave Brooks five years of probation on the condition that he participate in no public demonstrations, but Matthews, the primary spokesman of the Pensacola black community, received five years of hard labor in state prison. He served sixty-three days of his term before he received clemency, and left the state after his release. In 1979, he received a full pardon of all charges. The 1976 Pensacola riot, therefore, initiated a collapse of the area black freedom struggle and represented a nadir in race relations that still haunts the city.

J. Michael Butler

Philadelphia (Pennsylvania) Riot of 1964

Two weeks after President Lyndon Johnson signed the **Civil Rights Act of 1964** in the presence of Dr. **Martin Luther King, Jr.,** racially motivated riots exploded in several northeastern cities, including New York City (July 18–23); **Rochester,** New York (July 24–25); **Jersey City** (August 2–4), Paterson (August 11–13), and Elizabeth, New Jersey (August 11–13); and **Chicago,** Illinois (August 16–17). From August 28–30, 1964, Philadelphia erupted in violence and looting in response to the arrest and rumored death of Odessa Bradford in the predominantly black **ghetto** of North Philadelphia, marking a downturn in Philadelphia's population size, economic development efforts, and national reputation.

On the evening of August 28, 1964, Odessa Bradford's car stalled at Twenty-Third Street and Cecil B. Moore, formerly Columbia Avenue. Two police officers urged her to move the vehicle out of the way of traffic; however, unable to comply because the car was disabled, an argument began between Bradford and police officers, one white and one black. The officers attempted to remove her from the vehicle as a crowd gathered. One man, whose identity is unknown, attempted to help Bradford, but was also arrested with her. Rumors that Bradford and her would-be protector had been killed proliferated throughout the surrounding neighborhood and a riot ensued. Blacks, in a reversal, threw rocks from inside their apartments and on the street, physically challenged police officers outright. Outnumbered, the Philadelphia Police Department was forced to retreat. Over the next two days, the North Philadelphia neighborhood surrounding Temple University was battered and looted by thousands of people. When the riot officially ended, more than 300 people were injured, close to 800 had been arrested, and over 220 stores and businesses were damaged or permanently devastated. In addition to demonstrating the level of racial unrest in Philadelphia, the Bradford incident and the riot that followed mark the beginning of significant demographic, economic, political, and social changes in Philadelphia.

By 1970, in North Philadelphia, which extends to the Olney, East and West Oak Lane, and Mount Airy sections of the city, a considerable change in population had begun. The city's overall population dropped below two million as the city lost over 53,000 residents, most of them white. Blacks, who migrated from other parts of the city, suburban slums, and southern states, such as Virginia, Maryland, and Delaware, moved into homes sold, abandoned, or rented by whites in the North Philadelphia area. Whites moved to nearby and budding Bucks, Chester, and Montgomery counties, and as their employers followed, the city suffered an economic recession from which it has yet to recover. Although the 1964 race riots in North Philadelphia are not solely blamed for the shifts in population or the economic downturn of the city, the incident is historically noted for encouraging white majority voters to support Police Commissioner Frank L. Rizzo in his first run for mayor in 1971. Rizzo was known for not only leading Philadelphia politics with an iron hand, but also for being quick to use force when confronting blacks in the city. It was under his leadership as police commissioner that Bradford was arrested and the 1964 riot ensued, and it was under his mayoral administration that reported incidents of **police brutality** against Philadelphia's black residents dramatically increased.

By 2004, blacks were not only the racial majority of Philadelphia, but John F. Street, a black man, was in his second term as mayor. In the North Philadelphia neighborhood in which Bradford and residents confronted police in what was argued to be **black self-defense,** Temple University has spearheaded a new growth of businesses and a large portion of housing in the area has been rebuilt.

Further Readings: Boger, John Charles, and Judith Welch Wegner. *Race, Poverty, and American Cities*. Chapel Hill: University of North Carolina Press, 1996; Katz, Michael B., and Thomas J. Sugrue, eds. *W.E.B. Du Bois, Race, and the City: The Philadelphia Negro and Its Legacy*. Philadelphia: University of Pennsylvania Press, 1998; Weigley, Russell. *Philadelphia: A 300-Year History*. New York: W.W. Norton & Company, 1982.

Ellesia Ann Blaque

Police Brutality

Formal policing began in the United States in the major urban areas such as New York, Boston, and Philadelphia when these municipalities paid officials for crime control in the mid-nineteenth century, primarily in response to riots by newly arriving immigrants. Prior to this time, policing was mostly carried out through the "night watch" system, an idea borrowed from Europe in which local citizens were required to observe and report criminal behavior to authorities.

SNCC leader John Lewis cringes as a burly state trooper swings his club at Lewis' head, 1965. Courtesy of the Library of Congress.

Southern cities such as New Orleans, Louisiana, also began to develop professional police forces in the nineteenth century although southern slave patrols and vigilante committees continued to be the primary means of controlling slave escapes and revolts, which became increasingly common during the early and mid-nineteenth century. Racial conflicts did not end with the emancipation of slaves; the **lynching** of blacks continued at a startling rate, with the newly emerging police forces often ignoring the practice or even actively participating.

As an abuse of authority and power, agents of social control express police brutality through physical, emotional, or legal exploitation of those under their control. More than any other type of police misconduct, this type of violent behavior by police has resulted in calls for reforms by the public. In fact, local and national commissions have chronicled police excesses of force, including a report from the National Commission on Law Observance and Enforcement (1931), which resulted in a book titled *Our Lawless Police*. In addition, reports have been drawn up by the mayoral commission on police actions during the Harlem riots (1935), the President's Commission on Civil Rights (1947), the U.S. Civil Rights Commission (1961), the McCone Commission (1965), the Crime Commission (1967), the National Commission on Civil Disorders (commonly known as the **Kerner Commission Report** of 1968), the Knapp Commission (1972), and the Christopher Commission, which reported on the Rodney King beating (1991). Police brutality has occurred throughout police history and has been especially prominent, or at least visible, during race riots.

American policing as we know it today traces back primarily to England and the London Metropolitan Police. In the early years of the American police, the early 1800s, the departments were not as well organized as those of their British predecessors. Boston experienced a riot at the inception of its police department in 1837 when a mob of Protestants attacked the homes of the newly arrived Irish immigrants. In 1845, New York City formed its first police department. On July 12 and 13, 1863, the New York police had to quash the **New York City Draft Riot of 1863,** which occurred when a large group of whites rose in opposition to being drafted to fight in the Civil War.

One of the earliest documented accounts of unnecessary police force at the dawning of the twentieth century occurred in **New York City** in 1900 when a confrontation between a white officer and a black citizen erupted in mob activity that involved police and a large number of Irish immigrants, who together attacked blacks in the area. Riots at the beginning of the century also occurred in **Springfield,** Ohio (1904); **Greensburg,** Indiana (1906); and **Springfield,** Illinois (1908).

In 1917, a riot occurred in Houston, Texas, when a group formed to protest the practices of the city police department after an incident in which white police officers refused to turn over a suspect in compliance with the instructions of a black military officer. They placed another military officer in custody, beat him, and later shot at him when he attempted to escape. As word of the incident got out, several black citizens armed themselves and shot two white police officers. A firefight between the two groups resulted in the deaths of eleven to seventeen white officers and four black soldiers. The surviving black soldiers were either executed or given life sentences in prison.

The National Commission on Law Enforcement and Observance, which is more commonly known as the Wickersham Commission, released its well-known report in 1931. This document noted the use of excessive police force and intimidation by officials, commonly referred to as "the third degree" and suggested that it was widespread by the time of the report's release. Despite recommendations from the national commission report, police brutality continued.

In 1935, riots in Harlem, New York, broke out after rumors spread that a black youth had stolen a knife and was beaten to death by police. The effects of the Depression are often blamed as an underlying cause of the incident, but conditions of police brutality as a common way of life in the area are also cited as a factor. The Harlem Riot Commission Report was very condemning in its description of the police responses during the disruption.

In the 1940s, excessive police force was a common theme in the race riots of that decade. A major exodus of African Americans from the South to northern factories set the stage for confrontation. Serious complaints of police brutality occurred during the riots in **Detroit** in 1943 when a fight erupted between young black and white men in a predominantly recreational area of the city. Looting followed by rioting occurred and was so extensive that federal troops had to be called in to suppress the activity that left 34 people dead and over 1,000 injured. **Thurgood Marshall,** a young civil rights lawyer who later became a U.S. Supreme Court justice, rebuked the police actions during this riot by claiming that the police used undue force. Measures taken by the police to control white and black citizens in the riot were unequally represented, according to Marshall, as blacks were dealt with in an unnecessarily harsh manner while the violent actions of whites were ignored or condoned. A governor's commission report, however, stated that the actions of the police to contain the situation were appropriate.

The inner-city disturbances that occurred during the 1960s also brought many complaints of police brutality. A series of so-called **ghetto** riots occurred in several U.S. cities. In the 1960s, race riots erupted in large and small cities across the nation, such as Chicago, Illinois; **Philadelphia, Pennsylvania;** Savannah, Georgia; and Cambridge, Maryland. However, the most visible example of police brutality took place in Birmingham, Alabama, where officers under the supervision of city Police Commissioner **T. Eugene "Bull" Connor** attacked a group of young children and adolescents who were peacefully marching in the city. Dogs were unleashed on the crowd and high-pressure water hoses and cattle prods were used against the protesters even though they were not directly attacking anyone. This event is responsible for furthering public attention and outrage at police abuse of power.

In the Los Angeles area known as Watts, another example that is commonly cited as excessive and unnecessary police force occurred in 1965 (see **Los Angeles [California] Riot of 1965**). Like the 1943 encounter in Detroit, the riot, which in this case lasted almost a week, claimed the lives of 34 people and left over 1,000 injured. Police made approximately 4,000 arrests and rioters caused nearly $40 million of property damage. Many of the injured were police officers, firefighters, National Guard soldiers, and other government agents. Several sources reported that police brutality was used in the Watts riot. Although the McCone Commission cited the area's poor social and economic conditions as a cause of the event, the most salient factor leading to the riot involved a growing rupture in the relations between the black citizens and mostly white police. There was a particular dislike and distrust of Police Chief William H. Parker, who was viewed by black Watts residents as an advocate of police brutality due to police tactics and his insistence on his officers possessing a paramilitary presence in the community.

The **Long Hot Summer Riots of 1965–1967** involved over several hundred race riots in a number of cities and rural areas. It was reported that small events ignited the riots and one of the primary causes was poor police–community relations. The resulting police responses were seen by many as excessively violent or as possible contributors to already volatile conditions. Detroit, the home of the disastrous riots of 1945, had one of the worst riots of this period as well.

Newark, New Jersey, also saw major rioting during the summer of 1967. When an African American cab driver named John Smith was arrested and subsequently beaten by police on the way to the precinct, a crowd rioted was after an inaccurate report that the officers had killed him.

The 1970s did not see the same level of riotous behavior as the previous decades, but police misconduct was still at center stage, especially in regard to corruption, due in large part to the attention given Frank Serpico, the New York Police Department detective who exposed the high level of corruption that went on in that agency. One incident that occurred at the very end of the decade did, however, bring charges of police brutality. On December 17, 1979, police in Miami, Florida, gave chase to an African American man who supposedly was engaged in traffic violations on his motorcycle. Six white officers attacked Arthur McDuffie and proceeded to beat him until he was unconscious. He died a few days later. Three days of rioting followed his death; eighteen people were killed and much property was damaged.

Although there were not many serious race riots in the 1980s, an event in the early 1990s made an indelible mark on the issue of police violence. Perhaps the case most commonly connected with police brutality occurred on March 3, 1991, in Los Angeles when an African American named Rodney King was traveling at a high rate of speed in his car with two other men and was stopped after a chase by officers of the California Highway Patrol. King later claimed that he had refused to stop because he was on probation for robbery. Officers from the Los Angeles Police Department (LAPD) and from the Los Angeles Unified School District Police joined the chase. By the time King's vehicle was stopped, a host of officers, including twenty-three from the LAPD, had congregated on the scene, including officers hovering overhead in a police helicopter. King failed to exit the vehicle when ordered to do so by officers, although his passengers quickly complied. It is reported that King, acting in an erratic manner, ran at police. The officers believed that King was high on drugs and shocked him with a taser. Four officers began beating him with nightsticks and kicking him as he lay on the ground. King ended up with fractures to his skull, broken teeth, a broken ankle, internal organ damage, and brain damage as a result of the fifty-six blows that were dealt by the four officers.

A white amateur video camera operator who was watching from his apartment captured the King beating on film. The camera operator, George Holliday, attempted to provide this film to the LAPD the next day; a sergeant at the station was not interested in the tape, so Holliday went to local television stations that broadcast the video that night. The victim's brother, Paul King, also attempted to complain to the LAPD, but was turned away. By the next day, the ninety-second tape was shown on national television and interest in the case began to grow. When LAPD Chief of Police Daryl Gates and L.A. Mayor Tom Bradley, a former police officer, saw the video, they both displayed disgust over the brutal treatment of King.

The four officers who were directly involved in the beating—Stacey Koon, Laurence W. Powell, Timothy Wind, and Theodore J. Briseno—were indicted for assault. Due to the intense media exposure surrounding the case, a trial was scheduled in a new venue in Ventura County. A jury of ten whites, one Asian American, and one Latin-American acquitted the four officers of the charges against them. Within a few hours of the verdict, explosive rioting and looting broke out in Los Angeles, followed by disturbances in Atlanta, Georgia; Seattle, Washington; and Madison, Wisconsin. The violence in Los Angeles became extreme and the LAPD enlisted the assistance of county, state, and federal law enforcement to stop the riots (see **Los Angeles [California] Riots of 1992**). President George H.W. Bush intervened and ordered the military to establish order in the main hot spots of civil disruption. The massive violence, arson, and looting that accompanied the rioting resulted in over 54 deaths, 2,000 injuries, and great property loss, making it the largest outbreak of riot violence in the United States in the twentieth century.

The four officers were then charged with civil rights violations and were found guilty in federal court. A special commission to investigate the L.A. riots was assembled and Attorney Warren Christopher was called on to lead the investigation. Many have surmised that the LAPD, headed by Chief Daryl Gates, who was a young officer at the time of the 1965 riots, had an overly aggressive tone and a pervasive racist ethos.

Theorists have long speculated the potential causes of police brutality; however, the issue is complex and multifaceted. In many of the riot situations discussed above, the precipitating factors were essentially minor issues that were worsened by underlying social conditions. The cities where the violent activity occurred all have their own unique qualities that added fuel to the fire, or perhaps made conditions more amenable to compromise. Some cities saw more than their share of riots and police violence, including Harlem, which experienced major race riots in 1935, 1943, and

1964. Economic problems due to periods of depression, occupational competition, and poor housing, were often factors. And, of course, America's unique history of race relations, brought about by slavery, played a major part in all of the race riots. Regarding police brutality in relation to these riots, several factors also appear to present themselves and involve personal characteristics of the officers, agency philosophy, and police–community relations. Again, the issue of **racism** due to the nation's distinctive past is a recurring issue in police brutality in the United States.

Although excessive police force and intimidation has marred the history of American law enforcement, it should be noted that not all those who have been called to serve and protect have been guilty of this type of misbehavior. Most police officers believe in the law that they are required to uphold, and most understand that excessive force is unacceptable. It is important to note that commissions have always been formed to produce reports that not only describe the riot behavior and resulting police action, but also make recommendations for improvement. Greater police professionalism, through an increase in education and training programs, will hopefully reduce the amount of excessive force that is used by officers to control riots. *See also* Connor, T. Eugene "Bull"; Detroit (Michigan) Riot of 1943; Harlem (New York) Riot of 1935; Houston (Texas) Mutiny of 1917; Long Hot Summer Riots, 1965–1967; Los Angeles (California) Riot of 1965; Los Angeles (California) Riots of 1992; Newark (New Jersey) Riot of 1967; New York City Draft Riot of 1863; New York City Riot of 1900.

Further Readings: Barlow, David E., and Melissa Hickman Barlow. *Police in a Multicultural Society: An American Story*. Prospect Heights, IL: Waveland Press, Inc., 2000; Cannon, Lou. *Official Negligence: How Rodney King and the Riots Changed Los Angeles and the LAPD*. Boulder, CO: Westview Press, 1999; Kappeler, Victor E., Richard D. Skuder, and Geoffrey Alpert. *Forces of Deviance: Understanding the Dark Side of Policing*. 2nd ed. Prospect Heights, IL: Waveland Press, Inc., 1998; Platt, Anthony, ed. *The Politics of Riot Commissions 1917–1979: A Collection of Official Reports and Critical Essays*. New York: Collier Books, 1971; Skolnick, Jerome H., and James J. Fyfe. *Above the Law: Police and the Excessive Use of Force*. New York: Free Press, 1993; Stark, Rodney. *Police Riots: Collective Violence and Law Enforcement*. Belmont, CA: Wadsworth, 1972; Waskow, Arthur I. *From Race Riot to Sit-In, 1919 and the 1960s: A Study in the Connections between Conflict and Violence*. Garden City, NY: Doubleday & Company, 1966.

Leonard A. Steverson

Poverty

Despite the United States being one of the richest countries in the world, many people in the nation are affected by poverty, which has long been an important cause of race riots.

Currently, over 37 million people go without proper nutrition, adequate housing, access to health care, or a good education, and these people generally experience a grim quality of life. In other words, they receive or earn insufficient income to pay for life's basic necessities. The official poverty rate in 2004 was 12.7 percent, an increase from a 12.5 percent rate in 2003. While the poverty rate for non-Hispanic whites increased slightly (from 8.2 percent to 8.6 percent), and decreased for Asians (to 9.8 percent from 11.8 percent), the poverty rates for blacks and Hispanics remained unchanged between 2003 and 2004 (24.7 percent and 21.9 percent, respectively). The poverty rate for children under eighteen years of age is higher (17.8 percent) than for those from ages eighteen to sixty-four (11.3 percent) and for people ages sixty-five and older (9.8 percent). Over the decades, many of the differences between different groups in the United States have remained stable. For instance, women consistently face a greater risk of poverty than men, regardless of age, race, or ethnicity (i.e., the feminization of poverty) (DeNavas-Walt et al. 2005).

The most significant change in poverty rates has been among the nation's sixty-five-and-older population, reflecting the success of Social Security (including Medicare) and private pension plans. It is important to note that blacks are almost three times as likely to live in poverty as whites, just as they were in the 1960s. Today, about one million black children live in extreme poverty, and those who live in a household headed by a single parent are especially likely to be poor. The origins and persistence of poverty among blacks are not simple, but they are tied to the **racism** and exclusion experienced by blacks, especially in the labor and housing markets. Today, there are two different federal poverty measures: *poverty thresholds*, based on the U.S. Department of Agriculture's economy food plan, and *poverty guidelines*, which are a simplification of the poverty thresholds used to determine eligibility for a number of federal and state programs. Poverty thresholds are determined after the year is over, and are based on the U.S. Census Bureau's Current Population Survey from March of the current year. These thresholds are primarily used for statistical and research purposes. On the other hand, poverty guidelines are issued by the U.S. Department of Health and Human Services at the beginning of each year and, again, they are used to determine eligibility for a variety of programs. When we speak of the federal poverty level or poverty line, we are referring to poverty guidelines.

The nature and prevalence of poverty in the United States has been a source of political debate since the concept was officially defined and measured by the federal government in the early 1960s. The measure of poverty not only impacts public perceptions of the relative well-being of the U.S. population, but also impacts public policies and programs. The current poverty measure is based on a definition developed by the Social Security Administration in 1964 (revised in 1969 and 1981). After much debate, the first official measure of poverty was developed by Mollie Orshansky of the Social Security Administration. At this time, it was assumed that people experienced poverty on a temporary basis. Orshansky published an analysis of the poor population using poverty thresholds in a January 1965 *Social Security Bulletin* article. She based her poverty thresholds on the economy food plan, which was the cheapest of four food plans developed by the Department of Agriculture, which had based these plans on the 1955 Department of Agriculture's Household Food Consumption Survey that measured the amount of income families spent on food. Orshansky knew that families of three or more persons spent about one-third of their net income on food. She took this information and then multiplied the cost of the economy food plan by three to arrive at the minimal yearly income for a family. Using 1963 as the base year, she calculated that a family of four (two adults and two children) would spend $1,033 a year on food. Based on the 1955 survey, and using her formula, she concluded that $3,100 a year was the poverty threshold for a family of four in 1963.

The original poverty thresholds took into consideration family size, farm/non-farm status, the number of children in the family, the gender of the head of household, and the aged/non-aged status, resulting in a matrix of 124 poverty thresholds. In 1965, a year after declaring the **War on Poverty,** the Johnson administration's newly established Office of Economic Opportunity adopted Orshanky's poverty thresholds as the working definition of poverty. By 1969, the federal government recognized that because of inflation, the measure no longer accurately reflected the cost of living. Thus, that year the poverty thresholds were reexamined and adjusted for price changes. At this time it was decided that the poverty thresholds would be indexed by the Consumer Price Index rather than the per person cost of the economy food plan. The Bureau of the Budget (now called the Office of Management and Budget) designated the revised poverty thresholds as the government's official statistical definition of poverty. Since then, various committees and task forces have been charged with the task of examining whether, and how, the poverty thresholds need to be adjusted.

In 1992, the Panel on Poverty and Family Assistance was formed to conduct a study on measuring poverty. In 1995, the panel released its report called *Measuring Poverty: A New Approach*, which included a new way of determining an official poverty measure. Yet, the U.S. government has made no significant changes in the method it uses to measure poverty. Hence, each year, the U.S. Census Bureau updates the poverty thresholds accounting for inflation only. Once again, poverty guidelines are slightly different from poverty thresholds. They are a simplification of the poverty thresholds developed for administrative purposes. The Department of Health and Human Services issues poverty guidelines every year in the *Federal Register*, and they are designated by the year that they are issued. For instance, the 2006 poverty guideline for a family of four is $20,000 in the forty-eight contiguous states and the District of Columbia. Programs and policies that use poverty guidelines to determine eligibility include: Head Start, the Food Stamp Program, the Low-Income Home Energy Assistance Program, and the National School Lunch Program, among other programs. However, there are notable exceptions to federal, state, and local poverty programs that use the poverty guidelines to determine eligibility. For instance, the Federal Earned Income Tax Credit does not use the poverty guidelines, and public housing programs, like Section 8 Housing, use the area median income to determine eligibility.

The manner by which the federal government measures poverty has not gone without criticism. One criticism involves the types of income that are excluded from the poverty measure. Some argue that by not including the income from public assistance that many poor families receive (e.g., the cash value of food stamps and health insurance benefits), the extent of poverty in the U.S. is overstated. Another criticism involves expenses that many families consider critical to their budgets, but that are excluded from consideration in the poverty calculation. The cost of child-care, for instance, was not considered by Orshansky since the families that participated in the 1955 Department of Agriculture household survey involved one wage earner and a stay-at-home parent. Also, work-related expenses, such as commuting, are part of life today and have a significant impact on a family's budget. By ignoring these expenses, the poverty measure underestimates poverty. Also, the poverty measure still assumes that families spend one-third of their income on food, when in reality food makes up about one-sixth of families' expenditures. The costs of housing, utilities, and transportation are much greater today than they were in the 1960s. The key issue here is cost. If the government considered all of these factors in the way it measures poverty, the number of people falling below the poverty line would increase significantly, and the costs of providing assistance to these individuals would then be considerably higher than they are today. Recently, community-based organizations around the country have advocated for "living wages." These organizations argue that instead of using poverty as the standard measure for well-being, we should develop a measure of living wages, defined as the minimum hourly wage necessary for an individual to achieve a basic standard of living in a particular community. The basic argument is that limited public funds should not subsidize poverty-wage work. Rather, private enterprises that benefit from public funds (e.g., through service contracts and tax abatements) should pay their employees a living wage. Most people agree that poverty is a serious problem in our society. However, there is a lot of disagreement in what can be done about it. Some blame the poor for their own situation, pointing to cultural traits that are said to keep people in poverty. Others look at structural causes to explain poverty and focus on cycles and structural forces, such as racism and the restructuring of the U.S. economy, that are said to prevent people from escaping poverty.

Regardless of how we explain poverty, it has been seen as a major cause of racial violence in American history, particularly in terms of the urban race riots of the twentieth century. If not the main causes of race riots in the United States, the unemployment, poverty, and low-quality housing that large numbers of poor urban minorities experienced did contribute to the tinderbox. In the 1960s, two federal initiatives—the War on Poverty and the **Civil Rights Act of 1964**—were enacted and largely aimed at improving the well-being of blacks and, thus, reduced the racial tensions of the era. In fact, it was President **John F. Kennedy** who in 1963, at a time when racial issues were reaching a boiling point in the South, framed civil rights issues in economic terms. For instance, he revived an earlier request for educational and training programs that would benefit people of all races and that later became a significant part of President Johnson's antipoverty initiatives. Over the years, the condition for most blacks improved significantly, yet the gap between conditions for blacks and those of non-Hispanic whites in the United States remains significant, contributing greatly to the high level of inequality present in one of the richest nations in the world.

Further Readings: Citro, Constance, F., and Robert T. Michael, eds. *Measuring Poverty: A New Approach*. Washington, D.C.: National Academies Press, 1995; Danziger, Sheldon H., and Robert H. Haveman, eds. *Understanding Poverty*. New York: Russell Sage Foundation, 2001; DeNavas-Walt, Carmen, Bernadette D. Proctor, and Cheryl Hill Lee. *U.S. Census Bureau, Current Population Reports. Income, Poverty, and Health Insurance Coverage in the United States, 2004*. Washington, D.C.: U.S. Government Printing Office, 2005, 60–229; Fisher, Gordon M. "The Development and History of the Poverty Thresholds." *Social Security Bulletin* 55, no. 4 (Winter 1992): 3–14; Glasmeier, Amy K. *An Atlas of Poverty in America: One Nation, Pulling Apart, 1960–2003*. London: Routledge, 2006; Orshansky, Mollie. "Counting the Poor: Another Look at the Poverty Profile." *Social Security Bulletin* 28, no. 1 (January 1965): 3–29; Orshansky, Mollie. "How Poverty Is Measured." *Monthly Labor Review* 92, no. 2 (February 1969): 37–41; Orshansky, Mollie, Harold Watts, Bradley R. Schiller, and John J. Korbel. "Measuring Poverty: A Debate." *Public Welfare* 36, no. 2 (Spring 1978): 44–46; United States Department of Health and Human Services. "The 2006 HHS Poverty Guidelines." *Federal Register* 71, no. 15, January 24, 2006, 3848–3849.

Paulina X. Ruf

Powell v. Alabama (1932)

Powell v. Alabama was one of the U.S. Supreme Court's early opinions that expanded the scope of the Fifth Amendment. In this case, for the first time it was suggested that the right to counsel was a national right, if only in capital cases, and that aspect of the Bill of Rights was applied to the states. The case resulted in more trials, convictions, reversals, appeals, and retrials than any crime in American history.

The case revolved around nine black teenagers who were accused of raping two white girls on a train traveling through the South in 1931. The group became commonly known as the Scottsboro Boys (see **Scottsboro Case**). The incident stemmed from a fight that broke out on the train between the nine black youths and several whites. The confrontation ignited when a white youth crossing on top of the train stepped on the hand of Haywood Patterson, one of the black youths, who was hanging onto the side to the train. A stone-throwing fight then erupted between Patterson and his friends and the white youths. The result was that almost all of the whites were forced off the train, with the exception of one, Orville Gilley, whom Patterson saved. Some of the whites who were forced off the train complained to the stationmaster that they had been attacked by a gang of blacks. The next town was notified, and when the train arrived in Paint Rock, Alabama, an armed posse surrounded, tied up, and hauled the nine black youths off to jail in Scottsboro, Alabama.

However, it would turn out that the key element of that stop in Paint Rock was not the fight that had broken out, but the complaint of two white girls—Victoria Price and Ruby Bates—who had also been on the train. The girls claimed they had been raped by a gang of twelve blacks at pistol and knife point. Price positively identified six of the nine Scottsboro Boys.

The others were assumed guilty by association. Attempts by the boys to deny the accusations were met with violence, and the threat of a **lynching** materialized as the nine sat in jail. Several hundred local citizens gathered around the Scottsboro jail looking for quick justice on the night of their arrest. However, courage on the part of the local sheriff, and the order by Alabama's Gov. B.M. Miller to send the National Guard, quieted the crowd, which eventually dispersed.

Amidst this fear of potential violence and lynching, local officials in Alabama hurried through the legal proceedings. All but one of the trials was held and concluded in one day. The counsel afforded to the defendants was suspect at best, with one having no experience in criminal law at all. The lawyers and defendants met only right before the trials began, giving them no time to plan a defense, and both lawyers acted minimally in their appearance in court. The nine were quickly convicted and sentenced to death. The ruling was appealed to the Alabama Supreme Court, which ruled 6–1 that the trial was fair, and subsequently appealed to the U.S. Supreme Court. What was an obvious perversion of due process to many outside the Deep South, and even some within, became a national cause, hailed by diverse organizations from the **National Association for the Advancement of Colored People (NAACP)** to the Communist Party.

The Supreme Court agreed to hear the appeal combining *Weems v. Alabama* and *Patterson v. Alabama* into the case of Powell. Justice Sutherland explained that, in his opinion, the trial had been unfair. He concluded that the lack of effective counsel had violated the defendant's right to due process as required by the **Fourteenth Amendment**, and to counsel as guaranteed in the Fifth Amendment.

The decision overruled an earlier decision from 1884, *Hurtado v. California*, in which the Court ruled that the specific dictates of the Fifth Amendment did not apply to the states via the Fourteenth Amendment. *Powell* rejected that reasoning and represented a major step in extending the Bill of Rights to the states, which had begun not even a decade earlier in a series of cases referring to the First Amendment. This was the first time that, with the exception of free-speech guarantees, the Bill of Rights was impressed on state governments.

Justice Sutherland's opinion noted that the atmosphere around the case was unfriendly, unsettling, and downright hostile. With the threat of mob violence hanging over the proceedings, the defendants were escorted to and from the jail under armed guard. The judge made no effort to afford the defendants any help, including never asking them if they wanted counsel. The counsel that was eventually procured (with no help from the court), and paid for by concerned citizens was useless. One lawyer, from out of state, had no knowledge of Alabama law and was not even a member of the local bar. The other was so drunk he could barely stand. The Supreme Court noted that the trial court could have granted a delay to give the eventual counsel some time to prepare, or even find some effective counsel. In the end, the trial court did not even consider the issue of counsel as a vital and important component to the proceedings.

Sutherland made it clear that the counsel in this case was vital for justice to be achieved. The failure of the trial court to secure lawyers that were not in the least bit effective, or capable of being so, denied the defendants due process under the Fourteenth Amendment. However, Sutherland was careful to limit the ruling to capital cases, noting that whether there was such a need in other criminal cases was not at issue in this case. (That decision would take thirty more years; in *Gideon v. Wainwright*, the Court did extend the right to counsel to non-capital cases.) But the Court noted very specifically that in any capital case, when the defendant was not able to hire a lawyer and was incapable of making a proper defense because of a variety of circumstances, the demands of due process of law made it the duty of the Court, whether it was asked or not, to assign counsel. Any contrary decision would deny the basic "immutable principles of justice which inhere in the very idea of free government" (*Holden v. Hardy*, 169 U.S. 366, 389). *See also* Rape, as Provocation for Lynching.

Further Readings: Carter, Dan T. *Scottsboro: A Tragedy of the American South*. Baton Rouge: Louisiana State University Press, 1979; Goodman, James E. *Stories of Scottsboro*. New York: Pantheon Books, 1994; Linder, Douglas O. *Famous American Trials: The Scottsboro Boys 1931–1937*. See http://www.law.umkc.edu/faculty/projects/FTrials/scottsboro/scottsb.htm.

Gary Gershman

Press Coverage of Racial Violence

Historically, white press coverage of incidences of racial violence has often perpetuated racist beliefs about blacks, augmented racial tensions, and in some cases, generated more violence. There also exist examples of both black and white presses that have helped cover racial violence in a balanced and productive way.

Few crimes were covered as extensively as **lynchings** in the South. The *New York Tribune* reported on the lynching of **Sam Hose** on April 14, 1899, in the following way:

> In the presence of nearly 2,000 people, who sent aloft yells of defiance and shouts of joy, Sam Hose (a Negro who committed two of the basest acts known to crime) was burned at the stake in a public road, one and a half miles from here. Before the torch was applied to the pyre, the Negro was deprived of his ears, fingers, and other portions of his body with surprising fortitude. Before the body was cool, it was cut to pieces, the bones were crushed into small bits and even the tree on which the wretch met his fate was torn up and disposed of as souvenir. . . . Those unable to obtain the ghastly relics directly, paid more fortunate possessors extravagant sums for them. (Hine et al., 320)

This report is indicative of how southern journalists depicted lynchings. In these articles, the lynchings were graphically described and blacks were labeled as "wretches," "fiends," or "desperadoes" (Perloff, 315). The victims were invariably considered to be guilty, with or (more often) without benefit of trial or substantiated evidence. Although lynching was an extralegal activity, newspapers glorified and defended it as being right and proper, and necessary to achieve justice. Those who carried out the lynching were characterized as somber, duty-bound, upstanding leaders and members of the community. The victims of the alleged crimes were invariably portrayed as innocent. The advertisement of an impending lynching was written in language ranging from grave to celebratory.

These articles contributed also to the general miasma of racial tensions within the community. The portrayal of blacks in a derogatory fashion in local newspapers was one of the circumstances that, in 1919, fueled riots in **Washington, D.C.**; **East St. Louis,** Illinois; and **Chicago,** Illinois. Reed W. Smith claims that "by continually publishing stories and editorials about the supposed black threat," Georgia journalists "helped keep white Georgians agitated" and perpetuated fear among its readers (Smith, 83). Newspapers that presented blacks as being prone to crime further justified the rampant killings of innocent black men whose only offense was the color of their skin.

Although blacks spearheaded the large-scale attack on lynching in their own newspapers, white presses also made contributions. Notably, the *Chicago Tribune* was the first to keep statistics of the people lynched and the motives given for their executions. In his article "The Press and Lynchings of African-Americans," published in the *Journal of Black Studies*, Richard M. Perloff claimed that the *New York Times* severely criticized lynching but often did not question the alleged guilt of the blacks. Coverage from the black perspective emerged in numerous papers founded by **W.E.B Du Bois, Ida B. Wells-Barnett,** and others. These papers provided an unbiased record of numerous lynchings, arguments in defense of (or sympathetic to) the black victims, and positive representations of blacks, and were instrumental in combating anti-black violence.

The mainstream press played an essential role during the tumult of the **civil rights movement** of the 1950s and 1960s. Activists were assailed with violence during nonviolent protests and demonstrations, and several lost their lives in the struggle to obtain civil rights and eradicate **segregation**. The civil rights movement achieved many successes, mostly as a result of news and television coverage. At first, the press was not sympathetic to the movement, blaming the activists for white retaliatory violence. But as time passed, and the troubling accounts and images were projected for all the world to see, the pressure for federal legislation and enforcement mounted.

During the riots in the urban **ghettos** of the mid-1960s, as well as in the 1980s and 1990s, many blacks criticized the way the mainstream press portrayed racial violence. Blacks accused white reporters of portraying young blacks as criminals, hoodlums, and troublemakers. They also condemned the fact that their focus was on looting and the destruction of property rather than on the triggering circumstances such as **racism** and **poverty**. Authors David L. Paletz and Robert Dunn found fault with the press coverage of the Winston-Salem, North Carolina, riot in 1967. For example, the *Winston-Salem Journal*, although racially progressive, used mild language and excluded the perspective of the rioters. This practice was used by some newspapers to help quench racial conflict. *See also* Press Instigation of Racial Violence.

Further Readings: Hine, Darlene Clark, William C. Hine, and Stanley Harrold. "White Supremacy Triumphant: African-Americans in the South in the Late Nineteenth Century." Chap. 14 in *The African-American Odyssey.* Englewood Cliffs, NJ: Prentice Hall, 2000, 306–331; Jacobs, Ronald N. *Race, Media, and the Crisis of Civil Society: From Watts to Rodney King*. Cambridge, England: Cambridge University Press, 2000; Jean, Susan. "'Warranted' Lynchings: Narratives of Mob Violence in White Southern Newspapers, 1880–1940." *American Nineteenth Century History* 6 (2005): 351–372; Paletz, David L., and Robert Dunn. "Press Coverage of Civil Disorders: A Case Study of Winston-Salem, 1967." *Public Opinion Quarterly* 33 (1969): 328–345; Perloff, Richard M. "The Press and Lynchings of African-Americans." *Journal of Black Studies* (2000): 315–330; Smith, Reed W. "Southern Journalists and Lynching: The Statesboro Case Study." *Journalism & Communication Monographs* (2005): 51–92.

Gladys L. Knight

Press Instigation of Racial Violence

Press instigation concerns the proclivity of newspapers to provoke violence. The first newspaper was published in America in 1690. Since then, the press has provided a vital service, keeping the American people informed on events, whether local, national, or international. One of the most controversial aspects of newspaper publishing is its inherent ability to influence public emotion, opinion, and attitude, and to incite action. Throughout its history, the American press has frequently encouraged or directly instigated violent activities, just as it has also helped to end violence. This is particularly true in racial violence.

During **Reconstruction, white mobs** attacked and terrorized the newly freed slaves and their supporters. The **Ku Klux Klan (KKK)** was one of the most notorious organizations formed to control and oppress blacks through violence. Generally, the early conservative southern press encouraged violence by covering the activities of the Klan and condoning its practices. For example, the Richmond *Dispatch* listed the objectives of the Klan as follows: to "kill the kullered kuss" and "clean out the karpet-baggers" (Trelease, 61–62). There were also numerous newspapers published by the Ku Klux Klan itself.

Journalists in the North and the larger cities of the South generally opposed anti-black violence. The Kentucky *Courier-Journal* wrote: "This thing of serving notices of exile on Kentuckians at will, and hanging or shooting, at midnight and in their own door-yards, men who stand convicted of no crime, is a burning disgrace to the State" (Trelease, 282). The rebuttal to violence was often more fierce when it was against white supporters, rather than blacks. Sometimes, liberal presses, such as the *Atlanta Constitution*, inconsistently condoned violence against blacks in one issue and lambasted it in the next. When federal troops were positioned across the South in response to the massive violence inflicted on both blacks and whites, conservative presses toned down their support for organizations such as the Klan. This did not curtail the violent activities, however, and the occurrences of **lynching** and rioting increased and eventually swept across the nation.

Lynching was rampant between 1889 and 1932. Newspapers openly encouraged community involvement in lynching and sensationalized their accounts with lurid detail. Following a crime, conservative presses vilified the alleged lawbreakers, exaggerated the innocence of the white victims, and often hinted that swift justice was sure to follow. Reports thus embellished helped to justify and indeed spur on the incidence of lynching. In 1899, the *Atlanta Constitution* instigated a lynching when it "offered a $500 reward for the capture of Sam Holt, a black man that Georgia authorities were hunting for suspicion of raping a white woman and murdering her husband" (Smith, 58).

Ironically, the same medium used to provoke violence was frequently used to protest it. The *Chicago Tribune* was the first newspaper to publish statistics on lynching. It was followed by such organizations as the Tuskegee Institute and the **National Association for the Advancement of Colored People (NAACP). Ida B. Wells-Barnett** regularly castigated lynching in her newspaper, *Free Speech and Headlight*. When a **white mob** destroyed her office in retaliation to her outspokenness, she resumed her struggle in Chicago, Illinois. **Mary Church Terrell,** using the same gruesome descriptions previously printed in prominent pro-lynching newspapers, condemned lynching in a letter that was published. ***The Crisis*,** along with numerous anti-lynching women's associations, was also instrumental in exposing lynching and other atrocities against blacks. Although unsuccessful, the creation of the Dyer Anti-Lynching Bill illustrated how prominent this issue had become (see **Dyer, Leonidas C**.). The cumulative result was that large-scale press endorsements of lynching diminished. Some presses formerly in favor of lynching began criticizing violence against blacks. However, black journalists such as **W.E.B. Du Bois,** Ida B. Wells-Barnett, and **A. Philip Randolph,** as well as militant leaders of the 1960s, often used the press as a forum to advocate **black self-defense,** which often intensified already volatile situations.

The press was sometimes responsible for provoking riots. In the **Wilmington (North Carolina) Riot of 1898**, Alex Manly, the editor of a local black newspaper, published acerbic comments charging that the sexual crimes of white men against black women were equally as bad as those of black men against white women. This article triggered a riot that resulted in the destruction of the newspaper office and the murder of several black men. Some 1,500 blacks fled their homes, which were immediately purchased by whites at low cost. In the **Atlanta (Georgia) Riot of 1906,** three local papers, the *Constitution*, the *Journal*, and the *Georgian*, exaggerated and falsified reports of black crimes against white women. These accounts contributed to pre-existing racial tension, which erupted into a full-scale white riot after a white man, waving an Atlanta newspaper recounting another reputed black crime, challenged the locals to take law into their own hands. Some blame repeated televised broadcasts and heavy **press coverage** for the **Los Angeles (California) Riots of 1992** that ensued after white police officers escaped severe punishment for the beating of **Rodney King**. *See also* Police Brutality.

Further Readings: Jacobs, Ronald N. *Race, Media, and the Crisis of Civil Society: From Watts to Rodney King*. Cambridge, England: Cambridge University Press, 2000; Jean, Susan. "'Warranted' Lynchings: Narratives of Mob Violence in White Southern Newspapers, 1880–1940." *American Nineteenth Century History* 6 (2005): 351–372; Perloff, Richard M. "The Press and Lynchings of African-Americans." *Journal of Black Studies* (2000): 315–330; Smith, Reed W. "Southern Journalists and Lynching: The Statesboro Case Study." *Journalism & Communication Monograph* (2005): 51–92; Trelease, Allen W. *White Terror*. New York: Harper & Row, 1971.

Gladys L. Knight

Progressive Era (1890–1930)

The Progressive era (1890–1930) was a period of intense and wide-ranging reform, led primarily by middle- and upper-class whites. Milestones included the purging of corrupt businesses and government bodies, the development of factory standards, better work environments and child labor laws, and the campaign against **poverty** and prostitution. Also critical was the ratification of the Eighteenth Amendment, which outlawed the manufacture, transportation, import, export, and sale of alcoholic beverages, and the Nineteenth Amendment, which guaranteed women the right to vote. However, it was primarily blacks, not whites, who launched campaigns to demand equal rights and freedoms for blacks and to end the white-on-black violence that persisted throughout this era.

Although the 1890s marked the beginning of a period of great achievement for most of white America, it also witnessed the birth of **Jim Crow** laws and customs for blacks. Jim Crow put legally binding restrictions on nearly every aspect of black life. Particularly in the South, though to a small degree in the North, blacks were confined to black-only neighborhoods, restaurants, and schools. What the laws did not address, the rules and customs of **racial etiquette** covered. Racial etiquette prescribed how blacks were required to interact with whites. Blacks who violated the most minor of these rules were invariably beaten, torched, or lynched.

Lynching was a prominent means of punishing blacks during the Progressive era. Between 1889 and 1918, approximately 2,460 blacks were lynched in the southern states alone. Blacks were lynched over accusations of murder, rape, attack against a white woman, white racial prejudice, and for merely achieving some economic or social success. Among the infamous lynchings of this period were those of **Sam Hose** in 1899, **Jesse Washington** in 1916, and **Mary Turner** in 1918.

A surge of riots also engulfed black communities during this period. Racist **press coverage** detailing accusations of black attacks against white women instigated a riot in **Atlanta,** Georgia (1906), that resulted in the indiscriminate torture and beating of blacks, twenty-five black deaths, and one white death (Hine et al., 380). After a black man was accused of raping a white woman, a riot erupted in **Springfield,** Illinois (1908); "six black people were shot and killed, two were lynched, dozens were injured, and damage in the thousands of dollars was inflicted on black homes and businesses. About 2,000 black people were driven out of the community" (Hine et al., 380). The **National Association for the Advancement of Colored People (NAACP)** was established in the aftermath of this tragedy.

A riot in **East St. Louis**, Illinois (1917), was triggered when blacks replaced white workers on strike at the Aluminum Ore Company. Thirty-five blacks and eight whites died. In **Houston,** Texas (1917), a riot ensued when blacks from the North, unaccustomed to Jim Crow, attacked a police station in response to the beating and incarceration of a fellow soldier. Sixteen white and Hispanic residents, five police officers, four black soldiers, and two black civilians died. In a riot in **Chicago,** Illinois (1919), a young black man drifted into the white-only section of a beach and was stoned and drowned to death, triggering violent confrontations between white and black gangs. Twenty-three blacks and fifteen whites died. The **Elaine (Arkansas) Riot of 1919** began when white deputies tried to break up a black union meeting. Although whites murdered dozens of blacks without repercussions, twelve blacks were sentenced to death and sixty-seven were sent to prison. In the **Tulsa (Oklahoma) Riot of 1921,** blacks rallied to defend a black man accused of assaulting a white woman. This led to a deadly confrontation that spread to the nearby black **Greenwood Community**.

Despite the inequality and violence all blacks faced, the Progressive era saw the emergence of a rising black middle and upper class. A significant number of black leaders, such as **W.E.B. Du Bois** and **Mary Church Terrell,** emerged from this elite group. At the forefront of the anti-lynching movement were **Ida B. Wells-Barnett,** black publications such as ***The Crisis,*** and organizations such as the **National Association of Colored Women (NACW)** and the NAACP. Southern white liberal organizations and newspapers soon followed in their footsteps. These individuals and organizations also fought against Jim Crow and racial rioting. At the close of the Progressive era, **Marcus Garvey** heralded the call for black empowerment, thus initiating the turn toward a positive **racial consciousness** for the lower classes.

The most progressive changes for blacks during this era were the emergence of the black elite, the migration of blacks out of the tumultuous South, a burgeoning racial pride, and the marked decrease in the annual number of lynchings in the nation. On the other hand, the Progressive era did not bring about the elimination of discriminatory laws or the permanent abatement of race riots. *See also* Chester and Philadelphia (Pennsylvania) Riots of 1918; Dyer, Leonidas C.; Niagara Movement.

Further Readings: Brown, Richard Maxwell. "Living Together Violently: Blacks and Whites in America." In Richard Maxwell Brown, ed. *Strain of Violence: Historical Studies of American Violence and Vigilantism*. New York: Oxford University Press, 1975; Gatewood, Willard B. *Aristocrats of Color: The Black Elite, 1880–1920*. Fayetteville: University of Arkansas Press, 2000; Hine, Darlene Clark, William C. Hine, and Stanley Harrold. "Conciliation, Agitation, and Migration: African Americans in the Early Twentieth Century." Chap. 16 in *The African-American Odyssey*. Englewood Cliffs, NJ: Prentice Hall, 2000, 306–331.

Gladys L. Knight

R

Racial Consciousness

Racial consciousness is the awareness of genetically disposed differences based on skin color, facial features, ancestry, and genetics. At best, racial consciousness produces pride and dignity, as well as important artistic and intellectual work, and the appreciation thereof. At worst, racial consciousness is expressed in an intense fear, hatred, and prejudice of a group of a different race and, as a result, plays an enormous role in the perpetuation of racial violence. Numerous examples of racial brutality in America's past and present illustrate this point.

Racially conscious groups that have participated in racially motivated violence are characterized by narcissism, negative attitudes and beliefs about other races, racial obsession, self-imposed isolationism, and propensity for aggression. *Narcissism* is a term defined as more about "the human need to feel special, set apart, and touched by grace, than about hatred" (Dickerson, 55). Unfortunately, narcissism combined with the other traits mentioned can be destructive. Racial attitudes and beliefs, including prejudice and stereotyping, refer to the notion of vilifying and constructing generalizations about another race. Racial obsession concerns a preoccupation with viewing the world in terms of race. Self-imposed isolationism occurs when groups of one particular race separate themselves from a different race. Aggression is the tendency or willingness to engage in combative activities.

Black and white racial conflict in America originated long before the advent of slavery. Whites in America had negative stereotypes of Africa and its inhabitants. Africa was thought of as a savage country, and its people were considered equally barbarous. Many whites thought Africans were ignorant, and these whites looked down on African beliefs, culture, and traditions. Even the color black was synonymous with all things inferior, evil, and negative. Conversely, white Americans exalted in their **whiteness**, culture, and presumed purity and intelligence. The consequence of these racist stereotypes and prejudices facilitated the institution of slavery, which also furthered the dehumanization of Africans.

Africans also constructed stereotypes and prejudices about their white slaveholders. During the Middle Passage, the horrific journey from Africa to America, rumors abounded that the whites were cannibals. Although some Africans accepted the notion of white superiority, others, as a result of the system of slavery and the abuses and atrocities they suffered from it, saw all whites as oppressors. As a result, Africans often victimized whites indiscriminately during the slave uprisings of the 1700s.

Whites were the primary instigators of the majority of the violence against blacks from the mid-1800s to the 1960s, and white consciousness was at its most violent, unified, and powerful. The tradition of **vigilantism** played a significant role in the general aggressiveness of whites during this long period. Whites were quick to respond violently to any perceived injustice and felt it their duty and right to do so. Racial obsession was evident in the fact that the victims of violence were predominantly black, not white. Racist attitudes and beliefs, such as the inferiority and alleged inherent immorality of blacks, helped whites justify racial violence. The racial consciousness of local and federal authorities made it easy for them to neglect to protect blacks or to participate in anti-black violence themselves.

This phenomenon is evident in the anti-black and anti-abolition riots in the North during the mid-1800s. **White mobs** mercilessly attacked the growing population of free blacks that threatened all-white communities. Mobs also rioted against white abolitionists in pursuit of an integrated society. During the Civil War, President Abraham Lincoln emancipated black slaves. White abolitionists rejoiced, while many other whites, particularly in the South, were outraged. Many turned to violence and intimidation to maintain **white supremacy**. Numerous **vigilante organizations** and white mobs formed.

The effects of racial consciousness continued through the **Jim Crow** era, which lasted from the 1890s to the 1960s. During this period, whites violently enforced legally imposed **segregation** to maintain non-contact between the races. Many whites rampantly abused and murdered blacks to maintain black subservience to white dominance. Often, when one black was accused of raping or assaulting a white person, all black males, and indeed, the black community at large, were fair game. The primary motivations for violence during World War I and World War II were competition for housing and employment and general tensions resulting from racial hatred.

In the 1960s, black militant organizations formed in response to unremitting white violence. Blacks asserted a massive black consciousness. Although this was a positive phenomenon for most, segments of the population endorsed an intense hatred for whites. They believed all whites were racist and responsible for their systematic oppression. Blacks isolated themselves from whites and engaged in random attacks against whites. Nathan McCall, a reporter for the *Washington Post,* describes his participation in the beating of a white stranger who entered a black neighborhood in *Makes Me Wanna Holler* (1994). In the black rioting of the 1960s, 1980s, and 1990s, blacks, frustrated by the horrendous effects of two centuries of white racial consciousness, lashed out against unsuspecting whites and symbols of white power.

Although massive racial violence in the United States had abated considerably by the beginning of the twenty-first century, racial consciousness still thrives in the hearts of blacks and whites, and some believe its existence portends an impending race war. *See also* Racism; White Supremacy.

Further Readings: Dickerson, Debra. *The End of Blackness*. New York: Random House, 2004; Feagin, Joe R. *Racist America: Roots, Current Realities, and Future Reparations*. New York: Routledge, 2000; McCall, Nathan. *Makes Me Wanna Holler: A Young Black Man in America*. New York: Random House, 1994.

Gladys L. Knight

Racial Etiquette

Racial etiquette is a term used to describe the informal rules of conduct between blacks and whites. These rules reinforced **white supremacy** and black inferiority, and supported pre-existing discriminatory ordinances, such as the slave laws, the black laws in the North, the **black codes** during the **Reconstruction** period, and the **Jim Crow** laws. Enforcement of racial etiquette was at its peak during the Jim Crow era and was most prevalent in the South. Whites, embittered and threatened by the status of the newly emancipated blacks, often resorted to violence.

The rules of racial etiquette dictated the speech, manners, behaviors, and actions of whites and blacks. Blacks addressed whites with titles, such as *boss* or *cap'n*, *Mr.*, or *Miss*. Whites, on the other hand, referred to black men, regardless of their age, as *boy*, *uncle*, or *nigger*. They referred to black women as *girl*, *gal*, or *auntie*.

Racial etiquette also prescribed rules for blacks in public places. Blacks were not permitted to eat with whites in restaurants, although black women who took care of white children were an exception to this rule. Blacks were also not permitted to sit and eat in most restaurants. As a result, they often had to bring their own dishes to carry out their food. At department stores, blacks could only try on outfits over their street clothes. They could not try on shoes in most stores. Clerks assisted white customers before blacks. Blacks were forced to use back entrances of buildings and homes. Even on the western frontier, where blacks generally experienced more freedoms than those living in the South or the North, some saloons segregated their bars so that whites sat at one end and blacks at the other. Where Jim Crow laws were not enforced, racial etiquette demanded sections and places in town where blacks were allowed.

In all social interactions, whites expected blacks to show deference to them. Blacks could not assert themselves, even in self-defense. In many situations, blacks pretended to be less intelligent than whites and acted in ways that exaggerated their inferiority, made fun of themselves, or played on stereotypes. Blacks gave up seats on public transportation systems and moved aside to give whites the right of way on sidewalks. Although whites and blacks could talk openly in public, blacks were expected to remove their hats in the presence of whites. They were also expected to avoid eye contact with whites, and never shake hands. Touching whites, whether deliberately or by accident, was forbidden. Few actions were more perilous than for a black man to look at a white woman. Racial etiquette did not obligate whites to show blacks the same respect. Whites were not allowed to appear too congenial with blacks in public. For example, white conductors were prevented from helping black women with their bags.

Violence toward those who transgressed the rules of racial etiquette was often immediate and harsh. A black veteran who breached racial etiquette by refusing to step off a sidewalk for a passing white policeman was a catalyst for the **Memphis (Tennessee) Riot of 1866**. The ensuing violence spread to unarmed black veterans and a nearby black community. Whites robbed blacks, set churches, schools, and houses on fire, raped women, and beat children. Forty-six black men and two white men were killed. One of those white men was attacked because he was in violation of the racial etiquette that disallowed whites from talking amicably to blacks. In 1876, a black militia company marching through Hamburg, South Carolina, refused passage to two whites. A **white mob** confronted the militia, resulting in the executions of five of the black men. During the same period, white clergy killed a black man for defending another black man who had been removed from a church service. Another black man was murdered for asking for wages owed to him. A black man was killed in Texas for not removing his hat in the presence of a white woman. Blacks suffered numerous attacks whenever they resisted the rules of racial etiquette by showing themselves to be equal or superior to whites. This involved such acts as wearing better clothes, owning successful businesses, and acquiring wealth, education, and reputable positions.

A great number of violent events were triggered by perceived affronts to white women. **Lynching** was the most common punishment for black men who were accused of raping white women. Often, white mobs lynched not only the accused perpetrators but any black man, regardless of age, who crossed their path. Several riots began or were intensified as a result of unsubstantiated rumors or accusations that a black man looked at, touched, attacked, or raped a white woman. Whites angered by a series of perceived attacks on white women rioted in **Washington, D.C.,** in 1919. One of those attacks included a black man who bumped into a white woman. Racial etiquette prevailed with little change until it lost considerable strength after the **Civil Rights Act of 1964**. *See also* Black Church Arsons; Black Self-Defense; Castration; Frontier Justice; Racism; Rape, as Provocation for Lynching; Segregation; *Thirty Years of Lynching in the United States: 1889–1918*; Till, Emmett; Vigilante Organizations; Vigilantism; White Supremacy.

Further Readings: Cash, W.J. *The Mind of the South*. Reprint, New York: Vintage, 1991. Originally published 1941; Hale, Grace Elizabeth, and Joel Williamson. *A Rage for Order: Black-White Relations in the American South Since Emancipation*. New York: Oxford University Press, 1986.

Gladys L. Knight

Racial Stereotypes

Originally, a stereotype referred to a rigid and simplistic "picture in the head" (Lippmann 1922). In current usage, stereotypes are unreliable

Amos 'n Andy peforming "The Open Air Taxi Company," 1930. Courtesy of the Library of Congress.

generalizations about all members of a group without regard for individual differences. They can be positive (women are nurturers) or negative (athletes are dumb), but stereotypes are inaccurate when applied to every member—or most members—of a group. When applied to races, stereotypes are constructed beliefs claiming that all members of a race share given characteristics, usually negative. Stereotyping causes people to view Native Americans as alcoholics, Puerto Ricans as violent criminals, and white Americans as heartless bigots. A stereotype may contain a kernel of truth, but that kernel is exaggerated and too broadly applied.

There may be an innate tendency for humans to think categorically; however, stereotypes are learned. No child is born believing that blacks are naturally great athletes. That stereotype is acquired from many sources, including family, friends, books, television, and movies. A person may meet a talented black athlete and stereotypically conclude that 1) the person's athleticism is inherent, not the result of hard work; 2) the person is a good athlete *because* he or she is black; or 3) all blacks *must* be good athletes.

Humans have a tendency to overestimate the differences between their group and other groups, and to underestimate the differences than exist within their group. This we-they thinking is a crucial component of stereotyping. All Jews ("they") are seen as being preoccupied with money; whereas "we" have some people in our group who are infatuated with money—but they are few and not *as* obsessed—and "we" have many members who are not fixated with money. This stereotype is supported by anecdotal evidence, for example: "My uncle told me about a Jewish merchant who tried everything to sell him a car."

Stereotypes are often based on limited, inaccurate information. Blacks are stereotyped as drug users in movies, novels, and everyday conversations. In 1999, blacks constituted 13 percent of the country's drug users, roughly equal to their representation in the American population. Yet blacks made up 37 percent of those arrested on drug charges, 55 percent of those convicted, and 74 percent of all drug offenders incarcerated in prisons. Whites constitute 80 percent of the country's cocaine users; however, they are not collectively stereotyped as drug users, and law enforcement efforts are concentrated on drug use in inner cities (Schaefer 2004).

Stereotypes undergird racial discrimination. To justify the taking of Indian land, colonists propagated the stereotype of Native Americans as thieving, murdering savages. During the **Jim Crow** era, the stereotype of African Americans as ignorant, culturally deficient parasites was used to keep blacks at the bottom of a racial caste system, where they were not allowed to vote, compete for professional jobs, or attend white schools.

All stereotypes reduce individuals to an inflexible image, but with some racial stereotypes the targets have their worth as humans—even their humanness—assailed. When Chinese men arrived to work on the transnational railroad, they were seen as lesser humans with strange eyes, effeminate hair and clothes, and odd cultural patterns. Laws were passed that prohibited them from owning land and marrying American women.

Some stereotypes are relatively trivial—blacks do not like cold weather; whites smell bad when wet—but many stereotypes have significant consequences. During slavery, black men were often portrayed as Toms—physically weak, submissive servants—or Sambos—lazy, childlike buffoons. These portrayals were pragmatic and instrumental. Proponents of slavery created and perpetuated caricatures and stereotypes that justified slavery. If slaves were childlike, then a paternalistic institution where masters acted as quasi-parents to their slaves was humane. Neither the Tom nor the Sambo was a threat to whites. After slavery, many whites feared that the emancipated blacks would gain revenge. A new caricature of the black man—the brute—emerged. This portrayal stereotyped black men as innately savage, animalistic, destructive, and criminal—deserving punishment, maybe death. Between 1882 and 1951, whites lynched at least 3,437 blacks. Americans from all strata accepted **lynching** as a necessary evil to combat the black brute. In the 1990s, the brute caricature reemerged in the American psyche as young black males were portrayed as thugs, gangsters, and menaces to society.

Social scientific research on prejudice indicates that white Americans have become less willing to express prejudice openly. White Americans who believed blacks were innately less intelligent than whites declined from 53 percent in 1942 to about 20 percent in the 1960s to less than 10 percent in the 1990s. National surveys conducted from the 1950s through the 1990s, with few exceptions, showed less resistance among whites to racial **integration**. For example, 30 percent of the whites sampled in 1942 said that blacks should attend schools with whites, but by 1970, 74 percent of whites supported integrated schools, and in 1991, the number had risen to 93 percent

(Schaefer 2004). These statistics indicate racial progress; however, it is possible that traditional surveys underestimate negative racial views.

In research at Stanford University, black students performed worse than white students on standardized achievement tests when they were told that the test measured intelligence. When the test was presented as a problem-solving exercise, black students did as well as white students. Black students know that some whites believe that blacks are less intelligent than whites, but this research suggests that the mere awareness of the negative stereotype has negative consequences for the target individuals. This is the power of negative stereotyping.

Further Reading: Lippmann, Walter. *Public Opinion*. New York: Harcourt, Brace and Company, 1922; Schaefer, Richard T. *Racial and Ethnic Groups*. Upper Saddle River, NJ: Prentice Hall, 2004.

David Pilgrim

Racism

The term *racism* refers to prejudice and discrimination based on the belief that some races are intellectually, culturally, and/or biologically superior to other races.

As a theory, racism assumes that an individual's abilities and potential are directly related to his or her race. The term *racialism* was initially introduced, but in the 1930s the term was shortened to *racism*, and it was not until the 1950s that it became popular. Today, the use of the term *racialism* is often believed to be a less negative term and it is commonly utilized by those who argue that there are differences between racial and ethnic groups that can be scientifically substantiated.

Since it was first introduced, diverse definitions of racism have emerged. Some are broad and encompass several forms of racism, and other definitions are narrow and address specific forms that racism may take. *Overt racism* is often referred to as *traditional racism, old-fashioned racism*, or *Jim Crow racism*, and it is exemplified by obvious racist behavior such as **lynchings** or physical attacks. A close relative of overt racism is *scientific racism*, which implies that scientific research can substantiate claims that some groups are genetically inferior to others. Since the 1950s, these types of racism have become less common, yet they are still part of American culture. In 1998, for instance, three white men with ties to racist groups in Jasper, Texas, chained a black man, **James Byrd, Jr.**, to the back of their truck and dragged him to his death.

A recent example of scientific racism can be found in Herrnstein and Murray's book *The Bell Curve* (1994), in which the authors attempt to establish a genetic link between race and intelligence. A more subtle and elusive form of racism, known as *aversive* or *covert racism*, is more common today. This type of racism may involve avoiding contact with people of another race or ethnicity, or laughing at or telling jokes about other racial or ethnic groups, usually based on stereotypes about these groups. Another type of racism, referred to as *laissez-faire* or *symbolic racism*, has also become more popular since the 1950s. This form of racism involves blaming racial and ethnic minority groups themselves for lagging behind the dominant group (e.g., in educational attainment and socioeconomic status). It also tends to include the dominant group's resistance to policies that attempt to rectify past discrimination (e.g., affirmative action), and stereotypical portrayals of racial and ethnic minorities in the media. *Color-blind racism*, which is closely related to *laissez-faire racism*, involves the denial of the existence of racial differences and the belief that racial problems will only disappear when race is ignored altogether. This type of racism may not include any explicit intent to harm racial and ethnic minority groups, yet the idea that race and ethnicity are irrelevant tends to blind people to the very real effects race and ethnicity have on people's lives.

Institutional racism involves the negative and oppressive treatment of one race or ethnic group, presumed to be inferior, by institutions, including government agencies, corporations, and other organizations. *Racial profiling* and *redlining* are examples of this type of racism. Whatever the specific form racist ideology takes, its primary function is to justify the domination and exploitation of one racial or ethnic group by another based on its presumed biological, cultural, or intellectual inferiority. The connection between racism and race riots is quite obvious. Race riots reflect the anger and frustration among racial and ethnic minority groups that have endured decades of prejudice and discrimination and are often sparked by incidents involving racial profiling, **police brutality**, and other actions perceived as discriminatory.

Racism, and the many forms it can take, is the fundamental cause of riots and civil unrest in which race or ethnicity play a key role. The race riots that took place in many U.S. cities during and before the 1960s were fueled by the clash between the increasing aspirations for a better life among racial and ethnic minority groups and the racist and hostile opposition exhibited by the white majority. Further, these riots provide the backdrop to the **civil rights movement** and the legislative changes it brought about.

Further Readings: Bonilla-Silva, Eduardo. *White Supremacy and Racism in the Post-Civil Rights Era*. Boulder, CO: Lynne Rienner, 2001; Dovidio, J.F., and S.L. Gaertner, eds. *Prejudice, Discrimination, and Racism*. New York: Academic Press, 1986; Katkin, W., N. Landsmand, and A. Tyree, eds. *Beyond Pluralism: Essays on the Conception of Groups and Group Identities in America*. Urbana: University of Illinois Press, 1998; Kovel, Jonathan. *White Racism: A Psychohistory*. New York: Pantheon, 1970; Montagu, A. *Man's Most Dangerous Myth: The Fallacy of Race*. 5th ed. New York: Oxford University Press, 1974; Montagu, A. *Race, Science, and Humanity*. Princeton, NJ: Van Nostrand, 1963; Schumann, H., C. Steeh, L. Bobo, and M. Krysan. *Racial Attitudes in America: Trends and Interpretations*. Cambridge, MA: Harvard University Press, 1997; Wilson, W.J. *Power, Racism, and Privilege*. New York: Free Press, 1973.

Paulina X. Ruf

Racist Organizations

Racist organizations, groups based on anti-black or anti-white hatred, have historically been the primary instigators of racial violence in the United States, and their response to violence has generally been to generate more

The burning of the Henry Shepherd house by the Ku Klux Klan. Courtesy of the Library of Congress.

violence. Grassroots organizations, legislation, and law enforcement have all helped to dismantle a number of racist groups and to substantially lessen the violent outbreaks of extant organizations. Contemporary racial violence has decreased substantially and is largely incited by private individuals. However, the influence of racist organizations is strong.

White racist organizations originated in the South in the aftermath of the Civil War. The most notorious of these organizations was the **Ku Klux Klan (KKK)**, whose members dressed in ghostly white robes and cone-shaped masks and terrorized blacks with their eerie silent marches and infamous nightriding. Numerous Klan-like groups and **vigilante organizations** intimidated, terrorized, attacked, and murdered the newly freed black slaves and their white supporters. To white racist organizations, violence was an acceptable and glorified means of maintaining **white supremacy** and black oppression. In response, liberal Republicans insisted on federal intervention. The presence of federal troops, as well as the passing of the Enforcement Acts in 1870 and 1871, put a brief stop to the rampant violence.

While black and white Republicans passed legislation to ensure freedom for blacks during **Reconstruction**, conservative Democrats worked with organizations such as the Ku Klux Klan, the **White League**, and the Red Shirts to devise machinations to remove the liberals from power in the South. Through violence, the Democrats were able to seize power and once again dominate the South. At the same time, the federal government withdrew its troops and ended Reconstruction. However, this did not put an end to anti-black violence. In fact, **lynching** became the norm between the

1880s and 1930s, as racist organizations sought to enforce **Jim Crow**. Racist organizations regularly justified violence as a necessary means to control alleged black crimes and violence.

D.W. Griffith's film ***The Birth of a Nation*** and the **press coverage** of the trial and lynching of accused Jewish murderer Leon Frank were said to be responsible for the resurgence of the Ku Klux Klan in 1915. At its peak, the Klan comprised 15 percent of the nation's population. The Klan targeted blacks as well as Catholics, Jews, and immigrants, and endorsed white supremacy, **racism**, and lynching. Its activities included marches, rallies, and cross burnings. Its membership spread to the Midwest, the North, and Canada. The Klan disbanded as a result of scandals such as that involving Republican David Stephenson, a prominent leader, who was convicted of the rape and murder of Madge Oberholtzer; its association with Nazi organizations; its involvement in the **Detroit (Michigan) Riot of 1943**; and the 1944 revelation that the organization owed $685,000 in back taxes.

Klan activities were again revived in the 1950s in response to the emergence of the **civil rights movement**. The Klan was behind many of the violent attacks and threats against both black and white activists, particularly during the **Freedom Rides** and **Freedom Summer (Mississippi) of 1964**. It was also responsible for the infamous bombing of the Sixteenth Street Baptist Church in Birmingham, Alabama, which killed four young black girls. However, this surge of violence backfired on the Klan because it helped to win civil rights for blacks. As news spread of the senseless killings of black and white activists, public sentiment swung against racist organizations and support for civil rights burgeoned. The violence also forced the federal government to intervene on behalf of the civil rights activists and to accelerate the eradication of **segregation**.

Another outcome of the violence that occurred during the civil rights movement was the emergence of black militancy. The **Student Nonviolent Coordinating Committee (SNCC)** and the **Congress of Racial Equality (CORE)**, growing increasingly exasperated with the violent attacks, adopted the ideologies of **Black Power** and **black self-defense**. Other black militant groups included the **Nation of Islam** and the **Black Panther Party (BPP)**. These organizations were sometimes referred to as racist organizations because of their separatist views and willingness to use violence. However, only a small segment of black militants engaged in racial violence, which resulted in a number of crimes and violent attacks against innocent whites. The majority of the organizations were genuinely responding to perceived needs in the community and the day-to-day realities of **racism**.

Black militant groups were most popular in the cities of the North where crime, drugs, **police brutality**, unemployment, and **poverty** prevailed. These groups warned of black rebellion in response to oppressive conditions in the **ghettos**. When riots did erupt across the nation during the 1960s, black militant leaders were almost exuberant. Although these organizations were not directly responsible for the riots, their influence was evident. The Black Panthers formed during the 1960s to defend their community against racist police officers. This group eventually collapsed after it was infiltrated by the **Federal Bureau of Investigation (FBI)**.

The majority of hate crimes (including vandalism, violent attacks, and murders) are perpetrated by individuals, not racist organizations. Nonetheless, these individuals are often heavily influenced by contemporary racist organizations such as the National Alliance, Neo-Nazis, the Skinheads, the Council of Conservative Citizens, the Aryan Brotherhood, and the Ku Klux Klan. A number of these organizations believe that a global racial war is at hand and are actively preparing for it. Meanwhile, contemporary black racist organizations continue to advocate racial violence.

Numerous efforts have been made to quash hate crimes and racist organizations. The Southern Poverty Law Center has waged many legal battles against the Ku Klux Klan and, along with the Anti-Defamation League and the FBI, publicizes racial activities and crimes. Diversity and tolerance education is regularly taught in the workplace and in the classroom. **John Conyers**, Democratic representative of Michigan, along with a small group of politicians, introduced the Local Law Enforcement Hate Crimes Prevention Act of 2005.

Further Reading: Anti-Defamation League. "Extremism in America." ADL: Law Enforcement Agency Resource Network. See http://www.adl.org/learn/ext_us/.

Gladys L. Knight

Radio Free Dixie

Radio Free Dixie was a radio program broadcast from Havana, Cuba, on Friday evenings at 11:00 P.M. from 1962 to 1965. **Robert F. Williams**, helped by his wife, Mabel, was its conductor. The program's strong signal made it heard almost everywhere in the United States, although it was primarily aimed at African Americans living in the South because, as Williams put it, they did not have any voice. *Radio Free Dixie* called on African Americans to rise and free themselves. As Williams said, *Radio Free Dixie* was the first radio program on which black people could say whatever they wanted and did not have to worry about sponsors.

Although the program had its roots in African American cultural traditions, it was also highly innovative, for Williams was close to the black arts movement and the **Black Panther Party (BPP)**. His choice of music included such African American artists as Leadbelly, Joe Turner, Abby Lincoln and Max Roach, Otis Redding, Nina Simone, The Impressions, and Josh White. Selections heard on *Radio Free Dixie* included not only jazz (dubbed "freedom jazz"), but also blues and soul music. Among the well-known listeners were Amiri Baraka, Richard Gibson, Conrad Lynn, and William Worthy. Listeners sent Williams hundreds of records to be played. The show highlighted the anthems of the southern movement. Williams' use of jazz was intended as a new type of political propaganda. He saw *Radio Free Dixie* as much more than a radio program; for Williams, it was a political act meant to reassure African Americans and help them free themselves from an overly racist American society. Williams mixed music with news about racial violence or voter registration campaigns in the South. Music was intended to motivate people in their struggle.

Dixie was a familiar song composed in 1859 by Dan Emmett, a member of the Bryant's Minstrels troupe in New York. During the Civil War, the song reinforced and strengthened white identity in the South, which it pictured as a happy land. For a large number of Americans, the song retained its wartime and racial connotations in the twentieth century. During the **civil rights movement**, *Dixie* served as an anthem for white southerners and a reminder of **racism** and slavery for African Americans. Williams rejected the white southerner vision of the South as a happy land and used the word *Dixie* in an attempt to free the South from cultural, as well as political, **racism**. In a press conference after a trial in which a white man was acquitted for the attempted rape of a black woman, Williams said: "If the United States Constitution cannot be enforced in this social jungle called Dixie, it is time that Negroes must defend themselves" (Williams 1959).

Williams was at odds with the civil rights movement. He called for **black self-defense** and published ***Negroes with Guns***, although he also called for the continued pressure of nonviolent direct action. Williams believed in flexibility in the freedom struggle. For some time, he was leader of the local chapter of the **National Association for the Advancement of Colored People (NAACP)** and helped increase the membership from 6 to 200. He also formed the Black Guard, an armed group committed to the protection of the local black population, since calls of African Americans to law enforcement often went unanswered. He brought to the attention of national and international media the reality of **Jim Crow**.

Although Williams eventually went into exile, living in Cuba, the U.S.S.R., and Red China, he was neither a communist nor a black nationalist, but called himself an internationalist (see **Black Nationalism**). He realized that lack of freedom tainted communist regimes, and their view of the United Sates as imperialist distorted a political reality that was much more complex. Moreover, communist regimes did not understand the racism faced by African Americans, either because there were no important ethnic communities in their countries, or because such communities had already been marginalized and removed from the public consciousness.

Radio Free Dixie provided African Americans with a new way of grappling with **racial stereotypes** and lack of confidence. Williams was an influential figure in the struggle for civil rights, and his call for flexibility was followed by young black activists across the South who rejected the tactics of **nonviolence**. By broadcasting for the South, Williams intended to raise the level of confidence in African Americans. He gave new arguments to the **Black Power** movement and, although far from the United States for a number of years, he was an inspiration to, and a strong supporter of, the African American struggle for civil rights.

Eventually, CIA jamming and Cuban censorship ended *Radio Free Dixie*, but WBAI in New York and KPFA in Berkeley, California, often rebroadcast tapes of the shows. Bootleg tapes were also circulated in Watts and Harlem. The program ended in 1965 but Willams' influence has continued ever since.

Further Readings: Carmichael, S., and C.V. Hamilton. *Black Power: The Politics of Liberation in America*. London: Jonathan Cape, 1967; Carson, C. *In Struggle: SNCC and the Black Awakening of the 1960s*. Cambridge, MA: Harvard University Press, 1981; Tyson, Timothy B. *Radio Free Dixie: Robert F. Williams and the Roots* *of Black Power*. Chapel Hill: University of North Carolina Press, 1999; Williams, Robert F. Press conference, Monroe, NC, 1959.

Santiago Rodríguez Guerrero-Strachan

RAM *See* Revolutionary Action Movement

Randolph, A. Philip (1889–1979)

Asa Philip Randolph was an activist, union organizer, and civil rights leader. Born on April 15, 1889, in Crescent City, Florida, to Rev. James William and Elizabeth Robinson Randolph, he had one brother, James. When Randolph was two years old, the family moved to Jacksonville, Florida. He obtained his early education there and graduated from the Cookman Institute. He excelled academically. After graduating from high school, he decided that opportunities were limited for him in Jacksonville. Soon, he left for New York City. He settled in Harlem. His initial ambition was to study acting. Before long, he entered the City College of New York, where he became a student of economics and philosophy. He taught at the Rand School of Social Science. It was during this time that he met well-known socialists Eugene Debs and Norman Thomas. Socialism appealed to him, which led him to join the Socialist Party. While living in New York City, Randolph met and married Lucille Green. She was a widow from Virginia. She was a teacher by training, but when they met she was the owner of a thriving hair salon. Using resources from the business, she was able to provide financial and other support to her husband's efforts. Lucille Green

Asa Philip Randolph seated with President Lyndon B. Johnson. Courtesy of the Library of Congress.

Randolph shared many of her husband's ideals and they remained married until her death on April 12, 1963. There were no children born to the union.

To disseminate the vision that Randolph had regarding African Americans and the future of American society in general, he began publishing a new magazine. He cofounded and coedited it with his good friend Chandler Owen. First published in 1917, this new publication was called *The Messenger*. Later, the name was changed to *The Black Worker*. The publication mostly addressed issues surrounding socialism, **integration**, **nonviolence**, and unionism. Randolph believed that the condition of blacks in America at that time was not unlike that of other groups in the society. He believed that the source of the problem, which all poor and working-class people faced, was the uneven distribution of power, wealth, and resources. One issue of the magazine editorialized that "the employing class recognize no race lines. They will exploit a White . . . as readily as a Black" (Randolph, 11). Profit was the motive and it was more important than race. Thus, Randolph envisioned a critical role for unions to play. Unions could unite workers across the spectrum. Only then, he believed, would American society be changed.

On the throes of the United States entering World War I, Congress passed the Espionage Act. It called for a fine of $1,000 and twenty years in prison for interfering with military recruitment. It was during this time that Randolph's opponents often referred to him as "the most dangerous Negro in America" (Brinkley, 83). *The Messenger* carried articles that were staunchly against the war. Randolph rejected the claim that the war was "to make the world safe for democracy" (Wilson 1917). This was particularly unbelievable to him when he saw blacks being lynched and subjected to outright discrimination in the United States, the bastion of democracy. He became embroiled in a public dispute over the war issue with **W.E.B. Du Bois**, who urged blacks to participate in the war.

During one of the many trips that Randolph took around the country lecturing, organizing, and espousing his war views, he and his friend Owen were arrested in Cleveland, Ohio. The charge was treason. Seymour Stedman, a socialist lawyer, successfully got the pair released in his custody. This did not deter Randolph and Owen. They continued their antiwar crusade. Soon, Randolph himself was drafted to serve in the war. Just one day before he was scheduled to report for duty, the war ended.

In 1925, the dream of forming a union for workers was fulfilled. The Brotherhood of Sleeping Car Porters was formed. Amid ugly and vicious attacks, a union was finally organized. It was a momentous occasion in the history of unionism within the United States. The new union prevailed over one of the most powerful and richest companies in the country—the Pullman Company. Most of the workers were black men. In 1935, the union officially became a part of the American Federation of Labor (AFL). After the AFL joined with the Council of Industrial Organization (CIO), Randolph was appointed to the executive council and became a vice president in 1957. At many meetings, conferences, and conventions of the organization, Randolph often found himself out of step with many of the AFL-CIO leadership. His was the constant voice urging the unions to rid their ranks of discrimination. True to his earlier beliefs, he championed the rights of not only blacks, but poor whites, Puerto Ricans, Native Americans, Mexican-Americans and other minorities.

In 1940, just prior to World War II, Randolph embraced the problems of discrimination of blacks from wartime factory jobs. He was relentless in his efforts to change discriminatory practices in the industry. One strategy he proposed was a march on Washington. His hope was that the march would get the attention of the federal government and persuade Washington officials to abolish discrimination. Randolph's union had a natural constituency of black labor unionists and other sympathizers, and getting thousands of workers to descend on Pennsylvania Avenue in the nation's capital would send a powerful message. It is widely acknowledged that the prospect of a march of this magnitude weighed heavily on President Franklin D. Roosevelt to sign Executive Order 8802, which banned discrimination in defense plant jobs. It was no small feat that the most powerful leader of the world responded to the demands of the Brotherhood of Sleeping Car Porters, essentially a black labor union. The march was called off as a result of the president's proactive measures. The mission was accomplished.

On July 26, 1948, Randolph pursued and won another battle against discrimination. He called on blacks to refuse to serve in the military because it was segregated. He pressed another U.S. president, Harry Truman, to sign an order to end discrimination in the armed forces as well as in federal civil service jobs. The order also provided for blacks to enter the Army and Navy service academies. Although other blacks and their supporters pushed for these changes, Randolph was clearly in the forefront. He founded and served as president of the Afro-American Labor Council from 1960–1966.

In 1964, Randolph served as a pivotal figure in the legendary March on Washington where **Martin Luther King, Jr**., delivered the "I Have a Dream" speech. Joining him in organizing labor unionists to participate in the march was a seasoned civil rights warrior, Bayard Rustin. He had been involved in planning the 1940 March on Washington that had been abandoned. The AFL declined to support the march, but Randolph successfully recruited a number of rank and file members of unions to participate. By the time of the 1963 March on Washington, Randolph was recognized as the elder statesman of the **civil rights movement** and he was frequently referred to as such. After the March on Washington, which was held on August 28, 1963, he joined Dr. King, Whitney Young, **Roy Wilkins**, and other civil rights leaders in meeting with President **John F. Kennedy**. In 1964, President Lyndon B. Johnson presented Randolph with the Presidential Medal of Honor. The legacy of A. Philip Randolph is far-reaching. He was an indisputable pioneer in the American civil rights movement. He opened up unprecedented opportunities for blacks and other minorities in labor unions and other walks of life. One of his favorite quotes was "A quitter never wins and a winner never quits."

On May 16, 1979, A. Philip Randolph died in New York City. He had risen from being viewed as the most dangerous Negro in America to one of the most influential and respected black leaders in the United States. It seemed altogether fitting that President Jimmy Carter would attend his funeral. *See also* Lynching.

Further Readings: Brinkley, David. *Washington Goes to War*. New York: Alfred A. Knopf, 1988; Cwiklik, Robert. *A. Philip Randolph and the Labor Movement*. Minneapolis: Lerner Publishing Group, 1993; Harris, William. *Keeping the Faith: A. Philip Randolph, Milton P. Webster, and the Brotherhood of Sleeping Car Porters 1925–1937*. Blacks in the New World Series. Urbana: University of Illinois Press, 1991; Miller, Calvin Craig. *A. Philip Randolph and the African American Labor Movement*. Greensboro, NC: Morgan Reynolds Publishing, 2005; "Presidential Medal of Freedom Recipient A. Philip Randolph: 1889–1979." See http://www.medaloffreedom.com/APhilipRandolph.htm; Randolph, A. Philip. "Our Reason for Being." *The Messenger* (August 1919): 11–12; Reef, Catherine. *A. Philip Randolph: Union Leader and Civil Rights Crusader*. Berkeley Heights, NJ: Enslow Publishers, Inc., 2001; Tye, Larry. *Rising from the Rails: Pullman Porters and the Making of the Black Middle Class*. New York: Henry Holt and Company, 2004; Wilson, Woodrow. Speech, 65th Cong., 1st Sess., April 2, 1917, Senate Doc. 5.

Betty Nyangoni

Randolph, Benjamin Franklin (c. 1820–1868)

A state senator and Republican Party organizer in South Carolina, Benjamin Randolph was among the first African American political leaders to be murdered for speaking out against racial discrimination in the **Reconstruction** South.

Born free to mixed-race parents in Kentucky, Randolph grew up in Ohio, where he attended Oberlin College between 1857 and 1862. Having studied at the college's theological seminary, Randolph was ordained into the Methodist Episcopal Church shortly after graduation. Becoming chaplain with the 26th Colored Infantry Regiment, Randolph was posted to Hilton Head, South Carolina, in 1864. He returned to South Carolina in 1865 as an agent for the American Missionary Association. In 1866, he founded the Charleston *Journal* with Rev. E.J. Adams and, in 1867, became editor of the Charleston *Advocate*. In the latter year, Randolph also received a Freedmen's Bureau appointment, working first as a teacher and then becoming assistant superintendent of schools, a position he used to advocate complete **integration** of public education in South Carolina.

As a traveling minister who actively worked for the recently formed state Republican Party, Randolph encouraged political activism among the state's Methodist Episcopal congregations. In 1867, he was elected vice president of the Republican state executive committee, and became committee chairman in the following year. In 1868, he became one of 226 African American delegates elected to the South Carolina Constitutional Convention, where his powerful speeches on behalf of African American civil rights aroused the ire of Democrats. Elected to the state senate from Orangeburg County in 1868, Randolph demanded that no African American in South Carolina be discriminated against on the basis of race.

On October 16, 1868, while canvassing for the Republican Party in the mostly white upland counties of the state, Randolph, who had been warned of the risks of openly campaigning on behalf of the freedmen, was shot and killed by three white men as he stepped from a train at Hodges Depot in Abbeville County. Committed in broad daylight, the murder was rumored to have been the work of the **Ku Klux Klan (KKK)**. Although a mentally disturbed white man later confessed to involvement in the crime, he died, perhaps as a result of foul play, before he revealed who had paid him to kill Randolph. One of six black delegates to the South Carolina Constitutional Convention who were later slain by the Klan, Randolph was honored in 1871—a time when blacks were excluded from burial with whites—by the founding of Randolph Cemetery, a burial place for African Americans in Columbia, South Carolina. Randolph is today remembered as one of the most radical and influential African American leaders of the Reconstruction period. *See also* Disenfranchisement; Racism; Segregation.

Further Readings: Holt, Thomas C. *Black over White: Negro Political Leadership in South Carolina during Reconstruction*. Urbana: University of Illinois Press, 1977; Litwack, Leon, and August Meier, eds. *Black Leaders of the Nineteenth Century*. Urbana: University of Illinois Press, 1988; Rabinowitz, Howard N., ed. *Southern Black Leaders of the Reconstruction Era*. Urbana: University of Illinois Press, 1982; Williamson, Joel. *After Slavery: The Negro in South Carolina during Reconstruction, 1865–1877*. Chapel Hill: University of North Carolina Press, 1965.

John A. Wagner

Rape, as Provocation for Lynching

Lynching is the illegal killing of a person by mob action, which usually involved torture, mutilation, and hanging. It denotes mob action that takes place without due process of the law—no trial, no defense, no attorneys, no judge, no jury. The illegal action was particularly prevalent in the southern states during the late 1800s and into the early 1900s. African Americans were most often the victims of this vigilante movement carried out by **white mobs** and often witnessed by inhabitants of an entire town. **Vigilante organizations** such as the **Ku Klux Klan (KKK)** frequently initiated and executed the deadly practice, complete with torture and maiming of the individual prior to the hanging. A lynching would commonly be advertised in local newspapers and great crowds would appear to witness the event. The stereotype of the hypersexuality of the black male was central to the number of lynchings that used rape of white women as justification for the mob's brutality and killing. Body parts of the victim, including ears, noses, fingers, and genitalia were often given to members of the attending crowd as souvenirs. Authorities of the law did not intervene on the victims' behalf, and there are only rare cases in which the perpetrators were ever tried and punished for their illegal participation and actions in the execution of thousands of African Americans and supportive Caucasians.

Five hundred African Americans were lynched from the 1800s to 1955 in the state of Mississippi, while some nationwide estimates for the same time frame near 5,000 victims. Others report that between 1884 and the beginning of World War I, between 3,600 and 3,700 incidents of lynching occurred. The Tuskegee Institute reports that between the time when solid statistical data was available in 1882 to 1964, a total of 4,743 people died as a result of lynching, with 3,445 people being black and lynched by whites.

The term *lynch* was most likely derived from Colonel Charles Lynch (1736–1796) who fought in the American Revolution and was a torrid justice of the peace in the state of Virginia. Those Caucasians who publicly supported abolition or the eradication of the practice of lynching were also targeted by the mobs and lynched. Elijah Parish Lovejoy is an example of this form of Caucasian lynching. He, as a white man, wrote articles in 1837 expounding on the evils of slavery and calling for an end to lynching. He was, himself, lynched and killed for these actions.

Accusations of black men raping white women were but one of the many reasons given for lynching. It is commonly thought that rape constituted the most essential and popular provocation for lynching, but current research does not confirm this perspective. John Hope Franklin writes that "in the first fourteen years of the twentieth century only 315 lynch victims were accused of rape or attempted rape" (Franklin 1967). He notes that homicide, robbery, insulting whites, and other offenses constitute the bulk of justifications for lynching. The primary provocation for lynching was, instead, accusations of slave insubordination. The perception of an uppity attitude on the part of an African American person was sufficient mob justification for lynching. Black men were most often the victims, but many African American women were also lynched for allegedly displaying signs or attitudes of superiority—or the lack of humbleness, debasement, and subservience that was expected of blacks and desired by the dominant Caucasian population.

There are estimates that approximately one-fourth of the killings from 1880 to 1930 were motivated by accusations of rape (PBS Online). In 1933, Dr. Arthur Raper wrote a book titled *The Tragedy of Lynching* on the practice of lynching in the United States beginning in 1889. He reported that over four-fifths were of African American descent and less than one-sixth of the victims were accused of rape.

Concerns of rape across the black-white barrier remained an issue, regardless of the number or actual percentages of lynching provoked by accusations of rape. The threat of lynching was a horrific tool of the status quo used to maintain social dominance and control over emancipated or enslaved African Americans. White slave owners were known to rape black female slaves without reprisal or any sanctions. White men also feared the black man for his supposed virility, coupled with the stereotypical assumption that all black men possessed an intense desire and uncontrollable lust for white women. This fear was only intensified by the white man's perception of the white woman's returned attraction to African American men. Caucasian men of the time—especially in the South—would tolerate the image of the subservient, docile, unthreatening black man who happily expressed gratitude for the white man's paternalism. The counterimage of the virile, sexually superior black man seeking out white women for erotic pleasure or rape was an intolerable perception for the Caucasian slaveowner to endure . . . especially when he suspected reciprocity on the part of his Caucasian female partner. Some white women also falsely accused

African American men of rape, and although some women later recanted and told the truth that a rape was not committed, their confession often did nothing to nullify the mob's original intent and execution of a lynching.

In her 2003 book *Race, Ethnicity, and Sexuality: Intimate Intersections, Forbidden Frontiers*, Joane Nagel artfully describes the phenomenon in her chapter titled "Sex-Baiting and Race-Baiting: The Politics of Ethnosexuality":

> I have argued that there is no more potent force than sexuality to stir the passions and fan the flames of racial tension. Sex-baiting can be as provocative as race-baiting in conjuring up a vision of ethno-sexual threat. In fact, sex-baiting is a mechanism of race-baiting when it taps into and amplifies racial fears and stereotypes, and when sexual dangerousness is employed as a strategy to create racial panic. Sex-baiting and race-baiting often are used together by defenders of particular ethnosexual orders to maintain the status quo. It is the sexualized nature of things ethnic, racial, and national that heats up the discourse on the values, attributes, and moral worth of Us and Them, that arouses anger when there are violations of sexual contact rules, that raises doubts about loyalty and respectability when breaches of sexual demeanor occur, that provokes reactions when questions of sexual purity and propriety arise, and that sparks retaliation when threats to sexual boundaries are imagined or detected. (255)

The point of imagined actions driven by fear is also an important aspect of this phenomenon. Whether or not a black man really raped a white woman was often inconsequential and secondary to the fact that the action was considered reality by the lethal crowd. This accentuates the Thomas Theorem, which states that "If men define situations as real, they are real in their consequences" (Thomas and Thomas 1928). The alleged rapes did not have to be real to satisfy their function to the perpetrators of crimes such as lynching. They needed only be perceived as real in order for the consequences of lynching to become very real. Assigning hypersexuality to subordinate but threatening groups is not uncommonly used by the dominant society in order to justify horrendous behavior, including torture, bodily dismantlement, **castration**, and eradication of entire populations.

African American editor **Ida B. Wells-Barnett**, a strong social activist, found that consensual sex between black men and white women was prevalent at the time, even though it was forbidden. She also found that the accusations of rape used as rationale for lynching were but another form of the white male-dominant population seeking social control over the Caucasian female population. Historic legislation from 1870 to 1884 supports her finding, with eleven southern states passing laws to ban miscegenation, or marriage across racial and ethnic lines.

Wells-Barnett, a graduate of Rust College in Memphis, Tennessee, and teacher in 1888, sparked an intense campaign against lynching in the United States. She traveled to England to promote her cause on the world stage and became the editor of a local black newspaper titled *The Free Speech and Headlight*. She found it necessary to write editorials under the pen name of Iola. In 1895, Wells-Barnett published *A Red Record*, her study of race and the practice of lynching in the United States. She was particularly focused on the men who were hung due to accusations of rape. She found that in her own town of Memphis, African American men were being lynched, not predominantly because of accusations of rape, but because they were financially and independently established members of their newly thriving African American communities. **Reconstruction** had made African American affluence vibrant in many towns throughout the South. Wells-Barnett also joined forces with **W.E.B. Du Bois** in her fight for social justice and equality. She was forced to leave Memphis and took residency in Chicago.

For decades, strong opposition to lynching was not forthcoming from government or law enforcement agencies. Finally, in 1948, President Harry Truman supported legislation that posed a serious threat to the practice of lynching. The United States Senate—in particular, southern representatives—blocked the passage of Truman's bills. The determined intent of the federal government, however, could not be dismissed. Truman developed the **Civil Rights Commission** as a long-standing facet of the federal government to monitor the cessation of the crimes of lynching.

Caucasian women, predominantly from the South, formed an anti-lynching movement through an association named the Association of Southern Women for the Prevention of Lynching (ASWPL). This organization protested the violent practice of lynching perpetrated in name of protection of white women. It began in the 1920s and by the 1940s had impacted the end of this violent social action. In 1900, the African American Congressman George white brought forward the first anti-lynching bill, which died in the House Judiciary Committee. Lillian Smith is considered one of the most literate Caucasian females who wrote with the hope of ending lynchings. In her 1944 novel *Strange Fruit* and an anthology titled *Killers of the Dream*, Smith examines lynching in terms of the **racism** and sexism that was prevalent in the South. Actions of these individuals and other anti-lynching organizations eventually brought about the end of lynching in the United States. *See also* Dyer, Leonidas C.

Further Readings: Baker, Lee D. "Ida B. Wells-Barnett and Her Passion for Justice." In Vincent P. Franklin, ed. *Living Our Stories, Telling Our Truths: Autobiography and the Making of African American Intellectual Tradition*. New York: Scribner, 1995. See http://www.duke.edu/~ldbaker/classes/AAIH/caaih/ibwells/ibwbkgrd.html; Cardyn, Lisa. "Sexualized Racism/Gendered Violence: Outraging the Body Politic in the Reconstruction South." *Michigan Law Review* (2002); Davis, Ronald L.F. "Creating Jim Crow: In-Depth Essay." *The History of Jim Crow*. See www.jimcrowhistory.org/history/creating2.htm; Franklin, John Hope. *From Slavery to Freedom: A History of Negro Americans*. 3rd ed. New York: Knopf, 1967; Gibson, Robert A. *The Negro Holocaust: Lynching and Race Riots in the United States, 1880–1950*. New Haven, CT: Yale-New Haven Teachers Institute. See http://www.yale.edu/ynhti/curriculum/units/1979/2/79.02.04.x.html; LeMay, Michael C. *The Perennial Struggle: Race, Ethnicity, and Minority Group Relations in the United States*. 2nd ed. Upper Saddle River, NJ: Pearson, Prentice Hall, 2005; Nagel, Joane. *Race, Ethnicity, and Sexuality: Intimate Intersections, Forbidden Frontiers*. New York: Oxford University Press, 2003; PBS Online. "People & Events: Lynching in America." *American Experience: The Murder of Emmett Till*. See http://www.pbs.org/wgbh/amex/till/peopleevents/e_lynch.html; Raper, Arthur F. *The Tragedy of Lynching*. Chapel Hill: University of North Carolina Press, 1933; Steinhorn,

L., and B. Diggs-Brown. *By the Color of Our Skin: The Illusion of Integration and the Reality of Race*. New York: Plume, 2000; Thomas, William Isaac, and Dorothy Swaine Thomas. *The Child in America: Behavior Problems and Programs*. New York: A.A. Knopf, 1928; Women in History. "Ida B. Wells-Barnett." See www.lkwdpl.org/wihohio/barn-ida.htm; Zangrando, Robert L. "About Lynching." In *Modern American Poetry*. See http://www.english.uiuc.edu/maps/poets/g_l/lynching/lynching.htm.

Sheila Bluhm Morley

Reconstruction (1865–1877)

Reconstruction is the period that followed the Civil War (1861–1865) and ended with the reintegration of the Confederate States into the Union. It also produced a legal framework allowing African Americans to live as citizens in a post-slavery American society. This was done most notably through three amendments to the U.S. Constitution and several civil rights acts. The Thirteenth Amendment abolished all forms of slavery; the **Fourteenth Amendment** gave African Americans citizenship and promised them equal protection under the law; and the **Fifteenth Amendment** extended the right to vote to black men. On April 9, 1866, the Republican-dominated Congress overrode President Andrew Johnson's veto and passed the Civil Rights Act of 1866 (also known as the New Freedman Bureau Act), which gave citizenship to any person born in the United States, with rights and privileges such as voting; owning, selling, and inheriting property; and suing and giving evidence in court. President Johnson had questioned the qualification of former slaves to be citizens and had deemed the bill too favorable to blacks and unfair to whites. The act was essentially ignored and was only enforceable after the ratification of the Fourteenth Amendment, which reaffirmed citizenship rights and privileges to former slaves and the "equal protection of the laws."

A Thomas Nast cartoon, "Andrew Johnson's Reconstruction and How It Works," published in 1866. Courtesy of the Library of Congress.

Because of the relentless racism and violence of **vigilante organizations** such as the **Ku Klux Klan (KKK)**, and the continuous resentment of the South, which felt humiliated by defeat and by what it perceived as imposition by the northern victors, African Americans could not fully enjoy the rights promised by the 1866 Civil Rights Act and the Fourteenth Amendment. From 1870 to 1871, Congress passed three acts known as enforcement acts (the Enforcement Act of 1870, also known as the Ku Klux Klan Act of 1870, and two enforcement acts in 1871), mainly targeting the Ku Klux Klan, who were using violence to prevent African Americans and some whites from voting, holding office, serving on juries, or attempting to get educated.

African Americans hiding in the swamps of Louisiana, 1873. Courtesy of the Library of Congress.

In 1870, Massachusetts Congressmen Charles Sumner and Benjamin Butler introduced a bill to reaffirm equality and justice for all Americans as guaranteed by the Declaration of Independence and the Constitution. What became known, after years of negotiations, as the Civil Rights Act of 1875 sought to end discrimination and **segregation** against African Americans in the enjoyment of public places, facilities, and conveyances. In 1883, however, following southern legislatures' reversal of the legal achievement of Reconstruction and the general violence against blacks in the South, the U.S. Supreme Court declared the 1875 Civil Rights Act unconstitutional on the grounds that discrimination in public facilities was not within the power of Congress to legislate, nor was it a federal offense against the Thirteenth or Fourteenth Amendments.

Other problems that newly freed African Americans had to face included laws that had been in place in the past, such as the so-called **black codes**, a set of local and state laws already in place in the North before the Civil War and put in place by former slave states in the South to limit the civil rights and privileges that African Americans acquired as a result of the amendments and the civil rights acts. The Fourteenth and Fifteenth Amendments offered protection but did not completely shield African Americans from the intimidation and violence of white supremacists, the frequent burning of newly established black schools, and the beating and murder of teachers in those schools.

The promise of Reconstruction was further shattered by the violence of post-Reconstruction, which started after the Union Army pulled out of the South. Previously humiliated by the defeat in the Civil War, the South embarked on a steady and unapologetic course to reverse the achievement of Reconstruction. Tactics including the grandfather clause, literary test, the poll tax, and sheer violence led to the legal **disenfranchisement** of African Americans. The triumph of **Jim Crow** laws was sealed by the landmark Supreme Court decision *Plessy v. Ferguson* of 1896 that legalized segregation and discrimination, thus crushing the promise of racial harmony generated by the idealism of Reconstruction.

In spite of legal wrangling, the reconfiguration of the plantation system through the practice of **sharecropping**, and the continuing **racism** and discrimination against African Americans, Reconstruction brought hope to newly freed African Americans. Thousands of black and white volunteers, missionaries, and churches in or from both the North and the South established thousands of new schools and/or labored to educate the black population of all ages whom the institution of slavery had, by and large, forbidden to learn to read and write. Within three years of the end of the Civil War, several institutions of higher education were also launched; they included Fisk University, Hampton University, Howard University, and Morehouse College.

Even in the face of many daunting challenges, the amendments to the Constitution and the civil rights acts that followed the end of the Civil War allowed African Americans to vote, seek political office, own personal and real property, own the fruit of their labor, and use public facilities. Unfortunately, all of these achievements were legally suppressed by the triumph of post-Reconstruction Jim Crow laws. *See also* Disenfranchisement; Fifteenth Amendment; Fourteenth Amendment; Jim Crow.

Further Readings: Du Bois, W.E.B. *Black Reconstruction in America 1860–1880*. Introduction by David Levering Lewis. New York: Free Press, 1998; Foner, Eric. *Reconstruction: America's Unfinished Revolution, 1863–1877*. New York: HarperCollins, 1988; Smith, John David. *Black Voices from Reconstruction 1865–1877*. Gainesville: University Press of Florida, 1997.

Aimable Twagilimana

Redlining

Derived from the practice of banks, which drew red lines on city maps to mark areas and neighborhoods in which they did not want to lend money, the term *redlining* describes the refusal of banks and other institutions to provide services, such as banking and insurance, to residents of certain areas. Although this practice is illegal in the United States when it is based on race, religion, gender, disability, ethnic origin, or the presence or absence of children in a family, it has been used, especially against African Americans and other racial minorities, to restrict their ability to obtain affordable housing to only certain areas or parts of a city, and thus greatly increased residential **segregation** in the United States in the early and mid-twentieth century.

The practice of redlining was given major impetus by the Housing Act of 1934, which was passed to foster the development of affordable housing for the urban poor. Despite this basic aim, the act also required cities to designate certain areas and neighborhoods for particular racial groups, a practice that effectively prevented minorities from obtaining mortgages for housing outside their designated areas. In many cities, such as Philadelphia, Boston, and Kansas City, redlining forced African Americans into certain well-defined neighborhoods and preserved the all-white composition of others. Today, the federal government requires all banks to provide a map showing the locations of recent home loans it has made in a city to assure potential customers that no redlining is taking place. *See also* Ghettos; Integration.

Further Readings: Lang, William W., and Leonard I. Nakamura. "A Model of Redlining." *Journal of Urban Economics* 33, no. 2 (1993): 223–234; Schafer, Robert, and Helen F. Ladd. *Discrimination in Mortgage Lending*. Cambridge, MA: MIT Press, 1981; Tootell, Geoffrey M.B. "Redlining in Boston: Do Mortgage Lenders Discriminate against Neighborhoods?" *Quarterly Journal of Economics* 111, no. 4 (1996): 1049–1079; Zenou, Yves, and Nicolas Boccard. "Racial Discrimination and Redlining in Cities." *Journal of Urban Economics* 48 (2000): 260–285.

John A. Wagner

Red Scare and Race Riots

The term *red scare* refers to two periods in U.S. history, both marked by widespread and intense nationalist and anti-radical sentiment. During the first Red Scare, 1917–1920, the U.S. government, industry leaders, soldiers, and citizens attacked communists, socialists, anarchists, labor organizations, and recent immigrants, particularly German-Americans. The scare found U.S. blacks in the midst of both a regional and psychological shift, changes that served to further threaten a nation in the throws of hysteria. Blacks were both victims and actors in the events surrounding the Red Scare, as many of the blacks who sought to change the status quo by seeking economic opportunity in northern cities were included among accounts of the radicals who posed a threat to America. During the high tide of the scare, in 1919, there were seventy-eight **lynchings** and twenty-five race riots, phenomena that caused **James Weldon Johnson** to dub the summer and autumn of 1919 the "Red Summer." The rise of *the New Negro* (a termed coined by black philosopher **Alain Locke**), or the change in black self-understanding, was also a source of anxiety for whites, as blacks fought back against the mobs that attacked them.

Wars often serve to bolster nationalist sentiment in a nation. When groups of people, divided by race, class, gender, and region, can come together against a common enemy, they are able to forget the problems they have with their fellow citizens. President Woodrow Wilson put this social tendency in overdrive in the United States as he took extraordinary steps to manufacture national cohesion before American entry into World War I in 1917. Wilson created the Committee on Public Information, led by journalist George Creel, which distributed an enormous amount of pro-America propaganda—more than enough, it turns out, than was necessary to sustain the war effort; after the Great War, a violently nationalist populace, aided by industrial leaders, journalists, and the U.S. government, still hungry for a foe, turned its attention away from foreign enemies and took steps to root out the enemy within.

Anarchists were responsible for a series of bombing attempts throughout the country. Many Americans were concerned that these attempts might succeed, especially in the wake of Russia's Bolshevik Revolution. During the scare, Congress broadened the Espionage Act to include the Sedition Act of 1918, an act that made it illegal to speak out against the government and gave the Postmaster General the power to intercept dissenter mail. In November 1919, and on New Year's Day 1920, Attorney General Palmer authorized the infamous Palmer Raids. On January 1, officials arrested over 10,000 communists, left-wingers, and people with foreign-sounding names. Among the lay population, anarchist plots seemed illogical to many, and were unpredictable and shrouded in secrecy; workers, on the other hand, presented visible targets (Tuttle, 1970). With each passing strike, citizens began to more closely associate labor unrest with the ongoing plot to overthrow the U.S. government.

In 1919, the U.S. was also in the midst of massive labor unrest, as factories switched to peacetime production and soldiers returned to strained domestic labor markets. According to reports, there were as many as 3,000 labor disputes, strikes, and lockouts, involving over four million workers (Hallgren, 1933), as workers whose salaries had been frozen to help out with the war effort began to organize for better conditions. The Seattle General Strike, which took place from January 21 through February 11, began in earnest when 25,000 workers joined 35,000 striking shipyard workers and succeeded in shutting down the city. The Cleveland May Day Riot was also a major event, as local unionists, socialists, communists, and anarchists met at the behest of socialist leader Charles Ruthenberg to protest the detention of Eugene Debs. The September Steelworkers Strike grew to include 365,000 workers around the nation.

The communist and striker became intertwined in the American mind; industrialists, journalists, and officials only served to help Americans conflate the two. In addition to journalists' accounts that condemned strikers as un-American, Industrialists fighting collective bargaining efforts were not afraid to exploit nationalist sentiment. Although involved in a noble battle for fair working conditions, workers were not immune to **racism**. Labor leaders and industrialists alike mobilized anti-black sentiment, often with violent consequences.

As stated above, blacks were both actors and objects of violence during the Red Scare. As the conventional belief in black inferiority met the newfound hatred of foreigners and anyone who might upset the status quo, both attitudes merged against black efforts to realize the benefits of American society. Many of the 450,000 blacks who relocated to urban centers met angry whites who were afraid of what the influx of black workers would do to their economic and social standing. Any survey of the mobs that attacked blacks during the Red Summer found frustrated white workers and soldiers without a war to fight among the participants.

A change in attitude accompanied the black migration. The argument that blacks should not seek political and social equality, championed by **Booker T. Washington,** fell out of favor among the black population, as post-war blacks had reason to believe that they deserved full citizenship. The president's efforts to create national pride did not bypass the black community. African Americans were soldiers in the Great War, bought Liberty Bonds, and followed rationing restrictions (Tuttle, 1970). The Harlem Renaissance, the most well known of the New Negro efforts, and Carter G. Woodson's Association for the Study of Negro Life and History, founded in 1915, stand as evidence of a move to celebrate black historical and cultural achievements and the decision to reject the conventional belief in white superiority. Black newspapers, including **W.E.B. Du Bois**'s ***The Crisis*** and the ***Chicago Defender*,** encouraged blacks to hold their heads high as they relocated to cities across the country. Although many blacks lost their lives in the **Red Summer,** black people were no longer willing to believe that they deserved to die according to the whims of whites. Blacks heeded **Claude McKay**'s Red Summer call, and mobs met them, "pressed to the wall, dying, but fighting back!" (McKay, "If We Must Die," line 14). *See also* Black Self-Defense; Chicago (Illinois) Riot of 1919; East St. Louis (Illinois) Riot of 1917.

Further Readings: Hallgren, Mauritz A. "The Right to Strike." *The Nation* 137, no. 3566, November 8, 1933, 530; Rudwick, Elliott M. *Race Riot at East St. Louis, July 2, 1917*. Carbondale: Southern Illinois University Press, 1963; Tuttle, William M., Jr. *Race Riot: Chicago in the Red Summer of 1919*. New York: Antheneum, 1970.

Shatema A. Threadcraft

Red Summer Race Riots of 1919

The race riots of the Red Summer represent the height of **white mob** riot activity in the United States, never surpassed in frequency, breadth, or severity. In addition to the seventy-eight **lynchings** of black individuals by white mobs that year, white mobs also attacked entire black communities throughout the United States. The most well known of the Red Summer race riots are those that occurred in **Charleston,** South Carolina (May); **Chicago,** Illinois (July); **Longview,** Texas (July); **Washington, D.C.** (July); **Knoxville,** Tennessee (August); **Omaha,** Nebraska (September); and **Elaine,** Arkansas (October).

In May 1920, congressional Rep. **Leonidas C. Dyer** introduced an Anti-Lynching Bill in the House of Representatives. The bill contained a list of twenty-six riots, put together from the records of the **National Association for the Advancement of Colored People (NAACP)** and the Tuskegee Institute. The locations were Bisbee, Arizona; Elaine, Arkansas; New London, Connecticut; Wilmington, Delaware; Washington, D.C.; Blakely, Dublin, Millen, and Putnam County, Georgia; Chicago and Bloomington, Illinois; Corbin, Kentucky; Homer and New Orleans, Louisiana; Annapolis and Baltimore, Maryland; Omaha, Nebraska; New York City and Syracuse, New York; Philadelphia, Pennsylvania; Charleston, South Carolina; Knoxville and Memphis, Tennessee; Longview and Port Arthur, Texas; and Norfolk,

Virginia. Sen. Charles Curtis from Kansas introduced an anti-lynching bill to the Senate and used similar information.

Scholars have not yet determined the official total number of Red Summer riots, but the most often stated count is twenty-six. Several factors make it difficult to establish an accurate number. At the time of the incidents, local officials sometimes suppressed information, invoking a code of silence. As time went on, many people wanted to forget the incidents; consequently, much information has been lost. Alternately, it was common practice for newspapers at the time, both white and black, to sensationalize any news whatsoever. Exaggerating, or in some cases even inventing, racial conflicts sold papers, so newspaper accounts cannot be taken at face value.

These local, national, and international newspaper accounts and other reports do suggest additional locations. The black press in both the United States and Great Britain devoted attention to the reporting of race riots, often in more graphic detail and with a political edge. Using these sources, an extended list of possible incidents in the United States contains fifty-six entries. A verification model in which an incident must appear on one of the NAACP, Tuskegee, or Dyer lists, in addition to a newspaper account, or be referred to in official government accounts, either local or federal, adds these riot locations to the ones on the Dyer list: Mulberry, Florida; Berkeley, Milan, and Cadwell, Georgia; Camp Zachary Taylor, Kentucky; Gary, Indiana; Bogalusa, Louisiana; Youngstown, Ohio; and Donora, Pennsylvania.

Another factor affecting the count is the definition of terms. Incidents such as those in Chicago and Omaha involved mobs of hundreds of whites rampaging through black neighborhoods, looting and burning property and injuring people. These are clearly riots. In some incidents, however, such as those in Bisbee and New London, the mob comprised authorities of the law acting outside their official capacity while on duty. This type of situation requires interpretation as to whether, and at what point, the action became unlawful, thereby making it a riot. Other incidents involved smaller mobs, or the white mob was met with the resistance of an equal number of black people, and so these events may be considered by some sources or researchers to be fights or clashes, rather than riots.

The NAACP annual report from the years 1919 until 1923 uses the phrase *race riot* when reporting events in which white mobs targeted black communities. As the frequency of these events declined, the phrase fell out of common use, until, briefly, during the spate of riots after World War II. Then, during the riots in the 1960s, use of *race riot* was revived to describe events of destruction by mobs made up of black people. Such a transformation in meaning can generate confusion and can hide white responsibility for violence. Additionally, an alternate phrase, *white mob violence*, was used by many of the newspapers at that time as a euphemism for lynching.

In many ways, the Red Summer's anti-black riots were similar to lynchings. Both lynching mobs and rioting mobs used precipitating events as excuses to try to justify their violence, and in both cases these excuses were usually an alleged crime or social trespass of some sort by a black individual. Accusations of murder and rape were common, but sometimes it was an offense as minor as the failure to remove a hat. Both riots and lynchings were often inflamed by **rumors,** and were promoted and sensationalized in **press coverage**. The riots often included the murder of an accused person, and this murder was sometimes performed as a carefully enacted lynching ritual, with the riot preceding and/or following. Riots and lynchings produced a similar result—the targeted community was terrorized.

Yet the riots differed from lynchings in significant ways. Riot participation consistently crossed lines of age and gender. A riot targeted the entire community directly, while lynching targeted the community as a whole indirectly. Lynchings were highly ritualized, whereas riots, while conforming to a certain pattern, were less organized and more chaotic and random. Despite its popularity during the Red Summer, rioting never attained the level of societal approval that lynching did.

There was no one simple cause for this epidemic of white mob violence directed at black people. In some of the urban locations, there had been significant growth in the black population, resulting in overcrowding in the black neighborhoods and pressure on white neighborhoods to accommodate in various ways. World War I had just ended and many demobilized white troops returned home to find themselves competing with black workers for jobs and homes. Also, the war itself had acclimated people to the idea of using violence to solve problems, and had desensitized people to the horror of violence. Each of the Red Summer riots was a result of these overarching general factors combining with many other factors specific to each location.

The riots of the Red Summer can be sorted into four localized context categories. There were riots that occurred in relation to a labor dispute; involved military personnel as rioters or targets; related to local politics and a "boss" or political machine; and riots that rose out of a threatened, perceived, or actual rupture of the local racial caste system.

The Labor Riots

Lumber camps, textile mills, steel mills, mines, and waterfront docks were all sources of dangerous jobs requiring great numbers of strong laborers, and were places where black workers found employment during World War I. In 1919, unions were actively organizing in these industries, as they had been throughout the war. The racial composition of the unions varied. Many were all white, some were all black, some were biracial, with separate subdivisions by race, and a very few were beginning to be interracial, with membership recruitment from among both black and white workers. The high level of union activism heightened the tension among all parties in these industrial communities, adding yet another factor to the volatile post-war atmosphere, so it is no surprise that some of the Red Summer race riots occurred out of this context.

The labor-related riots took two forms. One pattern, by far the most common, was that of a mob of white strikers attacking black workers, regarding them as their enemy, competing for scarce jobs and status. During the Great Steel Strike, which affected much of the industrial Northeast for several months, as many as 40,000 black workers were brought in as strikebreakers. In Syracuse, New York, in July, striking iron molders attacked black workers at Globe Malleable Iron Works using clubs, stones, and firearms. Injuries to both workers and strikers occurred. Police made arrests and assigned all mounted officers, reserve patrolmen, and detectives to the area. Four white men were charged in the rioting.

In Gary, Indiana, the unions had excluded black workers who were already working in the mills. Once the steel strike began, they did try to get black workers to support it, but without success. U.S. Steel used local and non-local black strikebreakers, housing them in the plants or transporting them to and from work, for their safety. The riot in Gary occurred when several thousand strikers left a mass meeting and came on a streetcar bringing forty strikebreakers, many black, into town. The strikers attacked the streetcar with stones and bricks, beating the workers and dragging them through the streets. Witnesses said that two of the black workers fought back with razors. The governor ordered in the state militia and finally requested federal troops. General Leonard Wood, fresh from riot duty in Omaha, Nebraska, immediately declared martial law. The rioting in Gary broke the unions there.

For the *New York Times*, reporting the Great Steel Strike in Donora, Pennsylvania, the news was not that the strikers attacked the workers, or that most of those workers were black, but rather that the bulk of those attacked fought back. The first of two altercations occurred in the morning when black workers returned to work at the American Steel and Wire Company. They were attacked by strikers throwing bricks, and several of the workers were hurt. The workers then fired at the strikers with revolvers, wounding two men in the legs. State police broke up the incident. Then, that evening, strikers again threw bricks at the workers, injuring one woman and several men. Shots were fired without hitting anyone, and the workers fought back with fists and bricks.

In Youngstown, Ohio, also during the Great Steel Strike, black workers at Youngstown Sheet and Tube Company were attacked by strikers. Several workers were injured, one critically; one was killed. No injuries were reported among the strikers.

There were, on the other hand, industries and regions where black workers were union members. The other type of labor-related race riot took the form of a white mob, comprising company-hired assailants acting on behalf of an employer, attacking black union members out on strike. This type of riot was rare, and during the Red Summer happened only in Bogalusa, Louisiana, and Mulberry, Florida. In Bogalusa, the Great Southern Lumber Company, unhappy with unionizing in general, perceived the union of black lumber workers as a particular threat. A mob led by company men waged a violent campaign of fear and intimidation over a series of months, harassing the workers and their families, both white and black, in their homes. This campaign culminated in a riotous shoot-out in which four union men were killed.

In Mulberry, Florida, in what was probably an attempt to scare the black strikers back to work, a group of at least four white company guards from

Prairie Pebble Mine fired directly into the black section of town, reportedly as many as twenty-five rounds, from high-powered rifles. At least three black people were hit; one, a two-year-old black boy, was killed, and the woman holding him, possibly his mother, was seriously wounded. Another black man was killed the same night when the guards continued to fire into Mulberry's black neighborhood.

The Military Riots

The military subculture offered a particularly complex environment for interracial conflict to play out. While black troops had met with great success overseas during the war, and many had discovered a new definition of freedom, back in the United States during the Red Summer it was a different story. Many racist whites were threatened by the appearance of uniformed black men, and many white veterans were anxious to see any vestige of the temporarily esteemed status of their black compatriots restored to its pre-war marginality. After the war, the government was closely studying the performance and role of black troops in order to determine the future attitude of the military toward its racial composition. Due in part to these complicated factors, the riots of the Red Summer display a full range of military involvement, with black soldiers in different roles in various circumstances, being alternately targets of violence, upholders of the law, and activists for change. White soldiers, as well, were variously stopping riots and starting them, and the target of the violence was sometimes black soldiers and sometimes black civilians.

Mobs of white sailors started riots in Charleston, South Carolina, and Washington, D.C., targeting black residents and their property indiscriminately. In Washington, D.C., the mob's excuse was an alleged assault by two black men of a white woman, following a barrage of newspaper sensationalism promoting fear of a black crime wave, and the rioting continued for days. In Charleston, the alleged offense was the pushing of a sailor off the sidewalk. In both cases, Marines were called in to stop the rioting.

In New London, Connecticut, tension between white sailors and black sailors erupted in violence. Each side had accused the other of lying in wait for them as they crossed Long Cove Bridge after dark. When two white "bluejackets" were arrested for a fight, their comrades were unable to make the police turn them loose. In frustration, the white sailors raided the Hotel Bristol, a popular congregating spot for black sailors. A group of hotel patrons was thrown into the street and severely beaten. Reinforcements arrived on both sides and the fighting continued. The town's police, even with the help of the fire department, were unable to stop the riot. Marines with rifles came and restored order.

In Bisbee, Arizona, local officials and off-duty white infantrymen harassed and assaulted with gunfire the black 10th U.S. Cavalry. Five people were shot. George Sullivan, a white military policeman with the 19th Infantry, passed by Brewery Gulch, a club popular with black soldiers, and there were words between him and five 10th Cavalrymen. The black soldiers went to the police station and reported the incident, and the police chief tried to confiscate their weapons. When they refused to give up their guns, the police went up to Brewery Gulch to disarm any black troops with weapons. Gunfire was exchanged, repeatedly, until fifty black soldiers were placed in custody. During the melee, bystanders were shot as well, including Teresa Leyvas, a Mexican resident of Bisbee who was struck in the head.

A celebration honoring the return of Norfolk, Virginia's black veterans was halted because of rioting in which six people were injured. The Norfolk City Council had planned a week-long celebration, but on the first day of the festivities, a black soldier was arrested and a riot followed. Soldiers and Marines were sent in from the naval base to help restore order.

At Camp Zachary Taylor, tension simmered for months between the black soldiers stationed there and the white residents of Louisville, Kentucky, as well as between the white soldiers stationed there and the black residents. Many fractious incidents occurred, but one in particular stood out, involving many black soldiers and a large crowd of whites, both military and civilian. The fracas developed when local white authorities arrested a black soldier, and his compatriots reacted with resistance. Violent confrontation followed.

The Local Political Machine Riots

Political players vying for power have exploited social turmoil to reach their goals since time immemorial, and such appears to be the case in at least three of the Red Summer riots. A relationship between a key player in the incident and the mayor of the locality or some other community leader is a red flag to identifying riots in this local context category.

In Milan, Georgia, Berry Washington was a venerable figure in the black community. When two white men, John Dowdy and Levi Evans, came into the black neighborhood and attacked two girls, Washington shot and killed one of the men. That the dead man was the son of a local minister is no doubt of some importance in the events that followed. A mob of 75 to 100 people lynched Washington and subsequently forced the entire black community out of their homes for two days.

Another example is the riot in Knoxville, Tennessee. Maurice Mays was a politically active man about town. It was rumored that his real father was the mayor of Knoxville, and son or not, on the day the trouble started, Mays had been distributing campaign literature for the mayor's reelection. Mays had his enemies among the police, and it was one of these enemies who arrested him for the murder of a white woman. The mob in Knoxville did not want to wait for the trial and was set on lynching him. He was successfully protected by the authorities, who moved him to another town, but when the mob was unable to obtain Mays, they raged through the black part of town, burning homes and shooting people. Seven people were killed, and twenty were injured.

In Omaha, Nebraska, Mayor Ed Smith was nearly killed when he attempted to stop a mob, numbering more than 1,000, from lynching a black man, Will Brown, accused of assaulting a white woman. After burning the courthouse, hanging and shooting Brown, and burning his body, the mob cut a path of destruction through Omaha's black neighborhoods. The mob's actions may have been motivated, defined, and even paid for, by the political machine of Tom Dennison. From 1897, Dennison had a mayor of his choice in place for twenty-nine years, except for the 1918–1921 term, and he had a close relationship with the publisher of the *Omaha Bee*, which had been running sensationalized crime reports all summer. This, along with financial connections to certain leaders of the rioting mob, suggests that Dennison may have hoped to use the riot to discredit the local administration. In the next election, Smith was voted out of office, replaced with Dennison's man, James Dahlman.

The Caste Rupture Riots

The formal and informal structures of the binary black/white caste system, also known as the **Jim Crow** laws, were challenged in many ways after World War I, for the first time since **Reconstruction**. During the Red Summer, white mobs used these perceived caste ruptures as justification for violence.

One type of caste rupture, long at the heart of many racial conflicts, was demographic. The movement of black residents out of the neighborhoods allotted to them and into white neighborhoods heightened racial tension in many urban areas in the North. Demographic caste rupture was behind the rioting in Baltimore, Maryland, for example, where groups repeatedly clashed during the Red Summer as black residents moved into previously all-white neighborhoods. In one incident, white youths were harassing black residents with noise and taunts, and the residents complained to police many times without result. When the black residents confronted the youths, a mob of fifty whites, armed with bottles, bricks, and rocks, rioted. Police from two districts came to stop the disturbance.

The struggle of the black farmers in Phillips County, Arkansas, near the town of Elaine, represents economic caste rupture, as they began to try to break out of the peonage system by forming a Progressive Farmers and Household Union of America. The southern agricultural system was structured in such a way that most blacks worked as farmhands or sharecroppers. The landlord provided supplies in advance, receiving in payment a share of the season's crop. The situation was rigged so that the sharecropper would remain perpetually in debt. The landlord rarely gave a written statement of account to the sharecropper, which many illiterate sharecroppers would not have been able to read, and the crop was just never enough to pay off what the sharecropper owed for supplies. The whites in Phillips County were highly fearful of the Progressive Farmers and Household Union of America alliance, and rumors spread that an organized insurrection was imminent. On this pretext, white mobs, bolstered with people from nearby counties in Tennessee and Mississippi, hunted down, captured, and killed hundreds of black people, not only the farmers, but others as well. The highest-profile deaths were those of the four Johnston brothers, among them a doctor and a dentist, who were killed while in custody of the authorities.

Other riots occurred out of a more general context of caste rupture in which whites were threatened by perceived differences in quality of life. In both Millen and Cadwell, Georgia, a fear that Blacks were building a strong cultural alliance led whites to attack the symbols of the black community along with its leaders, burning a total of eleven church and lodge buildings and killing eight people. White locals in Corbin, Kentucky, ran black railroad workers out of town for challenging local social mores. Similarly, in Longview, Texas, whites were threatened by the economic success of the local black community and its increasingly expanded worldview inspired by the national black press. There, a mob of 1,000 white men, armed with rifles, pistols, and stolen ammunition, went to the black neighborhood, set several houses on fire, and shot several people.

Isolated incidents of caste rupture precipitated other riots. In Dublin, Georgia, black citizens fought against a mob to prevent a lynching. In New York City, a black man grabbed the straw hat of an off-duty white police officer. The officer retaliated by shooting his gun, and a racial melee ensued, involving large numbers of whites and blacks fighting one another.

Philadelphia, Pennsylvania, having had a huge race riot in 1918, suffered through the Red Summer with several racial clashes, one of which was reported as a riot. At a carnival, a crowd of whites fought a crowd of blacks, but most trouble was averted when 100 police officers showed up and made arrests.

In Wilmington, Delaware, a white mob formed in hopes of lynching two black men accused of killing a police officer, but the men had been moved to Philadelphia. Someone opened fire on the mob, which fired back and then proceeded to move through the black neighborhood vandalizing homes and other property.

The contagion theory of rioting has been applied to the Red Summer, the hypothesis being that many of these riots would not have happened without those that preceded, leading the way. This theory is practically impossible to test, but one riot was so lame in its triggering incident and weak in its execution that contagion is the most likely explanation. On a Port Arthur, Texas, streetcar, a black man was accused of smoking in the presence of a white woman. A white mob, estimated by witnesses as numbering forty, attacked him, and a group of black men, numbering about twenty, fought back. Port Arthur is located between Houston, which had a serious race riot in 1918, and Longview, a location of one of the major Red Summer riots, which had occurred only a week or so prior to the Port Arthur incident.

The Red Summer rioting in Chicago crosses the categories, because labor issues, political maneuvering, as well as demographic caste rupture, were all present. The incident that triggered the rioting there was the stoning and subsequent drowning of teenager Eugene Williams. Williams had, while swimming, strayed into the white part of the lake, and white people started throwing rocks at him. Unable to keep his head out of the water because of the rocks, he drowned. When a police officer at the scene refused to arrest the rock throwers, black citizens became angry, and the officer arrested them instead. Whites throughout the city used this as an opportunity to vent their rage, stoked that summer by competition for jobs and housing. White gangs, such as Regan's Colts, sought out trouble as a way of asserting power. Some scholars argue that labor unions played a large role, particularly in the meatpacking industry, while other scholars counter that if labor had gotten involved, things would then have been much worse, given meatpackers' skill with knives.

Analysis

Immediately after World War I, the entire world reeled with change. There had been the Bolshevik Revolution in Russia in 1917. In Peru, there were rebellions and a great climate of unrest as the indigenous people revolted in unprecedented number and uprisings were met with massacres and mob violence. There were labor strikes in Colombia; the British government killings of many protesters in the Amritsar province of India; and unrest in many Muslim populations. In South Africa, defiant demonstrations led to skirmishes between protesters and police, and later to conflict between groups of whites and blacks.

During the five-year span of World War I and subsequent post-war adjustment, from 1917 to 1921, the tenor of the times reverberated with increased nativism, racism, fear, suspicion, and economic uncertainty. A key feature of the political climate was the Red Scare, promoted and driven by Attorney General A. Mitchell Palmer. Promoting the fear of a *Red menace* made up of anarchists, radicals, Bolshevik propagandists, and revolutionaries, Palmer suspected the American labor movement was being infiltrated and polluted. Palmer used labor unrest and a series of letter bombs as evidence that sinister organizing was taking place nationally.

Palmer and his believers thought this radical trade unionism was gearing up to destroy capitalism in the United States and establish a new social order, ruled by the workers. Race was a focus of this Red Scare fear. The federal government was convinced that American blacks as a group were vulnerable to the persuasions of the Bolsheviks, and much money and resources were allotted to monitoring and infiltrating radical black activity. The Department of Justice, the **Federal Bureau of Investigation (FBI)**, the State Department, the General Intelligence Division, the Department of the Post Office, the Military Intelligence Division, and the Office of Naval Intelligence are all on record as being concerned with finding a link between Bolshevik propaganda and black militancy. Black publications, including the *Messenger*, the ***Chicago Defender***, the *Whip*, the *Crusader*, and the *Emancipator* were carefully watched for what was referred to as *Negro subversion*. Some of the weekly newspapers and monthly magazines were investigated and censured, and in some cases were withheld from distribution, or confiscated altogether. The Post Office sometimes revoked the second-class permit of a publication, forcing an underfunded publisher to pay first-class postage rates, effectively silencing the issue.

It was in this climate that race relations among the U.S. populace took on the volatility that allowed for the violence of the Red Summer. White violence increased and diversified. Black response became more active and focused. World War I had brought something new to the United States—that of the heroic return of the black soldier. One reaction was the revival of the **Ku Klux Klan (KKK)**, and the Red Summer race riots were akin to this spirit. This racism was not universal. Both the mayor of Knoxville and the governor of Tennessee, for example, went on record as repudiating the organization. The national black news magazine ***The Crisis*** summed up the situation by pointing out that the black soldier, after facing chemical warfare and artillery fire in the war, was not going to be intimidated by a bunch of cowards running around in bed linens. Rather, the article said, the war had taught black soldiers to face a danger and see it through.

The Red Summer race riots became a turning point in the history of race relations in the United States. White racists learned that the mob spirit methodology was not the powerful tool it may once have been, and that white mob violence would be met with both theoretical and practical resistance from black people, along with societal resistance, in the form of legislation and social policy lobbying and activism. Although ultimately the Dyer Anti-Lynching Bill was not enacted, the fight for its passage was part of a social and cultural force that laid the groundwork for the later rise of the **civil rights movement**.

Further Readings: Cortner, Richard C. *A Mob Intent on Death*. Middletown, CT: Wesleyan University Press, 1988; Flynt, Wayne. "Florida Labor and Political 'Radicalism,' 1919–1920." *Labor History* 9 (1968); Kitchens, John W., ed. *Tuskegee Institute News Clippings File*. Sanford, NC: Microfilming Corporation of America, 1981; Kornweibel, Theodore. *"Seeing Red": Federal Campaigns against Black Militancy, 1919–1925*. Bloomington and Indianapolis: Indiana University Press, 1998; Lakin, Matthew. "'A Dark Night': The Knoxville Race Riot of 1919." *Journal of East Tennessee History* 72 (2000): 1–29; Meier, August, ed. *Papers of the NAACP.* Part 7, Series A. Frederick, MD: University Publications of America, 1981; Murray, Robert K. *Red Scare: A Study of National Hysteria, 1919–1920*. Minneapolis: University of Minnesota Press, 1955; Norwood, Stephen. "Bogalusa Burning: The War Against Biracial Unionism in the Deep South, 1919." *Journal of Southern History* 63 (1997): 591–628; Palmer, A. Mitchell, Attorney General. *Investigation Activities of the Department of Justice*. 66th Congress, 1st Session, Senate Document 153, Vol. XII. 1919; Schmidt, Regin. *Red Scare: FBI and the Origins of Anticommunism in the United States, 1919–1943*. Copenhagen, Denmark: Museum Tusculanum Press, 2000; Stockley, Grif. *Blood in Their Eyes: The Elaine Race Massacres of 1919*. Fayetteville: University of Arkansas Press, 2001; Tuttle, William. *Race Riot: Chicago in the Red Summer of 1919*. Urbana: University of Illinois Press, 1996; Waskow, Arthur O. *From Race Riot to Sit-In, 1919 and the 1960s; A Study in the Connections between Conflict and Violence*. Garden City, NY: Anchor Books, 1966.

Jan Voogd

Reparations

Reparations are defined as the act or process of making amends through compensation or some other means. Efforts to allocate reparations to black slaves and their descendants in America have a long and thorny history. Early on, some whites made significant attempts to address the damage slavery had inflicted on freedmen and freedwomen, but they were thwarted at every turn. **White mobs,** particularly in the South, often used violence to suppress blacks, thus preventing them from seeking restitution. Significant black crusades for reparations did not occur until the 1950s. A number of individuals and organizations have since joined the movement, but they continue to face massive resistance. In 1994 and 2004, respectively, survivors of the **Rosewood** massacre and the **Tulsa** race riot received reparations.

During **Reconstruction**, several attempts were made to ameliorate the residual aftereffects of slavery on blacks. Congress established the Freedmen's Bureau to provide aid to former slaves. This aid focused on what the Bureau believed to be their most urgent needs—food, medical care, education, and land. The bureau, with the help of numerous blacks, was able to accomplish this goal to a limited degree. Their greatest contribution was the establishment of new schools. For the first time ever, black politicians were elected into office. However, by 1877, southern white Democrats had ousted all black politicians from office throughout the nation.

In 1865, Gen. William Tecumseh Sherman declared that the land confiscated during the war should be given to former slaves. Congress charged the Freedmen's Bureau to distribute that land. Word of the promise of "forty acres and a mule" spread quickly amongst blacks. However, President Andrew Johnson returned the land to the former slave owners instead. In 1866, opposition to Congress' Southern Homestead Act prevented all but 1,000 blacks from buying land at low cost. Thaddeus Stevens proposed a slave reparations bill, which would allot forty acres of land and $100 to build a home for every recently freed male, but it did not pass. A few proponents of **Black Nationalism,** such as **Henry McNeil Turner,** also advocated reparations. Turner sought financial assistance from whites to support black migrations to Africa. He believed blacks were owed remuneration as a result of several hundred years of forced slavery and unpaid wages. He received support from the American Colonization Society (ACS). In 1915, blacks failed to win a lawsuit against the U.S. Treasury Department for labor rendered during slavery.

Blacks benefited little from Reconstruction, as systematic subjugation and violence kept blacks in check. Landless, penniless, and denied the freedoms and opportunities they had anticipated after emancipation, blacks were disheartened. Nonetheless, with the exception of a few dauntless leaders, blacks did not openly demand retribution. White mobs squelched black opponents and white sympathizers through violence and intimidation. Following Reconstruction, race riots occurred throughout the nation. In these riots, whites often murdered and raped blacks, and burned down their homes, churches, and businesses. Among the decimated communities were Tulsa, Oklahoma, and Rosewood, Florida.

The **Tulsa (Oklahoma) Riot of 1921** was one of the most horrendous assaults on a black community in the nation. A young white woman charged that she had been raped in an elevator in a public building by a black youth, who was put in jail. Armed black men, hearing rumors that a white mob had formed to lynch the youth, gathered to guard him. A mob confronted the black men and a riot ensued. By the time the National

Guard arrived, the community had been ravaged: white mobs killed several hundred blacks, looted their homes, and burned down more than 1,200 buildings. Fifty whites were killed, and no members of the mob were charged with crimes.

On New Year's Eve, 1923, a white mob invaded the thriving black community of Rosewood after a white woman named Fannie Taylor falsely accused a black man of attacking her. During the seven days the riot lasted, the mob burned Rosewood to the ground and murdered eight to seventeen people (the actual numbers are not known). Many of the survivors narrowly escaped by hiding in nearby swamps. With help from local whites, they eventually managed to get out of Rosewood. Local law enforcement did not provide protection, and the perpetrators were never punished. Out of fear, the survivors did not attempt to return to Rosewood to reclaim their property, nor did they speak out against the violence against them.

The modern reparations movement occurred simultaneously with the nonviolent activism of the 1950s and 1960s. In 1955, Queen Mother Audley Moore founded the Reparations Committee of Descendants of the United States Slaves. On a Sunday morning in 1962, the committee filed a claim in California, without results. Seven years later, **James Forman,** a member of the **Student Nonviolent Coordinating Committee (SNCC)** proclaimed his Black Manifesto at the Riverside Church in Manhattan, New York. The manifesto demanded $500 million from the churches and synagogues and outlined how the money would be used to finance social programs, businesses, education, and other institutions to advance blacks. Surprisingly, the minister of the church was sympathetic. In a radio announcement, he acknowledged the abuses and degradations long suffered by blacks and defended Forman's demand for redress.

Reparations activism increased during the latter half of the twentieth century. The 1980s brought forth critical wins in reparations for other racial groups. For example, in 1980, the Supreme Court ordered the federal government to pay eight Sioux Indian tribes $122 million to compensate for the illegal seizure of tribal lands (in 1877). In 1988, the United States issued an apology and paid out $1.25 billion to 60,000 Japanese-Americans who had been forcefully placed into internment camps during World War II. As blacks continued to grapple with state and federal governments for reparations, the wins experienced by other races helped support their cause.

In 1989, Rep. **John Conyers** introduced the Commission to Study Reparation Proposals for African Americans Act, the first of several reparations bills he proposed to the House of Representatives. None of these bills passed. Also in 1989, Detroit City Council member Ray Jenkins requested $40 billion in federal education monies to form a fund for black college and trade school students. In *Cato v. United States* (1995), blacks were denied $100 million in reparations and an apology for slavery. In 1997, President Bill Clinton spoke of the evils of slavery and the need to resolve the effects it had on blacks. In 2000, Rep. Tony Hall proposed bill H.R. 356, which would acknowledge and apologize for slavery. This bill did not pass. In 2002, a former law student filed a federal lawsuit against several American corporations for their involvement in slavery. None of the companies has yet to pay reparations to blacks, but Aetna did make a formal apology for having insured slaves. Compensation is sought for the profits the companies gained at the expense of enslaved blacks, and for wages not paid to slaves. Many other individuals and organizations, such as the **Nation of Islam** and the Race Relations Institute at Fisk University, have contributed to the struggle for reparations. These groups regularly sponsor conferences and engage in marches to rally support.

Despite the repeated refusal to grant reparations, victims of the Tulsa, Oklahoma riot (1921) and the Rosewood massacre (1923) achieved significant victories in 1994 and 2004. In both of these incidents, white mobs either destroyed or stole property that had belonged to blacks. **White capping** was a common occurrence, particularly in the South and between 1900 and 1929 (Winbush, 48). The practice, which got its name from the white caps the participants wore, involved whites who terrorized and threatened blacks for the purpose of seizing their property. Between 1880 and the 1900s, there were at least 239 occurrences of white capping (Winbush, 49).

In 1997, the Oklahoma Legislature created the **Tulsa Race Riot Commission** to explore recommendations for reparations. In 2002, Tulsa race riot survivors received reparations payments totaling $28,000. After a two-year legal battle, Florida's Gov. Lawton Chiles approved the Rosewood Claims Bill, which provided more than $2 million in reparations for the survivors, as well as scholarships for their descendants. This win was an acknowledgement that the state was responsible for not protecting the lives and property of its constituents. Significantly, the Rosewood attorneys partially predicated the lawsuit on cases involving Japanese-Americans and Jewish Holocaust survivors.

Blacks believe reparations, whether in the form of monetary compensation, stock, land, a formal apology, or other actions, are crucial to righting the wrongs committed against—and still affecting—blacks. They argue that some whites unlawfully deprived their ancestors of freedom, life, property, equality, as well as social, economic, and political power, and that atonement is necessary.

The arguments against reparations movements are numerous. Former President Bill Clinton, although he empathized with the horrific history of blacks in America and took on a race relations initiative, commented that too much time had elapsed since slavery, and that the persons culpable for the suffering of blacks no longer existed. In place of reparations, he recommended that the country must come up with remedies to fix the disproportionate hardships experienced by blacks. Other individuals opposed to reparations point to the innumerable programs to alleviate current social problems for blacks and other disadvantaged groups. Clinton also suggested that America should work toward creating a more diverse and racially inclusive democracy. On the other hand, many supporters of reparations are not looking for corrective programs. They argue that programs such as affirmative action have better assisted other groups—not blacks—and do not make amends for the monies owed their ancestors for their slave labor, the indignities and hostilities inflicted on them, or their lost property.

Another prominent opponent is David Horowitz, a conservative author and political commentator who wrote *Uncivil Wars: The Controversy over Reparations for Slavery* (2002). One of his arguments against reparations is that they are racist. Opponents also argue that blacks are better off in America than they would have been in Africa. They also believe that the impoverished and crime-ridden inner cities—not slavery—are the cause of the current plight of blacks and point to the many blacks who have done well in America. Other popular arguments include the point that a reparations plan would be too expensive, and that slavery, though horrendous, was sanctioned, and, therefore, amends cannot legally be made.

Reparations adherents believe that expiations are more than reasonable and justifiable. They assert that the concept is not racist, and that reparations will actually help relieve the disillusionment many blacks feel toward the United States, and the feeling that America exhibits enmity toward them. They also point to the conditions of slavery that caused the so-called modern-day ills, such as broken families and poverty. They believe that life under **Jim Crow**, where blacks were denied the access, opportunities, and resources to better themselves, continues to affect them today, and that successful blacks make up only a small percentage of the population. Although slavery was legal, reparations activists claim that since Reconstruction, many whites have violated federal ordinances, such as the **Fourteenth Amendment,** to secure control over blacks.

Reparations proponents look to other groups and their causes to strengthen their arguments. For example, Holocaust survivors received reparations despite laws that enforced discrimination against Jews, and tort laws permit individuals who have been harmed by toxic waste to seek out compensation for medical care costs, lost wages, and pain and suffering, even if the exposure originated from an incident that occurred over 100 years ago. The recent triumphs of the Rosewood and Tulsa race riot survivors are two poignant cases in point. Reparations activists celebrated when, after many years of blatant, unrepentant, and uncensored crimes against blacks, the authorities finally acknowledged responsibility and made amends to the victims. *See also* Poverty.

Further Readings: Horowitz, David. *Uncivil Wars: The Controversy over Reparations for Slavery.* San Francisco: Encounter Books, 2002; Winbush, Raymond A. *Should America Pay?: Slavery and the Raging Debate on Reparations.* New York: HarperCollins, 2001.

Gladys L. Knight

Returning Soldiers (World War I)

Having fought for democracy abroad, black soldiers returning from service in World War I hoped that their participation in the war effort would mean better treatment and more respect for African American rights at home. Black soldiers thus became a metaphor for these rising expectations and helped spur within the African American community the civic engagement, political militancy, and sociocultural activities that marked the New Negro renaissance between 1918 and the Great Depression. Northern migrants and southern debt peons alike contributed 2.3 million African American men who registered for the draft. About 370,000 eventually served in all military branches, 200,000 overseas, mostly as stevedores and laborers, and 42,000 in combat duty.

W.E.B. Du Bois urged African Americans to "close ranks" (1918) in supporting the U.S. war effort while simultaneously pushing for the establishment of a training camp for black officers at Fort Des Moines, Iowa. Domestically, the racist film ***The Birth of a Nation*** (1915), the presidency of segregationist Woodrow Wilson, and the mistreatment of black military enlistees was partially offset when some white American soldiers praised black military bravery and the French celebrated African American heroism by awarding one of the four black regiments, New York's 369th (the "Harlem Hellfighters," the longest-serving U.S. regiment), the Croix de Guerre.

Soldiers returned, in the words of Du Bois in the May 1918 issue of ***Crisis*** magazine, "fighting," demanding that the United States "Make way for Democracy! We saved it in France, and by the Great Jehovah, we will save it in the United States of America, or know the reason why." They were instead greeted by escalating race violence. Some soldiers were lynched for wearing their uniforms. **Ku Klux Klan (KKK)** membership soared. African Americans—including many combat-trained veterans—fought back, literally and figuratively. The flood of northward migration momentarily slowed, then exploded. A decade-long explosion of activism included demands for southern voting rights and anti-**segregation** legislation, Pan-Africanism, anti-**lynching** campaigns, and the birth of the "Jazz Age," led by the 369th Regiment's band and its leader, James Reese Europe. *See also* Racism.

Further Readings: Du Bois, W.E.B. "Close Ranks." *The Crisis* (July 1918); Du Bois, W.E.B. "Returning Soldiers." *The Crisis* (May 1918); Robinson, Cedric J. *Black Movements in America*. New York: Routledge, 1997; Schneider, Mark Robert. *"We Return Fighting": The Civil Rights Movement in the Jazz Age*. Boston: Northeastern University Press, 2002; Slotkin, Richard. *Lost Battalions: The Great War and the Crisis of American Nationality*. New York: Henry Holt, 2005.

Gregory E. Carr

Revolutionary Action Movement (RAM)

The Revolutionary Action Movement (RAM) was a militant organization founded in the 1960s by Max Stanford (also known as Muhammad Ahmad). RAM was notorious for its reputed role in the conspiracies to assassinate civil rights leaders and in the ghetto riots of the 1960s.

Stanford fashioned RAM from an amalgam of the philosophies endorsed by **Malcolm X (Black Nationalism)**, **Robert F. Williams (black self-defense),** and Queen Mother Audley Moore (Marxism). RAM recruited youth from within black **ghettos,** prisoners, and ex-convicts as members. It influenced blacks who had rejected the nonviolent methodology and integrationism of the original **Student Nonviolent Coordinating Committee (SNCC)** and the **Congress of Racial Equality (CORE),** and supported the rise of like-minded militant organizations such as the **Black Panther Party (BPP),** the Black Liberation Army, and the League of Revolutionary Black

Workers. Stanford himself cofounded the African Liberation Support Committee and was instrumental in the struggle for **reparations**.

The violent orientation of RAM made it a target of the **Federal Bureau of Investigation (FBI),** which infiltrated the organization with its agents. In 1967, Stanford and several other members were arrested for allegedly plotting to assassinate several civil rights leaders. RAM claimed that the charges were never substantiated. RAM was also accused of plotting the violent rebellions within the nation's ghettos. Despite the fact that **Roy Wilkins** was one of the reputed targets of RAM's assassination plot, he stated in its defense that the riots were the independent responses of poor blacks who felt "abandoned by his government and his country" and "isolated, of no importance in the United States" (Wilkins, 324–326).

Further Readings: Ahmad, Muhammad, Ernie Allen, John H. Bracey, and Randolph Boehm, eds. *The Black Power Movement (Black Studies Research Sources)*. Bethesda, MD: Lexis Nexis, 2002; Wilkins, Roy, with Tom Matthews. *The Autobiography of Roy Wilkins: Standing Fast*. New York: Penguin Books, 1982.

Gladys L. Knight

Richardson, George (dates unknown)

George Richardson was an African American handyman whose arrest for the alleged rape of a white woman precipitated a series of events that led to the deadly **Springfield (Illinois) Race Riot of 1908**.

The 1908 Springfield riot was one of the worst to occur in the Midwest during the first decade of the twentieth century. On August 14, 1908, Mabel Hallam, the wife of a streetcar conductor, claimed that Richardson had raped her. On the evening of August 14, Richardson and another black man were arrested. Fearing for the safety of his prisoners, Sheriff Charles Werner, assisted by restaurant owner Harry Loper, removed them from jail and safely transported them to Bloomington. Enraged, a **white mob** attacked Loper's restaurant, destroying the building and the car used to drive Richardson and the other man out of town. The mob then invaded Springfield's black neighborhood, beating its residents and destroying its homes and businesses. One older black man who had been married to a white woman for over thirty years was lynched in a tree across the street from his house (see **Lynching**).

On August 15, Illinois Gov. Charles S. Deneen sent some 4,000 troops to restore calm, but they were slow to arrive. By the next day, eight blacks were dead, and seventy people, both black and white, were injured; the neighborhood was destroyed, and thousands of blacks had fled Springfield. Although no rioters were arrested, the violence embarrassed the white community because of the negative attention the riot brought the city. For this, whites blamed the black community. Several months later, Mabel Hallam admitted that she had falsely accused Richardson and had instead been beaten by a white man; George Richardson was then released from jail. In 1909, black and white activists met in New York to protest the Springfield riots. The meeting resulted in the founding of a new civil rights organization, the **National Association for the Advancement of Colored People (NAACP)**. *See also* Rape, as Provocation for Lynching.

Further Reading: Senechal, Roberta. *The Sociogenesis of a Race Riot: Springfield, Illinois, in 1908*. Urbana: University of Illinois Press, 1990.

Paulina X. Ruf

Rochester (New York) Riot of 1964

Like many race riots, the single cause of the one in Rochester, New York, on July 24–26, 1964, is not fully clear because the riot was a response to a larger set of issues and situations that were building. The conditions leading up to the weekend of rioting can shed light on the building tensions in the western portion of New York State. At the time, Rochester boasted the lowest unemployment rate for both blacks and whites in New York State, but many blacks felt disenfranchised with respect to their education and place within the economy.

In the decade and a half preceding the riot, there was a population explosion within Rochester's minority community. According to the 1950 census, there were 8,247 non-whites by 1960; that figure more than tripled to 25,067 residents. The population increase can be attributed to the settling of migrant workers and the arrival of professionally trained blacks to work at the city's industries (e.g., Bausch and Lomb, Eastman Kodak, and Xerox).

Integration of the new residents within the community did not occur. Residential **segregation** was vast. The housing discrimination against blacks was without regard to economic status or educational background. The 1955 census gives a picture of the socioeconomic situation within the black community. The census found that 56.9 percent of employed black men and 63.4 percent of working black women were classified as domestic workers, service workers, or unskilled laborers. Meanwhile, less than 11 percent of white men and 17 percent of white women were in the same positions.

With the influx of new black residents to Rochester, the education system became *de facto* segregated. Thirty percent of the public schools were predominantly black. By May 1962, the New York Chapter of **National Association for the Advancement of Colored People (NAACP)** filed a desegregation lawsuit on behalf of twenty parents. Interestingly, this was the first legal action against school segregation that was taken up by parents of both races.

Finally, in the years leading up to the Rochester riot, as was the case in many other cities around the country, there were a number of **police brutality** allegations within the black community. As a result of the allegations, the NAACP and the police department investigated; however, the police would not publish their report.

The tensions brewing in Rochester led to a confrontation late Friday, July 24, 1964. Police were called to pacify an inebriated black man who was reportedly causing a disturbance at a street dance in Rochester's Seventh Ward. When the police arrived, they were surrounded by those attending the dance. Bottles were thrown, the crowd grew, and every policeman in the city was called to the area. The crowd outnumbered the police and looting ensued. White businesses, even those that served the black community, were pillaged. Around 2:00 A.M., as white Rochester residents heard reports of the rioting, they began to amass in the area. The police stood between the two groups and, by 4:00 A.M., used fire hoses to break up the crowds. On Saturday morning, the city manager declared a state of emergency.

Black community leaders responded Saturday morning by calling for calm, but they were not successful. The violence continued that evening. An 8:00 P.M. to 7:00 A.M. curfew was imposed throughout the city and the county went dry for five days. Despite the curfew, the rioting continued, shots were fired into the air, rocks and bottles were thrown, and police reacted by using tear gas. By Sunday, Gov. Nelson Rockefeller ordered 250 National Guard troops to subdue the rioters. They were successful. In the end, the rioting in Rochester took place over approximately sixty hours, resulted in 4 deaths, some 350 injuries, more than 800 arrests (both black and white), and property damage costing more than $1 million.

By November 1964, Edward Rutledge, executive director of the National Commission Against Discrimination in Housing criticized Rochester for not conducting a public hearing or investigation on the social causes of the riots. As a result, by March 1965, Mayor Frank T. Lamb and Rev. St. Julian A. Simpkins, Jr., announced the formation of a new committee designed to promote interracial understanding. The committee was designed after Cincinnati's Friendly Relations Committee (later the Cincinnati Human Relations Committee) that was started after the **Detroit (Michigan) Riot of 1943**.

However, perhaps the most important outcome of Rochester's race riots was bringing together the black community and giving them a voice. After the riots, the Board of Urban Ministry (BUM), an assembly of Rochester's Protestant clergy, encouraged black religious leaders to organize the community. The ministers decided to invite the **Southern Christian Leadership Conference (SCLC)** to help organize the black religious community. The SCLC declined and suggested that the Industrial Areas Foundation (IAF) in Chicago be consulted.

As a result, a new community-based black-activist organization formed FIGHT (freedom, integration, god, honor, today; the "I" later changed to "independence"). FIGHT allowed Rochester's black community to speak for themselves on issues of civil rights. White civil rights supporters formed a sister organization, Friends of FIGHT (later Metro Act) to support the movement. FIGHT is best known for taking on Eastman Kodak and demanding that the company implement a job training program and hire 500 to 600 members of the black community. FIGHT was responsible for placing over 700 people in jobs by 1967. *See also* Civil Rights Movement.

Further Reading: *July '64*. Directed by Carvin Eison. Produced and written by Chris Christopher. Rochester, NY: ImageWordSound, Independent Television Service (ITVS), National Black Programming Consortium (NBPC), and WXXI-TV, 2004; Papers on the Rochester Race Riots are available at the University of Rochester Rush

Rhees Library Department of Rare Books, Special Collections and Preservation, D.185

Noah D. Drezner

Roosevelt, Eleanor (1884–1962)

Eleanor Roosevelt, the wife of President Franklin Delano Roosevelt (FDR), was a strong supporter of African American civil rights both during and after her husband's presidency.

Anna Eleanor Roosevelt was born in New York City on October 11, 1884, to Elliott Roosevelt and Anna Eleanor Hall, and had two younger brothers. The Roosevelt family was one of wealth and family lineage, yet not immune to marital tensions and alcohol abuse. After the death of her parents, a ten-year-old Eleanor went to live with her maternal grandmother. In 1899, Eleanor was sent away to the Allenswood Academy in London, where her liberal views flourished. In 1902, she returned to New York, where she joined the National Consumers League and volunteered as a teacher. That summer, she would be reintroduced to her distant cousin, Franklin Roosevelt. After a year of secret courtship, they became engaged on November 22, 1903. The couple was married on March 17, 1905. Her uncle, President Theodore Roosevelt, gave the bride, his favorite niece, away.

Within a year, Eleanor gave birth to Anna, followed closely by James, Franklin (who died at birth), Elliott, Franklin, and John. In 1908, FDR's mother gave the young family a townhouse, right next door to her own, in New York City. In 1911, when her husband was elected to the New York state senate, Eleanor eagerly agreed to move the family to Albany where she would not be under the close scrutiny of her mother-in-law. Two years later, Franklin joined Woodrow Wilson's administration and the family moved to Washington. In the years to follow, Eleanor became more independent and politically astute, stepping outside tradition and taking on a more public political role. In 1920, the family returned to New York.

Not satisfied with tea parties and luncheons, she joined the Women's Division of the Democratic State Committee and the New York chapters of the Women's Trade Union League and the League of Women Voters. After Eleanor discovered Franklin's affair with her social secretary, their marriage became one of professional collaboration and both sought support outside their marriage (PBS Online 1999). In March 1933, Eleanor accompanied her husband, who had been governor of New York, to the White House, not knowing that she would become the longest serving First Lady of the United States.

Throughout her husband's presidency, Eleanor was a vocal supporter of the American **civil rights movement** and of African American rights. She supported the **National Association for the Advancement of Colored People (NAACP)**, and joined local chapters of the NAACP and the **National Urban League**, becoming the first white Washington, D.C., resident to do so. Before the 1936 election, Franklin finally allowed her to address the NAACP and National Urban League annual conventions. After the election, she increased her activism, supporting anti-**lynching** legislation and

Eleanor Roosevelt and Roy Wilkins. Courtesy of the Library of Congress.

convening the National Conference of Negro Women at the White House. When opera singer Marian Anderson was not allowed to perform at Washington's Constitutional Hall, which was owned by the Daughters of the American Revolution, because she was black, Eleanor arranged her performance on the steps of the Lincoln Memorial with over 70,000 in attendance, and resigned her membership in the Daughters of the American Revolution. Despite these efforts, after the 1943 **Detroit** race riots, the *Jackson Daily News*, a Mississippi newspaper, blamed the riots on Eleanor's efforts toward social equality, suggesting that the riots were the result of an attempt to put into practice what she advocated. After her husband's death and the end of World War II, she played a significant role in the formulation of the United Nations' Universal Declaration of Human Rights. She continued to write and remained politically active until her death on November 7, 1962. Anna Eleanor Roosevelt was buried next to her husband in New York on November 10, 1962.

Further Readings: Beasley, Maurine H., Holly C. Shulman, and Henry R. Beasley. *The Eleanor Roosevelt Encyclopedia*. Westport, CT: Greenwood Press, 2001; Feldman, Glenn, ed. *Before Brown: Civil Rights and White Backlash in the Modern South*. Tuscaloosa: University of Alabama Press, 2004; PBS Online. "Franklin Delano Roosevelt, 1882–1945." *American Experience: People & Events* (1999). See http://www.pbs.org/wgbh/amex/eleanor/peopleevents/pande02.html; Roosevelt, Eleanor. *The Autobiography of Eleanor Roosevelt*. New York: G.K. Hall, 1984; Youngs, J. William T. and Oscar Handlin. *Eleanor Roosevelt: A Personal and Public Life*. 3rd ed. New York: Pearson/Longman, 2006.

Paulina X. Ruf

Rope and Faggot: A Biography of Judge Lynch (White, 1929)

Published in 1929, **Walter White**'s *Rope and Faggot: A Biography of Judge Lynch* was praised by **James Weldon Johnson** as the most comprehensive and authoritative treatise on **lynching** to date. Building on the important work of anti-lynching crusader **Ida B. Wells-Barnett,** *Rope and Faggot* explores the social, political, and economic motives behind lynching. According to White, less than 30 percent of African American men lynched in the South were actually accused of sexually assaulting white women. More often than not, lynching was used as a means of intimidation, as an attempt to control black labor. *Rope and Faggot* publicized these and other harsh truths about the phenomenon of lynching.

Walter White first experienced the dark, violent side of human nature at the tender age of thirteen during the Atlanta race riots (see **Atlanta [Georgia] Riot of 1906**). In his autobiography, *A Man Called White* (1948), White admits to being too naïve to fully appreciate the ramifications of the mounting racial tension that preceded the riots. He recalls reading the inflammatory headlines in the local newspapers, which fuelled the flames of racial hatred with their accounts of alleged rapes and other crimes committed by African Americans. Barricaded inside his home while an angry **white mob** marched through his neighborhood, White was enlightened to the fact that he belonged to a race condemned to suffering and abuse for no less a reason than the pigmentation of their skin. Yet, even as a boy, White recognized the inexplicable—that his skin was as white as the skin of those who sought to destroy him. With his blonde hair, blue eyes, and white skin, Walter White could have aligned himself with the dominant race. Instead, White chose to use his fair complexion to investigate crimes committed against members of his own race.

While working undercover for the **National Association for the Advancement of Colored People (NAACP),** White investigated more than thirty lynchings and eight race riots, the facts of which would later be published in *Rope and Faggot.* Within two weeks of joining the NAACP, White requested permission to investigate the lynching of an African American sharecropper in Tennessee named Jim McIlherron. The trepidation White felt as he embarked on his first planned attempt to pass as a white man was intensified by his knowledge of the severity of the penalty for such a trespass should he be caught. By feigning first ignorance of, and then a lack of interest in, the lynching, White successfully entrusted himself to the guilty parties. Boasting of more exciting lynchings, White was able to goad the participants into revealing the exact details of the murder. Despite the harrowing nature of this experience, White continued to pass for white in an attempt to expose the magnitude and severity of the lynching epidemic in the South. He even went so far as to infiltrate the most notorious white supremacist organization, the **Ku Klux Klan (KKK)**. Although his deception was eventually discovered and his life threatened, White was nonetheless successful in obtaining incriminating evidence against the Klan. With the assistance of an ex-Klan member, White was able to confirm the Klan's involvement in a triple lynching in South Carolina. Ironically, when it

"Judge Lynch" California Vigilants, 1848. Courtesy of the Library of Congress.

was revealed how he obtained the pertinent information, it was White who was threatened with prosecution. The culmination of more than a decade of hands-on research, *Rope and Faggot* was the first full-length indictment of lynching of its time. Through *Rope and Faggot*, Walter White hoped to expose the barbarity of lynching and to sway public opinion against the perpetrators of such heinous crimes.

Further Readings: Janken, Kenneth Robert. *White: The Biography of Walter White, Mr. NAACP.* New York: The New Press, 2003; White, Walter. *A Man Called White: The Autobiography of Walter White*. New York: Viking Press, 1948; White, Walter. *Rope and Faggot*. New York: Arno Press, 1969.

Carol Goodman

Rosewood (1997)

Rosewood is a riveting historical drama based on the true account of white rioting in the small black community of **Rosewood**, Florida, in 1923. Although debuted in 1997, the impetus for the movie began fifteen years prior with Gary Moore's article in the *St. Petersburg Times*. His article first exposed the public to the horrifying events that transpired in Rosewood. Shortly thereafter, the television news program *60 Minutes* aired a report featuring a few of the survivors and *Esquire Magazine* also featured an article on the tragedy. Attempts to produce a movie failed until 1994 when John Singleton, who received a 1991 Oscar nomination for *Boyz N the Hood*, accepted Peters Entertainment's offer to make *Rosewood*. Singleton interviewed a few of the survivors and enlisted Wynton Marsalis to compose the music, Gregory Poirer to write the screenplay, and assembled a remarkable cast.

The movie begins with a camera shot high above the town of Rosewood; the camera then pans across the various homes, a Mason hall, children happily playing, and a lush vegetable garden. Singleton casts the film in streaming golden sunlight, echoing the tranquility of the town and its people. Sarah Carrier (Esther Rolle), a resident, calls Rosewood "heaven on earth." Rosewood is one of numerous towns established by blacks.

Singleton depicts most of the individuals from the real-life Rosewood in his film. John Wright (Jon Voigt) owns a store in Rosewood. He is instrumental later in defending blacks against the **white mobs** from Sumner, a nearby white town. Sylvester Carrier (Don Cheadle) and his family are also portrayed. A fictional character, Mann, a World War I veteran, rides into town, looking to settle down. His budding love with the town's schoolteacher, Miss Scrappie (Elsie Neal), will soon be disrupted.

Singleton adroitly portrays two worlds. Blacks control and maintain one world, where they exhibit mutual respect and camaraderie. Whites dominate the nearby town, Sumner. Outside of Rosewood, blacks must wear the masks of inferiority. Bound to the rules of **racial etiquette,** the elderly Sarah Carrier refers to a white man as "Mr. Taylor," while he calls her by her first name. His wife calls her "Aunt Sarah." At an auction, Mann (Ving Rhames), the hero of this tale, and other blacks, are forced to stand in the back or off to the side. Whites scoff when Mann wins a bid for five acres of land. Racial tensions shade nearly every encounter. Even in the halcyon quiet of Rosewood, blacks are not exempt from feelings of hostility toward whites.

The film takes a catastrophic turn when a white woman, Fannie Taylor (Catherine Kellner), accuses a black man of beating her. The real perpetrator is a white man with whom she is having an affair. Whites retaliate by obliterating Rosewood, murdering innocent blacks, and hunting down survivors in the swamps. Mann evades death and rescues a few women and children. The movie ends with Rosewood—which had epitomized a refuge from **racism,** inhibiting laws, and violence—ablaze in flames.

Critics applauded Singleton for *Rosewood*. They also criticized it, mostly because Singleton strayed from the facts of the incident and omitted the detail that survivors and their descendants received **reparations** in 1994. The movie was not a success at the box office. Nevertheless, *Rosewood's* significance surpasses its flaws. It not only shows the prosperity of a town created by blacks, it brings national attention to the victims of racial violence.

Further Readings: *Rosewood*. Directed by John Singleton. Los Angeles: Warner Brothers, 1997; Singleton, John. "An Essay on Rosewood." In Michael D'Orso, ed. *Like Judgment Day*. New York: Warner Brothers, 1996.

Gladys L. Knight

Rosewood (Florida) Riot of 1923

The town of Rosewood, Florida, which had previously seen little racial conflict, erupted in racially motivated violence in January 1923. An accusation from a white woman from a nearby town about an assault by a black man caused Rosewood to experience mob behavior, collective amnesia, and many years later produced a movie and debate over reparations to the families of the Rosewood victims.

The town, now nonexistent, was located in Levy County on the western coast of the state of Florida, forty miles west of Gainesville, and nine miles east of Cedar Key. By 1923, Rosewood was comprised of approximately 120 to 150 residents, most of whom were African American. The small town consisted of approximately thirty homes, which were mostly small shanty shacks, a post office, a hotel, and a few small businesses, a school, a few churches, a Masonic lodge, a railroad depot, and a sawmill. One of the small businesses was a general store that was operated by the town's only white resident, John Wright.

The town received its name for the area's abundance of trees that were highly valued for furniture. When the trees had been exhausted, mill operations were moved from Rosewood to the predominantly white community of nearby Sumner, and many of the residents of Rosewood found work at the Sumner mill. The men who continued to work in Rosewood were primarily farmers, hunters, and trappers. The women of Rosewood often found work as domestic laborers for the white families of Sumner. According to reports, there had been a generally harmonious relationship between the blacks and whites of the area until January 1, 1923.

With the new year came an unusually cold spell of weather, causing frost to accumulate on the palmettos that covered the area. Although it was New Year's Day, the mill at Sumner continued to operate and the mill workers from Rosewood made their normal three-mile walk to their workplace. James Taylor, a white mill worker, was on the job at the mill that day, having left his young housewife, Fannie, and their two children at home. At one point that morning, Fannie came running out of the Taylor home, crying and shrieking that she had been assaulted, perhaps sexually, by an unidentified black man. Fannie Taylor told her neighbors of the attack and produced visible bruises, such as a bleeding mouth, as a confirmation of her story and was taken to a neighbor's house when she became faint. Several of Sumner's citizens gathered outside of the house and quickly spread the word of the attack. The white community became extremely angry and set out to find the perpetrator of this act. Although the young housewife was obviously assaulted by someone, no examination was ever performed on Taylor by a physician.

The black community, however, had a different version of the story. On hearing the accounts of the alleged attack, Sarah Carrier, a housekeeper for Mrs. Taylor, and her granddaughter both claimed that an unidentified white man visited Taylor at her home that morning. They believed that she and this unknown person were secretly having a romantic affair, and that morning they got into an argument and he physically assaulted her.

A group of white men from the Sumner area embarked on a hunt for the black man they believed was responsible for the attack. Robert Elias "Rob" Walker, the Levy County sheriff, had reported that an escapee from a prison work crew named Jesse Hunter was being sought and this person became the key suspect. The sheriff brought in tracking dogs and the trail was followed to Rosewood.

Aaron Carrier, a black resident from Rosewood, and a veteran of World War I, was questioned and coerced into providing information about the whereabouts of Jesse Hunter, the alleged attacker. After being tied to the back of a car and dragged, Carrier stated that Sam Carter, a local blacksmith, might be responsible for hiding the assailant. Carrier was delivered to a jail in Bronson, Florida, for his protection, and was later removed from the area. The bloodhounds carried the angry mob to Sam Carter's house. The whites became convinced that Carter was guilty of hiding the fugitive from the authorities. Carter, who was not at home, was found at a relative's house and abducted. The posse strung up Carter over a tree limb to get him to tell them where he hid the culprit.

Ernest Parham, a white citizen and an employee of the general store, later claimed that he implored the mob to release Carter, which they did. The posse began to cut him with knives to force him to give information as to where the wanted man was left by Carter. Seriously wounded by the knife cuts and beatings, Carter led the group to a place where he claimed to have left Hunter. The dogs failed to pick up a scent, however, and Carter was unexpectedly shot in the face and killed by one of the members of the mob. Authorities found Carter's mutilated body the next day. From reports, it seems possible that neither Sheriff Walker nor his deputy Clarence Williams were aware of this vigilante squad.

Three days had passed since Fannie Taylor made the accusations when the Sumner residents heard that Hunter was in Rosewood, in the care of a man named Sylvester Carrier, known locally as "man." Carrier was a large man who had an intense anger toward whites in the area. A mob of white men went to Carrier's residence that night, broke into the home, and was met with gunfire from Carrier. Two of the members of the mob, C.P. Wilkerson and Henry "Boots" Andrews, were killed when they tried to enter the residence; the other members of the party retreated from the house. Gunfire resumed by both groups, however, and Sarah Carrier was killed in the gunfight. The children in the house, who had been moved upstairs for protection, retreated into the woods with adult relatives. Sylvester Carrier was reportedly killed in the exchange of gunfire; however, some reports say that the person believed to be Carrier was actually someone else and that Carrier left that night and moved away from Rosewood. This version was believed by many, as it was claimed that Carrier sent cards and letters to Rosewood families years after the incident.

The violence increased the following day as people from other North Florida towns and cities such as Gainesville and Jacksonville, and even some people from towns in South Georgia, came to observe the situation playing out in Rosewood. It appears that they also came prepared to participate, if possible. Ailing widow Lexie Gordon was killed and her house was set ablaze, Mingo Adams was shot by an angry mob north of town, and James Carrier, who had been rescued from the swamp, was killed after being forced to dig his own grave.

Seeing the situation escalate, some whites from Sumner came to the aid of the blacks, hiding them and arranging for safe passage from the area. Two white conductors from Cedar Key, on hearing of the carnage in

Rosewood, sent railcars into the area to transport blacks. Only women and children were allowed to take the train ride because hauling the male passengers would be too risky for the conductors and crew as well as the women and children. The general store owner, John Wright, also hid several of the blacks in his expansive home until they could be rescued by the train and relocated to Gainesville. Homes in Rosewood were burned to the ground, but Wright's house was passed over since he was the only white resident in the town.

After five days, the racial violence sparked by Fannie Taylor's accusations in the small town of Rosewood ended. The remaining residents eventually moved away when the sawmill in Sumner burned and relocated to Pasco County. Rosewood survivors moved to Jacksonville, Miami, or out-of-state locales.

A special grand jury was convened on January 29, 1923, in Bronson at the request of Gov. Cary Hardee to investigate the incident at Rosewood. The grand jury found no evidence of criminal activity by law enforcement officials in the handling of the situation. Charges were never brought against any of the people who were involved in the Rosewood killings, participated in arson, or were a party to the alleged assault against Taylor. There are no records of the grand jury proceedings, except for descriptions that were given in local newspapers.

Newspapers, not only in Florida but those across the nation, reported the events of the Rosewood melee. For the most part, the issue left the public eye until 1982, when a journalist named Gary Moore investigated the history of the Rosewood situation and reported on it in a local publication called *The Floridian*, a magazine supplement for the *St. Petersburg Times* newspaper. The article gained national attention and, in 1983, CBS aired a segment of its *60 Minutes* news program on the events in Rosewood in 1923.

In 1993, largely due to the work of Arnett Doctor, a descendant of Rosewood survivor Philomena Goins, the matter appeared before the Florida state legislature in an attempt to recognize the event and to consider compensation to the families of the victims. As a result of House and Senate bills, an investigation was promulgated and a research team of scholars from three state universities, the University of Florida, Florida State University, and Florida A&M, were commissioned to provide additional information about the events. Issues were raised about possible reparations to the families of the Rosewood victims and connections were made between other complaints that ended up providing reparations, especially in the case of the evacuation and displacement of Japanese-Americans during World War II. Since both cases involved relocation without the ability to return to their homes (in the Rosewood situation, they were unable to return due to fear), the fact that law enforcement at the time did little to fully investigate the situation or arrest those responsible, and due to the failure of the legal system to investigate and prosecute the perpetrators of the violence, awards in the amount of $220 to $450,000 were given to 172 Rosewood survivors for emotional trauma. Also, funds were provided for demonstrated property loss as a result of the massacre. In addition, the Rosewood Bill required an investigation into any possible surviving perpetrators to consider criminal proceedings; this investigation occurred and there were no survivors located. The last provision of the bill was to provide a state university scholarship for the Rosewood descendants.

In 1996, a book about the incident titled *Like Judgment Day: The Ruin and Redemption of a Town Called Rosewood*, was published. It was followed by a movie version simply titled *Rosewood* that was released by Warner Brothers Motion Pictures in 1997. Many Americans who had never heard the story of a southern town that was wiped out because of racially motivated behavior that left several dead, many traumatized, and many more displaced, were stunned to learn of the event. The lives of those involved with the so-called massacre and their descendants would forever be changed as a result of the events in Rosewood, Florida, on New Year's Day in 1923.

Further Readings: D'Orso, Michael. *Like Judgment Day: The Ruin and Redemption of a Town Called Rosewood*. New York: G.P. Putnam's Sons, 1996; Hixson, Richard. "Special Master's Final Report." Letter to the Honorable Bo Johnson, Speaker of the House of Representatives, March 24, 1994. See http://afgen.com/roswood2.html; Jones, Daryl L. "Address to the Black Reparations & Self-Determination Conference." Washington Metropolitan A.M.E. Church, Washington, D.C., June 11, 1999. See http://www.directBlackaction.com/roserep.htm.

Leonard A. Steverson

Rumors

A rumor is a statement, usually unsupported by specific evidence, often exaggerated, that is widely repeated and discussed. Rumors have played critical roles in American race riots, even if their existence, effects, and meanings have generated important differences of opinion among scholars.

Most race riots can be traced not just to initiating events, but also to rumors—the varying accounts of the event that participants and bystanders, as well as those with no firsthand knowledge of the events in question, spread throughout the city or town. A race riot in **Houston**, Texas, in 1917 was sparked by two inaccurate rumors that surfaced after a black soldier, Charles Baltimore, was beaten and taken into custody by a white police officer. As Baltimore tried to escape, the police officer shot at him several times. A rumor began to spread that a black soldier had been killed, but Baltimore was actually still alive. The idea that one of their own men had been murdered made the rest of Baltimore's battalion want to retaliate. With the black troops already up in arms, another rumor surfaced that a white mob was coming to attack the black troops. Violence pervaded Houston as the black troops marched on the city. Over a dozen people were killed in just a few short hours.

The 1919 **Chicago** race riot began after large crowds of whites and blacks witnessed the murder of Eugene Williams. However, within hours of the event, rumors of far more extensive violence swept the city. In one case, the black-owned ***Chicago Defender*** alleged that a **white mob** had cut off a black woman's breasts (August 2, 1919). Both white-owned and black-owned newspapers printed stories, based on rumors, in which babies had been slaughtered by mobs of the other race.

Perhaps the best-documented single instance of a rumor inciting racial violence occurred in the 1943 **Detroit** race riot, in which a black man, after fighting with white youths at Detroit's Belle Isle park, made his way to a nightclub popular with African Americans, took the stage holding a briefcase, claimed he was a police officer, and told the crowd that white youths had thrown a black mother and baby off a bridge.

Finding that a pattern of rumors fuels race riots is perhaps not surprising. A riot is, by definition, a breakdown of public order, and a critical element in public order is the generation and dissemination of verifiable information. If a news reporter is unable to respond to a riot call until the riot is well underway, for example, that reporter may witness hundreds of people engaged in violent acts, but be essentially unable to get reliable information on how the melee began. However, this distance between verifiable information and rumor has caused no end of debate, not only for those individuals and communities who participated in and were victimized in race riots, but also for contemporary observers and scholars. Especially in the twentieth and twenty-first-century North, white and black commentators such as Terry Ann Knopf (*Rumors, Race, and Riots*, 1975) and Gary Alan Fine and Patricia A. Turner (*Whispers on the Color Line: Rumor and Race in America*, 2001) writing about race riots have linked the prevalence of rumors in riots to the irrationality of mobs. By contrast, in the eighteenth and nineteenth centuries, rumor often provided more direct justification for racial violence. In 1741, in New York, rumors claiming that slaves had set a series of fires in preparation for a large-scale revolt led to the arrest and forced confession—through torture—of 200 enslaved Africans. Today, historians dispute whether or not the conspiracy even existed. At the height of **lynching** in the United States, roughly 1880–1930, lynchings themselves would be cloaked in secrecy by white law officers, newspaper editors, and other elites by claims that the upcoming event was only a rumor being spread by shadowy figures. That newspaper accounts of these "rumors" mentioned committees appointed to oversee local arrangements for the events, attended by hundreds of white onlookers, only heightens the contrast between official denials of knowledge and rumors.

Rumors have been particularly problematic for scholars of riots as well. In attempting to understand rumor, scholars of riots have paid much attention to theories on the behavior of crowds. Some historians argue that, in the premodern period, crowds gathered and acted to enforce community norms against, for example, merchants believed to be hoarding foodstuffs in difficult economic times. In these cases, rumors serve as a kind of popular check on elite power. Scholars of race riots have, with good reason, avoided claiming any kind of rationality behind the rumors that fuel racial violence. Instead, many have argued, crowds or mobs in race riots behave in inherently irrational ways; charismatic leaders goad the crowd into increasingly violent acts, and participants in mobs lose their inhibitions against violent behavior because the mob itself undermines a sense of personal responsibility for one's actions. This dynamic, however, raises an important problem. On the one hand, scholarly consensus is that race riots occur as a result of tensions caused by real social, cultural, economic, and political changes. On the other, if fictitious information and exaggerated rumors cause and exacerbate riots themselves, how can we connect rumors with the reality of racism? *See also* Police Brutality; Rape, as Provocation for Lynching.

Further Readings: Fine, Gary Alan, and Patricia A. Turner. *Whispers on the Color Line: Rumor and Race in America*. Berkeley: University of California Press, 2001; Gilje, Paul. *Rioting in America*. Bloomington: Indiana University Press, 1999; Johnson, Marilynn S. "Gender, Race, and Rumors: Re-Examining the 1943 Race Riots." *Gender and History* 10, no. 2 (1990): 252–277; Knopf, Terry Ann. *Rumors, Race, and Riots*. New Brunswick, NJ: Transaction Books, 1975.

Jonathan S. Coit

S

Sainte Genevieve (Missouri) Riot of 1930

The Sainte Genevieve (Missouri) Race Riot was a four-day racial disturbance occurring between October 12 and 15, 1930, during which mobs of armed white vigilantes drove nearly all of the black residents from this small Mississippi River town, including several families whose ancestors had lived there for more than a century. The mob's action irrevocably changed the racial composition of the town and almost completely destroyed its long-standing African American community. Except for the double murder that triggered the unrest, no bloodshed or property destruction actually occurred during this incident, which might be more accurately described as a "near riot" or "averted riot." Nonetheless, **white mobs** succeeded in using racial terrorism, intimidation, and threats of violence to decimate Sainte Genevieve's African American population and to reinforce the community's traditional racial hierarchy.

Founded around 1750, Sainte Genevieve was one of the first French colonial outposts west of the Mississippi River; today it holds the distinction of being Missouri's oldest permanent white settlement. In 1930, on the eve of the riot, Sainte Genevieve was a lime-mining and agricultural center with a population of 2,658 residents, the overwhelming majority of whom were white Roman Catholics. Many of the town's adult male residents worked for one of the four lime-mining companies in the area, one of several stone quarries, or for the Missouri-Illinois Railroad, which maintained a roundhouse and shop just north of town. Approximately 160 African American residents also lived in the town, with an almost equal number scattered throughout the surrounding county. Race relations in Sainte Genevieve were complicated by the fact that, at the time, two distinct black communities actually existed within the town. One group consisted of approximately seventy longtime residents. Many of them were descended from Sainte Genevieve County slaves and free people of color, some of whom were of mixed French and African heritage. The other group consisted of about ninety southern migrants, chiefly from Tennessee, Mississippi, and Arkansas, who had arrived during the mid-1920s to work in the local lime mines and rock quarries. Most of these newcomers were Protestants, owned little or no property, and lived in a shantytown called the Shacks or in mining camps on the outskirts of town. Apparently, the two black communities seldom interacted.

The trouble that precipitated the four-day Sainte Genevieve race riot began on Saturday night, October 11, 1930, when two white lime kiln workers named Harry Panchot and Paul Ritter attended a black dance at the Shacks. At around 12:50 A.M., as the dance broke up, three black migrants—a quarry worker named Lonnie Taylor, originally from Tennessee; Columbus Jennings, a Mississippi native and also a quarryman; and Vera Rogers, from nearby Crystal City, Missouri—offered Panchot and Ritter $1.50 to drive them to a craps game at a boat landing located two miles north of town. According to Ritter, when the group arrived, the two black men drew .38-caliber revolvers, ordered them out of the automobile, and then robbed them of $45 in cash and a pocket watch. After collecting their valuables, Taylor fatally shot Panchot in the chest at point-blank range and then fired once at Ritter, wounding him in the abdomen. The bullet lodged in Ritter's spine, paralyzing him below the waist. Taylor and Jennings then dragged the white men to the edge of the riverbank and heaved them into the Mississippi River. The frigid water revived the unconscious Ritter, and, after realizing he was still alive, Taylor and Jennings hurled rocks at the wounded man, one of which fractured his skull. Thirty minutes later, federal prohibition agents, who were guarding a confiscated bootlegger's boat nearby, heard Ritter's cries for help. They rescued him and recovered Panchot's body from the river. Ritter was rushed by ambulance to St. Anthony's Hospital in St. Louis, where he was diagnosed to be in critical condition.

Within hours of the shootings, Sainte Genevieve County Sheriff Louis Ziegler and his deputies launched an intense manhunt for the alleged murderers. They soon arrested Taylor, Jennings, and Rogers, whom several witnesses had seen leaving the dance in Ritter's automobile. Meanwhile, news of Panchot's murder and Ritter's wounding spread throughout the town and the surrounding countryside. As Sunday Mass let out at the Sainte Genevieve Catholic Church, a crowd of more than 500 people assembled at the courthouse to await news of the ongoing investigation. Inside the courthouse, after more than four hours of intense questioning, Jennings and Rogers confessed to being at the boat landing the previous night. They both denied taking part in the shooting, and claimed that Taylor was the actual triggerman. Confronted with his accomplices' signed statements, Taylor confessed to shooting the two white men, but stated that he had done so in self-defense. He had shot the men, he told authorities, during a fistfight that broke out after Ritter insulted Rogers by offering her 50¢ to have sex with him. What actually transpired will probably forever remain a mystery, but after wringing confessions from the three prisoners, Sheriff Ziegler and two deputies whisked them away to Hillsboro, Missouri, located forty miles to the northwest, to prevent them from being lynched by the angry crowd gathered outside.

That Sunday night, armed bands of white men in automobiles visited the black districts in Sainte Genevieve and the outlying districts and warned black residents to leave town by 5:00 P.M. the next day, or else face serious reprisals. These self-appointed vigilantes, some of whom a St. Louis newspaper claimed belonged to the Knights of Columbus, made no distinction between longtime residents and recent newcomers; all African Americans, regardless of family background or social status, were banished from Sainte Genevieve. On Monday morning, October 13, the exodus began, and throughout the day, more than 200 terrified black residents fled the town and the surrounding area. Sheriff Ziegler, fearing possible mob violence, telephoned Missouri's Gov. Henry S. Caulfield to request the assistance of the National Guard in maintaining the peace during the mass exodus. Acting on the sheriff's request, the governor dispatched Companies M and H of the 140th Infantry from the towns of Festus and DeSoto, thirty miles and forty miles, respectively, to the northwest, to restore order in Sainte Genevieve and prevent any further disturbances. Approximately ninety national guardsmen arrived in Sainte Genevieve that evening, set up machine guns around the courthouse and on the roof of the City Hotel, and patrolled the town. By nightfall, only three black families remained in Sainte Genevieve, at least one of which sought protection with Fr. Charles Van Tourenhout, pastor of the local Catholic church.

On Tuesday afternoon, October 14, the National Guard withdrew from a quiet Sainte Genevieve. But when the second shooting victim, Paul Ritter, died at 1:15 P.M. in St. Anthony's Hospital, news of his death triggered renewed mob action in Sainte Genevieve. Around 10:30 P.M. that night, three carloads of white men armed with shotguns and rifles attempted to kidnap a mailcarrier named Louis "Cap" Ribeau, one of the few black residents who had refused to leave town. After seizing Ribeau, the mob huddled on the road in front of his home to discuss what to do with him. An approaching car accidentally collided with one of the mob's parked cars and then plowed into the group, knocking down Ribeau and several others. No one was seriously injured, but in the ensuing chaos Ribeau managed to escape into the woods and find safe harbor with a neighboring white family, who hid him in their well for the night.

Notified of the attempted kidnapping, Sheriff Ziegler and several deputies arrested six white Sainte Genevieve men (Russell Stockle, James Hurst, William Martin, J.A. Crowley, Herman Steiger, and Louis Ryan) on charges of unlawful assembly. Rumors soon circulated, however, that a mob might attempt to spring the six men from the Sainte Genevieve County Jail, and Sheriff Ziegler, fearing that he could not repel such an attack, again requested the National Guard's assistance. Companies M and H, whose members had only hours before returned to their homes, again rushed to Sainte Genevieve. When the troops arrived at 3:00 the next morning, they mounted machine guns in front of the jail and on the porch of the Ribeau home, and patrolled the streets of Sainte Genevieve.

On Wednesday morning, October 15, Cap Ribeau boarded a train for St. Louis under the armed guard of postal inspectors. According to the *St. Louis Argus* (October 17, 1930), he was in "a highly nervous state" from his traumatic encounter, and was admitted for treatment in a St. Louis sanitarium. Sainte Genevieve civic leaders and National Guard officers held a mass meeting at the courthouse that afternoon to discuss how best to end the racial disorder. Before a standing-room-only crowd, Fr. Van Tourenhout called on every citizen to cooperate in combating the racial strife that had wracked the town. That evening, the local post of the American Legion called an emergency meeting during which its members unanimously pledged to serve as sheriff's deputies in quelling any future mob outbreaks. The Legionnaires also adopted a resolution guaranteeing protection to "certain native, property owning blacks" (*Ste. Genevieve Herald,* October 18, 1930) if they wished to return to their homes. Absolutely no other African Americans would be permitted to return to Sainte Genevieve, however. By the following day, Thursday, October 16, the crisis in the community had subsided, and the National Guard troops, whose strong presence very likely prevented a full-blown race riot from erupting, returned to Festus and Desoto. Their departure marked the end of what one local newspaper called "one of the most serious situations ever experienced in Sainte Genevieve" (*Ste. Genevieve Herald,* October 18, 1930). But the aftershocks of the four-day racial disturbance reverberated in the community for decades to come.

On October 15, 1930, the six men arrested for attempting to kidnap Ribeau were tried in a Sainte Genevieve court and pled guilty. Each was fined $300 or sentenced to six months in jail, or both, but the judge stayed their sentences on promise of good behavior, and Wednesday evening the men were released. Two days later, however, U.S. postal inspectors rearrested the six men on federal warrants, charging them with conspiracy to prevent a federal employee from performing his duties, a crime punishable by a maximum sentence of six years in the penitentiary, a $5,000 fine, or both. In March 1931, all of them pled guilty in a U.S. district court in St. Louis and were paroled. Meanwhile, Lonnie Taylor and Columbus Jennings were tried for the first-degree murders of Panchot and Ritter in circuit court in Farmington, Missouri, on a change of venue. Both men were convicted of first-degree murder and sentenced to life imprisonment in the Missouri State Penitentiary in Jefferson City. Charges against their female companion, Vera Rogers, were eventually dismissed.

In the week following the riot, Sainte Genevieve civic leaders invited some seventy longtime black residents who had fled their homes to return to the community. Eventually, almost all of them did return, but the mobs succeeded in banishing the black migrants who had been recruited by the local lime plants and stone quarries, and the town's African American population never again reached pre-riot levels. In fact, in the decades following the riot, Sainte Genevieve gained a reputation as a town hostile to African Americans. By 1940, the number of black residents living in Sainte Genevieve had dwindled to only forty-five. By 1960, only sixteen remained. Today, Sainte Genevieve, a town dedicated to preserving and trading on its French colonial historical past, has largely forgotten this incident, which so dramatically affected its racial demographics. Indeed, the first historical account of the riot did not appear until 1999, almost seventy years after the incident. Meanwhile, Sainte Genevieve's African American population, which numbered slightly more than 120 in the 2000 census, is slowing beginning to increase.

Further Readings: Naeger, Bill, Patti Naeger, and Mark L. Evans. *Sainte Genevieve: A Leisurely Stroll Through History.* Sainte Genevieve, MO: Merchant Street Publishing, 1999; *St. Louis Argus,* October 17 and 24, 1930; *Sainte Genevieve Herald,* October 18 and 25, 1930; Sainte Genevieve *Fair Play,* October 18, 1930; Uhlenbrock, Tom. "Sainte Genevieve's Rich History Includes Indians and Blacks, Too." *St. Louis Post-Dispatch,* April 1, 2001.

Patrick Huber

San Francisco (California) Riot of 1966

In 1966, San Francisco experienced its only race riot, the result of a police shooting in the Hunters Point area of the city. However, leading up to the riot, many conditions for African Americans had become desperate. Overcrowded and segregated neighborhoods, insufficient and poor-quality housing, **police brutality,** and underemployment had grown worse since the end of World War II. By 1966 racial tensions were stretched tight.

Prior to the 1960s, San Francisco had one of the most proactive stances toward race relations of any city in the United States. As early as 1942, concerned citizens formed the Bay Area Council Against Discrimination (BACAD), an organization that would become the prototype for interracial societies during that time. Functioning as a pressure group and fact-finding agency, the BACAD forced city officials, business leaders and trade unions to implement nondiscriminatory policies. By 1944, the Council for Civic Unity (CCU) formed under the direction of Edward Howden and soon became the premier interracial organization working against discrimination in San Francisco. Its aim was to end discrimination in housing, employment, health, recreation, and welfare. It scored many victories throughout the 1950s.

However, organizations that combated racial discrimination were fighting an up-hill battle. For one, San Francisco's population was increasing faster than the housing market was able to accommodate. Between 1940 and 1950 the city's population increased by 22 percent and the African American population increased nearly 800 percent. Discrimination in housing was the norm and both **redlining** and restrictive covenants functioned to keep African Americans segregated primarily in just two enclaves: Hunters Point and the Western Addition. Further, employment prospects were grim, especially for African American youth. Shortly after World War II, many African Americans who had migrated to San Francisco for wartime employment were laid off their jobs. The combination of fewer jobs, poor-quality housing, and ever-increasing population proved volatile and it was under these conditions that San Francisco experienced its first race riot.

On September 27, 1966, police officer Alvin Johnson attempted to stop a car in the predominantly African American neighborhood of Hunters Point. The two teenagers who were in the vehicle fled the scene, and Johnson chased one youth, Matthew Johnson, across an empty lot. When Matthew Johnson ignored Officer Johnson's command to stop, the officer shot and killed him. Shortly thereafter, a crowd of residents gathered and demanded a meeting with Mayor John Shelley. However, by the time the mayor arrived at the Bayview Neighborhood Center, the crowd had grown both in size and discontent, and the mayor was forced to retreat as people threw bricks and a firebomb at him and the police. After the mayor's hasty departure, 200 police officers were called in to seal off a six-block area of Hunters Point. Although some youths managed to leave the area and smashed windows in other districts of the city, most of the disturbance was contained in Hunters Point.

One important aspect of the riot is that many of the leaders of the community, moderate middle-class residents, were totally unable to assuage the anger of the lower income younger residents. This would foreshadow an ongoing conflict between the two groups that would only deteriorate over the next decade.

The Hunters Point riot lasted 128 hours and, in contrast to the 1965 Watts riot (see **Los Angeles [California] Riot of 1965**), was characterized by only minor incidents of violence and looting, mainly directed at white- and Chinese-owned businesses. In the end, property damage was estimated around $100,000 and no one was killed; 146 people were arrested, 2 police officers were hurt, 42 African Americans were injured (10 from gunshot wounds) and many fire department vehicles and police cars were damaged.

City officials blamed the riots on unemployment among African American youth but failed to note that abysmal housing conditions in the area and ongoing tension between the police and the African American community were contributing factors as well. Following the riot, a presidential task force reported that a lack of good jobs for low-income minority youth was the primary cause of the disturbance. It urged local, state, and federal agencies to create employment opportunities for the residents of the area. After the riot, although unemployment remained high and police-community relations floundered, San Francisco's race relations remained relatively calm for the rest of the decade. *See also* Segregation.

Further Readings: Broussard, Albert. *Black San Francisco: The Struggle for Racial Equality in the West, 1900–1954*. Topeka: University Press of Kansas, 1993; Crowe, Daniel. *Prophets of Rage: The Black Freedom Struggle in San Francisco, 1945–1969*. New York: Garland Publishing, Inc., 2000; Fleming, Thomas. "Violence Hits the Streets." *Sun-Reporter,* October 1, 1966, p. 2; Hippler, Arthur. *Hunter's Point: A Black Ghetto*. New York: Basic Books, 1974.

Paul T. Miller

SCLC. *See* Southern Christian Leadership Conference

Scottsboro Case (1931)

In 1931, a series of court trials involving an alleged rape of two white teenage girls by nine youths in Scottsboro, Alabama, reflected the climate of racial relations in the South preceding the Great Depression. The allegations sparked violent responses that almost resulted in a **lynching** and spawned legal actions that spanned several decades. A hotly debated issue in the 1930s and 1940s, the controversy died down until a movie about the case, titled *Judge Horton and the Scottsboro Boys,* broadcast in the 1970s, brought the issue back to the nation's attention.

The effects of the Depression were evident by the poverty-stricken people who rode freight trains during the early 1930s in search of employment. On March 25, 1931, a fight broke out between several young people on the Chattanooga to Memphis train in Tennessee. A number of black boys threw a smaller group of white boys from the train. When the injured boys caught the attention of a train stationmaster, the sheriff of Jackson County, Alabama, was contacted about the incident. Sheriff W.L. Wann ordered his deputy to deputize as many men as possible in the town of Paint Rock and bring them to the next stop in Scottsboro. A posse was formed and met the train. After a search, they found nine black youths, one white boy, and two white girls dressed in caps and overalls. The girls were not immediately identified as females due to their dress. When Victoria Price and Ruby Bates were questioned, they stated that the black boys had raped them at knifepoint on the train. The boys were taken to jail and word of the incident quickly spread throughout the area. On March 26, a crowd gathered with the intention of lynching the nine boys, a common practice in the South at the time. Sheriff Wann was able to fend off the mob and tried to send the accused boys to another jail for their safety, even going as far as contacting the National Guard for assistance.

The nine defendants—Clarence Norris, Charlie Weems, Haywood Patterson, Olen Montgomery, Ozie Powell, Willie Roberson, Eugene Williams, Andrew Wright, and Roy Wright—ranged in age from twelve to twenty. On March 30, a grand jury indicted the youngsters for rape. On April 6, the first of a series of legal actions took place as the nine went on trial before Judge A.E. Hawkins. Eight of the nine "Scottsboro Boys" were found guilty and sentenced to death. Only Roy Wright, whose trial ended in a mistrial, escaped the death penalty. The pace of the trial process seemed to reflect the intensity of the prosecution and jury to convict the defendants.

The **National Association for the Advancement of Colored People (NAACP)** decided not to appoint an attorney to represent the boys due to the controversy over the case. The Communist Party decided to take the case and represent the youths through its legal arm, the International Labor Defense (ILD); this was seen as an opportunity to promote the party in America by connecting the issue to the oppression of workers nationwide. The trial drew not only national attention but international notice due to the details of the case, the obvious racial implications, the youthfulness of the defendants, and the swiftness of the disposition.

The case was appealed to the Alabama Supreme Court and the convictions were upheld except for that of Eugene Williams who was deemed to be a juvenile according to state law. In May 1932, The U.S. Supreme Court reviewed the case and reversed the decision due to inadequate representation of the defendants in the case.

In January 1933, Samuel S. Leibowitz was hired by the ILD as the Scottsboro Boys' defense attorney. In April of that year, a second trial again resulted in convictions and a sentence of the death penalty. The next month, there were many protests throughout the nation, including a large protest march in the nation's capital. Judge Edwin Horton, Jr., the new jurist in the case, overturned the verdict and granted a new trial. Shortly afterward, jurisdiction was transferred from Judge Horton to William Callahan. Judge Horton later lost a bid for reelection, most likely due to his perceived leniency on the Scottsboro defendants and would never return to the bench.

Over the next several years, there was a series of local court convictions followed by appeals, all the way to the U.S. Supreme Court. Even the recanting of the rape accusation by one of the victims failed to change the jury's mind about the boys' guilt. Although Governor Graves denied the parole applications in 1938, some of the defendants were later covertly granted parole in the 1940s. In 1976, Clarence Norris, the last of the Scottsboro Boys, was given a full pardon by Alabama's Gov. George Wallace, ending a series of legal actions dealing specifically with the defendants in the case.

However, that was not the last of the legal activity involving the alleged victims. When a made-for-television movie about the Scottsboro case called "Judge Horton and the Scottsboro Boys" was aired by NBC in 1976, both Ruby Bates Schut and Victoria Price Street filed lawsuits for libel, slander, and invasion of privacy. Ms. Bates Schut died before her case was completed and Ms. Price Street lost her case against the network. ***See also*** ***Powell v. Alabama*** (1932).

Further Reading: Carter, Dan. *Scottsboro: A Tragedy of the American South*. Baton Rouge: Louisiana State University Press, 1979.

Leonard A. Steverson

Segregation

Segregation is the separation of people from the dominant population, based on minority group status that may be established on issues of race, gender, age, class, sexual orientation, religious affiliation, disability, and other human or social variables. Two forms of segregation currently in use are *de jure* segregation and *de facto* segregation. *De jure* segregation is the formal, legal form of segregation that is both permitted and enforced by law. *De facto* segregation, on the other hand, is not dictated by law. It separates people through informal societal customs, norms, and personal decisions.

One of the most infamous examples of *de jure* segregation was established when the United States enacted the **Jim Crow** laws that stood from the 1870s to the 1950s when the modern **civil rights movement** was instrumental in repealing them. Under the Jim Crow laws, *de jure* segregation formed bilinear institutions and facilities throughout society. One system was established for the dominant Caucasian population and the other for African Americans.

Jim Crow laws affected nearly every aspect of social life, down to the most minute details. African Americans were often not allowed to walk through the front door of a building if a back door was available. Lunch counters and restaurants were segregated with either no place for African Americans and other minorities, or a subordinate location. The foremost seats of public

White students in class at the University of Oklahoma, and G.W. McLaurin, an African American, seated in an anteroom, 1948. Courtesy of the Library of Congress.

buses, trains, and planes were reserved for Caucasians. Any person of a minority group had to sit in the back of that form of public transportation. Segregation resulted in separate restrooms for Caucasians and African Americans. Separation along perceived racial lines was also established in churches, public schools, movie theaters, hotels, and many retail establishments.

Of course this segregation based on race meant that society would have to have definitive measures by which to ascertain if a person was Caucasian or African American. How was this to be accomplished when the concept of race is biologically insignificant and multitudes of people had backgrounds of mixed ethnicities? It was decided that the defining factor would be the One Drop Rule. In other words, if a person had one drop of African blood in their system, they were considered to be from a minority group and not allowed to enter the segregated white societal system.

In an effort to become even more technical on the matter, it was decided that if a person had a fraction of $1/32$ African blood in their bodies, they were to be considered black and they were to be segregated into the subordinate system of societal existence. This factor of attempting to determine racial identification by fractions is also known as the Rule of Hypodescent.

Jim Crow laws were first challenged in 1896 by a man named Homer Plessy who brought the *Plessy v. Ferguson,* 163 U.S. 537 (1896) case to the U.S. Supreme Court. The Court decided that the Jim Crow laws in place at that time were "not constitutionally impermissible under the **Fourteenth**

Amendment's Equal Protection Clause." In other words, the law was upheld and it was decided that the racially based dual systems were not illegal. Separate-but-equal facilities and social institutions were permissible. The states were legally allowed to racially segregate on the basis of race in all factions of life.

Of course, the facilities and social institutions afforded African Americans were substandard to those experienced by the Caucasian population. The *separate* part was in place, but things were not *equal*. In fact, the inequalities between the two systems were so significant that it remains a startling fact that the Jim Crow laws survived some eighty years of enforcement in the United States.

These decades of *de jure* segregation were challenged once again when in 1954 the U.S. Supreme Court heard the case of *Brown v. Board of Education,* 347 U.S. 483 (1954). The segregated educational system of the day was definitively unequal and presented an important and widespread form of discrimination in schooling. Supreme Court Chief Justice Warren of the U.S. Supreme Court determined that every faction of this well established dual system of segregation was "inherently unequal." The Supreme Court declared that segregation in any form was unconstitutional under the Equal Protection Clause of the Fourteenth Amendment.

Enacting the law was not, however, immediate. nor did it occur without major incidents. A year after the U.S. Supreme Court made its ruling, Jim Crow laws would still be upheld around the country. In Montgomery, Alabama, for example, Rosa Lee Parks publicly challenged the Jim Crow laws by defying their mandates. In 1955, she was taking a public bus home from an exhausting day at work. She was African American and knew that society and the Jim Crow laws dictated that she ride in the back of the bus. She sat in a front seat and refused to give up that seat to a white man who demanded it. Deputy Sheriff D.H. Lackey arrested and fingerprinted her for this violation of the Jim Crow laws. She was photographed by the law enforcement agency with her conviction number of "7053." Her arrest sparked a protest by the African American community who, in turn, refused to use the public transportation system for the next 380 days, under the boycott direction and guidance of **Martin Luther King, Jr.**

This courageous act is considered one of the great turning points that led to the modern civil rights movement. Rosa Lee Parks died Monday, October 24, 2005, at age 92. She is the first woman to lie in state at the U.S. Capitol Rotunda. The bus on which she refused to give up her seat is now preserved in a Detroit museum. On September 14, 1996, President Bill Clinton awarded the Presidential Medal of Freedom to Rosa Lee Parks for her brave, society-changing act of peaceful protest.

The civil rights movement was sparked, but as late as 1962 states were not complying with the 1954 Supreme Court ruling against segregation. In 1956, the University of Alabama received orders from the federal government stating that female African American student Autherine Lucy could not be denied admission to the university because of her race. She was admitted, but was assaulted by mobs. The university then suspended her, claiming it was for her own safety. When Lucy filed suit against the school for being unable to protect her and for supporting the **white mob**, the

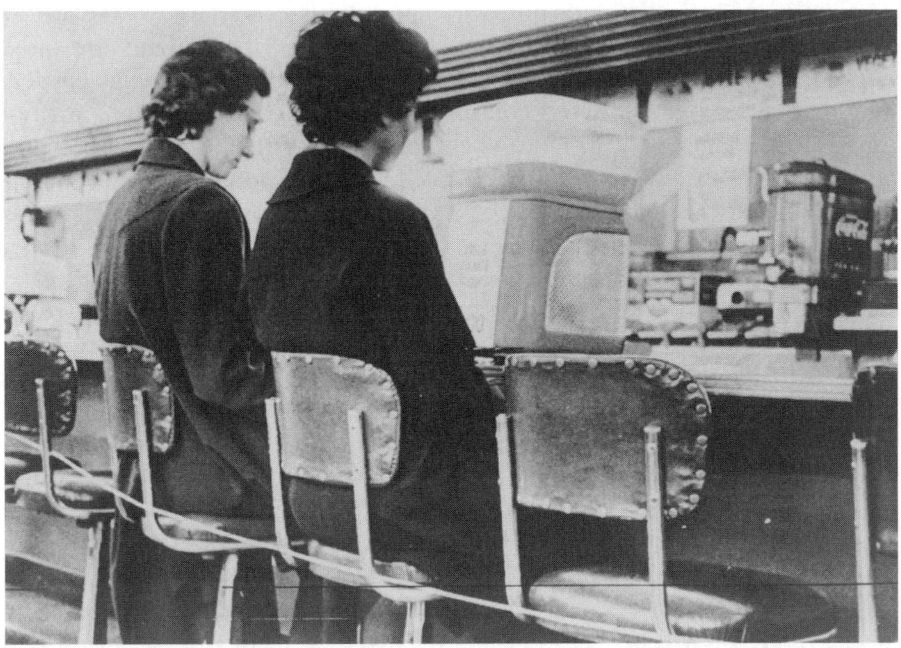

A Caucasian woman and an African American woman sitting side by side on stools at a lunch counter, protesting segregation, 1960. Courtesy of the Library of Congress.

university expelled her. The expulsion was not overturned by the University of Alabama Board of Trustees until the 1980s.

In 1957, President Dwight Eisenhower found it necessary to call in the National Guard to protect four African American students in Little Rock, Arkansas, trying to integrate the educational system. In 1962, President **John F. Kennedy** also used federal guardsmen to ensure the safety of African American student **James Meredith** as he began attendance at the University of Mississippi. In 1963, Gov. George Wallace of Alabama stood at the doors of the University of Alabama, deterring any African American students from attending the university.

By 1964, only 2 percent of southern African American children attended schools in which segregation did not exist. The U.S. Department of Health, Education, and Welfare decided in 1966 that it would establish very specific goals for each segregated school and cut off federal funding if the schools did not comply.

In the shadow of decades of *de jure* segregation, the practice of *de facto* segregation remains in place to this day. In the area of housing discrimination, **redlining** and gerrymandering are well-established practices. Despite the fact that the **Civil Rights Act of 1968** prohibits any form of discrimination in housing, members of minority populations are shown homes in the areas of a city in which realtors believe they would be residing with residents of their same racial or ethnic background.

In the current educational system, some 60 percent of elementary schools and 80 percent of secondary schools use *tracking* to segregate students. Incoming students are labeled as either *gifted* or *college prep* and given challenging work with positive expectations of success. These are by far the slots occupied by Caucasian students. Minority students are often tracked into special needs groups and are channeled in a general curriculum without expectations of continuation into higher education. African American students are also more likely than white students to be labeled as emotionally disturbed or learning disabled. The individual is held accountable for their own educational success or failure without regard to previous unequal educational opportunities or systems.

Occupational segregation also exists to this day, and is often measured by the Duncan's D tool. In 1992, the U.S. government called together a panel of experts to study American occupational trajectories. The commission discovered that women and racial minorities are often hired and allowed promotion to a certain mid-management level where they hit the "glass ceiling." They are stopped from obtaining top-level executive positions, but can still see through the ceiling to their Caucasian male counterparts progressing up the career ladder to higher and higher positions above them. Women are also still segregated into traditionally female jobs, which the majority of the time are low-paying, without benefits, and with little to no pension offers. Disparities can be tracked back to education on the university level, where the majority of nursing students are female and the majority of engineering majors are male. If multiple jeopardies are attached, we find the old, minority female on what is known as the *sticky floor,* unable to even reach the first rung of the career ladder, being segregated into the lowest-paying jobs.

The 2000 U.S. Census Bureau uses an "index of dissimilarity" (Community Research Partners 2005). It scores from zero to 100, with a score of zero indicating that no segregation exists and a score of 100 indicating total segregation within a city. Detroit currently holds the position of having the highest percentage at 84.7 percent. This means that 85 percent of whites or blacks would have to move to balance racial proportions of the total metropolitan area. In other words, the segregation fact is among the highest in the nation. Milwaukee, Wisconsin, stands in second place at 82.2 percent, followed by Chicago, Illinois (80.9 percent), and Newark, New Jersey (80.4 percent). Similar patterns for other minority groups have been found nationwide, as Latino and Asian percentages reflect high levels of segregation (Community Research Partners 2005).

Antidiscrimination laws (striking down most mandatory retirement laws) and social policies (such as Affirmative Action) are in place to break down walls of segregation, although their effectiveness in changing society is often challenged. Literally speaking, we segregate males and females by bathrooms. We segregate prisoners from the general population. We segregate the frail elderly in nursing homes, the mentally ill in psychiatric hospitals and wards, and the physically ill in hospitals. Many of these current forms of segregation, however, do not reflect the social injustices and inequality that exist when race, gender, class, ability, and age are used as the criteria for unequal treatment resulting in segregation. For example, Title I of the Americans with Disabilities Act of 1990 prohibited the segregation of people with physical disabilities from public buildings. Prior to this act becoming effective in 1992, anyone using a wheelchair or other walking aid could not gain access to numerous buildings, thus causing their direct segregation from service providers intended for all people.

Self-segregation also exists. This implies that women and minority groups may opt to segregate themselves from the dominant or general population. Many people choose to self-segregate in order to live in neighborhoods and join organizations in which their sex, age, race, ethnicity, or class are dominantly represented. In 2003, Dr. Beverly Daniel Tatum attempted to explain self-segregation in terms of the development of racial identity in her book *Why Are All the Black Kids Sitting Together in the Cafeteria?*

As American society continues to become more biracial and multiracial, many changes are expected, and it is hoped that segregation perpetrated for inequality will give way to positive forms of segregation that are self-selected and productive. *See also* Integration.

Further Reading: Community Research Partners. "Introduction & Overview: Population Indicators." *Community Indicators Database Report: Population* (October 2005). See http://www.communityresearchpartners.org/uploads/publications//CIDR-population.pdf.

Sheila Bluhm Morley

Sellers, Cleveland (1944–)

Cleveland Sellers is a civil rights organizer and activist, an advocate of Pan-Africanism, and a former **Student Nonviolent Coordinating Committee (SNCC)** executive board member.

Born in segregated Denmark, South Carolina, on November 8, 1944, Cleveland Sellers and his older sister Gwendolyn grew up in a working-class home. His father, a disciple of **Booker T. Washington,** was a farmer, restaurateur, taxi driver, and real estate owner, and his college-graduate mother was a teacher and dietician at Denmark's South Carolina Area Trade School.

Sellers became aware of class divisions in the black community when, among other things, he saw friends from the poor section of black Denmark eating out of trash cans. He had little contact with whites before his teenage years. By the late 1950s, Sellers was radicalized while following televised accounts of the Montgomery Bus Boycott, the **Emmett Till** murder, and **integration** of Little Rock High School, among other events.

Sellers graduated from Voorhees High School and Junior College, where he watched news accounts of the first sit-in, which occurred on February 1, 1960, in Greensboro, North Carolina. Two weeks later, Sellers helped plan a sit-in involving Voorhees students at a local drugstore. He expanded his protest activities to Rock Hill, North Carolina, where he met Ruby Doris Smith of the SNCC. Sellers subsequently founded a youth chapter of the **National Association for the Advancement of Colored People (NAACP)** in Denmark, South Carolina.

In September 1962, Sellers enrolled at Howard University, where he met **Stokely Carmichael** and joined the Nonviolent Action Group (NAG), a friends of SNCC affiliate. NAG assisted with logistics for the 1963 March on Washington, and Sellers went to Cambridge, Maryland, to assist Gloria

Richardson and the Cambridge Nonviolent Action Committee in organizing a protest against visiting Alabama Gov. George Wallace. The protesters were gassed and shot at by law enforcement, and Sellers was among those who were arrested.

Sellers recruited students for **Freedom Summer** (Mississippi) of 1964 and worked in the Mississippi Summer Project. He helped found the Mississippi Freedom Democratic Party, participating in the famous confrontation at the Democratic National Convention in August 1964. Sellers was named project director of SNCC Mississippi field operations, where he helped execute the Mississippi Challenge to congressional elections and helped provide SNCC logistical support for the Selma to Montgomery March of 1965.

In November 1965, Sellers was elected SNCC national program secretary, joining John Lewis (chairman) and **James Forman** (executive director) on the three-person Executive Committee of SNCC, which was rapidly moving in a black consciousness and internationalist direction. SNCC issued an anti–**Vietnam War** statement in January 1966. Sellers helped create the **Lowndes County Freedom Organization (LCFO)** in Alabama and was reelected as program secretary in the spring 1966 election that brought Carmichael to the chairmanship. As demonstrated by its support for **James Meredith**'s March Against Fear, SNCC thereafter shifted to a **Black Power** philosophy, which **Roy Wilkins** and Hubert Humphrey criticized at the July 1966 NAACP National Convention.

Heavily influenced by **Malcolm X,** by the work of Kwame Nkrumah and Frantz Fanon, and by international liberation struggles, Sellers refused to be drafted into the U.S. Army in May 1967. SNCC thereafter became more militant. The dismissal of white staffer Bob Zellner was followed by a series of increasingly violent confrontations with law enforcement, which culminated in the Cambridge, Maryland, shoot-out that resulted in the arrest of new SNCC Chairman **H. Rap Brown.** An SNCC position statement on anti-Zionism in Palestine also led to increasingly shrill criticism of the organization. In October 1967, Sellers, who with Carmichael had not stood for reelection to the SNCC executive board, moved to Orangeburg, South Carolina.

That same month, Sellers assisted the Black Awareness Coordinating Committee, a group of students from historically African American South Carolina State University, protest segregationist policies at a local bowling alley, which led to a series of increasingly violent confrontations with police. Shortly thereafter, on February 8, police, state troopers, and the South Carolina National Guard attacked the South Carolina State campus, wounding twenty-seven (most while attempting to flee) and killing three students. Shot during this "Orangeburg Massacre," Sellers was arrested and held on $50,000 bail as the principal organizer of the student protests. In 1970, a jury convicted him of inciting a riot and he spent seven months in jail as a consequence.

The April 1968 murder of Dr. **Martin Luther King, Jr.,** accelerated the deterioration of SNCC. In February 1968, Forman, Carmichael, and Brown entered into an alliance with the **Black Panther Party (BPP);** Sellers was jailed on a draft evasion charge (eventually dismissed) and a Louisiana weapons charge. In 1969, he took a position as lecturer in the Africana Studies

Program of Cornell University, enrolling at Harvard to pursue a master's degree in education the same year.

In the following year, he declared a Pan-Africanist philosophy and expanded his activities, working with the Student Organization for Black Unity, African Liberation Day, and Malcolm X Liberation University, among other efforts. He was also affiliated with Stokely Carmichael's (Kwame Ture's) All-African People's Revolutionary Party. In subsequent years, Sellers received a doctorate in history from the University of North Carolina at Greensboro (1987) and taught at both that university and the University of North Carolina at Chapel Hill and at Shaw. He is currently director of African American Studies for the University of South Carolina. On July 20, 1993, he finally received a pardon from the Parole Board of South Carolina for his conviction in the Orangeburg incident.

Further Readings: Nelson, Jack, and Jack Bass. *The Orangeburg Massacre.* New York: The World Publishing Co., 1970; Sellers, Cleveland. *The River of No Return: The Autobiography of a Black Militant and the Life and Death of SNCC.* New York: William Morrow and Company, 1973; University of South Carolina College of Arts and Sciences, African American Studies. "Cleveland Sellers." See www.cas.sc.edu/AFRA/sellers1.html.

Gregory E. Carr

Sharecropping

Sharecropping is a system of farming in which poor farmers (sharecroppers) work a parcel of land that they do not own in return for a portion of the crop raised or for a wage. Sharecropping arose in the American South

African American tenant farmer on his front porch in Oklahoma, 1939. Courtesy of the Library of Congress.

during **Reconstruction** in response to the abolition of slavery because it allowed the traditional subservient status of blacks to landowning whites to be maintained by legal means. With the abolition of slavery by the Thirteenth Amendment, African Americans had to be paid for their work in the fields. Labor contracts were issued that provided plant workers with wages, housing, clothing, and food in return for their work. African American workers lacked capital and resources and were forced to enter into labor agreements with their former masters. Normally, wages were a small share of the crop—one-eighth or even less—amounts that often permitted the sharecroppers to make only a subsistence living.

Sharecropping was a practice supported by the **Freedmen's Bureau** and originated in the **Black Codes** enacted during the period of presidential Reconstruction under the idea that freedmen could make their way in American society if they worked hard. As small, independent farmers, sharecroppers cultivated a plot of land that belonged to the landowners. In exchange, they were given a house, a mule, tools, seed, and a share of the crop, usually between one-third and a half. At first sight, it was a fair trade agreement, but in reality it proved a kind of neo-serfdom because the sharecropper in effect remained attached to the land and the owner. The sharecroppers did not raise enough of a crop to pay for their expenses. Most of the time they had to pay the plantation owners inflated prices for necessary supplies and equipment. When they did not have money to pay for these items, the sharecroppers were given the goods at extortionate rates of interest so that owners could sometimes claim 100 percent of the crop. In the end, African American fieldworkers were driven into subsistence farming to pay their debts, although they did not succeed in the endeavor. The result was that sharecropping limited black mobility and held a captive labor force at extremely low cost in the plantations that helped develop the South.

In an attempt to improve conditions, sharecroppers allied with poor white farmers in the People's Party in the 1890s. The alliance threatened the political supremacy of the white planter class. However, by the end of the decade, the People's Party had lost its challenging force as a consequence of racial enmity. Thus, African Americans were excluded from political life.

Sharecropping had some consequences in African American culture as well. It was not a communal working practice, instead it was based in a system that favored individualism. As a result, slave gangs were replaced by individuals who worked their plots of land. This resulted in the evolution of traditional ballads and worksongs into the Blues, a more individualistic form of music.

The heyday of sharecropping spanned the period from 1865 to 1930, when mechanization of fieldwork resulted in large numbers of unemployed workers. But there were other causes of sharecropping's decline. Although sharecropping favored African Americans staying in the South, many left anyway, fueling the **Great Migration** of the early twentieth century. Sharecropping was the economic form of a social system that enforced social subordination to whites with its consequent loss of home and work, and even led to **lynching**. The worsening economic conditions of agriculture in the early twentieth century, with a new insect pest, the boll weevil, was another cause for the decline of sharecropping. The boll weevil arrived in Texas in the 1890s and reached Georgia and the Carolinas in the 1920s. It destroyed the crops to the extent that African American workers could hardly subsist. Finally, the opportunities that the industrial boom in Detroit offered were much more attractive to younger generations than the repetition of a way of life that did not offer real opportunities.

Further Readings: Byres, T.J., ed. *Sharecropping and Sharecroppers*. Totowa, NJ: Biblio Distribution Center, 1983; Foner, E. *Reconstruction: America's Unfinished Revolution, 1863–1877*. New York: Harper and Row, 1988; Niemand, Donald G., ed. *From Slavery to Sharecropping: White Land and Black Labor in the Rural South, 1865–1900*. New York: Garland, 1994; Royce, Edward C. *The Origins of Southern Sharecropping*. Philadelphia: Temple University Press, 1993.

Santiago Rodríguez Guerrero-Strachan

Sharpton, Al (1954–)

Alfred (Al) Charles Sharpton, Jr., was born in Brooklyn, New York, to Alfred Sharpton, Sr., and Ada Richards Sharpton on October 3, 1954. Rev. Al Sharpton grew up in both Brooklyn and Hollis in Queens, New York. From the age of four, young Al began preaching in the pulpits of Pentecostal churches. From 1969 to 1971 Sharpton worked for two years with Operation Breadbasket, which was led by Rev. **Jesse Jackson.** Through this organization, he led protests against companies that discriminated against black people. Reverend Sharpton later founded the Brooklyn-based National Youth Movement. Through this organization he advocated against **police brutality** and racial discrimination, and organized civil protest demonstrations. He attended Brooklyn College during the 1970s, but later dropped out to work with the singer James Brown. While working with James Brown, he met his wife Kathy Jordan, who was a backup singer for Brown. He married Kathy Jordan in 1983, and the couple later had two daughters, Dominique and Ashley.

Al Sharpton appears on *Saturday Night Live*, 2003. Courtesy of Photofest.

Sharpton became known as a public persona during two controversial and significant cases involving two New York teenagers, Michael Griffith and Tawana Brawley. Griffith was a young African American man killed in a predominantly white area of **Howard Beach** in Queens in December

1986. The Howard Beach killing made national headlines and was considered one of the most significant racial hatred cases of the 1980s. Sharpton worked closely with two African American lawyers, Alton Maddox and C. Vernon Mason, to lead protest marches in Howard Beach. The leaders of the protest demanded that a special prosecutor be assigned to investigate the murder of Michael Griffith and prosecute his killers. The special prosecutor was eventually assigned in this case and three white youths from Howard Beach were convicted of manslaughter in Griffith's death.

Tawana Brawley was an African American teenager who alleged that she was beaten and sexually assaulted by white men in Wappinger Falls, New York. According to Brawley, the attack took place in November 1987. Sharpton became involved in the case and was a leading spokesperson in support of Brawley. Sharpton and others pressured the local police department and investigators in the case primarily because the incident involved the assault of a young African American woman and white male perpetrators. The case was later dropped by the police department and the state attorney general because after an intense investigation it was concluded that Tawana Brawley and her mother had fabricated the story to protect the girl from a harsh punishment by her stepfather.

These two incidents catapulted Al Sharpton into the national limelight. He became known as a brazen and loquacious advocate for social justice. In 1990, another African American teenager was killed in the Bensonhurst section of Brooklyn, New York. **Yusef Hawkins** was murdered by a group of whites. A leading activist and agitator, Sharpton again became actively involved in protest demonstrations to raise awareness of the case. During one of these protests, Sharpton was stabbed by a white man. After his recovery, Sharpton began to shift his political agenda and focused on running for political office. He ran in the Democratic primary for the U.S. Senate in 1992. Although he did not win the election, he did receive tremendous support in the African American community, including two-thirds of the black vote. He again ran unsuccessfully for the U.S. Senate in 1994.

Sharpton's political and professional career has been laced with controversy. At one time, he was labeled an informant for the **Federal Bureau of Investigation (FBI).** He was also sued for defamation of character and came under fire for both tax and financial fraud charges against his youth organization. Sharpton was acquitted of the tax and financial fraud charges but was required to pay $65,000 in a defamation suit by a white attorney he had accused of being involved in the rape of Tawana Brawley. These controversies have contributed to the public perception of Al Sharpton as a divisive figure who sometimes engages in self-aggrandizement and promotion.

Sharpton's most important contribution to the cause of civil rights and social justice came after the brutal murder of an innocent man that took place in New York. **Amadou Diallo,** an unarmed African immigrant was shot forty-one times by four white policemen in February 1999 in New York. This horrific killing led Sharpton to mobilize the city and organize many civil protests against police brutality within Manhattan. This significant event led hundreds of whites and African Americans to join together in civil protest to end the continued racial profiling and brutality that many African Americans were experiencing in New York City. Sharpton, along with many of his supporters, was arrested during some of these protests. Sharpton sought nomination as the Democratic candidate for the U.S. presidency in 2004. Although he did not receive the nomination, he did stimulate the election with his forthright speeches and his challenges to those candidates who would eventually receive their party's nominations.

Sharpton is both a controversial and passionate leader who has inspired debates on issues as important as police brutality, racial bigotry, and employment discrimination. His brash style and biting intellect are juxtaposed with his outward appearance (which includes a processed hairstyle reminiscent of James Brown) and the pedantic speech of a Baptist preacher. Al Sharpton has become one of the most notorious African American activists of the early twenty-first century.

Further Readings: Appiah, Kwame Anthony, and Henry Louis Gates, Jr., eds. *Africana Civil Rights: An A–Z Reference of the Movement That Changed America*. Philadelphia: Running Press, 2004; Howell, Ron. "Sharpton, Al." In Henry Louis Gates, Jr. and Evelyn Brooks Higginbotham, eds. *African American Lives*. New York: Oxford University Press, 2004.

Kijua Sanders-McMurtry

Shotgun Policy

The term *Shotgun Policy* refers to the violent exploits of conservative whites against blacks and Republicans to restore the Democrats to power in Mississippi in 1875. The tumultuous overthrow of Republican governments, also known as Redemption, took place throughout the South and inaugurated the ensuing years of unrestrained violence against blacks.

Prior to the Civil War, Mississippi, like other southern states, was dominated socially, politically, and economically by white landowners. At the bottom of the hierarchy were the black slaves. Conflicts in regional interests precipitated a split between the Union of the North and the Confederacy of the South and resulted in the Civil War.

In the aftermath of the Civil War, the federal government established the policy of **Reconstruction,** the purpose of which was to reintegrate the southern states into the Union, provide assistance to the newly freed slaves, and set up Republican-led state governments. Conservative Democrats were infuriated by these changes. **White mobs** and newly formed organizations, such as the **Ku Klux Klan (KKK)**, attacked and murdered black and white teachers who established schools for former slaves. They also terrorized black and white Republican politicians. In response, the federal government installed troops across the South to suppress the violence.

However, Democrats conspired to regain control of their state governments. Virginia, Tennessee, and North Carolina were the first states to seize back power. To do this, they resorted to fraudulence and violent intimidation. In 1870 and 1871, the federal government attempted to restore order by creating anti-Klan laws, but the success of these laws was short-lived. In

1874, white mobs murdered black and white Republican leaders and destroyed crops and homes. Violence erupted at the polls in Louisiana between 1868 and 1876.

In 1875, white Mississippians unleashed their infamous Shotgun Policy. In the same year, whites murdered thirty teachers, church leaders, and Republican officials in Clinton. Riots broke out in Vicksburg and Yazoo City, Mississippi, as well as in other southern states. White Mississippians also tormented and even lynched blacks to keep them from the polls. In response, politicians fled Mississippi in fear of their lives or were coerced to join the Democrats, and numerous blacks refrained from voting on election day.

Mississippi's Governor Ames appealed to President Ulysses S. Grant for assistance, but Grant was already preoccupied with problems of his own. Ames met with representatives from the Democratic Party, and they agreed to a peaceful election day in exchange for Ames' promise not to organize a black militia. Although Ames kept his bargain, the Democrats set homes on fire before election day and set up armed guards at the polls. While most blacks hid in the woods and stayed away from the polls, the Democrats celebrated their win. Following their return to power, conservative whites set about resuming their pre-Civil War life in Mississippi. Although blacks were legally free, they were bound by oppressive and discriminatory laws and practices (see **Black Codes**). Meanwhile, the violence against blacks continued unabated, and this time, the federal government did not intervene on the behalf of blacks.

Similar attacks against blacks and Republican politicians persisted throughout Redemption. In 1876, whites in South Carolina emulated Mississippi's Shotgun Policy. On the Democrat side were 600 Redshirts who beat and killed blacks to keep them from voting. Although President Grant sent federal troops, the Democrats retained power. By 1877, all of the southern states of the Confederacy were under Democratic control.

Further Readings: Perman, Michael. *The Road to Redemption: Southern Politics, 1869–1880*. Chapel Hill: University of North Carolina Press, 1984; Rable, George C. *But There Was No Peace: The Role of Violence in the Politics of Reconstruction*. Athens: University of Georgia Press, 1984.

Gladys L. Knight

Silent March of 1917. *See* New York City Silent March of 1917

Simmons, William J. (1882–1945)

William Joseph Simmons founded the second incarnation of the **Ku Klux Klan** in 1915. Simmons was born in 1880, to a country physician and former Klansman on a farm near Harpersfield, Alabama. He had little formal schooling. Simmons served in the Spanish-American War and attempted afterward to pursue a career in the ministry of the Methodist Episcopal Church, South. His several years of itinerant ministry in Florida and Alabama were not rewarded by a permanent church, sparking his departure from the group.

William Joseph Simmons, 1921. Courtesy of the Library of Congress.

Simmons joined over a dozen various Masonic orders, including the Woodmen of the World, where he—as did all his fellow Woodmen—received the honorific title of colonel. Simmons combined fraternal membership and personal career by becoming a field representative and salesman of fraternal insurance for the group. He sought the revival of what he called the original Klan of the lost era—the period of southern humiliation, defeat, and redemption starting with the original Klan's birth in 1866 in Pulaski, Tennessee.

According to Klan lore, Simmons swore at that time to found the Klan memorializing organization. According to Jonathan B. Frost, a fellow Woodman who joined the reborn Klan and later embezzled several thousand dollars from its beginning coffers, Simmons took the idea of restarting the Klan from a presentation he had made at a Woodmen's convention. A subsequent period of convalescence following an automobile accident led Simmons to develop detailed plans for rebuilding the Klan, an idea that had possessed him more firmly after having perhaps read of the March 1915 release of **D.W. Griffith**'s paean to the Klan, ***The Birth of a Nation.*** After the film opened in December in Atlanta, Simmons persuaded the theater owner to allow him to view it free and repeatedly.

On Thanksgiving Day in 1915, Simmons and fifteen others ascended Stone Mountain in Georgia, where he led them in the first initiation ceremony of a memorial organization to the original Klan, known as The

Invisible Empire, Knights of the Ku Klux Klan. The ceremony followed the general format of the initial Klan ceremony nearly fifty years before—an altar held an American flag, an open Bible, a sword, and a canteen of water. One major innovation was to become the lasting symbol of the various Klan and Klan-sympathizing groups—the erection and burning of a Christian cross. This symbol could be seen from nearby Atlanta.

The next week, Simmons incorporated the organization in Fulton County, pursuing yet another departure from original Klan procedure. Simmons, unlike his predecessors, sought to have the Klan protected by legal status and situated to assume a remunerative function as well. Drawing on research on the original Klan, he completed a fifty-four-page *Kloran,* a text of ritual, administrative rules, and coded jargon that was to serve as "the book" governing Klan business.

Simmons divided the country into eight administrative domains. Each domain was governed by a Grand Goblin, then a state (province) hierarchy, then intrastate provinces, and finally the local Klanverns. Many of these Klanverns assumed the names of preexisting or newly named organizations to avoid detection and to lend their efforts to ongoing work, such as the 100 percent Americanism movement in Colorado.

Until 1920, the Klan was confined almost exclusively to Georgia and Alabama. In 1920, however, Edward Young Clarke and Elizabeth Tyler formed the Southern Publicity Association and used it to parlay national anti-black, anti-Jewish, anti-Catholic, anti-Asian, and pro-Nativist sentiments into an explosion of Klan membership from 2,000 to 50,000 members by the time of congressional hearings on Klan activities in 1921. By 1924, 40 percent of the Klan's membership was in Indiana, Ohio, and Illinois, followed by a quarter in six southwestern states. Only 16 percent were in the southeast.

By 1923, Simmons had come into conflict with the organization by supporting Clarke and Tyler during a series of Tyler's indiscretions. Simmons' own incompetence and alcoholism led to his removal as Imperial Wizard in favor of Dallas' Hiram Wesley Evans. A series of legal battles ensued, leading to his banishment on January 5, 1924. He died in May 18, 1945, in Luverne, Alabama. The organization he restarted continues to hold sway in the popular imagination and to morph into other white supremacist organizations. *See also* Ku Klux Klan (KKK); White Supremacy.

Further Readings: Jackson, Kenneth T. *The Ku Klux Klan in the City: 1915–1930*. New York: Oxford University Press, 1967; Randel, William Pierce. *The Ku Klux Klan: A Century of Infamy*. Philadelphia: Chilton Books, 1965.

Gregory E. Carr

SNCC. *See* Student Nonviolent Coordinating Committee

South Carolina. *See* Charleston (South Carolina) Riot of 1919; Orangeburg (South Carolina) Massacre of 1968

Southern Christian Leadership Conference (SCLC)

The Southern Christian Leadership Conference (SCLC) was led by the Rev. **Dr. Martin Luther King, Jr.,** and was, if not the driving force of the

civil rights movement, often the most visible image of the movement. Reaching its peak in the mid-1960s, SCLC was formed in the aftermath of the 1955 bus boycott in Montgomery, Alabama. Because King was its leader from its inception until his death in 1968, the history of the two are closely intertwined.

SCLC was created to fill a gap left by the perceived shortcomings of other organizations. For example, by 1955, the **Congress of Racial Equality (CORE),** although committed to **nonviolence,** had failed to organize on a large scale, and its northern flavor and interracial board seemed to contradict what had created change in Montgomery—a southern-based black movement. It was into this apparent void that organizers stepped and created SCLC.

SCLC, on its founding, was also seen as distinctly different from the **National Association for the Advancement of Colored People (NAACP),** although there was much crossover. SCLC was exclusively southern. There were no individual memberships. SCLC acted as an umbrella organization, which, together with its regional flavor, would weaken it as it moved north after 1965. The organization consisted mainly of black ministers and seemed to operate in many ways as a political manifestation of the southern black churches. The first president of SCLC was King, and its first treasurer was Rev. Ralph Abernathy. The organization reflected King's commitment to nonviolent direct action as a technique to battle all forms of **racism.** SCLC, with King at the helm, tried to use these nonviolent tactics to pressure political forces in Washington, D.C., to create change at both the local and national levels.

In the years after Montgomery, King's efforts often came up short. By 1960, massive resistance from white southerners had limited the ability to extend equal rights to African Americans. Voting, the **desegregation** of public schools, and the **integration** of most public facilities had come to a standstill, despite the apparent progress in Montgomery and the integration of Central High School in Little Rock, Arkansas.

Galvanized by the sit-in movement, organized by students in places such as Greensboro, North Carolina, King seized another opportunity in 1961, in the midst of the **Freedom Rides,** to challenge the power structure of Albany, Georgia. King relished the opportunity because many SCLC actions had stalled in the wake of Montgomery and direct action initiatives had passed oftentimes to the activists of the **Student Nonviolent Coordinating Committee (SNCC)** and CORE. From December 1961 to July 1962, King went to jail three times along with thousands of others in the Albany movement, all to no avail. King and SCLC failed to break the intransigence of Albany Police Chief Laurie Pritchett, and without federal support—because black protestors appeared to be arrested without excessive force—the administration of **John F. Kennedy** refused to step in. Albany showed SCLC that direct confrontation was needed between civil rights demonstrators and segregationists.

SCLC became involved in the Voter Education Project (VEP) between 1962 and 1964 (together with organizations like the NAACP, SNCC, and CORE) to line up black voters and get them registered. However, because the federal government failed to really support the initiative with protection for workers, this effort met with mixed results.

By 1963, it was obvious to SCLC that direct confrontation was needed in the wake of previous failures. SCLC decided to provoke a confrontation in Birmingham with its police commissioner, **T. Eugene "Bull" Connor.** Protests, combined with what had already been going on under the direction of Rev. Fred Shuttlesworth, ignited federal involvement. Unlike Albany, news cameras highlighted the images of peaceful demonstrators being brutalized by Connor's police who used dogs and fire hoses. Although the forced confrontation by SCLC and its supporters initiated a compromise, it did not end the violence, and bombs ripped through the city. Several months later, the basement of a Birmingham church exploded and killed four young black girls (see **Black Church Arsons**).

In the wake of Birmingham, and tepid promises by the Kennedy administration regarding civil rights, SCLC joined with other organizations to help **A. Philip Randolph** lead a massive march on Washington, D.C., that he had first proposed twenty years earlier. The March on Washington featured a host of speakers, including King, who delivered his famous "I Have a Dream" speech. Despite the March and King's glowing rhetoric, the civil rights bill stalled in the House of Representatives. It was not until the assassination of President Kennedy that the bill finally managed to get passed into law.

SCLC's next big push came in 1965 in Alabama. King and SCLC helped orchestrate a march from Selma to Montgomery to highlight the lack of ability of blacks to vote in Alabama. The Selma march started with nationally televised violence and the black marchers were forced to retreat under the onslaught of the police (see **Bloody Sunday [1965]**). King, who missed the first march, attended the second one, and with federal protection, completed the march from Selma to Montgomery. Despite the protection, deadly acts persisted, as Viola Liuzzo, a white SCLC volunteer from Detroit, was ambushed and shot on the highway between Selma and Montgomery. The result of the violence-marred march was the Voting Rights Act of 1965, which marked a watershed in the black freedom struggle. It was the climax of SCLC's influence and the massive demonstrations that were used to pressure the federal government to act.

In the wake of Selma, the rise of **Black Power** advocates and the continued estrangement of SNCC from SCLC led to the diminution of the latter's influence. It oftentimes was left with the difficult job of trying to find the middle ground between the more traditional groups, such as the NAACP and the **National Urban League,** and aimed at integrating society via lobbying Congress and litigation. On the other side were SNCC and CORE, which rejected integration and nonviolence and espoused armed **black self-defense** and **Black Nationalism.** For example, **Stokely Carmichael,** the chairman of SNCC, championed Black Power. SCLC still tried to mobilize blacks to confront racism in the streets, and in 1966, as Carmichael's cries grew louder, King and SCLC moved the battle north and began to combat slum conditions and housing discrimination in northern cities.

By the time King was gunned down in Memphis in 1968, SCLC's message had become more radicalized as King campaigned for workers rights in Memphis, Tennessee, and against the **Vietnam War.** But SCLC's influence continued to wane in the North because of the lack of a cohesive religious organization as was seen in the South, and the southern nature of the organization failed to always reflect the needs of the northern urban population. After King's assassination in 1968, SCLC leadership was deeply divided over the organization's future. Nevertheless, led by King's family and friends, SCLC continued fighting segregation and discrimination. *See also* King, Martin Luther, Jr., Assassination of.

Further Readings: Branch, Taylor. *Pillar of Fire—America in the King Years, 1963–1965*. New York: Simon and Schuster, 1998; Fairclough, A. "The Preachers and the People: The Origins and Early Years of the Southern Christian Leadership Conference, 1955–1959." *The Journal of Southern History,* 52 (August 1986): 403–40; Fairclough, A. "Southern Christian Leadership Conference and the Second Reconstruction, 1957–1973." *The South Atlantic Quarterly* 80 (Spring 1981): 177–194; Fairclough, A. *To Redeem the Soul of America: The Southern Christian Leadership Conference and Martin Luther King, Jr.* Athens: University of Georgia Press, 1987; Garrow, David J. *Bearing the Cross: Martin Luther King, Jr., and the Southern Christian Leadership Conference*. New York: W. Morrow, 1986.

Gary Gershman

Southwest Missouri Riots (1894–1906)

Between 1894 and 1906, a series of race riots (or near riots) engulfed four southwest Missouri towns. During these disturbances, rampaging **white mobs** lynched at least eight African Americans and then expelled hundreds of others from the towns of Monett in 1894, Pierce City in 1901, Joplin in 1903, and, to a lesser degree, Springfield in 1906. Occurring within a span of twelve years and a radius of eighty miles, these four episodes represent the largest documented cluster of post-Civil War race riots in American history. The southwest Missouri riots resulted from a volatile combination of virulent **racism,** white fears of black sexual predations, growing African American urban populations, intense labor competition, and, in at least two cases, political rivalry between the races. In each case, the southwest Missouri riots originated with a **lynching** of at least one African American man accused of a violent crime, but bloodthirsty white mobs, unsatisfied with murdering only the black suspects, turned their racist fury on entire African American communities. These riots consequently led to mass exoduses of black residents from these four towns. In a particularly cruel twist of fate, some black refugees who escaped the Monett race riot fled to Pierce City, from which they were soon chased to Joplin or Springfield, where they would, for the third time, find themselves the targets of mob violence.

The first race riot in this cluster erupted in 1894 in the railroad town of Monett, a division point on the St. Louis and San Francisco Railroad established only seven years earlier. Most of the town's approximately 3,500 residents worked for the San Francisco Railroad or an affiliated industry. In

1894, on the eve of the riot, Monett was a rowdy boomtown on whose streets scenes of public drunkenness, knife fights, and gunplay were commonplace. Although fewer than 100 African Americans lived in Monett, bitter feelings existed between the races in large part because of job competition and an 1892 murder of a white man by a black waiter. The incident that triggered the Monett riot occurred at 10:00 P.M. on the night of June 20, 1894, when a group of five white railroad brakemen clashed with an equal number of black laborers outside a saloon. During the drunken altercation, one of the black men fatally shot Robert Greenwood, a San Francisco Railroad brakeman and the grandson of a Bentonville, Arkansas, judge. An intensive search resulted in the arrest of Ulysses Hayden eight days later in nearby Neosho, Missouri. Hayden admitted being among the group of black laborers the night of the murder, but he denied firing the shot that killed Greenwood, a conclusion a coroner's jury also reached in the days after Hayden's death. Nonetheless, later that night an enraged gang of between 50 and 100 white men, many of them railroad employees, boarded the train on which Hayden was being transported back to Barry County and forcibly removed the prisoner from the custody of law authorities. One mile south of Monett, the self-appointed executioners avenged Greenwood's death by hanging Hayden from a telegraph pole alongside the railroad tracks.

Later that night, following Hayden's lynching, the white mob ordered all African Americans to leave Monett or face serious reprisals. Fearing for their lives, black residents fled to Pierce City, Joplin, Springfield, and other nearby towns, and a few days later the *Carthage Press* reported, "Today there is not a darkey in Monett, nor does one dare to set foot in the town" (Stringer-Bishoff 1994). A coroner's inquest found that Hayden had died, as in so many other cases of lynching, at "the hands of unknown parties," and Barry County authorities made little effort to apprehend his murderers. (Stringer-Bishoff 1994). Although a few black porters who worked for the San Francisco Railroad continued to live in the town in the following decades, Monett largely became a "sundown town" in which African Americans were not welcome after dark. "Across the main street of Monett for years," reported the *Chicago Tribune* in 1901, "there has been a sign reading: 'Nigger, don't let the sun go down,' and no Negro has been permitted to remain inside the town after dark" (Stringer-Bishoff 1994).

Seven years later, an outbreak of collective racial violence rocked Pierce City, a railroad town established in 1870 and located five miles northwest of Monett, in adjoining Lawrence County. In 1900, Pierce City contained 2,151 residents, of which 175, or 8 percent, were African American. On the eve of the race riot, the town was reeling from a recent crime wave attributed to transients and an economic downturn resulting from a drought-induced crop failure. Under these conditions, the murder of a local white woman, allegedly by a black assailant, sparked a lynching and a full-blown race riot far deadlier than the one that had struck Monett.

Around 12:30 P.M. on August 18, 1901, a passerby discovered the body of Gisela Wild, the twenty-three-year-old daughter of a German farmer, under a railroad bridge on the outskirts of Pierce City. Her throat had been slashed, and her assailant had unsuccessfully attempted to rape her. Law enforcement officers found several witnesses who reported seeing an unidentified black man near the scene of the crime shortly before the murder, and suspicion soon fell on Will Godley, a thirty-two-year-old local black laborer with a criminal record. In 1891, Godley had been convicted of raping a local elderly white woman and was sentenced to ten years in the state penitentiary. At the time, only the protection of the National Guard and the decisive actions of a Pierce City marshal saved Godley from a lynch mob. In 1899, after serving seven and a half years of his sentence, Godley gained an early release for orderly and peaceable conduct and returned to Pierce City.

On August 19, the day after Wild's murder, police arrested Godley and Gene Barrett, a seventeen-year-old black railroad porter whom authorities believed was also involved in the crime. That evening, a mob of 1,000 men, some of whom had traveled to Pierce City from the surrounding countryside, stormed the jail with sledgehammers and removed both Barrett and Godley from their cells. Although the local National Guard unit stood prepared for mobilization, the Lawrence County sheriff refused to wire the Missouri governor to request assistance. Meanwhile, some members of the mob broke into the local armory and took 50 rifles and some 600 rounds of ammunition. In the downtown business district, the ringleaders of the mob attempted to extract confessions from the two suspects. Terrified, Barrett proclaimed his innocence and accused another black porter of committing the murder. His accusation probably saved his life. An unidentified man whisked Barrett through the mob, and law enforcement authorities transported the prisoner to the Mount Vernon jail for safekeeping. Godley, however, refused to speak. The frenzied mob hanged him from the balcony of the Lawrence Hotel and then riddled his dangling body with hundreds of rounds of gunfire.

After lynching Godley, scores of still-angry white men rampaged through a black neighborhood in search of Pete Hampton, described in accounts as Godley's half brother, who was suspected in the unsolved murder of a night watchman nine months earlier. Some black residents, seeking to protect their property and families, fired on the mob. The white men retreated, reorganized, and then launched a second invasion. The mob torched four black-owned homes before locating Hampton at the house of his seventy-year-old stepfather, French Godley. Barricaded inside the house, Hampton returned the mob's fire, and a deadly shoot-out ensued. When the gunfire from inside the house ceased, the mob set fire to the Godley home. According to the *Lawrence Chieftain* (August 22, 1901), "The attack on the Negroes continued as long as one of the hated race could be found," and it was six hours before the violence finally ended.

The next morning, law enforcement officers discovered the charred remains of Pete Hampton and French Godley in the smoldering ruins of the home. Rumors circulated in the aftermath of the riot that a black mob from surrounding towns was planning to attack Pierce City in retaliation, forcing the sheriff to request, finally, the assistance of the local National Guard. Fearing an invasion, some 500 armed white men stood guard around the town. The *Joplin Globe* headlined its account, "Race War Possible in Pierce

City," but the rumors proved false, and no assault occurred (Stringer-Bishoff 1991). During the six-hour riot the previous evening, virtually all of the town's black residents, as well as those who lived on the outskirts of town, fled Pierce City. Many of them went to Joplin, Carthage, and Springfield. "The citizens of Peirce [*sic*] City declare no Negro shall ever live there again," reported the *Chicago Tribune*. "Most of the refugees are making through the woods to Joplin, as Monett, the nearest town, has for years refused to permit a Negro to reside there" (Stringer-Bishoff 1994). The Pierce City race riot made front-page newspaper headlines and attracted sharp criticism across the nation, including from celebrated author Mark Twain. After reading a report of the incident in the *New York Weekly Post,* Twain wrote a scathing essay titled "The United States of Lyncherdom" (1923), in which he condemned the nation and his native Missouri in particular for the recent nationwide surge of violence against African Americans.

Less than two years after a white mob banished Pierce City's African American population, a deadly race riot engulfed nearby Joplin, Missouri. Located near the Kansas border, Joplin was, around the turn of the twentieth century, a bustling zinc and lead mining center plagued by public drunkenness, crime, and disorder. By 1900, 26,023 people inhabited the city, including a sizeable population of miners, railroad workers, and transient laborers. Joplin was segregated, and its 733 black residents, who comprised slightly less than 3 percent of the town's population, were restricted to living in two neighborhoods. A recent crime wave, which the *Joplin Daily Globe* attributed to "gangs of tramps" (April 15, 1903), had exacerbated racial tensions in Joplin.

On April 14, 1903, an unidentified black transient shot and killed thirty-four-year-old Officer Theodore Leslie, a one-year veteran of the Joplin Police Department, during a shootout in the Joplin rail yards. A group of men working nearby pursued the assailant and managed to wound him before he eluded them in the darkness. As news of Leslie's murder spread, a posse of 500 men organized an unsuccessful manhunt to find his killer. The following morning, April 15, two local men captured a twenty-three-year-old black man named Thomas Gilyard, who was suffering from a serious gunshot wound to the leg. A migrant worker from Mississippi, Gilyard told authorities that he had arrived in Joplin only two days earlier. Within a few hours of his arrest, a mob of 3,000 gathered outside the Joplin jail and, using large poles as battering rams, broke through one of the building's sidewalls and dragged Gilyard from his cell. Two blocks from the jail, mob ringleaders attempted to hang their prisoner from a telephone pole, but a dozen or so city leaders, including the mayor and prosecuting attorney, temporarily thwarted them. With the noose still around Gilyard's neck, the two groups of men engaged in what the *Joplin Daily Globe* described as "a tug-of-war" (April 16, 1903) struggle over control of the rope and the man ensnared by it. The mob prevailed and hanged Gilyard from a telephone pole.

Two and a half hours later, at around 8:00 P.M., the mob reformed and began its violent invasion of the African American neighborhood called

Kansas City Bottom. The mobsters stoned black pedestrians and torched several homes and businesses. When the Joplin Fire Department arrived to extinguish the blazes, members of the mob turned on the firefighters, slashing their hoses and forcing them to retreat. The mob then attacked residents and destroyed property in Joplin's other black neighborhood, but no one was killed. Roughly half of the city's African American residents fled for their lives, including, according to legend, future Harlem Renaissance writer Langston Hughes and his family. Most never returned again. The following month, an all-white grand jury made the highly unusual decision to indict three Joplin men for their alleged involvement in Gilyard's lynching. One of them was convicted of second-degree murder and sentenced to ten years imprisonment, but his conviction was overturned on appeal. In a second trial, he won acquittal, and the charges against the other two defendants were dropped.

In the aftermath of the 1903 riot, many of Joplin's dispossessed black residents sought sanctuary in Springfield, Missouri, located seventy-seven miles to the northeast, and it was here, three years later, that the final race riot of the southwest Missouri cluster occurred. In 1900, Springfield was a flourishing Ozarks city with a population of 23,267 residents, of whom 2,268, or fewer than 10 percent, were African American. Springfield's black community contained a prosperous and affluent middle class comprised of doctors, lawyers, dentists, and businessmen and, although segregated, African Americans wielded considerable influence in local Republican politics. Between 1870 and 1900, Springfield had enjoyed relatively harmonious race relations, but as the city entered the twentieth century, race relations became increasingly strained, particularly during municipal elections and in the local vice district of saloons, pool halls, and brothels where black and white working people often mingled. The recent unsolved murders of two white men, one in December 1905 and the other in January 1906, allegedly by African Americans, also inflamed racial animosity.

These smoldering tensions that gripped Springfield erupted into violence during the Easter holiday of 1906. On Good Friday, April 13, 1906, Mina Edwards, a white woman of dubious reputation who had moved to Springfield only a month before, claimed that two masked black men had sexually assaulted her. According to her and her companion, a twenty-two-year-old hotel clerk named Charles Cooper, Cooper was escorting Edwards to work when two black assailants knocked him down, dragged her into a field, and raped her. The next morning, police arrested two suspects, twenty-year-old Horace Duncan and twenty-one-year-old Fred Coker, both of whom were longtime Springfield residents and considered upstanding citizens. Neither had ever before been in trouble with the law. When their white employer told police that Duncan and Coker were at work at his livery stable and transfer company at the time of the alleged assault, authorities released them. But the two men were soon rearrested when Cooper swore out a complaint that they had stolen his pocket watch. That night, around 9:00 P.M., a mob of 1,000 white men, many of them drunk and indiscriminately firing guns into the air, stormed the jail and, in the absence of any resistance from law enforcement authorities, entered Duncan and Coker's cell and bludgeoned them with sledgehammers, probably killing Coker. The mob dragged the unconscious or already dead men through the streets to the Springfield city square and then hanged them from Gottfried Tower, a metal structure adorned with electric lights and crowned with a replica of the Statue of Liberty. Mob members then built a bonfire at the base of the tower, doused the dangling corpses with coal oil, and set them ablaze. A crowd of between 5,000 and 8,000 spectators, including hundreds of women and children, witnessed the ghastly spectacle. Local police officers, who were reported to have been standing around the edge of the mob, made no attempt to interfere. Still not satisfied, the bloodthirsty mob returned to the jail and removed Will Allen, a young black man charged with the recent murder of a Confederate veteran. The mob also dragged him to the city square, hanged him from the tower, and burned his body.

The following day, Easter Sunday, large crowds of churchgoers dressed in their Easter best converged on the scene of the lynchings, and some of them even sifted through the smoldering ashes for souvenirs of bone fragments and charred flesh with which to commemorate the previous night's orgy of violence. Meanwhile, rumors circulated that new mobs were forming for the purpose of invading Springfield's black neighborhoods and burning families out of their homes. The Greene County sheriff, fearing more bloodshed, telephoned Missouri's Gov. Joseph Folk, who sent five National Guard units to maintain order. National Guard troops patrolled the city's streets for ten days, but no other outbreaks of violence erupted, and Springfield's African American community was spared the fate suffered by those in Monett, Pierce City, and Joplin.

In the weeks following the bloodletting, as many African American families fled the area, Springfield drugstores and soda parlors sold postcards emblazoned with gruesome photographs of the dangling corpses. One enterprising local businessman even struck souvenir medals commemorating the triple lynching. One side of the medal read "Easter Offering," and the other side read "Souvenir of the hanging of 3 niggers, Springfield, Missouri, April 15, 1906" (Lederer 1981). Meanwhile, a grand jury determined that Duncan and Coker were innocent of any crime, and it was later revealed that Mina Edwards and Charles Cooper had fabricated the entire story about the rape. Governor Folk, for his part, publicly condemned the Springfield lynchings and offered a $300 reward for information leading to the arrest and conviction of the ringleaders. Eventually, eighteen men, including at least one policeman and the sons of two prominent local businessmen, were indicted for their alleged role in the triple lynching. The first of these court cases for second-degree murder ended in a mistrial, and the charges against the other defendants were eventually dismissed.

Springfield's Easter lynching marked the culminating race riot in southwest Missouri at the turn of the twentieth century. The contagion of bloodletting and violence in these four towns resulted in the following decades in the mass exodus of hundreds, perhaps even thousands, of African Americans from the region. According to the 2000 census, the black population in southwest Missouri nowhere near approaches what it was a century ago. Although African Americans comprise slightly more than 11 percent of Missouri's total population, they comprise between one-tenth of 1 percent and slightly more than 2 percent of the population in the four counties in which these race riots erupted. But this sharp decline in the African American population cannot be solely attributed to the riots. Historical patterns of black migration, which had begun in the 1890s, have also contributed to the current racial demographics of southwest Missouri.

The race riots of southwest Missouri represent defining historical events in these four communities but are often ignored in local city and county histories. Interestingly, though, both citizens of Pierce City and Springfield, reflecting a larger national trend, have recently acknowledged their community's shameful histories of racial violence and the lasting effects of the riots. In 2001, a group of Pierce City residents marked the centennial of their town's riot by erecting a monument in a local cemetery. The following year, the city of Springfield installed a bronze plaque in its downtown business district commemorating its Easter lynchings. *See also* Rape, as Provocation for Lynching.

Further Readings: Purrington, Burton L., and Panny L. Harter. "The Easter and Tug-of-War Lynching and the Early Twentieth-Century Black Exodus from Southwest Missouri." In George Sabo III and William M. Schneider, eds. *Visions and Revisions: Ethnohistoric Perspectives on Southern Cultures*. Athens: University of Georgia Press, 1987, 59–82; Capeci, Dominic J., Jr. *The Lynching of Cleo Wright*. Lexington: University Press of Kentucky, 1998; Lederer, Katherine. "And Then They Sang a Sabbath Song." *Springfield!* 2 (April, May, and June 1981): 26–28, 33–36, 24–26; Stringer-Bishoff, Murray. "The Lynching That Changed Southwest Missouri." *Monett Times,* August 14–16, 1991; Stringer-Bishoff, Murray. "Monett's Darkest Hour: The Lynching of June 28, 1894." *Monett Times,* June 27 and 28, 1994; Twain, Mark. "The United States of Lyncherdom." In *Europe and Elsewhere*. New York: Harper, 1923.

Patrick Huber

Springfield (Illinois) Riot of 1908

In August 1908, Springfield, Illinois, experienced three days of racial violence after the murder of a white man and the alleged rape of a white woman by black men. In response, an angry mob of white rioters wreaked havoc on the city, destroying black businesses, homes, and lives. Still, Springfield's black citizens, supported by their friends and families, defended themselves against the attack, killing and wounding several rioters. When the riot subsided, officials reported that two black men had been lynched, five white men had been killed, and hundreds had been wounded. In the end, the majority of rioters indicted for their crimes were acquitted of all charges.

Although the riot occurred in August, an incident that happened on July 4, 1908, initially led to the violence. That night, a black man allegedly entered the home of white mining engineer Clergy Ballard and attempted to assault Ballard's daughter. Ballard, awakened by his daughter's screams, grabbed the intruder and fought with him; however, the intruder managed to break away from Ballard by slashing him with a razor. Ballard's sons, also awakened during the fracas, chased the intruder but failed to catch him. Ballard later died from his wounds.

The next morning the city's newspapers printed stories about the attack on Ballard's daughter and the death of Clergy Ballard. As family and friends mourned, the police and community began their search for the attacker. The police scoured the black community questioning black men, but by late afternoon they still did not have any leads. However, before long they received their first break in the case. Four high school girls, schoolmates of Ballard's daughter, discovered a man asleep on the side of the road a few blocks from the Ballard home. Assuming this was Ballard's murderer, one of the girls immediately telephoned her father's saloon, the Ballard home, and the police. Within minutes, Ballard's sons, family, and friends arrived on the scene, grabbed the man and commenced to beat him brutally. The police arrived seconds later, saving him from sure death.

The man was identified as Joe James, a Negro drifter from Alabama who once was arrested in Springfield for vagrancy. According to officers, James had lived and worked for a year in East St. Louis before coming to Springfield in June. He also became a jail trustee, often running errands for the officers while serving out his time for the vagrancy charge. Now, James was the lead suspect in the murder of Clergy Ballard. The police questioned James about Ballard's murder, but he would not confess to the killing. James claimed to have passed out from drinking too much alcohol and could not remember anything from the previous night. Also, James was not in possession of the murder weapon. Nevertheless, the police charged James with Ballard's murder.

During the early twentieth century, in cities and towns across America, racially motivated crimes often led to **lynching** or a riot. Fortunately for Springfield, these did not occur after James was captured. Although racial tensions within the city did intensify, those initial, intense feelings of hatred toward blacks seemed to diminish before long. Through their actions and words, many of Springfield's citizens expressed their desire to grant James a fair trial. Springfield authorities appeared to be for law and order by quickly impaneling a special grand jury to hear the Ballard case. Unfortunately, many citizens did not share this spirit of fairness.

Throughout July and into early August, Springfield's mainstream newspapers printed racially intense stories. One told of a black man who was viciously attacked by a mob of white men near the Ballard residence. The victim escaped after police arrived; however, the newspaper remarked that he would have been lynched if it were not for the arrival of the police. The heated stories continued as one explained how a white woman was nearly assaulted by a black man and another story told how two black men fought with two Greek men, wounding one of the Greeks with a razor.

On Friday, August 14, largely because of the sensationalized stories printed in the newspapers, the growing racial tension within the city had reached its limit. The press headlined stories about the rape of a young white housewife, Mabel Hallam. Hallam claimed that a black man broke into her house and sexually assaulted her. The police immediately began their search, apprehending black men of suspicious character. In reality, the police were indiscriminately questioning and arresting a number of black men without provocation.

After the police questioned the men they apprehended, they were taken to Hallam's house. She would then confront the suspects with questions of her own. If she could not identify any of them as her attacker, they were released. This practice continued through the morning hours until officers picked up three laborers working near the Hallam's house. Like the others before them, the three men were subjected to the questioning process and were released after answering all questions; however, before they could leave the Hallams' yard, the police stopped them. **George Richardson** and a man named Rinehart were again questioned by Hallam; yet, she was still unsure if either of them was the rapist. Finally, after asking Richardson another question, she proclaimed that he was her attacker. Richardson was arrested and taken to the police station where Hallam officially identified him in a police lineup.

The news of Richardson's arrest caused fury throughout most of the white community. Calls for immediate justice where echoed by Hallam's husband, Ballard's friends, and many white residents. In front of the jail where Joe James and now George Richardson were being housed, a small group of angry men and boys began to form. As the crowd grew larger, so did the tension within the city. Increasingly, blacks were unsafe venturing into certain areas of Springfield. Reports circulated that blacks around town were being randomly attacked by whites. Initially, most of these reports were thought to be fabricated until it was confirmed that a group of white men did, in fact, beat an innocent black man with bricks and bats. As more people headed to the jail out of curiosity, rumors of lynching escalated. By mid-afternoon, the jail crowd numbered in the thousands.

Charles Werner, county sheriff and jail overseer, was responsible for the safety of the prisoners. He understood the situation was intensifying beyond his control and could possibly erupt into a riot. Still, Werner refused to contact the state militia for assistance. Instead, Werner believed he could devise a plan that would save James and Richardson from the lynch mob, protect the jailhouse from destruction, and save hundreds of lives by preventing a riot from occurring. He contacted Harry Loper, a local restaurant owner who owned a car, and asked for his assistance in transporting the prisoners to another town. Loper agreed. Hidden from the rowdy crowd, Richardson and James were secretly removed and driven a few miles from town to a train waiting for them. They were handed over to armed guards and taken by train seventy miles north of Springfield to a prison in Bloomington, Illinois.

By evening, the crowd had grown to approximately 5,000. As people left work and headed home, many whites proceeded to the jailhouse yard by way of the local saloons. Most of them, full of liquor and aroused to be a part of the excitement, joined the crowd in front of the jail, shouting insults at the authorities. On this Friday night, the city was filled with out-of-town visitors looking for weekend entertainment. The crowd in front of the jail was comprised mostly of men, women, and children of different classes, ages, and ethnicities. Although most were lower- and middle-class whites, there were a few upper-class whites among the group. The majority of the people present were native-born (American) citizens; however, there also were a few foreign-born (immigrant) residents in the crowd.

Blacks, after hearing about the day's earlier attacks on innocent black people and the constant rumors of lynching, stayed away from the jailhouse. Though some assumed there was no need for alarm, several believed that trouble was imminent and prepared for a possible mob attack. Several blacks, acting on their knowledge of previous race riots that occurred in various cities across America, secured their family, property, and neighborhoods by purchasing guns and ammunition for protection.

Unmistakably, the situation in Springfield was becoming worse. The unruly crowd at the jail continued to ridicule Werner, requesting that James and Richardson be released to them. Earl Hallam, Mabel Hallam's husband, was leading the taunts. Stubbornly, but strategically, Werner maintained his position, refusing to release the men to Hallam and the mob. As Hallam argued with Werner, it was rumored that the prisoners had been secretly removed. Prompted by these rumors, Hallam demanded that Werner allow him to tour the jail and prove these accusations to be false. Initially Werner refused, but after more heated debate he agreed to let Hallam enter the jail. After a few minutes, Hallam returned to the entrance and announced that James and Richardson were gone.

Werner, probably hoping that the confirmed absence of the prisoners would convince everyone to leave, was surprised by the crowd's reaction. In total disbelief, the crowd became extremely irate and threatened to destroy the prison. However, they were quickly distracted by the news that Harry Loper assisted on the removal of James and Richardson.

Immediately, the mob's attention shifted from destroying the jail to destroying Loper. The large mob marched toward Loper's restaurant shouting racial insults toward blacks and Loper. Several rioters expressed their desire to lynch Loper for saving the lives of James and Richardson and frustrating their plans to run blacks out of town. As they reached the restaurant, the mob rushed the building, throwing bricks through the window and demolishing Loper's car. Some members of the mob deliberately shot at Loper, but missed him. Others looted the cash register and burned down the building. After the destruction of Loper's restaurant, several people had suffered injuries and at least one person, a nineteen-year-old white man, was dead.

The mob, continuing on their rampage, quickly shifted their focus from Loper and his property, and headed to the Levee and Badlands. Through the years, the Levee and Badlands had gained reputations as heavy crime districts in Springfield. The shops, saloons, apartments, and homes in the area were mostly inhabited by poor blacks and members of Springfield's underclass. Both areas had long been viewed by most of the city's white and black upper- and middle-class residents as a disgrace to the city. Meanwhile, the Levee was actually Springfield's black business district while the Badlands was home to many impoverished blacks that were new to the city. Nonetheless, the mob, bent on destroying the black community, stormed through the Levee and Badlands looting and burning businesses and homes.

Rioters primarily targeted black saloons and barbershops because of their importance within the black community. Black-owned saloons in Springfield, as in most American towns and cities, were not only places of leisure, but often served as the headquarters for many black politicians. Moreover, the black barbershop was not only a place for a haircut and shave, but also a place where blacks could discuss and debate the issues of the day. While the mob destroyed these establishments, they also searched for any black person they could find. Blacks trying to escape were pulled off railcars and beaten while others were chased, caught, and beaten into unconsciousness. Only a few trapped by the mob got away, such as the black man who escaped by slashing people with an open razor as he ran through the crowd.

As the mob continued through the Levee, they were surprised at Eighth and Washington Streets by a group of armed blacks stationed on top of a saloon. The blacks fired into the mob, striking a few rioters and causing others to retreat behind buildings. By strategically placing themselves on top of the building, the black shooters gained an advantage over their attackers. Their elevated post allowed them to act as snipers, taking clear shots at rioters below. Simultaneously, one block away at Seventh and Washington Streets, another group of blacks positioned themselves similarly on top of a house and shot into the mob. The attempts by rioters to fight back by entering the saloon and the house failed as the black snipers forced them to retreat several times. Eventually, both black sniper groups, low on ammunition, escaped unharmed.

Notwithstanding, the mob pushed forward, furthering their work of death and destruction, displacing blacks all over the city. Some blacks sought refuge from their white employers, who hid them in their homes. Others headed to the state armory building or state fairgrounds, where the militia had established refugee camps for the victims. Several left the city seeking shelter and support from relatives or friends in surrounding towns. Many found protection with friends and relatives in a predominantly black enclave on the city's eastside. Still, most decided to stay and protect their homes from the mob.

Blacks living within the northeast and southeast sections of the city established armed patrols in order to keep rioters at bay. Most blacks on the eastside were upper- and middle-class residents who held responsible, good-paying jobs and owned their homes. They had worked hard to establish themselves and refused to let an angry **white mob** destroy their family, property, and future. Black men, women, and children organized a defense tactic that spanned across the neighborhood, placing groups of armed men and women in strategic locations. Some groups maneuvered among houses looking for intruders, and others even rode the railcars making sure rioters were not entering the neighborhood. The organized defense proved to be successful. Rioters never entered these carefully patrolled areas.

In other sections of the city, several black men, sending their families away, stayed at home to protect their property. Scott Burton, a black barber, was one of these men. After sending his family out of town to safety, he armed himself with a shotgun and prepared to defend his home. Ultimately, the mob reached his front porch. Burton was ready for the attack, shooting into the rushing mob and spreading buckshot into the rioters. But Burton's actions were not enough to stop the onslaught. The mob continued to push forward, forcing Burton to escape through a side door. Although quickly surrounded by the mob, he still attempted to get away, but was knocked unconscious. People spat in his face, punching and kicking him. Then someone slipped a rope around his neck and dragged him to the nearest tree. Burton was hoisted up and lynched in front of a saloon.

The rioters began to celebrate by dancing around the dangling corpse while riddling his body with bullets. Finally, the mob's celebration was halted by the arrival of the state militia, which had been called out by Gov. Charles S. Deneen, to end the violence and restore order. Unfortunately for Springfield, the arrival of the militia was too late. When the troops reached the city, most of the damage had been done, and Scott Burton had become the first known lynching death of the riot.

The following day, Saturday, August 15, the downtown area was filled with people wanting to view the destruction. The scene was almost carnival-like as curious sightseers toured the burned-out Levee district and posed for pictures in front of the tree where Burton was hanged. Many ripped bark from the tree to keep as souvenirs while others purchased photos of Mabel Hallam. The city's newspapers included stories of the Burton lynching, the burned-out Levee and Badlands, and the so-called black exodus from the city. In reality, the exodus was temporary, and the number of blacks leaving was much lower than reported. Still, the city's newspapers printed accounts of over 2,000 blacks fleeing Springfield with intentions of never returning. Adding to the stories being written by local reporters, journalists from various state and national news publications arrived in the city to write accounts of Friday night's mayhem.

William English Walling, a social activist from New York, had been in Chicago when he heard about the riot. He traveled from Chicago to Springfield to see the destruction and record people's reactions of the event. After interviewing several white residents, he was appalled by their statements. He concluded that most whites agreed with the actions of the mob. Walling noted how Governor Deneen assumed that the city's blacks were insane for challenging the rioters by fighting back, but Walling insisted that blacks were only defending themselves. Indeed, blacks were defending themselves and continued to prepare for the worst. During the rest of August 15, blacks were threatened and harassed as whites discussed plans for more attacks at nightfall. Many black residents, refusing to be affected by the threats, appealed to family and friends for armed support. Blacks from nearby towns and as far as Chicago arrived in Springfield with guns and ammunition to assist their relatives. Several blacks sent out messages to the white community that they were armed and ready to protect their families and property.

At dusk, gangs of whites began to gather. This time, the groups were smaller in size and more organized in their tactics. They had planned attacks on black homes located in the central western sections of the city. Although their target area was predominantly white, some blacks did live within the vicinity. The mob's movement indicated clearly that they did not intend to attack the heavily armed, predominantly black neighborhoods on the city's eastside. The gangs also had to contend with the militia that exchanged gunfire with rioters often throughout the evening. Yet, the militia was spread out around the city, mainly guarding intersections near the white business district as well as some residential areas. The positioning of the troops allowed rioters to employ hit-and-run tactics on black homes.

Such tactics were used against the home of William Donnegan, an eighty-six-year-old retired shoemaker, who had lived in Springfield for several years. Donnegan, who was married to a white woman, lived on Springfield's predominantly white central westside. As Donnegan and his family hid in the house, the mob stormed their residence, overtaking Donnegan and dragging him to the front yard. As one person slashed his throat, another wrapped some rope around his neck. He was strung up a tree and hanged. The militia, arriving within minutes of the lynching, realized Donnegan was still alive and cut him down. Unfortunately, his slashed throat proved fatal. Donnegan had officially become the second lynching death of the riot. For the rest of the night, small gangs of whites made attempts on black homes, but did not succeed in lynching anyone else. Several blacks who did not trust the militia's protection continued to arm themselves, defending their families and property.

On Sunday, August 16, Governor Deneen began ordering troops from the city. Although small disturbances would continue throughout the week, most state and city leaders agreed that the riot had been contained and further mob action was not probable. Almost immediately, the city began to move forward with the healing process. In the city's black and white churches, pastors stood in front of their congregations preaching repentance and reconciliation. They demanded that people stop the fighting and come together for law and order. From the death tolls and damage reports, everyone seemed to understand that enough harm had been done. The riot's casualty reports revealed more whites than blacks had been killed, with circulating rumors telling how thirty to forty whites had been killed and secretly buried. Within the downtown district, over $100,000 in damage had been inflicted on black and white businesses. Several black businesses had been totally destroyed. Moreover, black homes had been burned, black men lynched, and black people harassed by the militia. During the three days of rioting, the militia had been responsible for imposing curfews on black residents and confiscating their ammunition and guns, effectively disabling blacks from defending themselves against mob attacks. Regardless, it was obvious blacks and whites had suffered during the riot and now both races demanded justice.

By Monday, August 17, the riot was officially over. The city's leadership, embarrassed and outraged, vowed to bring all rioters to justice and restore the fair name of Springfield. White business leaders and professionals met to denounce the actions of the mob and offer resolutions confirming their allegiance to law and order. At the meeting, white leaders vowed to protect all citizens regardless of race or nationality; however, they refused to invite Springfield's black leadership to their meeting. While wanting to participate in the process, the city's black leaders felt slighted. They were left to denounce the riot and present their own resolutions for law and order. Still, many black leaders hoped to form an alliance with the city's white leadership. So, black leaders, within their resolutions, made it a point to announce their support for the actions taken by the city's white leaders.

Within days of the meetings, a special grand jury was impaneled to try members of the mob. With help from the city's white leaders, the assistant state attorney issued 107 indictments. The cases had to be handled in chronological order, so Joe James' case would be tried first.

Joe James, the alleged murderer of Clergy Ballard, attained representation from two black Springfield attorneys, O.V. Royall and A.M. Williams. After James pleaded not guilty, Royall and Williams attempted to move the trial to another county. They believed James could not receive a fair trial in Springfield, especially after the riot. However, their request for a change of venue was denied by Judge James A. Creighton. Creighton reasoned that James would receive a fairer trial in Springfield because, as he believed, the negative sentiments toward blacks within the city had subsided. Yet, minutes before the trial began, a black effigy of James had been strung up in the courthouse yard. Also, a letter was found that threatened more rioting if James did not hang for the murder of Ballard. Contrary to Creighton's rationalization, it was evident that negative feelings toward blacks had not subsided within Springfield. During the trial, the arguments posed by James' attorneys did not convince the jury of his innocence. Consequently, James was convicted of Ballard's murder and sentenced to death by hanging.

The next trial would have been George Richardson's, but the court dismissed his case. In preparation for the hearing, both Mabel Hallam and Richardson were examined by the state board of health's laboratory technician. Hallam's test results showed that she had contracted a sexually transmitted disease, presumably from the attack. The authorities, assuming that Richardson gave her the disease, were astonished by Richardson's test results. His exam showed that he did not have a sexually transmitted disease; therefore, he could not have raped Hallam. With this new evidence, detectives forced Hallam to admit that Richardson was not her attacker. Out of sheer embarrassment, Hallam lied again. She told police that she made a mistake, accusing another black man of the assault. After the police made a few inquiries, they concluded that the new suspect did not exist. Finally, it was revealed that Hallam had fabricated her story. She had actually been having an extramarital affair while her husband was at work, and it was Hallam's lover, a white man, who had assaulted her.

After Richardson's release, the prosecution shifted its focus to the 107 riot indictments. The assistant state attorney planned to present his case against the mobs' ringleaders and then the remaining riot participants. The ringleaders were identified by witnesses as "Bloody" Kate Howard, a proprietor of a brothel that led the mob in the destruction of Loper's restaurant; "Slim" Humphreys, a neighborhood huckster who guided rioters to the homes of blacks, specifically William Donnegan's home; and Abe Raymer, a Jewish man who was accused of lynching Donnegan, participating in the Scott Burton lynching, and helping in the destruction of Loper's restaurant.

Yet, Kate Howard never made it to trial; before the trials began, she committed suicide. Therefore, Abe Raymer would be tried first.

During Raymer's trial, witnesses placed him at the Donnegan lynching. They accused Raymer of slashing Donnegan's throat and lynching him. Although the testimonies against Raymer were damaging, the jury returned a verdict of not guilty. The court's ruling crippled the prosecution's case, setting a precedent for the remaining trials. Out of 107 indictments issued by the state, one person was convicted of theft.

The black community was appalled by the outcome of Raymer's trial and the acquittal of the other rioters, but most white residents, especially the city's white leadership, viewed the rulings as fair. The jury, unabashed by their decision, believed that they had done the right thing by allowing the rioters to go free. Many jurors expressed their approval of the mob's work by commenting how something had to be done to keep blacks in their place. Most jurors agreed that if they had convicted the rioters for their actions, Springfield's blacks would have believed they were as good as white people. The city's black leadership and community were devastated after realizing there would be no justice for them.

On October 23, 1908, Joe James was executed in front of a crowd of 147 witnesses. In a sense, his death symbolized the final chapter of the riot; however, it also symbolized the birth of increased **segregation** for Springfield's black community. Many white Springfield businesses had always practiced segregation, but segregation became a community norm after the riot. Several white businesses and homes that employed blacks fired their black employees. Blacks, who were previously allowed to patronize certain restaurants and theaters, were refused service or were forced to sit in theater balconies, away from white customers. Most blacks were not allowed to purchase homes in certain areas of the city. Some home developments contained specific clauses that disallowed the sale of these properties to blacks. On one hand, some whites were against segregating their places of business or releasing their black employees. On the other hand, serious threats from secret white organizations and other white groups directed at white business owners for employing or selling merchandise to blacks could not be ignored. Out of fear for their lives, these business owners acquiesced to the threats. City officials also felt pressure to obey anonymous threats. Mayor Roy Reece oversaw a city payroll that included an all-black fire department and four black police officers. During the riot, Reece received several intimidating letters urging him to remove all blacks from city employment. Also, several members of the mob had expressed their disgust with Reece for employing blacks. In response to the threats, Reece released the black firefighters from employment. Later, the city's black officers were removed from duty.

Through it all, Springfield's black residents continued to push forward and attempted to rebuild the black community. But the city's black leaders encountered great difficulties in convincing other blacks that Springfield was a good place to live. Unfortunately, segregation and memories of the riot atrocities eventually would take their toll. Before the riot, Springfield's black community was second only to Chicago's black community in population and had one of the fastest-growing black communities in the state. By 1920, Springfield's black population had significantly decreased to levels lower than its 1900 and 1910 population totals.

Conversely, Springfield's white community forged ahead with repairing the city's name and preparing for the centennial celebration of Springfield's favorite son, Abraham Lincoln. February 12, 1909, would mark the 100th anniversary of Lincoln's birth. Locally, many perceived that Springfield's white leadership had fixed the problems associated with the riot, and heaped praise on those white leaders for their immediate calls to action, although no one had been convicted for serious riot offenses.

Nationally, many whites applauded the work of the mob and approved of the outcomes. In contrast, many whites across the country were disgusted by the Springfield riots. Prominent among them was New York socialist and social worker Mary White Ovington. After reading William English Walling's article on the riot, Ovington wanted to prevent further senseless attacks on black communities across the nation. Ovington, along with prominent whites and blacks such as **W.E.B. Du Bois,** met in New York and formed the National Negro Committee, which ultimately changed its name to the **National Association for the Advancement of Colored People (NAACP).**

From the riot aftermath, one can clearly deduce that Springfield's white community blamed the black community for the riot. Most white residents believed that crimes perpetrated by blacks toward whites had gone too far, and the mob's work was justifiable in preventing further black-on-white crime. However, the true reasons for rioting went beyond black criminal activity or, as some scholars believe, the migration of blacks from the south to the north in search of white men's jobs. Actually, the progressive advancement of Springfield's blacks educationally, politically, and economically caused many white residents to express feelings of hatred and resentment toward blacks. Springfield's whites felt that the city's blacks had stepped out of their proper societal place by reaching a certain level of affluence within the community. The acquittal of the riot participants, regardless of the crime, and the increased segregation was a message to Springfield's black community that whites were still in control. *See also* Black Self-Defense; Rape, as Provocation for Lynching; Richardson, George (dates unknown); White Mobs.

Further Readings: Landis, Anthony M. "They Refused to Stay in Their Place: African American Organized Resistance During the Springfield, Illinois, Race Riot of 1908." Master's thesis, Southern Illinois University-Edwardsville, 2002; Senechal, Roberta. *The Sociogenesis of a Race Riot: Springfield, Illinois in 1908*. Urbana: University of Illinois Press, 1990.

Anthony M. Landis

Springfield (Massachusetts) Riot of 1965

The Springfield (Massachusetts) Riot of 1965 was a violent confrontation between blacks and white police officers. The 1960s and 1970s were a time when black riots in cities across the nation were an all-too-common occurrence. These riots, including the Springfield riot in Massachusetts, marked a significant change in the patterns of racial violence. Before the 1960s, whites were the primary instigators of riots. Whites destroyed black property and deliberately assaulted black citizens. Blacks generally targeted property in their own communities rather than individuals. White **racism,** particularly **police brutality** and harassment, was a major factor contributing to riots incited by blacks.

The riot in Springfield, Massachusetts, occurred on July 17, 1965. The incident was brief and did not result in any fatalities or damage to property. However minor the conflict, the riot epitomized the racial tensions between blacks and whites. The riot began when police attempted to break up a fight outside a black nightclub. Police later asserted that they had arrested eighteen of hundreds of black bystanders who threw rocks and bottles at them. Blacks insisted that they acted in self-defense in response to excessive police force. Nevertheless, the police officers were not charged with any crime. The local branches of the **Congress of Racial Equality (CORE)** and the **National Association for the Advancement of Colored People (NAACP)** organized a series of nonviolent protests, such as marches, at City Hall and in the downtown area throughout the summer. They demanded an official investigation of the incident. Their protests brought no change, no justice, and no official action to resolve the tense race relations. *See also* Black Self-Defense; Long Hot Summer Riots, 1965–1967; Nonviolence.

Further Readings: Harris, Fred R., and Roger W. Wilkins. *Quiet Riots: Race and Poverty in the United States: The Kerner Report Twenty Years Later.* New York: Pantheon Books, 1988; Horowitz, Donald L. *The Deadly Ethnic Riot.* Berkeley: University of California Press, 2001.

Gladys L. Knight

Springfield (Ohio) Riot of 1904

The Springfield (Ohio) Riot of 1904 was not an aberration in early-twentieth-century race relations. Not since the **Reconstruction** era (1865–1877) had race riots swept the nation as they did in the first decade of the twentieth century. The Reconstruction riots were confined to the South—**New Orleans,** Louisiana (1866), (1868), (1874); **Memphis,** Tennessee (1866); and Meridian (1870), Vicksburg (1874), and Yazoo City, Mississippi (1875). However, the turn of the twentieth century saw racial violence against blacks spread north to cities where many African Americans migrated in search of economic, social, and political opportunities.

Springfield, Ohio, was one city where blacks had established a vibrant community in the section of town known as the Levee. Many of the black industrial workers and day laborers resided in this section of Springfield, which included a black business sector and informal economy (prostitution, barrooms, and gambling parlors).

On March 6, 1904, an African American resident of Springfield, Richard Dixon (also reported as Richard Dickerson) went to the Jones hotel in the Levee to retrieve his clothes from a woman, Anna (a.k.a. Mamie) Corbin, who was purported to be his mistress. Dixon requested that a police officer, Charles Collis, accompany him to Corbin's room to reclaim his clothes. Various newspaper sources reported that Dixon and Corbin quarreled until Dixon took out a gun and shot the woman. The police officer attempted to subdue Dixon, only to be shot four times by the assailant. Dixon escaped and immediately turned himself in at police headquarters.

When news of the shooting and death of the white police officer reached the wider Springfield community, white men and boys gathered at the jail that next evening. Initially, some 300 male whites stood outside the jail demanding the release of Dixon, shouting "lynch the nigger." At one point, the police had dispersed the crowd, but a small group of men diverted police attention so that some 250 men could storm the jail and kidnap Dixon. An estimated mob of 2,000 to 2,500 men blocked the prison gates outside, preventing the police force from protecting Dixon. The white men took Dixon away and lynched him.

When news of the **lynching** reached the black community, African Americans prepared to defend themselves, as rumors circulated that the mob intended to invade the Levee. Springfield's Mayor G.J. Bowlus called Gov. Myron T. Herrick to send troops to subdue the potential rioters. Indeed, on March 9, some 2,000 white men shot bullets into the Levee and then set it ablaze, burning down mostly black-owned homes and businesses. Some newspaper sources numbered the mob that invaded the levee at 5,000. Springfield, Ohio, would experience another race riot in 1906.

Springfield was not the first city to experience race riots in the opening years of the new century. New Orleans and **New York City** both erupted in racial violence in 1900. During the same year as the second Springfield riot, "race wars" broke out in **Atlanta,** Georgia; **Greensburg,** Indiana; and **Brownsville,** Texas. In 1908, the **Springfield,** Illinois, race riot would lead to the creation of the **National Association for the Advancement of Colored People (NAACP).** All these riots had one element in common—white fear of a growing black presence.

Further Readings: Capeci, Dominic J., Jr., and Jack C. Knight. "Reckoning with Violence: W.E.B. Du Bois and the 1906 Atlanta Race Riot." *The Journal of Southern History* 62 (1996): 165–180; Murray, Percy E. "Harry C. Smith-Joseph Foraker Alliance: Coalition Politics in Ohio." *The Journal of Negro History* 68 (1983): 171–184.

Jeannette Eileen Jones

Strange Fruit (Allan, c. 1937)

In 1939, Abel Meeropol presented a song to blues and jazz performer **Billie Holiday** that he wrote. The song was titled *Strange Fruit*. Meeropol, a Jewish high school teacher and union activist from the Bronx, wrote the song to protest the **lynching** of black southerners and asked Holiday to perform his piece. She agreed, and her haunting version of *Strange Fruit* became an anthem against **racism** that the British magazine *Q* called "one of the ten songs that changed the world" (January 2003). Jazz writer Leonard Feather deemed *Strange Fruit* "the first significant protest in words and music, the first unmuted cry against racism," while record producer Ahmet

Ertegun declared it "a declaration of war" and "the beginning of the civil rights movement" (Margolick, 14, 10). In short, few songs have had the impact on race relations that *Strange Fruit* continues to possess.

The "strange fruit hanging from the poplar trees" that Meeropol referred to were African Americans who hanged after their execution at the hands of a lynch mob. Although the most active period of lynching in American history had passed, the practice continued to plague the south when Meeropol, who used the pseudonym Lewis Allan, wrote *Strange Fruit* in the mid-1930s. He wanted to bring attention to this injustice, in hopes that the federal government would pass a national anti-lynching law. Meeropol's powerful prose contrasted the horrors of lynching with the gentility of the "gallant south." A "pastoral scene" of "poplar trees" could not hide "the bulging eyes and the twisted mouth" of "black bodies swinging in the southern breeze." The song ended with the profound line, "Here is a strange and bitter crop."

Holiday first performed *Strange Fruit* at New York's only integrated nightclub, Café Society. When the song ended, Holiday later commented that "There wasn't even a patter of applause when I finished. Then a lone person began to clap nervously. Then suddenly everyone was clapping" (Margolick, 9). The song proved so powerful that she closed all performances with *Strange Fruit*. Word of the provocative song quickly spread throughout the city's liberal white elite, and Café Society mentioned the piece in its advertisements to attract customers. The *New York Post* reviewed Holiday's performance of *Strange Fruit* and said, "If the anger of the exploited ever mounts high enough in the South, it now has its Marseillaise" (Margolick, 62).

The song was so intense, its topic so unpleasant, that white nightclub patrons sometimes assaulted Holiday for performing *Strange Fruit*. Some theater owners prohibited her from including the song in her act, and the BBC and several American radio stations refused to play the record. Even Holiday's label, Columbia Records, refused to record the song. It was eventually produced and marketed by the smaller Commodore Records company. There is little evidence that performances including *Strange Fruit* ignited racially motivated riots. But the potential for violence existed every time Holiday performed the inflammatory song because of the genuine emotions, both positive and negative, it evoked. For instance, she told one newspaper that she was chased out of Mobile, Alabama, for singing *Strange Fruit*, but provided few details. Several stories also circulated of southern jukeboxes that were demolished because the tune appeared on their playlists.

The power *Strange Fruit* possesses is evident in the numerous artists who have performed the song. Josh White, Sidney Bichet, Tori Amos, Cassandra Wilson, Pete Seeger, Ella Fitzgerald, Lou Rawls, Diana Ross, Sting, and UB-40, among others, have recorded their version of the piece. The song still evokes the horrors of late-nineteenth and twentieth-century lynchings that took place in the United States, but it is also used to protest social injustices on a much broader scale. The fact, however, that *Strange Fruit* exposed the inhumanity of lynchings in such a troubling and intense manner made it both an anthem of the national anti-lynching movement and a timeless part of American popular culture.

Further Readings: Holiday, Billie, with William Dufty. *Lady Sings the Blues*. Garden City, NY: Doubleday & Company, 1956/1992; Margolick, David. *Strange Fruit: Billie Holiday, Café Society, and the Early Cry for Civil Rights*. Philadelphia: Running Press, 2000; Ward, Geoffrey C., and Ken Burns. *Jazz: A History of America's Music*. New York: Knopf, 2000.

J. Michael Butler

Student Nonviolent Coordinating Committee (SNCC)

The Student Nonviolent Coordinating Committee (SNCC) was a civil rights organization founded in 1960 by African American college students committed to the abolition of **segregation** and seeking to encourage African Americans to become more politically active in the **civil rights movement.** On February 1, 1960, four African American students entered the Woolworth Store on South Elm Street in Greensboro, North Carolina, and sat down at the counter reserved for whites only, and they refused to leave until they were served. The four students—Franklin McCain, Joseph McNeil, Ezell Blair, Jr., and David Richmond—were all freshman from North Carolina Agricultural and Technical State University. The waitress and manager refused to serve them, and the restaurant closed early to be rid of the students. Expecting to be beaten and arrested, all four students walked out of Woolworth's unharmed. Whether they realized it or not, their actions became the catalyst that helped change racial relations in the South because almost immediately, other students, black and white, participated in nonviolent sit-ins and direct-action demonstrations that challenged segregation not only in North Carolina but in fifty-four cities in nine states throughout the South.

Ella Josephine Baker (1903–1986) was one of those individuals. A former member of the **Southern Christian Leadership Conference (SCLC)** under the guidance of Dr. **Martin Luther King, Jr.,** Baker left SCLC after the Greensboro sit-ins. She was inspired by the courage of the student activists and wanted to do something to help further their cause. She organized a meeting at Shaw University in Raleigh, North Carolina, for student leaders, including representatives from SCLC, the **National Association for the Advancement of Colored People (NAACP),** and the **Congress of Racial Equality (CORE).** From that meeting, SNCC was born. Both SCLC and the NAACP wanted students to become part of their larger, more established organizations, but Ella Baker insisted that the students remain independent.

SNCC's significance to the civil rights movement cannot be overestimated, not only because of its myriad achievements, inventiveness, and determination in the struggle against segregation, but also because of the impressive array of young activists, like Julian Bond, who passed through its ranks. These men and women challenged the injustices, degradation, and violence that destroyed and distorted the hopes and dreams of generations of Americans, both black and white.

While Ella Baker preferred to remain in the background, quietly encouraging young activists, Fannie Lou Hamer (1917–1977), SNCC field secretary, took an active part in voter registration in the South. Hamer also helped found the Mississippi Freedom Democratic Party (MFDP) in 1964, which challenged the all-white Mississippi delegation to the Democratic National Convention. Diane Nash (1938–) and Ruby Doris Smith-Robinson (1942–1967) were SNCC members who participated in a demonstration at Friendship Junior College in Rock Hill, South Carolina, where the concept of *jail-no-bail* was first introduced. After being arrested, protesters refused to pay their fines or bail, preferring to serve their sentences instead.

Nash also participated in the **Freedom Rides.** In May 1961, members of SNCC and CORE organized bus trips throughout the South in an effort to test compliance of the Supreme Court ruling in *Boynton v. Virginia* (1960), which declared segregation in interstate transportation unconstitutional. Thirteen passengers, seven African Americans and six whites, who became known as freedom riders, boarded two buses, Greyhound and Trailways, in Washington, D.C., with the intent of traveling into the Deep South. The riders encountered few problems as they traveled through Virginia, North Carolina, and Georgia. However, in Rock Hill, South Carolina, John Lewis and another rider were beaten and kicked. In Anniston, Alabama, a group of white men, including members of the **Ku Klux Klan (KKK),** attacked the passengers and burned their bus. The riders ended their protest in Birmingham, Alabama, unable to find a driver willing to continue the trip. It was at this point that Diane Nash recruited another group of freedom riders to complete the trip. They too were victims of violence, including being arrested for entering a Whites Only waiting room. But this second venture attracted national attention, including that of Attorney General **Robert F. Kennedy.** Ultimately, the riders were forced to end their journey on the road. Those who wanted to complete the trip to New Orleans had to get there by plane.

Many other notable African Americans joined the ranks of SNCC. Marion Barry was the first chairperson of SNCC and established its headquarters in Atlanta, Georgia. Following Barry's departure, Charles McDew, a founding member of SNCC, was elected chairperson (1961–1963). He was replaced by John Lewis, one of the most influential members of SNCC. His influence was not only important inside SNCC but throughout the civil rights movement as a whole. He helped plan the March on Washington (1963), where Martin Luther King, Jr., made his famous "I Have a Dream" speech before a crowd of over 250,000 people. Lewis was also one of the keynote speakers. One of the most memorable moments in Lewis' career as a civil rights activist occurred in 1965 when he marched with King and 525 marchers from Selma to Montgomery, Alabama, in an effort to secure voting rights for African Americans. When they attempted to cross the Pettus Bridge in Selma, Alabama, the marchers were attacked and beaten by state troopers. The attack was so vicious that the incident became known as **Bloody Sunday.**

The five years between 1963 and 1968 were pivotal years for the members of SNCC. From its inception, SNCC was committed to the principles of **nonviolence.** The articles of the founding mission statement emphasized that the philosophical and religious principles of nonviolence would serve as the foundation of the organization's purpose, belief, and action. The founding members chose nonviolence as their sole course of action because they believed nonviolence created an atmosphere of reconciliation and justice. Nonviolence would be the weapon they would use to combat the violence of segregation and **racism** and achieve their ultimate goal of a racially integrated society based on the principles of justice and equality.

But the events of the mid-1960s challenged their commitment. It became increasingly difficult to practice nonviolence in a country that was being consumed by violence, and the struggle within the ranks of SNCC to come to terms with this paradox created dissension and conflict. It reached a point where every victory became bittersweet and every triumph was overshadowed by a sense of loss and defeat. Under these circumstances, it is a testimony of the strength and commitment of the individual members that they continued the struggle for civil rights. However, even though the struggle continued, many activists, not only within SNCC, but in the civil rights movement as a whole, began to contemplate more radical, militant, and nationalist or race-conscious approaches. The events of 1963 alerted many members of the civil rights movement that nonviolence might not be as effective a strategy as it was in the early part of 1960s during sit-in demonstrations. For example, on August 28, 1963, the March on Washington was an undisputed triumph and seemed to mark a positive turning point in the civil rights struggle. However, the murder of **Medgar Evers** on June 11, 1963, seemed to cast an ominous shadow over the events that took place in Washington, D.C. (see **Evers, Medgar, Assassination of**). And, coincidentally, the death of **W.E.B. Du Bois** on the eve of the March on Washington seemed equally ill-omened. To add to this sense of loss and triumph, on Sunday, September 15, 1963, a bomb exploded at the Sixteenth Street Baptist Church killing four African American girls—Carol Denise McNair, Cynthia Wesley, Carole Robertson, and Addie Mae Collins. Finally, President **John F. Kennedy** was assassinated on November 22, 1963.

The following year brought even more changes for SNCC. On July 2, President Lyndon B. Johnson signed into law the **Civil Rights Act of 1964.** In a passage that recalled the Greensboro sit-ins, the act declared the following:

> All persons shall be entitled to the full and equal enjoyment of the goods, services, facilities, privileges, advantages, and accommodations of any public accommodation . . . without discrimination or segregation on the ground of race, color, religion, or national origins. (Title II, Sec. 201, [a])

On July 18, 1964, a riot broke out in Harlem, a historic African American community in New York City. James Powell, a young African American, was fatally wounded by a white police officer. Members of CORE organized a peaceful protest but tempers flared and the demonstration turned violent. The riot raged two nights before erupting in the Bedford-Stuyvesant neighborhood in Brooklyn. More than just calling the philosophy of nonviolence into question, the Harlem riot foreshadowed insurrections, like the Watts (see **Los Angeles [California] Riot of 1965**) riot, which would erupt in African American communities throughout the late 1960s.

Harlem was not the only place where violence erupted. During the summer of 1964, thousand of activists came to Mississippi to participate in an intensive voter registration drive. It was called **Freedom Summer** and was, to a large extent, the brainchild of Robert Parris Moses. He had been one of the first SNCC workers to register black voters in Mississippi. Moses had also helped found the Council of Federated Organizations (COFO), a coalition of several civil rights organizations, including SNCC, the NAACP, and CORE. Because of the intensity of the project, Freedom Summer was considered to be one of the major milestones of the civil rights movement. Besides voter registration, Freedom Summer volunteers also established numerous Freedom Schools throughout the state in an effort to address some of the racial inequalities inherent in the educational system. Although the work was rewarding, Freedom Summer activists became targets for the police and white supremacists. Black churches, homes, and businesses were firebombed (see **Black Church Arsons**). Black and white volunteers were arrested and beaten by **white mobs** and the police (see **Police Brutality**).

But the tragic event that captured the attention of the nation was the murder of three Freedom Summer activists. On June 21, James Earl Chaney (1943–1964), Andrew Goodman (1943–1964), and Michael Schwerner (1939–1964) were arrested in Philadelphia, Mississippi. Six weeks later their bodies were discovered under a dam. Following the murders, many of the activists involved in the Freedom Summer were convinced that nonviolence was not the answer. Many members of SNCC voiced the opinion that workers should carry weapons. This shift away from the philosophy of nonviolence continued. During the Los Angeles (California) Riots of 1965, many members declared that the time had come for blacks to seize power and abandon their old policy of nonviolence. By May 1966, the transformation was complete. John Lewis, still an advocate of nonviolence, was replaced as chairperson of SNCC by **Stokely Carmichael** (Kwame Ture), who called for offensive violence to overthrow oppression. His rallying call was **Black Power** and **black self-defense.** SNCC severed ties with its white supporters and several civil rights organizations like SCLC and the NAACP. By 1967, SNCC began to suffer major internal problems. Its staff and membership dwindled and so did its funding. In June 1967, Carmichael left SNCC and became a member of the **Black Panther Party (BPP).** He was replaced by **H. Rap Brown,** who renamed the organization the Student National Coordinating Committee, deleting the word *nonviolent*. During the summer of 1967, Brown was arrested for inciting a riot. In May 1968, he left SNCC because of his legal problems. SNCC continued to function into the early 1970s, but it no longer possessed the power and enthusiasm of the student movement that Ella Baker helped found in 1960 during the Greensboro, North Carolina, sit-ins. *See also* Black Nationalism.

Further Readings: Carmichael, Stokely, with Ekwueme Michael Thelwell. *Ready for Revolution: The Life and Struggles of Stokely Carmichael (Kwame Ture)*. New York: Scribner, 2003; Carson, Clayborne. *In Struggle: SNCC and the Black Awakening of the 1960s*. Cambridge, MA: Harvard University Press, 1981, 1995; Lee, Chana Kai. *For Freedom's Sake: The Life of Fannie Lou Hamer*. Women in American History. Chicago: University of Illinois Press, 2000; Ransby, Barbara. *Ella Baker and the Black Freedom Movement: A Radical Democratic Vision*. Gender and American Culture. Chapel Hill: University of North Carolina Press, 2003.

John G. Hall

Sweet, Ossian H. (1894–1960)

Dr. Ossian Sweet, a former resident of Florida, migrated to Detroit during the **Great Migration** of African Americans from the South to major northern industrial cities in the United States (1910–1920s). His purchase of a home confronted racial **segregation** in Detroit, Michigan, and answered the question of whether an African American had the right to defend his or her property.

Most Detroit residents of apparent African American descent were forced to reside in an eastside location known as Paradise Valley. In May 1925, Dr. Ossian Sweet made arrangements to purchase 2905 Garland Street, a single home bungalow in what appeared to be an all-white eastside neighborhood in Detroit, Michigan. The immediate area included apartments, grocery store, and an elementary school. Sweet made himself visible as he inspected the property and its surroundings. The home's previous owners, Ed and Marie Smith, had occupied the Garland home for two years. Ed Smith was an African American with a light complexion and apparently the neighborhood Negro haters overlooked or were ignorant of his lineage. Nevertheless, once sale of the Garland house was known, Marie Smith received a threat for selling the house and was told that the caller would get Sweet as well.

Sweet graduated from Wilberforce College, followed by Howard University School of Medicine. Raised in a politically conscious and hardworking family with at least nine siblings, Ossian Sweet's father, Henry Sweet, believed in self-sufficiency for his sons. Consequently, Ossian Sweet financed his own education. After graduating with his medical degree in 1922, Sweet married Gladys Mitchell and both traveled to North Africa and Europe—Germany, France, Austria, Vienna, and England—where he received further specialized medical training. Sweet chose to practice gynecology and obstetrics at Detroit's progressive New Negro hospital, Dunbar Memorial Hospital (named after poet and writer Paul Laurence Dunbar). The Sweets had one child, Marguerite Iva Sweet, their daughter.

In 1925, the Detroit, Michigan, arm of the **Ku Klux Klan (KKK)** was large and active. In the 1923 Detroit mayoral election, KKK candidate Charles Bowles narrowly lost to John Smith. Commonly, during 1925, mobs of racist whites quickly formed to keep African Americans from integrating neighborhoods. On June 23, 1925, Dr. Alexander Turner, along with his wife and mother-in-law, were moving into their home on Spokane Street when they were met by the Tireman Avenue Improvement Association—hundreds of neighbors who gathered in front of them with rocks, potatoes, and garbage to throw at Turner's westside home. At gunpoint, two men forced Turner to sign his deed over to them and, with the help of the police, had the Turner family escorted from the premises. One block away from the *de facto* designated Negro neighborhood, Vollington Bristol constructed and moved into his apartment building on July 7, 1925, and refused to adjust his rent and choice of who could rent an apartment. Several days of violence ensued. On June 10, 1925, John Fletcher was preparing to have dinner with his wife and two children when a mob of neighbors began attacking the house. Two shots were fired from the Fletcher home, injuring a youth. Fletcher was jailed for an evening and the family later fled their home. Hence, Dr. Sweet knew what to expect from an angry **white mob** when he moved into his Garland home.

Sweet's pending move to Garland Street encouraged the formation of the Waterworks Park Improvement Association, which held at least one meeting at Howe Elementary School (named for abolitionist and composer of the *Battle Hymn of the Republic,* Julia Ward Howe), located across the street from Sweet's home. Sweet notified the Detroit Police Department of his intention to move into his home. On September 8, 1925, Dr. Sweet and his family and friends moved in their Garland home. On their first evening, it is estimated that a group of 500 to 800 individuals, led by the Waterworks Park Improvement Association, gathered in front of the Sweet home.

On September 9, 1925, another large crowd gathered and some individuals began chucking rocks into 2905 Garland. About 8:30 P.M., fearful occupants fired shots from the upper level of the home. Leon Breiner was shot and killed, and another neighbor, Eric Houghberg, was shot in the leg. Eleven occupants were taken into custody, including Gladys Sweet, and were charged with first-degree murder.

The **National Association for the Advancement of Colored People (NAACP)** hired famed attorney Clarence Darrow, assisted by Arthur Garfield Hays, to defend the eleven defendants. Judge Frank Murphy allowed Gladys Sweet to be released on bail on October 2, 1925. The other ten defendants were Dr. Ossian Sweet, Henry Sweet, Dr. Otis Sweet, William E. Davis, John Latting, Joe Mack, Leonard Morris, Morris Murray, Charles Wasington, and Hewitt Watson. On November 27, 1925, Judge Frank Murphy declared a mistrial and dismissed the jury when they were unable to reach a verdict after forty-six hours of deliberation. The defendants were released on bail in December 1925.

Henry Sweet fired the gun that killed Breiner. The trial, *Michigan v. Sweet* began on April 13, 1926. On May 13, 1926, after four hours of deliberation, Henry Sweet was found not guilty. Over a year later, in July 1927, the prosecutor dismissed all charges against the remaining defendants. The Sweet case reinforced the right of an African American to self-defense.

Tuberculosis claimed the lives of Sweet's daughter in 1926 and his wife in 1928. Dr. Sweet was unable to sell his home until 1944. He committed suicide on March 19, 1960. The Sweet home is listed in the *National Register of Historic Places. See also* Detroit (Michigan) Riot of 1943.

Further Readings: Boyle, Kevin. *Arc of Justice: A Saga of Race, Civil Rights, and Murder in the Jazz Age*. New York: Henry Holt, 2004; Vine, Phyllis. *One Man's Castle: Clarence Darrow in Defense of the American Dream*. New York: Amistad, 2004.

Regina V. Jones

T

Tampa (Florida) Riots of 1987

In Tampa, Florida, the months of February to April 1987 brought several nights of violence, citizens in fear, and heightened tension between police and citizens. Between November 1986 and April 1987, four black men died at the hands of white Tampa police. These incidents heightened already strained tensions between black citizens of Tampa and local police, and served as the impetus for angry citizens to take to the streets throwing rocks and bottles. Combined, these violent outbreaks are called the Tampa Riots of 1987.

Rioting began the night of February 19, when a white police officer used a controversial chokehold technique to subdue Melvin Eugene Hair, a black man in custody. As a result, Hair died of suffocation. On the same night, local television news stations reported the outcome of a city attorney's office investigation into the arrest of Dwight Gooden, star pitcher for the New York Mets and prominent black citizen of Tampa. Gooden was arrested the previous December after having been stopped for a traffic violation that escalated into a fight. As a result, Gooden was left visibly swollen and bruised. The city attorney's report blamed Gooden for starting the fight with police.

Both of these incidents came on the heels of the death of Franklin A. Lewis, a sixteen-year-old who was shot by police after allegedly shooting a gun into a crowd. The official investigative report following Lewis' death exonerated the officers, reporting that they had used necessary force to subdue their suspect. However, Tampa's black citizenry was not satisfied with this account, suspicious that no gun was found on Lewis' body. Many blacks in Tampa were becoming more and more incensed, alleging that police targeted them specifically, viewing them as criminals to be subdued and controlled rather than citizens to be protected. In that vein, they charged that police took liberties with young black men especially, brutalizing them without repercussion.

The news of Hair's death, coupled with the city attorney's report that reflected unfavorably on Gooden, was incendiary. Several black youths gathered outside, discussing the incidents. As they discussed the incidents, their discontent grew, and one of them set fire to a dumpster. That drew a crowd, which then began to throw bottles and rocks. The violence continued for the next three days, causing police to cordon off a section of the city where even media were not allowed. Similar incidents continued sporadically through April of that year, sparked by continuing tensions with police. Two more black men died at the hands of white police officers, inciting the city's youth, who were already tense and angry. During waves of violence, rioters threw bottles and rocks at police, whites driving through the neighborhood, and the media.

By April, Tampa was a hotbed of anger, frustration, and tension. The waves of violence ended, leaving in their wake an unmistakable outcry from the black citizens of Tampa, who resented the treatment they were receiving from the police. Response was swift—there were several **Federal Bureau of Investigation (FBI)** investigations into police department practices, Tampa's mayor pushed to substantially increase the number of black police officers on the force, and several task forces and city council committees were formed to look into racial tensions in the city. Both the police force and the local government pursued the reduction of **police brutality** and racial profiling.

Because police practices received the lion's share of attention and funding, the deeper, less visible issues received considerably less attention. By and large, the riots occurred in Tampa's College Hill and Ponce de Leon neighborhoods, two extremely impoverished sections of the city that are home to the majority of Tampa's public housing projects. In these areas, the overarching issues of extreme **poverty**, dwindling opportunities for social and economic growth, and insufficient housing fueled residents' unrest. For example, cuts in social programming left the housing authority grossly underfunded. While each apartment cost an average of $175 per month to maintain, the housing authority received less than $100 per month for each apartment, rendering adequate maintenance impossible. These same funding cuts resulted in decreased grant and loan programs in black communities. And those who did secure funding found it difficult to then obtain insurance. Such conditions, as outgrowths of poverty, have been shown to be predictors of high crime rates and citizen frustration.

Local authorities, however, responded with less action around the issues of poverty than around police practices. Although a summer job placement program for the community's youth was formed, and a task force was created to investigate community needs, this was considerably less programming than was set up for the Tampa Police Department. By giving less attention to the larger issues of poverty and economic growth for residents of these neighborhoods, the city was ineffective in addressing the very conditions that made it necessary for the police to be such a strong force in the affected neighborhoods. Indeed, the College Hill and Ponce de Leon neighborhoods continue to struggle with high poverty rates, high crime rates, and tension with the police.

Further Readings: Federal Emergency Management Agency and United States Fire Administration. "Report of the Joint Fire/Police Task Force on Civil Unrest:

Recommendations for Organization and Operation during Civil Disturbance." Publication No. FA-142. 1994. Retrieved from www.usfa.fema.gov/downloads/pdf/publications/fa-142.pdf; Waddington, David. *Contemporary Issues in Public Disorder: A Comparative and Historical Approach*. London: Routledge, 2001.

Stephanie Beard

Tennessee *See* Chattanooga (Tennessee) Riot of 1906; Knoxville (Tennessee) Riot of 1919; Memphis (Tennessee) Riot of 1866

Terrell, Mary Church (1863–1954)

Mary Church Terrell was a lecturer, political activist, and educator during the tumultuous **Jim Crow** era in the United States. As a black woman, Terrell enjoyed privileges and advantages not available to most blacks. Hers was a life that defied the constraints imposed by society on her race and gender. However, the **lynching** of a close friend propelled Terrell to relinquish the isolation of her immediate world and commit her life to public activism. Among the most critical issues confronted by Terrell were violence against blacks, **segregation**, and women's suffrage.

Mary Eliza Church was born free to former slaves on September 23, 1863, in Memphis, Tennessee, during the Civil War. On January 1, 1863, Abraham Lincoln issued the Emancipation Proclamation, which abolished slavery. While blacks were in the throes of adjusting to post-slavery life during **Reconstruction**, Mary was raised in the comfort, security, and safety of her parents' home. Mary's parents instilled in her the importance of education. Rather than send her to a segregated school, they enrolled her in the Antioch College Model School. Although she lived during this time with the Hunsters, a black family, she was the only black in her class. Two years later, she enrolled in a local public school. During this period, white southerners were seizing back political control across the South by violently assaulting both black and white opposition and engaging in other unscrupulous tactics. By 1877, all the southern states were under the tyrannical rule of the white Democrats. Once in power, they dismantled the rights and freedoms blacks had gained during Reconstruction. In their attempt to maintain **white supremacy**, whites instigated riots, and lynched, beat, and terrorized blacks on a regular basis. The federal government did nothing to relieve or remedy the situation.

In the midst of this turmoil, Mary graduated from a public high school and, afterward, attended Oberlin College, one of the few integrated universities at that time. Few women pursued higher education in that era. The few black women who attended college generally went to the historically black colleges that had been established during Reconstruction. Women who went to college usually did not aspire to careers. More often than not, women were denied employment and were restricted to being wives and homemakers. For women, education was a symbol of status within elite society, and only a few years of college were obligatory. Mary, on the other hand, earned a bachelor's degree in classics. She then took a teaching position at Wilberforce College in Ohio, while simultaneously pursuing a

Mary Church Terrell, circa 1890. Courtesy of the Library of Congress.

master's degree. Named after the abolitionist William Wilberforce, this college was the first of its kind to be owned and operated by blacks. Her father was devastated; like most of society, Mary's father believed her place was to marry and start a family. Mary's decision caused a rift with her father that lasted several years.

While Mary's professional career peaked, conditions in the South, and in the North to a lesser degree, steadily worsened. In the absence of slavery, whites found other ways to maintain social control. **White mobs** hunted down blacks who were purported to have committed crimes against white women or who challenged the laws of **racial etiquette**. Often, no reason was needed at all. Black men of all ages were the common target, and lynching was the common method of execution. Lynching was often accompanied by burning, maiming, or castrating the victim. Whites sometimes kept body parts for souvenirs. Lynching occurred without judge, jury, or trial, whether in the privacy of the mob or before a crowd ranting its encouragement. These executions often preceded unbridled violence against unsuspecting blacks and their communities. Whites were rarely, if ever, charged and punished for their crimes.

In 1886, as violence raged in the South and in the North, and discriminatory laws were established across the nation, Mary accepted another teaching position at the Colored High School in Washington, D.C. During this period, Washington had a large community of progressive and well-to-do blacks. Although they led more privileged lives than the majority of blacks, they were, as a whole, excluded from mainstream society and confined behind the color line of segregation and discrimination. At the high school, Mary met her soon-to-be husband, Robert Heberton Terrell, a graduate of Harvard University. In 1901, Terrell was appointed justice of the peace by President Theodore Roosevelt. The following year, he was appointed to the Washington, D.C., Municipal Court, the first black to hold that position.

On earning her master's degree, Mary traveled to Europe, as was the practice of both the white and black elite. She became fluent in French, German, and Italian. Two years later, in 1891, she returned and married Robert Terrell in Memphis, Tennessee. Under her new name, Mary Church Terrell, she returned to Washington, D.C., with her husband. She willingly surrendered her career and appeared to prepare for the life that her father had once envisioned. But high-society wives who had forgone professional careers were often privately active in meaningful philanthropic societies, organizations, and activities. Terrell might well have been one of them, but prompted by a personal tragedy, she did not follow this type of quiet activism.

In 1892, Terrell was pregnant with her first child when she heard the news that her friend from Memphis, Tennessee, Tom Moss, had been lynched by whites who were jealous of the success of his grocery store. Terrell was devastated. She was again grief-stricken when her baby died a few days after birth. To come to terms with the loss of the baby, she reasoned to herself that it might have been marred by her grief and mental preoccupation with the violent death of Moss. In the same year, Terrell turned her sorrow into activism. She spearheaded a campaign against lynching and eventually collaborated with Frederick Douglass. Together, they went to Washington, D.C., to galvanize support from President Benjamin Harrison, but to no avail.

Undeterred, Terrell pursued another issue—women's suffrage. She cofounded and was the president of the Colored Women's League. In 1896, the league joined with other black women's organizations to become the **National Association of Colored Women (NACW)**. Terrell was the founder and president of this association until 1904. In 1898, the year she gave birth to a daughter named Phyllis, Terrell was appointed honorary president for life. In 1905, she adopted a niece named Terrell Church.

The Colored Women's League went beyond working toward women's suffrage. It also established daycare centers for black children of working mothers and campaigned for improved working conditions for black women. It also fought for equal rights for blacks, and the elimination of Jim Crow laws. Despite their wealth, the accolades, and degrees, the black elite suffered greatly at the expense of Jim Crow legislation. Terrell herself had once, in her youth, challenged Jim Crow. Terrell's father had purchased a first-class seat for her, although Jim Crow sent segregated blacks to the second-class seats. Nevertheless, Terrell was allowed to keep her seat when she told the conductor that her father would sue the railroad if he made her move.

From 1892 to 1954, Terrell lectured on social and racial issues in the United States and abroad. During one presentation at the International Congress of Women in Berlin, Germany, she spoke in German, French, and English. In 1895, Terrell became the first black woman to be elected to the District of Columbia Board of Education. She was a member of the board from 1895 to 1901, and again from 1906 to 1911. Terrell's clout grew quickly, as did her network of influential friends. She befriended and collaborated with giants, such as **Booker T. Washington**, Mary McLeod Bethune, and Susan B. Anthony. In 1901, **W.E.B. Du Bois** invited her to become a charter member of the **National Association for the Advancement of Colored People (NAACP)**. She later founded the NAACP's Executive Committee and was a member of a group that investigated police harassment against blacks. She was also a member of Carter G. Woodson's Association for the Study of Negro Life and History. Terrell maintained her interests in intellectual pursuits by joining the Bethel Literary and Historical Association.

Meanwhile, as violence continued unabated across the nation, Terrell used her influence to champion the rights of the victims of violence and discrimination. She did not censor her opinions, no matter how powerful her opponents were. In 1904, Terrell wrote one of many articles to protest violence—lynching in particular—against blacks. In this article, she discussed the history of violence against blacks since the time of slavery, sparing no details. She wrote boldly that **racism** and lawlessness, not justice, were the real motivation behind the grievous executions of blacks. She also exposed the misconception that violence was limited to the South, proving that it was quickly intensifying across the nation.

Shortly after the **Brownsville (Texas) Riot of 1906**, she openly condemned President Theodore Roosevelt for dismissing three companies of black men from the Army without due process and without sufficient proof of involvement. The 167 black men were accused of having instigated a shoot-out on August 14 that injured a policeman and a resident. These men were also "barred from rejoining the military and from government employment, and were denied veterans' pensions or benefits" (Hine et al., 344). Nothing was done to the whites and Mexicans who had harassed and attacked the black soldiers prior to the riot.

Terrell continued to challenge lynching, as well as other adverse conditions besetting blacks, particularly in the South, such as chain gangs, peonage, and **disenfranchisement**. In 1920, Terrell's responsibilities expanded to include the supervision of all campaigns among black women on the East Coast.

Despite Terrell's active schedule, she and her husband made time to indulge in the pleasantries of the black upper class. Washington, D.C., was the dwelling place of some of the most prominent elite black families. Like the white upper class, blacks enjoyed the world of culture and a lavish lifestyle. The Terrells "attended balls, concerts, and parties, traveled extensively, and belonged to Washington's most exclusive black congregation, the Lincoln Temple Congregational Church, and she was active in Delta Sigma Theta sorority" (Hine et al., 372). In 1936, the Terrells were one of the first black families to move to LeDroit Park, which was originally an all-white suburb. Their house still stands today.

The 1940s and 1950s remained rigorous for Mary Church Terrell. In 1940, she wrote an autobiography titled *A Colored Woman in a White World*. In 1949, she chaired the Coordinating Committee for the Enforcement of District of Columbia Anti-Discrimination Laws. In the following year, she collaborated with a group of other blacks to challenge racial segregation. On February 28, they entered Thompson Restaurant, which was designated for whites only, to test the anti-discrimination laws that had been established in 1872 and 1873. When Terrell's group was denied service, they filed a lawsuit. The case, *District of Columbia v. John R. Thompson Co.*, went to the U.S. Supreme Court, where Terrell testified. While waiting for a decision, Terrell led and participated in several types of nonviolent protests that were commonly used in the **civil rights movement**, such as boycotts, picketing, and sit-ins. On June 8, 1953, the court ruled that segregated eating places in Washington, D.C., were unconstitutional. Other victories, such as the *Brown v. Board of Education* (1954) ruling, which eradicated segregation in public schools and prompted the complete annihilation of Jim Crow legislation, marked a significant change for blacks in American society. After many long and strenuous years of activism, Terrell witnessed the dawn of a new, albeit slowly improving, world. When she died on July 24, 1954, she knew her labor had not been in vain. *See also* Anti-Lynching Movement.

Further Readings: Hine, Darlene Clark, William C. Hine, and Stanley Harrold. *The African-American Odyssey.* New Jersey: Prentice Hall, 2000; Jones, Beverly Washington. *Quest for Equality: The Life and Writings of Mary Church Terrell.* New York: Carlson Publishers, 1990; Terrell, Mary Church. *A Colored Woman in a White World.* Washington, D.C.: Ransdell, 1940.

Gladys L. Knight

Texas. *See* Beaumont (Texas) Riot of 1943; Brownsville (Texas) Riot of 1906; Byrd, James, Jr. (1949–1998) Murder of (1998); Dallas (Texas) Disturbance of 1973; Houston (Texas) Mutiny of 1917; Longview (Texas) Riot of 1919; Palestine (Texas) Riot of 1910; Texas Southern University Riot of 1967

Texas Southern University Riot of 1967

The Texas Southern University (TSU) Riot (also referred to as the TSU Riot, TSU Police Riot, or TSU Disturbance) was a violent encounter between the Houston Police Department (HPD) and students on the TSU campus on the night of May 16–17, 1967. The riot had a number of causes, but stemmed mainly from sit-ins at a garbage dump and HPD's heavy-handed tactics.

On May 8, eleven-year-old Victor George fell into a garbage-filled pond and drowned at Houston's Holmes Road Dump. The city government traditionally placed landfills in segregated neighborhoods, and in 1967 most city dumps were located in black subdivisions. Beginning around May 15, students from TSU and other local universities sat down in front of the dump's entrance to stop the garbage trucks from entering the facility. The protestors hoped to convince the city to close the dump. Instead, the police responded by arresting large numbers of the students and their leaders. The students returned the following day and continued to sit-in at the dump. More arrests followed this protest. After these sit-ins, activists gathered for a number of rallies at local churches. At these rallies, militants called for battle with the police. When the police learned of this call to arms they assumed TSU students had issued it.

Police followed the students back to TSU, used squad cars to blockade the roads leading to the campus, and shut down the school. The mostly male students fought back by throwing rocks and bottles at the officers, and by setting fire to several garbage cans. Students then barricaded themselves in the dorm rooms and exchanged gunfire with the police, who had surrounded the dormitory. Mayor Louis Welch appealed to black civic leaders to convince the students to surrender. Police escorted Rev. William Lawson, who was one of the organizers of the dump protest, to TSU with the hope that he could entreat the students to yield to the police. He found the students unorganized but unwilling to disperse. After Lawson informed HPD officials that the students would not surrender, the police opened fire, charged the dormitory, ransacked the rooms, and arrested nearly 500 students. Only a few students were injured in the melee, but two police officers were wounded. Officer Louis Kuba was the only fatality.

Houston's daily newspapers reported that the police fired between 3,000 and 5,000 rounds of ammunition at the dormitory. The papers justified police actions by fabricating accounts that the students were armed with guns and Molotov cocktails. Other papers reported that students had shared one .22-caliber pistol—a .22 was the only gun found in the dorm rooms. The district attorney charged five students with the murder of Officer Kuba. The black community vigorously supported this TSU Five. After three years of legal wrangling, the judge dismissed the charges against the TSU Five. The judge decided that evidence needed to prove the case did not exist, and that Kuba probably died from a ricocheting police bullet.

The TSU Riot stands as the most violent episode in the struggle for black rights in Houston. The only other riot to occur in the city's history was the 1917 mutiny of black soldiers stationed in Houston. A congressional investigation blamed the TSU students for the riot, but the details of the disturbance indicate that the police were largely responsible. HPD blockaded the campus and effectively shut down the school without considering how the students might react. Combined with anger over the Holmes Road Dump incident and the general mistrust and fear that many blacks felt toward police, the students' resistance seems hardly surprising. *See also* Civil Rights Movement; Long Hot Summer Riots, 1965–1967; Houston (Texas) Mutiny of 1917; Police Brutality.

Further Reading: Justice, Blair. *Violence in the City*. Forth Worth: Texas Christian University Press, 1969.

Brian D. Behnken

Thirty Years of Lynching in the United States: 1889–1918 (Gruening and Boardman, 1919)

In an effort to investigate and expose the horrors of **lynching**, the **National Association for the Advancement of Colored People (NAACP)** published a book in 1919 titled *Thirty Years of Lynching in the United States: 1889–1918*, written by Martha Gruening and Helen Boardman. The NAACP's publication of this book was indicative of the organization's numerous and strenuous efforts to eradicate lynching in the United States.

Lynching was a heinous crime instigated by racial hostility and heightened during the **Jim Crow** era in the United States. Lynching peaked in the years after Emancipation in the late nineteenth century and in the early to mid-twentieth century. Lynch mobs often murdered Negro men and women whom they deemed guilty of a variety of crimes that could include verbally protesting mistreatment by whites or physically or verbally assaulting whites. These **white mobs** often did not require evidence of any crime; rather, they purposefully sought out individuals based on their status as Negroes.

The formation of the NAACP was rooted in an event that occurred in the hometown of President Abraham Lincoln. A race riot occurred in **Springfield**, Illinois, in 1908 and was preceded by race riots in several other cities, including **Wilmington**, North Carolina (1898); **New Orleans**, Louisiana (1900); and **Atlanta**, Georgia (1906). Vicious lynchings occurred in each of these cities during all of these riots and on numerous other occasions. The Springfield riots culminated in the deaths of both blacks and whites and led to such conferences as the National Negro Convention, which was considered the first official meeting of the NAACP. The NAACP was established by **W.E.B. Du Bois**, Mary White Ovington, and others in 1909 in the aftermath of the Springfield violence. Du Bois, a noted author, educator, and professor, was also considered one of the leaders of the Negro intellectual protest movement. Ovington was a descendant of New England abolitionists who had previously lived among poor Negroes in New York. These two individuals joined with others in an effort to fight social injustice and to establish an organization that would achieve this goal.

The NAACP was initially formed by an interracial group that was committed to speaking for Negroes in the United States. The organization spoke to Negroes and on behalf of Negroes, encouraging individuals and organizations to engage in activities that would advance the status and social and political conditions of Negroes in the United States. The NAACP laid the foundation for the **civil rights movement**, which would follow half a century later. The organization was also instrumental in obtaining civil and legal rights for Negroes well into the twentieth century.

In 1918, John Shillady became executive director of the NAACP. He is credited with greatly increasing the membership and encouraging and overseeing *Thirty Years of Lynching in the United States: 1889–1918*, the first book publication of the NAACP. Under his leadership, the NAACP decided to take a stance on lynching, one of the most pressing contemporary issues concerning the safety and well-being of blacks in the United States. The **Dyer Anti-Lynching Bill**, introduced by Congressman **Leonidas C. Dyer**, would have made participating in a lynch mob a federal crime. The NAACP publicly supported this bill and focused on pressuring the federal government to end lynching.

Since the NAACP was leading an anti-lynching movement and working to increase awareness and distaste for a practice that had become routinely tolerated, the organization determined to take an aggressive stance in the publication of a book on a thirty-year period of lynching. The focus of this historic work was to examine the 3,224 recorded lynchings that had occurred during this period and identify 100 of the most heinous documented lynchings. A three-pronged approach was essential to developing a cohesive summary of each identified lynching. Each documented lynching had to meet the following three criteria: articulate in extreme detail the rationale provided for the justification of the lynching, describe the procedure followed by the lynch mob to assault its victim, and explain the related activities associated with the lynching. Great care was used to ensure that the cases described were extremely disturbing and created an unsettling image for the reader. The purpose of the book was to cause even the most hardened individuals to reconsider their complacency in addressing lynching, which was an extralegal activity that had become routine in many areas of the country.

One of the most disturbing accounts included in the book was that of **Mary Turner** in Valdosta, Georgia. Her husband had been wrongfully lynched when a mob was unable to locate another black man who had allegedly killed a white planter. Ms. Turner publicly protested her husband's wrongful death and was subsequently punished for her outspokenness. Her execution was especially disturbing because she was eight months pregnant at the time. The lynch mob hanged her by her ankles, covered her with gasoline, and burned her alive. However, this did not satisfy the crowd, and during her ordeal, her stomach was cut open. Her unborn child fell to the ground, cried momentarily, and was subsequently stomped to death by onlookers. Other lynchings provided similar gruesome details about the deaths of persons who suffered acts of brutality, and in many cases the perpetrators were never brought to justice. The narration of these atrocities contributed greatly to the NAACP's ability to challenge individuals to examine their role in the promulgation of lynching in the United States.

Further Readings: Appiah, Kwame Anthony, and Henry Louis Gates, eds. *Africana Civil Rights: An A-Z Reference of the Movement that Changed America*. Philadelphia and London: Running Press, 2004; Berg, Manfred. *"The Ticket to Freedom": The NAACP and the Struggle for Black Political Integration*. Gainesville: University Press of Florida, 2005; Lewis, David Levering, ed. *W.E.B. Du Bois: A Reader*. New York: Henry Holt and Company, 1995; Raper, Arthur. *The Tragedy of Lynching*. New York: Dover Publications, 2003. Originally published in 1933.

Nia Woods Haydel and Kijua Sanders-McMurtry

Till, Emmett (1941–1955), Lynching of

Emmett Louis "Bobo" Till was a fourteen-year-old African American teenager from Chicago, Illinois, who was brutally murdered in the Mississippi Delta in the summer of 1955 for allegedly whistling at a white woman. National and international media attention surrounding the young man's death, his funeral, the trial, and the acquittal of Till's killers was remarkable for drawing attention from both black and white communities to the extent of the continuing racial violence in the United States. The episode had an immediate and ongoing impact in the United States, marking 1955 as the year that launched the modern **civil rights movement**, and continues to be cited as a reminder of the civil rights work still to be accomplished.

Born July 25, 1941, Emmett Till was the son of Mamie Carthan Till Bradley Mobley and Louis Till. Till was primarily raised by his mother, his parents having separated in 1942. Louis Till was drafted into the U.S. Army in 1943 during World War II, and was executed by the U.S. Army for raping two Italian women and murdering a third; this information was used to impugn young Till's character after the trial of his murder. Mamie Till Bradley, who held a good-paying job in the Chicago office of the Air Force Procurement Office, sent Emmett and his cousin, Curtis Jones, to Mississippi on vacation to stay with their uncle, Moses Wright. On August 21, 1955, the boys arrived in Money, Mississippi, a small town eight miles north of Greenwood, near the town of Drew, Sunflower County.

There are conflicting reports as to what precisely happened on the afternoon of August 24. One potential pitfall in rehashing the events of August 24 is that doing so potentially serves as justification for the punishment meted out to Till. What is also clear is that the events constituted a racial and sexual transgression that was also marked by North–South tensions, as well as big city–small town conflicts endemic to the United States.

Till apparently joined other teenagers as they went to Bryant's Grocery and Meat Market to get some refreshments after work in the cotton fields. Owned by Roy and Carolyn Bryant, the market mostly catered to the local black sharecropper population. Most accounts emphasize Till's naïveté about North–South differences in attitude regarding appropriate behavior for black Americans. Some accounts claim that Till pulled a picture of a white girl out of his wallet, boasting that she was his girlfriend. The idle bragging by a city boy from the North may have played poorly in the southern town; Till was encouraged to enter the store.

Most accounts indicate that Till spoke to or whistled at Carolyn Bryant; either action would have been considered a serious racial transgression at the time. Bryant, age twenty-one and the mother of two small boys, later stated at the trial that Till had grabbed her at the waist and asked her for a date. She testified that the young man also used "unprintable" words. He had a slight stutter from a childhood polio episode and some have conjectured that Bryant might have misinterpreted what Till said. Some say that he could have been mildly retarded and any unexpected behavior on his part might easily have been misconstrued. Others suggest that Bryant flirted with Till. Several black youths in the store at the time, all under the age of sixteen, reportedly forced him to leave the store for being rowdy.

Roy Bryant, age twenty-four, returned from a road trip three days after the episode; the gossip had spread throughout Tallahatchie County, and Bryant decided that he and his half brother, J.W. Milam, age thirty-six, would "teach the boy a lesson" (Crow). Bryant, Milam, and several others kidnapped Till from his uncle's house at gunpoint at about 2:30 A.M. on August 28. The men drove to a weathered plantation shed in neighboring Sunflower County, where they brutally beat Till, gouging out one eye. A witness heard Till's screams for hours until the men finally ended Emmett Till's life, shooting him with a .45-caliber pistol, then tying a seventy-five-pound cotton gin fan around his neck with barbed wire in an unsuccessful attempt to weigh down the body. They dropped him into the Tallahatchie River near the town of Glendora. A white teenage boy discovered the body three days later. When Till was removed from the river, the boy had been so badly beaten that Moses Wright could identify him only by his father's ring.

Although others were clearly involved, Milam and Bryant were soon under suspicion for Till's disappearance and were arrested on August 29. Both men admitted that they had taken the boy from his uncle's home, but they insisted that they turned him loose the same night. They argued that the body extracted from river was not Till's.

As word spread that Till was missing, two civil rights leaders from the **National Association for the Advancement of Colored People (NAACP)**—Medgar Evers, the state field secretary, and Amzie Moore, head of the Bolivar County chapter—disguised themselves as cotton pickers and went into the fields in search of information that would help locate Till. On the basis of the stories they collected, Moore later said that it was apparent that "more than 2,000 families" were murdered and lynched over the years, with their bodies thrown into the Delta's swamps and bayous, a much larger figure than official estimates (Wikipedia, "Emmett Till").

The Funeral

When Till's swollen body emerged from the Tallahatchie River after three days in the water, officials in Sumner County, Mississippi, wanted to bury it right away. Sheriff Harold Strider of Tallahatchie County ordered the body to be buried immediately in Mississippi. But Till's mother, Mamie Till Bradley, intervened to bring the body home. The Chicago funeral home offered to prepare the body for viewing, but Mamie chose to leave the body in its disfigured state, and to have an open-casket funeral, uttering the statement that has since become famous: "Let the people see what they have done to my boy" (*Pittsburgh Courier*, September 10, 1955). The funeral was held September 3–6, 1955, at the Roberts Temple Church of God in Christ. Bradley's decision to for an open-casket funeral was significant for fueling public knowledge about and sympathy for the victims of hate crimes. The **press coverage** of the murder now became press coverage of the funeral. More than 2,000 people attended the funeral, and a public-address system broadcast the service to the thousands more lining the streets outside the church. The popular black magazine, *Jet*, published a photograph of the body. Emmett Till was buried September 6 in Burr Oak Cemetery in Alsip, Illinois. The same day, Bryant and Milam were indicted in Mississippi by a grand jury.

The Trial

It took fewer than four weeks for the case to go to trial. The trial began on September 19. Scores of reporters descended on the Delta. Television networks chartered a plane to send footage to New York for the nightly news. Stories ran in all major national newspapers and magazines; the case was also an international news story, highlighting troubled U.S. race relations at a time of increasing international scrutiny. Initially, white southerners largely condemned the murder. Local lawyers demanded expensive fees that they knew Milam and Bryant could not afford, so initially, the two had no legal counsel. But as the press began referring to the incident as **a lynching**, white southerners reacted defensively, closing ranks. Local stores collected $10,000 in countertop jars for Bryant and Milam; all five attorneys from the town of Sumner, Mississippi, agreed to represent "the South" by representing them.

The trial was widely acknowledged to be a show, a false demonstration of justice designed to silence critics of southern **white supremacy**. The circus-like atmosphere of the trial proceedings heightened this sense. Snacks and soft drinks were sold to the crowd. Outside, the international press jockeyed for photographs and interviews that captured American southern folk ways. Inside, the courthouse echoed Mississippi social structure: a small number of black observers were permitted at a small segregated table; numerous white observers filled the seats; the defendants' families joked openly with prosecutors and jurors; each day, Milam and Bryant ate lunch with the sheriff at a café. Although Tallahatchie County was 63 percent African American, no African Americans were eligible to serve on the jury.

Although brief, the trial is noteworthy in a number of respects. First, Till's uncle, Moses Wright, identified the assailants in court—the first time a black person had testified against a white person in Mississippi. He was forced to leave town, but was later hired by the NAACP for speaking engagements. Second, that the verdict was a foregone conclusion was widely acknowledged; even the federal government failed to intervene to enforce justice. After the trial, the Bryant and the Milam families celebrated on camera, with smiles and cigars.

On September 23, an all-white, all-male jury of twelve acquitted Roy Bryant and J.W. Milam. The trial took only five days; jury deliberations took just sixty-seven minutes; one juror said the jurors took a break to stretch the time to over an hour. The hasty acquittal outraged people throughout the United States and Europe, and energized the nascent civil rights movement. No one else was ever indicted or prosecuted for involvement in the kidnapping or murder.

For eight weeks after the trial, protest rallies and lectures were staged around the country, drawing attention to the continuing injustices faced by African Americans. Numerous civil rights activists and leaders cite the Till murder as a consciousness-raising moment.

In a 1956 article for *Look* magazine, for which they were paid, J.W. Milam admitted that he and his half brother had killed Till. (The rule of double jeopardy, which protects defendants from being charged with the same crime twice, protected them from these admissions.) Milam claimed that their intention had been merely to scare Till by pistol-whipping him and threatening to throw him off of a cliff. But regardless of what they did to Till, he apparently never showed any fear, maintaining an unrepentant and defiant attitude toward them. Thus, the brothers felt they were left with no choice but to make an example of him. But the celebratory enthusiasm of a national magazine profile vanished when the local response to the story was to shun the brothers. Local blacks refused to shop at the store; local banks refused to lend them money; they eventually left Mississippi. Milam died of cancer in 1980, and Bryant died of the same cause in 1990.

Mamie Till Bradley became a crusader for civil rights and a teacher for the Chicago Public Schools. She founded the Emmett Till Foundation and the Emmett Till Players, a youth theater group. In her later years, she fought against the death penalty in Illinois, considering it "legal lynching." She died at age eighty-one on January 6, 2003. She is buried in a prominent location at Burr Oak Cemetery, Chicago, immediately inside the southeast entrance. That year her autobiography, *Death of Innocence: The Story of the Hate Crime That Changed America*, was published.

Federal Investigation

Till's story is far from over. On May 10, 2004, the U.S. Department of Justice announced that it was reopening the case to determine whether anyone other than Milam and Bryant was involved. They were prompted in part by information from filmmakers who found errors in the original investigation and concluded that several people, some still living, were involved in Till's abduction and killing. The decision was greeted enthusiastically by civil rights campaigners and some politicians.

Stanley Nelson, producer and director of *The Murder of Emmett Till* (2003), states that one witness, never sought by prosecutors, reportedly saw a black employee of Milam's laughing while cleaning Till's blood from the back of Milam's truck. Another said there were other people (in addition to Milam and Bryant) in the truck that took Till to his death Filmmaker Keith Beauchamp, while making his documentary, *The Untold Story of Emmett Louis Till* (2004), found more witnesses who did not testify at the trial and had not previously spoken in public—as many as ten more people involved in the murder than were previously indicated—five of whom are still alive today. At least one is believed to be black. Although the statute of limitations prevents charges from being pursued under federal law, they can still be pursued before the state court, and the **Federal Bureau of Investigation (FBI)** and officials in Mississippi worked jointly on the investigation.

On May 17, 2005, the FBI reported that one copy of the original Emmett Till court transcript had been found. Although in poor condition, its discovery was taken as a positive step, since the transcript had been presumed lost.

On June 1, 2005, Till's body was exhumed; the Cook County coroner conducted the autopsy. The body was reburied by relatives on June 4. On August 26, 2005, it was announced that the exhumed body had been positively identified as that of Emmett Till, thus contradicting the central argument in Bryant and Milam's case. This evidence is crucial to further prosecutions; bullet fragments were found, and DNA tests confirmed the identity of the body.

On September 14, 2005, the U.S. Senate passed the Unsolved Civil Rights Crimes Act (known as the "Till Bill"), forming a new federal unit within the Civil Rights Division of the Justice Department dedicated to probing and prosecuting unsolved civil rights–era murder cases. On November 23, 2005, the federal investigation was completed, and their findings were turned over to Mississippi officials. Possible defendants in the reopening of the case include Carolyn Bryant Donham, the ex-wife of Roy Bryant, and Henry Lee Loggins, the now eighty-two-year-old former plantation worker and Bryant employee, who is currently living in an Ohio nursing home.

Till's murder has inspired a wide range of artistic responses, including a poem by Langston Hughes; a song by Bob Dylan; the play *Blues for Mister Charlie* by James Baldwin; the novels *Your Blues Ain't Like Mine* (1992) by Bebe Moore Campbell; *Wolf Whistle* (1993) by Lewis Nordan; and the rap song "Through the Wire" (2003) by Kanye West. Additional acknowledgements of the boy's murder include the August 2005 renaming of a thirty-eight-mile stretch of U.S. Highway 49 North from Tutwiler, Mississippi, to

Greenwood, Mississippi. In November 2005, the Commission on Chicago Landmarks began considering landmark status for the Roberts Temple Church of God in Christ, the location of his momentous funeral.

Further Readings: Baldwin, James. *Blues for Mister Charlie*. New York: Vintage, 1995. Originally published in 1964; Campbell, Bebe Moore. *Your Blues Ain't Like Mine*. New York: Ballantine, 1992; Crow, Chris. "The Lynching of Emmett Till." *The History of Jim Crow*. See http://www.jimcrowhistory.org/resources/lessonplans/hs_es_emmett_till.htm; Metress, Christopher, ed. *The Lynching of Emmett Till: A Documentary Narrative*. Charlottesville: University of Virginia Press, 2002; *The Murder of Emmett Till*. Directed by Stanley Nelson. PBS, 2003. See http://www.pbs.org/wgbh/amex/till/; Norden, Lewis. *Wolf Whistle*. Chapel Hill, NC: Algonquin, 1993; West, Kanye. *Through the Wire*. Roc-a–Fella, 2004; Whitfield, Stephen. *A Death in the Delta: The Story of Emmett Till*. New York: Free Press, 1988; Wikipedia. "Emmett Till." See http://en.wikipedia.org/wiki/Emmett_Till.

Valerie Begley

Triggs, Clarence (1942–1966)

Clarence Triggs was slain by nightriders in Bogalusa, Louisiana, on July 30, 1966.

Born in 1942, Triggs had just moved to Bogalusa from Jackson, Mississippi, with his wife Emma. He had served in the armed forces and was working as a bricklayer. Triggs had never been active in the **civil rights movement**, but when he came to Bogalusa and saw that it was still a **Jim Crow** town, he joined civil rights marches and attended meetings organized by the **Congress of Racial Equality (CORE)**. It was believed that Bogalusa had more **Ku Klux Klan (KKK)** members per capita than any other region in the South during the mid-1960s. Triggs was one of the many blacks in the area who supported the movement for equality, yet he was never considered a leader in the movement; in fact, few people knew who he was in Bogalusa. Less than a month after marching at a civil rights demonstration, Triggs was found dead on the side of the road with a bullet wound in his head.

Believing that the police were covering up Triggs' murder—especially since his wife was not allowed to identify her husband's body at the scene—civil rights leaders organized nightly marches until someone was arrested. Two days later, the police arrested two white men, Homer Richard Seale and John W. Copling, Jr., and charged them with murder. Seale was never tried for this crime and a jury deliberated for less than an hour before finding Copling innocent. The motive for the deadly attack was never released and the death of Clarence Triggs remains a mystery.

Further Reading: "Civil Rights Memorial." See http://www.tolerance.org/memorial/memorial.swf.

Paulina X. Ruf

Trotter, William Monroe (1872–1934)

A newspaper publisher and militant civil rights activist, as well as a founder of the **Niagara movement** and the **National Association for the**

Advancement of Colored People (NAACP), William Monroe Trotter revived the black press and the tradition of organized protest as important components of the struggle for African American civil rights.

Born in Chillicothe, Ohio, on April 7, 1872, the son of a local politician and a former slave, Trotter was raised in Boston, where he graduated from Harvard University in 1895. The first African American to be elected to Phi Beta Kappa at Harvard, Trotter earned his master's degree before returning to Boston to enter the real estate field. Opening his own firm in 1899, Trotter was soon frustrated by the growing racial discrimination that he experienced in his own business and observed throughout the country, particularly the **segregation**, **disenfranchisement**, and violence that characterized race relations in the South. In 1901, Trotter and George Forbes founded the *Boston Guardian*, a crusading weekly that, under Trotter's direction, began to fearlessly and articulately demand full and immediate civil rights for African Americans.

Trotter made particular use of his newspaper to vehemently oppose the accommodationist policies of **Booker T. Washington**, whom Trotter believed was naively ignoring the country's worsening racial state. Through his frequent and eloquent editorials, Trotter made white Americans understand that not all black Americans adhered to Washington's conciliatory views. In July 1903, Trotter and a group of friends disrupted a speech that Washington delivered in Boston. By constantly heckling the speaker and shouting embarrassing questions, Trotter and his associates caused an uproar that came to be known as the Boston Riot. As a result of his actions, and at the insistence of Washington's supporters, Trotter was fined $50 and spent a month in jail, a punishment that Trotter later portrayed as the suffering of a martyr for the cause of civil rights.

In 1905, Trotter, **W.E.B. Du Bois**, and other prominent African Americans concerned with the increasing occurrence of **lynching** and other violence against blacks founded the Niagara movement. Although Trotter helped push Du Bois toward a greater militancy in his approach to civil rights, the two quarreled over tactics, with Trotter insisting that any national civil rights organization be led and financed entirely by African Americans. To this end, Trotter founded the all-black National Equal Rights League in 1908. In 1909, despite his disagreements with Du Bois, Trotter participated in the founding of the NAACP, although he continued to vehemently oppose white involvement in the organization.

A political independent, Trotter supported Democrat Woodrow Wilson for president in 1912. However, when Wilson supported increased segregation in federal offices, Trotter turned against the president, whom he confronted personally on the issue in the White House in November 1914. After forty-five minutes of argument, Wilson declared, "your manner offends me" (Jackson) and promptly ordered Trotter from his office.

In 1915, Trotter organized picket lines and demonstrations in an attempt to mobilize African Americans against **D.W. Griffith**'s racist film, ***The Birth of a Nation***. In one of the earliest African American protest marches in U.S. history, Trotter, who had been released from jail only two days before, led over 1,000 people in a march on the Massachusetts State House. In

1919, to Wilson's great annoyance, Trotter announced his intention to attend the Versailles Peace Conference to push for inclusion of a racial equality clause in the peace treaty ending World War I. When the U.S. government denied him a visa, Trotter took a job as ship's cook and so secured passage to France. Although he failed to obtain a hearing at Versailles, his trip and his militant editorials in the *Guardian* won worldwide publicity for his cause.

By the 1920s, Trotter was an increasingly isolated voice on the radical edge of the struggle for African American civil rights. Hit hard by the Great Depression, Trotter lost control of the *Guardian* in 1934. He died, an apparent suicide, on his sixty-second birthday, April 7, 1934, when he fell from the roof of a three-story Boston building. *See also* Racism.

Further Readings: Fox, Stephen R. *The Guardian of Boston: William Monroe Trotter*. New York: Atheneum, 1970; Jackson, Derrick Z. "About William Monroe Trotter." See the Trotter Group Web site at www.trottergroup.com.

John A. Wagner

TSU Riot, TSU Police Riot, or TSU Disturbance. *See* Texas Southern University Riot of 1967

Tulsa (Oklahoma) Riot of 1921

One evening in late April 1921, Henry Sowders, a white man who operated the motion picture machine in the Williams Dreamland Theatre in the black section of Tulsa, Oklahoma, overheard a heated discussion in an adjoining room. He removed the soda bottle that plugged a hole in the wall between the projection booth and a back room so that he could get a better sense of what was being said. Sowders, like the rest of white Tulsa, worried about the radicalism of Tulsa's blacks. Ever since the United States entered World War I in April 1917, blacks had been increasingly adamant in their calls for equal rights. Now, two leaders of Tulsa's black community, A.J. Smitherman, editor of the radical *Tulsa Star* and lawyer and real estate developer J.B. Stradford, who was famous for his opposition to **segregation**, were arguing about a fight between police officers and several black men in nearby Muskogee. The men had shot a police officer as they were freeing a prisoner, John McShane, from custody. The men feared McShane would be lynched.

Now Smitherman and Stradford were discussing the need to get the word out to the community as quickly as possible: another **lynching** has been avoided, through swift action. And once again the refrain was heard at the Dreamland's vaudeville shows, "Don't let any white man run it over you, but fight" (Brophy 2002). The economic success of Tulsa's black section, known as **Greenwood**, fostered ideas of pride and self-protection. In the jazz joints, as well as the illicit bars, Greenwood residents expressed their new freedom as white Tulsans gazed uneasily across the railroad tracks separating black and white Tulsa.

White Oklahomans saw the McShane story very differently, of course. They focused on the injuries the police officer suffered and the lawless

Smoke billowing over Tulsa, Oklahoma, during the 1921 race riot. Courtesy of the Library of Congress.

actions of the black men who freed McShane. There were, as *Invisible Man* author and Oklahoma native Ralph Ellison said, separate white and black views of law in Oklahoma around the time of World War I. The white view maintained that blacks must follow the dictates of law enforcement officers (called "laws") and the discriminatory statutes that left blacks with inferior accommodations on trains, streetcars, and in schools, and left them with little opportunity even to register to vote. Black Oklahomans had an optimism, though, that despite such discriminatory treatment, the Constitution's equal protection clause offered the promise of equal treatment—and that they were entitled to take action to make sure that vision was realized. In the pages of the Oklahoma City *Black Dispatch*, for example, editor Roscoe Dunjee urged lawsuits to ensure voting rights, equal funding for segregated schools, and the opportunity to live anywhere blacks wanted, not just where the city's segregation ordinance said they could live.

Other Oklahoma blacks had no faith in the laws. They had ample reason to fear both law enforcement officers and mobs. One dramatic lesson came on the last weekend of August 1920, when two men were lynched in Oklahoma: one in Tulsa and another in Oklahoma City. On August 28, Roy Belton, a white man accused of murdering a taxi driver, was taken from the jail on the top floor of the Tulsa County Courthouse by a mob. The sheriff in charge of the jail gave no resistance. The mob took the man out to Red Fork, a few miles from Tulsa, where a crowd was gathering. John

Gustafson, Tulsa's police chief, was there, as were uniformed police officers, white women, even some African American men were there, set to witness a lynching. The mob hung the man on a telephone post and a few minutes later he was dead. At the suggestion of an undertaker, the mob let the body hang there another fifteen minutes, then he was cut down. Men immediately ran to him to collect souvenirs: a coat button, a piece of rope, a shoe string. One witness, seeing everyone else with some memorial, took a shoe, which he brought back to his rooming house.

The next evening, men in Oklahoma City—not to be outdone by their cross-state rivals in Tulsa—went to the Oklahoma City jail. They cut off the lights, entered the jail, and a few minutes later, exited with Claude Chandler, a young black man accused of killing a white police officer. A few days earlier, police raided the Chandler home, where moonshine was being made. Both Chandler's father and an officer died during a subsequent gun battle. Two hours after Chandler's kidnapping, rumors began circulating in Oklahoma City's black community that Chandler had been taken from the jail. The community, knowing that a lynching was imminent, went into action. Perhaps 1,000 heavily armed black men assembled along Second Street, wondering how they might rescue Chandler. The police in Oklahoma City heard about the assembly. They headed off for Second Street, the heart of Oklahoma City's black district.

Fifty police surrounded a car full of black men that was about to go off to look for Chandler's kidnappers. They pointed riot guns at the car. One black man in the back seat moved to cock his gun. But another man in the car, a cooler head, warned "We are not fighting the police, hold a moment, let's submit, it will come out alright" (Brophy 2002). After a meeting with leaders of the black community and two black policemen, the mayor allowed the unarmed men to chase after Chandler, under the supervision of the two black officers. The mayor would allow the community to take some action to protect itself, but limited their ability to carry guns. They headed off, searched all night north and west of the city, near Chandler's home of Arcadia, trying to find him. At some point, they realized they would not find him alive. Still they searched, but found nothing. Around noon the next day, Claude Chandler's body was found hanging from a tree ten miles west of the city. He had been lynched the evening before, beaten, and shot twice.

Oklahoma City's *Black Dispatch* seized on the Chandler case as an example of how far the realities of life in the black community were from the promises of equal justice and equal protection. How could the jailers have been so easily overcome by three unmasked men, it asked? How could the sheriff have known where to go to find Chandler's body? The *Black Dispatch* highlighted the illegal actions of Oklahoma law enforcement. "And This Is the White Man's Law?" (Brophy 2002) was the incredulous title of the *Black Dispatch* editorial immediately following the lynching.

Chandler's lynching was only the most recent in a long series of nationwide examples of law enforcement denying equal protection to blacks. In the **East St. Louis (Illinois) Riot of 1917**, instead of protecting blacks, the police disarmed them. Then, the disarmed blacks "Got . . . a bullet out of the rifle of the man in uniform who had first disarmed him" (Brophy 2002). Such unequal treatment made people suspicious of law enforcement officers—and taught blacks not give up their arms. It also taught them that law did not mean equal protection for blacks. They did not follow the law, however. There was building tension between black views of justice and white views of law. Across years of editorials, the black press wrote about the myriad ways in which blacks received unequal treatment at the hands of police, in the arbitrary commands of police officers, and in capricious arrests of blacks, while whites insulted and attacked blacks with immunity. The unequal treatment continued in the courts and in the legislature. Oklahoma's blacks, therefore, developed a systematic, though straightforward interpretation of what *law* ought to mean. It ought to mean equal treatment. That idea, what we call today the equal protection of the law, existed in an intellectual realm, distinct from the harsh reality of life in Oklahoma. For whites, talk of law too often meant black obedience to the white commands and capricious and unequal treatment by the government. Blacks asked whether such unequal treatment actually could be *law*. They argued that something so different from justice and so different from the Constitution's promise of equal protection could not. There might be something called *law* by the Oklahoma courts; there might be what police officers called *laws*. But those statutes and the dictates of the law enforcement officers were not law. Sometimes the black vision of law won, as when the U.S. Supreme Court struck down Oklahoma's discriminatory voter registration statute in 1915. But, for the most part, the black view of law had to wait for another time, and blacks and whites continued to hold different understandings of what the word *law* meant.

In a series of editorials, A.J. Smitherman of the *Tulsa Star* chastised Oklahoma City blacks for not defending Chandler. Smitherman's first editorial criticized the Oklahoma City blacks who "got together after Claude Chandler had paid the penalty with his life, and as we are informed, permitted one lone policeman to take their guns away from them, and literally boot them off the street" (Brophy 2002). That failure to take a more aggressive stance was a commentary on the courage (and wisdom) of Oklahoma City's black community. The *Tulsa Star* maintained that blacks should have taken action sooner: "[T]he proper time to afford protection to any prisoner is before and during the time he is being lynched, and certainly not after he is killed" (Brophy 2002).

Arguments raged over the proper response to Chandler's lynching. Had the Oklahoma City black community acted with sufficient bravery? Was it proper to give up their guns to the police? Had the men taken the correct, measured steps? Some were willing to advocate direct confrontation with the police, but others were not willing to go so far. A split in opinion appeared between those who would use violence to protect the community members against lynchers and those who would go even further and pitch battle with the police. They thought that Oklahoma City blacks should have mobilized and gone to the jail to protect Chandler. Those radicals thought, despite the protestations that cool heads were needed when a lynching was imminent, that community members should have been more responsive to the danger to Chandler. Had the community done something, Chandler might still be alive.

The *Tulsa Star* urged aggressive action to combat lynching. It told of the legal right, even duty, to use violence to protect against lynching. "While the boy was in jail and while there was danger of mob violence any set of citizens had a legal right—it was their duty—to arm themselves and march in a body to the jail and apprize the sheriff or jailer of the purpose of their visit and to take life if need be to uphold the law and protect the prisoner" (Brophy 2002). The *Star* further urged that men could arm for self-protection or "to uphold the majesty of the law" (Brophy 2002); and that, in either of those cases, no officer has the right to disarm them and it would be cowardly to give up arms.

The Greenwood Community had experience with such aggressive action, designed to preserve life and—as some phrased it—the majesty of the law. In September 1919, when Jewel Davis, a black man, was arrested in Tulsa, leaders of the Greenwood Community allegedly showed up at the courthouse and demanded assurances that he would be protected. A few months later, in March 1920, Oklahoma blacks again took action to protect an accused man from a lynching. Some men from Shawnee armed themselves and stole a couple of cars to chase the mob that was forming to take a prisoner, Chap Davis (who had recently been convicted of attempted assault on a white teacher) from law enforcement officers. Under the heading "Mob Rule and the Law," the *Tulsa Star* praised the men who acted to avert a lynching as Davis was being transported to the state penitentiary:

> As to the Colored men of Shawnee who, it is alleged, stole an auto, armed themselves and went to protect the prisoner, aside from taking the auto which was manifestly wrong, but perhaps not without extenuating circumstances, since their intentions were to uphold the law of our state, they are the heroes of the story. If one set of men arm themselves and chase across the country to violate the law, certainly another set who arm themselves to uphold the supremacy of the law and prevent crime, must stand out prominently as the best citizens. Therefore, the action of the Colored men in this case is to be commended. We need more citizens like them in every community and of both races. (Brophy 2002)

Oklahoma's blacks spoke of law as they justified their armed actions. If the government would uphold the law, there would be no reason (or even justification) for the community to take action. But when the government failed to protect, Greenwood residents told themselves, they had the right—sometimes they even spoke about it as a duty—to take action.

The debate between the *Black Dispatch* and the *Tulsa Star* over Claude Chandler's lynching raised the consciousness of both communities about the need for vigilance. It also demonstrated the complex, sometimes conflicting, ideas that Oklahoma's blacks held about what it meant to uphold the law. Both papers agreed on the need for the community to take an active role in upholding the rule of law, but they disagreed on the steps to take. If the rule of law was going to prevail in Oklahoma, it would be through the actions of blacks, not the law officers.

A few weeks after the McShane incident, at the end of May 1921, the black men of Tulsa faced their own test. Nineteen-year-old Dick Rowland, who worked shining shoes, was arrested on charges that he attempted to assault Sarah Page, a white elevator operator in a downtown office building. When a headline on the front page of the *Tulsa Tribune* declared, "Nab Negro for Assault on White Girl" (Brophy 2002), lynch talk swept through white, as well as black, Tulsa. Soon, people were in Greenwood, talking about their next moves. By 7:00 P.M., people were gathered at the offices of the *Tulsa Star*. Stradford urged calm for the time being, but said he would take action if a lynching were imminent. He told the crowd at the newspaper's offices, "If I can't get anyone to go with me I will go single-handed and empty my automatic into the mob and then resign myself to my fate" (Brophy 2002). Getting people to go to the courthouse was no problem that evening. A few hours later, a group of veterans made their way from Greenwood to the courthouse, where Rowland was in jail. They were led, as a white Tulsa paper later reported, by a person named Mann, who had "come back from the war in France with exaggerated notions of social equality and thinking he can whip the world" (Brophy 2002). Those men had been schooled in ideas about democracy and freedom, fought for it on the fields of France, and then returned home. Reading radical literature like **W.E.B. Du Bois**' ***The Crisis***, Greenwood residents were reminded that they had closed ranks and helped defeat Germany in the recent war. But now, it was time to put an end to **racism** at home. Du Bois captured the militant stance of Tulsa's blacks when he observed of the soldiers in the spring of 1919, "We return. We return from fighting. We return fighting" (Brophy 2002). The veterans were also reading poetry that urged them to take aggressive action to protect their community and asked the ominous question:

And how can man die better,
Than facing fearful odds,
For the ashes of his fathers
And the temples of his gods? (Brophy 2002)

Many were about to find out, for within hours, dozens—perhaps hundreds—would be dead. At the courthouse, Mann and his comrades clashed with the **white mob** and the riot began. Within twenty-four hours, thirty-five blocks of Greenwood had been reduced to rubble, testimony to the clash between the ideas of justice motivating the black community and the fear and hatred of the white community.

And so, when there was news that a young black man was sitting in jail in the Tulsa County Courthouse on May 31, amidst charges of attempted rape, the Greenwood Community was electrified. They would not let another lynching happen on their watch. They marched in a body to jail twice that evening. The first time, the sheriff calmed them and told them there would be no lynching. The second time, around 10:00 P.M., ended in violence. As someone tried to disarm the black men, fighting began and all hell broke loose.

In the immediate aftermath of violence, Tulsa Police Chief John Gustafson worked with Mayor T.D. Evans and members of the police force and local units of the National Guard to put down what they believed was a "Negro uprising" (Brophy 2002). They devised a plan to deputize hundreds of men and provide them with weapons, then disarm the entire black population and take them into "protective custody" (Brophy 2002). They deputized several hundred men, perhaps as many as 250, then told them to each get a gun. Those who did not have access to guns were issued ones that had been confiscated from several sporting shops in downtown Tulsa. Then, throughout the night, the police chief coordinated efforts to take Greenwood residents into custody.

Throughout the night, there was shooting across the railroad tracks that separated Greenwood from the rest of Tulsa. In a lawsuit filed after the riot against insurance companies, one person testified about the violence that evening. He was near the boarder of Greenwood and had heard that the riot had begun:

> I ran across the street and there was some white boys on Boston [Avenue] with a light in their hands going toward the old shack that used to be down in there and somebody shot the first one that started and he did not get to the house. Then I ran up the street ... and on the east side of the street I got behind a telephone pole and then the people began firing, shooting, and I started over there and a guy came back toward me on the street ... he said, "Let's go in this house and go up stairs, and [we] won't be bothered," and I saw them coming out with another torch and something happened to him before he got there and a third man came out and set the little house afire. (Brophy 2002)

Shooting continued throughout the night and some officers and National Guard units were able to arrest a few people. But around dawn on the morning of June 1, a full-scale assault took place on Greenwood. At the sound of a police bell, hundreds of men—many of them special deputies, some uniformed officers, and many members of a mob—crossed the railroad tracks into Greenwood, amidst fire from Greenwood.

Much of what we know about the riot comes from testimony in several court cases. One case, filed by Native American William Redfearn, sought money from his insurance company. The insurance company refused to pay on his policy because there was a clause in their policy that excluded damage due to riot. But Redfearn sought to show that the damage was caused by police action, not rioters, and thus avoid the exclusion. Redfearn's lawyers introduced testimony that much of the damage arose from the special police officers. In deciding the case, the Oklahoma Supreme Court acknowledged that many of the people doing the burning were wearing deputy police badges. It stated simply, "the evidence shows that a great number of men engaged in arresting the Negroes found in the Negro section wore police badges, or badges indicating they were deputy sheriffs, and in some instances were dressed in soldier's clothes and represented to the Negroes that they were soldiers" (Brophy 2002). (The court, however, went on to deny Redfearn's claim, because the damage happened during a riot.)

The evidence of what happened comes from two sources: those who saw what was happening in white Tulsa and those who saw what was happening in Greenwood. Together the evidence presents a compelling case for the special deputies' involvement. Green E. Smith, a black man who lived in Muskogee and was in town for a few days to install a cooling system in the Dreamland Theater, testified during the trial about the role of the special deputies in Greenwood. He went to the Dreamland around five in the morning. He planned to install a fan, then catch a train back to Muskogee by nine. After the whistle blew at five, Smith heard shooting and watched out of the window. At one point it "looked like the world was coming to an end with bullets." By 8:00 A.M., the shooting had decreased in intensity, but it picked up again. By 9:30 A.M., "a gang came down the street knocking on the doors and setting the buildings afire." Smith did not know the men by face (he knew only the black officers), but they "had on what they call special police and deputy sheriff's badges." How could Smith have seen the badges? "They came and taken fifty dollars of money, and I was looking right at them." He had been close enough to them to "read the badge[s]." He saw "ten or twelve of them. Some *special police*, and others would be *deputy sheriff*.... Some had *ribbons* and some of them had *regular stars"* (Brophy 2002). Not all of the approximately fifteen men along Greenwood were wearing badges; some had "home guard" uniforms.

To know about what happened in white Tulsa, one needs to look at two other major sources of evidence: the July 1921 trial of Police Chief John Gustafson for neglect of duty and the lawsuit filed by J.B. Stradford against the American Central Insurance Company in Chicago in September 1921.

The July 1921 trial of Police Chief Gustafson focused on allegations of neglect of duty during the riot. One witness, Judge Oliphant, linked the police and their special deputies to burning, even murder. The seventy-three-year-old Oliphant went to Greenwood to check on his rental property there. He called the police department and asked for help protecting his homes. No assistance came, but shortly after his call, a gang of men—four uniformed officers and some deputies—came along. Instead of protecting property, "[t]hey were the chief fellows setting fires" (Brophy 2002). Oliphant tried to dissuade them from burning. "This last crowd made an agreement that they would not burn that property [across the street from my property] because I thought it would burn mine too and I promised that if they wouldn't ... I would see that no Negroes ever lived in that row of houses any more" (Brophy 2002). Gustafson, who had been suspended from duty after the riot, was found guilty of neglect of duty and never returned to office.

According to the testimony of Sheriff McCullough in Stradford's lawsuit, on the morning of June 1, many men were bent on murder.

> I told everyone I saw not to let them burn those houses, to keep them from it if they possibly could. My opinion in regard to the burning of those houses is that they were a bunch of looters and thieves who took part in it and saw a chance to get into the riot, after the shooting at the courthouse the white men who got their guns and did the shooting that night and the next day, the majority of them at least, I do not believe burned any houses.... They told me that the police gave everybody a gun who came in there and everybody had guns the next morning. There were a lot of good white men ... who were out ready to kill every Negro they saw, but that did not set fire to any houses. (Brophy 2002)

McCullough detected the hands of the police in the arrests and disarming that morning. When he heard shooting outside the courthouse, he went out to investigate and found some white men. They told him "We're hunting Negroes" (Brophy 2002), then added that they were helping the police.

> When I went down to the police station about nine o'clock the whole place was full; there was a big crowd; that was about the time the soldiers came and they were loading Negroes into trucks and everyway and making them come out with their hands up, including some old women who couldn't hurt anyone, and marched them into the police station, all the time with their hands up. (Brophy 2002)

Everyone had guns and the "police seemed to be engineering it" (Brophy 2002).

After the riot, black newspapers (and Greenwood residents suing the city) alleged that the police chief, mayor, and other city officials had planned an attack on Greenwood. An account of Van B. Hurley, who was identified as a former Tulsa police officer, was printed in the ***Chicago Defender*** in October 1921. Hurley described "the conference between local aviators and the officials. After this meeting Hurley asserted the airplanes darted out from hangars and hovered over the district dropping nitroglycerin on buildings, setting them afire" (Brophy 2002). Hurley said that the officials told their deputies to deal aggressively with Greenwood residents. "They gave instructions for every man to be ready and on the alert and if the niggers wanted to start anything to be ready for them. They never put forth any efforts at all to prevent it whatever, and said if they started anything to kill every b_ son of a b_ they could find" (Brophy 2002).

Around 10:00 A.M., units of the National Guard arrived from Oklahoma City and began to restore order. In the process, they killed some white rioters. By about noon on June 1, Greenwood residents were in custody; much of the community was in flames or already reduced to embers. As Tulsa and the nation began to take stock of what had happened, people began to realize that civilization had broken down for a time. Greenwood residents in custody were released only when a white employer or friend vouched for them. Some were released as early as the afternoon of the riot; many were in custody for several days. And when they returned to Greenwood, they saw thirty-five blocks of destruction.

The city began to take stock as well. It convened a grand jury to investigate the riot's origins and what happened during its course. Its foreordained conclusion was stated in the headline of the *Tulsa World*, which said the day after the report was released, "Negroes to Blame for Inciting Race Rioting; Whites Clearly Exonerated" (Brophy 2002). The report blamed the riot in part on "exaggerated notions of social equality" (Brophy 2002). The city passed a new fire ordinance, which required use of fireproof materials in rebuilding Greenwood. That made rebuilding prohibitively expensive. The mayor sought to get more "distance between the races" (Brophy 2002) by encouraging relocating the African American section further north, away from Tulsa. That would also leave Greenwood available for conversion to an industrial site. By the early fall, that ordinance had been overturned by the Tulsa courts as an interference with the property owners' rights. They ought, the reasoning seemed to go, to be permitted to rebuild what they had. Many others left Greenwood, never to return. Some leaders of the Greenwood Community, like newspaper editor A.J. Smitherman, fled to Boston and then, ultimately, to Buffalo, where he started the *Buffalo Star*. Others, like J.B. Stradford, fled to Chicago to avoid prosecution in Tulsa. He later filed a lawsuit, but it was dismissed when he refused to return to Tulsa to have his deposition taken. And yet others like O.W. Gurley went to Los Angeles. We know virtually nothing of Dick Rowland or Sarah Page, the two people initially at the center of the riot.

But that was one of the few victories in court for Tulsa riot victims. Subsequently, when they attempted to sue the city and insurance companies, they lost. For Oklahoma law was unfavorable to people who were injured by the government at the time. One could not expect the courts to be any more favorable than the mayor or the police chief to riot victims' claims. By the early 1930s, the victims abandoned their lawsuits and the riot was confined largely to the memory of Greenwood residents. A few stories persisted, passed down through the generations until it became impossible to tell fact from fiction. There are persistent stories that airplanes were used to bomb Greenwood. There are contemporary accounts of that in the black press. The white press says the airplanes were used for observation only. Perhaps they were limited to coordinating the attack on Greenwood. It is unlikely we will ever know the full story. And there is another rumor that the *Tulsa Tribune*, which published the front-page story about Dick Rowland's arrest, also had an editorial encouraging a lynching. There is some reason for skepticism about this story. For a few weeks after the riot, the Oklahoma City *Black Dispatch* ran a front-page story titled "The Story That Set Tulsa Ablaze" (Brophy 2002). It reprints the *Tribune*'s front-page story, but makes no reference to any other stories, which suggests that there was no other story in the *Tribune*.

For the most part, the riot was forgotten until 1997 when the Oklahoma legislature authorized the **Tulsa Race Riot Commission**. The commission brought the riot back to public attention and later helped place Tulsa in the center of the debate over **reparations** for slavery and **Jim Crow**. *See also* Greenwood Community (Tulsa, Oklahoma); Tulsa Race Riot Commission.

Further Readings: Brophy, Alfred L. *Reconstructing the Dreamland: The Tulsa Riot of 1921—Race, Reparations, Reconciliation*. Oxford: Oxford University Press, 2002; Brophy, Alfred L. "The Tulsa Race Riot in the Oklahoma Supreme Court." *Oklahoma Law Review* 64 (2001): 67–146; Ellsworth, Scott. *Death in a Promised Land: The Tulsa Race Riot*. Baton Rouge: Louisiana State University Press, 1982; Ellsworth, Scott, and John Hope Franklin, eds. *Tulsa Race Riot: A Report by the Oklahoma Commission to Study the Tulsa Race Riot of 1921*. 2001. See http://www.okhistory.org/trrc/freport.htm.

Alfred L. Brophy

Tulsa Race Riot Commission

In 1997, the Oklahoma legislature passed House Joint Resolution 1035, which provided modest funding for the 1921 Tulsa Race Riot Commission (see **Tulsa [Oklahoma] Riot of 1921**). The commission grew out of the lobbying efforts of state representative Don Ross. Ross, a lifelong resident of Oklahoma and a relative of riot survivors, first heard about the 1921 riot from a high school history teacher. He then made a career out of studying the riot and preserving its memory. In the aftermath of the 1995 Oklahoma City bombing, Ross wanted to bring attention to the act of terrorism in Tulsa, and so proposed legislation establishing and funding the commission.

The enacting legislation provided for an eleven-member board, appointed in part by the governor of Oklahoma and in part by the mayor of Tulsa. It was composed of riot survivors, local residents, community leaders, and several state legislators. They were to investigate the riot, look for hidden mass graves, and then make recommendations, including ones on **reparations**. The commission began work in 1998 under the direction of Scott Ellsworth, the leading historian of the riot. Dr. Ellsworth, author of the 1982 book *Death in a Promised Land*, the most comprehensive account of the riot, set about filling in some gaps in the historical record, as well as searching for additional sources, such as missing newspaper accounts of the riot (including an alleged editorial in the *Tulsa Tribune*, believed by some to be headlined "Lynch a Negro Tonight") and missing court records (including the grand jury testimony). The commissioners sought to investigate common beliefs about the riot, including what actually happened on the afternoon of May 30, 1921, in the Drexel Building, where Dick Rowland allegedly assaulted Mary Paige; what had become of Rowland and Paige; the role of the National Guard and local police forces in the riot, whether planes were used to bomb Greenwood (the black section of Tulsa); and how many people died in the riot.

The commission enlisted the help of volunteers throughout the Tulsa community and scholars throughout the nation to address issues of military technology, anthropology, and law. It raised many questions and fueled much discussion in Tulsa and the nation at large about a long-forgotten episode of racial violence and its aftermath. The commission's historians located the riot in the context of other racial violence in Oklahoma and the Southwest at the time, retold the story of the riot in greater depth than before, and explained the immediate aftermath of the riot, emphasizing the role of the Red Cross and white and black Tulsans in shaping the rebuilding (and sometimes the lack of rebuilding). It emphasized the culpability of the city government in the riot, the role of the *Tulsa Tribune* in stirring racial animosity, and the role of black and white World War I veterans in the riot.

As the commission worked, it steadily gained national attention. By 1999, people throughout the country were following the commission's deliberations through stories by the Associated Press and in the *New York Times*. At the same time, factions began to emerge on the commission, including those who strongly advocated paying reparations to survivors; those who wanted a more moderate result, such as a state-funded museum and perhaps scholarships for students from Tulsa (one might call them the reconciliation wing); and a final, small group that seemed to oppose reparations in any form. The latter group may have had only one member—a state senator. But the divisions that were emerging in 1999 and 2000 illustrated the problems the commission's recommendations would have when they reached the state legislature in 2001.

As the commission's historians and affiliated scholars began finishing their reports in 2000, the commission added University of Oklahoma history professor Danny Goble, an expert on Oklahoma history, to write an introduction. Professor Goble faced the task of trying to distill the findings of the commission's historians to arrive at some conclusions on the facts of the riot. His introduction discussed some of the key issues that would never be resolved, including the number of people killed. Much was known about the culpability of local government and the atmosphere of racial hatred, but much was also left unknown.

Following the presentation of the report at the end of February 2001, the focus shifted to the Oklahoma legislature, to see what steps it would take in terms of reparations or other action designed for reconciliation. Legislators feared discussion of reparations. Although the commission had voted to recommend some form of reparations, the Oklahoma legislature went in other directions. They passed a statute acknowledging the tragedy of the riot and authorizing medals for riot survivors. On one side of the medal was an image of the state seal; on the other was an image of burned Greenwood. Moreover, the legislature authorized (but did not fund) scholarships for Tulsa students to attend Oklahoma colleges. Subsequently, the legislature has donated land to be used for a riot museum.

In February 2003, a group of lawyers, including Harvard Law School professor Charles Ogletree, filed a civil rights lawsuit on behalf of Tulsa riot victims. The suit was based in part on the commission report. The suit was dismissed by the federal district court in Tulsa in March 2003, on the grounds that the plaintiffs waited too long. That dismissal was subsequently affirmed by the federal court of appeals and the U.S. Supreme Court declined to hear the case. Ogletree and his team of lawyers are continuing to advocate for riot survivors, who now number about 100, before Congress and the Oklahoma legislature. The commission's work continues to be part of reparations discussions throughout the country, such as Brown University's investigation of its connections to slavery. *See also* Greenwood Community (Tulsa, Oklahoma); Tulsa (Oklahoma) Riot of 1921.

Further Readings: Brophy, Alfred L. "The Functions and Limitations of a Historical Truth Commission: The Case of the Tulsa Race Riot Commission." In Elazar Barkan and Alexander Karn, eds. *Taking Wrongs Seriously: Apologies and Reconciliation*. Stanford, CA: Stanford University Press, 2006; Brophy, Alfred L. *Reconstructing the Dreamland: The Tulsa Riot of 1921—Race, Reparations, Reconciliation*. Oxford: Oxford University Press, 2002; Brune, Adrian. "Tulsa's Shame." *The Nation*, March 18, 2002; Ellsworth, Scott. *Death in a Promised Land*. Baton Rouge: Louisiana State University Press, 1982; Ellsworth, Scott, and John Hope Franklin, eds. *Tulsa Race Riot: A Report by the Oklahoma Commission to Study the Tulsa Race Riot of 1921*, 2001. See http://www.okhistory.org/trrc/freport.htm.

Alfred L. Brophy

Ture, Kwame. *See* Carmichael, Stokely

Turner, Henry McNeal (1834–1915)

Henry McNeal Turner was a leading proponent of black emigration to Africa as a response to the hostile conditions in the American South during the nineteenth century. Turner was a bishop of the African Methodist Episcopal (AME) Church, a delegate to the Georgia constitutional convention, a member of the Georgia state legislature, founder and president of Morris Brown College in Georgia, and founder of several newspapers. His life spanned a troubled period—slavery, the Civil War, **Reconstruction**, and the ensuing **Jim Crow** era. In his early years, an optimistic Turner joined the Union Army and was a member of the Freedmen's Bureau and the Republican Party. Rampant violence and **racism**, along with other critical events, caused Turner to launch an anti-America and pro-Africa campaign. Eventually becoming a bitter and disillusioned man, he turned to Africa as the only viable way for blacks to escape the mass violence and debilitating and racist laws in America, and to achieve dignity and self-empowerment.

Turner was born free in 1834 near Abbeville, South Carolina. In his youth, he worked in the cotton fields. After running away from home, he did janitorial work in a law office. Despite laws that forbade education for blacks, the white clerks taught him to read and write. In 1853, he received a preacher's license and evangelized throughout the South for the white-controlled Methodist Episcopal (ME) Church, South. In 1856, he married Eliza Preacher, the first of four wives. Only four of Turner's fourteen children survived into adulthood.

Exasperated by the constraints placed on him by the ME church, South, Turner joined the AME Church in 1858. He preached in St. Louis, Missouri; Baltimore, Maryland; and Washington, D.C. While on the East Coast, Turner studied Latin, Greek, Hebrew, and theology. In 1860, Turner formed the first black army troop from Washington, D.C., and was assigned by President Abraham Lincoln to be its chaplain. Turner was the first black to do so in the nation. He fought valiantly alongside his troops.

After the war, Turner, envisioning a grand future for blacks, accepted President Andrew Johnson's invitation to work with the Freedmen's Bureau in Georgia to assist the newly freed slaves. After encountering racism in the bureau, Turner resigned and spent the years from 1865 to 1867 organizing AME churches in Georgia. Turner was not discouraged, despite the escalating violence against blacks across the South during the aftermath of the Civil War. In 1866, the **Ku Klux Klan (KKK)**, one of many formal and informal **vigilante organizations**, was formed. The Klan terrorized and attacked blacks accused of crimes—or for no reason at all. Also in 1866, riots erupted in **New Orleans**, Louisiana, and **Memphis**, Tennessee. In the same year, Turner gave a roseate speech at the Emancipation Day Anniversary Celebration in Augusta, Georgia, in which he explained jubilantly that their new freedom had released blacks from living in turmoil, fear, and uncertainty, and that, in due time and with honest effort, they could attain equality with whites and eliminate racism.

Despite Turner's initial optimism, life after emancipation was precarious and brutal for blacks, and equality was as intangible as it had been during slavery. The first major event to squash Turner's faith in the future of blacks in the United States occurred in 1868 when whites refused to admit him and other black representatives into the legislature. He responded with a bold, impassioned, and eloquent speech, but to no avail. Turner was devastated. Compounding the situation was the fact that all across the South, white Democrats, abetted by private mobs, were violently seizing back political control, and the federal government was withdrawing Union troops. In 1883, the U.S. Supreme Court did away with seminal Civil Rights Act laws that forbade discrimination in hotels, trains, and other public places.

Infuriated, Turner unleashed a scathing attack on the United States, and on the heinous laws and atrocities inflicted on blacks, through numerous speeches, sermons, letters, and writings. He castigated America—and any individual, black or white—for withholding the protection, rights, and freedoms due to blacks. He lambasted **white mobs** for cruelly **lynching** blacks without due process of law. He discouraged **black self-defense**, since whites often outnumbered and outarmed their victims. He advocated the idea that blacks could only find peace, freedom, self-respect, and equality by establishing their own nation in Africa. He insisted that the American government should make **reparations** for the years blacks had toiled without pay during slavery by financing their emigration to Africa.

In 1893, Turner organized a national convention for blacks in Cincinnati, Ohio. The objective was to address the mob violence, lynchings, and other crimes against blacks, which had intensified. Turner advocated emigration, but the majority of blacks present were not interested in leaving the country to solve the problems that beset them. This was one of the major reasons that Turner's back-to-Africa strategy was not successful. Turner's **Black Nationalism** only interested a small number of poor farmers. It did not attract grand-scale support. Furthermore, blacks, unable to acclimate to life in Africa, often returned to the United States. Nevertheless, Turner was one of the most daring and outspoken black leaders of his time, a man who challenged the ruthless violence and injustices inflicted on blacks. *See also Thirty Years of Lynching in the United States: 1889–1918.*

Further Reading: Redkey, Edwin S., ed. *Respect Black: Writings and Speeches of Henry M. Turner*. New York: Arno Press, 1971.

Gladys L. Knight

Turner, Mary (d. 1918), Lynching of

Mary Turner was herself a victim of **lynching** after protesting the lynching of her husband, Hayes Turner, two days earlier. Turner's death is a popular point of reference for black human rights, and is mentioned in dozens of books and articles, discussed in academic conferences on the black American experience, and is often used to emphasize American **racism** against, and violence toward blacks.

In 1918 in Valdosta, Georgia, Hampton Smith and his wife were murdered by Sidney Johnson, a black field hand who worked on Smith's plantation to pay off a fine for gambling. After working a significant number of hours beyond what was required, Johnson demanded payment; however, Smith refused. Johnson withheld his services from Smith, who then pursued and physically accosted Johnson. After laying in wait a few days, Johnson shot Smith through his window. Mrs. Smith was also injured, but survived, but Hampton Smith was mortally wounded. After the shootings, a crowd of whites gathered, and giving no concern for who was killed in Johnson's absence, a **white mob** of men kidnapped and lynched two innocent black men, Will Head and Will Thompson. The next day, Hayes Turner was kidnapped and imprisoned. While allegedly being taken to a safe place away from the white mob, Turner, while handcuffed behind his back, was also lynched by the mob. In protest, Turner's wife, Mary, who was eight months pregnant at the time, publicly vowed to report the identities of the murderers to authorities. Members of the white mob kidnapped her, taking her to a densely forested area, where they bound her by the feet, hung her face-down, doused her with motor oil and gasoline, and burned her alive. Miraculously, the burning did not kill her, and while still alive, her clothing was sheared off and her unborn child was barbarically extricated from her womb, only to have its head crushed under the foot of one white person at the base of the tree from which Turner was hung. Finally, Turner was riddled with over 150 bullets. In addition to the lynchings of Head, Thompson, and the Turners during the racial fray, Eugene Rice, Chime Riley, Simon Schuman, and Sidney Johnson were also lynched.

The lynching and disembowelment of Mary Turner and the crushing of her child's head are a case of American racial violence that has reached beyond the original contextual borders, affecting other aspects of black culture and life, including politics, nationalism, and literature. Turner's death lent credibility to the increasing need for **black self-defense** by emphasizing the extreme violence against blacks in the South and the lack of legal redress afforded them, despite the **Fourteenth Amendment**. The details of the Turner lynching have made the Black Nationalist case for self-defense and unification of all Africans in the Diaspora. However, it is within black literature that Mary Turner has had considerable impact, particularly during the Harlem Renaissance.

Angela Grimké's story "Goldie" (the 1920 revised edition of "Blackness") treats the Turner incident, although Margaret Sanger was suspected of publishing the work in *Birth Control Review* to discourage black reproduction. Jean Toomer's *Cane* (Kabnis) also re-creates the death of Turner, changing the circumstances of the death, but not the motive. **National Association for the Advancement of Colored People (NAACP)** investigator **Walter White** wrote about the lynching of Turner after his probe into the lynching of blacks in general, and Turner's murder in particular, which was published in ***The Crisis*** in 1918.

The cruelty and barbarity of the killings of Mary Turner and her unborn child continue to be a reference point in arguments for human rights across the nation. Deleso Alford Washington, co-chair of the Legal Strategies Commission for the National Coalition of Blacks for Reparations in America used Turner's murder to make his argument for H.R. 40, the Commission to

Study Reparations Poposals for African Americn Act, before Congress in 2005, attesting to the political similarities between her murder and the 1998 lynching of **James Byrd, Jr.**, in Jasper, Texas. In his address to the 2005 audience at the NAACP's convention, Julian Bond discussed the lynching of Turner to bring to the foreground the American government's consistent refusal to pass anti-lynching laws, or to apologize for the treatment of blacks. *See also* Anti-Lynching Bureau; Anti-Lynching League; Black Nationalism; Dyer Anti-Lynching Bill of 1921; Griggs, Sutton; Hose, Sam, Lynching of; Parker, Mack Charles, Lynching of; Racism; Rape, as Provocation for Lynching; Reparations; *Thirty Years of Lynching in the United States: 1889–1918*; Till, Emmett, Lynching of; Washington, Jesse, Lynching of.

Further Readings: Als, Hilton, and James Allen. *Without Sanctuary: Lynching Photography in America*. Santa Fe, CA: Twin Palms Publishers, 2000; Brown, Mary. *Eradicating This Evil: Women in the American Anti-Lynching Movement, 1892–1940*. New York: Garland, 2000; Dray, Phillip. *At the Hands of Persons Unknown: The Lynching of Black America*. New York: Random House, 2002; Ginzburg, Ralph. *100 Years of Lynchings*. Baltimore: Black Classic Press, 1997.

Ellesia Ann Blaque

U

Urbanization

Urbanization is the growth of a population living in urban areas when an increasing proportion of an entire populace lives in cities and their suburbs. In the United States, urbanization has been closely connected with industrialization. Technological advances during the mid-1800s through the early decades of the 1900s shifted the main energy sources from humans and animals to machines. These changes enhanced human productivity and contributed to increased surpluses in both agriculture and industry and, given their condensed layout, cities became ideal places for businesses to locate factories and their workers. Thus, whereas 5 percent of the U.S. population lived in cities at the beginning of the nineteenth century, about 50 percent lived in urban areas by the first decades of the twentieth century. These shifts corresponded with rapid economic changes in the United States, especially those associated with the developing automobile industry, and the transition of technological leadership from Great Britain to the United States. Today about 80 percent of the U.S. population lives in urban areas.

Urbanization created a rapid change in the economies of local communities as agriculture, traditional local services, and small-scale industry gave way to big industry and related commerce. Industrialization created its own need for resources, particularly cheap human labor, and began drawing from an ever-widening area for its own sustenance. The decline of the agriculture industry in the rural South combined with the rise of the textile industries elsewhere to spawn a growth in urban areas throughout the United States.

In addition, post-Civil War political maneuverings, culminating in the presidential election of 1877, dismantled whatever political and economic gains black citizens enjoyed during the period of **Reconstruction**. Therefore, industrialism attracted poor southern black sharecroppers to urban areas where they believed they would enjoy greater economic opportunities. Significant geographic shifts in black U.S. residential patterns began as early as the late nineteenth century. However, the first two decades of the 1900s saw an increase in black urbanization, as large numbers of black families left the rural South for cities throughout the Midwest and along the eastern seaboard as part of the **Great Migration**.

Despite their optimism, African Americans found themselves largely concentrated in **ghettos**, subjected to **poverty**, and consigned to second-class citizenship. Unique features of urban life attendant to the growth of U.S. cities exacerbated these conditions and fostered racial tensions. For example, urbanization contributed to the spread of tenement living. Tenements are narrow multiunit buildings that contain few windows, limited plumbing and electricity, and small rooms. Tenements were the main housing available in the segregated areas occupied by multiple black and immigrant families who were forced to live in them because of poverty, **racism**, and, in some instances, law. They were incubators for disease, high infant mortality, and elevated levels of pollution. The hyper-dense living arrangements also fostered volatile social conditions and contributed to the eruption of race riots in major cities throughout the United States.

For example, in 1919 alone there were twenty-six race riots in the United States and in 1921 a **Tulsa**, Oklahoma, race riot resulted in the leveling of thirty-five square blocks in a predominantly black urban enclave and, by some estimations, more than 300 deaths. Both the pre–civil rights period of the 1940s and the post–civil rights period of the 1960s were punctuated by an increase in the number of race riots. Although each period was characterized by problems particular to its respective era, both shared similar social elements attendant to urbanization, immigration, wartime politics, and economic uncertainty.

Urbanization has changed over time, coming to a halt as cities and suburbs have become saturated with people. Changing social patterns and labor relations due to immigration have shifted the United States from an industrial to an information society. In addition, post-industrialism has resulted in massive job losses across the United States that disproportionately impact urban centers. In Philadelphia, Pennsylvania, for example, the expansion of service and high-tech industries resulted in a loss of over 100,000 jobs during the mid-1990s; in New York City, where nine out of ten jobs are currently in the service sector, 350,000 jobs were lost from 1989 to 1993. Changes in the economy have also created new geographic points of major human settlements and activity. Once concentrated around the downtown area of cities, residential areas and places for leisure and entertainment, such as malls, amusement parks, and sports facilities, have increasingly moved to largely white suburbs.

The consequences for urban centers have been severe, as suburbanization has resulted in a shift in tax bases, leaving city social goods, such as schools, hospitals, and local transportation, police and fire departments, understaffed and underfunded. Ironically, even as social changes attendant to post-industrialism have fostered conditions that contribute to racial tension and unrest, so have some of the measures employed to counter the demise of cities. For instance, city governments have provided increasingly generous incentives to lure mostly white professionals into their downtown areas to expand urban tax bases and to weed out blight. As a result, housing costs have skyrocketed and low-rent apartments have been supplanted by new developments, such as high-priced loft districts, that have displaced existing residents in historically black enclaves like Harlem, New York; Atlanta, Georgia; St. Louis, Missouri; and Oakland, California.

Further Readings: Population Reference Bureau. See http://www.prb.org/; Merrifield, Andy, and Erik Swyngedouw, eds. *The Urbanization of Injustice*. New York: New York University Press, 1997; U.S. Census Bureau. See http://www.census.gov/.

Garrett A. Duncan

V

Vietnam War and Race Riots

As the Vietnam War progressed, its connection to the **civil rights movement** became more pronounced. Race riots in the United States in the 1960s often reflected combined resentments—a perceived inequality of the impact of the war in Vietnam on African Americans and growing frustrations with discrimination and **racism** at home. Thus, riots and violence ensued among African Americans, both in the army in Vietnam and in the United States (see **Long Hot Summer Riots, 1965–1967**).

The home front saw riots both directly and indirectly connected to Vietnam. One of the more famous domestic episodes was the **Jackson State University Incident (1970)**. In the wake of the invasion of Cambodia and the violence at Kent State University, riots erupted at Jackson State University in Mississippi. The conflict at Jackson State was sparked by racial tensions in town and was brought to a head by **antiwar protests**. Two dead and twelve wounded signaled the volatile mix of race, frustration over civil rights, and antiwar agitation.

Racial tensions enveloped not only life at home, but within the armed services itself as the war expanded and became more unpopular in the late 1960s. The interracial violence coupled with Black Power that marked the home front also scarred the military. Discrimination was not alien to the military, and the same polarization that marked many breakdowns in American society was reflected in the rank and file of the armed services as many black soldiers sought to embrace their culture.

War showed strains in the system of military justice as the services tried to weed out what they noted as undesirables; a large number of these were black militants who challenged the system and the war. Because so many blacks served in the military, and were—especially in beginning of war—at a disproportionate number to whites, tensions increased. In addition, those normal stresses seen in society at large were heightened because of the military situation and the war. Punishment often fell more heavily on those categorized as black militants.

As the war expanded after 1965, opposition became an important issue among African American activists. For example, **Martin Luther King, Jr.**, especially in the last year of his life, broke with President Lyndon Johnson over the war. The riots that coursed through the Watts district of **Los Angeles** in 1965 and in Harlem in 1964 had negative effects on the military, but the widespread violent reaction to the 1968 assassination of King brought the greatest racial turmoil to the armed forces. Growing numbers of blacks were frustrated. Increased impatience with the war and the delays in racial progress in the United States led to race riots on a number of ships and military bases.

On August 30, 1968, the American prisoners in the Long Binh military stockade rioted. Blacks made up nearly 90 percent of the population. The prisoners voluntarily segregated themselves. The prison was incredibly dangerous with inhumane conditions and severe overcrowding that only worsened racial tensions. Prisoners often taunted the mostly white guards with Black Power signs. Racial tensions, combined with allegations of rampant drug use, were the primary causes of the uprising. In the end, one inmate was killed and fifty-eight inmates and five military policemen were injured before the military police used tear gas to break up the riot. Following a quick U.S. Army investigation, the U.S. command announced that racial tensions caused the riot. The command also claimed that most of the inmate injuries were caused by inmates fighting among themselves. Nearly a month later, twelve black inmates were still holding out in a section of the stockade. Eventually, six of the black inmates accused of starting the riot were charged with the murder or conspiracy to commit the murder of the white inmates.

Earlier in August, American prisoners in the Marine Corps brig at Danang rioted and set fire to cell blocks. Military police had to use tear gas to quell the riot. Two months later, in response to a weekend of incidents with racial overtones and tension between blacks and whites, the U.S. Navy imposed restrictions on movement in the Danang region.

At the Navy base at Cam Ranh Bay, white sailors donned **Ku Klux Klan (KKK)**–like outfits, burned crosses, and raised the Confederate flag. In February 1969, riots at Fort Benning, Georgia, followed when a black soldier awaiting discharge vented frustration over being assigned to menial labor and attacked white troops. That same summer in Camp Lejeune, North Carolina, forty-three men were charged when blacks and Puerto Ricans beat up white U.S. Marines. In March 1970, in Goose Bay, in Labrador, Canada, white airmen, apparently angered because local white women danced with blacks, stabbed a black man, thereby triggering random beatings of whites in retaliation.

The services dealt with issues by trying to grant concessions—both real and symbolic. For example, military brass accepted a modified afro, tolerated the Black Power salute, and cracked down on the use of racial epithets and offensive words. But these efforts did not resolve the problems. In October 1972, on the aircraft carrier *Kitty Hawk*, a series of incidents occurred that underscored the thin barrier that held back racial tensions. The *Kitty Hawk*, a mostly white ship, experienced trouble onboard after a brawl in an enlisted man's club in Subic Bay. The first confrontation, involving a group of black sailors and a detachment of Marines, was defused by the executive officer, an African American. However, this did not end the situation, and small groups of five to twenty-five blacks raged through the ship, attacking whites and pulling many sleeping sailors from their berths to beat them with their fists, chains, metal pipes, fire extinguisher nozzles, and broom handles. About 150 armed sailors moved through the ship spreading the hostility. The executive officer followed them and finally managed to end the threat of violence.

Although some men were charged, the *Kitty Hawk* incident, along with the other outbreaks of violence in the armed services, all reflected the fact the military was not immune from the stresses of society. The racial confrontations that raged across the United States were carried to the armed forces and did not subside until the war ended and changes were made. The military repeatedly provided a microcosm of the war's growing effect on race relations at home and how those tensions helped to exacerbate racial antagonism, at times culminating in violence. *See also* King, Martin Luther, Jr., Assassination of; Los Angeles (California) Riot of 1965.

Further Readings: Buckley, Gail. *Strength for the Fight: A History of Black Americans in the Military.* New York: Random House, 2001; Glines, C.V. "Black vs. White—Trouble in the Ranks." *Armed Forces Management* 16 (June 1970): 20–27; Rivera, Oswald. *Fire and Rain.* New York: Four Walls Eight Windows, 1990; Shields, Patrick M. "The Burden of the Draft: The Vietnam Years." *Journal of Political and Military Sociology* 9 (Fall 1982): 215–228; Terry, Wallace. *Bloods: An Oral History of the Vietnam War by Black Veterans.* New York: Random House, 1984; Tucker, Spencer C., ed. *Encyclopedia of the Vietnam War: A Political, Social, and Military History.* Santa Barbara, CA: ABC-CLIO, 1998.

Gary Gershman

Vigilante Organizations

Vigilante organizations are groups that are formed to extralegally enforce law and order and to protect life, community, and property. Whites established the first vigilante organizations in America in the 1700s. Vigilantism grew more violent and racist with the passage of time. Blacks also organized, both formally and informally, in response to the violence inflicted on them by the vigilantes and by spontaneously formed **white mobs**. Ultimately, white vigilante organizations outmatched blacks in terms of strength, number, influence, and brutality.

The earliest instances of **vigilantism** were not racist by nature. In 1767, white South Carolinians formed the Back Country Regulators. Like hundreds of organizations that followed it, the Regulators sought to provide an effective defense against a growing number of bandits, outlaws, and ne'er-do-wells in the absence of laws and law enforcement. Ostracizing, tarring and feathering, and whipping were initially employed as methods of punishment, but were soon largely replaced by **lynching**.

Vigilante organizations frequently developed elaborate organizational structures and procedures. For example, some organizations developed officers, hierarchical frameworks, constitutions, articles, and a manifesto. Others operated secretly, employing spies and passwords and using disguises to apprehend and execute criminals. In most cases, vigilantes executed offenders with or without the crude semblance of a trial. Common crimes during this period were the stealing of horses and gold, claim jumping, and shooting.

Vigilante organizations soon directed their wanton fury and vengeance on groups assumed to be inferior, such as sheep herders, Native Americans, immigrant groups, and blacks. Vigilante organizations systematically targeted these groups in response to deeply ingrained prejudices, as well as economic factors such as competition over land and resources. One of the earliest and most notorious vigilante organizations to appear after the Civil War was the **Ku Klux Klan (KKK)**. This organization was patterned after earlier vigilante groups. Numerous organizations similar to the Klan sprang up, including the Men of Justice, the Pale Faces, the Constitutional Union Guards, the White Brotherhood, the Order of the White Rose, and the **White League**.

The Ku Klux Klan was formed in 1866 in Pulaski, Tennessee. The original members were former Confederates who united to fight against liberal Republicans, black sympathizers, and blacks themselves. They were responsible for a large number of deaths, tortures, and burnings. They were instrumental in helping the conservative Democrats regain political power at the close of **Reconstruction** by subduing black suffrage through violence and intimidation. They also helped enforce the social, economic, and political oppression of blacks.

Klan members, or Clansmen, wore white robes and cone-shaped hoods to hide their identities. The all-white Klan united rich and poor, professional and laborer, landowner and landless against a common enemy. Disguised whites who rode on horses called themselves the Night Riders. The Klan frequently paraded silently through a town and devised mystical languages and disguises as scare tactics. They relied heavily on violence, such as lynching, torture, burning, and even rioting.

The Klan soon became a powerful entity. Despite occasional attempts to put a stop to their lawlessness, their actions went largely unchallenged. After Reconstruction, the federal government withdrew the troops, who had previously subdued such organizations, and no longer interfered in the affairs of the South. Indeed, many members of the government, as well as law enforcers, either supported or were members of the Klan. They helped enforce oppressive ordinances to maintain white domination over blacks. The Ku Klux Klan also incited or played a role in the riots that swept the nation in four major waves between 1866 and 1951, and participated in the violent opposition faced by both black and white protestors during the **civil rights movement**.

The earliest instances of black vigilantism occurred during slavery times. All the blacks who participated in the seven major uprisings and revolts of the eighteenth century, intending to take retribution on slave owners and on whites in general, lost their lives in the process. In response to the growing incidences of anti-abolitionist violence and riots in the North, blacks formed vigilante organizations. The most successful was William Still's Philadelphia Vigilance Association, an interracial organization that was active in the 1840s and 1850s. Their main objective was to aid slaves who had escaped to the North.

For the most part, blacks took a defensive, rather than an aggressive, approach to violence. Informal groups of armed men who patrolled their communities constituted the most common vigilante activity in the North and the South. These loosely organized groups were frequently overwhelmed by white violence, as was the case in the **Greenwood Community** destroyed during the **Tulsa (Oklahoma) Riot of 1921**. On the other hand, the **Deacons for Defense and Justice** were effective in staving off Ku Klux Klan attacks. When these organizations disbanded, Klan activity returned. Blacks were often murdered or otherwise thwarted when they attempted to confront racial violence. The **Black Panther Party (BPP)** was founded in the 1960s to better the condition of blacks in the **ghettos** and to protect black communities from **police brutality**. The BPP engaged in occasional violent confrontations, but the organization collapsed after the federal government infiltrated it.

Newspapers, both black and white, campaigned against specific vigilante organizations and violence in general. Legal cases, as well as decisive actions by the federal government, led to the elimination of racial violence. *See also* Frontier Justice.

Further Reading: Brown, Richard Maxwell. *Strain of Violence: Historical Studies of American Violence and Vigilantism*. New York: Oxford University Press, 1975.

Gladys L. Knight

Vigilantism

Vigilantism is an unlawful process whereby a community is purged of individuals who have allegedly committed crimes or other offenses. This phenomenon was first seen in the American West in 1767, where it was driven by noble intentions to maintain law and order and protect life, community, and property. But by the 1830s, vigilantism was being systematically used to justify brutal assaults against blacks. The horrendous practice did not end until the 1960s when the cumulative work of predominantly black leaders, the press, organizations, and federal intervention brought it to an end.

Vigilante activities against blacks followed the same patterns throughout the United States. Some whites formed spontaneous mobs or other more formal **vigilante organizations**. These vigilantes often collaborated with local law enforcement and were led or supported by prominent officials and community leaders. Whites, including young children, attending in droves, sometimes participated in the executions. Newspapers advertised impending executions and later printed sensational and gruesome accounts.

Vigilante crimes centered mostly around rioting and **lynching**. Beginning in the 1830s, whites rioted in black urban communities to discourage racial integration, black progress, and abolitionary activities. In the South after **Reconstruction**, whites rioted to regain political, social, and economic power. During the massive black migrations to the North, they also rioted to suppress black advancement and competition for jobs and housing.

Lynching was most frequent in the South but, in fact, it occurred in all but four states. The offenses blacks were alleged to have committed included assault, rape, robbery, and any number of violations of **racial etiquette**. Sometimes whites victimized blacks merely out of unadulterated racial prejudice. Lynching regularly included **castration**, dismemberment, and burning. *See also* Frontier Justice; Great Migration; Lynching.

Further Reading: Brown, Richard Maxwell. *Strain of Violence: Historical Studies of American Violence and Vigilantism*. New York: Oxford University Press, 1975.

Gladys L. Knight

Villard, Oswald Garrison (1872–1949)

Journalist, reformer, and pacifist, Oswald Garrison Villard, grandson of abolitionist William Lloyd Garrison, was born on March 13, 1872, in Wiesbaden, Germany, to U.S. citizens Henry and Helen Francis "Fanny" Garrison Villard on one of the couple's many foreign excursions. The junior Villard's philosophy of social justice was fostered by his mother's uncompromising commitment to equality, women's suffrage, and world peace; and his father's experiences as a Civil War battlefield correspondent. In his undergraduate years at Harvard University, Villard had no reputation for early political involvement. In writing for the *New York Evening Post* and *The Nation*, publications owned by his father, he wrote relatively conservative stances that assured him a teaching offer at his alma mater. There he received a master's degree without completing his thesis.

In 1897, Henry Villard arranged a brief, low-paying *Philadelphia Press* apprenticeship. At age twenty-four, the younger Villard refused an editor's position at the *New York Evening Post*, choosing instead to serve as feature editor to a Saturday supplement guided by anti-imperialist and pacifist editor Edwin L. Godkin, whose lead Villard followed on a variety of issues: condemnation of America's role in the Philippines and Cuba during the Spanish-American War, support of free trade, labor issues, and the elimination of political corruption. In 1900, Villard was a leader in the third-party movement and an assortment of support organizations for blacks and immigrants.

Having met his future wife, Julie Sanford, a former Kentucky Confederate officer's daughter, while still at Harvard, the couple produced three children. A fondness for sailing his thirty-five-foot sloop led to the creation of an elite magazine, *Yachting*. Throughout his life he belonged to exclusive New York social clubs and organizations, including the New York Philharmonic Society. In contrast, Villard helped in organizing a successful national conference on the plight of black people, which led to the founding of the **National Association for the Advancement of Colored People (NAACP)** in 1909. He held a position on its board for the rest of his life. His 1910 exposé of state Republican majority leader, Jotham L. Aulds, led to the first graft conviction of a New York legislator.

Villard's credits as a serious historical scholar resulted from his *John Brown, 1800–1859: A Biography Fifty Years After* (1910) and *Germany Embattled: An American Interpretation* (1940), in which Villard expressed competing loyalties between pride for his German ancestry and the militarism he so rejected. Respected, at first, by Woodrow Wilson for his isolationist policies, Villard lost favor with the president as World War I preparations escalated and the outspoken journalist criticized U.S. involvement. Villard lost much of his prestige and social standing by 1918 when he sold the parent publication and became editor of *The Nation*. The magazine served as an instrument for conveying Villard's ambitions and unswerving adherence to anti-imperialism, equal rights, opposition to lifetime terms for federal judges, congressional override of U.S. Supreme Court decisions, and establishment of a third political party, among other issues. Support for Socialist leader Eugene Debs' release from jail and bid for the U.S. presidency cemented the editor and the magazine as enemies of right-wing political groups. Villard's criticism of less-than-conclusive murder charges against Italian activists Sacco and Vanzetti, thought to be based on their anarchist viewpoints, prompted an angry Ohio mob of Legionnaires to attack the writer following a speech. He was blacklisted by the Daughters of the American Revolution.

After many years of hard-hitting radical journalism, he was still respected for his first-rate work. Villard suffered a heart attack in 1944, yet completed a lengthy attack on tariff systems. His righteous morality inspired the creation of the American Civil Rights Union, yet his last days of protest against World War II, during which he sided with ultra-conservative isolationists in the American First Committee, left him bitter about unrealized goals for his country. Villard died in 1949.

Further Reading: Humes, D. Joy. *Oswald Garrison Villard, Liberal of the 1920's*. Binghamton, NY: Syracuse University Press, 1960.

Millicent Ellison Brown

Virden, Pana, and Carterville (Illinois) Mine Riots (1898–1899)

The Illinois Coal Mine Riots were different incidents in three Illinois mining communities in 1898 and 1899 involving striking miners and black strikebreakers from the South. The Virden Riot occurred when miners and guards of the Chicago-Virden Coal Company exchanged gunfire when a train attempted to unload its black passengers. The Pana Riot occurred after a black strikebreaker and a deputy sheriff exchanged gunfire. The Carterville Riot was the result of black strikebreakers defending themselves against white miners.

In the second half of the nineteenth century, mining companies in Illinois used black strikebreakers with mixed results. Local townspeople generally assumed that blacks coming into their area were strikebreakers. While there was inherent **racism** in most Illinois residents—a carryover from the harsh black laws of the antebellum period—many low-paid workers additionally viewed blacks as an economic threat. The Illinois coal-mining industry illustrated these problems, and the growing discontent against black strikebreakers reached a climax in 1898 and 1899.

Coal miners worked long hours and earned low wages. In 1897, the United Mine Workers (UMW) called for a strike after negotiations between the union and mining operators broke down. Six months later, the operators agreed to concessions resulting in eight-hour days and six-day weeks. Most importantly, miners received forty cents per ton produced, a 60 percent increase in their pay.

Several mine operators complained that with the increase in pay, they would be unable to sell their coal in the Chicago market. Four operators and the UMW agreed to arbitration, which resulted in a favorable decision for the union. Several mines in Illinois, including the Chicago-Virden Coal Company in Virden; the Penwell Coal Company, the Pana Coal Company, and the Springside Mine in Pana; and the St. Louis and Big Muddy Coal Company in Carterville, decided to disregard the ruling, and the miners continued their strike against the operators. The central Illinois communities of Virden and Pana are twenty miles south and forty-five miles southeast of Springfield, respectively; Carterville is in southern Illinois, sixty miles north of Cairo. In all three communities, the operators recruited nonunion labor, but mass picket lines prevented laborers from working in Pana. Finally, the operators decided to bring in black strikebreakers from the South. The mining operators in Virden and Pana sent men to Alabama to recruit men who would receive twenty-five cents per ton. Samuel Brush, the operator in Carterville, secured the service of blacks from Tennessee. Some went north as individuals, and some brought their families.

In Pana, the operators built a stockade around the coal mines to prevent union miners from blocking work. Two hundred blacks arrived in Pana on August 24, 1898. By the beginning of October, nearly 700 blacks had arrived in Pana to work at the coal mine. Most blacks settled near the mines in the Flatham district. The sheriff supported the operators, and despite words and various incidents, most blacks were able to work in the mines with little to no opposition from the striking miners.

One incident caused Gov. John Tanner to call the Illinois National Guard to Pana. As a way to remove blacks from town, union miners attempted to pay train fare to Alabama for blacks who chose to leave. When several miners approached a black man on September 28, 1898, other blacks joined in to resist. A police officer arrested a black worker and began to move him to jail. A group of armed blacks, led by Henry Stevens, challenged the officers and armed miners, and the two groups exchanged gunfire, which injured a few blacks, but no one was seriously hurt. The police arrested Stevens, who received a fine for disturbing the peace and inciting a riot. The presence of the Illinois National Guard probably prevented more incidents from occurring.

In Virden, the situation was different. During the train ride from the Alabama to Virden, black strikebreakers received threats of violence when union miners boarded the train to convince them to return to the South. A small number did leave, but most remained on board. Miners from nearby communities arrived in Virden to prevent the company from bringing in the southern blacks. To protect the incoming black miners, the company built a stockade around the mine and moved other buildings within the stockade. Finally, the company hired ex-policemen and agents from a St. Louis detective agency to act as guards at the stockade.

On September 24, 1898, the first trainload of blacks approached Virden. The engineer noticed a large crowd but continued north to Springfield rather than stopping. In the next few weeks, rumors circulated throughout central Illinois about various trains carrying blacks, all of whom were under suspicion of being strikebreakers. Governor Tanner ordered the Illinois National Guard to move from Pana to Virden to stop any violence from occurring there.

On October 12, 1898, another train rolled into Virden with approximately fifty black coal miners. The company ordered the engineer to stop the train. The company's plan was to provide a guarded pathway for the strikebreakers to get inside the stockade. Once the train stopped in front of the stockade, someone fired a shot, and the guards and the striking miners began shooting at each other. The black strikebreakers crouched below the window-line to avoid the gunshots. After the twenty-minute gunfight, bullet holes covered the train cars, and none of the windows remained intact. The train quickly rolled off toward Springfield, leaving at least thirty wounded and seven dead striking miners, and five wounded and four dead guards. None of the blacks on board the train died, but several had received wounds.

After the riot, there were isolated incidents in which white miners attacked blacks. One black man escaped from the poor temporary housing conditions in Springfield only to be beaten by several whites. Another black man went to Virden to proclaim that he had a right to work as much as any other man, but he too was beaten. No blacks worked in the mines in Virden. Some returned to Birmingham, Alabama, while others settled in Springfield and St. Louis. By the middle of November, the Chicago-Virden Company capitulated, and the striking miners returned to work at the forty-cent-per-ton rate.

In Pana, however, the three coal companies refused to capitulate. In November, a pro-miner sheriff won election over the pro-operator incumbent. Minor skirmishes continued, but by February 1899, local townspeople grew tired of the Illinois National Guard presence. On March 23, 1899, Governor Tanner ordered the withdrawal of troops from Pana.

On April 10, 1899, Henry Stevens wanted to talk with several blacks who had been arrested. When police refused to let him do so and ordered him to leave, Stevens showed his gun. Deputy Sheriff Frank Cheney and Stevens exchanged shots, and Stevens fled as Cheney and other deputies chased him. During the chase, miners took up positions on rooftops to fire at blacks, and blacks took up positions in the stockade to fire at whites. Stevens made it to Penwell's Store, but the deputies continued their pursuit and shot him in the neck. Stevens' wound was not serious, and the police arrested him.

After the shooting, five blacks and two whites were dead, and six blacks and nine whites were wounded. Many of the killed and wounded were innocent bystanders, some of whom were simply working in their homes. Governor Tanner again ordered troops to Pana, and they quickly restored order. On April 13, the troops searched homes for weapons and collected several wagonloads. By June, the troops left Pana, and the mines shut down, leaving the black strikebreakers unemployed. They appealed to Governor Tanner for funds to return to Alabama, and Tanner responded by providing transportation at a cost of $1,600. Nearly all of the black strikebreakers left Pana. In October 1899, the Pana operators agreed to the forty-cent-per-ton rate.

In May 1898, Samuel Brush, the general manager of the St. Louis and Big Muddy Coal Company successfully recruited nearly 180 black strikebreakers to work with many of the remaining white miners. Despite the uneasiness between the strikers and strikebreakers, Brush's mine continued to operate without much trouble. The strikebreakers, however, produced less coal, and Brush had to spend additional money on guards and protection. In March 1899, Brush agreed to most of the union's demands, but he refused to recognize the union. At this time, the mine was the last large nonunion mine in the state. When Brush failed to concede to some of the miners' demands, the miners organized and called for a strike in May 1899. Brush knew of the departing strikebreakers from Pana and recruited them to work in Carterville.

On June 30, 1899, the train carrying black strikebreakers from Pana stopped a few miles northwest of Carterville. An armed man boarded the train, telling the conductor not to proceed. The conductor ordered the engineer to start the train, and men hiding in an adjacent field fired at the train, killing the wife of one of the black miners and wounding twenty other people on the train. The black miners on the train fired back into the field, but the train rolled on, preventing any more casualties. The black miners from Pana disembarked at Carterville without incident. Later in the week, the black miners fought back, but no one on either side received serious injuries. Governor Tanner ordered Spanish-American War veteran troops from nearby Carbondale to Williamson County to restore order. With the presence of the troops, there were no incidents for the rest of the summer.

On September 11, 1899, the troops left Carterville. On September 17, some white miners and black strikebreakers exchanged words. Later and unrelated, several black miners and family members walked to the Illinois Central Railroad station for personal business, and an armed group of blacks accompanied them. Believing that the armed black escort was responding to the exchange of words, an armed group of thirty white miners met them at the train station. Rather than face gunfire, the black families and their escorts left the station escaping along the tracks, but the white miners pursued them. One of the black men fired at their pursuers, and the miners responded by returning fire. Five of the blacks died instantly, and several others were injured. The remaining group made it back to the mine, and nearly 200 blacks stormed the mine's storehouse, where there were guns, but Brush's son prevented them from arming themselves. The troops returned shortly and restored peace. Three white men faced trial for the murder of the blacks, but a jury acquitted all three. Brush, who was known as a friend of the blacks, never capitulated to the union, and eventually sold his interest in the mine in 1906.

The Illinois General Assembly responded to the Virden Riot by passing a bill making it an offense for any person or company to induce workmen to come to Illinois to act as strikebreakers. One of the few dissenting votes was from William L. Martin, a black representative from Cook County. Governor Tanner enthusiastically supported the bill and signed it into law four days after the Pana Riot. In reality, the main purpose of the bill was to prevent black strikebreakers from entering the state.

Further Readings: Angle, Paul M. "Doctrinaire vs. Union." In *Bloody Williamson: A Chapter in American Lawlessness*. New York: Alfred A. Knopf, 1952, 89–116; Gutman, Herbert G. "Black Coal Miners and the American Labor Movement." In *Work, Culture, and Society in Industrializing America*. New York: Alfred A. Knopf, 1976, 119–208; Hicken, Victor. "The Virden and Pana Mine Wars of 1898." *Journal of the Illinois State Historical Society* 52 (1959): 263–278.

John A. Lupton

W

Waco Horror. *See* Washington, Jesse, Lynching of

War on Poverty

The War on Poverty was declared by President Lyndon B. Johnson during his first State of the Union address on January 8, 1964, and was a significant component of his Great Society campaign. Before President Johnson declared this metaphorical war, President **John F. Kennedy** had considered making the elimination of **poverty** a focus of his reelection campaign and second administration. In fact, Johnson's Great Society campaign was an extension of Kennedy's New Frontier initiatives, which included federal funding for education, health care for the elderly, as well as ending racial discrimination. Kennedy's initiatives assumed that by expanding access to health care, education, employment, and training opportunities, the poor would also benefit from the growth of the U.S. economy.

Michael Harrington's book *The Other America* (1962), the **civil rights movement**, and the urban unrest of the 1960s further supported the need for legislation that would address the economic and social problems faced by the poor. Certainly, the Watts riot in 1965 further demonstrated the need for such legislation and related programs (see **Los Angeles [California] Riot of 1965**). The War on Poverty involved legislation and social programs that were aimed at reducing or eliminating poverty in the United States, which at the time affected over 35 million people or 25 percent of the population. The War on Poverty speech encouraged the U.S. Congress to pass the Economic Opportunity Act (EOA) on August 20, 1964, which provided funds to combat unemployment and poverty. The EOA was the first government-sponsored attempt to include the poor and encourage their active participation in the planning and implementation of programs. The EOA established the since-disbanded Office of Economic Opportunity (OEO), which was to administrate the local application of federal funds aimed at poverty reduction. This legislation included several social programs designed to promote health, education, and the welfare of the poor. Further, this legislation was the basis for various initiatives, including: the Job

Corps; Volunteers in Service to America (VISTA), which was a domestic version of the Peace Corps; Upward Bound; Head Start; Legal Services, which provided legal services for the poor; the Neighborhood Youth Corps; the Community Action Program (CAP), which called for the establishment of community action agencies throughout the United States to focus on and improve a community's response to the needs of the poor by mobilizing resources and increasing sensitivity to their plight (the most controversial of all initiatives); the college Work-Study Program; Neighborhood Development Centers; small-business loan programs; rural programs; migrant worker programs; and community health care centers.

As part of Johnson's Great Society legislation, other important antipoverty measures included the Revenue Act of 1964, which called for an $11 billion tax cut; the Food Stamp Act (1964); the Social Security Amendments creating the Medicare and Medicaid programs (1965); the creation of the U.S. Department of Housing and Urban Development (1965); the Fair Housing Act (1968); various urban renewal projects; the **Civil Rights Act of 1964**; and the Voting Rights Act (1965). The latter two were a significant step for the civil rights movement. Originally introduced by Kennedy, the Civil Rights Act was the most extensive civil rights legislation enacted since **Reconstruction**. The Voting Rights Act eliminated several barriers to registration that had traditionally been utilized, especially in the South, to restrict black voting. After its enactment, black voter registration began a sharp increase, one reason why the Voting Rights Act has been referred to as the most effective piece of civil rights legislation ever passed by Congress.

Johnson's antipoverty programs were quickly the focus of criticism. Some argued that they did not do enough for the poor, while others argued that they did too much. Some argued that these programs demoralized the poor and others argued that they inspired the poor to riot. At the same time, Johnson began to rapidly increase U.S. involvement in Vietnam. By February 1965, U.S. fighter planes began bombing North Vietnam, and U.S. troops increased to more than 180,000 by the end of 1965, and to 500,000 by 1968. Racial tension at home sharpened, resulting in widespread race riots between 1965 and 1968. The racial unrest and the imperfections of some of the Great Society programs, including antipoverty measures, led to Republican gains in the 1966 elections, significantly limiting any hopes for further congressional cooperation with the Johnson administration. As a result, Johnson made two surprising announcements in 1968—he would stop bombing most of North Vietnam and attempt to negotiate an end to the war, and he would not run for reelection. Over the years, many of the War on Poverty programs have weathered attacks and the ill effects of underfunding and remain a significant component of U.S. antipoverty policy. *See also* Long Hot Summer Riots, 1965–1967; Urbanization; Vietnam War and Race Riots.

Further Readings: Clark, Robert F. *The War on Poverty: History, Selected Programs and Ongoing Impact*. Washington, D.C.: University Press of America, 2002; Divine, Robert A., ed. *Exploring the Johnson Years*. Austin: University of Texas Press, 1981; Gettleman, Marvin E., and David Mermelstein, eds. *The Great Society Reader: The Failure of American Liberalism*. New York: Random House, 1967;

Helsing, Jeffrey. *Johnson's War/Johnson's Great Society: The Guns and Butter Trap*. Westport, CT: Praeger Publishers, 2000; Katz, Michael B. *The Undeserving Poor: From the War on Poverty to the War on Welfare*. New York: Pantheon Books, 1989; Naples, Nancy A. *Grassroots Warriors: Activist Mothering, Community Work, and the War on Poverty*. London: Routledge, 1998; Zarefsky, David. *President Johnson's War on Poverty: Rhetoric and History*. Tuscaloosa: University of Alabama Press, 1986.

Paulina X. Ruf

Washington, Booker T. (1856–1915)

At the height of his power, just after the turn of the century, Booker T. Washington was one of the most famous people in North America and Europe. The United States was a **Jim Crow** society, yet Washington was an icon of progress operating at the highest levels. President Theodore Roosevelt consulted him, his books were best-sellers, universities gave him honorary degrees, and reporters quoted his policy statements. The school he directed, Tuskegee Institute in northeast Alabama, received donations from leading industrialists such as Andrew Carnegie, and the network of teachers, ministers, journalists, and federal workers that he coordinated—the *Tuskegee Machine*—stretched into almost every state. The muckraking writer Ray Stannard Baker observed after touring the South, "Whenever I found a prosperous Negro enterprise, a thriving business place, a good home, there I was almost sure to find Booker T. Washington's picture over the fireplace" (1908).

Booker T. Washington standing at an outdoor lectern speaking to a large audience in Pine Bluff, Arkansas. Courtesy of the Library of Congress.

His life was a deeply American story. He was born a slave in 1856, just before the Civil War. The barbarities of the "peculiar institution" he downplayed in his remembrances, but the conviction that evil would creep into people's souls whenever they lived in a system in which some worked and others did not became a central principle in his later thinking. Poor and humble, he made his way to school (Hampton Institute in Virginia), studied intensely, became a teacher, and devised a novel curriculum of vocational training and strict moral conduct. The ethic was a simple one. Hard work, thrifty spending, modest behavior—those were the ingredients of a successful life. For ex-slaves, opportunity was limited and racial passions were high. Best to learn a trade and save some money, he argued, to labor industriously and buy some land. Above all, do not provoke your white neighbors. You haven't the power to oppose them or the knowledge to outwit them. Because **racism** is rampant, the best relation to form with whites is a cooperative economic one—employer/employee, client/tradesman—and fulfill your end honorably.

Ambitious and energetic, he refined his gospel of work in lectures and writings. In 1895 came an invitation to speak at the **Cotton States and International Exposition** in Atlanta on September 18. His five minutes on stage in the September heat proved to be one of the landmark orations in U.S. history. It was an unusual occasion, a black man sharing a stage with white leaders in the Deep South. Introduced by Governor Bullock of Georgia as "a representative of Negro enterprise and Negro civilization," Washington strode forth and outlined a compact proposal of race relations in the United States. "The wisest among my race understand that the agitation of questions of social equality is the extremest folly," he assured the whites in the crowd. Black men and women would be a sound labor pool, starting at the bottom but ready to work cooperatively for mutual benefit. The choices were stark: "we shall contribute one-third to the business and industrial prosperity of the South, or we shall prove a veritable body of death, stagnating, depressing, retarding every effort to advance the body politic." At the same time, he assured the blacks, "No race that has anything to contribute to the markets of the world is long in any degree ostracized." American capitalism isn't color-blind, but it goes a long way toward defusing racial tensions. Anyone who works diligently will find employment; anyone who spends wisely will save money. And "when it comes to business, pure and simple, it is in the South that the Negro is given a man's chance in the commercial world."

The moment Washington stopped speaking, the onlookers erupted in cheers. Governor Bullock rushed to shake his hand, reporters jammed the stage, and word spread of a new black spokesman with a vision all could embrace. Newspapers echoed his message, and President Grover Cleveland wired him a note of congratulations. From that day forward, Washington was hailed as Leader of His Race, the Wizard of Tuskegee. The next twenty years would be a nonstop series of lecture tours, political meetings, writing assignments, negotiations with donors, secret protests, and public compromises.

But there was one aspect of American life that did not fit into Washington's design: racial violence. His work ethic might be an answer to illiteracy and vagrancy, and it might help one cope with white racism, but it was no defense against irrational aggression. Appealing to better feelings, or even to greed, may be wise, but white rage was part of the social landscape. Just as Washington was coming to power, a wave of "negrophobia" was sweeping the South. In the 1890s, initiatives to deny black men the right to vote, legalize separate facilities, and stock workhouses and chain gangs sprang up in every state. Worst of all, lynch law became a fact of life. **White supremacy** was the passion of southern politics, and in its ultimate expression took the form of mob rule. In **Wilmington**, North Carolina, in 1898, in **New Orleans** in 1900, and in **Atlanta** in 1906, **white mobs** seized downtown streets and attacked innocent black citizens, killing dozens and wounding thousands. Radical "negrophobes" justified the violence as a legitimate response to Negro crime and degeneracy, spurring further episodes in smaller communities and spreading terror throughout the land.

Washington's private actions were noble. He tried to hire detectives to discover the ringleaders of the outbreaks; he encouraged influential white moderates to speak out against **lynching**; and he lobbied quietly for colored regiments in the militia. But publicly, Washington adopted a conciliatory tone. He accused itinerant blacks of preying on white women, and he blamed vice dens in the city for corrupting black boys and girls. When black militants such as **Monroe Trotter** and fledgling groups such as the **Niagara movement** advocated stronger measures, Washington plotted a smear campaign. In the aftermath of the Atlanta riot, he claimed that the affair would actually improve relations between the races—an interpretation that struck those who endured the mobs as craven appeasement.

Washington's inability to address white violence proved a fatal weakness. In the last years of his life, African American activism shifted away from Tuskegee and toward the newly formed **National Association for the Advancement of Colored People (NAACP)** and the projects of **Marcus Garvey**. Washington died in 1915. *See also* Accommodationism; The Cotton States and International Exposition (Atlanta 1895); Du Bois, W.E.B.

Further Readings: Baker, Ray Stannard. *Following the Color Line*. New York: Doubleday, Page & Company, 1908; Harlan, Louis R. *Booker T. Washington: The Making of a Black Leader, 1856–1901*. New York: Oxford University Press, 1972; Harlan, Louis R. *Booker T. Washington: The Wizard of Tuskegee, 1901–1915*. New York: Oxford University Press, 1983.

Mark Bauerlein

Washington (D.C.) Riot of 1919

The five-day rioting in Washington, D.C., started on July 19, 1919, when a mob of several hundred off-duty white soldiers, sailors, and marines entered a black residential area to avenge the jostling of a white woman by two black men the night before. The jostled woman was described in some accounts as a sailor's wife, but was identified in the *New York Times* as Mrs. Elsie Stephnick, wife of an employee of the U.S. Naval Aviation Department, who had been on her way home from the Bureau of Printing and Engraving. The **white mob** assaulted several black people and vandalized the home of a black family. The next night, white mobs again rampaged, doing even more damage. Several black people were attacked by soldiers at Fifteenth Street and New York Avenue, NW. The third night, July 21, the tide turned, and blacks attacked whites and police. Black men in automobiles drove around the city shooting.

Key officials serving at the time were Chief of Police Major Pullman; Secretary of War Baker; Chief of Staff General March; Marine Corps Commandant Major General Barnett; and Navy Secretary Josephus Daniels. Maj. Gen. William G. Haan commanded 1,000 soldiers, marines, and cavalrymen to bring order. Although it was confirmed that uniformed troops had participated in the riots, General Haan attributed that to the large number of recently discharged soldiers in the area, and he was sure that no active-duty soldiers participated. With the perpetrators and the peacemakers wearing the same uniforms, stopping the riots was a complicated endeavor.

The rioting ended after four people had been killed, as many as thirty people were hospitalized, and finally, a powerful thunderstorm broke over the city, sending the rioters indoors. Dead were Detective Sergeant Harry Wilson and Kenneth Crall, both white, and Randall Neal and Thomas Armstrong, black. Some of the worst fighting had been at Seventh and T Streets in the black neighborhood, where police and soldiers confronted a large group of black rioters. During the fighting, black women stationed at windows and on rooftops threw bottles and other projectiles at the authorities.

Shortly after the turn of the century, social attitudes in Washington, D.C., had begun to change toward black residents. The city essentially became more southern, adopting **Jim Crow** policies and gradually eliminating black employees and members from the government and organizations. This strengthening of the racial divide flourished under the Wilson administration. Washington, D.C.'s black leadership reacted with a militant stance, achieving a first step in January 1919, when District Commissioner Brownlow established an all-black platoon in the fire department, ensuring promotions for the department's black veterans. This act, and the activism behind it, may have been a factor in the riots.

George E. Haynes, sociologist and founder of the Urban League, was the director of the Division of Negro Economics in the U.S. Department of Labor at the time. Haynes' article "Race Riots in Relation to Democracy" (1919) named four factors at work behind the rioting. Two factors were the new black militancy and the growing separation and antagonism between the races. A third was that the United States had become a world power, so U.S. race relations would now reflect on international relations, particularly regarding nations of color. Finally, the sensational journalism preceding the violence promoted and stoked the fear of black crime, providing the primary motivating undercurrent.

James Weldon Johnson agreed, and met with the city editor of the *Washington Post* to explain to him how the *Post* and the other daily newspapers were responsible. The city editor "stood as one struck dumb" (Johnson 1919). The D.C. branch of the **National Association for the Advancement of Colored People (NAACP)** had been active regarding the situation as far back as July 9, when it sent letters to the Washington, D.C., daily papers, telling them that their inflammatory headlines and articles had the potential to provoke a race riot. An article in the socialist black journal *The Messenger* said that the Washington newspapers incited the D.C. riot, U.S. soldiers and sailors started it, and the black people of D.C., determined to resist, finished it, demonstrating that they were not afraid to kill or die for liberty and home.

James Weldon Johnson also met with U.S. senators, including Sen. Charles Curtis from Kansas, asking for a congressional investigation of the riots. Johnson believed that black people had saved Washington by their determination not to run and to defend their lives and their homes. He felt that the

Chicago and D.C. riots marked a turning point in the nation's attitude toward race relations. Senator Curtis did sponsor a resolution requesting an investigation. *See also* Chicago (Illinois) Riot of 1919; Red Summer Race Riots of 1919.

Further Readings: Green, Constance McLaughlin. *The Secret City: A History of Race Relations in the Nation's Capital.* Princeton, NJ: Princeton University Press, 1967; Hawkins, W.E. "When Negroes Shot a Lynching Bee into Perdition." *The Messenger* 2, no. 9 (September 1919): 28–29; Haynes, George E. "Race Riots in Relation to Democracy." *Survey* 42 (1919): 697–699; Johnson, James Weldon. "The Riots: An N.A.A.C.P. Investigation." *The Crisis* 18, no. 5 (September 1919): 241–243; Kitchens, John W., ed. *Tuskegee Institute News Clippings File Microfilm.* Sanford, NC: Microfilming Corporation of America, 1981. Reel 10, Frame 986; "Race Riot at Capital: Soldiers and Sailors Make Raid on Negro Quarter." *New York Times.*, July 20, 1919, 4; Seligmann, Herbert. "Race War?" *New Republic* 20, August 13, 1919, 49; "Service Men Beat Negroes in Race Riot at Capital." *New York Times*, July 21, 1919, 1.

Jan Voogd

Washington (D.C.) Riots of 1968

Following the assassination of Dr. **Martin Luther King, Jr.**, in Memphis, Tennessee, on April 4, 1968, civil disorder broke out in nearly 110 U.S. cities. By far, the riot that occurred in Washington, D.C., between April 4 and 8 was the worst, bringing the city to a standstill. Schools closed, 1,000 buildings burned, 1,097 people were injured, 6,100 were arrested, and 12 people lost their lives. Damages exceeded $27 million.

The first place the rioting occurred was at Fourteenth and U Streets, in the northwest quadrant of the city. This area was at the heart of one of the black neighborhoods. It was a busy hub of activity, serving as a bus transfer point and the home of stores, businesses, theaters, and offices for such civil rights organizations as the **National Association for the Advancement of Colored People (NAACP)**, the **Student Nonviolent Coordinating Committee (SNCC)**, and the **Southern Christian Leadership Conference (SCLC)**.

When the news of the assassination was first broadcast over the airways, it was received in stunned silence and utter disbelief. Then it was announced that businesses were asked to close in respect for Dr. King. On Fourteenth and U Streets, a small band of young people, mostly black males, were gathering. They decided that they would go from business to business telling them that they should close. Soon the group was joined by **Stokely Carmichael**, who appeared on the scene. He was the West Indian-born former leader of SNCC who was known as a black activist. When he joined the crowd, it began to grow larger. The mood of the crowd changed. The crowd became angry and menacing. No longer were they asking the business owners to close—they were demanding that they do so. Carmichael left the area when anger turned to violence. Carmichael was well aware that he was being watched closely by local and federal authorities since he was viewed by them as a volatile agitator. But the violence escalated into breaking windows and widescale looting. Rioters threw rocks at motorists. The windshield of the first police car on the scene was broken in the melee. Eventually, local police quelled the rioters. As they secured the area around Fourteenth and U Streets, trouble erupted in other parts of the city. On the following morning, Walter Washington, the first black mayor of the city, had workers cleaning up the damage. For many in the city, this was presumed to be the end of the trouble. But it was not.

That day, Stokely Carmichael resurfaced and held a news conference in which he boldly declared that "America killed Dr. Martin Luther King Jr. last night." He continued, "We have gone full swing into the revolution" (Judge 2005). After the news conference, he went onto the campus of Howard University, which he had formerly attended. There were two activities in progress to commemorate Dr. King. There was a commemoration service in Cramton Auditorium and a rally a few steps away in front of Douglass Hall. At the rally, several speeches were given, including remarks by Carmichael. He drew a pistol, waved it over his head, and predicted that retaliatory action would occur to avenge the King assassination. Someone lowered the American flag and raised a flag of Ujamma. It symbolized a black nationalist student group. A reporter from the *Washington Post* newspaper interpreted the tone of the rally as "vehemently anti-white" (Judge 2005). When the attendees at the rally left and proceeded south on Georgia Avenue, the main street near the university, the crowd clashed with local police. A violent confrontation ensued.

By the afternoon, rioting, looting, and violence again erupted in other parts of the city. This happened mostly in black neighborhoods. In the areas where there was trouble, upwards of thousands of people roamed around with impunity. Stores, businesses, and a few homes were burned. When some storekeepers were forced to leave their stores for their own safety, many made signs that read *Soul Brother* or *I am a Brother*. These signs were displayed prominently in the windows and on doors of businesses owned by all races. They hoped that this would serve as a deterrent to having their businesses looted or burned. Sometimes it worked and sometimes it did not. Children and adults could be seen running up and down the street with clothes, shoes, food, furniture, appliances, liquor, and any other items that were easy to grab and carry away. Some stores had all of their merchandise taken and were then torched. Some rioters were seen using carts and suitcases to carry away their loot. On April 5, the rioters reached within a few blocks of the White House. A mob mentality reigned for nearly three days and nights in some parts of the city. In other parts of the city, where the rioters had not reached, many citizens huddled in their homes in fear that they and their neighborhood might fall victim to what was happening in the troubled neighborhoods. An eerie, smoldering silence fell over the city as the news media described the devastation that continued to mount.

In 1968, the full compliment of the Washington, D.C., Metropolitan Police Department was 3,100. Clearly, they were outnumbered and not fully prepared to deal with the rioters. They had never before faced a similar situation. Also, it was a sensitive matter of race, because the majority of police officers were white and the majority of rioters were black. Again, Mayor Walter Washington and other community leaders walked the streets and spoke through the media, pleading for calm. A curfew was imposed in the city. It began at 5:30 P.M. and ended at 6:30 A.M. President Lyndon B. Johnson issued an executive order to bring in 13,600 federal troops, including national guardsmen. They were immediately deployed to protect the U.S. Capitol, the White House, and various locations around the city. The federal military presence in Washington during the 1968 riots was the largest of any since the Civil War. President Johnson declared Sunday, April 8, 1968, a day of national mourning. Thirty-five years later, many of the areas struck by the riot had not been fully rebuilt. While some movement for rebuilding has begun, there remain scars and blight that can be traced directly to the riot of 1968.

Further Readings: Gilbert, Ben W., and the *Washington Post* staff. *Ten Blocks From the White House: Anatomy of the Washington Riots of 1968*. Washington, D.C.: Praeger Publishers, 1968; Judge, Mark Gauvreau. "Quiet Riots." *The American Spectator*, October 28, 2005. See http://www.spectator.org/dsp_article.asp?art_id=8940; Melder, Keith. *Magnificent Obsession*. 2nd ed. Washington, D.C.: Intac, 1997; "Nation's Capital Still Recovering from 1968 Riots." *CNN.com*, April 4, 1998. See http://www.cnn.com/Us/9804/04/mlk.dc.riots; Smith, Sam. *Multitudes: An Unauthorized Memoir*. See http://prorev.com/mmfire.htm.

Betty Nyangoni

Washington, Jesse (d. 1916), Lynching of

Jesse Washington, a seventeen-year-old illiterate black farm hand, was lynched in Waco, Texas, on May 15, 1916. Arrested on May 8, 1916, for murdering Robinson, Texas, resident Lucy Fryer, a fifty-three-year-old white woman, Washington confessed to Fryer's rape and murder. Despite the public outrage among whites, Sheriff Samuel S. Fleming safely transferred Washington to Dallas County to await trial. The trial began in Waco, a town of 25,000 located seven miles south of Robinson, on May 15, 1916, at the Fifty-Fourth District Court, Judge Richard I. Munroe presiding. A sea of white faces pushed into the court until it filled to capacity, and hundreds more gathered outside, anxious to render their own justice. Twelve white men served as the jury. After hearing the evidence, they deliberated for less than five minutes and returned with a guilty verdict, which carried with it the death penalty. What happened next became known as the Waco Horror.

The verdict ignited an already incensed court. Shouts rang out for Jesse's immediate execution. Men rushed Jesse, pushing aside security and Jesse's lawyers (who did not resist the onslaught), grabbed the frightened boy, and ripped off his clothes. Some had clubs, others bricks, still others had shovels, guns, and knives. They dragged him outside where they wrapped a chain around his neck. Jesse's plea for mercy did not phase the crazed mob, now 15,000 strong. They swarmed Jesse, the chain tightening around his neck. As they dragged him to the City Square to be hanged, they beat him, stabbed him, and mutilated him. His fingers were cut off, his ears, his toes—body parts taken as souvenirs.

No matter the verdict, the townspeople had already judged Jesse guilty, evident in their reaction to the verdict and the debris for a bonfire they had built in the City Square outside the courthouse. The boxes and wood that they had piled under a tree were doused in coal oil, as was Jesse. Then the fire was lit, the chain around Jesse's neck was looped over a branch, and Jesse was hoisted up. The onlookers' gaze bespoke anger, pride, and victory as Jesse was lowered into the blaze. His screams fell on the deaf ears of women, children, and men. Indeed, Waco's finest, many donned in their Sunday best, did not flinch at the sight or smell of the burning youth.

In fact, Jesse Washington's **lynching** drew a crowd of everyday, law-abiding, church-attending, educated citizens—Waco's mayor and police officials included. The popularity of lynching between 1880 and 1930 was often captured in photos depicting satisfied mobs smiling and posing with their kill. Waco photographer Fred Gildersleeve took pictures of Jesse's lynching as it was in progress. He photographed scenes of the mob torturing Jesse. Gildersleeve had planned to use the photos as postcards to sell commemorating the event. Although some of the photos were made into postcards, Gildersleeve did not expect his photos to stir a nation to outrage or to shame and tarnish Waco's image as the Athens of Texas. Yet his photographs shone a spotlight on what was sometimes called the New Negro Crime and was instrumental in bringing national attention to the crime of lynching.

The violence against blacks dubbed New Negro Crime emerged primarily to quell the upward mobility blacks gained during **Reconstruction** and reflected the stereotype of white females as prey of black men. Hence, merely accusing a black man of raping a white woman was reason for a black man, any black man, to be hanged. Although the accusations were mostly false, mobs could only be satisfied when a snapped-neck black victim paid with his life. Jesse's guilt was questionable, according to black journalist A.T. Smith. Smith alleged that George Fryer, Lucy Fryer's husband, murdered her, an allegation for which Smith was convicted of criminal libel and silenced.

Nevertheless, the New Negro Crime sealed Jesse's fate. His conviction, torture, mutilation, burning, decapitation; the bagging of his burnt body, dragging it back to Robinson, and hanging it in public as a warning to blacks occurred within an hour of his conviction. No one in the mob was charged. *See also* Rape, as Provocation for Lynching.

Further Readings: Bernstein, Patricia. *The Lynching of Jesse Washington and the Rise of the NAACP.* College Station: Texas A&M Press, 2005; Carrigan, William D. *The Making of a Lynching Culture: Violence and Vigilantism in Central Texas, 1836–1916.* Urbana: University of Illinois Press, 2004; Giddings, Paula. *When and Where I Enter: The Impact of Black Women on Race and Sex in America.* New York: Bantam Books, 1984.

Reginald Bruster

Watts Riots. *See* Los Angeles (California) Riot of 1965

Wells-Barnett, Ida B. (1862–1931)

Ida Bell Wells-Barnett was born July 16, 1862, in Holly Springs, Mississippi, to James Wells, a carpenter, and Elizabeth Warrenton Wells, a cook. She was the eldest of eight children, four girls and four boys, two of whom died in early childhood. Her father was respected as a community leader and was known locally as a *race man* because of his commitment to civil rights, community development, and educational opportunity. Both of her parents offered strong role models for hard work, responsible citizenship, and positive living, and they instilled into their children a keen sense of duty to God, family, and community.

Ida B. Wells-Barnett, 1891. Courtesy of the Library of Congress.

Wells-Barnett attended elementary and high school at Shaw University, later renamed Rust College. She was well on her way to laying a solid foundation for life when both her parents and her youngest brother died suddenly in the yellow fever epidemic that struck her area in 1878. To keep her siblings together and sustain their family, she left school and secured a teaching position in the public schools of rural Mississippi. This career path took her to Shelby County, Tennessee, and to the city of Memphis.

As a teacher in the Memphis area, she interacted with African American people who were centrally involved in creating a brighter day for African Americans, just as her parents had worked to do in Holly Springs. The community took pride generally in being forward-looking and culturally and intellectually vibrant. They worked aggressively to take advantage of opportunities and to function as productive and responsible citizens. Wells-Barnett also continued to be active in her church, the African Methodist Episcopal (AME) Church, as well as in others, and she was able to hear and meet many nationally renowned people, including Frederick Douglass, Blanche K. Bruce, **Henry McNeal Turner**, and Frances Ellen Watkins Harper.

Wells-Barnett also became active in the local literary clubs. Through these activities, she became a contributor and later editor of the *Evening Star* and columnist for the *Living Way*, both periodicals in Memphis. In 1884, she brought a lawsuit against the Chesapeake, Ohio, and Southwestern Railroad Company for **Jim Crow** practices that resulted in her being physically thrown off a train. She won, but the ruling was overturned by the Tennessee Supreme Court. Her first editorial was an invitation from the *Living Way* to write about her ordeal. The editorial was well received by the African American community, and Wells-Barnett was invited to write a column.

Using the pen name "Iola," Wells-Barnett was fiercely dedicated to justice and social reform. Her popularity as a journalist grew, and her column was syndicated in several papers across the nation. By 1889, she had left her teaching job and become co-owner of a newspaper, *Free Speech and Headlight*, with Rev. F. Nightingale and J.L. Fleming. In 1891, she and Fleming bought out Nightingale and shortened the name of the paper to *Free Speech*. By this point, Wells-Barnett was firmly established as a successful businesswoman and a highly respected journalist with a well-deserved reputation as a sharp-tongued political observer.

From this springboard, Wells-Barnett fashioned a remarkable career as a political activist and as an investigative journalist, especially with regard to the **lynching** of African American men, women, and children. Her list of accomplishments is long. She made two speaking tours of England, Scotland, and Wales, in 1893 and 1894. She was active over the next decades in several political organizations and movements, including the National Afro-American League, Afro-American Council, National Association of Colored Women (NACW), National Equal Rights League, Ida B. Wells Woman's Club, National American Woman's Suffrage Association, the **Niagara movement**, the woman's suffrage movement, and the international peace movement. She was a cofounder of the **National Association for the Advancement of Colored People (NAACP)** in 1910, and founder of the Negro Fellowship League in 1910 and the Alpha Suffrage Club in 1913. She ran for Illinois state senate in 1930 and lost. She worked arduously until her death as a self-determined crusader for justice and died of uremic poisoning on March 25, 1931 in Chicago.

A Time of Challenge

Thomas Moss, Calvin McDowell, and Henry Stewart, three enterprising and well-respected African American men in Memphis, owned and operated a grocery store, the People's Grocery Company, in a suburban area of the city that was popularly called the Curve because the streetcar line curved sharply at that point (Wells-Barnett, 47–76). Moss, a mail carrier, was the president of the company and worked in the store at night, while his partners operated the business during the day. In this mostly African American neighborhood, their store was able to compete successfully for business with a store that was white-owned and -operated. Before the People's Grocery, the white-owned store had held a monopoly, and the owner was much agitated by the success of his competition. He became openly hostile.

According to Wells-Barnett in *Crusade for Justice*, one incident that became violent was a quarrel between white boys and African American boys over a game of marbles. A fight ensued between the two groups that escalated into a fight between the fathers of the boys. The African American father won the fight, but the white father, the grocery store owner, swore out a warrant for the arrest of the African Americans. The People's Grocery owners were drawn into the tense dispute. The case was dismissed with nominal fines, but the victory for the African Americans was met by a threat that the People's Grocery would be forcibly closed by the white contenders on the next Saturday night.

In the face of such direct threats, Moss, McDowell, and Stewart sought legal counsel and found that, because the Curve was outside of the city limits of Memphis, they would be justified in protecting themselves. They did. They armed several men and stationed them at the rear of the store in preparation for repelling any attack that might occur. As threatened, that Saturday night, armed whites came to the rear of the store. The guards fired on them and wounded three. Others of the attacking group fled. The next morning, Moss, McDowell, and Stewart were dragged from their homes, and they and over 100 other African American men were arrested and jailed.

According to Wells-Barnett, the next morning the white newspaper reported that on the evening before, white law enforcement officers had been wounded while discharging their duty to hunt down criminals who were being harbored in the People's Grocery. Instead of being described as a successful grocery, the store was presented as an unsavory hangout for thieves and thugs who engaged in drinking and gambling. This account and others sensationalized the incident and enflamed **racism**. Groups of white men were permitted throughout the day on Sunday to view the imprisoned African American men, and white men gathered on the streets and in other meeting places to discuss the insurrection and its remedies. Although Memphis had not been a site of lynchings since the Civil War, the African American community became alarmed. Several African American men volunteered to stand guard at the jail to ensure the safety of those incarcerated. By the third night, they thought that the situation had calmed down and that the crisis had ended. They went home.

That night, March 9, 1892, a **white mob** was admitted to the jail. They took Moss, McDowell, and Stewart from their cells, loaded them on a train car that ran in back of the jail, carried the men a mile north of the city limits, and shot them to death. Wells-Barnett explained that the white newspaper reported the following details:

> "It is said that Tom Moss begged for his life for the sake of his wife and child and his unborn baby"; that when asked if he had anything to say, told them "tell my people to go West—there is no justice for them here"; that Calvin McDowell got hold of one of the guns of the lynchers and because they could not loosen his grip a shot was fired into his closed fist. When the three bodies were found, the fingers of McDowell's right hand had been shot to pieces and his eyes were gouged out. This proved that the one who wrote that news report was either an eyewitness or got the facts from someone who was. (Wells-Barnett, 50–51)

The deaths of the three men were reported as "by hands unknown," with no attempt by law enforcement to actually find the killers. The African American community was outraged by both the lynchings and the fact that the men who were lynched were clearly upstanding citizens rather than criminals of any kind. Their agitation fed rumors that spread through the white community indicating that African Americans were congregating at the Curve. A judge of the criminal court issued an order to the sheriff to "take a hundred men, go out to the Curve at once, and shoot down on sight any Negro who appears to be making trouble" (Wells-Barnett, 51). The white male community responded accordingly. They gathered, obtained weapons, went to the Curve, fired arbitrarily into groups of African Americans, and achieved their objective. They took possession of the People's Grocery Company and consumed and destroyed its contents at will. In the days that followed, creditors sold the remaining stock at auction, and the rivalry of the People's Grocery with the white-owned store was summarily ended.

When these incidents occurred, Ida B. Wells-Barnett was in Natchez, Mississippi, on a marketing development trip for her newspaper. By the time she returned home, Moss had already been buried. The death of Moss and his two business partners was quite a blow to Wells-Barnett. Moss and his wife Betty were personal friends, and she was godmother to their daughter Maurine. Wells-Barnett was incensed by the injustice. She wrote editorials against the conditions for African Americans in Memphis and urged African Americans, as Moss had recommended, to "save our money and leave a town which will neither protect our lives and property, nor give us a fair trial in the courts, but takes us out and murders us in cold blood when accused by white persons" (Wells-Barnett, 52). African Americans started leaving Memphis in large numbers, especially with the opening of Oklahoma (Indian Territory) for settlement. When the white backlash to this migration sought to discourage the departures with stories of danger and distress, Wells-Barnett went to Oklahoma to investigate and discover the truth. She sent letters to the *Free Speech* reporting her findings, and the migration continued, drawing people, not only from Memphis, but also Arkansas, Mississippi, and other parts of Tennessee.

In addition to migration as a political strategy, Wells-Barnett also understood the power of economic leverage. She made speeches in local churches and wrote editorials that encouraged a boycott of the streetcar system, a business that benefited greatly from African American patronage. This campaign stands historically as an important precursor of the more contemporary Montgomery bus boycott.

Friends warned Wells-Barnett that such activities were dangerous. Wells-Barnett, however, was unrelenting in her campaign for justice. Instead of modifying her approach, shortly after the three lynchings, she bought a gun. In *Crusade for Justice*, she stated the following:

> I expected some cowardly retaliation from the lynchers. I felt that one had better die fighting against injustice than to die like a dog or a rat in a trap. I had already determined to sell my life as dearly as possible if attacked. I felt if I could take one lyncher with me, this would even up the score a little bit. But fate decided that the blow should fall when I was away. (Wells-Barnett, 62)

Wells-Barnett continued to write editorials and to conduct investigations, not only on African American settlement in Indian Territory and on the streetcar boycott, but also on lynchings. She paid particular attention to the fact that lynchings were typically not a reaction of whites to the criminal behavior of African Americans. Instead, she documented that they were acts of terrorism designed to intimidate and oppress African American victims (men, women, and children) who were making political or economic progress. Most provocatively, however, Wells-Barnett also found that lynchings were used, not just for political and economic control, but also for social control. She discovered that several lynchings were the violent reaction of whites to the voluntary romantic liaisons between white women and African American men. Wells-Barnett felt compelled to speak the truth.

Three months after the lynchings of her friends, on May 21, 1892, Wells-Barnett quickly wrote a short editorial before departing for travel to the East. She wrote the following:

> Eight Negroes lynched since last issue of the *Free Speech*: one at Little Rock, Ark., last Saturday morning where the citizens broke (?) into the penitentiary and got their man; three near Anniston, Ala.; one near New Orleans; and three at Clarksville, Ga., the last three for killing a white man, and five on the same old racket—the new alarm about raping white women. The same programme of hanging, then shooting bullets into the lifeless bodies was carried out to the letter. Nobody in this section believes the old threadbare lie that Negro men assault white women. If southern white men are not careful, they will over-reach themselves and public sentiment will have a reaction; a conclusion will then be reached which will be very damaging to the moral reputation of their women. (Royster, 1997, 79)

With this editorial, Wells-Barnett set off a dramatic response from the white community in Memphis that would have significant consequences for her personal safety. However, there was a simultaneous effect. She also set herself on a rising trajectory of public activism that would propel her through the remainder of her life as a local, national, and international leader against lynching and mob violence and in support of general social justice.

A Time of Opportunity

Two days after the editorial appeared, the *Commercial Appeal*, a white newspaper in Memphis, reproduced it and, according to Wells-Barnett, published its own editorial, calling on

> the chivalrous white men of Memphis to do something to avenge this insult to the honor of their women. It said, "The Black wretch who had written that foul lie should be tied to a stake at the corner of Main and Madison Streets, a pair of tailor's shears used on him and he should then be burned at a stake." (Wells-Barnett, 66)

In other words, Mr. Carmack, whom Wells-Barnett names as the author of the editorial, called for yet another lynching. The white community of Memphis responded accordingly. An extralegal committee was formed and mob violence was again unleashed. On May 27, 1892, the committee ransacked the offices of the *Free Speech* and destroyed all of the equipment, and they had every intention of torturing and killing the owners. They were foiled in this latter pursuit, however. Wells-Barnett's business partner, J.L. Fleming, received a timely warning from a sympathetic white citizen that he should leave the city. Having been in a similar crisis with an earlier paper, the *Marion Headlight* in Marion, Arkansas, Fleming left immediately, barely escaping before the committee reached the *Free Press* offices.

As indicated above, as the female writer of the editorial rather than the male writer that Carmack presumed her to be, Wells-Barnett was not in Memphis when the attack occurred. She had written the editorial before leaving for her trip East. Her itinerary was in support of multiple interests. Her first stop was Philadelphia, where she attended the annual meeting of the AME Church. At the end of the conference, she went on to New York at the invitation of **T. Thomas Fortune**, editor of the *New York Age*, a paper in which her newspaper column was syndicated. Her Memphis editorial was published during the first leg of her trip.

When Wells-Barnett reached New York, Fortune informed her of the details of the mob violence and the threats of more violence that were occurring in Memphis. He impressed on her that it was not safe for her to return to her home and that the threat was quite specific. After the white leaders of Memphis discovered that Wells-Barnett, not her male partner, was actually the author of the editorial, they let it be known that if she ever set foot in Tennessee again, she would be tortured and killed on sight. In effect, the clear and present danger to Wells-Barnett expressed openly by the white citizens of Memphis forced her into an exile from the South that lasted thirty years.

This exile, however, was not the end of the story. It was the beginning of a provocative new page in Wells-Barnett's career as a journalist, political activist, and community leader. She became a reporter for the *New York Age*, where she told her story of exile in a feature article on June 25, 1892. As she stated in her autobiography,

> Having lost my paper, had a price put on my life, and been made an exile from home for hinting at the truth, I felt that I owed it to myself and to my race to tell the whole truth now that I was where I could do so freely. (Wells-Barnett, 69)

After the publication of this article, two African American women, Maritcha Lyon of Brooklyn and Victoria Earle Matthews of New York, hosted a testimonial dinner for Wells-Barnett. Lyon, an educator and writer, was one of the first African American women to be named assistant principal in a Brooklyn public school. Matthews was a fellow journalist who wrote for several newspapers, including the *New York Age*. She was also well known as the founding director of the White Rose Mission, a shelter for the increasing number of African American women and girls who were migrating to northern cities from the South in search of better opportunities. In New York, the White Rose Mission functioned as a community center for women and children, offering educational opportunities focused on self-improvement and Christian living. New and inexperienced in an urban environment filled with danger, especially to women alone, the women were particularly vulnerable to sexual assault and exploitation and to what was perceived to be lifestyles that were inappropriate for pious and respectable women. The mission helped to keep these southern migrants off the streets, involved with more positive activities, and focused on developing skills that helped them to secure adequate employment.

As women leaders who were active in social reform and experienced in community development activities, both Lyon and Matthews were very much attuned to the need to support Wells-Barnett and to bring attention to the ongoing need across the nation for social justice. On October 5, 1892, at Lyric Hall in New York, they brought together 250 African American women from the New York area, Philadelphia, and Boston. The group included some of the most recognizable and notable African American women leaders of the day. Among them, for example, were Josephine St. Pierre Ruffin, Gertrude Bustill Mossell, Susan Smith McKinney Steward, and Sarah Smith Garnet.

Josephine St. Pierre Ruffin and her husband George were prominent citizens of Boston. He was a lawyer and politician who served as a city councilman, a state legislator, and a municipal judge. Ruffin was noted for her work across racial lines through numerous organizations in Massachusetts, including the Associated Charities of Boston, the Massachusetts State Federation of Women's Clubs, and the Boston Kansas Relief Association, an organization that supported African American migrants. She was also a journalist and a member of the New England Women's Press Association, composed largely of white women.

Gertrude Bustill Mossell developed a national reputation as a writer and journalist, with her articles and columns appearing in newspapers across the nation. Ultimately, she became particularly well known for the publication of *The Work of the Afro-American Woman* (1894). Her family was among the free-black elite of nineteenth-century Philadelphia. For many generations, the female members of the Bustill family had built a remarkable record of social and political activism, as noted by their work as pioneering educators and as leaders of the Female Anti-Slavery Society. Mossell continued this tradition as an educator, activist, and journalist, a career choice that was facilitated by her ongoing affluence in being the wife of physician Nathan F. Mossell.

Susan Smith McKinney Steward and Sarah Smith Garnet were sisters who were also present at the testimonial. They were the daughters of Sylvanus and Ann S. Smith, both active in social and political reform and members of the African American elite of Brooklyn. Steward was a physician, the first African American woman to practice medicine in New York State and the third in the nation. Her highly successful practice was with the Brooklyn Woman's Homeopathic Hospital and Dispensary and with the Brooklyn Home for Aged Colored People. In addition, she served as president of the Women's Christian Temperance Union Number 6 in Brooklyn and was active in various social causes. The widow of clergyman William S. McKinney and later the wife of Theophilus Gould Steward, chaplain of the 25th U.S. Colored Infantry, Steward was also a prolific writer across a range of her professional interests as well as her religious and spiritual interests.

Her sister, Sarah Smith Tompkins Garnet, was a prominent educator, the first African American woman to be appointed principal of a public school in the borough of Manhattan. She was the widow of James Tompkins, an Episcopal minister, and later married Henry Highland Garnet, a Presbyterian minister, abolitionist, and diplomat. Garnet was an impassioned opponent of discrimination in education and a civil rights advocate. She was a member of many charitable and reform organizations, and she and her sister often served as delegates to national and international meetings.

Many such women of high energy and commitment across three states attended the testimonial for Wells-Barnett and heard her story. They presented her with $500 to enable her work and a gold, pen-shaped brooch to commemorate the occasion. From this gathering, Wells-Barnett went on two anti-lynching tours in England, Scotland, and Wales; published three pamphlets against lynching (*Southern Horrors: Lynch Law in All Its Phases*, 1892; *A Red Record*, 1895; *Mob Rule in New Orleans*, 1900), and came to be acknowledged as a steadfast champion of justice. Settling in Chicago, she married Ferdinand L. Barnett, an attorney, and raised a family, but her activism did not end. Wells-Barnett founded a suffrage club for women and a community development organization, ran for public office, and continued to speak and write in support of social justice.

Simultaneously, the New York gathering also firmly planted the seeds of organized political reform at a national, rather than just the local level for African American women in general. The leaders who attended, Wells-Barnett included, went on with like-minded women from across the nation to form in 1896 the National Association of Colored Women (NACW), an organization through which they were able to engage actively in the social and political discourses that surrounded them, nationally and internationally, and to accomplish the vital work of social and political reform. This organized, socially conscious, politically active moment constituted the inception of what has since been named the Black Clubwomen's movement. The point to be emphasized is that the Black Clubwomen's movement was well connected to all of the major social movements of the time: civil rights, women's rights, labor rights, settlement, international peace, and more, and Wells-Barnett was very active in all of them.

The turn of the twentieth century, in fact, was a time in which trials and challenges for the African American community were great, which, in effect, provided even more inspiration for African American women to use their talents and abilities well at every occasion that presented itself for remedy and reform. Wells-Barnett, therefore, was not alone in the energy that she brought to the cause of social justice, but she was, nevertheless, distinctive. In the 1890s, after her Memphis press was destroyed, she rose to national and international fame as the most visible and outspoken African American woman in the world and as the person who sustained the most active of the anti-lynching campaigns of her era, directing attention against lynching and other causes for the next four decades.

Coda

Despite her record of achievements as a journalist and highly visible community activist, historical accounts about this era for most of the twentieth century were not particularly inclusive of Wells-Barnett's accomplishments. In effect, she almost literally disappeared from the public record and from public consciousness within her own lifetime. Her achievements did not go down in either national lore or in history books. She was not celebrated as the darling of the black press, a central investigator and spokesperson against lynching, or as a courageous crusader across the United States and Great Britain for truth and justice. By the second decade of the twentieth century, her involvement in the public sphere seemed a faint shadow of her earlier prominence.

While Wells-Barnett retained public regard in the city of Chicago and in the state of Illinois, as indicated by the fact that the city of Chicago named a housing project in her honor, her national presence waned, not to be rejuvenated until decades after her death when the research and scholarship of the late twentieth century in women's studies and African American studies reclaimed and reinstated her contributions. Today, she is recognized as a tireless champion against lynching and a stellar exemplar of socially and politically conscious activism despite the racist and sexist conditions that surrounded her. Moreover, her life and work as a community activist and journalist have been instrumental in raising provocative questions about the impact of race, sex, and class on achievement and on how such achievements are publicly acknowledged and valued or not. The effect of this renewal of interest is that justice prevails. Wells-Barnett's contributions in several areas of achievement have been documented, and she is indeed celebrated as an astute businesswoman, a provocative investigative journalist, a passionate proponent of civil and women's rights, a champion of truth and justice, and a national and international leader. *See also* Anti-Lynching League; Lynching; National Association of Colored Women (NACW).

Further Readings: *The American Experience: Ida B. Wells—A Passion for Justice*. Directed by William Greaves. PBS, 1989; Aptheker, Bettina, ed. *Lynching and Rape: An Exchange of Views*. New York: American Institute for Marxist Studies, 1977; DeCosta-Willis, Miriam. *Ida B. Wells: The Memphis Diaries*. Boston: Beacon Press, 1994; Diggs-Brown, Barbara. "Ida B. Wells-Barnett: About the Business of Agitation." In Susan Albertine, ed. *A Living of Words: American Women in Print Culture*. Knoxville: University of Tennessee Press, 1995; Duster, Alfreda M. *Crusade for Justice: The Autobiography of Ida B. Wells*. Chicago: The University of Chicago Press, 1970; Harris, Trudier, compiler. *Selected Works of Ida B. Wells-Barnett*. New York: Oxford University Press, 1991; Hendricks, Wanda. "Ida B. Wells-Barnett and the Alpha Suffrage Club of Chicago." In Marjorie Spruill Wheeler, ed. *One Woman, One Vote: Rediscovering the Woman Suffrage Movement*. Troutdale, OR: New Sage Press, 1995; Humrich, Shauna Lea. "Ida B. Wells-Barnett: The Making of a Reputation." Master's thesis, University of Colorado, 1989; Hutton, Mary M.B. "The Rhetoric of Ida B. Wells: The Genesis of the Anti-Lynch Movement." Ph.D. dissertation, University of Indiana, 1975; Logan, Shirley W., ed. *With Pen and Voice: A Critical Anthology of Nineteenth-Century African American Women*. Carbondale: Southern Illinois Press, 1995; McMurry, Linda O. *To Keep the Waters Troubled: The Life of Ida B. Wells*. New York and Oxford: Oxford University Press, 1998; Newkirk, Pamela. "Ida B. Wells-Barnett." In Robert Giles and Robert Snyder, eds. *Profiles in Journalistic Courage*. New Brunswick, NJ: Transaction Publishers, 2001; Royster, Jacqueline Jones. "Ida B. Wells-Barnett." In Cary D. Wintz and Paul Finkelman, eds.

Encyclopedia of the Harlem Renaissance. 2 vols. New York: Routledge, 2004, 98–101; Royster, Jacqueline Jones. *Southern Horrors and Other Writings: The Anti-Lynching Campaign of Ida B. Wells, 1892–1900*. Boston: Bedford Books, 1997; Royster, Jacqueline Jones. "To Call a Thing by Its True Name: The Rhetoric of Ida B. Wells." In Andrea Lunsford, ed. *Reclaiming Rhetorica*. Pittsburgh: University of Pittsburgh Press, 1995, 167–84; Rydell, Robert W., ed. *The Reason Why the Colored American Is Not in the World's Columbian Exposition*. Urbana: University of Illinois Press, 1999; Schechter, Patricia. "Unsettled Business: Ida B. Wells against Lynching, or How Antilynching Got Its Gender." In Fitzhugh Brundage, ed. *Under Sentence of Death: Lynching in the South*. Chapel Hill: University of North Carolina Press, 1997; Thompson, Mildred I. "Ida B. Wells-Barnett: An Exploratory Study of an American Black Woman, 1893–1930." In Darlene Clark Hine, ed. *Black Women in United States History, vol. 15*. New York: Carlson Publishing Inc., 1990; Tucker, David M. "Miss Ida B. Wells and Memphis Lynching." In Darlene Clark Hine, ed. *Black Women in American History: From Colonial Times Through the Nineteenth Century, vol. 4*. New York: Carlson Publishing Inc., 1990, 1085–1095; Wells-Barnett, Ida. *Crusade for Justice: The Autobiography of Ida B. Wells*. Edited by Alfreda M. Duster. Chicago: University of Chicago Press, 1970, 47–76.

Jacqueline Jones Royster

White Capping

The term *white capping* refers to the violent intimidation of blacks to rob them of their property. The individuals responsible for this violence were known as White Caps, nightriders named for the distinctive headgear they used to disguise themselves. The term seems to have originated in Indiana in 1887. The stated aim of the White Caps was to regulate the morality of the community, and their most common form of intimidation was whipping.

Between 1900 and 1929, the white capping epidemic reached its peak, chiefly in southern rural areas. In addition to whipping, the White Caps terrorized, beat, and lynched blacks to unlawfully take their land. The phenomenon often occurred during periods when the competition for land was high. At other times, the purpose was to crush prosperous landowning blacks or to simply confiscate desirable property. Between 1887 and 1900, 239 incidences of white capping were reported. Despite the fact that White Caps violated black rights under the **Fourteenth Amendment**, the federal government did little, if anything, to protect blacks or their property.

Exacerbating the phenomenon of white capping was the fact that for blacks to acquire land in the first place was a Sisyphean task. Although rumors abounded of blacks being awarded "forty acres and a mule" after the Civil War, the majority of blacks received no land. In their everyday lives, blacks were forced to surmount gargantuan obstacles—**poverty**, **racism**, and discrimination—making it nearly impossible for them to eke out the most meager of existences. Nevertheless, blacks did manage to purchase land as a result of their own efforts.

In 1999, steps were taken by organizations such as the Race Relations Institute of Fisk University to address land theft and to locate its victims.

The ultimate goal was to submit these cases to the court system in the hope that **reparations** might be forthcoming. *See also* Lynching.

Further Reading: Holmes, William F. "Whitecapping: Agrarian Violence in Mississippi, 1902–1906." *Journal of Southern History* 35 (1969): 165–185.

Gladys L. Knight

White Citizens' Council

The White Citizens' Council was born in Mississippi in response to the 1954 *Brown v. Board of Education* ruling by the U.S. Supreme Court and the subsequent urgings of Mississippi Circuit Court Judge Thomas Pickens Brady. Acting on Brady's call, Robert Patterson organized the first chapter in Indianola, Mississippi, in July 1954. Membership soared as black challenges to southern **segregation** increased. The Council gave white southerners a way to channel their ire into a new movement organized around opposition to **integration** and the Supreme Court decision. It focused on two main goals: maintaining a segregated school system and preventing southern blacks from exercising their right to vote.

Members of the Council viewed themselves as the "uptown **[Ku Klux] Klan [KKK]**" (PBS Online). Although the goals of the two groups were often the same, techniques were different and membership varied. Whereas the Klan was a **vigilante organization** that primarily used violence and terror to accomplish its goals, the council used economic reprisals and manipulation of the law in an effort to intimidate and undermine civil rights activists and supporters. By galvanizing public opinion, the council hoped to stop the **civil rights movement** and preserve the pre-*Brown* southern way of life.

The Council met openly and was seen as a reputable and respectable organization. Rather than the rabble that populated the Klan, the Council was often led by some of the most prominent, responsible, respected, and influential citizens in their respective communities and states. Included on the list of eminent members were national politicians like U.S. Sen. Allen Ellender of Louisiana and Sen. Herman Talmadge of Georgia, and local politicians like George Wallace, governor of Alabama; Marvin Griffin, governor of Georgia; and Ross Barnett, governor of Mississippi.

In some states, the Council almost completely controlled the political process. It secured passage of numerous bills, defeated politicians who refused to cooperate with it, and secured important positions for various members. In Mississippi, where Governor Barnett was seen by many as a front man for the organization, the council acquired quasi-governmental status and received thousands in state funds. This gave the Council a legitimacy that increased when institutions like the State Sovereignty Commission in Mississippi contributed money to council chapters and helped create informal connections between state organizations, like the State Sovereignty Commission, the Klan, and the Council. The staffs of important state agencies often mirrored council membership. As a result, the White Citizens' Council used state agencies like the commission to spread its influence throughout the state government and to work in partnership with the Klan.

The State Sovereignty Commission contributed money and helped fund the council. The commission helped the council accomplish its goals by creating a covert network that tracked blacks and whites, noting which should receive negative treatment. Economic reprisals were common forms of punishment. Blacks who favored integration or were observed attempting to register black voters lost their jobs, their homes, and, in some cases, their lives. White businessmen faced boycotts. Politicians deemed sympathetic to integration of blacks lost votes and hence their jobs. The White Citizens' Council was so successful in places like Mississippi that **desegregation** failed to occur for more than ten years after the *Brown* decision.

The various Council chapters functioned as independent and autonomous units. This, in part, inhibited the organization's ability to establish strong footholds in states like Florida, Virginia, Arkansas, Texas, North Carolina, or Tennessee, although the council still managed to create a regional network of some strength, especially in the Deep South. Despite sporadic attempts to unite the chapters under a single banner, they remained largely independent. Still, unity was promoted in council literature and on television shows and radio programs distributed and broadcast in the South. In the latter case, a fifteen-minute broadcast, sponsored by the Mississippi congressional delegation, was shown on fifty stations. In another case, the Council published a tape of a man, supposedly a black professor at Howard University, giving a highly provocative speech appealing to southerners' deepest fears of social equality and miscegenation.

Despite these apparently peaceful means, the Council's actions often inspired white violence against blacks. Council activity contributed heavily to the violent animosity that permeated the South. The Rev. George Washington Lee, a strong advocate for black suffrage, was shot to death in May 1955. Gus Court, who helped Lee lead voter registration drives, was evicted from his store and was eventually called before a three-member Council committee, where he was questioned about his voter-registration activities, which he refused to stop. After being wounded in a shooting, he eventually left the state for Chicago.

The Council reached its zenith in the late 1950s. In 1956, not a single black voter in Mississippi cast a ballot. However, by the early 1960s, the council's demise began as African Americans openly challenged the Council and its grassroots structure began to crumble as white southerners began to begrudgingly accept desegregation. In addition, as black economic power increased, white businessmen were more reluctant to be associated with a group like the Council. These two events combined to undercut its effectiveness and signaled the end of its reign. Despite an attempt to move its message north, by 1964 it had all but disappeared in peripheral states and was demoralized and in disarray in the Deep South. As its power weakened after 1964, it began to focus on segregated private schools. It still lingers today under such different names as the Council of Conservative Citizens.

Further Readings: Bartley, Numan V. *The Rise of Massive Resistance*. Baton Rouge: Louisiana State University Press, 1969; Geyer, Elizabeth. "The 'New' Ku Klux Klan." *The Crisis* (1956): 139–148; McMillen, Neil R. *The Citizens Council: Resistance to the Second Reconstruction 1954–1964*. Champaign: University of Illinois Press, 1994; PBS Online. "People & Events: Citizens' Councils." *American Experience:*

The Murder of Emmett Till. See http://www.pbs.org/wgbh/amex/till/peopleevents/e_councils.html; Thayer, George. *The Farther Shores of Politics: The American Political Fringe Today*. New York: Simon and Schuster, 1967.

Gary Gershman

White Flight

White flight originally denoted the post-World War II movement of Caucasian Americans out of inner cities that were predominantly African American and into the homogeneity of white suburbs. The term is synonymous with *white flux*. Although the mobility pattern is commonly believed to be racially based, arguments have been made (Bickford) that issues of wealth and class (not race and ethnicity) may be at the root of this social phenomenon. Other studies (Farley) find substantial **segregation** patterns after adjusting for both educational achievement and income, confirming the hypothesis that suburban segregation cannot be explained by socioeconomic status alone, and may well be based on racial bias.

This massive emigration of whites also had a grave snowball effect on the economy of the inner city. As wealthier residents moved out of the inner city, higher tax dollars and property taxes followed the mobile Caucasian. When this happens on a broad scale, inner cities are eventually left devoid of essential financial resources. Inner-city schools suffer, crime rises, and buildings deteriorate, making it even less desirable for middle- and upper-class residents to remain in the city's core.

As minority affluence rises, the African American family becomes much more economically mobile and is able to migrate from urban, inner-city residential settings into the more lucrative suburbs of the United States. Middle- and upper-class African Americans are able to buy homes in previously all-white neighborhoods.

Closely tied to the term *white flight* are the phrases *racial steering* and ***redlining***. Racial steering is a practice used by realtors to direct clients only to homes and neighborhoods of their own perceived racial category. Whites are shown homes in white neighborhoods, blacks are shown homes in all-black neighborhoods, Latinos are shown homes in Hispanic neighborhoods. Redlining occurs when realtors circle in red pen the areas of the city that are considered too risky to provide mortgages for homes, most likely homes of minority populations.

White flight also has an opposing trend surfacing throughout American cities today. **Gentrification** denotes the process by which many cities have put forth extreme efforts and money to revitalize their inner cities and downtown areas. Old buildings are refurbished into elegant apartments. Abandoned storefronts become occupied by high-end stores. A portion of the affluent white population returns to the inner city. Although this process brings higher revenue to the city and improves the aesthetics of the urban area, there are social consequences. Cheap housing is razed and eliminated, driving thousands of economically fragile people into the state of homelessness. Single-room occupancy hotels that once provided substandard, yet financially affordable housing for the poor are either refurbished into luxury condominiums or leveled to provide space for new high-end residential structures.

Further Readings: Bickford, Eric. "White Flight: The Effect of Minority Presence on Post World War II Suburbanization." See www.eh.net/Clio/Publications/flight.shtml; Farley, Reynolds. "Components of Suburban Population Growth." In Barry Schwartz, ed. *The Changing Face of the Suburbs*. Chicago: University of Chicago Press, 1976.

Sheila Bluhm Morley

White Flux. *See* White Flight

White League

The White League was an all-white paramilitary group that formed during **Reconstruction** in the nineteenth century to remove Republicans from office and restore Democrats to power in states across the South. The league is best known for its role in the political ferment that followed the contentious election of 1872 in Louisiana. It played a significant role in three major disturbances in Colfax, Coushatta, and Liberty Place.

The conditions that gave rise to the formation of the White League were manifold. Soon after the Civil War, white southerners formed militias, ostensibly to protect whites from the threat of black violence and crime. This gave whites opportunity to unlawfully seize property and weapons from blacks and mutilate and murder them. It is out of this tradition that the White League formed, but it directed violence against the black population as a whole, as well as against Republican officials.

In the election of 1872, Louisiana Democrats attempted to usurp power by running John D. McEnery for governor and claiming victory. However, the Republicans claimed that William Pitt Kellogg had won the election, and President Ulysses S. Grant recognized Kellogg as Louisiana's new governor. Trouble followed when, in 1873, Kellogg appointed one white Republican and one black to fill positions previously assigned to white conservatives at the Colfax courthouse. A black militia, sanctioned by Kellogg, formed to protect the Republican officials. A group of whites, including some members of the White League, attacked the courthouse, killing more than sixty-nine people. Participants of the massacre at Colfax were charged with violating the civil rights of those they had murdered and of infringing on the Enforcement Acts. Their case went to the U.S. Supreme Court, where it was decided that the states were responsible for the enforcement of civil rights. Conservative whites interpreted this ruling to mean they were free to terrorize blacks and Republicans at will, as long as they were careful not to provoke the federal government into sending in troops.

In 1874, many conservatives joined the White League. These new members used the local press to recruit members and to brandish threats to the Republicans. They held regular rallies inciting men, women, and even children to participate in acts against the Republicans and blacks. Adding fuel to the sweltering hostility were **rumors**, instigated by the local press, of black schemes to attack whites (see **Press Instigation of Racial Violence**).

The league threatened to lynch Republicans in Natchitoches, St. Martin, Avoylles, Winn, and elsewhere, effectively vacating seats for the Democrats. In the summer of 1874, violence erupted in Coushatta when league members murdered several blacks who had attacked whites. It was assumed that the league was behind the brutal murders of six white Republicans who had been acquitted of accusations that they had masterminded the black uprisings. In September, federal troops arrived in Shreveport, Louisiana.

On September 14, 1974, 3,500 armed members of the White League faced off against 3,600 police officers and black militia troops in what is known as the Battle of Liberty Place. A one-hour fight ensued, resulting in thirty-eight men killed and seventy-nine wounded. The triumphant White League overran the city hall, the statehouse, and the arsenal, and installed John McEnery as governor. After three days, federal troops arrived in New Orleans and restored Kellogg to power. The league surrendered and dispersed, but not before they had inspired other southern states to engage in similar tactics. In the election of 1876, political violence, intimidation, and fraud secured the Democratic victory and, consequently, brought an end to Reconstruction in Louisiana. *See also* Lynching.

Further Reading: Taylor, Joe Gray. "Louisiana: An Impossible Task." In Otto H. Olsen, ed. *Reconstruction and Redemption in the South*. Baton Rouge: Louisiana State University Press, 1980, 202–230.

Gladys L. Knight

White Mobs

White mobs were disorderly crowds that ruthlessly terrorized and victimized blacks and their supporters, particularly between the 1800s and 1960s. Unlike **racist organizations**, white mobs were loosely organized, spontaneous, and ephemeral. Nevertheless, they exhibited similar motives, activities, and characteristics, and were equally frightful. **James Weldon Johnson**, author and activist, aptly described his confrontation with a mob when he said: "On the other side of the fence, Death was standing. Death turned and looked at me and I looked at Death" (Dray, 84).

The motives of white mobs varied throughout history. During the period of growing opposition to the anti-slavery movement, white mobs formed to riot and, if necessary, even kill sympathetic whites and free blacks in the North. After the Civil War, white mobs sporadically formed to attack newly freed blacks and anyone else committed to advancing their cause. White mobs worked independently of, and concurrently with, **vigilante organizations** like the **Ku Klux Klan (KKK)** to destroy the Freedmen's Bureau's schools, to beat black and white teachers, and to intimidate and kill Republican politicians during **Reconstruction** in the South.

Between the 1880s and 1930s, numerous blacks were lynched. White mobs were largely responsible for these **lynchings**, as well as for the anti-black riots that occurred. Violence was to the mob a tool to enforce the racist and discriminatory **Jim Crow** laws, to maintain **white supremacy** and black oppression, and to thwart black resistance. White mobs attacked any black person who violated Jim Crow or **racial etiquette** or threatened the status quo. White mobs, feeding off their fear that black men were a threat to white women, lynched numerous black men on hearing accusations of gazing at, speaking to, touching, and assaulting white women. Sometimes they created rumors of rape to create an opportunity to destroy prosperous black communities. Many, if not most, of the rape accusations were unfounded and untried in a court of law. Due to rampant **racism** in the judicial court system and biased all-white juries, just trials were an anomaly.

In the 1940s, white mobs rioted in black communities as a result of competition for housing and employment opportunities. In the 1950s and 1960s, white mobs were responsible for the violent opposition to the forced integration of formerly all-white schools and to the demonstrations of the **civil rights movement**. The motives of the white mobs often stemmed from a deep and unsatiated racial animosity toward blacks. This racial hatred was what unified and solidified the white mobs.

White mobs employed an assortment of violent methods, which frequently resulted in death. Specific targets rarely survived to tell their tales. Hence Johnson's fear as he faced a white mob, though he was one of the few who escaped unharmed. When a white mob was on the rampage, it targeted any available black men, women, and children. White mobs were known to lynch the elderly as well as pregnant women. When the black community at large was the target, homes and property were seized or destroyed, and more than a few lives were lost. The common methods of violence between the 1860s and 1930s were beating, shooting, burning, and lynching. Sometimes the lynchings involved all the above. During the civil rights movement, white mobs were notorious for pelting objects at demonstrators and bombing.

White mobs had common characteristics. They were generally male-dominated (with more female involvement during the mid-twentieth century) and were not necessarily affiliated with a racist organization. The size of the mob ranged from a dozen to several thousand and comprised a mixture of economic backgrounds. Most of the participants lived next door to the black community they targeted and brazenly pursued their victims without disguises. Sometimes, men from outside the community were enlisted or willingly participated without invitation. Although many mobs formed spontaneously, others were organized several days, weeks, or months prior to the culminating activity. Furthermore, most mob activities were not isolated, self-sustaining affairs.

Although formal racist organizations and white mobs sometimes worked privately and in disguise, a number of mobs relied heavily on outside sources and unabashedly acted out their crimes. On several occasions, mob activities were not random, spontaneous events, but deliberate plots devised by whites with economic, social, or political power. During Reconstruction, conservative Democrats often masterminded white mob activities. In the **Memphis (Tennessee) Riot of 1866**, the affluent whites of the neighborhood manipulated and controlled the middle-class white rioters. State and local officials rarely challenged white mob violence. By neglecting to act, they allowed the mob to carry out its will without fear of penalty. Some officials even encouraged anti-black violence, just as police and elected officials would later warn white mobs of impending black demonstrations and permitted their violent attacks during the civil rights movement in the 1960s. In this atmosphere of tolerance and approval, white mobs assaulted blacks openly and shamelessly.

The press also helped fuel the activities of white mobs by providing an effective means of communicating imminent lynchings to the local community and beyond. Whites traveled from afar on trains and set up camps in anticipation of the event. As many as several thousand people were known to attend a single lynching. Food was served; children played; photos were taken, and the press stood ready with pen and paper to report the events. The audience, usually (but not necessarily) all white, often participated in the chilling torture and death of the victim. Men, women, and children were known to stab or beat the victims. After the death of the victim, the community sometimes rushed on the body and severed fingers, toes, organs, or any other part of the body for a keepsake. Afterward, the mob, and sometimes members of the community, small children included, posed proudly beside the ravaged body for the camera. *See also* Rape, as Provocation for Lynching; Vigilante Organizations.

Further Readings: Dray, Philip. *At the Hands of Persons Unknown: The Lynching of Black America*. New York: Random House, 2002; Pfeifer, Michael J. *Rough Justice: Lynching and American Society, 1874–1947*. Urbana: University of Illinois Press, 2004.

Gladys L. Knight

White Supremacy

White supremacy is an ideology of racial and cultural superiority according to which people of European, Christian, and mainly Anglo-Saxon heritage, as well as ethnicity, are superior to all others. It is important to focus on the intellectual history of white supremacy as a concept to properly situate and understand not only the various forms it has assumed for close to a millennium, but also what motivates its adherents and promoters. Next, one can discuss the modern expressions—obvious and otherwise—of this powerful ideology that has shaped our current world.

White supremacy is informed by ideas of genetic and cultural purity and religious and spiritual exclusivity. Its vision of the world is often apocalyptic, intolerant, triumphalist, and hegemonic. It has had ardent, charismatic, and articulate promoters who have organized themselves into political parties and pressure groups to advance their causes. In Nazi Germany, white supremacist ideology actively promoted the concept of *Herrenvolk*, or master race. This ideology held that people of Nordic and Germanic heritage exemplified a pure race, and that all others were congenitally inferior. It also proclaimed the right of the master race to dominate the world. Herrenvolk itself is a product of nineteenth-century racial theories of Count Arthur de Gobineau, who, in his book, *The Inequality of Human Races* (1853–1855), categorized the peoples of the world into a hierarchy of

Klan members marching in Nazi uniforms, circa 1940. Courtesy of the Library of Congress.

black, white, and yellow races. Gobineau argued that cultures become degenerate when these distinct races intermingle. He also viewed this racial mixing as a form of contamination, which he called "semiticization," because he believed that Semitic peoples were a hybrid race resulting from the mixing of the three distinct races. Thus, Gobineau saw Semitic peoples as an impure, polluted version of the white race. He placed southern Europeans, Jews, and Arabs at the bottom of the racial hierarchy, while white Europeans were at the top. Other white supremacists have placed black people and indigenous Australians at the bottom of this racial ladder. It must be noted that today's white supremacists' vehement opposition to any form of racial interaction, such as mixed marriages, ethnic diversity, and multiculturalism can be traced to this almost pathological fear of racial contamination or impurity.

Before Gobineau, white supremacy seems to have been part of the Western Christian heritage. It arguably goes back to the Middle Ages when white Christians from Western Europe waged war against Moslems to stop Islam, which had been gaining ground since the seventh century on the southern and eastern borders of Europe. The ultimate goal was to recapture the Holy Land. Although this was a war between two competing religions, it was also motivated by attitudes of white supremacy, which were fueled by false **rumors** already widespread in Christendom about peoples of Arab-Islamic identity. For example, in 1095, Pope Urban II castigated Moslems as a godless, inferior race utterly alienated from God. In his book *The First Crusade: Accounts of Eyewitnesses and Participants*, August C. Krey quotes the pope as describing the Moslems as "a barbaric fury [that] has deplorably afflicted and laid waste the churches of God in the regions of the Orient" (42–43). Urban accused the Moslems of seizing the churches of Jerusalem, mutilating Christians, and desecrating churches by spreading blood on altars. Urban used these rumors to demonize Arabs and other Moslems of color and to rally Europeans for the First Crusade.

For African Americans, white supremacy has it roots in the *Romanus Pontifex* issued by the Vatican in 1455. This document authorized the Portuguese monarchy to subdue, enslave, or conquer any "pagan or Muslim people" to convert them to Christianity. By the mid-1500s, the Church gave full moral and spiritual support to the enslavement of black peoples along the west coast of Africa by crusading Spanish and Portuguese monarchists who were focused on creating what Anthony Pagden calls the *Monarchia Universalis*, or a universal Christian empire. Millions of Africans were uprooted from their homes and sold as slaves in the Americas. Accompanying the slavers were missionaries from Spain, Britain, France, and Portugal who went to foreign lands with the belief that theirs was a superior culture that brought a superior faith and civilization to the new lands. Here again, religion and notions of racial superiority informed centuries of Western European domination of peoples of color.

Slavery was followed by a period of massive colonization, plunder, and the violent destruction of indigenous cultures in Africa, Asia, and the Americas by imperialist Western European nations such as Britain, France, Spain, Portugal, Holland, and Germany. Although discovery and exploration constituted the primary rationale for Western Europe's intrusion into these lands, an ideology of racial superiority was the driving force behind it, fueled by Christian-inspired white supremacy. Through their writings, prominent philosophers and thinkers of the Enlightenment, such as G.W.F. Hegel, David Hume, Immanuel Kant, and John Locke, among others, provided the moral, intellectual, and political justifications for white supremacy. They encouraged ideas of the racial superiority of white people. For example, Montesquieu, the French political philosopher and contributor to Denis Diderot's *Encyclopédie* project, described Africans as physically gifted, but unintelligent. In his *Spirit of the Laws* (book 15, chapter 5), Montesquieu remarked about the spiritual and physical inferiority of blacks: "These creatures are all over black, and with such a flat nose that they can scarcely be pitied. It is hardly to be believed that God, who is a wise Being, should place a soul, especially a good soul, in such a black ugly body."

These thinkers used all manner of scientific and pseudo-scientific theories to reinforce notions of white supremacy and non-white inferiority. For example, Hegel gave justifications for colonialism and imperialism that will astound today's readers. In his *Lectures on the Philosophy of World History*, he questioned the very humanity of Africans:

> It is characteristic of the blacks that their consciousness has not yet even arrived at the intuition of any objectivity, as for example, of God or the law, in which humanity relates to the world and intuits its essence.... He [the black person] is a human being in the rough. (Hegel, 138)

Furthermore, Hegel gave justifications for colonialism (especially in India) and imperialism that will astound today's readers. The attitudes of these thinkers were clearly influenced mainly by travelers' stories, geographical location, and utter ignorance of other cultures besides their own. By the same token, Kant and Hume portrayed Africans as genetically inferior to whites.

In the twentieth century, white supremacy found legitimacy as a political expression in Nazism, which became the most egregious form of white supremacy. It is responsible for the deaths of over six million Jews, most sent to die in gas chambers. White supremacy under Adolf Hitler became Germany's state policy and identity. The ultimate goal was to build an Aryan master race. Right after the defeat of Nazi Germany in 1945, South Africa became the next country where white supremacy was state policy and identity. *Apartheid*, or racial **segregation**, was practiced for almost half a century; close to 90 percent of South Africa's population was denied legal and political rights during these decades. Just like Nazi Germany, legislation was promulgated making racial discrimination official state policy. Mixed marriages and interracial sex were banned. Every individual was classified by race. The Group Areas Act of 1950 became the heart of the apartheid system because efforts were made to geographically separate the racial groups. The Separate Amenities Act created, among other things, separate beaches, buses, hospitals, schools, and universities. Blacks and Coloreds were forced to carry identity documents to be able to move around within the country. The resistance efforts of Nelson Mandela, among others, and those of the international community, eventually ended this white supremacist régime.

In the United States, white supremacy played a major role in the Civil War of 1861–1865 because the institution of slavery, which had been the economic backbone of the South, was threatened by the election of Abraham Lincoln as president in 1860. The end of this war did not end white supremacy. Several organizations arose in the southern states with the sole aim of returning to antebellum enslavement of black people because they were considered inferior—fit only to be bought, sold, and used as beasts of burden on sugar and cotton plantations. The most prominent white supremacist organization was the **Ku Klux Klan (KKK)**. It was established in Tennessee in 1866, barely a year after the end of the Civil War. Most Klan leaders were former members of the Confederate Army. For several years, Klansmen wearing masks, white cardboard hats, and white sheets, tortured, maimed, and killed African Americans and sympathetic whites in orgies of racial hatred. From 1868 to 1870, the Ku Klux Klan was mainly responsible for restoring white rule in North Carolina, Tennessee, and Georgia. The key goal of white supremacist groups was to perpetuate the denial of civil and political rights to recently freed black people.

In the modern United States, white supremacist groups continue to proliferate. They are very militaristic and violent in outlook. They do not hesitate to use force and violence to achieve their ends. Just as Hitler had his Gestapo and stormtroopers, groups like the KKK, Skinheads, and Aryan Nation have hundreds of white youth in gangs whose sole purpose is to do bodily harm to people of color, either as the expression of their hatred, or out of loyalty to white supremacy. Targets of their hatred also include Jews who, with black people, are called *mud people* by these modern American white supremacists.

Sociologists and other scholars have studied what propels individuals to support these supremacist groups. Members are candid in expressing their belief that the American political system is being controlled by a Jewish cabal led by the Zionist Occupational Government (ZOG), whose aim is to create a one-world government intent on curtailing the rights of white Americans. They tend to see Jewish or multiculturalist conspiracies in almost every action taken by the government. They are also highly suspicious of international multilateral organizations such as the United Nations.

Michael Barkun, in his *Religion and the Racist Right: The Origins of the Christian Identity Movement* (1996), discusses a particularly frightening white supremacist group that uses all elements previously described—ideology of racial superiority, ultra-conservative Christian fundamentalism, intolerance, militarism, and violence—to achieve the ultimate goal of a white homeland. The group is called Christian Identity. It is opposed to cultural diversity, affirmative action, and other government policies that its members label as *liberal* or *leftist*. According to Barkun, Christian Identity groups trace their origins to an obscure nineteenth-century religious movement in England known as British-Israelism. This movement claimed Britons as the descendants of the ten lost tribes of Israel. Through some linguistic sleight-of-hand, they managed to establish their connection to the Jews to claim as theirs the heritage of a chosen people. However, the original British-Israelist movement was neither anti-Semitic nor racist. Indeed, the latter actually recognized a kinship with Jews.

For scholars of American politics, Christian Identity supremacist groups have been quite successful in co-opting and dominating the political right. They have seductively and insidiously spread their message and ideology—even among groups not even distantly linked to them—by using the discourse and rhetoric of conservatism, such as family values, self-reliance, personal responsibility, and patriotism. Christian Identity is also believed to have been rather adept in strategically using the current political system to put in office, and in policy-making positions, people sympathetic to its vision of society, but who do not necessarily espouse white supremacist ideas.

Further Readings: Barkun, Michael. *Religion and the Racist Right: The Origins of the Christian Identity Movement*. Durham: University of North Carolina Press, 1996; Bushart, Howard L., and Myra Edwards Barnes, eds. *Soldiers of God: White Supremacists and Their Holy War for America*. New York: Kensington Publishing Corporation, 2000; Cohler, Anne M., Basia Carolyn Miller, Harold Samuel Stone, Raymond Geuss, and Quentin Skinner, eds. *Montesquieu: The Spirit of the Laws*. Cambridge Texts in the History of Political Thought. Cambridge, England: Cambridge University Press, 1989; Dobratz, Betty A. *The White Separatist Movement in the United States: "White Power, White Pride!"* Baltimore: The Johns Hopkins University Press, 2000; Eze, Emmanuel Chukwudi. *Race and the Enlightenment: A Reader*. Malden, MA: Blackwell Publishers, 1997; Ferber, Abby L. *White Man Falling: Race, Gender, and White Supremacy*. Lanham, MD: Rowman & Littlefield Publishers, Inc., 1998; Gay, Peter. *The Enlightenment: The Rise of Modern Paganism*. New York: W.W. Norton & Company, 1995; Gobineau, Arthur de. *The Inequality of Human Races*. New York: Howard Fertig, Inc., 1999; Hegel, G.F.W. *Hegel, Lectures on the Philosophy of World History, Introduction: Reason in History*. Translated by H. B. Nisbet. Cambridge, England: Cambridge University Press, 1975; Krey, August C. *First Crusade*. Magnolia, MA: Peter Smith Publisher Inc., 1986; Krey, August C. *The First Crusade: The Accounts of Eyewitnesses and Participants*. Princeton, NJ: Princeton University Press, 1921; Nieli, Russ, and Carol M. Swain, eds. *Contemporary Voices of White Nationalism in America*. New York: Cambridge University Press, 2003; Pagden, Anthony. *Lords of All the World: Ideologies of Empire in Spain, Britain* *and France c. 1500–c. 1800*. New Haven, CT: Yale University Press, 1998; Swain, Carol M. *The New White Nationalism in America: Its Challenge to Integration*. New York: Cambridge University Press, 2004.

'BioDun J. Ogundayo

White, Walter (1893–1955)

Walter Francis White, a civil rights leader, authority on American race riots and **lynchings**, and writer who published his first works during the Harlem Renaissance, was born on July 1, 1893, in Atlanta, Georgia.

White was one of seven children born to George White, a postman, and his wife, Madeline (nee Harrison) White, a schoolteacher. The family lived on the border between the African American and white neighborhoods. After graduating from the high school located on the Atlanta University campus, White matriculated at Atlanta University and graduated in 1916. In the summer of 1915, White began working at Standard Life Insurance Company, where he accepted full-time employment after earning his college degree.

In 1916, White became secretary of the newly formed Atlanta branch of the **National Association for the Advancement of Colored People (NAACP)**, which was founded in response to the Atlanta school board's recent decisions to eliminate the seventh and eighth grades in African American schools to provide more funding for white schools. The first president of the Atlanta NAACP was Harry Pace, who was an officer at Standard Life. In 1918, White accepted **James Weldon Johnson**'s offer to become assistant secretary of the NAACP's New York office, and, in 1929, White succeeded Johnson as the NAACP's executive secretary.

In addition to White's work as a preeminent civil rights leader, he was a prolific author. White wrote two novels—*Fire in the Flint* (1924) and *Flight* (1926)—which focus on lynching and "passing" for white, respectively, and a non-fiction work about lynching, *Rope and Faggot: The Biography of Judge Lynch* (1929). White also helped promote the work of other Harlem Renaissance writers such as poets Countee Cullen and **Claude McKay** as well as of such novelists as Rudolph Fisher, Nella Larsen, and Dorothy West. After the Harlem Renaissance, White wrote three additional book-length works: *A Rising Wind: A Report on the Negro Soldier in the European Theatre of War* (1945); *A Man Called White: The Autobiography of Walter White* (1948); and *How Far the Promised Land?* (1955), which was published posthumously and chronicles African American achievement. White, who contributed articles to such publications as ***The Crisis***, *American Mercury, Saturday Evening Post*, and *Reader's Digest*, was a war correspondent for the *New York Post* from 1943 to 1945, and a columnist for the ***Chicago Defender***. White continued his work as executive secretary of the NAACP and as a writer until he suffered a heart attack and died at his New York home on March 21, 1955. At his funeral four days later, 1,500 individuals filled St. Martin's Protestant Episcopal Church to capacity, and an additional crowd of 1,500 people listened to the service on loudspeakers outside the church.

White, who was arguably the leading expert on American race riots and lynchings during the first half of the twentieth century, retained boyhood memories of the 1906 **Atlanta** riot. When he was thirteen, White rode with his father as he performed his postal duties. They reached Peachtree Street where one of the establishments was The Crystal Palace, a barbershop that catered to a non-black clientele and was owned by Alonzo Herndon, a prominent African American. White and his father saw a lame African American employee from The Crystal Palace try in vain to outrun a mob of white men. After the mob caught the man, he was beaten with clubs and fists and left dead on the street in a pool of blood. As White and his father continued riding through the streets of Atlanta, the mail cart and their light skin protected them; the mob was not bold enough to attack the cart, which was government property, and the rioters assumed that the cart's driver and passenger were white. The mail cart then collided with a carriage from which clung three African Americans, while the white driver lashed both the horses and the rioters who pursued the carriage. After White and his father kept their cart from turning over, they rescued an elderly African American woman who was being chased by the mob; White's father handed the reins to him as he lifted the lady into the cart, and White lashed the horse to run faster.

The next day, friends of White's father warned him that the rioters were going to march from Peachtree Street to Houston Street, where the Whites lived. That night, the rioters stood outside White's home with torches. The son of the Whites' grocer identified their residence as the home of "that nigger mail carrier" and urged the mob to burn the house down because it was "too nice for a nigger to live in!" (White, 11). White and his father, possessing firearms, waited for the men to step onto their lawn. As the rioters moved to the front of the lawn, White, with his light skin, blonde hair, and blue eyes, claimed his identity as an African American. White writes, "In that instant there opened up within me a great awareness; I knew then who I was. I was a Negro, a human being with an invisible pigmentation" (White, 11). Friends of White's father, who were barricaded in a nearby building, fired shots at the mob, causing the rioters to retreat.

Twelve years after the Atlanta riot, White moved to New York to become the NAACP's assistant secretary, and twelve days after he began working at the civil rights organization where he performed clerical and office tasks, a racial crime diverted his attention away from his office work. Jim McIlherron, an African American sharecropper, who defended himself when his employer physically attacked him, was slowly burned to death by a mob in Estill Springs, Tennessee. White and the other NAACP officials realized that if they sent a telegram protesting the lynching to the governor of Tennessee, it would have minimal effect. White then volunteered to travel to Tennessee to investigate the incident. According to David Levering Lewis, "With his eyes and hair, refined accent, and nervous energy, he looked and behaved far more the Wall Street broker than a man destined to be director of the nation's principal civil rights organization" (131). Posing as a white man interested in buying farmland, White gained the trust of the Estill Springs residents who admitted that McIlherron's employer was not justified in beating him, yet they asserted that McIlherron had to be murdered because he hit a white man, and they had to keep other African Americans from getting out of hand. White returned to New York and published his findings.

The Estill Springs lynching marked the first of more than forty lynchings as well as eight race riots that White personally investigated between 1918 and 1929, and it established a pattern that he followed in subsequent investigations. White traveled to the troubled areas; passed as a white reporter, land speculator, etc.; gained the confidence of white individuals who spoke candidly about the horrific racial events; and then returned to New York to publish his findings. White, who took a pay cut when he gave up his job at Standard Life Insurance to work with the NAACP, sacrificed his comfortable lifestyle to put himself in harm's way during his undercover investigations. After three members of the Lowman family were murdered near Aiken, South Carolina, White's investigation revealed that the **Ku Klux Klan (KKK)** was responsible for the lynchings of the young woman and two men. When several local newspapers criticized the lynchers, the sheriff's response was to announce his intention to request that the grand jury indict White for "bribery and passing for white" (White, 59). On other occasions, White received death threats from the Klan.

In 1919, race riots occurred in such places as **Washington**, D.C.; **Chicago**, Illinois; **Omaha**, Nebraska; Philadelphia, Pennsylvania; and **Elaine**, Arkansas. The Chicago riot taught White that when a **white mob** is out of control, a northern city could be as dangerous as a southern town such as Estill Springs. The Chicago violence also taught him not to assume that he was well known by other African Americans. Although appearing white proved to be an advantage for him when he was among whites, his light complexion nearly ended his life when an African American, assuming he was white, shot at him.

In October 1919, White traveled to Phillips County, Arkansas, after a meeting held by African American sharecroppers at a local church erupted into chaos as an armed mob and some of the sharecroppers exchanged gunfire. After more than 200 African Americans were killed, many black men, women, and children fled the county. The rest were placed in stockades and awaited their appearance before a kangaroo court. White arrived in Phillips County and introduced himself to the governor of Arkansas as a reporter for the *Chicago Daily News* who had little knowledge of African Americans. The governor, assuming White was white, welcomed him; the politician, who described White as brilliant, gave him a letter of recommendation to use in case he ran into trouble in Phillips County. As White was conducting his investigation, an African American man warned him that white men were after him. White quickly boarded a train. As the conductor collected White's fare, he told him that he was leaving "just when the fun is going to start" (White, 51) because the lynching of a man who was passing for white was imminent. When White's train arrived in Memphis later that evening, he heard that he had been lynched in Arkansas that afternoon. Among the tributes to White's work as an investigator are the Spingarn Medal, which he received in 1937, and the *Ballad of Walter White*, a poem by Langston Hughes.

Although White became too well known to continue conducting his undercover investigations, he continued to seek justice for the victims of lynchings and riots. White also attempted to help restore law and order to the troubled areas. When the local and state officials did not halt the rioting in **Detroit** in 1943, White asked the governor of Michigan to request federal troops. Noticing Gov. Harry Kelly's reluctance, White contacted the War Department in Washington and was told that a Michigan official would have to contact the commanding general of the area, who was stationed in Chicago. After White shared that information with Kelly, the governor finally requested the federal troops, and order was restored after thirty hours of rioting. During that period, 34 people were killed, and more than 600 were injured.

White was a peacemaker during the Harlem Riot in August 1943 (see **New York City Riot of 1943**). The riot was the result of a rumor that an African American soldier died after he had been shot in the back by a white police officer. White rode with Mayor Fiorello LaGuardia through the streets of Harlem before he convinced the mayor to allow well-known African Americans to ride through Harlem in sound trucks. As objects were thrown at them, White and at least two other prominent black men rode through Harlem proclaiming that the soldier was only slightly injured and urging the residents to return to their homes; eventually the crowd dispersed.

During Walter White's tenure with the NAACP, he worked diligently to end racial discrimination in education, employment, and voting, as well as in the arts and military. Armed with courage and tenacity, White sought justice for the victims of hate crimes and equal rights for African Americans. His deeds as assistant secretary and executive secretary of the NAACP during the first half of the twentieth century helped pave the way for subsequent victories in the **civil rights movement**.

Further Readings: Janken, Kenneth R. "Walter Francis White." In Henry Louis Gates, Jr., and Evelyn Brooks Higginbotham, eds. *African American Lives*. New York: Oxford University Press, 2004, 879–881; Janken, Kenneth R. *White: The Biography of Walter White, Mr. NAACP.* New York: New Press, 2003; Johns, Robert L. "Walter White." In Jessie Carney Smith, ed. *Notable Black American Men*. Detroit: Gale Research, 1998, 1209–1212; Lewis, David Levering. *When Harlem Was in Vogue*. New York: Knopf, 1981; Meier, August, and Elliott Rudwick. "Walter White." In Rayford W. Logan and Michael R. Winston, eds. *Dictionary of American Negro Biography.* New York: W.W. Norton & Company, 1982, 646–650; "Walter White, 61, Dies in Home Here." *New York Times*, March 22, 1955; White, Walter. *A Man Called White: The Autobiography of Walter White*. New York: Viking Press, 1948.

Linda M. Carter

Whiteness

Whiteness is a concept designed to emphasize the socially constructed nature of race as a category that organizes daily life and society. Critical white studies, a subdivision of critical race studies, traces the historical development of concepts such as "white" and "black," and interrogates the function of those concepts in the historical and contemporary United

States, ultimately seeking to denaturalize these concepts as a means toward the end of racial justice. Furthermore, critical race studies seek to destabilize the intellectual hegemony, or centrality, of white consciousness. Such efforts are directed toward ending racially based injustices by revealing the socially constructed nature of categories of social organization that are typically imagined to be *natural*.

White and *black*, like the terms *race* and *gender*, seem to point to fixed, stable biological attributes. But cultural studies and critical theory teach us to interrogate these seemingly natural conditions and reveal them to be in fact socially and culturally constructed, produced, and maintained in a wide variety of ways, from the language that we use to the images that we see daily and accept as normal or natural. It is our generally uncritical acceptance and use of categories of difference that perpetuate their value and sustain their seeming normalcy, obscuring the historical processes by which such ideas have developed. Whiteness, then, is not a stable category, but a product of specific historical and ideological conditions, and hence, social effects. Terms such as *race* refer not to skin color, but to sets of practices that reveal the differential relations of power and experience that are frequently, though not necessarily, connected to biological and anatomical attributes. It is this seeming connection to the biological that provides the ongoing essentialist justification for the naturalness of ideas such as *white*. By critically interrogating social categories considered natural, we can examine the many ways in which societies rely on these categories to distribute their goods and privileges, usually in a disproportionate manner.

Whiteness, like other racial categories, is a fluid category, falsely homogenizing, and implies a reified set of privileges. That is, whiteness seems to be something fixed and real, and therefore something automatically conferred on anyone who looks white. To say that race categories are not natural is not to say that they are not real; they are real in their effects, and in the way we experience them. But the meaning of whiteness changes throughout time and place, and the privileges of whiteness are unevenly distributed, particularly at the intersection of race and class—the economically disadvantaged tend to experience whiteness differently than the wealthy do. An elitist category, it offers benefits and power to those who can claim its mantle; therefore the category's boundaries undergo frequent struggle to expand or strengthen the category and its meanings.

Critical race theory shares assumptions and methods with interdisciplinary work in sociology, legal theory, history, and literary and cultural studies (see Crenshaw et al. and Omi and Winant; for literary treatments of the concept, see Wonham; for a study of the concept in film history, see Cripps). Ignatiev, Jacobsen, and Roediger have examined the historical adoption of white identities by immigrant ethnic groups as compensation for economic and political exclusion from power. Feminist and critical race theorists have developed increasingly detailed understandings of the ways in which **racism** and racial ideologies enable white women to negotiate their subordinated social, political, and economic positions (see Frankenberg, Hill, and Ware).

Contemporary ethnic studies have relied on theories of whiteness in order to emphasize the diversity and complexity of ethnic identities within and between ethnic groups; to examine the ways in which such identities are unwillingly mapped onto social subjects; to examine the ways in which ethnic groups have adopted and shaped whiteness as compensation for economic and political exclusion from power; to challenge ethnocentric perspectives on immigration; interrogate models of ethnic assimilation; and open up for examination areas of political and economic contest previously unexamined under the weight of assimilationist theories (see Romero et al.; Scott-Childress; and Yans-McLaughlin).

Further Readings: Crenshaw, Kimberle, Neil Gotanda, and Garry Peller, eds. *Critical Race Theory: The Key Writings That Formed the Movement*. New York: New Press, 1996; Cripps, Thomas. *Making Movies Black*. New York and Oxford: Oxford University Press, 1993; Frankenberg, Ruth. *White Women, Race Matters: The Social Construction of Whiteness*. Minneapolis: University of Minnesota Press, 1983; Hill, Mike, ed. *Whiteness: A Critical Reader*. New York and London: New York University Press, 1997; Ignatiev, Noel. *How the Irish Became White*. New York: Routledge, 1994; Jacobson, Matthew Frye. *Whiteness of a Different Color: European Immigrants and the Alchemy of Race*. Cambridge, MA: Harvard University Press, 1998; Omi, Michael, and Howard Winant. *Racial Formation in the United States: From the 1960s to the 1990s*. 2nd ed. New York: Routledge, 1994; Roediger, David. *Wages of Whiteness: Race and the Making of the American Working Class*. New York: Verso, 1991; Romero, Mary Romero, Pierrette Hondagneu-Sotelo, and Vilma Ortiz, eds. *Challenging Fronteras: Structuring Latina and Latino Lives in the U.S: An Anthology of Readings*. New York and London: Routledge, 1997; Scott-Childres, Reynolds J., ed. *Race and the Production of Modern American Nationalism*. Wellesley Studies in Critical Theory, Literary History and Culture. New York and London: Garland, 1998; Ware, Vron. *Beyond the Pale: White Women, Racism, and History*. London: Verso, 1992; Wonham, Henry B., ed. *Criticism and the Color Line: Desegregating American Literary Studies*. New Brunswick, NJ: Rutgers University Press, 1996; Yans-McLaughlin, Virginia, ed. *Immigration Reconsidered: History, Sociology and Politics*. New York and Oxford: Oxford University Press, 1990.

Valerie Begley

Wilkins, Roy (1901–1981)

Roy Wilkins was a prominent leader in the **civil rights movement**. He remained a staunch supporter of **nonviolence** in the face of white retaliatory violence and the rise of black militancy during the 1960s. His reaction to the uprisings that were endemic to the urban black communities of the time illustrate the magnitude of his sympathy toward oppressed blacks and his unwavering resolve to attack injustice through peaceable means.

Wilkins was born on August 30, 1901, in St. Louis, Missouri. He obtained a degree in sociology and worked as a journalist at the *Minnesota Daily* and as the editor of *St. Paul Appeal* and *Kansas City Hall*. In 1929, he married a social worker named Amanda "Minnie" Badeau. In 1963, he served as the executive secretary of the **National Association for the Advancement of Colored People (NAACP)** and replaced **W.E.B. Du Bois** as the editor of ***The Crisis***, the official magazine of the NAACP, when the latter left the organization. Wilkins was more conservative than his predecessor, who eventually migrated to Ghana, West Africa, so disillusioned was he with the United States.

Roy Wilkins displays a hangman's noose sent to the NAACP's national headquarters from Florida, circa 1959. Courtesy of the Library of Congress.

Among Wilkins' numerous accomplishments were his testimonials at Congressional hearings, his influence with U.S. presidents, such as **John F. Kennedy**, Lyndon B. Johnson, and Richard Nixon, and his prominent role in such civil right triumphs as *Brown v. Board of Education* and the **Civil Rights Act of 1964**. As a result of these victories, Wilkins strongly believed "that if you pushed the government long enough, hard enough, and in enough of the right places, change could be accomplished" (Wilkins, 127). Wilkins picketed on several occasions and did not limit himself to behind-the-scenes activism.

Wilkins was not only concerned with ending **segregation**; he also tackled the issue of white violence against blacks. In the 1930s, he and other NAACP members attempted unsuccessfully to encourage Franklin D. Roosevelt to support anti-lynching legislation. Although he supported the **Freedom Rides**, because of the dangers they would inevitably meet in the Deep South, he called the riders' strategy "desperately brave" and "reckless" (Wilkins, 283). While the freedom riders indeed met with violence at the hands of the **Ku Klux Klan (KKK)** and **white mobs**, Wilkins convinced President John F. Kennedy and his brother, Attorney General **Robert F. Kennedy**, to provide federal protection for the riders. Wilkins realized that the whites who attacked the activists afforded him an opportunity to press for greater involvement from the Kennedy administration, which had previously believed that there was no immediate need for civil rights.

But the brutality against blacks continued: at the University of Mississippi, where whites opposed the registration of **James Meredith**; in Birmingham, Alabama, where demonstrators were met with vicious dogs and **police brutality**; and in Jackson, Mississippi, where protestors encountered truculent whites. Following these events, when Kennedy gave a televised speech announcing his support for immediate social change, Wilkins finally received the affirmation he had so longed to hear. On the following day, Wilkins received a phone call telling him that **Medgar Evers**, whom Wilkins described as "one of the bravest, most selfless men ever to throw in his lot with the N.A.A.C.P." had been murdered (Wilkins, 290). A week later, Kennedy informed the nation of his impending civil rights legislation.

But the violence continued and manifested in unexpected ways. On November 22, 1963, Kennedy was assassinated. President Johnson, Kennedy's former vice president, signed the Civil Rights Act of 1964. The youthful members of the **Student Nonviolent Coordinating Committee (SNCC)** and the **Congress of Racial Equality (CORE)**, with whom Wilkins had collaborated, became increasingly disheartened after each episode of violence and with the plodding or nonexistent response from the local and federal government. They eventually succumbed to the militant and separatist ideologies of **Black Power**. To Wilkins' horror, the erstwhile nonviolent civil rights organizations began to advocate violence. He believed this ideology was detrimental to the cause of civil rights and further widened the gulf between blacks and whites.

Early in 1967, a bomb exploded in the car of Wharlest Jackson, the former treasurer of the NAACP. Wilkins asserted that "through the murder, God had offered the United States Senate a second chance to enact a civil rights bill allowing the federal government to punish such assassins," but Congress continued to hold up essential legislation (Wilkins, 324). In the summer of 1967, the New York Police Department told Wilkins that the **Revolutionary Action Movement (RAM)** was plotting to assassinate him and other civil rights leaders who promoted passive resistance and cooperation with whites and their institutions. The militants planned to blame whites for the murders to incite violence in the black **ghettos**. Guards were immediately assigned to Wilkins, who was accustomed to being intimidated by whites, but was bewildered that members of his own race would threaten his life. Soon after, RAM members were incarcerated for planning the assassinations.

Throughout that summer and after, black ghettos throughout the nation went up in flames as a result of riots triggered largely by incidences of police brutality and injustice (see **Long Hot Summer Riots, 1965–1967**). But the origins of the violence were far more deeply rooted and included such issues as **racism**, unemployment, **poverty**, lack of opportunities, and alienation. Although Wilkins strongly opposed violence as a means of protest, he sympathized with the black rioters, as illustrated in the following excerpt from his autobiography, which was written with Tom Matthews:

> The change of the early sixties had come perilously late. In those months after the Harlem and Watts ghettos went up in flames, the ordinary ghetto dweller elsewhere could see little improvement in his daily life. The new laws passed by Congress applied mostly to the South and meant very little to him. It was easy for him to feel that he had been abandoned by his government and his country, that he was isolated, of no importance in the United States. Nobody could stand those feelings. So he leaned over, picked up a rock, and heaved it at the biggest plate-glass window he could see. (326)

Wilkins died in New York on September 8, 1981.

Further Reading: Wilkins, Roy, with Tom Matthews. *The Autobiography of Roy Wilkins: Standing Fast*. New York: Penguin Books, 1982.

Gladys L. Knight

Williams, Robert F. (1925–1996)

Robert Franklin Williams was born on February 26, 1925, in Monroe, North Carolina. One of his early memories was witnessing the violent beating and arrest of a black woman by "Big" Jesse Alexander Helms, a white policeman and father of U.S. Sen. Jesse Helms. Five years later, Williams and a friend enrolled in a National Youth Administration job training program near Monroe, where he organized a protest of unequal training curriculum and segregationist camp policies that activated a **Federal Bureau of Investigation (FBI)** file in his name. The next year, he witnessed the northern face of race violence when, while living in Detroit with his brother Edward and working briefly for the Ford Motor Company, he was caught up with his brother and sister-in-law in a racial fight at Belle Isle during the Detroit race riot (see **Detroit [Michigan] Riot of 1943**).

Returning to Monroe, Williams graduated from Winchester Street High School in 1944 and served eighteen months as an Army draftee at the end of World War II, where his exposure to the fears and weaknesses of his fellow white soldiers disabused him of any notion that whites had any well-organized or powerful superiority to blacks. Williams received weapons training and took a creative writing course that developed the two major icons—the gun and the pen—that became his signature weapons. He spent much of his Army time in the brig for a variety of acts of defiance, including failure to obey orders, disrespect toward officers and being AWOL several times.

His political career began in 1956 when he was elected president of the Monroe branch of the **National Association for the Advancement of Colored People (NAACP)**, a group that at the time had only six members. Williams recruited furiously from the working and poor classes of Monroe's African American community, swelling the branch membership to over 250. That same year, he organized the Black Militia, an armed self-defense group, in response to threats he had received as a consequence of efforts to integrate local recreational facilities and in defense of Dr. Albert E. Perry, a local physician and leader.

In 1958, Williams advocated on behalf of eight-year-old David Exell "Fuzzy" Simmons and ten-year-old James Hanover Grissom Thompson, who had been found guilty and sent to reform school for playing a kissing game with white girls. Williams' work clearing the boys' names and bringing national and international attention to what became known as the Kissing Case embarrassed the U.S. government and was followed by the branch's protest of the acquittal of Louis Medlin, a white Monroe resident charged in 1959 with assaulting and intending to rape a black woman who was eight months pregnant. Williams argued that African American women and men would defend themselves with arms if necessary in the wake of the acquittal, saying, "If it's necessary to stop **lynching** with lynching, then we must be willing to resort to that method" (Mayfield 1961). This led to his suspension and subsequent expulsion from the national NAACP, but endeared him to many in the radical left as well as to those drawn to the more confrontational politics of voices such as **Malcolm X**. He was reelected to his position as president of the Monroe NAACP branch.

In 1961, the freedom riders came to Monroe, and Williams assisted them, although he refused to accept the philosophy of **nonviolence** that they observed (see **Freedom Rides**). When a **white mob** began to attack them, African Americans—some armed—rose to their defense. In the resulting conflict and turmoil, a white couple was given refuge in the Williams home. As a result, local law enforcement charged Williams with kidnapping and used the incident to raid the homes of other African Americans, disarming them as a consequence. To escape the trumped-up charge, Williams, his wife Mabel, and their two sons (John and Franklin) fled Monroe, then the country.

The Williams family took up residence in Cuba, where, over the course of the next five years, they broadcast ***Radio Free Dixie***, a music, news, and commentary show advocating armed self-defense and black self-determination; published *The Crusader* (a newsletter Williams had started in 1959); and networked with an international coterie of revolutionaries, theoreticians, and activists. During their first year there, Williams published his signature manifesto, ***Negroes with Guns***, which detailed the Monroe movement and the philosophy that had grown out of it. **Black Panther Party (BPP)** cofounder **Huey P. Newton** credited the book with having a great influence on his political philosophy. After his ongoing differences with Fidel Castro caused him to move his family to Mao Tse Tung's China in 1966, Williams spent three years touring Asia and Africa from his base there. Considering himself a "militant revolutionary nationalist" ("In Memory"), Williams was made chairman of Max Stanford's **Revolutionary Action Movement (RAM)** and president-in-exile of Milton and Richard Henry's Republic of New Africa (RNA). His legacy lies in the impact his philosophy of self-determination and self-defense had on groups such as RAM, the RNA, the **Deacons for Defense and Justice**, and the Black Panthers, among others.

In 1969, after negotiations with the U.S. government, Williams returned from exile, settling in Baldwin, Michigan. Seven years later, after a protracted struggle to avoid extradition to North Carolina, the kidnapping charges against him were dropped. He spent the last decade and a half of his life as an elder statesman, college and community lecturer, and local activist with groups such as Baldwin's People's Association for Human Rights. Williams died of Hodgkin's Disease on October 15, 1996. His papers are housed at the University of North Carolina. *See also* Black Power; Black Self-Defense; Lynching.

Further Readings: Freedom Archives, ed., and Robert F. Williams. *Robert F. Williams: Self Respect, Self Defense and Self Determination (An Audio Documentary as Told by Mabel Williams)*. Edinburgh, Scotland: AK Press, 2005; "In Memory of Robert F. Williams: A Voice for Armed Self-Defense and Black Liberation." *Revolutionary Worker* 882, November 17, 1996. See http://rwor.org/a/firstvol/882/willms.htm; Mayfield, Julian. "Challenge to Negro Leadership." *Commentary* 31, no. 4 (April 1961); Tyson, Timothy. *Radio Free Dixie: Robert F. Williams and the Roots of Black Power*. Chapel Hill: University of North Carolina Press, 1999; Williams, Robert F. *Negroes with Guns*. Detroit, MI: Wayne State University Press, 1998. Originally published in 1962.

Gregory E. Carr

Wilmington (North Carolina) Riot of 1898

The Wilmington (North Carolina) Riot of 1898 was a violent coup d'état engineered by the North Carolina Democratic Party, resulting in the death

A nineteenth-century depiction of scenes from the Wilmington Riot. Courtesy of the Library of Congress.

of hundreds of African American residents of Wilmington, the forceful expulsion of thousands of others, and the removal of a democratically elected government of black and white Republicans and Fusionists. The ultimate goal of this **white supremacy** rebellion was to reverse the political and economic progress African Americans had made since **Reconstruction** (1865–1877).

The broad context of the riot is to be found in the post-Reconstruction period that started in 1877 when the federal army pulled out of the South, giving southern legislatures the opportunity to start a steady course of disenfranchising the newly freed black population. During Reconstruction, a number of legal tools had given hope to African Americans, notably the Thirteenth, **Fourteenth**, and **Fifteenth** Amendments to the U.S. Constitution that respectively abolished slavery, gave citizenship and equal protection of the law to African Americans, and extended the right to vote to black men. In addition, the Civil Rights Act of 1866, the Force Acts of 1870 and 1871, and the Civil Rights Act of 1875, among other laudable efforts, sought to protect African Americans against the increasing violence of white supremacist groups in the South and the general discrimination and **segregation** that followed the end of the Civil War. Reconstruction had seen a number African Americans occupying positions of power in elected office. On the other hand, post-Reconstruction was characterized by a relentless effort on the part of southern legislatures to disenfranchise the black population, especially the elected officials and professionals. The grandfather clause, literary tests, poll taxes, **sharecropping** (a reconfiguration of the plantation system), and violence were some of the strategies used by white **vigilante organizations** to defraud the promises of the three amendments and prevent African Americans from enjoying the rights and privileges conferred by citizenship, including the right to vote and hold office. In a revealing decision, in 1883 the U.S. Supreme Court pronounced the Civil Right Act of 1875 unconstitutional, thus legalizing discrimination and segregation against blacks in transportation and public facilities. The 1896 Supreme Court decision known as *Plessy v. Ferguson* further consolidated the **Jim Crow** laws of the South and thus sanctioned the segregationist and discriminatory principle of separate but equal. The **lynching** of African Americans in the last two decades of the nineteenth century reached the thousands. It is in this context of violence, white supremacy rule, and political **disenfranchisement** of blacks that the Wilmington, North Carolina, race riot has to be understood.

The immediate cause of the riot is found in the result of the 1894, 1896, and 1898 elections in Wilmington, which white democrats lost to Republicans and Fusionists, a relatively large number of whom were black. As a result of these democratic elections, blacks were appointed to various positions in the administration of the city, leading white Democrats to cry foul over what they called *Negro domination*. If a number of African Americans had achieved real economic and political power, this constituted a threat to white supremacists, who could not tolerate such a rise to power. This was a tradition inherited from a long period of slavery, in which the only suitable position for the supposedly inferior blacks was to serve the superior white man. Thus, the idea of a black man in power summoning a white man, giving orders to a white man, or inspecting a white man's home, or simply questioning a white man, was an affront to the ideology of white supremacy. A contemporary novelist, Charles Chesnutt, dramatized the coup d'état of 1898 in Wilmington, in his 1901 novel ***The Marrow of Tradition***.

The North Carolina newspapers played a critical role in the campaign to disenfranchise African Americans in Wilmington. For example, the *Raleigh News and Observer* and the *Wilmington Messenger* ran a ruthless campaign demeaning African Americans in general but reserving the most severe disparagement for black civil servants and professionals. In the months leading to the 1898 elections, newspapers were saturated with articles that depicted lawlessness, black self-assertion and takeover, and sexual crimes by blacks, a favorite pretext for white supremacists to start mass violence against blacks in the post-Reconstruction South. In the days leading to the 1898 election, Alex Manly, the mixed-race editor of a local black-owned newspaper, the *Wilmington Daily Record*, claimed that "poor white men [were being] careless in the matter of protecting their women," further claiming that "our experience among poor white people in the country teaches us that women of that race are not any more particular in the matter of clandestine meetings with colored men than the white men with the colored women" (August 18, 1898). Manly's editorial was a reaction to a speech delivered the previous year by Rebecca Latimer Felton, the first woman ever to become a U.S. senator, in which she forcefully sanctioned the lynching of black men to protect white women from black men, whom she referred to as "ravening human beasts" (quoted in Sundquist, xvii). In reality, Manly's editorial condemned lynching and the ideology of white supremacy and its deceptive and violent ways bent on galvanizing racial strife. Manly also condemned the hypocrisy of white supremacists, who did not hesitate to ruin the morality of black women but cried foul at the idea of a black man being intimate with a white woman. The Democratic newspapers seized on what they fanatically characterized as an attack against white womanhood to mount a campaign aimed at provoking race tensions. In doing so, they deliberately focused on one aspect of Manly's editorial, namely the fact that white women were attracted by black men whose own fathers were white. For white supremacists, it was inconceivable to condone the sin of amalgamation. The irony was that many blacks in the Wilmington population were descendants or sons and daughters of such relationships through rape (in the period of slavery) or even love. Instead of lynching Manly for his editorial, the white supremacists calculated to use it for political purpose: to forcibly remove the interracial coalition of black and white Republicans and Fusionists from power.

On November 9, 1898, the day after the election that the Democrats had lost to Republicans and Fusionists, the Secret Nine at the forefront of the violence presented what they called the "White Declaration of Independence," rejecting the black man's right to vote and hold office and calling for the government to be given to the white population paying most of the taxes. For the Secret Nine, only whites had the right to a job in the city. They also reiterated their earlier condemnation of Manly's editorial for its affront on white womanhood and they demanded his expulsion from the city. Alfred Moore Waddell, a former Confederate officer and congressman, along with a committee he headed, brought the declaration to thirty-two black leaders in Wilmington and requested a reply the next day, with the expectation of submission to total white control. Mailed, instead of being carried in person, the reply missed the November 10 deadline.

When a mob of armed white men from Wilmington and surrounding towns and farms gathered on November 10 at 8:00 A.M., Waddell led them to offices of the *Daily Record*. From 500 white men, the group quickly grew to 2,000 men as the mob progressed through town. The office was ransacked and fire broke out, burning the office down. In an act that speaks of the spectacle-like nature of race riots, the mob had a picture taken in front of the building.

The riot spread within hours, and because of superior weapons, ample supply of guns and ammunition, and the help of the state militia, the white supremacy mobs defeated the blacks who had resolved to defend themselves. The rioters quickly spread their criminality throughout the city. The white Republican mayor of the city, Dr. Silas P. Wright, and the city council members of both races were forced to resign. Waddell, with the support of the prominent members of the city, proclaimed himself mayor. Alexander Manly and other blacks, who were expecting violence to erupt, had already left town. The **white mob** was intent on driving the blacks in general, but specifically black jobholders and professionals, out of town.

The white Democrats, who took over the reigns of government after overthrowing the democratically elected Republicans and Fusionists, put the death toll to twelve or fourteen, but more objective estimates put the death toll in the hundreds. Another result of this mass violence against blacks led to many leaving the city, and to property being illegally seized. The Wilmington race riot of 1898 made national headlines, but neither Congress nor the president intervened to protect the black population of Wilmington, North Carolina, as indeed both branches of government generally did little or nothing against the violence that accompanied the Jim Crow laws, in spite of the Fourteenth Amendment's promise of "equal protection of the laws."

The Wilmington, North Carolina, race riot was dramatized in a number of fictional works, including Celia Bland's *The Conspiracy of the Secret Nine*, Philip Gerard's *Cape Fear Rising*, and Charles W. Chesnutt's *The Marrow of Tradition*. Chesnutt's 1901 novel is a complex commentary on white violence, the undying galvanizing power of race, and the virulent segregation and discrimination that characterized the post-Reconstruction South, all of which produced tense racial relations that contemporaries of Chesnutt, such as **W.E.B. Du Bois** in his *Souls of Black Folk* (1903), also chastised in their own works.

In a way of commenting on Manly's editorial, Chesnutt complicates the situation by exploring the entangled family history of the leading white supremacist in the novel, the white newspaper editor General Carteret. His wife Olivia learns that she is the sister of Janet Miller, wife of a prominent black doctor in the city (named Wellington in the novel). Olivia's father fathered Janet with a black woman. Through this sub-story, Chesnutt's work avoids the easy taxonomy of race by showing the complexity of race relations in the South as complicated by white-black sexual relations, including the rape of black women by white slave owners, but also free love affairs between the two races, thus reaffirming the truthfulness of Manly's editorial. As the story of Olivia Carteret and Janet Miller shows in *The Marrow of Tradition*, this was a reality that the white supremacists were not ready to accept when they overthrew the government of the interracial political coalition of black and white Republicans and Fusionists. Chesnutt's novel also highlights the class issue that the mob mentality of the 1898 race riot obfuscates. While the riot was the work of a white mob that resulted in the triumph of white supremacy and the disenfranchisement of African Americans in both the real riot and the novel, in both cases the class issue is an important part of the process. In the real riot, it is the political elite of the North Carolina Democratic Party that engineered the riot, while in the novel, Carteret and Belmont are the brains of the riot; McBane, whom the two aristocrats despise because of his low class, follows in the name of white supremacy.

All in all, the Wilmington, North Carolina, race riot of 1898 was the culmination of the ideology of white supremacy. It disenfranchised the black population of the city, thus betraying the promises of both the Fourteenth and Fifteenth Amendments to the U.S. Constitution. The riot definitely established the Jim Crow tenets of **racism**, separation, and discrimination in North Carolina, and these would prevail until the civil and voting rights acts were enacted by Congress in the 1960s.

Further Readings: Cecelski, David S., and Timothy B. Tyson, eds. *Democracy Betrayed: The Wilmington Race Riot of 1898 and Its Legacy.* Chapel Hill: University of North Carolina Press, 1998; Hossfeld, Leslie H. *Narrative, Political Unconscious and Radical Violence in Wilmington, North Carolina.* New York: Routledge, 2005; Sundquist, Eric J. "Introduction." In Charles W. Chesnutt, *The Marrow of Tradition.* New York: Penguin Books, 1993, vii–xliv. Originally published in 1901.

Aimable Twagilimana

Y

York (Pennsylvania) Riots of 1969

The race riots during the late 1960s engulfed cities and towns throughout the United States. In November 1967, this pandemic prompted hearings before the U.S. Senate Subcommittee on Investigation of the Committee on Government Operations. According to "Riots, Civil and Criminal Disorders," a document generated during the hearings, race riots were endemic to both large and small cities and each localized riot appeared to start for a combination of unique reasons. There are different versions of what ignited the race riots in York, Pennsylvania, in the summer of 1969. However, the bouts of violence in York streets left 2 people killed, over 100 residents injured, dozens arrested, and several homes and businesses damaged or destroyed. Local and state officials declared a state of emergency before it was all over.

To date, most written accounts suggest that a false **rumor** concocted by a black teenager, Clifford Green, caused the York race riots. On July 17, 1969, Green told York police and blacks in the community that members of a local white gang, the Girarders, doused and burned him with gasoline. Consequently, many black youth retaliated against the Girarders. Later, it was revealed that Green had accidentally burned himself playing with lighter fluid. Even though many sources pinpoint Green's fabrication as the impetus, other factors contributed heavily to racial violence that summer as well. York mayor, John D. Snyder and other authorities had ignored discriminatory practices surrounding housing, recreational facilities, education, employment, and police abuse in the black community for some time. Officials paid little attention to warnings and recommendations from community leaders to help improve the social and economic climate in York to head off rising tensions.

Factors Contributing to Racial Tensions

During the winter of 1967, the Pennsylvania Human Relations Commission (PHRC) released its findings from the investigatory hearings. The report indicated that there was racial—black versus white—polarization and tension in the city of York. The **Federal Bureau of Investigation (FBI)** had informants in the black and white communities and was also aware of the social unrest in York. Several factors contributed to the climate. According to the 1960 census, 4,747 blacks, or 8.8 percent of York's population, lived in **ghettos**. **Segregation** and unwritten real estate practices (see **Redlining**) relegated blacks to rudimentary houses in unpaved alleyways and side streets, such as Newberry Street, Mason Alley, or Cherry Lane. York's blacks lived in rodent- and roach-infested shacks. Some houses had no shower, bathtubs, or hot water. Despite available recourse, city officials did little to address the housing situation. As one of few cities statewide to have a full-time housing inspector and an assistant, the supposed oversight yielded only one fine for violating building codes during that time period. The mayor even refused to accept federal monies to assist the poor in rehabilitating homes and to enable redevelopment.

The dilapidated communities occupied by blacks were also not allocated funds by York officials for recreational facilities, and unfair restrictions were placed on black gatherings. The Crispus Attucks Community Center, the Three-Ten (3:10) Club, and Freddy's, a combination grocery store and restaurant, were popular black teenage hangouts. Black youth also congregated in Penn Commons, a park located on the south end of the city. It was common for white youth to loiter a few blocks away in downtown York. Police illegally imposed a 9:15 P.M. curfew for black youth at the park. On the other hand, white youth could remain on the town square until midnight.

Such biased treatment was also evident in educational practices. Like many northern cities, schools in the York Public School District were racially integrated. However, traceable racial discrimination existed via the de facto segregation practices. According to the *Investigatory Hearing Report* (1968) published by the PHRC, York High School's administrators subscribed to strict disciplinary practices that treated black students unfairly. It was reported that there was "frequent recourse to corporal punishment of students. Instances wherein this corporal punishment was a reflection of a racist attitude on the part of teacher(s)." Likewise, instead of encouraging post-secondary education, white guidance counselors recommended general or vocational-track programs for black male students and business or clerical-track programs for black female students. They also advised black students to enlist in the armed services. Overall, educational neglect often left black youth unprepared to meet the needs of employers after graduation.

This lack of preparedness, in addition to unfair employment practices, made it difficult for York blacks to secure jobs. According to a study conducted by the York County Council for Human Relations, blacks did not have the same job opportunities as their white counterparts. The report also indicated that the majority of York's white employers did not have any black employees. Employers that did not have black employees indicated that they would not hire blacks or were reluctant to do so. Therefore, many blacks filled domestic services and unskilled labor positions and earned one-third the wage paid to white laborers.

Existing hostilities in the community born from employment, housing, recreational, and educational disparities were further agitated by what the

PHRC reported as harassment and excessive force by police toward blacks. Even though local officials refused to address legitimate concerns of **police brutality** in the black community, Mayor Snyder did create a K-9 unit to handle York's "Negro problem." The K-9 unit was commonly used to instill fear and to disperse crowds of juveniles. The police unfairly used canines to arrest non-white citizens.

On Friday, July 19, 1963, police arrested two black men, James Padgett and McCoy Moore. While Padgett and Moore were in the custody of the police, the officers allowed their canines to maul the two men. Outraged by the brutal attack, approximately 250 black community members protested at City Hall. Black community leaders submitted a petition with 800 signatures, which demanded that the arresting officer be relieved of duty, the K-9 unit be disbanded, and a police oversight board be created. To counter the efforts of to the blacks, some white citizens circulated a petition that supported the police officers and called for an expansion of the K-9 unit. The result was that Mayor Snyder suspended both officers involved for five days, eventually expanded the K-9 unit, and refused to create an oversight board.

In July 1965, police arrested a black woman, Mary Brown, and two black men. During the arrest, Brown was beaten in the face with a club and a police dog mauled one of the men. Over 100 members of the black community protested the officer's mistreatment, but to no avail—nothing happened.

On November 11, 1965, two days after police arrested Carl Williams, his body was found near Smalls Athletic Field. A police blackjack was discovered near Williams' bloodied and swollen corpse. The arresting officers in the case lied about detaining Williams and falsified police records. York City Council found the two officers guilty of misconduct and neglect of duty; however, the officers retained their jobs.

Tension between blacks and white authorities continued to intensify on July 11, 1968, when Officer Wayne Toomey fired his service revolver while chasing two black youths. Conflicting testimonies were presented during city council investigation. Officer Toomey and white witnesses indicated that shots were fired but they went over the heads of the assailants. On the other hand, blacks testified that the shots were fired directly at the black youths. Again, both the black and white communities rallied and circulated respective petitions in the case. Six months after the incident, Toomey was reprimanded but remained on the force.

Blacks were not only terrorized by members of the York Police Department; white residents also tormented blacks in York. On August 4, 1968, Chester Roach fired shots at black youths from his apartment window above Hoffman's Meat Market on South Penn Street, a predominantly black neighborhood. During the melee on Penn Street, Roach inflicted gunshot injuries to ten blacks while the blacks hurled bricks and bottles through Roach's second-story apartment window. Police did not arrest Roach when they responded to the disturbance; instead, they rescued Roach's wife and permitted the fracas to continue. After the police failed to apprehend Roach, black youths torched the meat market in order to smoke out the sniper. Finally, out on the street, black residents confiscated Roach's weapons. Three days later, police arrested Roach and charged him with aggravated assault with intent to kill and aggravated assault and battery. After the Roach incident, Hoffman, the white store owner, told the black youths in the area that they could take what they wanted from the debris. However, as the police arrived to investigate, Cpl. Peter Chantiles fired his weapon to scare away black children. After an outcry from the black community, Chantiles was suspended for ten days.

In the early 1960s, black leaders in York attempted to work with the city's governing structure to curb racial tensions. Maurice Peters, former leader of the local chapter of the **National Association for the Advancement of Colored People (NAACP)** and the Peaceful Committee for Immediate Action, challenged individuals, institutions, and systems that sanctioned **racism** toward blacks. Peters suggested that "if the situation does not improve, there will be many a long, hot summer. . . . Negroes will find ways to make their plight known public" (Rappold, "1966").

Peters' prophecy came closer to reality during the mid-1960s. A group led by Theodore Holmes established the local chapter of the **Congress of Racial Equality (CORE).** Conservative Negroes and whites perceived CORE as a militant organization. Despite this, the local branch played a vital role instilling a sense of pride in black youth. CORE also attracted blacks who grew frustrated with conservative organizations that did not address the issues. Theodore Holmes, cochairman of the York Chapter of CORE, offered, "We've been beating our drum, asking for police review boards, more jobs, better housing, and being accepted" (Rappold, "Militancy").

Shortly after the establishment of CORE, some members splintered to form the Black Unity Movement (BUM). The organization sponsored a conference in York with workshops on self-defense, guerilla warfare, and black history. The organization was modeled after the **Black Panther Party (BPP)** and encouraged blacks not to talk to police if questioned and to defend each other by any means necessary. Young militants stressed that patience, reasoning, and nonviolence did nothing to address the so-called Negro problem. In *Crisis in Black and White*, author Charles Silberman agreed. He wrote that white people were not troubled by the justice denied to black people. Instead, whites were concerned that their peace was being shattered and their business interrupted.

The Summer That Changed York, Pennsylvania

While the debate continues over what ignited the riots in York, several reports confirm that both white and black youths engaged in gang warfare after 11:00 P.M. on July 17, 1969. On the first night of the riots, youths hurled rocks, bottles, and Molotov cocktails in the predominantly white North Newberry Street neighborhood. A few blocks away, near the corner of Philadelphia Street and Pershing Avenue, plainclothes detective George Smith stopped two black youths about curfew violations. While the detective questioned the youths, John Washington and Taka Nii Sweeney, the youths were hit by sniper fire. It was later discovered that Robert

Messersmith fired the shots. Black and white retaliatory violent measures occurred after the incident.

On July 18, police attempted to seal off areas of the city where violence was reported. To prevent blacks from entering the white neighborhood, the police blockaded the intersection of Philadelphia and Newberry Streets. In addition, the police barricaded six intersections surrounding York's southwest black community. To protect themselves from sniper fire, police kenneled their canines and wore bulletproof vests. Police patrol cruisers were abandoned for bank delivery vans with gun ports on the sides. In the makeshift armored vehicles, police patrolled troubled neighborhoods and exchanged gunfire with blacks. During a shoot-out, a black gunman fired a high-powered Krag .30–.40-caliber rifle at the armored van. The bullet pierced the 1/8- inch steel-plated van and injured rookie policeman Henry C. Schaad inside. Thirteen days later, Schaad died. In response to the Schaad shooting, police opened fire on the homes suspected in the shooting.

By July 19, 1969, every member of the ninety-six-man police unit was ordered into emergency duty. Mayor Snyder declared a state of emergency. Snyder imposed a strict curfew for youths. He also restricted the sale of guns, ammunition, and gasoline, and closed liquor stores and malt shops. Thirty-five state troopers were called in to reinforce York police.

It was firebomb attacks from both sides that caused the York riots to further escalate. The Myers, a black family that lived on Cottage Hill Road in an all-white neighborhood near North Newberry Street, had their home frequently firebombed by members of the Newberry Street Boys (NSB).

The next day, in broad daylight, James and Sherman Spells confronted NSB gang leader Bobby Messersmith on his porch for firebombing black residences. Resolute, the Spells brothers threatened to return to Newberry Street and wreak havoc if the firebombing did not stop. Later that day, while police manned the barricade at the intersection of Philadelphia and Newberry Streets, a group of black young men in a gray Cadillac breached the white neighborhood through a side alleyway. As the white gang members confronted the carload of blacks, the driver opened the trunk and a gunman sprung out and hailed gunfire at the white youth. Caught off guard, the white gang members scattered. The carload of blacks escaped the white neighborhood without sustaining injuries.

After the surprise attack, Messersmith gathered several local white gangs—Newberry Street Boys, Swampers, Girarders, and Yorklyns—at a White Power rally at Farquhar Park. Prior to this meeting, the white gangs fought one another over turf. Messersmith convinced the rival gang members that militant blacks were a common enemy. White police officers also attended the rally. As Officer Schaad lay dying, police stepped up their efforts and made allegiances with white gangs in York.

The rally organizers and police told the attendees to bring all of their weapons to Newberry Street. The Messersmith family, led by Robert's father John, coordinated the effort to protect the neighborhood from the black insurgency. Armed white youth congregated at the Messersmith home for ammunition and instructions. The senior Messersmith strategically placed young gunmen on balconies, rooftops, and back alleys surrounding the

Newberry Street neighborhood. A few gang members were posted on the corner of Philadelphia and Newberry Streets, where police stationed a barricade, to signal when blacks approached. In addition to signalers, the senior Messersmith monitored his own police scanner. Several people called police about the overwhelming presence of young people with guns, but officers did nothing to interfere with Messersmith's operation.

On the evening of July 21, 1969, police permitted a black family in a white Cadillac to pass through the barricade. The unsuspecting family was attempting to take the Newberry Street shortcut to JM Fields grocery. Officers at the barricade dispatched a message over the radio that a carload of blacks in a light-colored Cadillac entered Newberry Street. Even though the streetlights were blown out, the driver, Hattie Dickson, was able to see snipers on roofs as well as armed white youths on the street ahead. As the Cadillac crossed the railroad tracks at Newberry Street and Gay Avenue, Dickson attempted to turn the vehicle around and flee. During the U-turn, Dickson stalled the Cadillac on the railroad tracks. In an attempt to get her family out of harm's way, unarmed backseat passenger Lillie Belle Allen decided to take over the wheel. Immediately after Allen got out of the car, the armed white youths launched a barrage of gunfire. The defenseless passengers crouched below the window line as the Cadillac was riddled with bullets. However, outside the vehicle, Allen was blown out of her sneakers. On a family visit from Aiken, South Carolina, Allen was the first civilian casualty in the York race riots. As police arrived on the murder scene, young, armed vigilantes dispersed and avoided arrest.

Unable to control the situation in York, Public Safety Director Jacob W. Hose requested assistance from the Pennsylvania National Guard. On Tuesday, July 22, 1969, at 2:05 A.M., Gov. Raymond Shafer declared a state of emergency in York. Over 200 national guardsmen in tanks, trucks, and jeeps moved into York. The presence of the heavily armed troops, as well as the torrential rainfall, restored calm to the city.

On Wednesday, July 23, 1969, Elmer Woodyard, one of six black officers on the force, resigned from the York Police Department. Woodyard referred to an incident during the riots where officers inside armored vehicles fired recklessly in an attempt to damage and destroy black property. He also claimed that some white officers' hatred toward blacks superceded their responsibility to protect and serve.

During the next few days, the police and National Guard seized guns and ammunition. The fighting dramatically decreased. On July 24, 1969, Governor Shafer and Mayor Snyder relaxed the curfew for all residents from 11:00 P.M. to 6:00 A.M. The governor and mayor assessed the situation in York and prepared to pull the national guardsmen out of York. By July 26, the first 100 troops departed from York. The next day, Governor Shafer lifted the state of emergency over York. No longer under martial law, York remained calm. The last of the state troopers and national guardsmen retreated from York on July 28, 1969. According to FBI files, the police made 108 arrests: 78 curfew violations, 7 disorderly conduct charges, 2 furnishing false information charges, and 11 violations of the uniform firearms act. In addition, $30,625 of property damage was reported.

Further Reading: Rappold, R. Scott. "Militancy Grows in City's Slums: Black, White Leaders Under Fire in '66–67." *York Dispatch*. See http://www.yorkdispatch.com/yorkriots/beforetheriots/ci_00011203700; Rappold, R. Scott. "1966: The First Long, Hot Summer: Police Issues Fester for York's Black Community; Violence Breaks Out." *York Dispatch*. See http://www.yorkdispatch.com/yorkriots/beforetheriots/ci_00011201150; Silberman, Charles. *Crisis in Black and White*. New York: Random House, 1964; "York City Riots Investigation." *York Dispatch* (2005). See www.yorkdispatch.com/riotsinvestigation.

Dwayne Wright

PRIMARY DOCUMENTS

1. Excerpts from the Report of the Select House Committee on the Memphis Riots of May 1866, July 25, 1866

Reproduced below are excerpts from the report of the House Select Committee charged with investigating the Memphis, Tennessee, race riots of 1866. The passages contain eyewitness testimony regarding the atrocities committed during the Memphis violence.

RAPE

The crowning acts of atrocity and diabolism committed during these terrible nights were the ravishing of five different colored women by these fiends in human shape, independent of other attempts at rape. The details of these outrages are of too shocking and disgusting a character to be given at length in this report, and reference must be had to the testimony of the parties. It is a singular fact, that while this mob was breathing vengeance against the Negroes and shooting them down like dogs, yet when they found unprotected colored women they at once "conquered their prejudices," and proceeded to violate them under circumstances of the most licentious brutality.

FRANCES THOMPSON

The rape of Frances Thompson, who had been a slave and was a cripple, using crutches, having a cancer on her foot, is one to which reference is here made. On Tuesday night, seven men, two of whom were policemen, came to her house. She knew the two to be policemen by their stars. They were all Irishmen. They first demanded that she should get supper for them, which she did. After supper the wretches threw all the provisions that were in the house which had not been consumed out into the bayou. They then laid hold of Frances, hitting her on the side of the face and kicking her. A girl by the name of

LUCY SMITH

about sixteen years old, living with her, attempted to go out the window. One of the brutes knocked her down and choked her. They then drew their pistols, and said they would shoot them and fire the house if they did not let them have their way. The woman, Frances Thompson, was then violated by four of the men, and so beaten and bruised that she lay in bed for three days. They then took all the clothes out of the trunk, one hundred dollars in greenbacks belonging to herself, and two hundred dollars belonging to another colored woman, which had been left to take care of her child, besides silk dresses, bed-clothing, &c. They were in the house nearly four hours, and when they left they said they intended "to burn up the last God damned nigger, and drive all the Yankees out of town, and then there would be only some rebel niggers and butternuts left." The colored girl, Lucy Smith, who was before the committee, said to be sixteen or seventeen years old, but who seemed, from her appearance, to be two or three years younger, was a girl of modest demeanor and highly respectable in appearance. She corroborated the testimony of Frances Thompson as to the number of men who broke into the house and as to the policemen who were with them. They seized her (Lucy) by the neck and choked her to such an extent that she could not talk for two weeks to anyone. She was then violated by one of the men, and the reason given by another for not repeating the act of nameless atrocity was, that she was so *near dead he would not have anything to do with her*. He thereupon struck her a severe blow upon the side of the head. The violence of these wretches seemed to be aggravated by the fact that the women had in their room some bed-covering or quilting with red, white, and blue, and also some picture of Union officers. They said, "You niggers have a mighty liking for the damned Yankees, but we will kill you, and you will have no liking for anyone then." This young girl was so badly injured that she was unable to leave her bed for two weeks.

Another case is that of

REBECCA ANN BLOOM

who was ravished on the night of the 2nd of May. She was in bed with her husband, when five men broke open her door and came into her house. They professed to have authority to arrest Mr. Bloom, and threatened to take him to the station house unless he should pay them a forfeit of twenty-five dollars. Not having the money, he went out to raise it, and while absent one of the men assaulted the wife and threatened to kill her if she did not do as he wished. Brandishing his knife, and swearing she must submit to his wishes, he accomplished his brutal purpose. This is from the testimony of Mrs. Bloom, taken before the Freedmen's Bureau commission, and is corroborated by the testimony of Elvira Walker, taken before the committee, and also by Mrs. Bloom's husband, Peter Bloom.

Another case is that of

LUCY TIBBS

A party of seven men broke into her house on Tuesday night and demanded to know where her husband was. She had with her two little children of the ages of five and two years, respectively. She implored them not to do anything to her, as she was just there with her "two little children." While the others of the party were plundering the house, one man threatened to kill her if she did not submit to his wishes; and although another man, discovering her situation, interfered, and told him to let that woman alone—that she was not in a situation for doing that, the brute did not desist, but succeeded in violating her person in the presence of the other six men. She was obliged to submit, as the house was full of men, and she thought they would kill her, as they had stabbed a woman the previous night in her neighborhood.

WHAT LUCY TIBBS SAW

This woman lived in the immediate neighborhood, and was in the situation to see, and did see, a great deal that transpired during the riotous proceedings. This witness was intelligent and well-appearing, and the committee was strongly impressed with the truth and fairness of her testimony. She saw two colored soldiers shot down on Tuesday night, not ten rods apart. One of the men, she states, was killed by John Pendergrast, who keeps a grocery in her neighborhood. She was looking right at him when he shot the man. After being shot, the soldier made an effort to get up the bayou, and Pendergrast went to a policeman, got another pistol and shot him in his mouth. This man had no sooner been killed by Pendergrast—the witness being within a few feet at the time—than another colored man came in sight. *They beat him and kept him down until they loaded their pistols then they shot him three times, burst his head open and killed him*. She knew of four colored people being killed, their bodies lying within two hundred yards of her house for two days and nights, beside the body of Rachel Hatcher, to whom allusion is made in another part of this report. She testifies to other matters, and particularly to the conduct of Policeman Roach, one of the most murderous of them all, and who is understood still to be in Memphis. She testifies also to the shooting of a colored man by a white man of the name of Galloway, and of another colored man by the name of Charley Wallace, being shot by a Mr. Cash. Her brother, Robert Taylor, a member of the 59th Regiment, was killed on Tuesday afternoon. He had $300 in possession of his sister, the witness, of which she was robbed. She states further, in regard to a man who lives in the next house to her, that he was called outside of his house and shot down. They shot him three times and then said, "Damn you, that will learn you how to leave your old master and mistress," and took $25 from his pocket. His name was Fayette Dickerson. The white men she knew in this crowd of murderers and robbers were the old man Pendergrast and his two sons, Mr. Cash, a boy called Charley Toller, and also a wretch by the name of

Charley Smith, who professed to have belonged to the Union army, and who had been teaching a school of colored people, but who had now joined these other men in their robberies and murders. Another case of rape is that of

HARRIET ARMOR

On Wednesday morning, in open day, two men came into her room. One of them, by the name of Dunn, living on South street, under the pretext of hunting for arms, entered and barred the door, and both of them violated her. This outrage was attended with circumstances of too disgusting and shocking a character to be mentioned except by the most distant allusion. The testimony of this witness is substantially corroborated by other witnesses.

SHOOTING AND BURNING OF RACHEL HATCHER

The shooting and burning of a colored girl by the name of Rachel Hatcher was one of the most cruel and bloody acts of the mob. This girl Rachel was about sixteen years of age. She was represented by all to be a girl of remarkable intelligence, and of pure and excellent character. She attended school, and such had been her proficiency that she herself had become a teacher of the smaller scholars. Her mother, Jane Sneed, testified before the committee that on Tuesday night the mob came to her house, took a man out, took him down to the bridge and shot him. They then set fire to the house of an old colored man by the name of Adam Lock, right by the house of the witness. Her daughter, Rachel, seeing the house of a neighbor on fire, proposed to go and help get the things out. While in the house, enraged in an act of benevolent heroism, the savages surrounded the burning building, and with loaded revolvers threatened to shoot her. In piteous tones she implored them to let her come out; but one of the crowd—the wretched Pendergrast—said, "No; if you don't go back I will blow your damned brains out." As the flames gathered about her, she emerged from the burning house, when the whole crowd "fired at her as fast as they could." She was deliberately shot and fell dead between the two houses. Her clothes soon took fire and her body was partially consumed, presenting a spectacle horrible to behold. The mother of Rachel was, in the meantime, inside her own house trying to get out a man who was wounded that night, and who she was afraid would be burnt up. When she came back, she saw the dead body of her daughter, the blood running out of her mouth. There was an Irishman about her house at this time by the name of Callahan, with the largest pistol in his hand she had ever seen. He demanded that her husband should come out until he could shoot him. But his life was saved at that moment by the appearance of two regulars, who told them to go to the fort.

CALLAHAN AND M'GINN

Among the parties who robbed the houses of Sneed and Adam Lock were Callahan, one George McGinn, and a young man whose name witness did not know. Callahan was seen to go off with a feather-bed on one arm and a pistol in the other hand, and the young man was seen to have the hoop skirt and the Balmoral skirt of the girl Rachel who was killed the night before.

These facts are testified to by a German woman of the name Garey, whose husband was a confectioner. At the time these things were carried off, a large crowd ran into Callahan's store, and he came out with bottles and things and treated them. The crowd was very noisy, and made a great many threats. They said the next night they wanted to kill there "d—d Yankee niggers"—calling such people as this German witness "Yankee niggers."

OTHER BURNINGS AND SHOOTINGS

Witnesses testified as to the circumstances of other burnings and shootings. A house containing women and little children was set on fire, and was then surrounded by armed men. Scorched by the extending flames the terrified inmates rushed out, but only to be fired upon when fleeing from their burning dwelling. It was reported that the arm of a little child was shot off. A woman and her little son were in a house which was fired. She begged to be permitted to come out, but the murderer (Pendergrast) shot at her. She got down on her knees and prayed him to let her out. She had her little son in there with her. They told her that if she did not go back they would kill her. McGinn was in this crowd, and the scene moved even his adamantine heart to mercy. He said, "This is a very good woman; it is a pity to burn her up. Let her come out." She came out with her boy; but it happened he had on *blue clothes*. That seemed to madden them still more. They pushed him back and said, "Go back, you d—n son of a b—h." Then the poor heart-broken mother fell on her knees and prayed them to let her child out; *it was the only child she had*; and the boy was finally permitted to escape from the flames. Pendergrast went into a grocery and gave ammunition to a policeman to load his pistol. They then started up a Negro man who ran up the bayou, and told him to come to them. He was coming up to them, when they put a pistol to his mouth, shot his tongue off, killing him instantly. This man's name was Lewis Robertson.

ATTEMPT TO BURN LUCY HUNT

One Chris. Pigeon, an Irishman, went with others to the house of Lucy Hunt, a colored woman, and threatened if they could not get in they would burn them all up. They did set fire to the house in which Lucy lived, and when she attempted to come out they pushed her back into the fire three or four times. One of them caught her by the throat and said he was going to burn her up. One of the gang put his pistol to her head and said, "G—d d—n you, if you leave I will shoot you." She thinks she owes her life to the appearance of some soldiers. They broke open her trunk and robbed her of $25, the proceeds of sixteen months' work at the fort, where she had been cooking for a company of soldiers. And they not only robbed her of her money, but of all her clothes, and everything she had, leaving her nearly naked and penniless.

MARY BLACK AND MARIA SCOTT

They also broke into the house of Mary Black on Wednesday night. This same Pigeon was in the crowd. They poured turpentine on the bed and set the house on fire. There was in the house opposite Mary Black, at the time, a little girl twelve years old, and an old colored woman by the name of Maria Scott. After they had set fire to the house, they attempted to keep them in, and when asked to let them out they replied, they intended to burn them up. Witness had no doubt they would have done so had it not been for the appearance of the regulars.

SHOOTING OF JOSEPH WALKER

Among the instances of shooting and killing was that of Joseph Walker, a colored man who was returning home from his work during the riotous proceedings, and going round by way of the Tennessee and Mississippi railroad depot. The depot agent, a man by the name of Palmer, ordered him to halt, while Palmer's brother, from the top of a car called out, "Shoot the d—n son of a b—h." He thereupon pulled out his pistol and shot at him three times, but hit him only once. The ball was in the body of witness at the time he was before the committee, the doctor having been unable to extract it. He was so badly injured that he has been unable to work since. He has a wife, sister, mother, brother and child, all of whom are dependent on him for support. The ruffians who shot this man hold responsible positions under the Tennessee and Mississippi Railroad Company, and the attention of the others of that company is called to that fact, so that if the laws cannot be vindicated in bringing them to punishment, it may be seen whether they will be employed by a railroad company that seeks support from the public. The testimony is, that after Joseph Walker had escaped from these men they went after another black man whom they saw dodging round the bayou.

THE KILLING OF BEN. DENNIS

Perhaps there is nothing that can more fully illustrate the feeling in the city of Memphis than the impunity with which the most brutal and dastardly crimes were committed upon white persons also, and upon those not even remotely connected with the riotous proceedings than the murder of Dennis on Thursday, after the riots were substantially at an end. It seems that Dennis was a man of respectable connections, and of a good disposition, who had served a year in the rebel army; that he went into a saloon to take a drink, and while there met a colored barber, who was an old acquaintance, and spoke to him in a kind and friendly manner. At this time an Irishman was sitting behind a screen, eating his dinner, and when he heard the kind words of Dennis to the Negro he rushed out and demanded to know how Dennis dared to talk that way to a Negro. Dennis made some reply, then the Irishman deliberately shot him. He fell on the floor and died in ten minutes. The murderer was escorted to the station-house, and according to the testimony of the station-keeper was retained there for a term of *five or ten minutes*, and no one appearing against him, he was set at liberty. The statement is, though not in proof, that while at the station-house, someone made the remark that he had "only shot a nigger," and that was no cause for his detention. No further effort has been made to bring this murderer to justice.

ATTEMPT TO BURN MARY JORDAN AND HER CHILDREN

There are but few acts of the mob which equal in barbarism that of the outrage committed upon Mary Jordan. She had just lost her husband, and was in her house with her three children, the youngest of which being seven months old and very sick. They had been shooting down colored people in her neighborhood, and she was very much frightened, expecting that she would herself be shot down. While she and her three children, the oldest of which being only sixteen years, were in her house, the mob set fire to a house adjoining, and the flames communicated to her dwelling. They refused to allow her or her children to come out. She started out, and told her children to follow her. Her eldest daughter said, "Mother, you will be shot." She replied she had rather be shot than burned. While she was escaping from the flames into the streets it was raining, and she could get no shelter. Her child got wet, and afterwards died. She states there were policemen in that crowd, as she knew them by the stars they wore. She lost everything she had. When, however, the house was all in flames, she ran out with her little children, with her baby in her arms. They fired at her, the bullets coming all around her, and she would have been hit had she not ran around the corner of the house and got out of the way. While running away with her baby in her arms a man put a pistol to her breast and asked her what she was doing. She told him she was trying to save her baby.

THE MURDER OF LONG

Scarcely a more brutal murder was committed than that of Shade Long. He with his wife and two children were in their house while a mob of twenty or thirty men came to it and demanded admittance. Long was very sick, and had been in bed for two weeks. They broke into the house, and told him to get up and come out, that they were going to shoot him. He told them he was very sick. They replied that they did not "care a d—n." They took him out of doors, and told him that if he had anything to say, to "say it very quick;" that they were going to kill him. They asked him if he had been a soldier. He replied that he had not, but had been in the employ of the government. Then one of them stepped back and shot him, putting a pistol to his head and firing three times. He scuffled about a little and looked as if he was trying to get back to the house, when they told him that if he did "not make haste and die" they would shoot him again. Then one of them kicked him, and another shot him after he was down. They shot him through the head every time. They then robbed the poor woman of fifty-five dollars in paper money and fifteen dollars in silver, and went away.

THE SHOOTING OF WOMEN AND CHILDREN

The shooting of Rachel Hatcher and the subsequent burning of her body has already been alluded to in detail. Adeline Miller, a colored girl, about twenty years old, on the first evening of the mob was standing at the door of a family grocery kept by an Italian named Oicalla. She seems to have been discovered by some person in the mob at a distance, who deliberately fired at her, the ball taking effect and killing her instantly.

Rhoda Jacobs, a young girl twenty years old, lived with her mother, who had three other young children living with her. On one night during the riots a gang of five or six men came to the door and demanded admittance. They pretended to be looking for some man. One of the ruffians pulled out his pistol and told the mother that if she did not light the candle quick he would shoot her brains out. The light disclosed that there was somebody in a bed behind the door, and it turned out to be this girl Rhonda, with her little sister, who was eight years old. Seeing the man with the pistol she screamed out, "O! I am a woman! I am a woman! Don't shoot!" But that did not stay the hand of the assassin, who deliberately fired into the bed. The witness was before the committee, and in answer to the question, "Where did he shoot you?" says, "The ball came into my arm, grazed two of my fingers, went through between the lips of my little sister lying in bed with me, entered my breast, *and the bullet is right there now*."

This girl could not identify any of the parties. She looked at the pistol in the hands of a man and said she was so afraid they would shoot her mother that she did not think of herself at all; that he had his pistol at her mother's head, and had it cocked. The little girl was not much hurt, the ball only grazing her lips. After accomplishing this brilliant feat they left the house. The mother then describes the scene as follows:

> I looked at my daughter and thought that death was upon her. The ball had gone through her arm, had hit her fingers, and shot into her breast, and, what I did not see till afterwards, the ball had glanced the child's lips. I fixed up my daughter's wounds by the *light of the burning house* on the other side of the street, and put them all to bed. I put out my lamps for fear they would come back again. It was a fuss all the time, and I dared not put my head out. . . .

A gang consisting, among others, of Mike Cotton, S. D. Young, and Billy Barber, together with a policeman, went to the house of Richard Lane, colored man, in which he kept a salon. They demanded a light, and while Mrs. Lane was getting one they asked her husband for arms, and upon his denying that he had any they deliberately shot him through the shoulder, the ball being afterwards cut out below in his back. As they were going out one of the fiends deliberately shot their little girl through the right arm. In the language of the mother, the little child "screamed dreadfully and bled awfully, and looked just as though she had been dipped in a tub of blood." The mother seeing her husband and child thus wounded and bleeding, commenced screaming, whereupon the crowd left.

Jane Goodloe testified before General Stoneman's commission that the mob shot into her house on the evening of that first of May and wounded her in the breast.

ATTEMPTS TO BURN WHITE CHILDREN

The vindictive and revengeful feelings of the mob were not limited to the colored people, but they extended to such white people as had manifested particular friendship to the colored race by interesting themselves in their schools and churches, and in their welfare generally. Mr. and Mrs. Cooper were English people; they had put up a building, a portion of which was to be let for a colored school, which was to be taught by a Mr. Glasgow, who had been a soldier in the Union Army. Mr. Cooper was called an "abolitionist," because they said he was doing too much for the colored people, and spoke occasionally in their chapel. A gang of policemen and citizens came into the neighborhood in a threatening attitude. Being appealed to by Mrs. Cooper to know what they were going to do, they said they were going to kill her husband and Mr. Glasgow, for they would have no abolitionists in the South. While they were talking to her, at some distance from her house, and assuring her that they would not hurt her or her children, the house, with her four little children in it, was deliberately set on fire, and while her husband and Mr. Glasgow attempted to put it out the mob fired at them several times. A policeman headed this crowd of incendiaries, whose intention, Mrs. Cooper thinks, was to burn up her children. The building and all the furniture was burned, and Mr. Cooper fled from the city to save his life.

TEACHERS OF COLORED SCHOOLS

The most intense and unjustifiable prejudice on the part of the people of Memphis seems to have been arrayed against teachers of colored schools and against preachers to colored people. They would not teach the colored people themselves, and seemed to think it a reflection upon them that benevolent persons and societies outside should undertake the work. The preachers seemed to be men of earnest piety and sincere convictions, and to be actuated by the highest and best motives. Many of the teachers of the schools were young ladies from the northern states, graduates of the best northern schools, of intelligence, of education, and of the most unblemished characters, and who, responding to convictions of duty, had, at the call of benevolent individuals and societies, left their homes, gone to Memphis, and entered upon the task of educating and elevating a down-trodden and oppressed race. In the face of scorn and obloquy they proceeded, even at the peril of their own lives, to the work assigned them; and with consciences so void of offense and lives so pure and blameless, that while subject to persecution and insult, neither hatred nor calumny was ever able to stain their reputations or to blacken their characters; and yet these people, guilty of no crime, engaged in a work of benevolence and Christianity, were themselves obliged to flee from the city for personal safety; and as they left, they were guided in their pathway by the light reflected from their burning school-houses.

THE SCHOOLS

At the breaking out of the riots the number of schools was twelve, and the number in attendance was about 1,200, taught by twenty-two teachers. The superintendent of these schools was a Mr. Orin E. Waters, whose testimony was taken by the committee, and is hereby referred to. The teachers were employed by the American Baptist Missionary Association, the Western Freedmen's Aid Commission, the American Missionary Associations, two or three independent associations, and two or three were established independent of any associations. Twelve school-houses, or places where schools were taught, were burned during the riot, and the value of each was estimated at $2,500, besides the apparatus, furniture, &c. Mr. Waters testifies as to the teachers leaving on account of the threats of the mob that they would burn them out and kill them. Their offense was that they were teaching colored children; and although these schools had been going on for three years, there had never been a single instance in which any difficulty had been created on the part of any person connected with them, and the character and conduct of the scholars had been uniformly good. The progress of the scholars in their studies was said to be remarkable. The colored children evinced very great eagerness and interest in their studies. As an instance of the low prejudice against the teachers, your committee quote the following anonymous communication which was sent three or four days after the riots:

MEMPHIS, TENNESSEE, May 6, 1866.

To — — :

You will please to notice that we have determined to rid our community of Negro fanatics and philanthropic teachers of our former slaves. You are one of the number, and it will be well for you are absent from the city by the 1st of June. Consult you safety.

ANONYMOUS.

It might also be stated that the mob were not satisfied with burning school-houses and churches, but they burned also a building belonging to the government, used by the Western Freedmen's Aid Commission as a storehouse for supplies for freedmen. The total amount of stores destroyed, and of property belonging to that commission was $4,597.35. Your committee were glad to learn that, to supply the place of the school-houses burned by the mob, Major General Fisk had, on behalf of the Freedmen's Bureau, with commendable energy, built a large school-house for the use of colored schools.

THE CHURCHES BURNED

Four churches were burned during the riots. One was a large brick building; another was a large frame structure, with a brick basement, and two others were used as churches and school-houses. And although all the churches and places of worship of the colored people were destroyed by the mob, no effort whatever seems to have been made by the people of Memphis to supply, even temporarily, the want created. So far as your committee were able to ascertain, no church within the control of the white people was open for their worship...

THE CAUSE OF THE RIOT—THE NEWSPAPERS

As has been stated in this report, the riotous proceedings had their immediate cause in a difficulty between Irish police and colored soldiers. The more remote cause may be found in the prejudice which has grown up between the two races. The feelings of hatred and revenge toward the colored race, which have been fostered by the Irish and by large numbers of people in the south, seem to have been intensified since the Negro became free. The colored race have been subject to great abuse and ill-treatment. In fact, they have no protection from the law whatever. All the testimony shows that it was impossible for a colored man in Memphis to get justice against a white man. Such is the prejudice against the Negro that it is almost impossible to punish a white man by the civil courts for any injury inflicted upon a Negro. It was in the testimony before the committee that several months prior to their arrival in Memphis a Negro was most brutally and inhumanly murdered publicly in the streets by a policeman by the name of Maloney. The officer in command at Memphis, Major General John E. Smith, knowing full well that Maloney would not be punished through the civil tribunals, had him tried by a military commission, by which he was found guilty and sentenced to imprisonment in Nashville. It appears that afterwards the murderer Maloney was brought before United States Judge Trigg, at Nashville, on a writ of *habeas corpus*, and the judge, without giving any notice whatever to General Thomas, that there might be a fair hearing of the question, made haste to discharge him from imprisonment, and he is now at large, "unwhipt of justice." There can be no doubt that the feeling which led to the terrible massacres at Memphis was stimulated by the disloyal press of that city. Judge Hunter states that he has no doubt but that the mob was stimulated by the newspapers. Reverend Mr. Tade says the effect of the press was to incite the riotous proceedings; and expresses the opinion that the Irish have been used as mere cat's-paws; that the papers published there had every day incited them to the deeds of violence which they committed. He states that the Avalanche is the worst, and that the Argus and Ledger are echoes of it. Witness believed that much of the ill-feeling against men of northern birth, entertaining what are called "radical sentiments," is due to the conduct of the press. Out of the seven daily papers there, five were controlled, in a greater or less degree, by men who have been in the rebel army. He states that the Avalanche, which is the most violent, vindictive, and unscrupulous of all the papers there, and which has done the most to exasperate the people against the Negroes and northern people, claims to have the largest circulation and most patronage of any paper in the city, and to most truly represent the sentiments and opinions of the mass of the people. Your committee caused extracts to be made from these papers, which they have carefully read over. Many of the articles were characterized by a bitter hostility to the government, and by appeals to the lowest and basest prejudices against the colored population; by bitter personal attacks upon northern people residing in Memphis; and, in fact, the whole tenor of the disloyal press was a constant incitation to violence and ill-feeling.

CONDUCT OF THE COLORED SOLDIERS

As great efforts had been made to justify the massacre of the colored people on account of the conduct of the colored soldiers who have been so long stationed at Fort Pickering, your committee deemed it their duty to take much testimony on this subject in order to satisfy themselves as to the facts in the case. That there was bad conduct on the part of some of the soldiers there can be no doubt, and the riotous and lawless conduct of a portion of them on the evening of the 1st of May is without excuse. General Stoneman, in answer to the question as to how these colored troops compared with white troops under similar circumstances, answered as follows:

"I must say, in justice to the colored troops, that their conduct compared very favorably with that of the same number of white troops under similar circumstances."

Lieutenants Garrett and Hastings, and others, who had been officers in the colored regiment stationed at Fort Pickering, testified as to their general good conduct, and it was testified that there was no disposition on the part of the colored soldiers to maltreat white people, or to attack them in any way, and that whenever it became necessary for them to make arrests of white citizens it was done in an orderly and proper manner.

The testimony of Captain Thomas J. Dornin, of the 16th regular infantry, is referred to as being particularly full and explicit in regard to the character and conduct of the colored soldiers. He was in Fort Pickering with them during the days of the riot, and was in a position to know the facts in regard to which he testified. The behavior of these colored men under the trying circumstances in which they were placed, seeing their families murdered and their dwellings burned, was such as to extort admiration from all the officers in the fort. With the exception of a feeble attempt on the part of a few to seize some arms to defend their families from the butcheries of the mob, there was the most complete subordination among them, although they had been in point of fact mustered out of the service. In answer as to what he had seen in regard to the riotous conduct of these soldiers, Captain Dornin states:

> I never saw any riotous act among them, and one thing I will say for them, that there is no number of white soldiers that I ever saw that could be held in such subjection as they were when their houses were being burned as they were. I could not have expected it; never could have believed it could be done.

In speaking of this matter, Captain Dornin, with the instincts which belong to the true soldier, states that he sympathized with the colored people, and was sorry that the men could not get their arms to defend their wives and families. He said he "sympathized with them as things were going, for they could not defend themselves, and it seemed like a brutish laughter on the part of the mob." Captain D. further states that there were policemen leading the mob and shooting down the colored people, and he himself saw them engaged in carrying off everything they could lay their hands on, and inciting others to do the same.

Captain Allyn, of the sixteenth regular infantry, commanding the post at Memphis, testified before the committee, and gave a very full and detailed account of the riotous proceedings, and the operations of the force under him. His report to the general commanding will be found in the appendix. Captain A. seems to have made the best and most judicious use of the small forces under his command. He states, in regard to the conduct of the colored soldiers, that if his own regiment had been there he does not think it would have been possible to keep them from interfering in favor of the negroes with their arms; and if the negroes had been a regiment of regulars, they would have rushed out unless it could have been prevented by previous knowledge, and by placing a heavy guard over it. Speaking his feelings, he said he should not have blamed them.

THE FEELING TOWARD THE GOVERNMENT

General Stoneman states, in answer to a question as to what was his opinion of the loyalty of the people of Memphis toward the United States, that if the desire to be restored to the Union was considered loyal, he should consider a large majority of the people of Memphis loyal, that far; but if a love of the Union and the flag was considered loyal he would look *upon a large majority of the people of Memphis as not being loyal.* He said there was not that disposition now on the part of the people of Tennessee to recognize existing facts that there was six months previous; that, so far as he could get at it from the press and from the meetings of the people for various purposes, he did not consider them as loyal, if loyalty was to be defined as love for the Union, *as they were six months ago, and that it was growing worse and worse every day.* He states that he knows of only three points where the United States flag is displayed—one at his own headquarters, another at the Freedmen's Bureau, and another is in front of the building used as the printing office for the Memphis Post. He had never seen it displayed at public meetings or places of amusement or theatres, and only sometimes on steamboats coming down the river. Information was conveyed to the general that at the theatre such national airs as "Hail Columbia," "Star-spangled Banner," and "Yankee Doodle" were hissed by the audience, and that the rebel airs were received with applause; he was obliged to write to the manager of the theatre that if national airs were to be met with disapprobation, and the "so-called confederate national airs" should be received with applause by the audience, it would compel him to interfere.

Mr. Stanbrough says that he would no more have raised the United States flag over his mill than he would think of putting a match to his property to burn it up; that he would not for his life think of taking the American flag and marching down Main Street with it; that if a band should go through the streets playing the national airs it would be received with a hiss and a groan. Everybody residing in Memphis knew the flag of our country was not respected, and that while national airs are hissed, when "Dixie" is struck up there is always a shout, and if played for the twentieth time, for every time there is a shout; but there is no "Yankee Doodle" or "Hail Columbia" in Memphis. He says there is not a bit more love for the laws, the Constitution of the United States, or the Union in Memphis than there was in the hottest days of the rebellion, and that the fires of hate burn as hot and as deep down as ever.

General Runkle, of the Freedmen's Bureau, speaks of having seen pictures of rebel generals in all the shop-windows, but of never having seen those of such men as Lincoln, Grant, Sherman, or Farragut displayed, nor even the picture of the name printed in gold letters on the sign-board; that such was the feeling there the people hated the sight of the uniform of a Union officer, and he would not consider it safe for him to be on the streets alone at night in his uniform.

GENERAL CONCLUSIONS

From the testimony taken by your committee, from personal observation and from what they could learn in regard to the state of feeling in Memphis, and, indeed, through that entire section of the country, they are of opinion that there is but little loyalty to the government and flag. The state of the things in the city of Memphis is very much now as it was before the breaking out of the rebellion. Many of the same newspapers published there then are published now, and by many of the same men—by who, during the war, were in the rebel armies fighting for the overthrow of the government. Professing to accept the situation, they seem inspired with as deadly hatred against the government as ever, and are guilty of the same incitation to violence, persecution, and oppression toward the men holding opinions obnoxious to them, that they were towards the men who were well disposed toward the Union men in 1861. Your committee say, deliberately, that, in their judgment, there will be no safety to loyal men, either white or black, should the troops be withdrawn and no military protection afforded. They believe that the riots and massacres of Memphis are only a specimen of what would take place throughout the entire south, should the government fail to afford adequate military protection. There is everywhere too much envenomed feeling toward the blacks, particularly those who served in the Union armies, and against northern men and Union people generally who love the government, and who desired to see it sustained, its authority vindicated, and who believe that treason is a crime that should be punished. There is no public sentiment in the south sufficiently strong enough to demand and enforce protection to Union men and colored people. The civil-rights bill, so far as your committee could ascertain, is treated as a dead letter. Attorney General Wallace, in flagrant violation of his oath and duty, whose name has been heretofore alluded to in this report, has, according to the newspapers, proclaimed that he will utterly disregard the law.

The hopes based upon this law that the colored people might find protection under it are likely to prove delusive; for, where there is no public opinion to sustain law, but, on the other hand, that public opinion is so overwhelmingly against it, there is no probability of its being executed. Indeed, your committee believe the sentiment of the south which they observed is not a sentiment of full acquiescence in the results of the war, but that there is among them a lingering hope that their favorite doctrine of succession may yet be vindicated. It is the same idea that Jeff. Davis expressed. When he was seeking safety in flight, a traveler remarked to him that the cause was lost. Davis replied: *"It appears so; but the principle for which we contended is bound to reassert itself, though it may be at another time, and in another form."* (Pollard's Southern History of the War, vol. 2, page 582.) They believe in the principle and doctrine of succession. Though they have been beaten by arms, they assert and maintain that the principle is the same, and hope for its vindication hereafter in some way. Recognizing the friendship to them of what was called the "democratic party" in the north during the war, and their efforts to embarrass the government in the prosecution of the war against them, they hope, by combining with them in their political movements, finally to secure by the ballot what they dialed to achieve by arms.

The fact that the chosen guardians of the public peace, the sworn executors of the law for the protection of the lives, liberty, and property of the people, and the reliance of the weak and defenseless in time of danger, were found the foremost in the work of murder and pillage, gives a character of infamy to the whole proceeding which is almost without a parallel in all the annals of history. The dreadful massacre of Fort Pillow, which excited the horror of the country and of the civilized world, was attempted to be palliated on the ground that the garrison was taken after the most desperate resistance, and after having been repeatedly summoned to surrender; that the blood of the assailants had been heated to such a degree and their passions so aroused that there was no controlling them, though it is alleged that some of their officers vainly attempted to do so. But no such ground of palliation can be advanced in the case of the Memphis massacres. After the first troubles on the first evening, there was no pretense of any disturbance by the colored people, or any resistance to the mob, calculated to excite their passions, and what subsequently took place was the result of a cool and mature deliberation to murder and destroy the colored people. Like the massacre of St. Bartholomew, the Memphis massacre had the sanction of official authority; and it is no wonder that the mob, finding itself led by officers of the law, butchered miserably and without resistance every negro it could find, and regretting that death had saved their victims from further insult, exercised on their dead bodies all the rage of the most insensate cruelty.

In view of the fact that the state of public sentiment is such in Memphis that is it conceded that no punishment whatever can be meted out to the perpetrators of these outrages by the civil authorities, and in view of the further fact that the city repudiates any liability for the property, both of the government and individuals, destroyed by the mob, your committee believe it to be the duty of the government to arrest, try, and punish the offenders by military authority; and also by the same authority levy a tax upon the citizens of Memphis sufficient to cover the losses for all property destroyed.

Source: "Memphis Riots and Massacres." U.S. House of Representatives, 30th Congress, 1st Session, Report No. 101, Report of the Select Committee on the Memphis Riots. Washington, D.C., 1866, pp. 13–21, 30–34.

2. Report of the Federal Grand Jury on the Activities of the Ku Klux Klan in South Carolina, 1871

The activities of the Ku Klux Klan in South Carolina in the years 1868–1871 were so notorious as to lead President Ulysses Grant to suspend the right of habeas corpus in nine South Carolina counties in October 1871. The military was sent in to arrest perpetrators and a grand jury was convened in Columbia, South Carolina, to investigate Klan activities and Klan organization throughout these counties. Below is an excerpt of the grand jury's report to the judges of the U.S. Circuit Court. *See also the entry* Ku Klux Klan.

In closing the labors of the present term, the grand jury begs leave to submit the following presentment.

During the whole session we have been engaged in investigations of the most grave and extraordinary Character—investigations of the crimes committed by the organization known as the Ku Klux Klan. The evidence elicited has been voluminous, gathered from the victims themselves and their families, as well as those who belong to the Klan and participated in its crimes. The jury has been shocked beyond measure at the developments which have been made in their presence of the number and character of the atrocities committed, producing a state of terror and a sense of utter insecurity among a large portion of the people, especially the colored population. The evidence produced before us has established the following facts:

1. That there has existed since 1868, in many counties of the state, an organization known as the "Ku Klux Klan," or "Invisible Empire of the South," which embraces in its membership a large proportion of the white population of every profession and class.
2. That this Klan is bound together by an oath, administered to its members at the time of their initiation into the order, of which the following is a copy:

Obligation

I [name], before the immaculate Judge of Heaven and Earth, and upon the Holy Evangelists of Almighty God, do, of my own free will and accord, subscribe to the following sacredly binding obligation:

1. We are on the side of justice, humanity, and constitutional liberty, as bequeathed to us in its purity by our forefathers.
2. We oppose and reject the principles of the Radical Party.
3. We pledge mutual aid to each other in sickness, distress, and pecuniary embarrassment.
4. Female friends, widows, and their households shall ever be special objects of our regard and protection.

Any member divulging, or causing to be divulged, any part of the foregoing obligations, shall meet the fearful penalty and traitor's doom, which is Death! Death! Death!

That, in addition to this oath, the Klan has a constitution and bylaws, which provides, among other things, that each member shall furnish himself with a pistol, a Ku Klux gown, and a signal instrument. That the operations of the Klan were executed in the night, and were invariably directed against members of the Republican Party by warnings to leave the country, by whippings, and by murder.

3. That in large portions of the counties of York, Union, and Spartanburgh, to which our attention has been more particularly called in our investigations during part of the time for the last eighteen months, the civil law has been set at defiance and ceased to afford any protection to the citizens.
4. That the Klan, in carrying out the purposes for which it was organized and armed, inflicted summary vengeance on the colored citizens of these counties by breaking into their houses at the dead of night, dragging them from their beds, torturing them in the most inhumane manner, and in many instances murdering them; and this, mainly, on account of their political affiliations. Occasionally, additional reasons operated, but in no instance was the political feature wanting.
5. That for this condition of things, for all these violations of law and order and the sacred rights of citizens, many of the leading men of those counties were responsible. It was proven that large numbers of the most prominent citizens were members of the order. Many of this class attended meetings of the Grand Klan. At a meeting of the Grand Klan held in Spartanburgh County, at which there were representatives from the various dens of Sparatanburgh, York, Union, and Chester Counties, in this state, besides a number from North Carolina, a resolution was adopted that no raids should be undertaken or anyone whipped or injured by members of the Klan without orders from the Grand Klan. The penalty for violating this resolution was 100 lashes on the bare back for the first offense; and for the second, death.

This testimony establishes the nature of the discipline enforced in the order, and also the fact that many of the men who were openly and publicly speaking against the Klan, and pretending to deplore the work of this murderous conspiracy, were influential members of the order and directing its operations, even in detail.

The jury has been appalled as much at the number of outrages as at their character, it appearing that 11 murders and over 600 whippings have been committed in York County alone. Our investigation in regard to the other counties named has been less full; but it is believed, from the testimony, that an equal or greater number has been committed in Union, and that the number is not greatly less in Spartanburgh and Laurens.

We are of the opinion that the most vigorous prosecution of the parties implicated in these crimes is imperatively demanded; that without this there is great danger that these outrages will be continued, and that there will be no security to our fellow citizens of African descent.

We would say further that unless the strong arm of the government is interposed to punish these crimes committed upon this class of citizen, there is every reason to believe that an organized and determined attempt at retaliation will be made, which can only result in a state of anarchy and bloodshed too terrible to contemplate.

SOURCE: 42nd Congress, 2nd Session, House Report No. 22, Pt. 1, pp. 48–49.

3. Excerpts from Ida B. Wells' Exposé on Lynching, *The Red Record*, 1895

Noted anti-lynching crusader Ida B. Wells published *The Red Record* in 1895. The book, as shown in the excerpt reproduced below, not only provided statistics on lynching, which were mainly gathered from mainstream press accounts, but also offered a detailed overview of the history of lynching in the United States since the Civil War.

Offenses Charged for Lynching

Suspected arson, 2; stealing, 1; political causes, 1; murder, 45; rape, 29; desperado, 1; suspected incendiarism, 1; train wrecking, 1; enticing servant away, 1; kidnapping, 1; unknown offense, 6; larceny, 1; barn burning, 10; writing letters to a white woman, 1; without cause, 1; burglary, 1; asking white woman to marry, 1; conspiracy, 1; attempted murder, 1; horse stealing, 3; highway robbery, 1; alleged rape, 1; attempted rape, 11; race prejudice, 2; introducing smallpox, 1; giving information, 1; conjuring, 1; incendiarism, 2; arson, 1; assault, 1; no offense, 1; alleged murder, 2; total (colored), 134.

Lynching States

Mississippi, 15; Arkansas, 8; Virginia, 5; Tennessee, 15; Alabama, 12; Kentucky, 12; Texas, 9; Georgia, 19; South Carolina, 5; Florida, 7; Louisiana, 15; Missouri, 4; Ohio, 2; Maryland, 1; West Virginia, 2; Indiana, 1; Kansas, 1; Pennsylvania, 1.

Lynching by Month

January, 11; February, 17; March, 8; April, 36; May, 16; June, 31; July, 21; August, 4; September 17; October, 7; November, 9; December, 20; total colored and white, 197.

Women Lynched

July 24, unknown woman, race prejudice, Sampson County, Miss.; March 6, unknown, woman, unknown offense, Marche, Ark.; Dec. 5, Mrs. Teddy Arthur, unknown cause, Lincoln County, W.Va.

Chapter X. The Remedy

It is a well-established principle of law that every wrong has a remedy. Herein rests our respect for law. The Negro does not claim that all of the one thousand black men, women and children, who have been hanged, shot and burned alive during the past ten years, were innocent of the charges made against them. We have associated too long with the white man not to have copied his vices as well as his virtues. But we do insist that the punishment is not the same for both classes of criminals. In lynching, opportunity is not given the Negro to defend himself against the unsupported accusations of white men and women. The word of the accuser is held true and the excited bloodthirsty mob demands that the rule of law be reversed and instead of proving the accused to be guilty, the victim of their hate and revenge must prove himself innocent. No evidence he can offer will satisfy the mob; he is bound hand and foot and swung into eternity. Then to excuse its infamy, the mob almost invariably reports the monstrous falsehood that its victim made a full confession before he was hanged.

With all military, legal and political power in their hands, only two of the lynching States have attempted a check by exercising the power which is theirs. Mayor Trout, of Roanoke, Virginia, called out the militia in 1893, to protect a Negro prisoner, and in so doing nine men were killed and a number wounded. Then the mayor and militia withdrew, left the Negro to his fate and he was promptly lynched. The businessmen realized the blow to the town's financial interests, [and] called the mayor home. The grand jury indicted and prosecuted the ringleaders of the mob. They were given light sentences, the highest being one of twelve months in State prison. The day he arrived at the penitentiary, he was pardoned by the governor of the State.

The only other real attempt made by the authorities to protect a prisoner of the law, and which was more successful, was that of Gov. McKinley, of Ohio, who sent the militia to Washington Courthouse, O., in October, 1894, and five men were killed and twenty wounded in maintaining the principle that the law must be upheld.

In South Carolina, in April, 1893, Gov. Tillman aided the mob by yielding up to be killed, a prisoner of the law, who had voluntarily placed himself under the Governor's protection. Public sentiment by its representatives has encouraged Lynch Law, and upon the revolution of this sentiment we must depend for its abolition.

Therefore, we demand a fair trial by the law for those accused of crime, and punishment by law after honest conviction. No maudlin sympathy for criminals is solicited, but we do ask that the law shall punish all alike. We earnestly desire those that control the forces which make public sentiment to join with us in the demand. Surely the humanitarian spirit of this country which reaches out to denounce the treatment of the Russian Jews, the Armenian Christians, the laboring poor of Europe, the Siberian exiles and the native women of India—will no longer refuse to lift its voice on this subject. If it were known that the cannibals or the savage Indians had burned three human beings alive in the past two years, the whole of Christendom would be roused to devise ways and means to put a stop to it. Can you remain silent and inactive when such things are done in our own community and country? Is your duty to humanity in the United States less binding?

What can you do, reader, to prevent lynching, to thwart anarchy and promote law and order throughout our land?

1st. You can help disseminate the facts contained in this book by bringing them to the knowledge of every one with whom you come in contact, to the end that public sentiment may be revolutionized. Let the facts speak for themselves, with you as a medium.

2d. You can be instrumental in having churches, missionary societies, Y.M.C.A.'s, W.C.T.U.'s and all Christian and moral forces in connection with your religious and social life, pass resolutions of condemnation and protest every time a lynching takes place; and see that they are sent to the place where these outrages occur.

3d. Bring to the intelligent consideration of Southern people the refusal of capital to invest where lawlessness and mob violence hold sway. Many labor organizations have declared by resolution that they would avoid lynch infested localities as they would the pestilence when seeking new homes. If the South wishes to build up its waste places quickly, there is no better way than to uphold the majesty of the law by enforcing obedience to the same, and meting out the same punishment to all classes of criminals, white as well as black. "Equality before the law," must become a fact as well as a theory before America is truly the "land of the free and the home of the brave."

4th. Think and act on independent lines in this behalf, remembering that after all, it is the white man's civilization and the white man's government which are on trial. This crusade will determine whether that civilization can maintain itself by itself, or whether anarchy shall prevail; whether this Nation shall write itself down a success at self government, or in its deepest humiliation admit its failure complete; whether the precepts and theories of Christianity are professed and practiced by American white people as Golden Rules of thought and action, or adopted as a system of morals to be preached to heathen until they attain to the intelligence which needs the system of Lynch Law.

5th. Congressman Blair [Henry W. Blair, a New Hampshire Republican] offered a resolution in the House of Representatives, August, 1894.* The organized life of the country can speedily make this a law by sending resolutions to Congress endorsing Mr. Blair's bill and asking Congress to create the commission. In no better way can the question be settled, and the Negro does not fear the issue. . . .

The belief has been constantly expressed in England that in the United States, which has produced Wm. Lloyd Garrison, Henry Ward Beecher, James Russell Lowell, John G. Whittier and Abraham Lincoln there must be

*Blair's Resolution would have authorized and funded a Department of Labor inquiry into all alleged assaults of males upon females in the preceding 10 years, as well as into all acts of organized violence perpetrated during the same period on anyone accused of such crimes.

those of their descendants who would take hold of the work of inaugurating an era of law and order. The colored people of this country who have been loyal to the flag believe the same, and strong in that belief have begun this crusade.

SOURCE: Ida B. Wells. *The Red Record: Tabulated Statistics and Alleged Causes of Lynchings in the United States, 1892–1893–1894*. Chicago: The Author, 1895.

4. Thomas Dixon's Preface to His Novel, *The Clansman*, 1905

Published in 1905, Thomas Dixon's *The Clansman*, which was both a novel and a play, became the basis for the pro-Klan view displayed in the second part of D.W. Griffith's controversial 1915 film, *The Birth of a Nation*. That viewpoint is amply illustrated in Dixon's Preface to *The Clansman*, which is reprinted here. Through *The Clansman*, Dixon hoped to support the continuance of racial segregation, which he viewed as vital to the maintenance of stable race relations. *See also the entries The Birth of a Nation; The Clansman*; Griffith, D.W.; Ku Klux Klan.

TO THE READER

"THE CLANSMAN" is the second book of a series of historical novels planned on the Race Conflict. "The Leopard's Spots" was the statement in historical outline of the conditions from the enfranchisement of the Negro to his disfranchisement.

"The Clansman" develops the true story of the "Ku Klux Klan Conspiracy," which overturned the Reconstruction régime.

The organization was governed by the Grand Wizard Commander-in-Chief, who lived at Memphis, Tennessee. The Grand Dragon commanded a State, the Grand Titan a Congressional District, the Grand Giant a County, and the Grand Cyclops a Township Den. The twelve volumes of Government reports on the famous Klan refer chiefly to events which occurred after 1870, the date of its dissolution.

The chaos of blind passion that followed Lincoln's assassination is inconceivable to-day. The Revolution it produced in our Government, and the bold attempt of Thaddeus Stevens to Africanize ten great states of the American Union, read now like tales from "The Arabian Nights."

I have sought to preserve in this romance both the letter and the spirit of this remarkable period. The men who enact the drama of fierce revenge into which I have woven a double love-story are historical figures. I have merely changed their names without taking a liberty with any essential historic fact.

In the darkest hour of the life of the South, when her wounded people lay helpless amid rags and ashes under the beak and talon of the Vulture, suddenly from the mists of the mountains appeared a white cloud the size of a man's hand. It grew until its mantle of mystery enfolded the stricken earth and sky. An "Invisible Empire" had risen from the field of Death and challenged the Visible to mortal combat.

How the young South, led by the reincarnated souls of the Clansmen of Old Scotland, went forth under this cover and against overwhelming odds, daring exile, imprisonment, and a felon's death, and saved the life of a people, forms one of the most dramatic chapters in the history of the Aryan race.

Thomas Dixon, Jr.
Dixondale, Va., December 14, 1904.

SOURCE: Thomas Dixon, Jr., *The Clansman: An Historical Romance of the Ku Klux Klan*. New York: Doubleday, Page & Company, 1905.

5. Excerpts from Various Newspaper Accounts of Disorders Following the Jack Johnson–James Jeffries Fight, July 4, 1910

When African American boxer Jack Johnson, then current heavyweight champion, defeated former white champion Jim Jeffries in Reno, Nevada, on July 4, 1910, news of the decision caused racial disorders to erupt in almost a dozen cities across the country as both blacks, proud of their fighter's victory, and whites, angry at their fighter's defeat, responded to the outcome and to each other. *See also the entry* Johnson–Jeffries Fight of 1910, Riots Following.

Baltimore

Seventy negroes, half the number women, were arrested tonight in the "black belt" of this city for disorderly celebration of Johnson's victory. One negro was badly cut by another, and two other negroes were assaulted and severely injured by whites in arguments over the big fight.

SOURCE: "Racial Clashes Follow Victory of Jack Johnson." The *Atlanta Constitution*, July 5, 1910, p. 2.

Bluefields, West Virginia

Negroes are boisterous at Keystone, W. Va., tonight and are said to be in possession of the town, the police being powerless.

SOURCE: "Racial Clashes Follow Victory of Jack Johnson." The *Atlanta Constitution*, July 5, 1910, p. 2.

Little Rock, Arkansas

Although there have been a number of fights in Little Rock in which whites and blacks clashed, with the latter receiving the worst of the argument in practically all cases, following the announcement of the result of the Jeffries–Johnson fight, no fatalities have occurred ... Several fights between whites and negroes started at a local theater, where fight returns were received, but were quickly stopped.

SOURCE: "Racial Clashes Follow Victory of Jack Johnson." The *Atlanta Constitution*, July 5, 1910, p. 2.

Mounds, Illinois

One dead and one mortally wounded is the result of an attempt by four negroes to shoot up the town in honor of Jack Johnson's victory at Reno tonight. A negro constable was killed when he attempted to arrest them.

SOURCE: "Eight Killed in Fight Riots." The *New York Times*, July 5, 1910, p. 4.

Philadelphia

The announcement of Johnson's victory over Jeffries was followed by numerous clashes in this city between colored men and crowds of white men and boys. In some cases, the blacks, exulting the victory, were the aggressors, but in other cases inoffensive colored men were attacked by riotous whites ... Lombard Street, the principal street in the negro section, went wild in celebrating the victory, and a number of fights, in which razors were drawn, resulted. In the suburb of Germantown a crowd of negroes paraded the streets and there were several clashes with white men.

SOURCE: "Race Clashes in Many Cities." The *Washington Post*, July 5, 1910, p. 11.

Pittsburgh

Less than half an hour after the decision of the fight was announced here three riot calls were sent into two police precincts in the negro hill district. Street cars were held up and insulting epithets were hurled at the passengers. The police beat the crowds back with their clubs to permit the passage of street cars. Patrolmen have been summoned to this district from all sections of the city.

SOURCE: "Racial Clashes Follow Victory of Jack Johnson." The *Atlanta Constitution*, July 5, 1910, p. 1.

Roanoke, Virginia

Six negroes with broken heads, six white men locked up and one white man, Joe Chockley, with a bullet wound through his skull and probably fatally wounded, is the net result of clashes here tonight following the announcement that Jack Johnson had defeated James J. Jeffries. The trouble started when a negro, who had just heard the news from Reno, said: "Now I guess the white folks will let the negroes alone." A white man replied: "No!" and the two clashed.

SOURCE: "Racial Clashes Follow Victory of Jack Johnson." The *Atlanta Constitution*, July 5, 1910, p. 2.

St. Joseph, Missouri

S.I. Sawyer, a white man who took the part of a negro when the latter was struck by another white man, was mobbed by a crowd of whites immediately following the Johnson–Jeffries fight. Sawyer was rescued by a policeman, and charges that the latter struck him in the face and broke his nose.

SOURCE: "Racial Clashes Follow Victory of Jack Johnson." The *Atlanta Constitution*, July 5, 1910, p. 2.

St. Louis

Rioting in a negro section of St. Louis, at Market Street and Jefferson Avenue, followed quickly upon the announcement that Jack Johnson was the victor in the Reno prize fight. The eighth district police responded to a riot call, but were powerless to cope with the negroes who were blocking traffic and making threats. A second call to the Central district brought out a score of policemen. The negroes were clubbed into submission and dispersed.

SOURCE: "Eleven Killed in Many Race Riots." The *Chicago Tribune*, July 5, 1910, p. 4.

Shreveport, Louisiana

L.E. Roberts, a conductor of the Iron Mountain railroad is dead; John Anderson, a negro, is dead; his son, Henry Anderson, is dead; an unknown negro woman is dying, shot through the head; one or two negroes are injured, and a race riot is imminent. The authorities have no control over the situation in Madison and East Carroll parishes, and posses are scouring the whole country tonight.

SOURCE: "Eleven Killed in Many Race Riots." The *Chicago Tribune*, July 5, 1910, p. 4.

Wilmington, Delaware

A serious race riot occurred here tonight as the result of an argument over the victory of Johnson. Michael Brown, a white man, was attacked by a gang of negroes and severely injured about the head and cut with a razor. A mob of whites then chased the negroes several blocks. One of the negroes, Benjamin White, fled into a negro apartment house. The mob of whites, which by this time numbered several thousand, bombarded the place with stones.

SOURCE: "Race Clashes in Many Cities." The *Washington Post*, July 5, 1910, p. 11.

6. Account of the Riots in East St. Louis, Illinois, July 1917

The National Association for the Advancement of Colored People (NAACP) commissioned W.E.B. Du Bois and Martha Gruening to investigate and report on the riots that had convulsed East St. Louis during the summer of

1917. The following excerpts from their report, which was published in *The Crisis*, summarize eyewitness accounts of the horrible atrocities perpetrated on the African American residents of East St. Louis by the white rioters. *See also the entries* Du Bois, W.E.B.; East St. Louis (Illinois) Riot of 1917; National Association for the Advancement of Colored People (NAACP).

A Negro, his head laid open by a great stone-cut, had been dragged to the mouth of the alley on Fourth Street and a small rope was being put about his neck. There was joking comment on the weakness of the rope, and everyone was prepared for what happened when it was pulled over a projecting cable box, a short distance up the pole. It broke, letting the Negro tumble back to his knees, and causing one of the men who was pulling on it to sprawl on the pavement.

An old man, with a cap like those worn by street car conductors, but showing no badge of car service, came out of his house to protest. "Don't you hang that man on this street," he shouted. "I dare you to." He was pushed angrily away, and a rope, obviously strong enough for its purpose, was brought.

Right here I saw the most sickening incident of the evening. To put the rope around the Negro's neck, one of the lynchers stuck his fingers inside the gaping scalp and lifted the Negro's head by it, literally bathing his hand in the man's blood.

"Get hold and pull for East St. Louis!" called a man with a black coat and a new straw hat, as he seized the other end of the rope. The rope was long, but not too long for the number of hands that grasped it, and this time the Negro was lifted to a height of about seven feet from the ground. . . .

A Negro weighing 300 pounds came out of the burning line of dwellings just north and east of the Southern freight house. His hands were elevated and his yellow face was speckled wit the awful fear of death.

"Get him!" they cried. Here was a chance to see suffering, something that bullets didn't always make.

So a man in the crowd clubbed his revolver and struck the Negro in the face with it. Another dashed an iron bolt between the Negro's eyes. Still another stood near and battered him with a rock.

Then the giant Negro toppled to the ground. "This is the way," cried one. He ran back a few paces, then ran at the prostrate black at full speed and made a flying leap.

His heels struck right in the middle of the battered face. A girl stepped up and struck the bleeding man with her foot. The blood spurted onto her stockings and men laughed and grunted.

No amount of suffering awakened pity in the hearts of the rioters. . . . A few Negroes, caught on the street, were kicked and shot to death. As flies settled on their terrible wounds, the gaping-mouthed mobsmen forbade the dying blacks to brush them off. Girls with blood on their stockings helped to kick in what had been black faces of the corpses on the street.

The first houses were fired shortly after 5 o'clock. These were back of Main Street, between Broadway and Railroad Avenue. Negroes were "flushed" from the burning houses, and ran for their lives, screaming and begging for mercy. A Negro crawled into a shed and fired on the white men. Guardsmen started after him, but when they saw he was armed, turned to the mob and said:

"He's armed, boys. You can have him. A white man's life is worth the lives of a thousand Negroes."

A few minutes later matches were applied to hastily gathered debris piled about the corner of one of the three small houses 100 feet from the first fired. These were back of the International Harvester Company's plant. Eight Negroes fled into the last of the houses and hid in the basement. When roof and walls were about to fall in, an aged Negro woman came out. She was permitted to walk to safety. Three Negro women followed and were not fired upon. Then came four Negro men, and 100 shots were fired at them. They fell. No one ventured out to see if they were dead, as the place had come to resemble No Man's Land, with bullets flying back and forth and sparks from the fires falling everywhere.

A Negro who crawled on hands and knees through the weeds was a target for a volley. The mob then burned back to Main Street and another Negro was spied on a Main Street car. He was dragged to the street and a rioter stood over him, shooting.

The crowd then turned to Black Valley. Here the greatest fire damage was caused. Flames were soon raging and the shrieking rioters stood about in the streets, made lurid by the flames, and shot and beat Negroes as they fled from burning homes.

They pursued the women who were driven out of the burning homes, with the idea, not of extinguishing their burning clothing, but of inflicting added pain, if possible. They stood around in groups, laughing and jeering, while they witnessed the final writhings of the terror and pain wracked wretches who crawled to the streets to die after their flesh had been cooked in their own homes.

Mrs. Cox saw a Negro beheaded with a butcher's knife by someone in a crowd standing near the Free Bridge. The crowd had to have its jest. So its members laughingly threw the head over one side of the bridge and the body over the other.

A trolley-car came along. The crowd forced its inmates to put their hands out the window. Colored people thus recognized were hauled out of the car to be beaten, trampled on, shot. A little twelve-year-old colored girl fainted—her mother knelt beside her. The crowd surged in on her. When its ranks opened up again Mrs. Cox saw the mother prostrate with a hole as large as one's fist in her head.

SOURCE: W.E.B. Du Bois and Martha Gruening. "Massacre at East St. Louis." *The Crisis*, XIV, 1917, pp. 222–238.

7. A Southern Black Woman's Letter Regarding the Recent Riots in Chicago and Washington, November 1919

The Washington riot gave me the thrill that comes once in a lifetime. I was alone when I read between the lines of the morning paper that at last our men had stood like men, struck back, were no longer dumb, driven cattle. When I could no longer read for my streaming tears, I stood up, alone in my room, held both hands high over my head and exclaimed aloud: "Oh, I thank God, thank God!" When I remember anything after this, I was prone on my bed, beating the pillow with both fists, laughing and crying, whimpering like a whipped child, for sheer gladness and madness. The pent-up humiliation, grief and horror of a life time—half a century—was being stripped from me. Only colored women of the south know the extreme in suffering and humiliation.

We know how many insults we have borne silently, for we have hidden many of them from our men because we did not want them to die needlessly in our defense; we know the sorrow of seeing our boys and girls grow up, the swift stab of the heart at night to the sound of a strange footstep, the feel of a tigress to spring and claw the white man with his lustful look at our comely daughters, the deep humiliation of sitting in the Jim Crow part of a street car and hear the white man laugh and discuss us, point out the good and bad points of our bodies. God alone knows the many things colored women have borne here in the South in silence.

And, too, a woman loves a strong man, she delights to feel that her man can protect her, fight for her, if necessary, save her.

No woman loves a weakling, a coward, be she white or black, and some of us have been near to thinking our men cowards, but thank God for Washington colored men! All honor to them, for they first blazed the way and right swiftly did Chicago men follow. They put new hope, a new vision in their almost despairing women.

God grant that our men everywhere refrain from strife, provoke no quarrel, but that they protect their women and homes at any cost.

A Southern Colored Woman

I'm sure the editor will understand why I cannot sign my name.

SOURCE: *The Crisis*, XIX, November 1919, p. 339.

8. Excerpts from the NAACP Report *Thirty Years of Lynching in the United States: 1889–1918*, 1919

Published by the NAACP in 1919, the report *Thirty Years of Lynching in the United States: 1889–1918* was an important part of the organization's strenuous ongoing effort to eradicate the crime of lynching by educating the public to the frequency and brutality of the crime. Written by Martha Gruening and Helen Boardman, *Thirty Years of Lynching* presents facts, figures, and anecdotes on lynching collected by the NAACP. The two excerpts below offer statistics on the types of crimes that were given as reasons for lynchings and the opening of the section from newspaper accounts describing 100 lynchings that had occurred between 1894 and 1918. *See also the entries* Lynching; National Association for the Advancement of Colored People (NAACP); *Thirty Years of Lynching in the United States: 1889–1918.*

Alleged Offenses Which Appear as "Causes" for the Lynchings

Table No. 6 sums up the known facts regarding the alleged offenses committed by the men and women lynched. It is to be remembered that the alleged offenses given are pretty loose descriptions of the crimes charged against the mob victims, where actual crime was committed. Of the whites lynched, nearly 46 per cent were accused of murder; a little more than 18 per cent were accused of what have been classified as miscellaneous crimes, *i.e.*, all crimes not otherwise classified; 17.4 per cent were said to have committed crimes against property; 8.7 per cent crimes against the person, other than rape, "attacks upon women," and murder; while 8.4 per cent were accused of rape and "attacks upon women."

Among colored victims, 35.8 per cent were accused of murder; 28.4 per cent or rape and "attacks upon women" (19 per cent of rape and 9.4 per cent of "attacks upon women"); 17.8 per cent of crimes against the person (other than those already mentioned) and against property; 12 per cent were charged with miscellaneous crimes and in 5.6 per cent of cases no crime at all was charged. The 5.6 per cent, classified under "Absence of Crime," does not include a number of cases in which crime was alleged but in which it was afterwards shown conclusively that no crime had been committed. Further, it may fairly be pointed out that in a number of cases where Negroes have been lynched for rape and "attacks upon white women," the alleged attacks rest upon no stronger evidence than "entering the room of a woman" or brushing against her. In such cases as these latter the victims and their friends have often asserted that there was no intention on the part of the victim to attack a white woman or to commit rape. In many cases, of course, the evidence points to *bona fide* attacks upon women.

The Story of One Hundred Lynchings[‡]

To give concreteness and to make vivid the facts of lynching in the United States, we give below in chronological order an account of one hundred lynchings which have occurred in the period from 1894 to 1918. These "stories," as they are technically described in newspaper parlance, have been taken from press accounts and, in a few cases, from the reports of investigations made by the National Association for the Advancement of Colored People. Covering twenty-five years of American history, these accounts serve to present a characteristic picture of the lynching sport, as was picturesquely defined by Henry Watterson.

The last of the stories describes one of the rare events in connection with lynchings, that of the conviction of members of a mob involved in such affairs. In this case no lynching was consummated, it having been

Table No. 6

	Murder	Rape	Attacks upon Women*	Other Crimes Against the Person	Crimes Against Property	Miscellaneous Crimes	Absence of Crime†	Total
Total	1,219	523	250	315	331	438	148	3,224
White	319	46	13	62	121	135	6	702
Per cent. of total whites lynched	45.7	6.6	1.8	8.7	17.4	18.1	1.4	100.0
Negro	900	477	237	253	210	303	142	2,522
Per cent. of total Negroes lynched	35.8	19.0	9.4	9.5	8.3	12.0	5.6	100.0

*This classification includes all cases in which press accounts state that attacks upon women were made, but in which it was not clear whether rape was alleged to have been consummated or attempted.

†Under this heading are listed such causes as "testifying against whites," "suing whites," "wrong man lynched," "race prejudice," "defending himself against attack," etc.

prevented by the prompt and public-spirited action of the mayor of the city (Winston-Salem, North Carolina), and members of the "Home Guard" and Federal troops who defended the jail against the mob.

Alabama, 1894

Three Negroes, Tom Black, Johnson Williams and Tony Johnston, were lynched at Tuscumbia, Alabama. They were in the local jail, awaiting trial on the charge of having burnt a barn. A mob of two hundred masked men entered the jail, after having enticed away the jailer with a false message, took the keys from the jailer's wife and secured the three prisoners. They were carried to a near-by bridge. Here a rope was placed around the neck of each victim, the other end being tied to the timbers of the bridge, and they were compelled to jump.

SOURCE: *New York Tribune*, April 23, 1894.

‡ One hundred *persons* lynched, not one hundred occasions on which lynching occurred.

SOURCE: NAACP. *Thirty Years of Lynching in the United States*. National Association for the Advancement of Colored People, 1919, pp. 9, 10, 11, 36.

9. Excerpts from the "Anti-Lynching" Hearings Held before the House Judiciary Committee, January 1920

Reproduced below are excerpts of testimony given before the House Judiciary Committee in January 1920. Responding to the many serious race riots that had erupted over the previous three years, and especially during the "Red Summer" of 1919, the committee heard testimony regarding the need for anti-lynching legislation to protect African Americans from the growing racist violence being offered them throughout the country. The hearings accompanied the House's consideration of the Dyer Anti-Lynching Bill, which was introduced into the House in 1918 by Congressman Leonidas Dyer, a Republican from a heavily black district in St. Louis. Although passed by the House in January 1922, the Dyer bill, which made participation in a lynch mob a federal crime, was defeated in the Senate shortly thereafter. No federal anti-lynching legislation was ever passed by Congress. *See also the entries* Anti-Lynching Legislation; Dyer, Leonidas C.

Statement of Mr. Neval H. Thomas

Mr. Thomas. In the first place, I am representing the National Association for the Advancement of Colored People. Locally we have 7,000 members whom I am representing, and nationally we have 100,000 members in 310 branches, which are organized to oppose just such a recommendation as has been presented here to-day. I do not know where this man comes from—

Mr. Dyer. He says he comes from St. Louis. How long have you lived in St. Louis, Mr. Madden?

Mr. Madden. About two years: I came there from Oklahoma.

Mr. Dyer. I thought so.

Mr. Thomas. I am acquainted with the leaders of thought among colored people all over this country, and I never even heard of this man before. He represents nothing but himself. Beware of any Negro who comes recommending a segregation scheme to you: he is simply seeking to be head of the group if we are segregated. When Woodrow Wilson became President, there were some venal Negro politicians who asked him to segregate the colored clerks in one department, and at the same time everyone presented an application for the leadership of that department; so pay no attention to them. The masses of the colored people are unalterably opposed to segregation. Civilization has been spread and prejudices softened by the contact of peoples with each other. Even President Wilson is on record as saying that you can not hate a man whom you know, although he has segregated men to keep them from knowing, so that they can hate.

We recognize, in the first place that every man is lord of his castle; complete master of his own home. We seek no association, but cooperation with the white people of this country in the up-building of the things which belong to us all. When we go upon a common carrier, we are not seeking contact with the other people, we simply want to travel from place to place; we do not even expect another passenger to say "Good morning" to us. This is an ordinary civil right. The common carrier, like all other institutions, belongs to all of us alike. They are supported by our taxes, protected by the police power of our State, and every one is a taxpayer because the ultimate consumer is the taxpayer. The owner of property does not pay the taxes. He charges enough rent to make a profitable return on his investment, plus the insurance, water rent, and all other expenses, and the tenant pays it. The owner of the property is simply a messenger through whom the tenant sends his taxes to the taxgatherer. Therefore, we have equal rights to all public places, such as the common carrier, the theaters, restaurants, and hotels, and we will never cease to clamor for our rights until we gain admission. What we want the Congress to do, and also the Department of Justice, is to enforce the thirteenth, the fourteenth, and the fifteenth amendments to the Constitution. Even the thirteenth amendment, forbidding slavery and involuntary servitude, is violated in the Southern States by the infamous system of peonage. We demand the ballot, for in a Government where men vote the voter is king, and the disfranchised man is the victim of the man who does vote. We demand the abolition of the infamous "Jim-Crow" car, which was simply made to insult us. We demand admission to all public places, in fact, we demand equality of treatment everywhere, and equality before the law. Again, I say that segregation keeps men apart and is opposed to all sound principles of Government. My own experience in this country and Europe with white people has taught me how segregation works against my people. I have met people in this country and in Europe who were surprised that I could write; that I knew history; that I knew what I was traveling for; could explain a painting or a piece of sculpture or a great work of architecture. They had lived side by side with me for all these years, the segregation had kept them from knowing me. Suppose there were no prejudices in this country, the races would mingle and discover their common humanity, and learn that color is the least of differences among men, and we would have no resulting friction. There are people living right in Boston who have gone over Boston Common, the most historic park in this country, where there is a statue of Crispus Attucks, a Negro, the first to shed his blood in the American Revolution. Nearby is the famous Robert Gould Shaw statue, dedicated to the Fifty-fourth and Fifty-fifth regiments of Negroes in the Civil War, who died like men at Fort Pillow for the preservation of the Union, and yet have never looked up to find how much the colored men of this country have done for it. The system of segregation prevents that mutual interest that should exist between the races; we are all opposed to segregation. The African Methodist Episcopal Church is the largest institution among the Negroes, with 700,000 members. This church issued a declaration of 14 points, the number of which is in imitation on the President's 14 points, and the strongest point in it is a declaration against segregation. This church supports 24 institutions in the South and collects from the pockets of washerwomen $350,000 every year for the education of the Negro youth, and this is in addition to the expense to which colored people are put for education of their own in the South because all the people are taxpayers.

As this great church is against segregation, so are the Baptists and other denominations. The great organization for which I am talking to-day is opposed to it. We are all opposed to it, and this man is simply seeking his own personal gain. The gentleman from Oklahoma asked if we were willing to leave this country and said he believed three-fourths of us would not leave. No. Nine hundred and ninety-nine out of every thousand would not leave. This man has falsely stated that this is a white man's country. He knows nothing of the history of his people. The Negro came here when the white man did, and he has contributed to the upbuilding of this country by this labor, by his suffering, by his sacrifices and blood. There are none of the highest callings he has not entered. In art, the highest calling of man, the greatest name is Henry O. Tanner, a Negro, whose paintings the French Government seeks and purchases and puts in her great art galleries as soon as they are painted. So it is foolish to talk about Americans, and we are not going to leave in spite of our sufferings, but we are going to work out our destiny right here in our own land. We have almost enough law in this country. What we want is enforcement of the law. We have a Constitution with 19 amendments, and with its imperfections, it is the greatest political document that has ever come from the hand of man. What we want Congress to do is to enforce it. Think of it: even the House of Representatives has closed its public restaurants to Negroes, where we have been going for 50 years without friction. This was done at the very time that brave black boys were dying in the trenches in France. This is a new reward to give the returning black soldier for his heroic sacrifices in every part of far-off France. . . .

Statement of Prof. George William Cook, Howard University, Washington, D.C.

Mr. Cook. I have been coming to the Capitol appearing before committees for nigh onto 20 years. I must say that I have never been before a committee where the occasion was of such vast and deep importance as this appearance to-day. You may read it through the inference or read where the inference is given, or you may read it out of the logic of events, that this committee representing the judiciary of the United States in Congress assembled is to-day challenged. The presentation of facts and conditions here to-day are such that if the committee does not take a very serious consideration of it it is scarcely up to the level of its own duty.

We did not come here to-day simply for the purpose of talking to you. We came here to convince you as we know it, and as we hope to show it to you that this awful carnage of lynching and injustice in so many different ways must be stopped or we have our backs to the wall. My family is broken to-day and let me give you the circumstances. As my wife and I motored from Washington last July, we heard in Baltimore that there was a race riot in Washington. It was Tuesday after Monday the last day of the riot. We hastened here because we had one son, our only child, a young boy whom we found home, and I asked him. "Where were you, George?" "I was in it." "Why were you in it?" "You can not take me out and shoot me like a dog. I am going to die fighting if I have to die." There is an 18-year-old boy. He contemplated that thing, and he said finally, "Papa, I am not going to stay here." He is somewhat of a law unto himself. I said, "Where are you going?" "I am going out of the country." "Where do you propose to go first?" "I think that I will go to Canada and go to school." He went to Canada. These holidays he returned to Washington on a visit and he was not home two days before he said, "I smelt it as soon as I reached Baltimore and I am going away again."

Now, you may consider that as an isolated case or you may consider it trivial. I have been teaching young colored men for 40 years. I have tested the opinion and growing conviction. I want to say if you want to drive out a pure unadulterated loyalty that has existed in the colored man, just allow this lynching to continue. You are all men of spirit and courage and belong to the Anglo-Saxon race. You would not stand it. You did not stand taxation without representation with very little personal violence attached to it and you were right, and I want to say here as far as I can gauge my people they are loyal to the backbone, they want no disturbance, and they will accept none until forced to. This is our position in the matter.

Why did I speak of that boy? Do you want to drive citizens who are loyal from your shores? You have sent away the undesirables. We are not undesirable; no. You want the labor, but we are going to say and can say that along with that response and the giving of labor we are going to ask for our God-given rights, and it is our duty as far as possible to demand them.

There was a question raised this morning as to loyalty. There seems to be some little idea that possibly the Negro is not quite as loyal as he used to be. The Attorney General of the United States shows that in 30 pages, I read almost all of it night before last and there are some in the South who feel the same way.

Mr. Sumners. Just a moment. I made the statement that there was no evidence. I made the statement that there was no general evidence of disloyalty on the part of the colored man toward the Government. I made that upon my own responsibility.

Mr. Cook. I meant simply the question that came before us. I want to say now, sir, that the colored man is loyal. He is loyal in secret and he is loyal openly, and there is but one way to shake that loyalty. He sings, "My Country, 'Tis of Thee," with all the luster and all of the sincerity that you sing, and there is now but one way to shake that, and that is to continue the lawlessness against him, and when you find him raising his hand in defense it is against the mob. He never voluntarily raises his hand against the Government, never has, never was an assassin, political assassin or menace, never was a traitor, there is not one that betrayed the confidence in all of the wars, and in all you have had he has engaged. There never was one. Therefore, I appeal to you now to help us because we are a weak people, financially, economically, but with all the opposition we have had we are stronger that we were 50 years ago, and it is not only in strength that we would come and ask you, we would come and ask you in our helplessness, that we, as American citizens, in the Thomas Jefferson declaration sense, are willing to die rather than continue our serfdom.

It is only necessary to be a little honest. You gentlemen who have studied the Elaine case understand it. These four brothers were not in the riot. They were out hunting when that treacherous gang came to them and told them they had better go home because they might get into trouble, and "let us have your guns in order that you will not be considered in the mob." They got their guns and then shot them to death. They had not done anything and did not even know a riot was going on in the town. I appeal to every man on this committee and I am sorry they are not here to hear these other gentlemen speak. I am only taking up the raveled ends and appeal to you upon pure justice first, and then on the lower ground of political necessity, to give us our rights. Do not allow your communities to deny the colored man an accounting when he has given his sweat toward the cultivation of the crop. Let him have an accounting and treat him fairly.

We bring this general proposition to you and we can support every one of them by cases upon cases. The most horrible thing of it all in that lynching, when they shot these four brothers to death, that they scarcely knew for what they were being shot. That was a lynching. Now, it is too late, and I am glad to see by the public press, the white press, that the white man is half ashamed of bringing attacks upon women as the great cause for lynching. The record has been too well kept by the *Chicago Tribune* and by *The Crisis*. We know why it is. Men have been lynched for nothing else but wearing the uniform of the United States Government. It was but yesterday that a young man in my class in commercial law said to me: "I will tell you something." I went to him when I came out of the classroom. He said: "I was simply standing in the street down in South Carolina talking when a young white man came up and said, "What are you doing with this on?" He says, "I just came out of the Army." "Well, you can not wear that down here." Can not wear the uniform of the United States Government down there? Just a few feet away they brought up another one and he left for nothing but wearing the uniform. He said he went to the post office for his father's mail and the postmaster said to him, "Do you want the package that is here?" He said, "No, I can not carry that, I will wait for the car to come in." This young man said, "What did you say to me?" I said, "No, I will not take that now." He said, "I want you to know you can not talk that way to me. You must say 'sir' to me, if you propose to stay about here," and started to come out to him. He talked up and said, "If you come after me on a charge like that, one or both of us will report to God to-day."

That is just yesterday. Do you blame the man for saying it. No security from attack upon a colored man even though he had the uniform of the United States Government upon him; this young man in the post office assuming to chastise a man who had given his all for the life of the Government, offered his all, for the protection of the flag of the United States. He said his father said to him, "You had better go. They might take out revenge on me and burn us out." He was not wrong in telling that young man to go away. The other young men had gone away. These cases are not imaginary cases. These have happened.

Now, there are two points I wanted to make. One is will you continue to teach the younger element of 12,000,000 people to ask the question, Is loyalty worth while? One you have driven out of the country. We are bereft of our son, as I have told you. He made up his mind that he would not die like a dog and that he would get out of it. Are you anxious to lose loyal citizens? If the economic condition of the Negro was such, hundreds of them, would migrate upon economic grounds, you may say, and go out as pioneers, but we have been chained down in America for over 300 years, the sweat of our brow has gone into the wealth of the Nation; it is undeniable because the statistics of your own department records will show it. What we ask now is protection under the flag that we have fought to keep aloft in as many wars as you have engaged in. Well might we repeat what Carney said when he returned at Fort Wagner, "The old flag never touched the ground," you have never heard of a Negro color bearer of the United States going to the rear unless ordered there. That is a sample of the feeling of the colored people.

We are born here. "My Country, 'Tis of Thee," I sing. You will find some few colored people, and probably with just convictions, who will not sing it. I sing it. Why? It is my country. Born here, my mother and father before me and my grandmother and grandfather. And what they added in honest industry went to help build up this Nation and to make it strong. It is my country. I will not forsake it. Why? I will treat it very much as I will a leaking house. I will repair the roof. I will not abandon it. The United States to the black man has a leaky roof, and we are here to-day to ask you to repair that roof in order that we may live in comfort and in peace, and the challenge that I spoke of to you was a challenge to you who have not thought the matter out to think it out and come on the side of justice. Let no man go out of here and say the Negroes are arguing for social equality. What some people call social equality we call disdain. I want my company and I never seek other company, which does not want me, and so it is with every self-respecting colored man, but I tell you what else I want, whether you want me or not, I want my civic political rights, and if you call that social equality, I say that you have made a misrepresentation and you give a wrong distinction. For me to be driven to travel from here to New Orleans and forced to ride and sit in a dirty car is what I protest against. I do not protest for social equality. I protest for civil rights, for civic privileges, for a discharge of the contract on the part of the railroad people to give me what I have paid for, and when you allow, as was done Sunday night, a man to step up and put a pistol to the body of an attorney of the District of Columbia and say to him, "You get out of this car or I will shoot you," when you allow that, gentlemen, you are only inviting the downfall of the Republic, because not only will the 12,000,000 finally be affected by that, but the whole Nation will be affected.

Some people speak of the unrest of the Negro. The Negro has always been the most quiet man in the United States. There are a few criminals who are among us, naturally, just like the white criminals, but the unrest in this Nation is not only with Negroes, and I pray to Almighty God that when the time comes for you to put down unrest in the form of anarchy, that the 12,000,000 of Negroes will have a just cause to be on the side of the United States, and if that is not realized, then may God help, for my country is lost. Do not misunderstand us. We are here to ask you to attempt to do something, even though there is a doubt as to the constitutionality of it. Don't I remember when I walked down to pay my income tax? There were men who said it was unconstitutional before you passed it, and you put it up to the Supreme Court of the United States, and you remember there was some little juggling up there and finally it was declared unconstitutional. Somebody changed. The inveighed against it because there was some doubt. They all said let us do it, and to-day what have you? An amendment to the Constitution for an income tax to be operated. Now, let us for the hope of our common good and of justice to all and for a fair understanding, let us pass some bill that will look toward stopping the greatest crime that you have in the land, that of lynching.

SOURCE: "Anti-Lynching Hearings." Hearings Before the Judiciary Committee, House of Representatives, 66th Congress, 2nd Session, on House Judiciary Resolution 75; House Resolutions 259, 4123, and 11873, Serial No. 14. January 14 and 29, 1920. Part II, Anti-Lynching. Washington, DC: Government Printing Office, 1920, pp. 8–10, 72–75.

10. Excerpt from the Cook County Coroner's Report Regarding the 1919 Chicago Race Riots, 1920

Reproduced below is an excerpt from one of several reports by the Cook County Coroner's Office on the causes and results of a series of race riots that occurred in Chicago in 1917, 1918, and 1919. The passage given here is from the report of the Coroner's Jury investigating the particularly serious riot of July and August 1919. The jury finds the main causes of the riot to be criminal activity on the part of both whites and African Americans, as well as, to a lesser extent, the friction created by a greater mixing of the races resulting from a great influx of African Americans from the South, who came North during the World War I seeking work.

The true facts regarding the race riots in the City of Chicago in July and August, 1919, should be presented to set at rest the many grossly exaggerated tales and rumors and the misrepresentations which have been broadcast throughout the City of Chicago and the United States. The number of lives lost, the manner of losing the same, the causes of the riots, and all known facts attending the dark and frightful days beginning July 27, 1919, are matters of vital interest to all orderly citizens who live and work in Chicago and for Chicago. That these facts may become known and studied and analyzed is the purpose of this report.

Five days of terrible heat and passion let loose cost the people of Chicago thirty-eight lives, wounded and maimed several hundred, destroyed property of untold value, filled thousands with awful fright, blemished the good name of our City, and left in its wake fear and apprehension for the future.

Race feeling and distrust reaches far back into the history of the past. While new, perhaps, to Chicago, other cities and communities have tasted of its frightfulness, and yet race antagonism in itself rarely gets beyond bound and control. The real danger lies with the criminal and hoodlum element, white and colored, who are quick to take advantage of any incipient race riot conditions to spread the firebrands of disorder, thieving, arson, lust and murder—and under the cover of large numbers, to give full sway to cowardly animal and criminal instincts.

The riot jury was impaneled July 28, 1919, and our investigations and inquiry have proceeded continuously through one form and another, to the present time.

We have visited hospitals, undertakers, and scenes of the rioting, received statements from the relatives and friends of the victims, attended the exhumation of one body at Lincoln Cemetery for fuller confirmation as to the course of the bullet wound; have held seventy day sessions and twenty night sessions on inquest work, examining approximately four hundred and fifty witnesses, the testimony taken amounting to fifty-five hundred and eighty-four folio pages, typewritten. Twenty men were held to the Grand Jury for murder or manslaughter, one held to court martial for murder. There were seven cases of justifiable homicide. Recommendation that unknown rioters be apprehended and punished was made in eighteen cases. One Police Officer was killed, three men were killed by Police Officers. One case—that of Joseph Lovings, a colored man—is still under investigation.

Homicides, due to the riots, occurred in widely separated localities, on the south, southwest and west sides of the city.

Particularly atrocious and cruel murder was committed on the persons of Morris Parel, Walter Parejko, Eugene Temple, David Marcus, Morris Lazzeroni and George L. Wilkins (white men), and Robert Williams, B.F. Hardy, John Mills, William H. Lozier, Oscar Lozier, Louis Taylor, Paul Hardwick and Joseph Lovings (colored men)....

We have no thought of, or desire, to criticize any of the city officials, the State's Attorney or the Police Department. In the grave emergency and riot conditions, we believe they all did their duty, as we conscientiously tried to do ours; nor do we believe that politics, so-called, or catering to the white or colored vote, had much if anything to do with the production of race rioting.

The riots began on the afternoon of July 27, 1919, when Eugene Williams, a colored boy, was drowned at the 29th street bathing beach, having been prevented from landing by stones thrown by a mob of white men and boys. Prior to that afternoon, this beach had been used exclusively by white people. The colored people contested the right of the white people thereto, and a pitched battle was fought with stones thrown between two mobs, the drowning of Williams being the result. The report of his death spread with great rapidity through the colored residence district, and the report was in general that he had been stoned to death in the water. Evidence disclosed that no stones struck the boy, that an attempt was made to stone him and stones were thrown in his direction. He was drowned—probably by reason of exhaustion due to the inability to land. However, the reports caused a white heat of passion and desire for reprisal among a large proportion of the colored population, and the riot spread.

July 27, 2 men were killed or sustained injuries causing death.
July 28, 17 men were killed or sustained injuries causing death.
July 29, 11 men were killed or sustained injuries causing death.
July 30, 5 men were killed or sustained injuries causing death.
July 31, 1 man was killed or sustained injuries causing death.

One George R. Fleming, white, was slain by a soldier, white, August 5th.

By August the 1st, the riots had subsided, the situation being well under control of the police and the soldiery, normal conditions being in part restored.

Incomplete police reports covering the five days of the rioting, show that one police officer was killed and thirty-nine wounded or injured; twenty-three colored men and fourteen white men killed; two hundred and ninety-one white and colored citizens wounded or injured. We have no report of white or colored women outraged and but few women were mistreated during the rioting. No evidence of drunkenness was presented.

To review the circumstances of all the thirty-eight homicides would be tiresome to the reader and serve no good purpose. As illustrating all of them we will review briefly the cases of Eugene Temple, a white man, and Joseph Lovings, a colored man. All verdicts rendered are on record in the Coroner's Office.

Eugene Temple, a reputable citizen and proprietor of the Columbia Laundry, located at 3642 South State Street, stepped from the doorway of his place of business, accompanied by his wife and another lady, and was thus upon the sidewalk about to enter his automobile. He was leisurely approached by three colored men, who grabbed him, one on either side, at his back. While securely held by two of the men, the third man lifted up Mr. Temple's left arm and plunged a sharp and long knife, evidently a stiletto, through his heart. Then they as leisurely walked away, leaving their victim dead upon the sidewalk. Apparently, this was a cold blooded, calculated murder, without the element of race passion. There was evidence that some attempt had been made to rob him at the same time. These men have not been apprehended and presumably are walking the streets of Chicago, a constant and continual menace.

The slaying of Joseph Lovings, colored, was an atrocious, savage crime. He, a defenseless man, caught like a rat in a trap, by a surrounding mob, was dragged from his place of concealment and refuge, beaten, skull fractured, and shot fourteen times—left lying a bruised and broken semblance of a man, on the grass plot in front of a city home in the heart of the west side. This crime has not a single redeeming feature. It particularly illustrates the savage animal nature of a mob. To hunt down, apprehend and punish the dastardly criminals who killed this man, is the duty, not alone of the Police Department, but of every citizen who values the security of life. No wonder that reports of this crime grew to large proportions as it spread. It was published by the press of this and other large cities that he had been sprayed with gasoline and burned alive. Comments were made in Congress at Washington regarding the rumor. It gives us satisfaction to say that this rumor, from our investigation, is false and unsubstantiated—but the subtraction of this rumor mitigates the crime but a very slight degree.

Persistent reports have been circulated that the total number of deaths far exceeded thirty-eight. Intelligent citizens have approached the Coroner and members of this jury and gave their opinion that the number of deaths was far in excess of the number found. These reports were freely handed about and believed.

We have made a thorough investigation to verify or disprove these reports. Bubbly Creek has been the favorite cemetery for the undiscovered dead, and our inquiry has been partly directed to that stream. In our inquiry we have been assisted by the Stock Yard officials and workers, by adjacent property owners and residents, by private detective bureaus, the Police Department, Department of Health, State's Attorney's Office, by observing and intelligent colored citizens, and by other agencies, and we are firmly of the opinion that these reports, so widely circulated, are erroneous, misleading and without foundation in fact, the race riot victims numbering thirty-eight, and no more, nor are there any colored citizens reported to us as missing.

It has been said that the importation of colored labor from the South, congesting the south side residence district, caused ill feeling and friction, and was one of the causes of the rioting. The labor situation was a war condition; at the same time taking thousands of young men from the factory and shop for war service. Labor was needed, and employers turned to the South as their source of supply. Neither the Government, the employer nor the southern laborer is to be criticized for that condition. And while some friction was produced, we doubt very much whether it was in any considerable measure productive of the rioting.

Nevertheless, it was unfortunate that negroes in large numbers, and unacquainted with northern ways, were induced to come or did come to the City of Chicago without adequate steps being taken to properly house and care for them. Naturally they gathered in the south division, where others of their race were to be found, and where there was congestion, abominable housing, and bad sanitary conditions. This, with the inadequate transportation facilities, notably in the rush hour, which resulted daily in the mixing of white and colored in the overcrowded street cars and elevated trains, tending to friction and bad feeling, can be readily understood.

These conditions can and should be changed. We believe that a representative committee of white and colored people, working together, could suggest and bring about the necessary and advisable changes.

The movement of the southern negro to the North, and mainly to the large northern cities, has brought the race problem to the North. It is serious indeed, but not necessarily a great danger, unless we allow it to become so. The problem is new to the North and must be solved by northern people. This problem is so large and entails such serious consequences that this jury feels itself powerless to do more than suggest its seriousness to the civilized thinking people of the North, both white and colored, in the hope that the initiative may be taken in the solution of the race problem, which is here now and here to stay.

In our investigations, numerous visits were made to the home district of the colored population, and we observed the housing conditions of which we had heard much.

Overcrowded and unmistakably bad living conditions were found, and we were impressed with the fact that the colored people justifiably for cleanliness and health had moved in considerable numbers to the east of Michigan Avenue and to the south of 39th Street, encroaching on the residence districts of the white people. The streets mentioned have been the boundaries voluntarily accepted by the colored population to within the past few years. The inrush of colored labor from the South caused congestion and resulted in a movement of considerable extent into the white neighborhoods where homes were purchased or leased.

Unquestionably this movement was encouraged by unscrupulous dealers in real estate, both white and colored, who were interested solely in the profits to be derived.

In our opinion the situation described was not a vital or material cause of the riot, but the rioting certainly awakened the public to the changing conditions of the south side residence district, and thoughtful men must consider that unless some remedy is found and applied, the situation is fruitful of unsettled and inharmonious relations in the future.

SOURCE: Cook County (Illinois) Coroner. *The Race Riots: Biennial Report 1918–1919 and Official Record of Inquests on the Victims of the Race Riots of July and August, 1919, Whereby Fifteen White Men and Twenty-three Colored*

Men Lost Their Lives and Several Hundred Were Injured. Chicago, 1920, pp. 19–22.

11. Final Report of the Grand Jury on the Tulsa Race Riot, June 25, 1921

In this excerpt from their final report, the grand jury charged with investigating the causes of the 1921 Tulsa riot places full blame for the violence on African Americans and completely exonerates whites of any part in starting the disorders. *See also the entries* on Tulsa (Oklahoma) Riot of 1921; Tulsa Race Riot Commission.

To the Honorable Judge Valjean Biddison, of the District Court, Tulsa County:

We, the grand jurors summoned by you to make an investigation of the cause of the recent riot, and other violations of the law in Tulsa and Tulsa County, beg leave to submit to you the following report, in addition to indictments and accusations which are already in your hands.

We first desire to state that we have examined a great many witnesses in our effort to arrive at the facts; we have advertised that we desired the full information of every citizen who knew facts: We have heard every one who requested to be heard in addition to the many who were summoned to appear; we have weighed the evidence impartially; we have sought to do justice to every individual and to carry out the instructions of the honorable court.

We find that the recent race riot was the direct result of an effort on the part of a certain group of colored men who appeared at the courthouse on the night of May 31, 1921, for the purpose of protecting one Dick Rowland then and now in the custody of the sheriff of Tulsa County for an alleged assault upon a young white woman. We have not been able to find any evidence either from white or colored citizens that any organized attempt was made or planned to take from the sheriff's custody any prisoner; the crowd assembled about the courthouse being purely spectators and curiosity seekers resulting from rumors circulated about the city. There was no mob spirit among the whites, no talk of lynching and no arms. The assembly was quiet until the arrival of armed negroes, which precipitated and was the direct cause of the entire affair.

While we find the presence of the armed negroes was the direct cause of the riot, we further find that there existed indirect causes more vital to the public interest than the direct cause. Among these were agitation among the negroes of social equality, and the laxity of law enforcement on the part of the officers of the city and county.

We find that certain propaganda and more or less agitation had been going on among the colored population for some time. This agitation resulted in the accumulation of firearms among the people and the storage of quantities of ammunition, all of which was accumulative in the minds of the negro which led them as a people to believe in equal rights, social equality and their ability to demand the same. We are glad to exonerate the great majority of the colored people who neither had knowledge of or part in either the agitation or the accumulation of arms or ammunition, and recognize the possibility of such a fact as even in as public a place as a church without the rank and file of the people having knowledge of the same. We have sought to ascertain the names of the particular parties who took part and the indictments returned show our findings.

SOURCE: *Tulsa World*, June 26, 1921, pp. 1, 8.

12. Excerpts from the Transcripts of *Bee Publishing Company v. State of Nebraska* Regarding a Lynching That Occurred in Omaha in September 1919, November 17, 1921

Filed on November 17, 1921, *Bee Publishing Company v. State of Nebraska* concerns an appeal by the publisher of the *Omaha Bee* of his conviction for constructive contempt of court in publishing an article that allegedly attempted to sway public opinion on behalf of a *Bee* reporter who was awaiting trial on charges of arson. The charges against the reporter arose from his alleged activities during a September 1919 riot that concluded with the lynching of a black man being held on a rape charge and the subsequent burning of the courthouse from which he was taken by the mob. The excerpts from the trial transcripts that are reproduced below describe the riot and the events following that led to the arrest of the *Bee* reporter and the publication of the offending article.

On November 11, 1919, the Bee Publishing Company, a corporation, Victor Rosewater, and John H. Moore, defendants, were jointly informed against by the county attorney for Douglas County, under Section 8236, Rev. St. 1913, and charged with a willful attempt to obstruct the proceedings and hinder the due administration of justice in a suit, then lately pending and undetermined, by the publication of a certain article in the *Omaha Sunday Bee*, November 9, 1919. Moore was acquitted, but the Bee Publishing Company and Rosewater were both found guilty of contempt and were each separately fined $1,000 and costs. They have brought the case here for review.

The exhibits and the evidence tend to show that the facts out of which this suit arose, and which form the basis of the newspaper story in question, are substantially these:

On the afternoon and night of Sunday, September 28, 1919, the Douglas County courthouse in Omaha was beset by a riotously assembled mob made up of several thousand persons who came together for the unconcealed purpose of lynching an inmate of the jail, who was suspected of having made an attempt to commit a heinous offense against a defenseless woman. The mob overpowered the police force and other of the city officials, all of whom were assisted by many law-abiding citizens, but to no avail, in an endeavor to restore order. The object of the mob's fury was seized and lynched, the courthouse was fired and in large part destroyed, and with it most of its contents, before the mob dispersed. Within a short time after the fire, namely, November 6, 1919, John H. Moore, a *Bee* reporter, was indicted by a grand jury specially called by the district court to inquire into the facts leading up to and connected with the riot and the fire. The indictment charged Moore with conspiring with others to commit arson. Two boys, named Morris and Thorpe, were suspected of being implicated in the riot and were arrested. While under arrest they testified before the grand jury and informed that body that they saw Moore, on the afternoon of the riot, leading a gang of boys to the courthouse, carrying gasoline and oils for the purpose of aiding in the conflagration. It was mainly on this evidence that the indictment against Moore was based.

Subsequently, and while the Moore case, pursuant to the indictment, was pending and undetermined in the district court, Morris and Thorpe furnished affidavits which in effect stated that their testimony before the grand jury with respect to Moore was false, and that it was obtained by coercion and intimidation practiced upon them, while under arrest, by certain members of the Omaha police force, and by promise of immunity from prosecution. The article that is set out in the information and that appears as an exhibit in the *Omaha Bee* of Sunday November 9, 1919, and other like exhibits, purport to give an account of some of the circumstances attending the fire and the alleged unfair methods under which the testimony that implicated Moore was obtained. The article, or newspaper story in question, covers about two columns of the newspaper exhibit of Sunday, November 9, and about six pages of legal cap in the information. It is too extended to be fully reproduced in this opinion.

The following headlines that precede the article that is incorporated in the information are in large display type:

> **Boys Disclose the Frame-up—Promised Freedom by Police—Captain Haze Offered Liberty to Prisoners for False Testimony Before Grand Jury, They Declare in Affidavits—Rotten Police Methods Laid Bare by Youths—Admit They Never Saw Bee Man They Testified Against Until After Case Had Been Framed by Detectives.**

The excerpts in ordinary brevier type follow:

> Captain of Police Henry P. Haze "framed up" the malicious and false testimony submitted to the grand jury upon which J. Harry Moore, reporter for the Bee, was indicted Friday, on a charge of conspiracy to commit arson in connection with the riot of September 28th. This statement was made to a reporter for the *Bee,* in the county jail yesterday by Ernest Morris and Harold Thorpe, confessed members of the mob, upon whose evidence the indictment against the reporter was returned. Both Morris and Thorpe made affidavits to the effect that Haze prevailed upon them to perjure themselves in order to convict Moore, whose investigations as a newspaper man have resulted in sensational and startling revelations against the Omaha police department, upon a

> promise that they would not be required to serve their full sentences in jail for rioting. They were told they would be released from jail as soon as the reporter had been tried and sent to the penitentiary. When the boys told Captain Haze they never had laid their eyes on the Bee reporter, the policeman replied that he would arrange it so they could see the man.

The article goes on to say that the boys changed their minds, and that Morris informed a reporter that after they got to thinking about it in jail they agreed they "did not want to be a party to a frame-up on an innocent man," and decided to "expose Captain Haze and the other detective." The writer of the article then observed that the other witness who testified against reporter Moore before the grand jury was a notorious bootlegger and a former policeman. Then follow the affidavits of Morris and Thorpe, that were printed as a part of the objectionable article, that purport to substantiate the foregoing statements, and many other statements of like import that appear in the article in question. Besides the foregoing excerpts, the article elsewhere, as it appears in the information, proceeds to vilify the police department generally, and the police officers who testified before the grand jury, and who would of necessity be witnesses at the coming trial against Moore in the district court. It proceeds to say that whether the police commissioner or the chief of police "had a hand in the frame-up on the reporter (Moore) Morris and Thorpe were unable to say." Continuing, the article observed that the commissioner always approved of Captain Haze's methods, and that the chief of police was known to have offered to promote a certain police officer if he succeeded in "getting" the Bee reporter.

Taylor Kennerly was the managing editor of the *Bee* when the objectionable article was published, and as the head of the editorial department he directed the news policy of the paper. He said that Rosewater never gave him any orders with respect to his work, and if he, the witness, was absent the city editor or the news editor determined what articles should appear. He testified that as a general proposition a communication or a reporter's story, before publication, was edited by one of six or seven men called copy readers, day editors, night editors, or telegraph editors.

It plainly appears that the article seriously reflected upon the integrity of the witnesses who appeared before the grand jury and who would in all probability testify in the district court. It took sides as between the state and the defendant, and opinions in respect of the merits were expressed. Violent comment was indulged in respecting the evidence, and the innocence of the accused was declared. Upon its face it is apparent that a bold attempt was made to mold public opinion favorable to Moore in advance of his trial, the Bee having an extensive circulation, not only throughout the state, but in the city and in Douglas County as well, the vicinity from which the jurors would be drawn and before whom Moore would be subsequently tried. Clearly an inflammatory harangue, in the locality where the trial was to be had, so worded, would tend to hinder the due administration of justice. That a publication so worded and so circulated, under the circumstances that prevailed at the place of its publication, constitutes constructive contempt of court is well settled.

SOURCE: *Bee Publishing Company v. State of Nebraska; Victor Rosewater v. State of Nebraska*, Nos. 21314, 21315, Supreme Court of Nebraska, 107 Neb. 74; 185 N.W. 339 (1921).

13. Excerpts of Testimony from *Laney v. United States* Describing Events During the Washington, D.C., Riot of July 1919, December 3, 1923

Decided on December 3, 1923, *Laney v. United States* involved an appeal by William Laney, an African American man convicted of manslaughter in the death of a white man during the July 1919 riots in Washington, D.C. Laney sought a new trial based on the trial court's refusal to allow him to assert a defense based on self-defense. The excerpts of testimony reproduced below include Laney's description of what happened on the night of July 21, 1919, as well as the supporting statement of his lady friend, Mattie Burke. The appeals court refused to overturn Laney's conviction, believing that he could have escaped without further incident, but instead deliberately exposed himself to the crowd to provoke further violence.

VAN ORSDEL, Associate Justice. This appeal is from a verdict and judgment of the Supreme Court of the District of Columbia, adjudging appellant, defendant below [William Laney], guilty of the crime of manslaughter. The indictment charged the defendant with the crime of murder in the first degree, growing out of the killing of one Kenneth Crall, during a race riot in Washington on July 21, 1919.

The defense interposed was self-defense, and a large number of assignments of error are based upon the refusal of the court to grant certain prayers offered by the defendant relating to the law of self-defense. The court instructed the jury on this subject, but we think it will be unnecessary for us to consider the assignments of error in relation to the prayers offered, since in our opinion, viewing the evidence in the most favorable aspect, self-defense does not enter into the case.

Defendant testified as follows:

> On the night of the 21st of July, 1919, I went to the theater with Mattie Burke, and came back and went up on Seventh Street at the request of Teresa Dobbins, to get Florence and Garfield Wood. On my return to 617 Massachusetts Avenue, as I got to the corner where the Home Savings Bank is located, a large crowd that was there started to yelling "Catch the nigger!" and "Kill the nigger!" and started to chase me. I ran ahead of them down Massachusetts Avenue. When I got near to 617 Massachusetts Avenue, I pulled out my gun and the crowd stopped chasing me. I went into the back yard, and while trying to fix the safety on my gun it went off. I then put the gun in my pocket

> and went to the front again, intending to go back to my place of employment. The mob was attacking a house across the street, and were coming both ways on Massachusetts Avenue, from the direction of Sixth and from the direction of Seventh Street. While I was in the areaway between 617 and 619, the mob came across from the south side of the street, firing and hollering "Let's kill the nigger!" The mob was firing at me, and I shot in the direction towards Seventh Street. I fired to protect my life. I fired three shots. My pistol had eight bullets in it at first. There were four bullets in it when it was taken by the officials; three bullets having been fired in the front yard and one in the back yard.

The witness Mattie Burke testified, in relation to the movements of the defendant, as follows:

> Later he came running back, with a mob chasing him, throwing sticks and stones at him, hollering "Catch the nigger!" I think Mr. Laney had his gun in his hand while he was running, but I did not see him do anything with it. He ran into the areaway between 615 and 617. The crowd, consisting of 100 or more men, then started after a house on the opposite side of the street. At that time William Laney went into the back yard and tried his gun. I was with him in the back yard at the time. Then we came out to the front again. After attacking the house on the opposite side of the street, the mob gathered in the car track as though they were coming toward 617, and then Laney fired his gun. After Laney had escaped through the back way, the crowd began to break into the house, and then I escaped myself over the back fence, and I did not see any more.

It is clearly apparent from the above testimony that, when defendant escaped from the mob into the back yard of the Ferguson place, he was in a place of comparative safety, from which, if he desired to go home, he could have gone by the back way, as he subsequently did. The mob had turned its attention to a house on the opposite side of the street. According to Laney's testimony, there was shooting going on in the street. His appearance on the street at that juncture could mean nothing but trouble for him. Hence, when he adjusted his gun and stepped out into the areaway, he had every reason to believe that his presence there would provoke trouble. We think his conduct in adjusting his revolver and going into the areaway was such as to deprive him of any right to involve the pleas of self-defense. Of course, the extent to which a person assailed may go, under a given state of facts involving self-defense, is always a question of fact for the jury; but whether or not self-defense can be invoked under the evidence adduced is a question of law for the court to determine. If the facts, in the judgment of the court, are not such as to admit of this defense, the issue should not be left to the mere speculation of the jury.

SOURCE: *Laney v. United States*, No. 4000, Court of Appeals of the District of Columbia, 54 App. D.C. 56; 294 F. 412 (1923).

14. Excerpts on "Sex and Lynching" from Walter White's *Rope and Faggot*, 1929

The following excerpt from "Chapter 4: Sex and Lynching" of Walter White's 1929 book, *Rope and Faggot*, explores the reasons why sex was such a big factor in the prevalence of lynching in the American South. The book was based on information gathered by White, whose light skin enabled him to pass for white, during the investigations of numerous lynchings and race riots that he undertook for the National Association for the Advancement of Colored People (NAACP). White became executive director of the NAACP in 1929.

With the most intransigent Negrophobe it is possible to conduct a conversation on certain phases of the race question and do so with a measured calmness of manner. But when one approaches, however delicately or remotely, the question of sex or "social equality," reason and judicial calm promptly take flight. Berserk rage usually seizes one's conversational *vis-à-vis*. One can count with mathematical certainty upon the appearance of the fiercely challenging: "How should *you* like to have your daughter marry a nigger?" as the answer to any attempt at sane discussion of this phase of the race question. It is of no avail to point out that there is but a tenuous connection between sex relations or intermarriages on the one hand and ordinary justice and decency on the other. Sex with all its connotations so muddies the waters of reason that it is impossible to bring the conversation back to its more unimpassioned state.

Of all the emotional determinants of lynching none is more potent in blocking approach to a solution than sex, and of all the factors, emotional or otherwise, none is less openly and honestly discussed. Even the most fair-minded Southerner keeps away from the topic, fearing the tempest which follows its introduction as a topic of discussion. As a result, this element in the race problem and specifically in lynching is distorted by the conspiracy of semi-silence into an importance infinitely greater than the actual facts concerning it would justify. From the time of its introduction as a defense of lynching, which, as we shall see, was simultaneous with the elevation of cotton through inventions to one of the premier crops of the world, sex and alleged sex crimes have served as the great bulwark of the lyncher. . . .

This Southern excitability over so universal a fact as sex has many causes. It is impossible to trace them all to their source. But a few of them can be separated from the fabric of many patterns and weavings which is the race problem. Perhaps statement of these may serve to bring some light where there has been little but heat.

There are at least a half-dozen reasons why sex harasses the South, and especially the rural South and the anti-Negro South. The first is one that is common to most regions which are predominantly rural—the dullness of life and the lack of such diversions as theatres, moving-pictures, parties, concerts, shop-windows, and the like, which in the city leave less time for concupiscent desires and thoughts. The South has suffered more than other sections because of the fact noted in the preceding chapter—the preponderance of Methodists and Baptists to whom such diversions as card-playing, dancing, and theatre attendance are forbidden. In many parts of the South this circumstance has elevated attendance at church, sex escapades, and lynching into the principal escapes from the grim and sordid reality of work.

A second reason for over-emphasis on sex in the lynching states is that the creation of the bogy of sex crimes as a defense of lynching has made the South the terrified victim of the fears of its own conjuring. Despite the evidence of the figures showing that only a small percentage of lynched Negroes were even accused of rape, the vast majority of whites in the states where lynchings are most frequently staged really believe that most mob murders are the results of sex crimes. Having created the Frankenstein monster (and it is no less terrifying because it is largely illusory), the lyncher lives in constant fear of his own creation and, at the same time, has by means of his creation caused more crimes against the women of his race than there would have been in a more sane and normal environment.

The vast amount of advertising which lynchings have given to allegations of sex crimes has induced subnormal Negroes to attempt crimes of rape, the power of suggestion being as potent as it is. Such an aftermath to lynchings has been noted in certain instances—the idea of successfully consummating sex crimes having been implanted by the news of a lynching. The mentally deficient individual who would thus be impregnated with the thought of being able to escape punishment would obviously not be deterred by fear of a horrible death in expiation of his crime. Thus it is not at all improbable that lynching has added to sex crimes or attempts at such crimes. There is some foundation for such a surmise when one considers how infrequently Negroes are charged with such crimes in the states where lynchings have been very infrequent.

Third in the list of causes of sex-obsession in the South is the Southern white woman's proneness to hysteria where Negroes are concerned; and this is an aspect of the question of lynching which needs investigation by a competent psychologist. It is appropriate here only to report observations and conclusions based upon a fairly extensive experience with the statistics and literature of lynching. My own experience in investigating forty-one lynchings and the study of several thousand others reveals that in the great majority of cases where rape or attempted rape was alleged, the women can be divided into four classes: young girls ranging from the ages of twelve or thirteen to nineteen or twenty years of age, passing through the difficult period of adolescence; second (and this includes a considerable percentage of the alleged victims of attacks), women who range in age from the middle forties upwards; third, women who have been married for many years and usually to rather unattractive husbands; fourth, spinsters.

Fourth among the reasons is the intense religiosity of the lynching states and the primitiveness of their religion. Psychologists have long since established the intimate relation between the emotions of sex and of religion, and that the more primitive the religion, the greater is the part played by sex. Critics of the American scene from Frances Trollope to H.L. Mencken have observed in the frenzy of Methodist revivals what comes dangerously close to being a species of sex indulgence. Certainly one can find in many parts of the South numerous counterparts, male and female, white and Negro, of the woman William James describes in his *Varieties of Religious Experience* who could induce a state of rapture by dwelling upon the thought that "she could always cuddle up to God."

It is also a familiar phenomenon that the sex instinct figures in religious ecstasy in somewhat the same proportions that illiteracy and ignorance afflict the religious-minded. Given an elaborate system of taboos that label as "sinful" even relatively innocent diversions, which would absorb at least a part of the time otherwise given to erotic thoughts and desires, subjected to the explosive experiences attendant upon religious experiences, deprived by ignorance, geographical isolation, and poverty from books and other intellectual releases, and victims of a bogy of the Negro as a *bête noire*—all these handicaps reveal vividly the state of mind which turns devout Christians into lynchers, especially when sex enters the equation. . . .

A fifth reason for preoccupation with sex in the lynching states is the traditional attitude towards colored women and the price now being paid for that attitude. For two and a half centuries of slavery slave women had no control over or defense of their bodies. As chattels, their bodies were their own only in so far as their owners were men of moral integrity. In codes and practices these owners ranged from those who permitted neither themselves, their overseers, nor male members of their families to tamper with the persons of their female slaves, down to owners who deliberately used slave women as breeders of half-white slaves—combining, as it were, pleasure with business. Midway between these poles of conduct were those who permitted and even urged their sons to take Negro mistresses and thus protect the chastity of white women, a somewhat analogous practice to that of ancient Rome when Solon caused female slaves "to be brought to the city and exposed to save other women from assaults on their virtue."

Whatever may be the current interpretation of virtue, it is axiomatic that an individual or society cannot maintain for any great length of time dual standards of personal conduct which are diametrically opposed to each other. The man who attempts to maintain a fixed respect towards one group of women and indulges meanwhile in all manner of immoralities with another group may seek ever so hard to maintain such a balanced dual standard. Inevitably and imperceptibly he finds it impossible, to the detriment of his respect for the first group. And that is precisely what has happened to the South, the white South, both male and female. For more than two hundred years this moral deterioration has affected the Southern states, and from that decay arises the most terrifying of all the aspects of the race problem to the white man.

SOURCE: Walter White. *Rope and Faggot*. Reprint ed. New York: Arno Press and the *New York Times*, 1969, pp. 54–59, 62–63. Originally published 1929.

15. Excerpts from the Mayor's Commission on Conditions in Harlem, 1935

In response to the race riots that erupted in Harlem in March 1935, New York Mayor Fiorella LaGuardia appointed a commission to investigate the cause of the violence. Including among its members the distinguished African American sociologist E. Franklin Frazier, the commission dismissed the notion that communists and other outside agitators had started the riots, and concluded instead that the main causes of the disorders were racial discrimination, unemployment, and police brutality. Because Mayor LaGuardia refused to release the report, it was first made public by the *New York Amsterdam News*, a leading African American newspaper.

At about 2:30 on the afternoon of March 19, 1935, Lino Rivera, a 16-year-old colored boy, stole a knife from a counter in the rear of E.H. Kress and Company on 125th Street. He was seen by the manager of the store, Jackson Smith, and an assistant, Charles Hurley, who were on the balcony at the time. Mr. Hurley and another employee overtook the boy before he was able to make his escape through the front door. When the two men took the knife from Rivera's pocket and threatened him with punishment, the boy in his fright tried to cling to a pillar and bit the hands of his captors. Rivera was finally taken to the front entrance, where Mounted Patrolman Donahue was called. The boy was then taken back into the store by the officer, who asked the manager if an arrest was desired. While Mr. Smith, the manager, instructed the officer to let the culprit go free—as he had done in many cases before—an officer from the Crime Prevention Bureau was sent to the store.

This relatively unimportant case of juvenile pilfering would never had acquired the significance which it later took on had not a fortuitous combination of subsequent events made it the spark that set aflame the smoldering resentments of the people of Harlem against racial discrimination and poverty in the midst of plenty. Patrolman Donahue, in order to avoid the curious and excited spectators, took the boy through the basement to the rear entrance on 124th Street. But his act only confirmed the outcry of a hysterical Negro woman that they had taken "the boy to the basement to beat him up." Likewise, the appearance of the ambulance which had been summoned to dress the wounded hands of the boy's captors not only seemed to substantiate her charge, but, when it left empty, gave color to another rumor that that the boy was dead. By an odd trick of fate, still another incident furnished the final confirmation of the rumor of the boy's death to the excited throng of shoppers. A hearse which was usually kept in a garage opposite the store on 124th Street was parked in front of the store entrance while the driver entered the store to see his brother-in-law. The rumor of the death of the boy, which became now to the aroused Negro shoppers an established fact, awakened the deep-seated sense of wrongs and denials and even memories of injustices in the South. One woman was heard to cry out that the treatment was "just like down south where they lynch us." The deep sense of wrong expressed in this remark was echoed in the rising resentment which turned the hundred or more shoppers into an indignant crowd.

The sporadic attempts on the part of the police to assure the crowd within the store that no harm had been done the boy fell upon unbelieving ears, partly because no systematic attempt was made to let representatives of the crowd determine the truth for themselves, and partly because of the attitude of the policemen. According to the testimony of one policeman, a committee of women from among the shoppers was permitted to search the basement, but these women have never been located. On the other hand, when the crowd became too insistent about learning the fate of the boy, the police told them that it was none of their business and attempted to shove them towards the door. This only tended to infuriate the crowd and was interpreted by them as further evidence of the suppression of a wronged race. At 5:30 it became necessary to close the store.

The closing of the store did not stay the rumors that were current inside. With incredible swiftness the feelings and attitude of the outraged crowd of shoppers was communicated to those on 125th Street and soon all of Harlem was repeating the rumor that a Negro boy had been murdered in the basement of Kress' store. The first sign of the reaction of the community appeared when a group of men attempted to start a public meeting at a nearby corner. When the police ordered the group to move from the corner, they set up a stand in front of Kress' store. A Negro who acted as chairman introduced a white speaker. Scarcely had the speaker uttered the first words of his address to the crowd when someone threw a missile through the window of Kress' store. This was the signal for the police to drag the speaker from the stand and disperse the crowd. Immediately, the crowd reassembled across the street and another speaker attempted to address the crowd from a perch on a lamp-post. He was pulled down from his post and arrested along with the other speaker on a charge of "unlawful assemblage."... the extreme barbarity which was shown towards at least one of these speakers was seemingly motivated by the fact that these policemen who made derogatory and threatening remarks concerning Negroes were outraged because white men dared to take the part of Negroes.... These actions on the part of the police only tended to arouse resentment in the crowd which was increasing all the time along 125th Street. From 125th Street the crowds spread to Seventh Avenue and Lenox Avenue and the smashing of windows and looting of shops gathered momentum as the evening and the night came on...

From its inception, as we have pointed out, the outbreak was a spontaneous and unpremeditated action on the part, first, of women shoppers in Kress' store and, later, of the crowds on 125th Street that had been formed as the result of the rumor of a boy's death in the store. As the fever of excitement based upon this rumor spread to other sections of the community, other crowds, formed by many unemployed standing about the streets and other on-lookers, sprang up spontaneously. At no time does it seem that these crowds were under the direction of any single individual or that they acted as a part of a conspiracy against law and order. The very susceptibility which the people in the community showed towards this rumor—which was more or less vague, depending on the circumstances under which it was communicated—was due to the feeling of insecurity produced by years of unemployment and deep-seated resentment against the many forms of discrimination which they had suffered as a racial minority.

While it is difficult to estimate the actual number of persons who participated in the outburst, it does not seem, from available sources of information, that more than a few thousand were involved. These were not concentrated at any time in one place. Crowds formed here and there as the rumors spread. When a crowd was dispersed by the police, it often reformed again. These crowds constantly changed their make-up. When bricks thrown through store windows brought the police, the crowds would often dissolve, only to gather again and continue their assaults upon property. Looting often followed the smashing of store windows. The screaming of sirens, the sound of pistol shots and the cracking of glass created in many a need for destruction and excitement. Rubbish, flowerpots, or any objects at hand were tossed from windows into the street. People seized property when there was no possible use which it would serve. They acted as if there were a chance to seize what rightfully belonged to them, but had long been withheld. The crowds showed various needs and changed their mood from time to time. Some of the destruction was carried on in a playful spirit. Even the looting, which has furnished many an amusing take, was sometimes done in the spirit of children taking preserves from a closet to which they have accidentally found the key. The mood of these crowds was determined in many cases by the attitude of the police toward their unruly conduct. But, in the end, neither the threats nor the reassurances of the police could restrain these spontaneous outbursts until the crowds had spent themselves in giving release to their pent-up emotions.

SOURCE: Mayor's Commission on Conditions in Harlem. *The Negro in Harlem: A Report on the Social and Economic Conditions Responsible for the Outbreak.* New York, 1935.

16. Lyrics to Billie Holiday's Anti-Lynching Song *Strange Fruit*—First Performed 1939

Although often misattributed to Billie Holiday, an inaccuracy that she fostered, the words and music to *Strange Fruit* were written in the mid-1930s by Abel Meeropol writing under the pseudonym "Lewis Allan." Horrified by the brutality and frequency of lynchings, particularly in the South, Meeropol wanted to draw attention to the crime and thereby spur passage of a federal anti-lynching law. Meeropol brought the song to Holiday, who first performed it at Café Society, New York's only integrated nightclub, in 1939. So powerful was Holiday's rendition of the song, a British journal later described it as "one of the ten songs that changed the world." *See also the entries* Holiday, Billie; *Strange Fruit*.

Strange Fruit

Southern trees bear strange fruit,
Blood on the leaves and blood at the root,
Black bodies swinging in the southern breeze,
Strange fruit hanging from the poplar trees.

Pastoral scene of the gallant south,
The bulging eyes and the twisted mouth,
Scent of magnolias, sweet and fresh,
Then the sudden smell of burning flesh.

Here is fruit for the crows to pluck,
For the rain to gather, for the wind to suck,
For the sun to rot, for the trees to drop,
Here is a strange and bitter crop.

SOURCE: Words by Lewis Allan (Abel Meeropol) and first published in *New Masses*, 1937.

17. Excerpts from the Moynihan Report, March 1965

In March 1965, Daniel Patrick Moynihan, the undersecretary of labor policy planning in the Johnson administration, published a study titled *The Negro Family: The Case for National Action*. The study, which was informally known as the Moynihan Report, looked at the potential for social advancement available to contemporary African Americans and found that the social and familial structures of African Americans were weak and highly dependent on white society. The following excerpts from the Moynihan Report look at what Moynihan and his researchers saw as the causes of the problem and some possible means for improvement. *See also the entries* Moynihan, Daniel Patrick; *The Negro Family: The Case for National Action*.

The United States is approaching a new crisis in race relations.

In the decade that began with the school desegregation decision of the Supreme Court, and ended with the passage of the Civil Rights Act of 1964, the demand of Negro Americans for full recognition of their civil rights was finally met.

The effort, no matter how savage and brutal, of some State and local governments to thwart the exercise of those rights is doomed. The nation will not put up with it—least of all the Negroes. The present moment will pass. In the meantime, a new period is beginning.

In this new period the expectations of the Negro Americans will go beyond civil rights. Being Americans, they will now expect that in the near future equal opportunities for them as a group will produce roughly equal results, as compared with other groups. This is not going to happen. Nor will it happen for generations to come unless a new and special effort is made.

There are two reasons. First, the racist virus in the American blood stream still afflicts us: Negroes will encounter serious personal prejudice for at least another generation. Second, three centuries of sometimes unimaginable mistreatment have taken their toll on the Negro people. The harsh fact is that as a group, at the present time, in terms of ability to win out in the competitions of American life, they are not equal to most of those groups with which they will be competing. Individually, Negro Americans reach the highest peaks of achievement. But collectively, in the spectrum of American ethnic and religious and regional groups, where some get plenty and some get none, where some send eighty percent of their children to college and others pull them out of school at the 8th grade, Negroes are among the weakest.

The most difficult fact for white Americans to understand is that in these terms the circumstances of the Negro American community in recent years has probably been getting worse, not better.

Indices of dollars of income, standards of living, and years of education deceive. The gap between the Negro and most other groups in American society is widening.

The fundamental problem, in which this is most clearly the case, is that of family structure. The evidence—not final, but powerfully persuasive—is that the Negro family in the urban ghettos is crumbling. A middle-class group has managed to save itself, but for vast numbers of the unskilled, poorly educated city working class the fabric of conventional social relationships has all but disintegrated. There are indications that the situation may have been arrested in the past few years, but the general post-war trend is unmistakable. So long as this situation persists, the cycle of poverty and disadvantage will continue to repeat itself.

The thesis of this paper is that these events, in combination, confront the nation with a new kind of problem. Measures that have worked in the past, or would work for most groups in the present, will not work here. A national effort is required that will give a unity of purpose to the many activities of the Federal government in this area, directed to a new kind of national goal: the establishment of a stable Negro family structure.

This would be a new departure for Federal policy. And a difficult one. But it almost certainly offers the only possibility of resolving in our time what is, after all, the nation's oldest, and most intransigent, and now its most dangerous social problem. What Gunnar Myrdal said in *An American Dilemma* remains true today: "America is free to chose whether the Negro shall remain her liability or become her opportunity.

CHAPTER III. THE ROOTS OF THE PROBLEM

Slavery

The most perplexing question abut American slavery, which has never been altogether explained, and which indeed most Americans hardly know exists, has been stated by Nathan Glazer as follows: "Why was American slavery the most awful the world has ever known?" The only thing that can be said with certainty is that this is true: it was.

American slavery was profoundly different from, and in its lasting effects on individuals and their children, indescribably worse than, any recorded servitude, ancient or modern. The peculiar nature of American slavery was noted by Alexis de Tocqueville and others, but it was not until 1948 that Frank Tannenbaum, a South American specialist, pointed to the striking differences between Brazilian and American slavery. The feudal, Catholic society of Brazil had a legal and religious tradition which accorded the slave a place as a human being in the hierarchy of society—a luckless, miserable place, to be sure, but a place withal. In contrast, there was nothing in the tradition of English law or Protestant theology which could accommodate to the fact of human bondage—the slaves were therefore reduced to the status of chattels—often, no doubt, well cared for, even privileged chattels, but chattels nevertheless.

Glazer, also focusing on the Brazil–United States comparison, continues.

> In Brazil, the slave had many more rights than in the United States: he could legally marry, he could, indeed had to, be baptized and become a member of the Catholic Church, his family could not be broken up for sale, and he had many days on which he could either rest or earn money to buy his freedom. The Government encouraged manumission, and the freedom of infants could often be purchased for a small sum at the baptismal font. In short: the Brazilian slave knew he was a man, and that he differed in degree, not in kind, from his master.
>
> [In the United States,] the slave was totally removed from the protection of organized society (compare the elaborate provisions for the protection of slaves in the Bible), his existence as a human being was given no recognition by any religious or secular agency, he was totally ignorant of and completely cut off from his past, and he was offered absolutely no hope for the future. His children could be sold, his marriage was not recognized, his wife could be violated or sold (there was something comic about calling the woman with whom the master permitted him to live a "wife"), and he could also be subject, without redress, to frightful barbarities—there were presumably as many sadists among slaveowners, men and women, as there are in other groups. The slave could not, by law, be taught to read or write; he could not practice any religion without the permission of his master, and could never meet with his fellows, for religious or any other purposes, except in the presence of a white; and finally, if a master wished to free him, every legal obstacle was used to thwart such action. This was not what slavery meant in the ancient world, in medieval and early modern Europe, or in Brazil and the West Indies.
>
> More important, American slavery was also awful in its effects. If we compared the present situation of the American Negro with that of, let us say, Brazilian Negroes (who were slaves 20 years longer), we begin to suspect that the differences are the result of very different patterns of slavery. Today the Brazilian Negroes are Brazilians; though most are poor and do the hard and dirty work of the country, as Negroes do in the United States, they are not cut off from society. They reach into its highest strata, merging there—in smaller and smaller numbers, it is true, but with complete acceptance—with other Brazilians of all kinds. The relations between Negroes and whites in Brazil show nothing of the mass irrationality that prevails in this country.

Stanley M. Elkins, drawing on the aberrant behavior of the prisoners in Nazi concentration camps, drew an elaborate parallel between the two institutions. This thesis has been summarized as follows by Thomas Pettigrew:

> Both were closed systems, with little chance of manumission, emphasis on survival, and a single, omnipresent authority. The profound personality change created by Nazi internment, as independently reported by a number of psychologists and psychiatrists who survived, was toward childishness and total acceptance of the SS guards as father-figures—a syndrome strikingly similar to the "Sambo" caricature of the Southern slave. Nineteenth-century racists readily believed that the "Sambo" personality was simply an inborn racial type. Yet no African anthropological data have ever shown any personality type resembling Sambo; and the concentration camps molded the equivalent personality pattern in a wide variety of Caucasian prisoners. Nor was Sambo merely a product of "slavery" in the abstract, for the less devastating Latin American system never developed such a type.
>
> Extending this line of reasoning, psychologists point out that slavery in all its forms sharply lowered the need for achievement in slaves... Negroes in bondage, stripped of their African heritage, were placed in a completely dependent role. All of their rewards came, not from individual initiative and enterprise, but from absolute obedience—a situation that severely depresses the need for achievement among all peoples. Most important of all, slavery vitiated family life... Since many slaveowners neither fostered Christian marriage among their slave couples nor hesitated to separate them on the auction block, the slave household often developed a fatherless matrifocal (mother-centered) pattern.

The Reconstruction

With the emancipation of the slaves, the Negro American family began to form in the United States on a widespread scale. But it did so in an atmosphere markedly different from that which has produced the white American family.

The Negro was given liberty, but not equality. Life remained hazardous and marginal. Of the greatest importance, the Negro male, particularly in the South, became an object of intense hostility, an attitude unquestionably based in some measure of fear.

When Jim Crow made its appearance towards the end of the 19th century, it may be speculated that it was the Negro male who was most humiliated thereby; the male was more likely to use public facilities, which rapidly became segregated once the process began, and just as important, segregation, and the submissiveness it exacts, is surely more destructive to the male than to the female personality. Keeping the Negro "in his place" can be translated as keeping the Negro male in his place: the female was not a threat to anyone.

Unquestionably, these events worked against the emergence of a strong father figure. The very essence of the male animal, from the bantam rooster to the four-star general, is to strut. Indeed, in 19th century America, a particular type of exaggerated male boastfulness became almost a national style. Not for the Negro male. The "sassy nigger [sic]" was lynched.

In this situation, the Negro family made but little progress toward the middle-class pattern of the present time. Margaret Mead has pointed out that while

> In every known human society, everywhere in the world, the young male learns that when he grows up one of the things which he must do in order to be a full member of society is to provide food for some female and her young.

This pattern is not immutable, however: it can be broken, even though it has always eventually reasserted itself.

> Within the family, each new generation of young males learn the appropriate nurturing behavior and superimpose upon their biologically given maleness this learned parental role. When the family breaks down—as it does under slavery, under certain forms of indentured labor and serfdom, in periods of extreme social unrest during wars, revolutions, famines, and epidemics, or in periods of abrupt transition from one type of economy to another—this delicate line of transmission is broken. Men may flounder badly in these periods, during which the primary unit may again become mother and child, the biologically given, and the special conditions under which man has held his social traditions in trust are violated and distorted.

E. Franklin Frazier makes clear that at the time of emancipation Negro women were already "accustomed to playing the dominant role in family and marriage relations" and that this role persisted in the decades of rural life that followed.

Urbanization

Country life and city life are profoundly different. The gradual shift of American society from a rural to an urban basis over the past century and a half has caused abundant strains, many of which are still much in evidence. When this shift occurs suddenly, drastically, in one or two generations, the effect is immensely disruptive of traditional social patterns.

It was this abrupt transition that produced the wild Irish slums of the 19th Century Northeast. Drunkenness, crime, corruption, discrimination, family disorganization, juvenile delinquency were the routine of that era. In our own time, the same sudden transition has produced the Negro slum—different from, but hardly better than its predecessors, and fundamentally the result of the same process.

Negroes are now more urbanized than whites.

Negro families in the cities are more frequently headed by a woman than those in the country. The difference between the white and Negro proportions of families headed by a woman is greater in the city than in the country.

The promise of the city has so far been denied the majority of Negro migrants, and most particularly the Negro family.

In 1939, E. Franklin Frazier described its plight movingly in that part of *The Negro Family* entitled "In the City of Destruction":

> The impact of hundreds of thousands of rural southern Negroes upon northern metropolitan communities presents a bewildering spectacle. Striking contrasts in levels of civilization and economic well-being among these newcomers to modern civilization seem to baffle any attempt to discover order and direction in their mode of life.
>
> In many cases, of course, the dissolution of the simple family organization has begun before the family reaches the northern city. But, if these families have managed to preserve their integrity until they reach the northern city, poverty, ignorance, and color force them to seek homes in deteriorated slum areas from which practically all institutional life has disappeared. Hence, at the same time that these simple rural families are losing their internal cohesion, they are being freed from the controlling force of public opinion and communal institutions. Family desertion among Negroes in cities appears, then, to be one of the inevitable consequences of the impact of urban life on the simple family organization and folk culture which the Negro has evolved in the rural South. The distribution of desertions in relation to the general economic and cultural organization of Negro communities that have grown up in our American cities shows in a striking manner the influence of selective factors in the process of adjustment to the urban environment.

Frazier concluded his classic study, *The Negro Family*, with the prophesy that the "travail of civilization is not yet ended."

> First, it appears that the family which evolved within the isolated world of the Negro folk will become increasingly disorganized. Modern means of communication will break down the isolation of the world of the black folk, and, as long as the bankrupt system of southern agriculture exists, Negro families will continue to seek a living in the towns and cities of the country. They will crowd the slum areas of southern cities or make their way to northern cities where their family life will become disrupted and their poverty will force them to depend upon charity.

In every index of family pathology—divorce, separation, and desertion, female family head, children in broken homes, and illegitimacy—the contrast between the urban and rural environment for Negro families is unmistakable.

Harlem, into which Negroes began to move early in this century, is the center and symbol of the urban life of the Negro American. Conditions in Harlem are not worse, they are probably better than in most Negro ghettos. The social disorganization of central Harlem, comprising ten health areas, was thoroughly documented by the HARYOU report, save for the illegitimacy rates. These have now been made available to the Labor Department by the New York City Department of Health. There could hardly be a more dramatic demonstration of the crumbling—the breaking—of the family structure on the urban frontier.

Unemployment and Poverty

The impact of unemployment on the Negro family, and particularly on the Negro male, is the least understood of all the developments that have contributed to the present crisis. There is little analysis because there has been almost no inquiry.

Unemployment, for whites and nonwhites alike, has on the whole been treated as an economic phenomenon, with almost no attention paid for at least a quarter-century to social and personal consequences.

In 1940, Edward Wight Bakke described the effects of unemployment on family structure in terms of six stages of adjustment. Although the families studied were white, the pattern would clearly seem to be a general one, and apply to Negro families as well.

The first two stages end with the exhaustion of credit and the entry of the wife into the labor force. The father is no longer the provider and the elder children become resentful.

The third stage is the critical one of commencing a new day-to-day existence. At this point two women are in charge:

> Consider the fact that relief investigators or case workers are normally women and deal with the housewife. Already suffering a loss in prestige and authority in the family because of his failure to be the chief bread winner, the male head of the family feels deeply this obvious transfer of planning for the family's well-being to two women, one of them an outsider. His role is reduced to that of errand boy to and from the relief office.

If the family makes it through this stage Bakke finds that it is likely to survive, and the rest of the process is one of adjustment. The critical element of adjustment was not welfare payments, but work.

> Having observed our families under conditions of unemployment with no public help, or with that help coming from direct [*sic*] and from work relief, we are convinced that after the exhaustion of self-produced resources, work relief is the only type of assistance which can restore the strained bonds of family relationship in a way which promises the continued functioning of that family in meeting the responsibilities imposed upon it by our culture.

Work is precisely the one thing the Negro family head in such circumstances has not received over the past generation.

The fundamental, overwhelming fact is that Negro unemployment, with the exception of a few years during World War II and the Korean War, has continued at disaster levels for 35 years.

Once again, this is particularly the case in the northern urban areas to which the Negro population has been moving.

The 1930 Census (taken in the spring, before the Depression was in full swing) showed Negro unemployment at 6.1 percent, as against 6.6 percent for whites. But taking out the South reversed the relationship: white 7.4 percent, nonwhite 11.5 percent.

By 1940, the 2 to 1 white-Negro unemployment relationship that persists to this day had clearly emerged. Taking out the South again, whites were 14.8 percent, nonwhites 29.7 percent.

Since 1929, the Negro worker has been tremendously affected by the movements of the business cycle and of employment. He has been hit worse by declines than whites, and proportionately helped more by recoveries.

From 1951 to 1963, the level of the Negro male unemployment was on a long-run rising trend, while at the same time following the short-run ups and downs of the business cycle. During the same period, the number of broken families in the Negro world was also on a long-run rise, with intermediate ups and downs.

[The data reveal] that the series move in the same directions—up and down together, with a long-run rising trend—but that the peaks and troughs are 1 year out of phase. Thus unemployment peaks 1 year before broken families, and so on. By plotting these series in terms of deviation from trend, and moving the unemployment curve 1 year ahead, we see the clear relation of the two otherwise seemingly unrelated series of events; the cyclical swings in unemployment have their counterpart in increases and decreases in separations.

The effect of recession unemployment on divorces further illustrates the economic roots of the problem. The nonwhite divorce rates dipped slightly in high unemployment years like 1954–55, 1958, and 1961–62.. . .

Divorce is expensive: those without money resort to separation or desertion. While divorce is not a desirable goal for a society, it recognizes the importance of marriage and family, and for children some family continuity and support is more likely when the institution of the family has been so recognized.

The conclusion from these and similar data is difficult to avoid: During times when jobs were reasonably plentiful (although at no time during this period, save perhaps the first 2 years, did the unemployment rate for Negro males drop to anything like a reasonable level) the Negro family became stronger and more stable. As jobs became more and more difficult to find, the stability of the family became more and more difficult to maintain.

This relation is clearly seen in terms of the illegitimacy rates of census tracts in the District of Columbia compared with male unemployment rates in the same neighborhoods.

In 1963, a prosperous year, 29.2 percent of all Negro men in the labor force were unemployed at some time during the year. Almost half of these men were out of work 15 weeks or more.

The impact of poverty on Negro family structure is no less obvious, although again it may not be widely acknowledged. There would seem to be an American tradition, agrarian in its origins but reinforced by attitudes of urban immigrant groups, to the effect that family morality and stability decline as income and social position rise. Over the years this may have provided some consolation to the poor, but there is little evidence that it is true. On the contrary, higher family incomes are unmistakably associated with greater family stability—which comes first may be a matter for conjecture, but the conjunction of the two characteristics is unmistakable.

The Negro family is no exception. In the District of Columbia, for example, census tracts with median incomes over $8,000 had an illegitimacy rate one-third that of tracts in the category under $4,000.

The Wage System

The American wage system is conspicuous in the degree to which it provides high incomes for individuals, but is rarely adjusted to insure that family, as well as individual needs are met. Almost without exception, the social welfare and social insurance systems of other industrial democracies provide for some adjustment or supplement of a worker's income to provide for the extra expenses of those with families. American arrangements do not, save for income tax deductions.

The Federal minimum wage of $1.25 per hour provides a basic income for an individual, but an income well below the poverty line for a couple, much less a family with children.

The 1965 Economic Report of the President revised the data on the number of persons living in poverty in the United States to take account of the varying needs of families of different sizes, rather than using a flat cut off at the $3,000 income level. The resulting revision illustrated the significance of family size. Using these criteria, the number of poor families is smaller, but the number of large families who are poor increases, and the number of children in poverty rises by more than one-third—from 11 million to 15 million. This means that one-fourth of the Nation's children live in families that are poor.

A third of these children belong to families in which the father was not only present, but was employed the year round. In overall terms, median family income is lower for large families than for small families. Families of six or more children have median incomes 24 percent below families with three. (It may be added that 47 percent of young men who fail the Selective Service education test come from families of six or more.)

During the 1950–60 decade of heavy Negro migration to the cities of the North and West, the ratio of nonwhite to white family income in cities increased from 57 to 63 percent. Corresponding declines in the ratio in the rural nonfarm and farm areas kept the national ratio virtually unchanged. But between 1960 and 1963, median nonwhite family income slipped from 55 percent to 53 percent of white income. The drop occurred in three regions, with only the South, where a larger proportion of Negro families have more than one earner, showing a slight improvement.

Because in general terms Negro families have the largest number of children and the lowest incomes, many Negro fathers literally cannot support their families. Because the father is either not present, is unemployed, or makes such a low wage, the Negro woman goes to work. Fifty-six percent of Negro women, age 25 to 64, are in the work force, against 42 percent of white women. This dependence on the mother's income undermines the position of the father and deprives the children of the kind of attention, particularly in school matters, which is now a standard feature of middle-class upbringing.

The Dimensions Grow

The dimensions of the problems of Negro Americans are compounded by the present extraordinary growth in Negro population. At the founding of the nation, and into the first decade of the 19th century, 1 American in 5 was a Negro. The proportion declined steadily until it was only 1 in 10 by 1920, where it held until the 1950's, when it began to rise. Since 1950, the Negro population has grown at a rate of 2.4 percent per year compared with 1.7 percent for the total population. If this rate continues, in seven years 1 American in 8 will be nonwhite.

These changes are the result of a declining Negro death rate, now approaching that of the nation generally, and a fertility rate that grew steadily during the postwar period. By 1959, the ratio of white to nonwhite fertility rates reached 1:1.42. Both the white and nonwhite fertility rates have declined since 1959, but the differential has not narrowed.

Family size increased among nonwhite families between 1950 and 1960—as much for those without fathers as for those with fathers. Average family size changed little among white families, with a slight increase in the size of husband-wife families balanced by a decline in the size of families without fathers.

Negro women not only have more children, but have them earlier. Thus in 1960, there were 1,247 ever children born per thousand ever-married nonwhite women 15 to 19 years of age, as against only 725 among white women, a ratio of 1.7:1. The Negro fertility rate overall is now 1.4 times the white, but what might be called the generation rate is 1.7 times the white.

This population growth must inevitably lead to an unconcealable crisis in Negro unemployment. The most conspicuous failure of the American social system in the past 10 years has been its inadequacy in providing jobs for Negro youth. Thus, in January 1965 the unemployment rate for Negro teenagers stood at 29 percent. This problem will now become steadily more serious.

During the rest of the 1960's the nonwhite civilian population 14 years of age and over will increase by 20 percent—more than double the white rate. The nonwhite labor force will correspondingly increase 20 percent in the next 6 years, double the rate of increase in the nonwhite labor force of the past decade.

As with the population as a whole, there is much evidence that children are being born most rapidly in those Negro families with the least financial resources. This is an ancient pattern, but because the needs of children are greater today it is very possible that the education and opportunity gap between the offspring of these families and those of stable middle-class unions is not closing, but is growing wider.

A cycle is at work; too many children too early make it most difficult for the parents to finish school. (In February, 1963, 38 percent of the white girls who dropped out of school did so because of marriage or pregnancy, as against 49 percent of nonwhite girls.) An Urban League study in New York reported that 44 percent of girl dropouts left school because of pregnancy.

Low education levels in turn produce low income levels, which deprive children of many opportunities, and so the cycle repeats itself.

CHAPTER V. THE CASE FOR NATIONAL ACTION

The object of this study has been to define a problem, rather than propose solutions to it. We have kept within these confines for three reasons.

First, there are many persons, within and without the Government, who do not feel the problem exists, at least in any serious degree. These persons feel that, with the legal obstacles to assimilation out of the way, matters will take care of themselves in the normal course of events. This is a fundamental issue, and requires a decision within the government.

Second, it is our view that the problem is so inter-related, one thing with another, that any list of program proposals would necessarily be incomplete, and would distract attention from the main point of inter-relatedness. We have shown a clear relation between male employment, for example, and the number of welfare dependent children. Employment in turn reflects educational achievement, which depends in large part on family stability, which reflects employment. Where we should break into this cycle, and how, are the most difficult domestic questions facing the United States. We must first reach agreement on what the problem is, then we will know what questions must be answered.

Third, it is necessary to acknowledge the view, held by a number of responsible persons, that this problem may in fact be out of control. This is a view with which we emphatically and totally disagree, but the view must be acknowledged. The persistent rise in Negro educational achievement is probably the main trend that belies this thesis. On the other hand our study has produced some clear indications that the situation may indeed have begun to feed on itself. It may be noted, for example, that for most of the post-war period male Negro unemployment and the number of new AFDC [Aid to Families with Dependent Children] cases rose and fell together as if connected by a chain from 1948 to 1962. The correlation between the two series of data was an astonishing .91. (This would mean that 83 percent of the rise and fall in AFDC cases can be statistically ascribed to the rise and fall in the unemployment rate.) In 1960, however, for the first time, unemployment declined, but the number of new AFDC cases rose. In 1963 this happened a second time. In 1964 a third. The possible implications of these and other data are serious enough that they, too, should be understood before program proposals are made.

However, the argument of this paper does lead to one central conclusion: Whatever the specific elements of a national effort designed to resolve this problem, those elements must be coordinated in terms of one general strategy.

What then is that problem? We feel the answer is clear enough. Three centuries of injustice have brought about deep-seated structural distortions in the life of the Negro American. At this point, the present tangle of pathology is capable of perpetuating itself without assistance from the white world. The cycle can be broken only if these distortions are set right.

In a word, a national effort towards the problems of Negro Americans must be directed towards the question of family structure. The object should be to strengthen the Negro family so as to enable it to raise and support its members as do other families. After that, how this group of Americans chooses to run its affairs, take advantage of its opportunities, or fail to do so, is none of the nation's business.

The fundamental importance and urgency of restoring the Negro American Family structure has been evident for some time. E. Franklin Frazier put it most succinctly in 1950:

> As the result of family disorganization a large proportion of Negro children and youth have not undergone the socialization which only the family can provide. The disorganized families have failed to provide for their emotional needs and have not provided the discipline and habits which are necessary for personality development. Because the disorganized family has failed in its function as a socializing agency, it has handicapped the children in their relations to the institutions in the community. Moreover, family disorganization has been partially responsible for a large amount of juvenile delinquency and adult crime among Negroes. Since the widespread family disorganization among Negroes has resulted from the failure of the father to play the role in family life required by American society, the mitigation of this problem must await those changes in the Negro and American society which will enable the Negro father to play the role required of him.

Nothing was done in response to Frazier's argument. Matters were left to take care of themselves, and as matters will, grew worse not better. The problem is now more serious, the obstacles greater. There is, however, a profound change for the better in one respect. The President has committed the nation to an all out effort to eliminate poverty wherever it exists, among whites or Negroes, and a militant, organized, and responsible Negro movement exists to join in that effort.

Such a national effort could be stated thus:

> The policy of the United States is to bring the Negro American to full and equal sharing in the responsibilities and rewards of citizenship. To this end, the programs of the Federal government bearing on this objective shall be designed to have the effect, directly or indirectly, of enhancing the stability and resources of the Negro American family.

SOURCE: *The Negro Family: The Case for National Action*, Office of Planning and Research, United States Department of Labor (March 1965), www.dol.gov/oasam/programs/history/webid-meynihan.htm.

18. Excerpt from the Governor's Commission Report on the Watts Riots, December 1965

Reproduced here is an excerpt from the report, titled *Violence in the City—An End or a Beginning*? compiled by the Commission appointed by California Governor Edmund G. Brown to investigate the causes and course of the riots that erupted in the Watts district of Los Angeles in August 1965. The governor also charged the Commission, which was chaired by John A. McCone, with developing recommendations for how to avoid similar violence in the future. The following excerpt describes how the riot started and grew.

---

144 HOURS IN AUGUST 1965

The Frye Arrests

On August 11, 1965, California Highway Patrolman Lee W. Minikus, a Caucasian, was riding his motorcycle along 122nd Street, just south of the Los Angeles City boundary, when a passing Negro motorist told him he had just seen a car that was being driven recklessly. Minikus gave chase and pulled the car over at 116th and Avalon, in a predominantly Negro neighborhood, near but not in Watts. It was 7:00 P.M.

The driver was Marquette Frye, a 21-year-old Negro, and his older brother, Ronald, 22, was a passenger. Minikus asked Marquette to get out and take the standard Highway Patrol sobriety test. Frye failed the test, and at 7:05 P.M., Minikus told him he was under arrest. He radioed for his motorcycle partner, for a car to take Marquette to jail, and a tow truck to take the car away.

They were two blocks from the Frye home, in an area of two-story apartment buildings and numerous small family residences. Because it was a very warm evening, many of the residents were outside.

Ronald Frye, having been told he could not take the car when Marquette was taken to jail, went to get their mother so that she could claim the car. They returned to the scene about 7:15 P.M. as the second motorcycle patrolman, the patrol car, and tow truck arrived. The original group of 25 to 50 curious spectators had grown to 250 to 300 persons.

Mrs. Frye approached Marquette and scolded him for drinking. Marquette, who until then had been peaceful and cooperative, pushed her away and moved toward the crowd, cursing and shouting at the officers that they would have to kill him to take him to jail. The patrolmen pursued Marquette and he resisted.

The watching crowd became hostile, and one of the patrolmen radioed for more help. Within minutes, three more highway patrolmen arrived.

Minikus and his partner were now struggling with both Frye brothers. Mrs. Frye, now belligerent, jumped on the back of one of the officers and ripped his shirt. In an attempt to subdue Marquette, one officer swung at his shoulder with a night stick, missed, and struck him on the forehead, inflicting a minor cut. By 7:23 P.M., all three of the Fryes were under arrest, and other California Highway Patrolmen and, for the first time, Los Angeles police officers had arrived in response to the call for help.

Officers on the scene said there were now more than 1,000 persons in the crowd. About 7:25 P.M., the patrol car with the prisoners, and the tow truck pulling the Frye car, left the scene. At 7:31 P.M., the Fryes arrived at a nearby sheriff's substation.

Undoubtedly the situation at the scene of the arrest was tense. Belligerence and resistance to arrest called for forceful action by the officers. This brought on hostility from Mrs. Frye and some of the bystanders, which, in turn, caused increased actions by the police. Anger at the scene escalated and, as in all such situations, bitter recriminations from both sides followed.

Considering the undisputed facts, the Commission finds that the arrest of the Fryes was handled efficiently and expeditiously. The sobriety test administered by the California Highway Patrol and its use of a transportation vehicle for the prisoner and a tow truck to remove his car are in accordance with the practices of other law enforcement agencies, including the Los Angeles Police Department.

The Spitting Incident

As the officers were leaving the scene, someone in the crowd spat on one of them. They stopped withdrawing and two highway patrolmen went into the crowd and arrested a young Negro woman and a man who was said to have been inciting the crowd to violence when the officers were arresting her. Although the wisdom of stopping the withdrawal to make these arrests has been questioned, the Commission finds no basis for criticizing the judgment of the officers on the scene.

Following these arrests, all officers withdrew at 7:40 P.M. As the last police car left the scene, it was stoned by the now irate mob.

As has happened so frequently in riots in other cities, inflated and distorted rumors concerning the arrests spread quickly to adjacent areas. The young woman arrested for spitting was wearing a barber's smock, and the false rumor spread throughout the area that she was pregnant and had been abused by police. Erroneous reports were also circulated concerning the treatment of the Fryes at the arrest scene.

The crowd did not disperse, but ranged in small groups up and down the street, although never more than a few blocks from the arrest scene. Between 8:15 P.M. and midnight, the mob stoned automobiles, pulled Caucasian motorists out of their cars and beat them, and menaced a police field command post which had been set up in the area. By 1:00 A.M., the outbreak seemed to be under control but, until early morning hours, there were sporadic reports of unruly mobs, vandalism, and rock throwing. Twenty-nine persons were arrested.

A Meeting Misfires

On Thursday morning, there was an uneasy calm, but it was obvious that tensions were still high. A strong expectancy of further trouble kept the atmosphere tense in the judgment of both police and Negro leaders. The actions by many individuals, both Negro and white, during Thursday, as well as at other times, to attempt to control the riots are commendable. We have heard many vivid and impressive accounts of the work of Negro leaders, social workers, probation officers, churchmen, teachers, and businessmen in their attempts to persuade the people to desist from their illegal activities, to stay in their houses and off the street, and to restore order.

However, the meeting called by the Los Angeles County Human Relations Commission, at the request of county officials, for the purpose of lowering the temperature misfired. That meeting was held beginning about 2:00 P.M. in an auditorium at Athens Park, eleven blocks from the scene of the arrest. It brought together every available representative of neighborhood groups and Negro leaders to discuss the problem. Members of the press, television, and radio covered the meeting. Various elected officials participated and members of the Los Angeles Police Department, Sheriff's Office and District Attorney's Office were in attendance as observers.

Several community leaders asked members of the audience to use their influence to persuade area residents to stay home Thursday evening. Even Mrs. Frye spoke and asked the crowd to "help me and others calm this situation down so that we will not have a riot tonight." But one Negro high school youth ran to the microphones and said the rioters would attack adjacent white areas that evening. This inflammatory remark was widely reported on television and radio, and it was seldom balanced by reporting of the many responsible statements made at the meeting. Moreover, it appears that the tone and conduct of the meeting shifted, as the meeting was in progress, from attempted persuasion with regard to the maintenance of law and order to a discussion of the grievances felt by the Negro.

Following the main meeting, certain leaders adjourned to a small meeting where they had discussions with individuals representing youth gangs and decided upon a course of action. They decided to propose that Caucasian officers be withdrawn from the troubled area, and that Negro officers in civilian clothes and unmarked cars be substituted. Members of this small group then went to see Deputy Chief of Police Roger Murdock at the 77th Street Station, where the proposals were rejected by him at about 7:00 P.M. They envisaged an untested method of handling a serious situation that was rapidly developing. Furthermore, the proposal to use only Negro officers ran counter to the policy of the Police Department, adopted over a period of time at the urging of Negro leaders, to deploy Negro officers throughout the city and not concentrate them in the Negro area. Indeed, when the proposal came the police had no immediate means of determining where the Negro officers on the forces were stationed. At this moment, rioting was breaking out again, and the police felt that their established procedures were the only way to handle what was developing as another night of rioting. Following those procedures, the police decided to set up a perimeter around the center of trouble and keep all crowd activity within that area.

An Alert Is Sounded

About 5:00 P.M. Thursday, after receiving a report on the Athens Park meeting, Police Chief William H. Parker called Lt. Gen. Roderic Hill, the Adjutant General of the California National Guard in Sacramento, and told him that the Guard might be needed. This step was taken pursuant to a procedure instituted by Governor Brown and agreed upon in 1963 and 1964 between the Los Angeles Police Department, the Governor and the Guard. It was an alert that the Guard might be needed.

Pursuant to the agreed-upon procedure, General Hill sent Colonel Robert Quick to Los Angeles to work as liaison officer. He also alerted the commanders of the 40th Armored Division located in Southern California to the possibility of being called. In addition, in the absence of Governor Brown who was in Greece, he called the acting Governor, Lieutenant Governor Glenn Anderson, in Santa Barbara, and informed him of the Los Angeles situation.

The Emergency Control Center at Police Headquarters—a specially outfitted command post—was opened at 7:30 P.M. on Thursday. That day, one hundred and ninety deputy sheriffs were asked for and assigned. Between 6:45 and 7:15 P.M., crowds at the scene of the trouble of the night before had grown to more than 1,000. Firemen who came into the area to fight fires in three overturned automobiles were shot at and bombarded with rocks. The first fire in a commercial establishment was set only one block from the location of the Frye arrests, and police had to hold back rioters as firemen fought the blaze.

Shortly before midnight, rock-throwing and looting crowds for the first time ranged outside the perimeter. Five hundred police officers, deputy sheriffs and highway patrolmen used various techniques, including fender-to-fender sweeps by police cars, in seeking to disperse the mob. By 4:00 A.M. Friday, the police department felt that the situation was at least for the moment under control. At 5:09 A.M., officers were withdrawn from emergency perimeter control.

During the evening on Thursday, Lt. Gov. Anderson had come to his home in suburban Los Angeles from Santa Barbara. While at his residence, he was informed that there were as many as 8,000 rioters in the streets. About 1:00 A.M. Friday, he talked by phone to John Billett of his staff and with General Hill, and both advised him that police officials felt the situation was nearing control. About 6:45 A.M., at Lt. Gov. Anderson's request, Billet called the Emergency Control Center and was told by Sergeant Jack Eberhardt, the intelligence officer on duty, that "the situation was rather well in hand," and this information was promptly passed on to Anderson. Anderson instructed Billett to keep in touch with him and left Los Angeles at 7:25 A.M. for a morning meeting of the Finance Committee of the Board of Regents of the University of California in Berkeley, and an afternoon meeting of the full Board.

Friday, the 13th

Around 8:00 A.M., crowds formed again in the vicinity of the Frye arrests and in the adjacent Watts business area, and looting resumed. Before 9:00 A.M., Colonel Quick called General Hill in Sacramento from the Emergency Control Center and told him riot activity was intensifying.

At approximately 9:15 A.M., Mayor Sam Yorty and Chief Parker talked on the telephone, and they decided, at that time, to call the Guard. Following this conversation, Mayor Yorty went to the airport and boarded a 10:05 flight to keep a speaking engagement at the Commonwealth Club in San Francisco. Mayor Yorty told our Commission that "by about 10:00 or so, I have to decide whether I am going to disappoint that audience in San Francisco and maybe make my city look rather ridiculous if the rioting doesn't start again, and the mayor has disappointed that crowd." The Mayor returned to the City at 3:35 P.M.

The riot situation was canvassed in a Los Angeles Police Department staff meeting held at 9:45 A.M. where Colonel Quick, of the California National Guard, was in attendance, along with police officials. At 10:00 A.M., according to Colonel Quick, Chief Parker said, "It looks like we are going to have to call the troops. We will need a thousand men." Colonel Quick has said that Chief Parker did not specifically ask him to get the National Guard. On the other hand, Chief Parker has stated that he told Colonel Quick that he wanted the National Guard and that Quick indicated that he would handle the request.

In any event, at 10:15 A.M., Colonel Quick informed General Hill by telephone that Chief Parker would probably request 1,000 national guardsmen. General Hill advised Colonel Quick to have Chief Parker call the Governor's office in Sacramento. At 10:50 A.M., Parker made the formal request for the National Guard to Winslow Christian, Governor Brown's executive secretary, who was then in Sacramento, and Christian accepted the request.

By mid-morning, a crowd of 3,000 had gathered in the commercial section of Watts and there was general looting in that district as well as in adjacent business areas. By the time the formal request for the Guard had been made, ambulance drivers and firemen were refusing to go into the riot area without an armed escort.

Calling the Guard

At approximately 11:00 A.M., Christian reached Lt. Gov. Anderson by telephone in Berkeley and relayed Chief Parker's request. Lt. Gov. Anderson did not act on the request at that time. We believe that this request from the chief law enforcement officer of the stricken city for the National Guard should have been honored without delay. If the Lieutenant Governor was in doubt about conditions in Los Angeles, he should, in our view, have confirmed Chief Parker's estimate by telephoning National Guard officers in Los Angeles. Although we are mindful that it was natural and prudent for the

Lieutenant Governor to be cautious in acting in the absence of Governor Brown, we feel that, in this instance, he hesitated when he should have acted.

Feeling that he wished to consider the matter further, Lt. Gov. Anderson returned to Los Angeles by way of Sacramento. A propeller-driven National Guard plane picked him up at Oakland at 12:20 P.M., and reached McClellan Air Force Base, near Sacramento, at 1:00 P.M. Anderson met with National Guard officers and civilian staff members and received various suggestions, ranging from advice from Guard officers that he commit the Guard immediately to counsel from some civilian staff members that he examine the situation in Los Angeles and meet with Chief Parker before acting. Although Anderson still did not reach a decision to commit the Guard, he agreed with Guard officers that the troops should be assembled in the Armories at 5 P.M., which he had been told by General Hill was the earliest hour that it was feasible to do so. Hill then ordered 2,000 men to be at the armories by that hour. Anderson's plane left Sacramento for Los Angeles at 1:35 P.M. and arrived at 3:35 P.M.

At the time Lt. Gov. Anderson and General Hill were talking in Sacramento, approximately 856 Guardsmen in the 3rd Brigade were in the Long Beach area 12 miles to the south, while enroute from San Diego, outfitted with weapons, to summer camp at Camp Roberts. We feel it reasonable to conclude, especially since this unit was subsequently used in the curfew area, that further escalation of the riots might have been averted if these Guardsmen had been diverted promptly and deployed on station throughout the riot area by early or mid-afternoon Friday.

Friday afternoon, Hale Champion, State Director of Finance, who was in the Governor's office in Los Angeles, reached Governor Brown in Athens. He briefed the Governor on the current riot situation, and Brown said he felt the Guard should be called immediately, that the possibility of a curfew should be explored, and that he was heading home as fast as possible.

Early Friday afternoon, rioters jammed the streets, began systematically to burn two blocks of 103rd Street in Watts, and drove off firemen by sniper fire and by throwing missiles. By late afternoon, gang activity began to spread the disturbance as far as fifty and sixty blocks to the north.

Lieutenant Governor Anderson arrived at the Van Nuys Air National Guard Base at 3:35 P.M. After talking with Hale Champion who urged him to call the Guard, Anderson ordered General Hill to commit the troops. At 4:00 P.M., he announced this decision to the press. At 5:00 P.M., in the Governor's office downtown, he signed the proclamation officially calling the Guard.

By 6:00 P.M., 1,336 National Guard troops were assembled in the armories. These troops were enroute to two staging areas in the rioting area by 7:00 P.M. However, neither the officials of the Los Angeles Police Department nor officers of the Guard deployed any of the troops until shortly after 10:00 P.M. Having in mind these delays, we believe that law enforcement agencies and the National Guard should develop contingency plans so that in future situations of emergency, there will be a better method at hand to assure the early commitment of the National Guard and the rapid deployment of the troops.

The first death occurred between 6:00 and 7:00 P.M. Friday, when a Negro bystander, trapped on the street between police and rioters, was shot and killed during an exchange of gunfire.

The Worst Night

Friday was the worst night. The riot moved out of the Watts area and burning and looting spread over wide areas of Southeast Los Angeles several miles apart. At 1:00 A.M. Saturday, there were 100 engine companies fighting fires in the area. Snipers shot at firemen as they fought new fires. That night, a fireman was crushed and killed on the fire line by a falling wall, and a deputy sheriff was killed when another sheriff's shotgun was discharged in a struggle with rioters.

Friday night, the law enforcement officials tried a different tactic. Police officers made sweeps on foot, moving en masse along streets to control activity and enable firemen to fight fires. By midnight, Friday, another 1,000 National Guard troops were marching shoulder to shoulder clearing the streets. By 3:00 A.M. Saturday, 3,356 guardsmen were on the streets, and the number continued to increase until the full commitment of 13,900 guardsmen was reached by midnight on Saturday. The maximum commitment of the Los Angeles Police Department during the riot period was 934 officers; the maximum for the Sheriff's Office was 719 officers.

Despite the new tactics and added personnel, the area was not under control at any time on Friday night, as major calls of looting, burning, and shooting were reported every two to three minutes. On throughout the morning hours of Saturday and during the long day, the crowds of looters and patterns of burning spread out and increased still further until it became necessary to impose a curfew on the 46.5 square-mile area on Saturday. Lieutenant Governor Anderson appeared on television early Saturday evening to explain the curfew, which made it a crime for any unauthorized persons to be on the streets in the curfew area after 8:00 P.M.

The Beginning of Control

Much of the Saturday burning had been along Central Avenue. Again using sweep tactics, the guardsmen and police were able to clear this area by 3:30 P.M. Guardsmen rode "shotgun" on the fire engines and effectively stopped the sniping and rock throwing at firemen. Saturday evening, road blocks were set up in anticipation of the curfew. The massive show of force was having some effect although there was still riot activity and rumors spread regarding proposed activity in the south central area.

When the curfew started at 8:00 P.M., police and guardsmen were able to deal with the riot area as a whole. Compared with the holocaust of Friday evening, the streets were relatively quiet. The only major exception was the burning of a block of stores on Broadway between 46th and 48th Streets. Snipers again prevented firemen from entering the area, and while the buildings burned, a gun battle ensued between law enforcement officers, the Guard, and the snipers.

During the day Sunday, the curfew area was relatively quiet. Because many markets had been destroyed, food distribution was started by churches, community groups, and government agencies. Governor Brown, who had returned Saturday night, personally toured the area, talking to residents. Major fires were under control but there were new fires and some rekindling of old ones. By Tuesday, Governor Brown was able to lift the curfew and by the following Sunday, only 252 guardsmen remained.

Coordination between the several law enforcement agencies during the period of the riot was commendable. When the California Highway Patrol called for help on Wednesday evening, the Los Angeles Police Department responded immediately. When the situation grew critical Thursday evening, the Los Angeles Sheriff's Office committed substantial forces without hesitation. Indeed, the members of all law enforcement agencies—policemen, sheriff's officers, highway Patrolmen, city Marshals—and the Fire Departments as well—worked long hours, in harmony and with conspicuous bravery, to quell the disorder. However, the depth and the seriousness of the situation were not accurately appraised in the early stages, and the law enforcement forces committed and engaged in the several efforts to bring the riots under control on Thursday night and all day Friday proved to be inadequate. It required massive force to subdue the riot, as demonstrated by the effectiveness of the Guard when it moved into position late Friday night and worked in coordination with the local law enforcement units.

Other Areas Affected

As the word of the South Los Angeles violence was flashed almost continuously by all news media, the unrest spread. Although outbreaks in other areas were minor by comparison with those in South Central Los Angeles, each one held dangerous potential. San Diego, 102 miles away, had three days of rioting and 81 people were arrested. On Friday night, there was rioting in Pasadena, 12 miles from the curfew zone. There, liquor and gun stores were looted and Molotov cocktails and fire bombs were thrown at police cars. Only prompt and skillful handling by the police prevented this situation from getting out of control.

Pacoima, 20 miles north, had scattered rioting, looting, and burning. There was burning in Monrovia, 25 miles east. On Sunday night, after the curfew area was quiet, there was an incident in Long Beach, 12 miles south. About 200 guardsmen and Los Angeles police assisted Long Beach police in containing a dangerous situation which exploded when a policeman was shot when another officer's gun discharged as he was being attacked by rioters. Several fires were set Sunday night in the San Pedro-Wilmington area, 12 miles south.

Was There a Pre-established Plan?

After a thorough examination, the Commission has concluded that there is no reliable evidence of outside leadership or pre-established plans for the rioting. The testimony of law enforcement agencies and their respective intelligence officers supports this conclusion. The Attorney General, the District Attorney, and the Los Angeles police have all reached the conclusion that there is no evidence of a pre-plan or a pre-established central direction of the rioting activities. This finding was submitted to the Grand Jury by the District Attorney.

This is not to say that there was no agitation or promotion of the rioting by local groups or gangs which exist in pockets throughout the south central area. The sudden appearance of Molotov cocktails in quantity and the unexplained movement of men in cars through the areas of great destruction support the conclusion that there was organization and planning after the riots commenced. In addition, on that tense Thursday, inflammatory handbills suddenly appeared in Watts. But this cannot be identified as a master plan by one group; rather it appears to have been the work of several gangs, with membership of young men ranging in age from 14 to 35 years. All of these activities intensified the rioting and caused it to spread with increased violence from one district to another in the curfew area.

The Grim Statistics

The final statistics are staggering. There were 34 persons killed and 1,032 reported injuries, including 90 Los Angeles police officers, 136 firemen, 10 national guardsmen, 23 persons from other governmental agencies, and 773 civilians; 118 of the injuries resulted from gunshot wounds. Of the 34 killed, one was a fireman, one was a deputy sheriff, and one a Long Beach policeman.

In the weeks following the riots, Coroner's Inquests were held regarding thirty-two of the deaths. The Coroner's jury ruled that twenty-six of the deaths were justifiable homicide, five were homicidal, and one was accidental. Of those ruled justifiable homicide, the jury found that death was caused in sixteen instances by officers of the Los Angeles Police Department and in seven instances by the National Guard.

The Coroner's Inquest into one of the deaths was canceled at the request of the deceased's family. There was no inquest into the death of the deputy sheriff because of pending criminal proceedings.

A legal memorandum analyzing the procedures followed in the inquests, which was prepared at the request of the Commission, has been forwarded to the appropriate public officials for their consideration.

It has been estimated that the loss of property attributable to the riots was over $40 million. More than 600 buildings were damaged by burning and looting. Of this number, more than 200 were totally destroyed by fire. The rioters concentrated primarily on food markets, liquor stores, furniture stores, clothing stores, department stores, and pawn shops. Arson arrests numbered 27 and 10 arson complaints were filed, a relatively small number considering that fire department officials say that all of the fires were incendiary in origin. Between 2,000 and 3,000 fire alarms were recorded during the riot, 1,000 of these between 7:00 A.M. on Friday and 7:00 A.M. on Saturday. We note with interest that no residences were deliberately burned, that damage to schools, libraries, churches and public buildings was minimal, and that certain types of business establishments, notably service stations and automobile dealers, were for the most part unharmed.

There were 3,438 adults arrested, 71% for burglary and theft. The number of juveniles arrested was 514, 81% for burglary and theft. Of the adults arrested, 1,232 had never been arrested before; 1,164 had a "minor" criminal record (arrest only or convictions with sentence of 90 days or less); 1,042 with "major" criminal record (convictions with sentence of more than 90 days). Of the juveniles arrested, 257 had never been arrested before; 212 had a "minor" criminal record; 43 had a "major" criminal record. Of the adults arrested, 2,057 were born in 16 southern states whereas the comparable figure for juveniles was 131. Some of the juveniles arrested extensively damaged the top two floors of an auxiliary jail which had been opened on the Saturday of the riots.

Those involved in the administration of justice—judges, prosecutors, defense counsel, and others—merit commendation for the steps they took to cope with the extraordinary responsibility thrust on the judicial system by the riots. By reorganizing calendars and making special assignments, the Los Angeles Superior and Municipal Courts have been able to meet the statutory deadlines for processing the cases of those arrested. Court statistics indicate that by November 26, the following dispositions had been made of the 2,278 felony cases filed against adults: 856 were found guilty; 155 were acquitted; 641 were disposed of prior to trial, primarily by dismissal; 626 are awaiting trial. Of the 1,133 misdemeanor cases filed, 733 were found guilty, 81 were acquitted, 184 dismissed and 135 are awaiting trial.

The Police and Sheriff's Department have long known that many members of gangs, as well as others, in the south central area possessed weapons and knew how to use them. However, the extent to which pawn shops, each one of which possessed an inventory of weapons, were the immediate target of looters, leads to the conclusion that a substantial number of the weapons used were stolen from these shops. During the riots, law enforcement officers recovered 851 weapons. There is no evidence that the rioters made any attempt to steal narcotics from pharmacies in the riot area even though some pharmacies were looted and burned.

Overwhelming as are the grim statistics, the impact of the August rioting on the Los Angeles community has been even greater. The first weeks after the disorders brought a flood tide of charges and recriminations, Although this has now ebbed, the feeling of fear and tension persists, largely unabated, throughout the community. A certain slowness in the rebuilding of the fired structures has symbolized the difficulty in mending relationships in our community which were so severely fractured by the August nightmare.

Source: Governor's Commission on the Los Angeles Riots. *Violence in the City—An End or a Beginning?* Los Angeles: The Commission, 1965.

19. Excerpts from Cyrus R. Vance's Report on the Riots in Detroit, July–August 1967

Cyrus R. Vance, a special assistant to the secretary of defense, was sent to Detroit by the Johnson administration in July 1967 to coordinate the federal response to the riot with state and local authorities. The following excerpts from Vance's official report on his activities describe the actions taken by authorities to quell the disorders; it is not a description of the disorders themselves or an attempt to determine the causes of the riot. After three years of what would be known as the Long Hot Summer Riots (1965–1967), Vance's purpose was to gather information that could help the government respond more effectively to similar urban disorders in the future.

I. Introduction

This report covers the Federal activities connected with the riots in Detroit, Michigan, during the period 23 July through 2 August 1967. Its purpose is to recount the sequence of events, to summarize the experience gained, and to focus upon the problems encountered, both resolved and unresolved, for consideration in planning for or conducting future operations of a similar nature. This report does not treat with the underlying causes of the loss of law and order in Detroit, which required Federal intervention.

My participation commenced shortly after 1100 on Monday, 24 July. The facts with respect to the period prior to my participation have been taken from the records of the Department of Justice and the Department of Defense.

II. Narrative of Events

The first contact between city and state officials in Detroit and Attorney General Clark occurred Sunday night, 23 July at 2355. Mayor Cavanagh, who was with Governor Romney at the time, called the Attorney General at his home and said a very dangerous situation existed in the city. The Attorney General promptly relayed this information to Secretary of the Army Resor.

At 0240 on Monday, Governor Romney called the Attorney General at his home and said he thought he might need Army troops to quell the rioting. Mr. Clark said he would begin the alert so that the Army could make preparations and be ready promptly if needed. Immediately upon the completion of this conversation, the Attorney General again called Secretary Resor to inform him of the situation and of the need for the Army to commence preparations.

The Attorney General called the President, at about 0300, to advise him of the disorders in Detroit.

At 0340 the Attorney General called Governor Romney, who reported that the situation was about the same and that he still might need help from the Army. The Attorney General said the Army could be present by late morning, if necessary.

At this point, the Attorney General proceeded to his office, where he called Secretary Resor at 0420. The Army Secretary stated that General Moore, of the Michigan National Guard, believed the Guard could handle the situation. Secretary Resor also said that the Army could place troops in Detroit before noon, if necessary.

The Attorney General called Secretary Resor at 0450 to review the situation and again at 0500. On this latter occasion, Secretary Resor said General Simmons, the Commanding General of the 46th Infantry Division, Michigan National Guard, had toured the riot area and believed that the Guard could handle the situation. Secretary Resor said he was informed that 2,000 Guardsmen were in the area, 3,000 more would be there by noon and another 3,000 were not yet called from a reserve force. The Secretary also reported again that General Moore believed the Guard could handle the situation. He reported that Inspector Gage of the Detroit Police was of the same view.

Attorney General Clark called Governor Romney at 0515 and relayed the information that General Simmons, General Moore and Inspector Gage felt the situation was under control and could be handled locally. The Governor replied that rather than take any chance, he should get Federal help. He said he had just told the press that Federal troops were requested. The Attorney General said that a written request for Federal troops would be desirable before their commitment. He advised the Governor that he would have to exhaust his resources and be prepared to say that there was a state of insurrection in Michigan or that there was domestic violence he was unable to suppress. The Governor replied that he would talk to General Simmons and advise the Attorney General later of his decision. He said the situation at that time was not as bad as it had been in Watts or Newark. He also said he appreciated the assistance he had been given.

The Attorney General called Secretary Resor at 0535 to report this conversation with Governor Romney. At 0550 Secretary Resor called the Attorney General to say that 2,400 troops from Fort Bragg, North Carolina, and 2,400 from Fort Campbell, Kentucky, were in a position to move into Selfridge Air Base, Michigan, by noon, if ordered to do so within the next 10 or 15 minutes. At 0640 the Secretary informed Mr. Clark that 2,190 National Guardsmen were in Detroit and it was estimated 5,000 would be there by noon.

Governor Romney called the Attorney General at 0650 to say that major looting continued and new fires were breaking out. He stated that no one could say whether the situation was contained or not. He said he was going out to look the situation over and would call back in an hour. The Attorney General told Governor Romney that if Federal troops were used, it would probably be necessary to Federalize the National Guard. The Attorney General went on to say that the Governor should not ask for the troops unless they were needed. He also stated that the Army had troops in a state of readiness to move and that the Governor would need to decide within three hours to ask for the troops if they were to arrive in daylight.

Mr. Clark called Secretary Resor at 0700 to report his conversation with Governor Romney.

At 0855 the Governor called the Attorney General and read a statement *recommending* the use of Federal troops. Mr. Clark replied that, under the Constitution and other laws, it would be necessary for the Governor to *request* the use of Federal troops, and to give assurances that a full commitment of State resources had been made and that he was unable to suppress the violence. Governor Romney answered that he understood and would get in touch with the Attorney General as soon as he could.

At 0915 Secretary Resor informed Mr. Clark that General Throckmorton would be in command of the Army troops if they were to be used.

At 0935 the Attorney General briefed the President.

At 0945 Governor Romney called the Attorney General and read a draft of a telegram to the President requesting troops. The Attorney General said the telegram was adequate and that if the Governor decided to send it, he should do so quickly. The Governor said a decision would be made promptly.

Mr. Clark relayed the gist of this conversation to Secretary Resor at 1000 and then to the President at 1010. The President instructed the Attorney General to tell Secretary Resor to move full speed ahead. Mr. Clark did so at 1015.

At 1046 Governor Romney sent the President the telegram he had read to the Attorney General. The telegram was received by the President at 1056 and he replied at 1105 with a wire informing Governor Romney that he was dispatching Federal troops.

At 1155 the Attorney General, then at the White House, reached Governor Romney and read the President's telegram to him. The Governor said it was very helpful. The Attorney General informed him that I would be in charge of the Federal operations. Thereupon I took the phone and talked briefly with the Governor.

At approximately 1100 I had received a telephone call at home from Secretary McNamara who said that he was at the White House with the President and wished to know whether it would be possible for me to go to Detroit in connection with the riots which had started on Sunday. I replied affirmatively, and told him that I would come to the White House as soon as possible.

I arrived at the White House at about 1150 and went to the Cabinet Room where a meeting was in progress. Among those present at the meeting were the President, Secretary McNamara, Attorney General Clark, Deputy Attorney General Christopher, Assistant Attorney General Doar and Mr. Wilkins, the Director of the Department of Justice Community Relations Service.

Secretary McNamara summarized the situation and gave me two telegrams to read. One was from Governor Romney; the second was the response from the President.... Governor Romney's telegram stated that as Governor of the State of Michigan he was officially requesting the immediate deployment of Federal troops into Michigan to assist state and local authorities in re-establishing law and order in the City of Detroit. His telegram stated "there is reasonable doubt that we can suppress the existing looting, arson and sniping without the assistance of Federal troops. Time could be of the essence." The President's telegram stated that he had directed the troops, which had been requested by the Governor, to proceed at once to Selfridge Air Force Base. The President's telegram further stated that these troops would be available for immediate deployment as required to support and assist city and state police and Michigan National Guard forces. The telegram also stated that I was being sent as Special Assistant to the Secretary of Defense to confer with Governor Romney and Mayor Cavanagh and to make specific plans for providing such support and assistance as might be necessary.

At 1155, as reported above, Attorney General Clark read to Governor Romney over the telephone the text of the telegram from the President which had been dispatched. I spoke briefly to Governor Romney and told him I would be catching a special military aircraft as soon as possible, and hoped to be in Detroit within 1½ to 2 hours. I asked if he could have a car available at Selfridge Air Force Base to take me to downtown Detroit immediately to meet with him and Mayor Cavanagh. He said he would arrange this.

The President made it very clear to me that he was delegating to me all the responsibility which he could under the Constitution and laws enacted by the Congress and that I should take such action as I believed necessary after I evaluated the situation in Detroit. He asked that I keep Secretary McNamara informed. Secretary McNamara then asked me to designate the individuals whom I wished to take with me to Detroit. I designated Mr. Christopher, Mr. Doar, Mr. Wilkins, Mr. Fitt, General Counsel of the Army; Mr. Henkin, Deputy Assistant Secretary of Defense for Public Affairs; and Colonel Elder.

At approximately 1220 I reached General Throckmorton by telephone at Fort Bragg, and told him to commence as soon as possible the deployment of the already alerted and waiting troops from Fort Bragg, and Fort Campbell, to Selfridge Air Force Base, approximately 25 miles outside of Detroit. I asked General Throckmorton to meet me at Selfridge, and told him we would then proceed together to meet with the Governor and Mayor and their staffs in downtown Detroit.

At 1335, as soon as we could assemble our team, the other members and I departed National Airport for Selfridge. On the plane, we reviewed the facts which were then available and the mission that had been assigned to us. Specific assignments were made to each member of the team for the collection of detailed information which would be needed to form the basis of an objective, comprehensive and independent appraisal of the situation in Detroit and of the Federal support and assistance which might be required. Members of my team present at this time included Mr. Christopher, Mr. Doar, Mr. Wilkins, Mr. Henkin, Mr. Fitt, and Colonel Elder.

I arrived at Selfridge at 1510 and was met by General Throckmorton, who had arrived shortly before from Fort Bragg. We conferred briefly and agreed to put all incoming troops on a 30-minute alert so they would be able to move instantly into Detroit if required. We also confirmed that the necessary transportation was being assembled to move the troops rapidly into the city should they be needed. This transportation consisted primarily of city buses which had been hired by the Fifth Army. We placed a telephone call to find out where Governor Romney and Mayor Cavanagh were located. I was informed that they were at the Detroit Police Headquarters in downtown Detroit. General Throckmorton changed into civilian clothes and we immediately proceeded by police car to that building, arriving at about 1625.

We met at Police Headquarters with Governor Romney and Mayor Cavanagh; Detroit Commissioner of Police Girardin; Colonel Davids of the Michigan State Police; Major General Simmons, Commanding General of the 46th National Guard Division; and Major General Schnippke, Adjutant General of the State of Michigan, and other members of the Governor's and Mayor's staffs.

Mayor Cavanagh reported that there had been 483 fires with 23 still burning on the west side and 6 on the east side; that 1,800 arrests had been made and that detention facilities where being strained. He said that between 800 and 900 Detroit policemen were on the streets at that time (3,000 of the Detroit Police Force normally being assigned to street duty, all shifts). Mayor Cavanagh further stated that he believed local forces were inadequate to cope with the situation, and that there had been intelligence reports that there would be attacks on Monday night on the homes of middle-class Negroes, and that they, in turn, were arming themselves.

Governor Romney asked General Simmons to brief me on the deployment of the Michigan National Guard. General Simmons reported that a substantial number of Guardsmen had not been deployed into the streets and that they were awaiting instructions. I asked him what they were waiting for, and was informed that they were waiting for us. General Throckmorton and I recommended that they immediately deploy additional Guard units into the streets. General Simmons left the room to take such action.

Governor Romney further indicated there were 730 State Police available in Detroit. He said that he felt Federal troops would be necessary to quell the riots. I asked Governor Romney whether he was stating that there was a condition of insurrection or domestic violence which state and local law enforcement forces could not control. Governor Romney replied that he was not prepared to so state but had said "there was reasonable doubt" as to whether the situation could be controlled by state and local law enforcement agencies. He said that he did not wish to state that there was an insurrection because he had been advised that such action might result in the voiding of insurance policies. I pointed out that the commitment of Federal troops to the streets presented grave legal issues and that it was necessary, under the law, to have a finding that a condition of insurrection or domestic violence existed and that local law enforcement agencies could not control the situation prior to the commitment of Federal troops. He did not state that either of those conditions existed. I then requested that space be made available for our headquarters and that it be as close as possible to offices being used by the Mayor and the Police Commissioner. This request was filled immediately.

Governor Romney and Mayor Cavanagh suggested that we take a tour of the city with them to assess the situation. I concurred in this suggestion and said that I wished to make a personal evaluation of the situation on the ground in the riot-torn areas of the city.

At about 1730, Governor Romney, Mayor Cavanagh, General Throckmorton, Mr. Christopher, Mr. Doar and I departed on an automobile tour of the areas of the city which had suffered the most from the rioting, looting and burning. This tour covered a period of about an hour and three-quarters. Our tour took us through all the hardest-hit areas.

In a few areas, fires were burning but they appeared to be coming under the control of fire fighting equipment on the scene. Furthermore, there were large areas of the city where only an occasional window was broken or store burned out. In the downtown business district there was no evidence of lawlessness. The only incident during our tour of the city was a flat tire.

Upon our return to Police Headquarters, I received preliminary reports from the local Federal agencies (i.e., the FBI, the U.S. Attorney's Office and the Community Relations Service) and the members of my party.

These reports indicated that the situation was much quieter than the preceding day. The information available at this time was fragmentary and in oral form, and left much to be desired. Colonel Elder soon thereafter began to assemble data from all sources—principally the local police—on the number of incidents, both current and for the period prior to our arrival, in order to provide a sounder basis for our subsequent assessments of the situation. This compilation proved invaluable.

I was informed that there was a delegation of community leaders who wished to meet with Governor Romney, Mayor Cavanagh and me. We met with this group at about 1930. The group consisted of approximately 15 community leaders, including Congressman Diggs and Congressman Conyers. The meeting was chaired by Mr. Damon Keith, a lawyer and Chairman of the Michigan Civil Rights Commission. Mr. Keith stated at the outset of the meeting that time was short and that the fundamental issue on which the community leaders wished to express their views was the question of whether Federal troops should be deployed in the city. To the best of my recollection, about eight of those present spoke. Congressman Diggs was the first to speak, stating he believed the situation demanded immediate deployment of Federal troops into the city. Congressman Conyers then spoke, saying he did not believe the situation was sufficiently critical to justify the deployment of Federal troops at that time, and that he felt the deployment of Federal troops into the city might inflame rather than quiet the situation. He also said that he believed the rioting had passed its peak and was on the downturn. Of those who spoke, the majority were in favor of the immediate deployment of troops and the remainder were opposed. I closed the meeting by thanking the community leaders for the expression of their views on this critical question and stated that while I tended to agree with Congressman Conyers, I had not finally made up my mind and wished to meet briefly with my staff to review all available evidence prior to making a decision.

General Throckmorton and I and the members of my staff, after reviewing the available evidence, concluded unanimously that there was an insufficient basis at that time to justify the deployment of Federal troops into the city. We gave special weight to two points. First, the incident rate as reflected in the figures now available was about one-third of what it had been the previous day and was holding approximately level.... Second, there were now three times as many National Guard troops in the city as on the previous day and it was not clear that law and order could not be re-established with this additional force.[1]

At approximately 2015 Governor Romney, Mayor Cavanagh and I held a joint press conference. I stated publicly that I had just met with a group of community leaders and also had completed a tour of the city with Governor Romney and Mayor Cavanagh. I said with respect to the evening we hoped very much that the situation would quiet down and that by tomorrow morning people would be able to return to work. I told the newsmen that Federal troops were moving into Selfridge Air Force Base and that we hoped it would not be necessary for them to be used. I said that the City of Detroit and the State of Michigan had an excellent police force and National Guard. I noted that these forces were on the streets at the present time, and said I was hopeful that it would be possible to contain the situation during the night without the necessity of using Federal troops. I further said the Governor, the Mayor and I would continue to follow the situation throughout the entire night and that I would take whatever action might be required.

Governor Romney then stated that he thought the situation was more hopeful that night as a result of these basic facts—number one, the Army was at Selfridge and available to give assistance if necessary; number two, the effort throughout the community, including the police and National Guard, was better organized than the night before; number three, about three times as many National Guardsmen were available for duty in the streets as the night before; and, number four, the fire fighting organization, including units from adjacent communities, unlike the preceding night, was ... available to deal with that aspect of the situation. He also cited a rising desire on the part of people throughout the community to see the disorder and lawlessness ended. The Governor urged everyone in the community to work for the restoration of law and order and the reestablishment of community life on a peaceful basis, and suggested it might be possible the next day to lift the emergency bans. Mayor Cavanagh stated that although he saw some hopeful signs that didn't exist yesterday, he would still like to see the Federal troops committed at this point.

Following the news conference, we returned to our headquarters room, which was located immediately adjacent to the Press Room and to the Police Commissioner's office, from which Mayor Cavanagh was operating. Governor Romney had an office a few doors away on the same floor. Shortly after the press conference at about 2030, Governor Romney came into my office and stated privately that it would soon be dark and that he felt strongly that Federal troops should be deployed into the city before nightfall. I told him that I was still not satisfied that the situation could not be controlled by the local law enforcement agencies but that we would follow the matter on a continuous basis as the evening developed. General Throckmorton and I continued to follow the reports of incidents, both by type and number, on a one-half hour basis as reports were received from the police and other sources. Between this time and 2100, the incident rate data began to climb.[2]... Most of the incidents, as reported over the police net, were cases of arson or looting. As the incident rate continued to increase, General Throckmorton and I decided at about 2130 that we should move three battalions of paratroopers to the Fairgrounds within the Metropolitan area of Detroit so they might be more readily available in case they should have to be deployed into the streets. General Throckmorton gave the necessary orders to implement this decision. During the next hour and one-half the incidents throughout the city, as reported over police radio, continued a steady rise. Just before 2300, General Throckmorton and I, after further consultation with Governor Romney and Mayor Cavanagh, determined that the local law enforcement agencies could not control the situation. The Governor and the Mayor both now informed me that they had committed all available police and National Guard forces. At approximately 2310, I recommended to the President, with the concurrence of all of the members of my team, that Federal troops be deployed into the streets.

At 2320, the President signed the Proclamation and Executive Order authorizing the use of Federal troops in the City of Detroit and Federalizing the Army and Air National Guard of the State of Michigan. I made a public statement at a news conference about 2325 announcing the action which was being taken; General Throckmorton immediately took command of all the military forces. He ordered the deployment of Regular U.S. Army forces into the eastern half of the city, with the responsibility for the western half assigned to the Michigan National Guard. The rules of engagement issued to all troops under Federal control were to use the minimum force necessary to restore law and order. Specifically the troop commanders were instructed to apply force in the following order of priority:

a) Unloaded rifles with bayonets fixed and sheathed
b) Unloaded rifles with bare bayonets fixed
c) Riot control agent CS—tear gas
d) Loaded rifles with bare bayonets fixed

Immediately after the President signed the Executive Order, General Throckmorton called Major General Simmons to inform him that he was under General Throckmorton's command and requested him to stand by at his headquarters for a visit, and to send a liaison officer to General Throckmorton's office at Police Headquarters. General Throckmorton then drove to the Fairgrounds where he contacted Major General Seitz, Commander of the Federal troops (Task Force 82) and instructed him to assume responsibility from the 46th Division (National Guard) for the restoration of law and order in the eastern half of the city—east of Woodward Avenue. The time of changeover would be mutually agreed upon by the commanders concerned.

From the Fairgrounds, General Throckmorton preceded to the 46th Division CP at the Artillery Guard Armory where he issued instructions to General Simmons, relieving him of responsibility for the east side of town and charged him with retaining responsibility for the west side. Prior to General Throckmorton's departure from the 46th Division CP, General Seitz arrived to coordinate with General Simmons.

During the inspection tour which we had taken with the Mayor and Governor commencing at 1730, we visited three areas which had been harder hit by the disturbances than any others. These were in the 2d Precinct along Grand River Avenue, the area around 12th Street north of Grand River Avenue in the 10th Precinct and the area around Mack Avenue in the 5th Precinct in the eastern part of the city.... Of the three areas, 12th Street had been the hardest hit; however, as it became dark the incidents in the eastern half of the city began to increase over those in the western part of the city. Thus, at the time the decision was made to assign TF 82 to the eastern portion of the city, it appeared that the Regular troops were taking over the most active sector. Other factors influencing the decision to assign the eastern portion to TF 82 were the closer proximity of eastern Detroit to Selfridge and the proximity of the 46th Division CP to western Detroit.

At 0410 on Tuesday, 25 July, TF 82 completed relief of the 46th National Guard Division elements in that portion of the city east of Woodward Avenue, and the remainder of the Federal troops were moved from Selfridge to the Fairgrounds....

At 0225, General Throckmorton and I made a statement to the press outlining the situation and delineating the areas of responsibility of the Federal and National Guard troop units. General Throckmorton and I made another tour of the city beginning at 0330. On our return we held another press conference at 0520 at Police Headquarters. Our objective was to keep the public fully informed of all developments connected with the restoration of law and order to Detroit.

Based on the situation as I saw it then, I proposed to Governor Romney and Mayor Cavanagh that a joint announcement be made to the effect that Detroit industrial plants, businesses and offices should be reopened that day. They concurred and such a statement was released at 0703.

Throughout the morning of Tuesday, 25 July, the members of my group and I participated in a series of discussions with state and city officials and community leaders concerning health and medical problems; food distribution; emergency shelter needs, processing, confinement and disposition of persons in arrest; and other matters which required consideration at once in order to begin and expedite the return to normal.

Early Tuesday morning, on the basis of a deteriorating situation in other parts of Michigan, Governor Romney requested the release of 250 National Guard troops for use outside of the Detroit area. He said he also wanted to remove 250 State Police for use elsewhere in the State. These actions were taken. Throughout Tuesday and Wednesday further releases of National Guard and police to State control were made. Adjustments also were made in troop dispositions within the city to take account of changes in the situation in Detroit and nearby areas.

The incident rate on Tuesday during daylight hours ran at about half the rate for Monday. Although it rose sharply again in the evening, the peak rate at 2300 was only 166 per hour versus 231 at the same hour on Monday. There were 11 deaths between noon on Tuesday and daylight Wednesday and about 60 fires were reported between 2100 and midnight, a rate well above normal.

On Wednesday night, Mayor Cavanagh, Governor Romney and I all agreed that it was essential that we assure the leadership of the city that law and order was being re-established and that we urge the leadership to mobilize to take the necessary steps to begin to rebuild the city. A list of those to be invited to attend a meeting on Thursday was prepared by the staffs of the Mayor and the Governor and telegrams were sent out asking them to attend a meeting on Thursday at 1500.

In view of the improved situation which existed early Thursday morning, the first steps of restoring full responsibility for the maintenance of law and order to the state and local authorities were initiated. As an initial step, General Throckmorton and I agreed that an order should be issued that bayonets be sheathed and ammunition removed from the weapons of the Regular Army and National Guard troops. This was done. An announcement of the lifting of the curfew and the easing of gasoline restrictions was made by the Governor at 1000 Thursday, 27 July. The lifting of curfew, however, was withdrawn later that day by the Governor because of the congestion caused by "spectators, gawkers and photographers" in the damaged areas.

On Thursday, additional attention was given to the definition of the tasks that needed to be performed to get the stricken city moving again. The meeting of several hundred community leaders was held at 1615 that day for the purpose of discussing how best to organize to meet this challenge. General Throckmorton and I gave brief situation reports on the status of law and order and on Federal actions being taken to provide for emergency food, health and safety needs. Following remarks made by a number of participants, Governor Romney announced the appointment of Mr. Joseph L. Hudson, Jr. to head a broadly based committee of community leaders to proceed with the development of recovery plans for the city.

By Friday morning, the situation had improved sufficiently so that, after coordination with Governor Romney and Mayor Cavanagh, the first steps could be taken in the withdrawal of Federal troops from Detroit. Units of TF 82 were withdrawn from the First, Seventh and Thirteenth Precincts and were assembled at City Airport and the Fairgrounds. Their sectors were taken over by National Guard troops of the 46th Infantry Division. The 5th precinct remained under the responsibility of the Regular U.S. Army forces.

I met with Governor Romney and Mayor Cavanagh on Friday morning, in accordance with the President's telegram of 27 July to discuss further the emergency health, food and safety needs of the citizens of Detroit. At 1200 we announced results of these discussions at a joint press conference. These matters are discussed further in a later section of the report.

At 1230, Mr. Christopher, Mr. Doar and I met with Governor Romney, Mayor Cavanagh and state, city and county legal and judicial authorities to review the problems associated with the large numbers of persons in custody and awaiting disposition. These matters are discussed in some detail later in the report.

On Saturday morning, 29 July, I returned to Washington to report to the President and to attend the first meeting of the President's National Advisory Commission on Civil Disorders.

Following my meeting with the Commission, a news conference was held at which I announced the Small Business Administration's declaration of Detroit as a disaster area. This declaration had the effect of authorizing low interest (3%) long-term (30 year) loans for repairing or replacing small businesses, homes and personal property destroyed or damaged by the riots.

I returned to Detroit at 2040 that night and met with my group to discuss further plans. Deputy Attorney General Christopher returned to Washington upon my arrival in Detroit.

On Sunday, I met with Mr. Phillips, Regional Director of the SBA with responsibility for the Detroit area, to discuss the actions needed to carry out the previous day's SBA declaration of Detroit as a disaster area. Mr. Phillips agreed to open a temporary office in the riot-torn 12th Street area, to consider opening an additional office in the most heavily damaged area on the east side, to supplement his personnel in the Detroit area, and to hold a press conference with me in Police Headquarters on Monday morning to announce the special arrangements which had been made. These arrangements were completed on Sunday and an announcement was made at 0935 on Monday morning. On Wednesday, 2 August, Mr. Moot, Administrator designate of the SBA, visited Detroit with members of his staff for further discussions of the SBA program and its potential contribution to the city's recovery.

During Monday, Tuesday and Wednesday, Federal troops were withdrawn progressively from the Detroit area and the TF 82 sectors were taken over by the 46th Division. On Monday, the last units of TF 82 were withdrawn from the streets of Detroit and three battalions were moved to Selfridge Air Force Base with the remaining four held in assembly areas at the City Airport and the Fairgrounds. On Tuesday, four battalions were airlifted to their home stations at Fort Campbell and all remaining battalions were assembled at Selfridge Air Force Base from which they were airlifted to Fort Bragg on Wednesday. The 46th National Guard Division was de-Federalized and returned to the control of the State of Michigan (to operate under the State Police Director) at 1200 on Wednesday, 2 August, as the last units of TF 82 were being returned home.

The curfew was relaxed concurrently with the withdrawal of Federal troops; the effective period was 2400 to 0530 on Monday night–Tuesday morning and it was discontinued entirely on Wednesday. Liquor sales, which had been suspended, were resumed outside curfew hours beginning on Monday. The return of the control of the city to the National Guard and local authorities, and the relaxation of curfew and the restriction on liquor sales, did not result in any increase in incident rates. These rates had lessened each day, reaching a low of 280 incidents in 24 hours on Tuesday, 1 August.

On Monday, 31 July, I met with Mr. Crook, Director of Volunteers in Service to America (VISTA) and Mr. Brabson, VISTA Program Officer, to review the VISTA program in support of Detroit's recovery. . . .

My principal activities and those of my staff on Monday, Tuesday, and Wednesday, 31 July–2 August, were to meet and talk with as wide a segment of the citizens of Detroit as possible in order to gain additional insights into the problems which had caused the riots and those which had grown from them. Although these meetings proved highly productive, they did not lead me to any simple conclusions with respect to the problems which Detroit must meet and overcome; they convinced me anew of the tangled economic, sociological, and psychological origins of the riots and of the enormity of the related tasks to be performed.

At 0935 on Wednesday, 2 August, General Throckmorton and I held a final press conference in the Police Headquarters press room. At that time we announced that "law and order have been restored to Detroit ... responsibility for maintaining law and order in Detroit will be returned at noon to state authorities."

At 2110 I departed from Detroit, arriving in Washington with my mission completed at 2310....

Notes

1. Some uncertainty now exists regarding the deployment status of the Michigan National Guard during the afternoon of Monday, 24 July. There are several accounts.

First is the account given to us at the initial conference at about 1625 by General Simmons, the Commander of the 46th National Guard Infantry Division. His report stated that approximately half of the Guard units were not deployed at that time. Governor Romney stated that these deployments were being held up pending arrival of the Federal troops.

Second is the report given to Colonel Elder by Colonel Phillips, Chief of Staff of the 46th National Guard Infantry Division, at about 1915. According to this account, the division had about 7,000 troops then in the Detroit area with another 700 (2 tank battalions and a Signal unit) enroute from Camp Grayling. Of the 7,000 in Detroit, 2,240 were in the Central High School area and 1,810 were in the Southeast High School area; 85% of both groups were reported deployed. Of the approximately 2,950 remaining, 300 were beginning to be sent out to accompany the fire department to provide security and the remainder were overhead, in reserve, resting or feeding.

Other accounts are based on a reconstruction of events after the fact. One was developed between the staffs of Task Force Detroit and the 46th Division on 31 July and 1 August through a detailed survey of journals, morning reports and other available documents. According to this account, there were 2,725 troops deployed under the 2d Bde, 46th Div (headquarters at Central High School), 1,319 deployed under the 3d Bde, 46th Div (headquarters at Central High School), 905 allocated or functioning, as guards to accompany fire trucks, 392 involved in command and support tasks, 1,900 in reserve or being prepared for commitment, 713 in rear detachments at Camp Grayling, and 243 enroute (at Flint)....

It is clear from the above accounts that at 1630 on 24 July there were between 2,000 and 3,000 additional Army National Guard troops available for deployment into Detroit's streets. In addition, none of the Air National Guard units were being used to control the riots. The total strength of the Michigan Air National Guard was 2,137 of which 660 were deployed after the National Guard was federalized.

2. The incident rate data must be used with caution. Although an incident was at all times described as "an event requiring police action," a review of the specific incidents logged reveals a wide range of variation and apparent validity. Substantial numbers of individual incidents which were surveyed did not bear any relation to the riot. Hence, these data may be useful to identify trends, and were used in that way, but should not be considered an absolute indicator.

SOURCE: *Final Report of Cyrus R. Vance, Special Assistant to the Secretary of Defense, Concerning the Detroit Riots, July 23 through August 2, 1967*, pp. 1–27. See http://www.lbjlib.utexas.edu/johnson/archives.hom/oralhistory.hom/Vance-C/DetroitReport.asp.

20. Excerpts from the Kerner Commission Report, 1968

In July 1967, President Lyndon Johnson created the National Advisory Commission on Civil Disorders, an eleven-member commission chaired by Illinois governor Otto Kerner, Jr., and thus known as the Kerner Commission. The Commission was charged with explaining why race riots had erupted in major American cities every summer since 1964 and with offering recommendations for avoiding such disorders in the future. Published in 1968, the Kerner Report concluded that the country was dividing into "two societies, one black, one white—separate and unequal." In the two report excerpts reprinted here, the Commission lists what it sees as the basic causes of the disorders, and assesses the role of the news media in the riots. *See also the entries* Kerner Commission Report (1968); Kerner, Otto; Long Hot Summer Riots, 1965–1967.

Excerpt from the Report Summary

PART II—WHY DID IT HAPPEN?

Chapter 4—The Basic Causes

In addressing the question "Why did it happen?" we shift our focus from the local to the national scene, from the particular events of the summer of 1967 to the factors within the society at large that created a mood of violence among many urban Negroes.

These factors are complex and interacting; they vary significantly in their effect from city to city and from year to year; and the consequences of one disorder, generating new grievances and new demands, become the causes of the next. Thus was created the "thicket of tension, conflicting evidence and extreme opinions" cited by the President.

Despite these complexities, certain fundamental matters are clear. Of these, the most fundamental is the racial attitude and behavior of white Americans toward black Americans.

Race prejudice has shaped our history decisively; it now threatens to affect our future.

White racism is essentially responsible for the explosive mixture which has been accumulating in our cities since the end of World War II. Among the ingredients of this mixture are:

Pervasive discrimination and segregation in employment, education and housing, which have resulted in the continuing exclusion of great numbers of Negroes from the benefits of economic progress.

Black in-migration and white exodus, which have produced the massive and growing concentrations of impoverished Negroes in our major cities, creating a growing crisis of deteriorating facilities and services and unmet human needs.

The black ghettos[1] where segregation and poverty converge on the young to destroy opportunity and enforce failure. Crime, drug addiction, dependency on welfare, and bitterness and resentment against society in general and white society in particular are the result.

At the same time, most whites and some Negroes outside the ghetto have prospered to a degree unparalleled in the history of civilization. Through television and other media, this affluence has been flaunted before the eyes of the Negro poor and the jobless ghetto youth.

Yet these facts alone cannot be said to have caused the disorders. Recently, other powerful ingredients have begun to catalyze the mixture:

Frustrated hopes are the residue of the unfulfilled expectations aroused by the great judicial and legislative victories of the Civil Rights Movement and the dramatic struggle for equal rights in the South.

A climate that tends toward approval and encouragement of violence as a form of protest has been created by white terrorism directed against nonviolent protest; by the open defiance of law and federal authority by state and local officials resisting desegregation; and by some protest groups engaging in civil disobedience who turn their backs on nonviolence, go beyond the constitutionally protected rights of petition and free assembly, and resort to violence to attempt to compel alteration of laws and policies with which they disagree.

The frustrations of powerlessness have led some Negroes to the conviction that there is no effective alternative to violence as a means of achieving redress of grievances, and of "moving the system." These frustrations are reflected in alienation and hostility toward the institutions of law and government and the white society which controls them, and in the reach toward racial consciousness and solidarity reflected in the slogan "Black Power."

A new mood has sprung up among Negroes, particularly among the young, in which self-esteem and enhanced racial pride are replacing apathy and submission to "the system."

The police are not merely a "spark" factor. To some Negroes police have come to symbolize white power, white racism and white repression. And the fact is that many police do reflect and express these white attitudes. The atmosphere of hostility and cynicism is reinforced by a widespread belief among Negroes in the existence of police brutality and in a "double standard" of justice and protection—one for Negroes and one for whites.

To this point, we have attempted to identify the prime components of the "explosive mixture." In the chapters that follow we seek to analyze them in the perspective of history. Their meaning, however, is clear:

In the summer of 1967, we have seen in our cities a chain reaction of racial violence. If we are heedless, none of us shall escape the consequences.

Note

1. The term "ghetto" as used in this report refers to an area within a city characterized by poverty and acute social disorganization, and inhabited by members of a racial or ethnic group under conditions of involuntary segregation.

Excerpt from the Commission's Assessment of Media Coverage of the Riots Coverage of the 1967 Disturbances

We have found a significant imbalance between what actually happened in our cities and what the newspaper, radio and television coverage of the riots told us happened. The Commission, in studying last summer's disturbances, visited many of the cities and interviewed participants and observers. We found that the disorders, as serious as they were, were less destructive, less widespread, and less a black-white confrontation than most people believed.

Lacking other sources of information, we formed our original impressions and beliefs from what we saw on television, heard on the radio, and read in newspapers and magazines. We are deeply concerned that millions of other Americans, who must rely on the mass media, likewise formed incorrect impressions and judgments about what went on in many American cities last summer.

As we started to probe the reasons for this imbalance between reality and impression, we first believed that the media had sensationalized the disturbances, consistently overplaying violence and giving disproportionate amounts of time to emotional events and "militant" leaders. To test this theory, we commissioned a systematic, quantitative analysis, covering the content of newspaper and television reporting in 15 cities where disorders occurred. The results of this analysis do not support our early belief. Of 955 television sequences of riot and racial news examined, 837 could be classified for predominant atmosphere as either "emotional," "calm," or "normal." Of these, 494 were classified as calm, 262 as emotional, and 81 as normal. Only a small proportion of all scenes analyzed showed actual mob action, people looting, sniping, setting fires, or being injured, or killed. Moderate Negro leaders were shown more frequently than militant leaders on television news broadcasts.

Of 3,779 newspaper articles analyzed, more focused on legislation which should be sought and planning which should be done to control ongoing riots and prevent future riots than on any other topic. The findings of this content analysis are explained in greater detail in Section I. They make it clear that the imbalance between actual events and the portrayal of those events in the press and on the air cannot be attributed solely to sensationalism in reporting and presentation.

We have, however, identified several factors which, it seems to us, did work to create incorrect and exaggerated impressions about the scope and intensity of the disorders.

First, despite the overall statistical picture, there were instances of gross flaws in presenting news of the 1967 riots. Some newspapers printed "scare" headlines unsupported by the mild stories that followed. All media reported rumors that had no basis in fact. Some newsmen staged "riot" events for the cameras. Examples are included in the next section.

Second, the press obtained much factual information about the scale of the disorders—property damage, personal injury, and deaths—from local officials, who often were inexperienced in dealing with civil disorders and not always able to sort out fact from rumor in the confusion. At the height of the Detroit riot, some news reports of property damage put the figure in excess of $500 million.[1] Subsequent investigation shows it to be $40 to $45 million.[2]

The initial estimates were not the independent judgment of reporters or editors. They came from beleaguered government officials. But the news media gave currency to these errors. Reporters uncritically accepted, and editors uncritically published, the inflated figures, leaving an indelible impression of damage up to more than ten times greater than actually occurred.

Third, the coverage of the disorders—particularly on television—tended to define the events as black-white confrontations. In fact almost all of the deaths, injuries and property damage occurred in all-Negro neighborhoods, and thus the disorders were not "race riots" as that term is generally understood.

Closely linked to these problems is the phenomenon of cumulative effect. As the summer of 1967 progressed, we think Americans often began to associate more or less neutral sights and sounds (like a squad car with flashing red lights, a burning building, a suspect in police custody) with racial disorders, so that the appearance of any particular item, itself hardly inflammatory, set off a whole sequence of association with riot events. Moreover, the summer's news was not seen and heard in isolation. Events of these past few years—the Watts riot, other disorders, and the growing momentum of the civil rights movement—conditioned the responses of readers and viewers and heightened their reactions. What the public saw and read last summer thus produced emotional reactions and left vivid impressions not wholly attributable to the material itself.

Fear and apprehension of racial unrest and violence are deeply rooted in American society. They color and intensify reactions to news of racial trouble and threats of racial conflict. Those who report and disseminate news must be conscious of the background of anxieties and apprehension against which their stories are projected. This does not mean that the media should manage the news or tell less than the truth. Indeed, we believe that it would be imprudent and even dangerous to downplay coverage in the hope that censored reporting of inflammatory incidents somehow will diminish violence. Once a disturbance occurs, the word will spread independently of newspapers and television. To attempt to ignore these events or portray them as something other than what they are, can only diminish confidence in the media and increase the effectiveness of those who monger rumors and the fears of those who listen.

But to be complete, the coverage must be representative. We suggest that the main failure of the media last summer was that the totality of its coverage was not as representative as it should have been to be accurate. We believe that to live up to their own professed standards, the media simply must exercise a higher degree of care and a greater level of sophistication than they have yet shown in this area—higher, perhaps, than the level ordinarily acceptable with other stories.

This is not "just another story." It should not be treated like one. Admittedly, some of what disturbs us about riot coverage last summer stems from circumstances beyond media control. But many of the inaccuracies of fact, tone and mood were due to the failure of reporters and editors to ask tough enough questions about official reports, and to apply the most rigorous standards possible in evaluating and presenting the news. Reporters and editors must be sure that descriptions and pictures of violence, and emotional or inflammatory sequences or articles, even though "true" in isolation, are really representative and do not convey an impression at odds with the overall reality of events. The media too often did not achieve this level of sophisticated, skeptical, careful news judgment during last summer's riots.

The Media and Race Relations

Our second and fundamental criticism is that the news media have failed to analyze and report adequately on racial problems in the United States and, as a related matter, to meet the Negro's legitimate expectations in journalism. By and large, news organizations have failed to communicate to both their black and white audiences a sense of the problems America faces and the sources of potential solutions. The media report and write from the standpoint of a white man's world. The ills of the ghetto, the difficulties of life there, the Negro's burning sense of grievance, are seldom conveyed. Slights and indignities are part of the Negro's daily life, and many of them come from what he now calls "the white press"—a press that repeatedly, if unconsciously, reflects the biases, the paternalism, the indifference of white America. This may be understandable, but it is not excusable in an institution that has the mission to inform and educate the whole of our society.

Ghetto Reactions to the Media Coverage

The Commission was particularly interested in public reaction to media coverage; specifically, what people in the ghetto look at and read and how it affects them. The Commission has drawn upon reports from special teams of researchers who visited various cities where outbreaks occurred last summer. Members of these teams interviewed ghetto dwellers and middle-class Negroes on their responses to news media. In addition, we have used information from a statistical study of the mass media in the Negro ghetto in Pittsburgh.[8]

These interviews and surveys, though by no means a complete study of the subject, lead to four broad conclusions about ghetto, and to a lesser degree middle-class Negro, reactions to the media.

Most Negroes distrust what they refer to as the "white press." As one interviewer reported:

> The average black person couldn't give less of a damn about what the media say. The intelligent black person is resentful at what he considers to be a totally false portrayal of what goes on in the ghetto. Most black people see the newspapers as mouthpieces of the "power structure."

These comments are echoed in most interview reports the Commission has read. Distrust and dislike of the media among ghetto Negroes encompass *all* the media, though in general, the newspapers are mistrusted more than the television. This is not because television is thought to be more sensitive or responsive to Negro needs and aspirations, but because ghetto residents believe that television at least lets them see the actual events for themselves. Even so, many Negroes, particularly teenagers, told researchers that they noted a pronounced discrepancy between what they saw in the riots and what television broadcast.

Persons interviewed offered three chief reasons for their attitude. First, they believed, as suggested in the quotation above, that the media are instruments of the white power structure. They thought that these white interests guide the entire white community, from the journalists' friends and neighbors to city officials, police officers, and department store owners. Publishers and editors, if not white reporters, supported and defended these interests with enthusiasm and dedication.

Second, many people in the ghettos apparently believe that newsmen rely on the police for most of their information about what is happening during a disorder and tend to report much more of what the officials are doing and saying than what Negro citizens or leaders in the city are doing and saying. Editors and reporters at the Poughkeepsie conference acknowledged that the police and city officials are their main—and sometimes their only—source of information. It was also noted that most reporters who cover civil disturbances tend to arrive with the police and stay close to them—often for safety, and often because they learn where the action is at the same time as the authorities—and thus buttress the ghetto impression that police and press work together and toward the same ends (an impression that may come as a surprise to many within the ranks of police and press).

Third, Negro residents in several cities surveyed cited as specific examples of media unfairness what they considered the failure of the media:

To report the many examples of Negroes helping law enforcement officers and assisting in the treatment of the wounded during disorders;
To report adequately about false arrests;
To report instances of excessive force by the National Guard;
To explore and interpret the background conditions leading to disturbances;
To expose, except in Detroit, what they regarded as instances of police brutality;
To report on white vigilante groups which allegedly came into some disorder areas and molested innocent Negro residents.

Some of these problems are insoluble. But more first-hand reporting in the diffuse and fragmented riot area should temper any reliance on police information and announcements. There is a special need for news media to cover "positive" news stories in the ghetto before and after riots with concern and enthusiasm.

A multitude of news and information sources other than the established news media are relied upon in the ghetto. One of our studies found that 79 percent of a total of 567 ghetto residents interviewed in seven cities[9] first heard about the outbreak in their own city by word of mouth. Telephone and word of mouth exchanges on the streets, in churches, stores, pool halls, and bars, provide more information—and rumors—about events of direct concern to ghetto residents than the more conventional news media.

Among the established media, television and radio are far more popular in the ghetto than newspapers. Radios there, apparently, are ordinarily listened to less for news than for music and other programs. One survey showed that an overwhelmingly large number of Negro children and teenagers (like their white counterparts) listen to the radio for music alone, interspersed by disc jockey chatter. In other age groups, the response of most people about what they listen to on the radio was "anything," leading to the conclusion that radio in the ghetto is basically a background accompaniment.

But the fact that radio is such a constant background accompaniment can make it an important influence on people's attitudes, and perhaps on their actions once trouble develops. This is true for several reasons. News presented on local "rock" stations seldom constitutes much more than terse headline items which may startle or frighten but seldom inform. Radio disk jockeys and those who preside over the popular "talk shows" keep a steady patter of information going over the air. When a city is beset by civil strife, this patter can both inform transistor radio-carrying young people where the actions is [sic], and terrify their elders and much of the white community. "Burn, baby, burn," the slogan of the Watts riot, was inadvertently originated by a radio disc jockey.

Thus, radio can be an instrument of trouble and tension in a community threatened or inundated with civil disorder. It can also do much to minimize fear by putting fast-paced events into proper perspective. We have found commendable instances, for example, in Detroit, Milwaukee, and New Brunswick, of radio stations and personalities using their air time and influence to try to calm potential rioters. In Section II, we recommend procedures for meetings and consultations for advance planning among those who will cover civil disorders. It is important that radio personnel, and especially disc jockeys and talk show hosts, be included in such preplanning.

Television is the formal news source most relied upon in the ghetto. According to one report, more than 75 percent of the sample turned to television for national and international news, and a larger percentage of the sample (86 percent) regularly watched television from 5 to 7 P.M., the dinner hours when the evening news programs are broadcast.

The significance of broadcasting in news dissemination is seen in Census Bureau estimates that in June 1967, 87.7 percent of nonwhite households and 94.8 percent of white households had television sets.

When ghetto residents do turn to newspapers, most read tabloids, if available, far more frequently than standard size newspapers and rely on the tabloids primarily for light features, racing charts, comic strips, fashion news and display advertising. . . .

Negroes in Journalism

The journalistic profession has been shockingly backward in seeking out, hiring, training, and promoting Negroes. Fewer than 5 percent of the people employed by the news business in editorial jobs in the United States today are Negroes. Fewer than 1 percent of editors and supervisors are Negroes, and most of them work for Negro-owned organizations. The lines of various news organizations to the militant blacks are, by admission of the newsmen themselves, almost nonexistent. The complaint is "We can't find qualified Negroes." But this rings hollow from an industry where, only yesterday, jobs were scarce and promotion unthinkable for a man whose skin was black. Even today, there are virtually no Negroes in positions of editorial or executive responsibility and there is only one Negro newsman with a nationally syndicated column.

News organizations must employ enough Negroes in positions of significant responsibility to establish an effective link to Negro actions and ideas and to meet legitimate employment expectations. Tokenism—the hiring of one Negro reporter, or even two or three—is no longer enough. Negro reporters are essential, but so are Negro editors, writers and commentators. Newspaper and television policies are, generally speaking, not set by reporters. Editorial decisions about which stories to cover and which to use are made by editors. Yet, very few Negroes in this country are involved in making these decisions, because very few, if any, supervisory editorial jobs are held by Negroes. We urge the news media to do everything possible to train and promote their Negro reporters to positions where those who are qualified can contribute to and have an effect on policy decisions. . . .

The Negro in the Media

Finally, the news media must publish newspapers and produce programs that recognize the existence and activities of the Negro, both as a Negro and as part of the community. It would be a contribution of inestimable importance to race relations in the United States simply to treat ordinary news about Negroes as news of other groups is now treated.

Specifically, newspapers should integrate Negroes and Negro activities into all parts of the paper, from the news, society and club pages to the comic strips. Television should develop programming which integrates Negroes into all aspects of televised presentations. Television is such a visible medium that some constructive steps are easy and obvious. While some of these steps are being taken, they are still largely neglected. For example, Negro reporters and performers should appear more frequently—and at prime time—in news broadcasts, on weather shows, in documentaries, and in advertisements. Some effort already has been made to use Negroes in television commercials. Any initial surprise at seeing a Negro selling a sponsor's product will eventually fade into routine acceptance, an attitude that white society must ultimately develop toward all Negroes.

In addition to news-related programming, we think that Negroes should appear more frequently in dramatic and comedy series. Moreover, networks and local stations should present plays and other programs whose subjects are rooted in the ghetto and its problems.

Notes

1. As recently as February 9, 1968, an Associated Press dispatch from Philadelphia said "damage exceeded $1 billion" in Detroit.

2. Michigan State Insurance Commission Estimate, December, 1967. See also *Meeting the Insurance Crisis of Our Cities*, a Report by the President's National Advisory Panel on Insurance in Riot-Affected Areas, January, 1968.

8. The Commission is indebted, in this regard, to M. Thomas Allen for his document on *Mass Media Use Patterns and Functions in the Negro Ghetto in Pittsburgh*.

9. Detroit, Newark, Atlanta, Tampa, New Haven, Cincinnati, Milwaukee.

SOURCE: United States. Kerner Commission. *Report of the National Advisory Commission on Civil Disorders*. Washington, D.C: U.S. Government Printing Office, 1968.

21. Progress Report of the Presidential Task Force on Los Angeles Recovery, May 1992

Reproduced below is the initial progress report of the task force of cabinet undersecretaries and other federal officials appointed by President George H.W. Bush to assess how the federal government could best assist the recovery process in Los Angeles in the first weeks following the 1992 riots. Released barely two weeks after the end of the riots, this report mainly describes conditions in the riot zone immediately after the disorders ended and the first steps taken by federal, state, and local officials to begin the economic recovery of the affected areas.

Members of the Task Force:

David T. Kearns, Co-chairman
Deputy Secretary
U.S. Department of Education
Washington, D.C.

Alfred A. DelliBovi, Co-chairman
Deputy Secretary
U.S. Department of Housing and Urban Development
Washington, D.C.

Robert E. Grady
Deputy Director-designate
Office of Management and Budget
Executive Office of the President
Washington, D.C.

Delbert Spurlock
Deputy Secretary
U.S. Department of Labor
Washington, D.C.

Arnold Tompkins
Assistant Secretary for Management and Budget
U.S. Department of Health and Human Services
Washington, D.C.

Robert S. Mueller, III.
Assistant Attorney General
Criminal Division
U.S. Department of Justice
Washington, D.C.

Oscar Wright
Regional Administrator
Small Business Administration
San Francisco, California

Linda Peterson
Regional Administrator
Office of Personnel Management
Los Angeles, California

Jay Lefkowitz
Office of Cabinet Affairs
The White House
Washington, D.C.

William Medigovich
Federal Coordinating Officer
Federal Emergency Management Agency
Los Angeles, California

Earl Fields
Chairman
Federal Executive Board
Long Beach, California

Gretchen Pagel
Office of National Service
The White House
Washington, D.C.

Presidential Task Force on Los Angeles Recovery
May 12, 1992

The President
The White House

Dear Mr. President:

On Monday, May 4, 1992, in response to the civil unrest in the city of Los Angeles and Los Angeles County, California, you directed that a task force of Cabinet Deputy Secretaries and other key Federal officials be sent immediately to Los Angeles to assist in the recovery process.

Attached is a progress report on what that task force has accomplished in the past eight days. We hope that our efforts to date have assisted in easing the effects of this tragedy, and in ensuring the prompt delivery of Federal, state, county, and city services.

We have been struck in conducting our work by the genuine desire for prompt recovery, and by the cooperative spirit that has sprung from the ashes of the Los Angeles fires.

The work of this task force is ongoing and will continue. We will report again to you in the weeks and months ahead. While our work has been focused on process and implementation issues, we would be pleased to give you and your Cabinet impressions and input as you develop programs and legislation to assist large urban centers. Thank you for the opportunity to serve in this important mission.

Respectfully,
Alfred A. DelliBovi
Co-chairman

David T. Kearns
Co-chairman

Progress Report of the Presidential Task Force on Los Angeles Recovery

I. OVERVIEW AND HIGHLIGHTS

On Monday, May 4th, the President established a task force of Cabinet Deputies and other key Federal officials to assist in the recovery of Los Angeles. The purpose of the task force was limited and straightforward: to knock down barriers to the speedy delivery of services to the citizens of greater Los Angeles who suffered as a result of the disturbances there, and to bring quickly to the area those Federal resources and programs which could help address the immediate problems facing the affected area.

The Federal role represented by the task force was not to supplant state and local efforts to rebuild Los Angeles, but rather to ensure a coordinated response and to make the Federal government a helpful partner—assisting in every way possible the state, county, and city governments, and the private sector, in rebuilding their community.

Examples of the work accomplished by the task force include:

- Assisting in the establishment of 7 Disaster Application Centers (DACS) to provide "one-stop shopping" for residents and businesses in need of disaster assistance and Federal, state, or local services. As demand for the services grew, the task force helped arrange for a mobile facility to expand the space available at one DAC and for the opening of an eighth DAC in an area in need.
- Removing roadblocks to the provision of FEMA and SBA assistance to those who suffered fire or looting losses due to the disturbance.
- Cutting red tape and providing special assistance to small businesses in the provision of SBA disaster loans. The task force brought in minority business specialists to help small businesses prepare loan applications and IRS personnel to assist in the prompt recovery of tax returns. The task force helped create a special expedited process at the Treasury Department for clearing SBA loan checks, and removed a hurdle for very small businesses by creating a much simplified test of the requirement that they seek credit elsewhere before applying to the SBA.
- Responding to the language problem which naturally arises in a diverse community such as Los Angeles. The task force helped arrange for the hiring of about 60 bilingual aides to assist applicants. When a shortage of Spanish-speaking assistants arose, ten were hired on the same day.
- Helping to speed the delivery of a full array of Federal services to the Los Angeles area, including rental assistance for those who were displaced from their homes, unemployment assistance for those who lost their jobs, food for those in areas with shortages, emergency funds for those who did not receive Social Security checks, and crisis counseling for those affected by the disturbance. On Monday, May 11th, three days after the opening of the application centers, FEMA mailed the first disaster housing assistance checks to applicants.

II. THE MISSION OF THE TASK FORCE

One might think of the Federal response to the civil unrest that occurred in Los Angeles as encompassing three phases. One phase was the restoration of peace and the rule of law in the immediate term. A second phase is the provision of necessary assistance and services to those who suffered losses or disruption of services as a result of the disturbance. A third phase is the crafting of a long-term policy strategy for addressing the underlying problems facing urban America.

The work of this task force has been focused on the second phase. The task force did not participate in or direct any law enforcement activities, although in the aftermath of the disturbance, the task force leadership has worked closely with Robert Mueller, the Assistant Attorney General, Criminal Division, and with Governor Wilson to coordinate appropriately with law enforcement. Nor is the task force a policy-making body.

This task force has sought to work with the state, county, and city governments, as well as private sector and non-profit entities, in speeding the delivery of services to the people of Los Angeles. The task force worked to bring quickly to the Los Angeles area those programs which the Federal government can deliver right now, under existing statutory authority and using existing funds, to help those victimized by the violence.

Most importantly, the mission of the task force has been to knock down any extraneous barriers to the efficient delivery of services to the people of Los Angeles city and county. Too often, the processes and paperwork of the Federal government are a source of frustration to citizens who confront them. The goal of this task force was to ease that frustration in every way possible—and to deliver assistance to the people who need it in record time.

III. THE PROCESS

Meeting Schedule

Upon arrival in Los Angeles on Monday night May 4th, members of the task force met with Governor Pete Wilson and his staff. Governor Wilson also met with the full task force on Tuesday morning May 5th to offer his assessment of the situation. At that meeting, he designated the State of California's Director of Emergency Services, Richard Andrews, as liaison with the task force.

Also on Tuesday morning, task force representatives met with Los Angeles Mayor Tom Bradley and Deputy Mayor Linda Griego. Bradley appointed Deputy Mayor Griego as liaison and she met with the full task force on Tuesday to identify specific problems the city had encountered that could be addressed by task force actions.

The task force coordinated by telephone on Tuesday with Los Angeles County Chief Administrative officer Richard Dixon, who designated Sheriff's Lieutenant Ben Nottingham as the County's liaison with the task force. On Wednesday, May 6th, representatives of the task force met with the Chairman of the Los Angeles County Board of Supervisors, Supervisor Deane

Dana, Los Angeles County Sheriff Sherman Block, Supervisor Michael Antonovich, Mr. Dixon, and other representatives of the county.

On the afternoon of Tuesday, May 5th, the task force met with Mr. Peter Ueberroth, who had been appointed by Mayor Bradley and Governor Wilson to chair Rebuild L.A., a long-term effort to promote recovery by encouraging private sector investment in affected areas of greater Los Angeles.

On Friday, May 8th, at the invitation of its President, Councilman John Ferraro, representative of the task force presented a briefing to the Los Angeles City Council, and subsequently met with various members of the Council.

Throughout the week, members of the task force took the opportunity to meet with members of the community, including the mayors of Compton, Inglewood, Long Beach, and Linwood, City of Los Angeles Superintendent of Schools Bill Anton, Los Angeles County Superintendent of Schools Stuart Godholt, President of the Los Angeles Urban League John Mack, various members of the clergy, representatives of the police and firefighting forces, and affected businessmen and women. In addition, members of the task force toured affected areas and neighborhoods at various times throughout the week.

The task force briefed the President on two occasions: upon his arrival in Los Angeles on Wednesday night, May 6th, and again on Thursday evening, May 7th. Also in attendance at one or both of these briefings was Governor Wilson, Mayor Bradley, U.S. Senator John Seymour, Supervisor Dana, Councilman Ferraro, Secretary of Health and Human Services Louis Sullivan, Secretary of Housing and Urban Development Jack Kemp, and Administrator of the Small Business Administration Patricia Saiki.

Coordination Mechanisms

The task force has coordinated its activities closely with the state, county, and city governments. Since Tuesday, May 5th, senior task force representatives have participated in a daily conference call with officials of the state, city, county, the Small Business Administration (SBA) and FEMA. This conference call has made possible an immediate, coordinated response, on a daily basis, to problems that are occurring in the field. This daily conference call will continue for the foreseeable future.

For the past week in Los Angeles, the task force met at the beginning and at the end of each working day.

IV. ASSESSMENT OF THE SITUATION IN LOS ANGELES

While the greater Los Angeles community sustained significant damage as a result of the rioting, the task force was impressed by the pervasive signs of hope that have arisen in the wake of this tragedy. Every member of the task force was struck by the genuine desire, at every level of government and throughout the community, to cooperate in working toward the quick recovery of Los Angeles.

The nature of the damage which resulted from the thousands of fires set during the rioting was different from that sustained in Watts, Detroit, and other riots in the 1960s. While the damage was extensive and indeed staggering, relatively few residences were burned: HUD estimates that approximately 250–300 families lost their homes as a result of fires related to the disturbance.

The principal physical damage sustained during the rioting was the destruction and/or looting of several thousand businesses. Preliminary estimates by city and county building and safety experts are that 5,000 structures in the greater Los Angeles area were either damaged or destroyed. The businesses housed in these structures provided essential services to the citizens of South Central, Crenshaw, Koreatown, Compton, Inglewood, Long Beach and other areas of greater Los Angeles. The task force believes that an urgent priority is to encourage re-investment in these neighborhoods.

Because many of the businesses which were destroyed or looted were small, family-owned businesses, without the staff or facilities for extensive recordkeeping, the task force recognized that these businesses might encounter special difficulties in completing the paperwork necessary to apply for SBA disaster loans and FEMA disaster assistance.

Further, given the emotionally charged nature of the disaster and the attendant tensions in the community, the task force was eager to minimize any additional frustration which might result from delays in processing and receiving disaster assistance. Two key objectives of the task force were therefore to assist in the application process and to streamline the approval process for these types of assistance.

The record-keeping problems of small business had the potential to be exacerbated by language barriers in the culturally diverse community of Los Angeles. The languages spoken by affected business owners ranged from English to Korean to Spanish to Persian to Armenian to Thai to Mandarin Chinese. Throughout the week, the task force worked to surmount this barrier by marshalling the resources necessary to provide effective translation services.

V. DISASTER ASSISTANCE

On Saturday, May 2nd, in response to a request from Governor Wilson on that same date, the President declared that a major disaster exists in the County and City of Los Angeles. This declaration made Federal disaster-related funding available for individuals, businesses' and local governments who had suffered as a result of the civil disturbance.

Specifically, as a result of the President's declaration, SBA is making available direct, low-interest loans to homeowners, renters, businesses and non-profit organizations who suffered losses. These include physical disaster loans to help rebuild and replace uninsured property, and economic industry loans to provide small businesses with the working capital to replace inventory and otherwise resume normal operations.

FEMA is providing temporary housing and grants to individuals and families whose homes and property were damaged in the disaster, and who cannot qualify for SBA loans. In addition, FEMA provides grants to local governments to cover the costs of repairing public buildings and facilities and the overtime salaries of state and local workers who had to respond to the disaster.

This SBA and FEMA assistance constitutes the lion's share of the Federal assistance made available to respond to urgent, short-term recovery needs. In the past, the application and approval process for these programs has been the source of some frustration. The task force was and is committed to removing any unnecessary bureaucratic barriers to the efficient functioning of this process. The specific goal of the task force is to provide this FEMA and SBA assistance in record time.

To aid in the task of minimizing confusion for a local population already under stress, the task force worked with the state, county, and city governments to establish centers that would provide all key services under one roof. Under this "one stop shopping" approach, a citizen could find information on and make application for SBA loans; FEMA grants; emergency food, clothing, shelter, and medical assistance; individual and family grants; tax assistance; and crisis counseling—all at one location.

On Friday, May 8th, seven DACS were opened throughout the affected areas of greater Los Angeles to provide this "one-stop shopping" service. One measure of the success of the task force is this: on Monday, May 11th, three days after the opening of the application centers, FEMA mailed its first disaster housing assistance checks to victims of the disturbance.

Breaking Down Language Barriers

The task force recognized that language differences could constitute an important barrier to the efficient delivery of services in such a culturally diverse community as Los Angeles. As a result, FEMA, SBA, and the task force worked to tap a range of resources to provide sufficient numbers of linguistic specialists in the DACS. FEMA and SBA enlisted the services of Korean-speaking assistants to aid the many Korean-American business owners affected by the disaster. On Friday, May 8th, it became clear that a shortage of Spanish-speaking assistants existed at the Ardmore DAC site. FEMA redeployed several assistants to that site, and hired ten additional Spanish speaking aides that day.

In total, approximately 60 bilingual aides have been hired to date to ease the language problem.

In order to minimize the time between the actual disaster and the receipt of disaster assistance, the task force took several actions to reduce red tape and assist applicants.

Speeding Delivery of SBA Disaster Assistance Loans

Many of the businesses affected by the rioting were small businesses without extensive records. In order to receive disaster assistance loans, businesses must furnish tax returns from the past three years; an itemized list of losses; proof of operation of a business at a particular location, such as a copy of a deed, lease, or mortgage; a brief history of the business; and financial statements for the past three years.

For many of the businesses in the affected areas of Los Angeles, it is difficult to meet these requirements. To help such applicants, the task force:

- Arranged for the placement of specialists from the Minority Business Development Agency (MBDA) in each of the DACS. These specialists are providing technical assistance to businesses in preparing such required items as the business history and the profit and loss statements from the past three years. MBDA arranged to have its services provided in several languages.
- Arranged for the placement of representatives of the IRS in each of the DACS, to speed the process of recovering tax returns from IRS headquarters in those cases in which the applicants' copies of the tax returns are missing or destroyed. In addition, the task force worked with the IRS headquarters in Washington to ensure that expedited treatment is given to any request to retrieve tax returns in cases related to the situation in Los Angeles.

Another requirement of the SBA for disaster loan applicants is that they demonstrate that they sought and were unable to secure credit elsewhere. In the case of many of the small businesses in South Central and other affected areas of Los Angeles, it is safe to assume that availability of credit was a major difficulty for them even prior to the disturbance—that they would be unable to secure such credit. In response, the task force:

- Developed through SBA a simplified "credit elsewhere" test. This is a major time saver in the application process, which for thousands of businesses will cut weeks from the time it takes to receive an SBA disaster loan.

The length of time required to process SBA disaster loan applications and actually provide checks to affected businesses has been a source of frustration in past disasters. To reduce that frustration, the task force:

- Established a special expedited process with the U.S. Treasury Department to speed approval of check writing for the Small Business Administration.

Delivering FEMA Assistance Fairly and Efficiently

The city and state governments expressed concern that, due to the wording of the disaster declaration, FEMA and SBA might be in the position of providing disaster assistance to those who had suffered losses or damage due to fire, but not to those who had suffered losses or damage due to looting. The task force:

- Worked with FEMA to clarify the interpretation of the President's disaster declaration. Under the clarification, FEMA declared that, "'Fires during a period of civil unrest means all *fire-related damages or hardships* which occurred during the major disaster." (emphasis added) Further, FEMA stated that "where it is not feasible to differentiate among the causes of civil unrest . . . or where it appears that damages or hardships may be in any way the effect of fires or fire-related circumstances, all damage is considered to be related to fires." This interpretation should allow agencies to provide assistance to all those who suffered damages as a result of the civil disturbance.

Creating Additional DACs

The task force has sought to be flexible in accommodating the demand for assistance in the community and to reduce undue waiting time in the DACS.

When indications of long waiting times at the Ardmore Recreation Center DAC in Koreatown arose on Friday, May 8th, the task force:

- Worked with FEMA and the state government to move a mobile DAC to the site, expanding the available space by 720 square feet.

When the need for additional application facilities in the Crenshaw area was identified during the first weekend of operations of the DACS, the task force:

- Worked to establish a new DAC site at 4030 Crenshaw Boulevard in Los Angeles. This new DAC was opened at 10:00 am on Monday, May 11th.

The task force is prepared to remain flexible as new demand for disaster recovery services arises.

VI. ASSISTANCE PROVIDED BY OTHER FEDERAL AGENCIES

In addition to FEMA and SBA, other Federal agencies have worked to provide quickly a range of other services and types of assistance in response to the disturbance in Los Angeles. Some examples follow.

Agriculture

In response to spot shortages of food in certain neighborhoods, the U.S. Department of Agriculture (USDA) sent over 27,000 boxes of cereal, over 58,000 cans of infant formula, over 1,500 six-pound boxes of nonfat dry milk, and other foodstuffs to Los Angeles area food banks.

A USDA survey revealed that private sector donations to food banks soared in the wake of Los Angeles disturbance, and that distribution outlets in the area had been increased, thanks to the participation of churches and other non-profit institutions in the community.

The USDA survey revealed that there was no marked increase in food stamp demand in the wake of the disturbance. Nevertheless new requests from individuals affected by the disturbances will be put on a special fast track. Because several outlets authorized to accept food stamps were closed or destroyed, red tape was cut so that new food stamp authorization applications from retail outlets are being processed in one day.

At least fifty stores authorized to receive vouchers in the Women, Infants and Children (WIC) program were closed or destroyed. In response, USDA issued instructions to allow WIC coupons to be valid at any authorized vendor.

Commerce

The Department of Commerce has provided both business and economic development assistance in the wake of the Los Angeles disturbance.

In addition to placing its representatives in the DACs to assist in the preparation of applications by small minority businesses, the Minority Business Development Agency (MBDA) operates two Minority Business Development Centers in the Los Angeles areas.

The Commerce Department is in the process of making available approximately $25 million in Economic Development Administration (EDA) funds to assist in the recovery process. Six to ten million dollars will be made available to the county and city governments for bridge loans to businesses to be used for purposes such as cleanup, demolition, and restoration of inventory, machinery and equipment, or building structures.

Another $2 to 3 million is expected to be provided to Rebuild LA, chaired by Peter Ueberroth, to help set up and operate this non-profit organization, whose mission is to assist in the economic recovery of greater Los Angeles by attracting job-creating private sector investment.

Approximately $1 to 2 million is expected to be provided to the Los Angeles Convention and Visitors Bureau, to help reinvigorate international tourism to the Los Angeles area. This is the second largest industry in the area, employing 360,000 southern Californians, eighty percent of whom are minorities.

Finally, EDA is discussing $5.5 million in defense adjustment grants for Los Angeles County, to assist areas where defense contracts were terminated. Some of these grants could be used for seed capital for technology companies which are spinoffs from defense-related companies.

Education

The Department of Education is taking steps to speed the availability of-approximately $1.2 billion in formula grants to the State of California, and to work with the state to optimize the suballocation of these grants in order to address conditions related to the disturbances.

Education is working with college student aid administrators to allow them to use "special condition" procedures in the Pell Grant program to take into account any loss of family income due to the disturbances.

In addition, a special desk has been set up at Education's Federal Student Aid Information Center to handle inquiries from Los Angeles students on how to apply for student aid or how to reflect loss of assets or income due to the disturbances in the application. This desk will be serviced by an "800" phone number.

Health and Human Services

Within 24 hours of the disturbance, the Department of Health and Human Services (HHS), through the Social Security Administration, ordered the use of emergency check-writing authority to make payments of up to $200 for those elderly poor or low income, disabled children whose Supplemental Security Income (SSI) checks were not received as a result of the disturbance. HHS also put in place procedures to speed the replacement of any welfare or disability check lost as a result of the disturbance.

HHS dispatched experts from the National Institute of Mental Health to assess mental health assistance needs and requirements. Mental health and crisis counseling is available in the DACS. Epidemiologist from the Centers for Disease Control were brought in to investigate the health effects of the disturbance—including those related to environmental safety (chemical and biohazards), health control (sanitation and clean water), and other questions.

Housing and Urban Development

The Department of Housing and Urban Development (HUD) immediately made available Section 8 rental assistance vouchers to those families who have been displaced by fires related to the disturbance.

HUD is also making available 32 HUD-owned homes, with a dollar value of $2.3 million, for use in the affected areas. These homes will be leased to the city for one dollar per month. HUD issued a new rule this past week to provide priority contracting for businesses that are at least 51 percent resident owned. This means that a higher proportion of contracts for work performed for HUD will go to businesses which are representative of the area in which the work is to be performed.

On Wednesday, May 6th, HUD announced that it will approve requests to allow the early release of over $92 million in Community Development Block Grant (CDBG) funds to the city and County of Los Angeles that were scheduled to be released on July 1st.

On Thursday, May 7th, HUD signed an interagency memorandum of understanding with the Department of Labor to better coordinate Labor's job training efforts with HUD's HOPE and other public housing initiatives.

On Friday, May 8th, HUD announced the availability of $1.5 million in Technical Assistance program grants for low- and moderate-income young people (between the ages of 14 and 21) to help them acquire the skills and knowledge they need to start and operate successful small businesses.

The Resolution Trust Corporation (RTC) has made available to HUD a list of properties available in the affected area of Los Angeles. HUD has been working to match these properties to local needs, and leases could be signed later this week.

Labor

The Department of Labor provided $2 million in emergency grants to hire and pay the wages of workers who were dislocated as a result of the disturbance.

Labor also launched a demonstration project to use unemployment insurance benefit payments to support entrepreneurship efforts by unemployment insurance claimants.

Labor also provided about $2 million for several types of training assistance. One grant would establish "one-stop shopping" skill centers to provide vocational training and employment-related assistance to affected areas. Another would finance an expansion of a program operated by the Community Youth Gang Services which allows area youth to participate in community service projects as an alternative to incarceration. A third would finance youth apprenticeship model programs for African-American and Hispanic males. And a fourth would provide training funds to supplement local economic development efforts.

Office of Personnel Management

The Director of the Office of Personnel Management (OPM) authorized the conduct of a special Combined Federal Campaign effort among Federal employees in the Los Angeles area to help generate contributions to non-profit organizations involved in the recovery effort. OPM has also taken steps in the past week to increase job opportunities and to provide job counseling and stress counseling in the Los Angeles area.

VII. CONTINUATION OF THE WORK OF THE TASK FORCE

The work of the task force will continue beyond the efforts of this first week. The task force is committed to implementing fully the President's directive to work with the state, county, and city, and with the private sector, to ensure the swift delivery of needed assistance and services to the people of Los Angeles.

The task force has established a structure and a set of processes to see that this directive is carried out in the weeks and months ahead.

With the return of most Deputy Secretaries to Washington, the conference calls with State, county, city, and on-site Federal representatives are nevertheless continuing. Deputy Secretary DelliBovi has returned to Los Angeles this week. Deputy Secretary Schnabel will arrive later in the week. The task force co-chairs, Deputy Secretaries Kearns and DelliBovi, plan to continue alternate visits to Los Angeles for as long as such visits are helpful.

Each of the agencies represented on the task force has stationed a representative to remain in Los Angeles. Some of these representatives will be moved to the site of the current Federal/State/Local coordinating office in Pasadena to ensure maximum coordination.

The task force co-chairmen are now in the process of identifying a task force leader to lead the task force in Los Angeles on a day-to-day basis. This leader will report regularly to the co-chairmen.

In six weeks, the task force has agreed to reconvene in Los Angeles to assess the state of the recovery effort, to meet again with state, local, and private sector officials, and to determine what additional actions are necessary.

The task force will work diligently to support state, county, city, and private sector efforts to help Los Angeles recover, and to make sure that the Federal government is a constructive partner in that recovery.

VIII. CONCLUSION

Throughout greater Los Angeles, members of the task force witnessed inspiring signs of hope in the wake of the tragic violence. Store owners whose shops had been looted only days earlier rushed to replace inventory, placed plywood over their shattered windows, and proudly painted "Open for Business" in bold letters on their newly installed plywood facades.

Volunteers poured into the affected areas from all over the city—indeed from all over the country. Mayor Bradley estimated that 50,000 volunteers had assisted in the cleanup of Los Angeles in the days following the disturbances.

On one street corner in South Central, against a backdrop of a burned out shopping center, a man opened a flower stand, in one first small step of hope and recovery.

One firefighter who had served 27 years earlier in combating the fires of Watts, predicted and observed "a much quicker recovery" than that which followed the Watts disturbances, because, he said, of "the total commitment to cleanup and recovery on the part of the local people."

From the ashes of this recovery, the members of the task force found blossoming a springtime of hope. Its most important feature was a near-consensus on the types of measures that are needed not only to restore Los Angeles but to make its neighborhoods stronger than they were before this incident happened.

While there is much about which to be encouraged, the task force found that this is a *very* tough situation. It is estimated that unemployment in the affected area *prior* to the disturbance was far higher than the national average, perhaps more than triple the national rate. Mayor Bradley estimates that many thousands of jobs were lost as a result of the disturbance—some permanently.

Virtually everyone the task force spoke to believed that private sector investment in these neighborhoods, investment which can create jobs in the community, was the most urgent priority. Virtually everyone the task force spoke to believed that residents of these affected areas must be given a greater equity stake in success—the opportunity to accumulate assets without penalty—from the welfare system, the opportunity to own and manage their own homes, the opportunity to live in neighborhoods free from crime and drugs. What the Federal government can provide is incentives to encourage investment that will create jobs and build local assets.

The members of the task force believe that in this emergent consensus lie the seeds of a truly complete recovery for Los Angeles, and for all of America's cities.

SOURCE: Los Angeles—A City in Stress Web Site: http://www.usc.edu/isd/archives/cityinstress/.

22. Excerpts from the Preliminary and Final Reports of the Oklahoma Commission to Study the Tulsa Race Riot of 1921, 2000, and 2001

Formed in 1997, the Tulsa Race Riot Commission was charged with determining exactly what happened during the May 1921 riot that devastated the African American Greenwood district of Tulsa, Oklahoma. The Commission undertook both an historical and an archeological analysis of the event and, as indicated below in the cover letter to its preliminary report released in 2000, recommended that reparations be paid to survivors of the riot. Also reproduced below are excerpts of the final report of the Commission, which was compiled by Danney Goble and released in 2001.

Letter Introducing the Commission's Preliminary Report, February 7, 2000

The Honorable Frank Keating
Governor of the State of Oklahoma
State Capitol Building
Oklahoma City, OK 73105

Dear Governor Keating:

The Tulsa Race Riot Commission, established by House Joint Resolution No. 1035, is pleased to submit the following preliminary report.

The primary goal of collecting historical documentation on the Tulsa Race Riot of 1921 has been achieved. Attachment A is a summary listing of the record groups that have been gathered and stored at the Oklahoma Historical Society. Also included are summaries of some reports and the full text of selected documents to illustrate the breadth and scope of the collecting process. However, the Commission has not yet voted on historical findings, so these materials do not necessarily represent conclusions of the Commission.

At the last meeting, held February 4, 2000, the Commission voted on three actions. They are:

1) The Issue of Restitution

Whereas, the process of historical analysis by this Commission is not yet complete,

And Whereas, the archeological investigation into casualties and mass burials is not yet complete,

And Whereas, we have seen a continuous pattern of historical evidence that the Tulsa Race Riot of 1921 was the violent consequence of racial hatred institutionalized and tolerated by official federal, state, county, and city policy,

And Whereas, government at all levels has the moral and ethical responsibility of fostering a sense of community that bridges divides of ethnicity and race,

And Whereas, by statute we are to make recommendations regarding whether or not reparations can or should be made to the Oklahoma Legislature, the Governor of the State of Oklahoma, and the Mayor and City Council of Tulsa,

That, we, the 1921 Tulsa Race Riot Commission, recommend that restitution to the historic Greenwood Community, in real and tangible form, would be good public policy and do much to repair the emotional as well as physical scars of this most terrible incident in our shared past.

2) The Issue of Suggested Forms of Restitution in Priority Order

The Commission recommends

1) Direct payment of reparations to survivors of the Tulsa Race Riot

2) Direct payment of reparations to descendants of the survivors of the Tulsa Race Riot
3) A scholarship fund available to students affected by the Tulsa Race Riot
4) Establishment of an economic development enterprise zone in the historic area of the Greenwood District
5) A memorial for the reburial of any human remains found in the search for unmarked graves of riot victims

3) The Issue of an Extension of the Tulsa Race Riot Commission

The Commission hereby endorses and supports House Bill 2468, which extends the life of the Commission in order to finish the historical report on the Tulsa Race Riot of 1921.

We, the members of the Tulsa Race Riot Commission, respectfully submit these findings for your consideration.

COMMISSIONERS:

Currie Ballard, Coyle

Dr. Bob Blackburn, Oklahoma City

Joel Burns, Tulsa

Vivian Clark, Tulsa

Rep. Abe Deutschendorf, Lawton

Eddie Faye Gates, Tulsa

Jim Lloyd, Tulsa

Sen. Robert Milacek, Wauikomis

Jimmie L. White, Jr., Checotah

CHAIRMAN:

T. D. "Pete" Churchwell, Tulsa

SPONSORS:

Sen. Maxine Horner, Tulsa

Rep. Donn Ross, Tulsa

ADVISORS:

Dr. John Hope Franklin, Durham NC

Dr. Scott Ellsworth, Portland OR

Final Report of the Oklahoma Commission to Study the Tulsa Race Riot of 1921

Compiled by Danney Goble

The 1921 Tulsa Race Riot Commission originated in 1997 with House Joint Resolution No. 1035. The act twice since has been amended, first in 1998, and again two years later. The final rewriting passed each legislative chamber in March and became law with Governor Frank Keating's signature on April 6, 2000.

In that form, the State of Oklahoma extended the commission's authority beyond that originally scheduled, to February 28, 2001.

The statute also charged the commission to produce, on that date, "a final report of its findings and recommendations" and to submit that report "in writing to the Governor, the Speaker of the House of Representatives, the President Pro Tempore of the Senate, and the Mayor and each member of the City Council of the City of Tulsa, Oklahoma." This is that report. It accounts for and completes the work of the 1921 Tulsa Race Riot Commission.

A series of papers accompanies the report. Some are written by scholars of national stature, others by experts of international acclaim. Each addresses at length and in depth issues of expressed legislative interest and matters of enormous public consequence. As a group, they comprise a uniquely special and a uniquely significant contribution that must be attached to this report and must be studied carefully along with it.

Nonetheless, the supporting documents are not the report, itself. The scholars' essays have their purposes; this commission's report has another. Its purpose is contained in the statutes that first created this commission, that later extended its life, and that each time gave it the same set of mandates. That is why this report is an accounting, presented officially and offered publicly, of how Oklahoma's 1921 Tulsa Race Riot Commission has conducted its business and addressed its statutory obligations.

Its duties were many, and each presented imposing challenges. Not least was the challenge of preparing this report. Lawmakers scheduled its deadline and defined its purpose, and this report meets their requirements. At the same time, four years of intense study and personal sacrifice surely entitle commission members to add their own expectations. Completely reasonable and entirely appropriate, their desires deserve a place in their report as well.

Together, then, both the law's requirements and the commissioners' resolves guide this report. Designed to be both concise and complete, this is the report that law requires the 1921 Tulsa Race Riot Commission to submit to those who represent the people. Designed to be both compelling and convincing, this also is the report that the 1921 Tulsa Race Riot Commission chooses to offer the people whom both lawmakers and the commissioners serve.

The Commission shall consist of eleven (11) members ...

The legislative formula for commission membership assured it appropriate if unusual composition. As an official state inquiry, the state's interest was represented through the executive, legislative, and administrative branches. The governor was to appoint six members, three from names submitted by the Speaker of the House, three from nominees provided by the Senate President Pro Tempore.

Two state officials—the directors of the Oklahoma Human Rights Commission (OHRC) and of the Oklahoma Historical Society (OHS)—also were to serve as ex officio members, either personally or through their designees.

Reflecting Tulsa's obvious interest, the resolution directed the city's mayor to select the commission's final three members. Similar to the gubernatorial appointments, they were to come from names proposed by Tulsa's City Commission. One of the mayor's appointees had to be "a survivor of the 1921 Tulsa Race Riot incident"; two had to be current residents of the historic Greenwood community, the area once devastated by the "incident." The commission began with two ex officio members and ended with two others. After Gracie Monson resigned in March 2000, Kenneth Kendricks replaced her as OHRC's interim director and its representative to the commission. Blake Wade directed the historical society until Dr. Bob Blackburn succeeded him in 1999. Blackburn had been Wade's designated representative to the commission anyway. In fact, the commission had made him its chairman, a position he would hold until June 2000.

Governor Frank Keating's six appointees included two legislators, each from a different chamber, each from an opposite party, each a former history teacher. Democrat Abe Deutschendorf's participation in the debate over the original house resolution echoed his lingering interest in history and foretold his future devotion to this inquiry. As a history teacher, Robert Milacek had included Tulsa's race riot in his classes. Little did he know that he, himself, would contribute to that history as a Republican legislator, but he has.

Governor Keating turned to metropolitan Tulsa for two appointees. T.D. "Pete" Churchwell's father serviced African-American businesses in the Greenwood district, and Churchwell has maintained concern for that community and with the 1921 riot that nearly destroyed it. He was Blackburn's replacement as chairman during the commission's closing months. Although born in Oklahoma City, Jim Lloyd and his family moved to Turley (the community just north of Greenwood) when he was three. Raised in Tulsa, he graduated from Nathan Hale and the University of Tulsa's College of Law. He now practices law in Sand Springs and lives in Tulsa.

The governor's other appointees entered the inquiry less with geographical than with professional connections to Tulsa and its history. Currie Ballard lives in Coyle and serves neighboring Langston University as historian-in-residence. Holding a graduate degree in history, Jimmie White teaches it and heads the social science division for Connors State College.

Tulsa Mayor Susan Savage appointed the commission's final three members. If only five in 1921, Joe Burns met the law's requirement that one mayoral appointee be a survivor of the 1921 "incident." He brought the commission not faint childhood memories but seasoned wisdom rooted in eight decades of life in the Greenwood community and with Greenwood's people.

As the resolution specified, Mayor Savage's other two appointees live in contemporary Greenwood, but neither took a direct route to get there. Eddie Faye Gates's path began in Preston, Oklahoma, passed through Alabama's Tuskegee Institute, and crisscrossed two continents before it reached Tulsa in 1968. She spent the next twenty-four years teaching its youngsters and has devoted years since researching and writing her own memoirs and her community's history. Vivian Clark-Adams's route took nearly as many twists and turns, passing through one military base after another until her father retired and the family came to Oklahoma in 1961. Trained at the University of Tulsa, Dr. Vivian Clark-Adams serves Tulsa Community College as chair of the liberal arts division for its southeast campus.

In the November 1997, organizing meeting, commissioners voted to hire clerical assistants and expert consultants through the OHS. (The legislature had added $50,000 to the agency's base appropriations for just such purposes.) They then scheduled their second meeting for December 5 to accommodate the most appropriate and most eminent of all possible authorities.

John Hope Franklin is the son of Greenwood attorney B.C. Franklin, a graduate of Tulsa's Booker T. Washington High School (Fisk and Harvard, too), and James B. Duke Professor of History Emeritus at Duke University. Recipient of scores of academic and literary awards, not to mention more than a hundred honorary doctorates, Franklin came back for another honor. He received the Peggy V. Helmerich Distinguished Author Award on December 4 and stayed to meet and help the commission on the fifth.

Commissioners were delighted to learn that Franklin was anxious to serve, even if he confessed the contributions limited by age (he was eighty-two at the time) and other obligations. They enthusiastically made John Hope Franklin their first consultant, and they instantly took his advice for another. Dr. Scott Ellsworth, a native Tulsan now living in Oregon, was a Duke graduate who already had written a highly regarded study of the riot. Ellsworth became the second consultant chosen; he thereafter emerged first in importance.

As its work grew steadily more exacting and steadily more specialized, the commission turned to more experts. Legal scholars, archeologists, anthropologists, forensic specialists, geophysicists—all of these and more blessed this commission with technical expertise impossible to match and unimaginable otherwise. As a research group, they brought a breadth of vision and a depth of training that made Oklahoma's commission a model of state inquiry.

Ten consultants eventually provided them expert advice, but the commissioners always expected to depend mostly on their own resources, maybe with just a little help from just a few of their friends. Interested OHS employees were a likely source. Sure enough, a half-dozen or so pitched in to search the agency's library and archives for riot-related materials.

That was help appreciated, if not entirely unexpected. What was surprising—stunning, really—was something else that happened in Oklahoma City. As the commission's work attracted interest and gathered momentum, Bob Blackburn noticed something odd: an unusual number of people were volunteering to work at the historical society. Plain, ordinary citizens, maybe forty or fifty of them, had asked to help the commission as unpaid researchers in the OHS collections.

At about that time, Dick Warner decided that he had better start making notes on the phone calls he was fielding for the Tulsa County Historical Society. People were calling in, wanting to contribute to the inquiry, and they just kept calling. After two months, his log listed entries for 148 local calls. Meanwhile, Scott Ellsworth was back in Oregon, writing down information volunteered by some of the three hundred callers who had reached him by long distance.

Most commission meetings were in Tulsa, each open to any and all. Oklahoma's Open Meetings Law required no less, but this commission's special nature yielded much more. It seemed that every time the commissioners met at least one person (usually several) greeted them with at least something (usually a lot) that the commission needed.

Included were records and papers long presumed lost, if their existence had been known at all. Some were official documents, pulled together and packed away years earlier. Uncovered and examined, they took the commission back in time, back to the years just before and just after 1921. Some were musty legal records saved from the shredders. Briefs filed, dockets set, lawsuits decided—each opened an avenue into another corner of history. Pages after pages laid open the city commission's deliberations and decisions as they affected the Greenwood area. Overlooked records from the National Guard offered overlooked perspectives and illuminated them with misplaced correspondence, lost after-action reports, obscure field manuals, and self-typed accounts from men who were on duty at the riot. Maybe there was a family's treasured collection of yellowed newspaper clippings; an envelope of faded photographs; a few carefully folded letters, all hand written, each dated 1921.

One meaning of all of this is obvious, so obvious that this report pauses to affirm it.

Many have questioned why or even if anyone would be interested now in events that happened in one city, one time, one day, long ago. What business did today's state lawmakers have in something so old, so local, and so deservedly forgotten? Surely no one cares, not anymore.

An answer comes from hundreds and hundreds of voices. They tell us that what happened in 1921 in Tulsa is as alive today as it was back then. What happened in Tulsa stays as important and remains as unresolved today as in 1921. What happened there still exerts its power over people who never lived in Tulsa at all.

How else can one explain the thousands of hours volunteered by hundreds of people, all to get this story told and get it told right? How else can one explain the regional, national, even international attention that has been concentrated on a few short hours of a mid-sized city's history? As the introductory paper by Drs. Franklin and Ellsworth recounts, the Tulsa disaster went largely unacknowledged for a half-century or more. After a while, it was largely forgotten.

Eventually it became largely unknown. So hushed was mention of the subject that many pronounced it the final victim of a conspiracy, this a conspiracy of silence.

That silence is shattered, utterly and permanently shattered. Whatever else this commission has achieved or will achieve, it already has made that possible. Regional, national, and international media made it certain. The *Dallas Morning News*, the *Los Angeles Times*, the *New York Times*, National Public Radio (NPR), every American broadcast television network, cable outlets delivering Cinemax and the History Channel to North America, the British Broadcasting Corporation—this merely begins the attention that the media focused upon this commission and its inquiry. Many approached it in depth (NPR twice has made it the featured daily broadcast). Most returned to it repeatedly (the *New York Times* had carried at least ten articles as of February 2000). All considered it vital public information.

Some—including some commission members—thought at least some of the coverage was at least somewhat unbalanced. They may have had a point, but that is not the point.

Here is the point: The 1921 Tulsa Race Riot Commission is pleased to report that this past tragedy has been extensively aired, that it is now remembered, and that it will never again be unknown.

The Commission shall undertake a study to [include] the identification of persons. . . .

No one is certain how many participated in the 1921 riot. No one is certain how many suffered how much for how long. Certainty is reserved for a single quantifiable fact. Every year there remain fewer and fewer who experienced it personally.

Legislation authorizing this commission directed that it seek and locate those survivors.

Specifically, it was to identify any personable to "provide adequate proof to the Commission" that he or she was an "actual resident" of "the 'Greenwood' area or community" at the time of the riot. The commission was also to identify any person who otherwise "sustained an identifiable loss . . . resulting from the . . . 1921 Tulsa Race Riot." Some considered this the commission's most difficult assignment, some its most important duty, some its most compelling purpose. They all were right, and had Eddie Faye Gates not assumed personal and experienced responsibility for that mandate, this commission might have little to report. Because she did, however, it principally reports what she and those who worked with her were able to accomplish in the commission's name.

Commissioner Gates's presence gave this commission a considerable and welcomed head start. She already had included several riot victims among the early pioneers whom she had interviewed for *They Came Searching: How Blacks Sought the Promised Land in Tulsa*. The book finished, she had an informal list of survivors, but the list kept changing.

Death erased one name after another. Others appeared. Many were of old people who had left Oklahoma years, even decades, ago; but she heard about them and patiently tracked them down. As lawmakers were authorizing this inquiry, the count stood at thirteen, nineteen if all the leads eventually panned out. No one presumed that even nineteen was close to final, but no one knew what the accurate total might be either.

At its very first organizing meeting on November 14, 1997, this commission established a "subcommittee on survivors," headed by Commissioner Gates and including Commissioner Burns and Dr. Clark-Adams. From that moment onward, that subcommittee has aggressively and creatively pursued every possible avenue to identify every possible survivor.

Letters sent over Dr. Ellsworth's signature to *Jet* and *Ebony* magazines urged readers to contact the commission if they knew of any possibilities. From *Gale's Directory of Publications*, Commissioner Gates targeted the nation's leading African-American newspapers (papers like the *Chicago Defender* and the *Pittsburgh Courier*), appealing publicly for survivors or to anyone who might know of one. The commission's website, created and maintained by the Oklahoma Historical Society, prominently declared a determination to identify and register every survivor, everywhere. For affirmation, it posted the official forms used as the subcommittee's records, including instructions for their completion and submission.

An old-fashioned, intensely personal web turned out to be more productive than the thoroughly modern, entirely electronic Internet.

Like historical communities everywhere, modern Greenwood maintains a rich, if informal, social network. Sometimes directly, sometimes distantly, it connects Greenwood's people, sometimes young, sometimes old. Anchoring its interstices are the community's longest residents, its most active citizens, and its most prominent leaders.

One quality or another would describe some members of this commission. After all, these are the very qualifications that lawmakers required for their appointments. Others share those same qualities and a passion for their community's history as well. Curtis Lawson, Robert Littlejohn, Hannibal Johnson, Dr. Charles Christopher, Mable Rice, Keith Jemison, Robert and Blanchie Mayes—all are active in the North Tulsa Historical Society, all are some of the community's most respected citizens, and all are among this commission's most valuable assets.

The initial published notices had early results. Slowly they began to compound upon themselves. The first stories in the national and international media introduced a multiplying factor. Thereafter, each burst of press attention seemed to increase what was happening geometrically. People were contacting commissioners, some coming forward as survivors, more suggesting where or how they might be found. Names came in, first a light sprinkle, next a shower, then a downpour, finally a flood.

Old city directories, census reports, and other records verified some claims, but they could confirm only so much. After all, these people had been children, some of them infants, back in 1921. After eighty years, could any one remember the kind of details—addresses, telephone numbers, property descriptions, rental agreements, business locations—someone else could verify with official documents? Not likely. In fact, these were exactly the kind of people most likely to have been ignored or lost in every public record. Officially, they might have never existed.

Except that they did, and one who looked long enough and hard enough and patiently enough could confirm it—that is, if one knew where to look and whom to ask.

That is what happened. Name-by-name, someone found somebody who actually knew each person. In fact, that is how many names surfaced: a credible figure in the community knew how to find older relatives, former neighbors, or departed friends. Others could be confirmed with equal authority. Maybe someone knew the claimant's family or knew someone that did. If a person claimed to be kin to someone or offered some small detail, surely someone else knew that relative or remembered the same detail as well. Some of those details might even be verified through official documents.

It was a necessary process but slow and delicate, too. As of June 1998, twenty-nine survivors had been identified, contacted, and registered. (The number did not include sixteen identified as descendants of riot victims.) It took another fourteen months for the total to reach sixty-one. It would have been higher, except that three of the first twenty-nine had died in those months. This deadline had an ominous and compelling meaning.

Work immediately shifted through higher gears. In March 2000, the identification process finished for forty-one survivors then living in or near Tulsa. Just a few more still needed to be contacted. The real work remaining, however, involved a remarkable number of survivors who had turned up outside of Oklahoma. Following a recent flurry of media attention, more than sixty out-of-state survivors had been located. They lived everywhere from California to Florida, one in Paris, France! All of that work is complete. As the commission submits its report, 118 persons have been identified, contacted, and registered as living survivors of the 1921 Tulsa Race Riot. (Another 176 persons also have been registered as descendants of riot victims.) The 1921 Tulsa Race Riot Commission thereby has discharged the mandate regarding the identification of persons.

The Commission shall . . . gather information, identify and interview witnesses . . ., preserve testimony and records obtained, [and] examine and copy documents . . . having historical significance

Whatever else this commission already has achieved or soon will inspire, one accomplishment will remain indefinitely. Until recently, the Tulsa race riot has been the most important least known event in the state's entire history. Even the most resourceful of scholars stumbled as they neared it for it was dimly lit by evidence and the evidentiary record faded more with every passing year.

That is not now and never will be true again.

These few hours—from start to finish, the actual riot consumed less than sixteen hours—may now comprise the most thoroughly documented moments ever to have occurred in Oklahoma. This commission's work and the documentary record it leaves behind shines upon them a light too bright to ignore.

The Oklahoma Historical Society was searching its existing materials and aggressively pursuing more before this commission ever assembled. By the November 1997, organizing meeting, Bob Blackburn was ready to announce that the society already had ordered prints from every known source of every known photograph taken of the riot. He was contacting every major archival depository and research library in the country to request copies of any riot-related materials they might hold themselves. Experienced OHS professionals were set to research important but heretofore neglected court and municipal records.

This was news welcomed by commission members. It assured early momentum for the job ahead, and it complemented work that some of them were already doing. Eddie Faye Gates, for one, had pulled out every transcript of every interview that she had made with a riot witness, and she was anxious to make more. Jim Lloyd was another. Lloyd already had found and copied transcripts from earlier interviews, including some with Tulsa police officers present at the riot. He also had a hunch that a fellow who knew his way around a court house just might turn up all sorts of information.

That is how it began, but that was just the beginning. In the months ahead, Larry O'Dell and other OHS employees patiently excavated mountains of information, one pebble at a time, as it were. They then pieced together tiny bits of fact, carefully fitting one to another.

One by one, completed puzzles emerged. Arranged in different dimensions, they made magic: a vision of Greenwood long since vanished.

Master maps, both of the community on the eve of the riot and of the post-riot residue, identified every single piece of property. For each parcel, a map displayed any structure present, its owner and its use. If commercial, what firms were there, who owned them, what businesses they were in. If residential, whether it was rented or owned. If the former, the landlord's name. If the latter, whether it was mortgaged (if so, to whom and encumbered by what debt). For both, lists identified each of its occupants by name.

It was not magic; it was more. Larry O'Dell had rebuilt Greenwood from records he and other researchers had examined and collected for the commission. Every building permit granted, every warranty deed recorded, every property appraisal ordered, every damage claim filed, every death certificate issued, every burial record maintained—the commission had copies of every single record related to Greenwood at the time of the riot.

Some it had only because Jim Lloyd was right. Able to navigate a courthouse, he ran across complete records for some 150 civil suits filed after the race riot. No one remembered that they even existed; they had been misplaced for thirty-five years. When Jim Lloyd uncovered and saved them, they were scheduled for routine shredding.

The commission gathered the most private of documents as well. Every form registering every survivor bears notes recording information taken from every one of 118 persons. With Kavin Ross operating the camera, Eddie Faye Gates videotaped interviews with about half of the survivors. Each is available on one of nine cassettes preserved by the commission; full transcripts are being completed for all. Sympathetic collectors turned over transcripts of another fifty or more. Some had been packed away for twenty, even thirty years.

Others, including several resourceful amateur historians, reproduced and gave the commission what amounted to complete documentary collections. There were sets of municipal records, files from state agencies, reports kept by social services, press clippings carefully bound, privately owned photographs never publicly seen.

People who had devoted years to the study of one or more aspects of the riot supplied evidence they had found and presented conclusions they had reached. Beryl Ford followed the commission's work as a Tulsan legendary for his devotion to his city and its history. William O'Brien attended nearly every commission meeting, sometimes to ask questions, sometimes to answer them, once to deliver his own full report on the riot. Robert Norris prepared smaller, occasional reports on military topics.

He also dug up and turned over files from National Guard records. Others located affidavits filed with the State Supreme Court. The military reports usually had been presumed lost; the legal papers always had been assumed unimportant.

Commissioners were surprised to receive so much new evidence and pleased to see that it contributed so much. They were delighted to note that so much came from black sources, that it documented black experiences and recorded black observations.

It had not always been that way. Too many early journalists and historians had dismissed black sources as unreliable. Too few early librarians and archivists had preserved black sources as important. Both thereby condemned later writers and scholars to a never ending game of hide-and-go-seek, the rules rigged so no one could win.

This commission's work changes the game forever. Every future scholar will have access to everything everyone ever had when the original source was white. In fact, they will have a lot more of it. They also will have more from sources few had before when the original source was black.

Because they will, the community future scholars will behold [that] the property they will describe was a community of black people, occupied by black people. The public records they will examine involved black people and affected black people. Objects they will touch came from black people. Interviews they will hear and transcripts they will read were recorded from black people. The evidence they will explore reveals experiences of black people.

Consider what so much new information and what so many new sources can mean for future historians. Consider what it already has meant for one.

Read closely Scott Ellsworth's accompanying essay, "The Tulsa Riot," a rather simple title, as titles go. Much more sophisticated is the title he gave the book he wrote in 1982, *Death in a Promised Land: The Tulsa Race Riot of 1921*.

It is fair that they have different titles. They tell somewhat different stories in somewhat different ways. The chief difference is that the one titled so simply tells a tale much more sophisticated.

For one thing, it is longer. The report attached here filled 115 typed pages in the telling; the comparable portion of the book prints entirely in 25 pages. The report has to be longer because it has more to report, stories not told in the first telling. It offers more because it draws upon more evidence. The report packs 205 footnotes with citations for its story; 50 did the job for the first one.

Within that last difference is the difference that causes every other difference. To write this report, Scott Ellsworth used evidence he did not have—no one had it—as recently as 1982. He cites that new evidence at least 148 times. He had information from black sources accessible now because of this commission.

That knowledge contributed to Scott Ellsworth's citations from black newspapers, black interviews, or black writings. He cites black sources at least 272 times.

No wonder the two are different. From now on, everything can be different. They almost have to be.

Before there was this commission, much was known about the Tulsa race riot. More was unknown. It was buried somewhere, lost somewhere, or somewhere undiscovered. No longer.

Old records have been reopened, missing files have been recovered, new sources have been found. Still being assembled and processed by the Oklahoma Historical Society, their total volume passed ten thousand pages some time ago and well may reach twenty thousand by the time everything is done.

The dimensions of twenty thousand pages can be measured physically. Placed side-by-side, they would reach across at least ten yards of library shelving, filling every inch with new information. The significance of these twenty thousand pages has to be gauged vertically and metaphorically though. Stacked high, they amount to a tower of new knowledge. Rising to reach a new perspective, they offer visions never seen before.

The 1921 Tulsa Race Riot Commission thereby has discharged the mandate to gather and preserve a record of historical significance.

The Commission shall … develop a historical record of the 1921 Tulsa Race Riot.…

The commission's first substantive decision was to greet this obligation with a series of questions, and there was compelling reason why.

Eighty years after the fact, almost as many unresolved questions surround the race riot as did in 1921—maybe even more. Commissioners knew that no "historical record" would be complete unless it answered the most enduring of those questions—or explain why not. That was reason enough for a second decision: Commissioners agreed to seek consultants, respected scholars, and other experts to investigate those questions and offer answers.

Their findings follow immediately, all without change or comment, each just as the commission received it. Accompanying papers present what scholars and others consider the best answers to hard questions. The reports define their questions, either directly or implicitly, and usually explain why they need answers. The authors give answers, but they present them with only the confidence and exactly the precision they can justify. Most retrace the route they followed to reach their positions. All advance their positions openly. If they sense themselves in hostile territory, some stake their ground and defend it.

The commissioners harbor no illusion that every reader will accept their every answer to every question. They know better. Why should everyone else? None of them do. All eleven have reservations, some here, some there. Some dispute this point; some deny that one. Some suggest other possibilities. Some insist upon positions squarely opposite the scholars'.

None of that matters. However they divide over specifics, they also are united on principles. Should any be in need, they endorse and recommend the route they took to reach their own consensus. The way around an enraged showdown and the shortest path to a responsible solution is the line that passes through points ahead. Each point marks a big question and an important answer. Study them carefully.

What was the total value of property destroyed in the Tulsa race riot, both in 1921's dollars and in today's? Larry O'Dell has the numbers. Any one of them could be a little off, probably none by very much. Could a lawyer argue, and might a judge decree, that citizens living now had a duty to make that good, had to repay those losses, all because of something that happened eighty years ago? Alfred Brophy can make the case, and he does.

Over eight decades, some Tulsans (mostly black Tulsans) have insisted that whites attacked Greenwood from the air, even bombed it from military airplanes. Other Tulsans (mostly white Tulsans) have denied those claims; many have never even heard them. In a sense, it is a black-or-white question, but Richard S. Warner demonstrates that it has no black-or-white answer.

He proves it absolutely false that military planes could have employed military weapons on Greenwood. He also proves it absolutely true that civilian aircraft did fly over the riot area. Some were there for police reconnaissance, some for photography, some for other legitimate purposes.

He also thinks it reasonable to believe that others had less innocent use. It is probable that shots were fired and that incendiary devices were dropped, and these would have contributed to riot-related deaths or destruction. How much? No one will ever know: History permits no black-or-white answer.

Can modern science bring light to old, dark rumors about a mass grave, at least one, probably more, somewhere in Tulsa? Could those rumors be true? If true, where is one? Robert L. Brooks and Alan H. Witten have answers. Yes, science can address those rumors. Yes, there are many reasons to believe that mass graves exist. Where? They can point precisely to the single most likely spot. They can explain why scientists settle on that one—explain it clearly enough and completely enough to convince non-scientists, too. Without making a scratch on the ground, they can measure how deep it has to be, how thick, how wide, how long. Were the site to be exhumed and were it to yield human remains, what would anyone learn? Quite a bit if Lesley Rankin-Hill and Phoebe Stubblefield were to examine them.

How many people were killed, anyway? At the time, careful calculations varied almost as much as did pure guesses—forty, fifty, one hundred, two hundred, three hundred, maybe more. After a while, it became hard to distinguish the calculations from the guesses. By now, the record has become so muddied that even the most careful and thorough scientific investigation can offer no more than a preliminary possible answer.

Clyde Collins Snow's inquiry is just as careful and just as thorough as one might expect from this forensic anthropologist of international reputation, and preliminary is the word that he insists upon for his findings. By the most conservative of all possible methods, he can identify thirty-eight riot victims, and he provides the cause of death and the burial site for each of them. He even gives us the names of all but the four burned beyond recognition.

That last fact is their defining element. Thirty-eight is only the number of dead that Snow can identify individually. It says nothing of those who lost their lives in the vicious riot and lost their personal identities in records never kept or later destroyed. An accurate death count would just begin at thirty-eight; it might end well into the hundreds. Snow explains why as many as 150 might have to be added for one reason, 18 more for an other reason. What neither he nor anyone can ever know is how many to add for how many reasons. That is why there will never be a better answer to the question of how many died than this: How many? Too many.

For some questions there will never be answers even that precise. Open for eighty years and open now, they will remain open forever because they are too large to be filled by the evidence at hand.

Some of the hardest questions surround the evidence, itself. Evidence amounting to personal statements—things said to have been seen, heard, or otherwise observed—raises an entire set of questions in itself. Surely some statements are more credible than others, but how credible is that? Most evidence is incomplete; it may be suggestive but is it dispositive? Evidence often inspires inference, but is the inference reasonable or even possible? Evidence is usually ambiguous, does it mean this or does it mean that? Almost every piece of evidence requires an interpretation, but is only one interpretation possible? Responsibilities will be assigned, decisions will be evaluated, judgments will be offered—on what basis?

These are not idle academic musings. On the contrary: This small set of questions explains why so many specific questions remain open. They explain how people—reasonable, fair-minded, well-intended people—can disagree so often about so much.

Consider a question as old as the riot itself. At the time, many said that this was no spontaneous eruption of the rabble; it was planned and executed by the elite. Quite a few people—including some members of this commission—have since studied the question and are persuaded that this is so, that the Tulsa race riot was the result of a conspiracy. This is a serious position and a provable position—if one looks at certain evidence in certain ways.

Others—again, including members of this commission—have studied the same question and examined the same evidence, but they have looked at it in different ways. They see there no proof of conspiracy. Selfish desires surely. Awful effects certainly. But not a conspiracy. Both sides have evidence that they consider convincing, but neither side can convince the other.

Another nagging question involves the role of the Ku Klux Klan. Everyone who has studied the riot agrees that the Klan was present in Tulsa at the time of the riot and that it had been for some time. Everyone agrees that within months of the riot Tulsa's Klan chapter had be come one of the nation's largest and most powerful, able to dictate its will with the ballot as well as the whip.

Everyone agrees that many of the city's most prominent men were klansmen in the early 1920s and that some remained klansmen through out the decade. Everyone agrees that Tulsa's atmosphere reeked with a Klan-like stench that oozed through the robes of the Hooded Order.

Does this mean that the Klan helped plan the riot? Does it mean that the Klan helped execute it? Does it mean that the Klan, as an organization, had any role at all? Or does it mean that any time thousands of whites assembled—especially if they assembled to assault blacks—that odds were there would be quite a few Klansmen in the mix? Does the presence of those individuals mean that the institution may have been an instigator or the agent of a plot? Maybe both? Maybe neither? Maybe nothing at all? Not everyone agrees on that.

Nor will they ever. Both the conspiracy and the Klan questions remain what they always have been and probably what they always will be. Both are examples of nearly every problem inherent to historical evidence. How reliable is this oral tradition? What conclusions does that evidence permit? Are these inferences reasonable? How many ways can this be interpreted? And so it must go on. Some questions will always be disputed because other questions block the path to their answers. That does not mean there will be no answers, just that there will not be one answer per one question. Many questions will have two, quite a few even more. Some answers will never be proven. Some will never be disproved. Accept it: Some things can never be known.

That is why the complete record of what began in the late evening of May 31 and continued through the morning of June 1 will never quite escape those hours, themselves. They forever are darkened by night or enshrouded by day.

But history has a record of things certain for the hours between one day's twilight and the next day's afternoon. These things:

- Black Tulsans had every reason to believe that Dick Rowland would be lynched after his arrest on charges later dismissed and highly suspect from the start.
- They had cause to believe that his personal safety, like the defense of themselves and their community, depended on them alone.
- As hostile groups gathered and their confrontation worsened, municipal and county authorities failed to take actions to calm or contain the situation.
- At the eruption of violence, civil officials selected many men, all of them white and some of them participants in that violence, and made those men their agents as deputies.
- In that capacity, deputies did not stem the violence but added to it, often through overt acts themselves illegal.
- Public officials provided firearms and ammunition to individuals, again all of them white.

- Units of the Oklahoma National Guard participated in the mass arrests of all or nearly all of Greenwood's residents, removed them to other parts of the city, and detained them in holding centers.
- Entering the Greenwood district, people stole, damaged or destroyed personal property left behind in homes and businesses.
- People, some of them agents of government, also deliberately burned or otherwise destroyed homes credibly estimated to have numbered 1,256, along with virtually every other structure—including churches, schools, businesses, even a hospital and library—in the Greenwood district.
- Despite duties to preserve order and to protect property, no government at any level offered adequate resistance, if any at all, to what amounted to the destruction of the neighborhood referred to commonly as "Little Africa" and politely as the "Negro quarter."
- Although the exact total can never be determined, credible evidence makes it probable that many people, likely numbering between one and three hundred, were killed during the riot.
- Not one of these criminal acts was then or ever has been prosecuted or punished by government at any level, municipal, county, state, or federal.
- Even after the restoration of order it was official policy to release a black detainee only upon the application of a white person, and then only if that white person agreed to accept responsibility for that detainee's subsequent behavior.
- As private citizens, many whites in Tulsa and neighboring communities did extend invaluable assistance to the riot's victims, and the relief efforts of the American Red Cross in particular provided a model of human behavior at its best.
- Although city and county government bore much of the cost for Red Cross relief, neither contributed substantially to Greenwood's rebuilding; in fact, municipal authorities acted initially to impede rebuilding.
- In the end, the restoration of Greenwood after its systematic destruction was left to the victims of that destruction.

These things are not myths, not rumors, not speculations, not questioned. They are the historical record.

The 1921 Tulsa Race Riot Commission thereby has discharged the mandate to develop a historical record of the 1921 Tulsa Race Riot.

The final report of the Commission's findings and recommendations . . . may contain specific recommendations about whether or not reparations can or should be made and the appropriate methods. . . .

Unlike those quoted before, these words give this commission not an obligation but an opportunity. Nearly every commissioner intends to seize it.

A short letter sent to Governor Frank Keating as a preliminary report in February, 2000 declared the majority's view that reparations could and should be made. "Good public policy," that letter said, required no less. This report maintains the same, and this report makes the case.

Case, reparations—the words, themselves, seem to summon images of lawyers and courtrooms, along with other words, words like culpability, damages, remedies, restitution. Each is a term used in law, with strict legal meaning.

Sometimes commissioners use those words, too, and several agree—firmly agree—that those words describe accurately what happened in 1921 and fit exactly what should happen now.

Those, however, are their personal opinions, and the commissioners who hold them do so as private citizens. Even the most resolute of its members recognizes that this commission has a very different role. This commission is neither court nor judge, and its members are not a jury.

The commission has no binding legal authority to assign culpability, to determine damages, to establish a remedy, or to order either restitution or reparations. In fact, it has no judicial authority whatsoever.

It also has no reason or need for such authority. Any judgments that it might offer would be without effect and meaning. Its words would as well be cast to the winds. Any recommendations that it might offer neither have nor need judicial status at all. Statutes grant this commission its authority to make recommendations and the choice of how—or even if—to exercise that authority.

The commission's majority is determined to exercise its discretion and to declare boldly and directly their purpose: to recommend, independent of what law allows, what these commissioners believe is the right thing to do. They propose to do that in a dimension equal to their purpose. Courts have other purposes, and law operates in a different dimension. Mistake one for the other—let this commission assume what rightly belongs to law—does worse than miss the point. It ruins it.

Think of the difference this way. We will never know exactly how many were killed during the Tulsa race riot, but take at random any twenty-five from that unknown total. What we say of those we might say for everyone of the others, too.

Considering the twenty-five to be homicides, the law would approach those as twenty-five acts performed by twenty-five people (or thereabouts) who, with twenty-five motives, committed twenty-five crimes against twenty-five persons. That they occurred within hours and within a few blocks of each other is irrelevant. It would not matter even if the same person committed two, three, ten of the murders on the same spot, moments apart. Each was a separate act, and each (were the law to do its duty) merits a separate consequence. Law can apprehend it no other way.

Is there no other way to understand that? Of course there is. There is a far better way.

Were these twenty-five crimes or one? Did each have a separate motive, or was there a single intent? Were twenty-five individuals responsible, those and no one else? The burning of 1,256 homes—if we understand these as 1,256 acts of arson committed by 1,256 criminals driven by 1,256 desires, if we understand it that way, do we understand anything at all? These were not any number of multiple acts of homicide; this was one act of horror. If we must name the fires, call it outrage, for it was one. For both, the motive was not to injure hundreds of people, nearly all unseen, almost all unknown. The intent was to intimidate one community, to let it be known and let it be seen. Those who pulled the triggers, those who struck the matches—they alone were law breakers. Those who shouted encouragement and those who stood silently by—they were responsible.

These are the qualities that place what happened in Tulsa outside the realm of law—and not just in Tulsa, either. Lexington, Sapulpa, Norman, Shawnee, Lawton, Claremore, Perry; Waurika, Dewey, and Marshall—earlier purges in every one already had targeted entire black communities, marking every child, woman, and man for exile.

There is no count of how many those people numbered, but there is no need to know that. Know that there, too, something more than a bad guy had committed something more than a crime against something more than a person. Not someone made mad by lust, not a person gripped by rage, not a heartbroken party of romance gone sour, not one or any number of individuals but a collective body—acting as one body—had coldly and deliberately and systematically assaulted one victim, a whole community, intending to eliminate it as a community. If other black communities heard about it and learned their lessons, too, so much the better; a little intimidation went a long way.

All of this happened years before, most fifteen or twenty years before Dick Rowland landed in jail, but they remained vivid in the recent memories of Greenwood's younger adults.

This, or something quite like it, was almost always what happened when the subject was race.

Here was nothing as amorphous as racism. Here were discrete acts—one act, one town—each consciously calculated to have a collective effect not against a person but against a people.

And is that not also the way of Oklahoma's voting laws at the time? The state had amended its constitution and crafted its laws not to keep this person or that person or a whole list of persons from voting. Lengthen that list to the indefinite, write down names to the infinite—one still will not reach the point. For that, one line, one word is enough. The point was to keep a race, as a race, away from the polls.

Jim Crow laws—the segregation commands of Oklahoma's statutes and of its constitution—worked that way, too. Their object was not to keep some exhausted mother and her two young children out of a "white car" on a train headed somewhere like Checotah and send them walking six miles home. (Even if John Hope Franklin could recall that about his own mother and sister and himself as he accepted the Helmerich Award some three-quarters of a century afterwards.) No, the one purpose was to keep one race "in its place." When Laura Nelson was lynched years earlier in Okemah, it was not to punish her by death. It was to terrify the living. Why else would the lynchers have taken (and printed and copied and posted and distributed) that photograph of her hanging from the bridge, her little boy dangling beside her?

The lynchers knew the purpose; the photographer just helped it along. The purpose had not changed much by 1921, when another photographer snapped another picture, a long shot showing Greenwood's ruin, smoke rising from fires blazing in the background. "RUNING THE NEGRO OUT OF TULSA" someone wrote across it, candor atoning for misspelling. No doubt there. No shame either.

Another photograph probably was snapped the same day but from closer range. It showed what just days before must have been a human being, maybe one who had spent a warm day in late May working and talking and laughing. On this day, though, it was only a grotesque, blackened form, a thing, really, its only sign of humanity the charred remains of arms and hands forever raised, as if in useless supplication.

Shot horizontally, that particular photo still turns up from time to time in the form of an early use: as a postcard. People must have thought it a nice way to send a message.

It still sends a message, too big to be jotted down in a few lines; but, then, this message is not especially nice either. The message is that here is an image of more than a single victim of a single episode in a single city. This image preserves the symbol of a story, preserves it in the same way that the story was told: in black-and-white.

See those two photos and understand that the Tulsa race riot was the worst event in that city's history—an event without equal and without excuse. Understand, too, that it was the worst explosion of violence in this state's history—an episode late to be acknowledged and still to be repaired. But understand also that it was part of a message usually announced not violently at all, but calmly and quietly and deliberately.

Who sent the message? Not one person but many acting as one. Not a "mob"; it took forms too calculated and rational for that word. Not "society"; that word is only a mask to conceal responsibility within a fog of imprecision. Not "whites," because this never spoke for all whites; sometimes it spoke for only a few. Not "America," because the federal government was, at best, indifferent to its black citizens and, at worse, oblivious of them. Fifty years or so after the Civil War, Uncle Sam was too complacent to crusade for black rights and too callous to care. Let the states handle that—states like Oklahoma.

Except that it really was not "Oklahoma" either. At least, it was not all of Oklahoma. It was just one Oklahoma, one Oklahoma that is distinguishable from another Oklahoma partly by purpose. This Oklahoma had the purpose of keeping the other Oklahoma in its place, and that place was subordinate. That, after all, was the object of suffrage requirements and segregation laws. No less was it the intent behind riots and lynchings, too. One Oklahoma was putting the other Oklahoma in its place.

One Oklahoma also had the power to effect its purpose, and that power had no need to rely on occasional explosions of rage. Simple violence is, after all, the weapon of simple people, people with access to no other instruments of power at all. This Oklahoma had access to power more subtle, more regular, and more formal than that. Indeed, its ready access to such forms of power partially defined that Oklahoma.

No, that Oklahoma is not the same as government, used here as a rhetorical trick to make one accountable for the acts of the other. Government was never the essence of that Oklahoma. Government was, however, always its potential instrument. Having access to government, however employed, if employed at all—just having it—defined this Oklahoma and was the essence of its power.

The acts recounted here reveal that power in one form or another, often several. The Tulsa race riot is one example, but only an example and only one. Put along side it earlier, less publicized pogroms—for that is what they were—in at least ten other Oklahoma towns. Include the systematic disfranchisement of the black electorate through constitutional amendment in 1910, reaffirmed through state statute in 1916.

Add to that the constitution's segregation of Oklahoma's public schools, the First Legislature's segregation of its public transportation, local segregation of Oklahoma neighborhoods through municipal ordinances in Tulsa and elsewhere, even the statewide segregation of public telephones by order of the corporation commission. Do not forget to include the lynchings of twenty-three African-Americans in twelve Oklahoma towns during the ten years leading to 1921. Stand back and look at those deeds now.

In some government participated in the deed.
In some government performed the deed.
In none did government prevent the deed.
In none did government punish the deed.

And that, in the end, is what this inquiry and what these recommendations are all about.

Make no mistake about it: There are members of this commission who are convinced that there is a compelling argument in law to order that present governments make monetary payment for past governments' unlawful acts. Professor Alfred Brophy presses one form of that argument; there doubtless are others.

This is not that legal argument but another one altogether. This is a moral argument. It holds that there are moral responsibilities here and that those moral responsibilities require moral responses now.

It gets down to this: The 1921 riot is, at once, a representative historical example and a unique historical event. It has many parallels in the pattern of past events, but it has no equal for its violence and its completeness. It symbolizes so much endured by so many for so long. It does it, however, in one way that no other can: in the living flesh and blood of some who did endure it.

These paradoxes hold answers to questions often asked: Why does the state of Oklahoma or the city of Tulsa owe anything to anybody? Why should any individual tolerate now spending one cent of one tax dollar over what happened so long ago? The answer is that these are not even the questions. This is not about individuals at all—not anymore than the race riot or anything like it was about individuals.

This is about Oklahoma—or, rather, it is about two Oklahomas. It must be about that because that is what the Tulsa race riot was all about, too. That riot proclaimed that there were two Oklahomas; that one claimed the right to push down, push out, and push under the other; and that it had the power to do that.

That is what the Tulsa race riot has been all about for so long afterwards, why it has lingered not as a past event but lived as a present entity. It kept on saying that there remained two Oklahomas; that one claimed the right to be dismissive of, ignorant of, and oblivious to the other; and that it had the power to do that.

That is why the Tulsa race riot can be about something else. It can be about making two Oklahomas one—but only if we understand that this is what reparation is all about. Because the riot is both symbolic and singular, reparations become both singular and symbolic, too.

Compelled not legally by courts but extended freely by choice, they say that individual acts of reparation will stand as symbols that fully acknowledge and finally discharge a collective responsibility.

Because we must face it: There is no way but by government to represent the collective, and there is no way but by reparations to make real the responsibility.

Does this commission have specific recommendations about whether or not reparations can or should be made and the appropriate methods? Yes, it surely does.

When commissioners went looking to do the right thing, that is what nearly all of them found and what they recommended in last year's preliminary report. To be sure they had found the right thing, they have used this formal report to explore once more the distant terrain of the Tulsa race riot and the forbidding territory in which it lies. Now, they are certain. Reparations are the right thing to do.

What else is there to do? What else is there to find?

SOURCE: Final Report of the Oklahoma Commission to Study the Tulsa Race Riot of 1921 at http://www.ok-history.mus.ok.us/trrc/freport.htm.

23. Excerpt from the Draft Report of the 1898 Wilmington Race Riot Commission, December 2005

Created by the North Carolina Legislature in 2000 to initiate and review research on the causes and course of the race riot that occurred in Wilmington in November 1898, the Wilmington Race Riot Commission issued its 600-page draft report on December 15, 2005. The excerpt from that report reproduced below describes the initial violence that occurred on November 10, 1898. The thirteen-member Commission concluded that the riot was not a spontaneous event, but was instead fomented by white businessmen and Democratic leaders who sought to overthrow the political power local blacks had won in the elections of 1894 and 1896, when an alliance between local Republicans and local Populists had broken the political dominance the Democrats had exercised in the town since the end of Reconstruction. Democrats had won the election held on November 8, two days before the disorders began, by stuffing ballot boxes and keeping African Americans from the polls through intimidation. The riots only sealed the return to power of white supremacist forces.

Eye of the Storm—Fourth and Harnett Streets

The bloodshed began when black workers from the waterfront industrial yards and Brooklyn residents confronted with armed whites. The point where the peace was fractured was at the corner of Fourth and Harnett Streets in Brooklyn, a mixed race neighborhood on the edge of the predominantly black section of Wilmington.

A group of blacks were gathered on the southwest corner of Fourth and Harnett near Brunje's Saloon in George Heyer's store when armed whites returned to the neighborhood. A streetcar also entered the area loaded with men direct from burning the Record. As the groups exchanged verbal assaults from opposite street corners, whites and blacks alike sought to calm fellow citizens.

Norman Lindsay encouraged his fellow blacks to go home: "For the sake of your lives, your families, your children, and your country, go home and stay there!" After Lindsay's plea, the group of blacks moved to the opposite corner at W.A. Walker's store while the whites took up a position between Brunje's store and St. Matthew's English Lutheran Church. Aaron Lockamy, a newly deputized white police officer, also tried to diffuse the problem by going between the two groups and trying to get them to disperse. He recalled that, while serving as a special policeman during the aftermath of the election, he was stationed in Brooklyn to ensure that the opening of two bars on Fourth Street would be peaceful. Instructed not to arrest anyone by Chief Melton, Lockamy asked the blacks to disperse and go home for their own safety. They refused but moved as a group a bit further away from the corner. Lockamy's inability to disperse the crowd angered the white men at the opposite corner. Lockamy felt he had done all he could in the turf war and went back to his post on Fourth near Brunswick. From this point forward, gunshots rang throughout the city for the next several hours.

White and black witnesses of the activities at the intersection of Fourth and Harnett both claimed that the other side was the responsible party for firing the first shots. There are conflicting viewpoints on first shots and an affidavit, probably taken by Rountree [Attorney George Rountree] was used in the newspapers to counter accounts from black witnesses such as George H. Davis, a black man wounded at Fourth and Harnett and interviewed by reporter Thomas Clawson for the Wilmington *Messenger*. Lockamy went back and forth between the clusters of whites and blacks on opposing corners at Fourth and Harnett at least two times and later said that the only people on the corner that were armed were whites. Nothwithstanding the point of origin, once the first shot was fired, whites launched a fusillade of bullets towards the blacks near Walker's store. Several black men fell injured but most were able to get up and run away from the scene. Most accounts agree that three men died instantly at Walker's while two injured men ran around the corner into a home at 411 Harnett. One of these men by the surname of Bizzell died in the house while the other, George H. Davis, was later taken to the hospital on the 11th and survived his wounds. Davis apparently lived at the residence and was wounded in his left thigh and had a bullet lodged between his shoulders. He was found in the house along with a dead black man and three women by reporter Clawson and taken to the hospital on the eleventh. Although Davis recovered, Clawson recalled that after he sent for a white doctor, W.D. McMillan, and a black doctor, T.R. Mask, he thought that "it appeared impossible for one so desperately wounded ever to recover." The rest of the men fled west on Harnett, reportedly firing at whites as they ran. Although it was difficult for black men to purchase weapons in the weeks and months just prior to the election, many already owned weapons for hunting or personal safety. Men identified in papers as wounded at Fourth and Harnett intersection: Alfred White, William Lindsay, Sam McFarland. Men identified as dead at Fourth and Harnett: John Townsend (Townsell?), Charles Lindsay (aka Silas Brown), William Mouzon, John L. Gregory. Whites identified as being at the scene: S. Hill Terry (armed with double-barrel shot gun loaded with buck shot), Theodore Curtis, N.B. Chadwick (armed with a 16-shot Colt or Remington rifle), Sam Matthews (armed with a .44 caliber Navy rifle), and George Piner.

After the first shots were fired, a streetcar entered the business section in downtown from Brooklyn and the conductor told men gathered there that blacks had shot into the car. Men crowded into the car bound for Brooklyn at the stop on Fourth and Harnett. One of the "first responders" was Captain Donald MacRae of Company K, fresh from the tense situation at Sprunt's Compress [Sprunt's Cotton Compress, where a standoff between whites and blacks had occurred earlier in the day]. MacRae recalled that once he arrived in Brooklyn after hearing reports of fighting, he began to establish a skirmish line with other white men in the area. He was stopped by another man because he was still a Captain of Company K in the U.S. Army and white leaders thought that he should not be involved in case the President investigated the participants.

Having feared the worst in the weeks prior to the election, leaders Roger Moore and Walker Taylor had developed a strategy for quelling violence by stationing contacts throughout the city with instructions to notify Taylor and Moore if trouble ignited. The contact in the Fourth Street area near Harnett was Bernice Moore at his drug store at 901 North Fourth Street. Moore was instructed by J. Alan Taylor of the Secret Nine to sound the "riot alarm" to alert the WLI [Wilmington Light Infantry] and Naval Reserves in the event of violence. As soon as shots were heard, Moore called the armory to inform the leaders there that shots were being fired in Brooklyn. Once the "riot alarm" was sounded, as leader of the WLI, Walker Taylor declared martial law and the WLI and the Naval Reserves began to make their way into the Brooklyn neighborhood.

Taylor had authority to take control because just before Moore's call for backup was received at the armory, a telegram arrived from Governor Russell through the state's Adjutant General that instructed Taylor to "take command of Captain James' company . . . and preserve the peace."

Before the Governor's telegram arrived, Commander George Morton of the Naval Reserves sought approval from a city official to grant the military authority to take over but claimed he could not locate the mayor or police officer. Instead, Morton's men found Deputy Sheriff G.Z. French in his room at the Orton Hotel and requested permission to march his men from his headquarters in Brooklyn. French complied, possibly under duress, and wrote out an order instructing Morton to "use all force at your disposal to quell the existing violation of the peace in this city."

Morton then sent a telegram to the Governor informing him of his plan of action as well as notifying Walker Taylor of his intentions. The Governor later ordered Morton to place his men under the command of Taylor although the transfer of power had already taken place by the time the telegram was received. Morton's men, equipped with Lee magazine rifles and a Hotchkiss rapid firing gun, assembled at the corner of Third and Princess.

As soon as the first shots were fired, a "running firefight" erupted on Harnett, with scores of men, black and white, running in all directions from the intersection, some firing at the opposite side as they ran. William Mayo, a white man who lived at 307 Harnett, was seriously wounded by a stray bullet.

Mayo's wounding presented a rallying point for the whites who then began to retaliate. Because of Mayo, whites fired in unison into a group of black men and another five or six died near the intersection of Harnett and Fourth Streets. Mayo was taken to a nearby drug store for treatment by Dr. John T. Schonwald who lived close to the scene. Mayo's injury was serious but since he received quick care, he survived an otherwise life-threatening injury. Additionally, two other white men, Bert Chadwick and George Piner, were injured and treated alongside Mayo. Mayo's wounding rallied the white men involved in the first scuffle and they began to avenge Mayo as they aimed for any blacks that came into sight. The whites also sought to identify the individual who shot Mayo, perhaps as a means to stop random shootings. Later in the afternoon they pointed to Daniel Wright, who lived nearby at 810 North Third, as the culprit responsible for shooting Mayo as well as shooting George Piner. A manhunt was launched for Wright.

As large groups of white men gathered in the vicinity of Fourth and Harnett—milling about, angry and eager to avenge Mayo's shooting—Wright was identified by a "half breed Indian" who told J. Alan Taylor that he knew who had shot Mayo. Taylor was shown a house where he was told Wright was hiding and that he could be identified by "a missing thumb on his right hand and the possession of an outmoded rifle with a large bore." Captain MacRae remembered the incident with the Indian, saying that he felt the man had a grudge against local blacks. Taylor then sent a group of men led by John S. Watters to capture and identify Wright. Once his house was surrounded, white witnesses claimed Wright went into the attic and shot into the approaching crowd, wounding Will Terry and George Bland.

Wright's home was set afire and he tried to escape but was captured while his wife watched from the street. Once captured, Wright was marched into the street and hit in the head with a length of gas pipe. When he stood back up, someone in the crowd suggested that Wright be hanged from a nearby lamp post. Before a rope could be found, a member of the Citizen's Patrol drove up and suggested that Wright be given the chance to run for his freedom. Wright was given this opportunity but, after he ran about fifty yards, "at least forty guns of all descriptions turned loose on him." Wright was left in the street bleeding and severely wounded with about thirteen gunshot wounds, five of which entered through his shoulders and back, for about a half hour before he was picked up and carried to the hospital. Doctors at the hospital observed that they had never seen anyone with as many gunshot wounds live for as long as Wright did. He held onto life until early the next morning and his body was handed over to undertaker Thomas Rivera for burial after a formal inquest by coroner David Jacobs.

More shots rang throughout the area as more and more whites and blacks filtered into the Brooklyn area. Among the white onlookers was attorney George Rountree. Having just mediated the safety of blacks at Sprunt's Compress, Rountree went to investigate so that if a governmental inquiry took place, he would be prepared to answer questions. Rountree is probably the person responsible for filing the sworn affidavit of William McAllister that was published repeatedly in local and statewide newspapers indicating that a black man was responsible for firing the first shots. Rountree recalled that he and several others attempted to "quiet the situation and to prevent any further shooting," but acknowledged that "at this time I had no influence whatever with the rioters" and was pleased that the arrival of the military "quieted the matter down as quickly as possible."

SOURCE: Wilmington 1898 Race Riot Commission Web site at http://www.ah.dcr.state.nc.us/1898-wrrc/report.

APPENDIX: A SELECT HISTORIOGRAPHY OF RACE RIOTS

The modern study of rioting began with the application of social science to the new social history of the 1960s, including African American studies and, within that field, racial violence. Otto Dahlke (1952) posited a hypothesis of rioting that black assaults on the color line drew white backlash. Expanding on this premise, Allen D. Grimshaw (1959) produced an in-depth study of urban riots since the Civil War, advancing topologies of disorder and theories of suppression. Grimshaw's work (*see also* 1969, 1999) affected everyone after him, notably Elliott M. Rudwick, author of the first modern study, *Riot in East St. Louis, July 2, 1917* (1964), which combined primary documents and comparative analysis of riots in 1919 Chicago and 1943 Detroit. With the 1960s disorders, Grimshaw's work took on new significance, particularly for scholars assisting federal endeavors to deal with the violence, including Rudwick and August Meier (1983) and Morris Janowitz (1983). Their studies for the National Commission on Causes and Prevention of Violence remain among the best on "rhetoric and retaliation" and patterns of racial violence. Other influential analyses include Robert M. Fogelson, *Violence as Protest* (1972); Joe R. Feagin and Harlan Hahn, *Ghetto Revolts* (1973); Terry A. Knopf, *Rumors, Race, and Riot* (1975); and Russell Dynes and E.L. Quarantelli, "What Looting in Civil Disturbances Really Means" (1968). Leonard L. Richards, *Gentlemen of Property and Standing* (1971) addressed pre–Civil War anti-abolition rioting.

Meanwhile, drawing from this body of work, including that of the National Advisory Commission on Civil Disorders, William M. Tuttle, Jr., penned his classic *Race Riot* (1970). His inspired writing, with an emphasis on ordinary people, dissection of riot conditions, sociopsychological analysis, and comparison of Chicago's outburst in 1919 with those of the 1960s is the model of scholarship that benefited a generation of riot studies, including those by Christina S. Haynes (1976), Dominic J. Capeci, Jr. (1977/1981), and Scott Ellsworth (1982). In 1989, Sidney Fine closed this era with a detailed account of the 1967 Detroit riot.

Thereafter, riot scholars began addressing new queries and using class and gender theory, sampling methods, and oral and legal history. For example, Iver Bernstein (1990) placed the New York draft riots within the Civil War, party politics, and class antagonisms. Roberta Senechal (1990) focused on participants and victims in the Springfield, Illinois, riot of 1908, stressing the outburst's class dimension, while Dominic J. Capeci, Jr., and Martha Wilkerson (1991) established similarities between those white rioters and their counterparts in the Detroit riots of 1943 and 1967. They provided the only sample of black male, white male, and black female participants and victims, including white women victims, for any riot, challenging the stereotype of rioters as largely riffraff and criminals. Gail Williams O'Brien (1997) demonstrated in the Columbia, Tennessee, riot of 1946 the reconfiguration of extralegal violence and its limitations in the postwar era; police replaced the mob in white attacks on blacks and avoided federal prosecution, while black arrestees avoided state prosecution. She indicated, too, that, ultimately, lynching declined as both races departed the rural South, and legal protection for African Americans reemerged in the civil rights era. And, for the pre–Civil War years, David Grimstead (1998) compared 600 northern and southern riots.

Significantly, historians, lawyers, and officials in the 1990s also revisited the 1920s pogroms in Rosewood and Tulsa, linking them to the reparation issue. Their findings appeared in the studies of Michael D'Orso (1996) and Alfred L. Brophy (2002). The subject of memory and history for the Tulsa pogrom was addressed by James S. Hirsch (2002), while the Philips County, Arkansas, pogrom was examined by Grif Stockley (2001) and Nan Elizabeth Woodruff (2003). Given the revelations of wholesale slaughter and scholarship on holocausts, Tuttle, speaking at the Mid-America Conference on History (2004), considered these pogroms acts of genocide and called upon historians to reinvestigate racial violence from 1917 to 1923 with "fresh lenses," undertake studies in comparative racism, and "reconceptualize the field." He also contended that previous riot scholarship should be analyzed.

Almost simultaneously, Charles Tilly (2003) rethought his earlier analysis of uprisings in the 1960s (1975), concluding that looters possessed grievances, but were hardly protesters. He deemed their actions opportunism, and omitted "riot" from his refashioned typology of interpersonal violence worldwide because it connotes "a political judgment rather than an analytical distinction"; authorities use the term disapprovingly, while participants never use it.

Although the contrasting theories of Tuttle and Tilly refer to different types and periods of rioting, they draw on international comparisons and signal that the study of collective racial violence—including lynching—is at a crossroads similar to the 1960s. Building on data compiled by anti-lynching organizations and analytical studies published by Walter F. White (1929), James H. Chadbourn (1933), and Arthur F. Raper (1933), among others, lynching scholarship experienced a renaissance in the mid-1970s. It began with three works on the anti-lynching crusade by Donald L. Grant (1975), Jacquelyn Dowd Hall (1979), and Robert L. Zangrando (1980). These were followed by Hall's seminal article on rape and racial violence (1983) and by

James R. McGovern's and Howard Smead's respective monographs on the lynching of Claude Neal (1982) and Mack Charles Parker (1986). In 1990, George C. Wright published his insightful study of racial violence in Kentucky.

Thereafter, W. Fitzhugh Brundage, Stewart E. Tolnay, and E.M. Beck, energized the field further. Brundage (1993, 1997) published his model study of lynching in Georgia and Virginia, while Tolnay and Beck (1995) produced the most accurate lynching database compiled for ten southern-border states from 1882 to 1930. Two years later, Brundage edited a book on new lynching perspectives. Since then, many scholars have expanded upon them, including Grace Elizabeth Hale on whiteness and spectacle lynching and legal precedent (1998), Dominic J. Capeci, Jr., on the Cleo Wright lynching and legal precedent (1998), James Allen on lynching photography (2000), Dora Apel on lynching photography and protest (2004), and Jonathan Markovitz on lynching and memory (2004).

Christopher Waldrep (2002) recently questioned the definition of lynching, its use historically and by scholars, as well as the tendency to ignore the subject outside the South. To this, Michael J. Pfeifer (2004) responded in his study of lynching in several regions over nearly seventy-five years. Thus lynching and rioting scholarship have entered new stages of debate that continue to advance our understanding of collective racial violence.

To date, however, the standard syntheses of racial violence that provide incisive analyses and bibliographies beyond each encyclopedic entry remain: Richard Maxwell Brown, *Strain of Violence* (1975); Herbert Shapiro, *White Violence and Black Response* (1988); and Paul A. Gilje, *Rioting in America* (1996). Brown's work includes reports for the National Commission on Causes and Prevention of Violence (1968), *No Duty to Retreat* (1991), and "Overview of Violence in the United States" (1999). Shapiro plans a second volume on the civil rights era and aftermath. Gilje also wrote *The Road to Mobocracy* (1987). Further information appears in reference books, the most useful companion to this is an edited work by Ronald Gottesman, *Violence in America: An Encyclopedia* (1999).

References

Allen, James, Hilton Als, Jon Lewis, Leon F. Litwack. 2000. *Without Sanctuary: Lynching Photography in America*. Santa Fe, NM: Twin Palms.

Apel, Dora. 2004. *Imagery of Lynching: Black Men, White Women, and the Mob*. New Brunswick, NJ: Rutgers University Press.

Bernstein, Iver. 1990. *The New York City Draft Riots: Their Significance for American Society and Politics in the Age of the Civil War*. New York: Oxford University Press.

Brophy, Alfred L. 2002. *Reconstructing the Dreamland: The Tulsa Riot of 1921, Race, Reparations, and Reconciliation*. New York: Oxford University Press.

Brown, Richard Maxwell. 1969. "Historical Patterns of Violence in America" and "The American Vigilante Tradition" in *Violence in America: Historical and Comparative Perspectives*. Ed. Leon Friedman. New York: Chelsea, Volume III, pp. 35–64 and 121–169. The National Commission on the Causes and Prevention of Violence Report of 1969.

——. 1975. *Strain of Violence: Historical Studies of American Violence and Vigilantism*. New York: Oxford University Press.

——. 1991. *No Duty to Retreat: Violence and Values in American History and Society*. New York: Oxford University Press.

——. 1999. "Overview of Violence in the United States" in *Violence in America: An Encyclopedia*, ed. Ronald Gottesman. New York: Scribner, I, 1–20.

Brundage, Fitzhugh, ed. 1993. *Lynching in the New South: Georgia and Virginia, 1880–1930*. Urbana: University of Illinois Press.

——. 1997. *Under Sentence of Death: Lynching in the South*. Chapel Hill: University of North Carolina Press.

Capeci, Dominic J., Jr. 1977. *The Harlem Riot of 1943*. Philadelphia: Temple University Press.

——. 1984. *Race Relations in Wartime Detroit: The Sojourner Truth Controversy of 1942*. Philadelphia: Temple University Press.

——. 1998. *The Lynching of Cleo Wright*. Lexington: University Press of Kentucky.

Capeci, Dominic J., Jr., and Martha Wilkerson. 1991. *Layered Violence: The Detroit Rioters of 1943*. Jackson: University Press of Mississippi.

Chadbourn, James H. 1933. *Lynching and the Law*. Chapel Hill: University of North Carolina Press, 1933.

D'Orso, Michael. 1996. *Like Judgment Day: The Ruin and Redemption of a Town Called Rosewood*. New York: G.P. Putnam's Sons.

Dahlke, Otto. 1952. "Race and Minority Riots—A Study in the Typology of Violence." *Social Forces* 30 (May): 419–425.

Dynes, Russell, and E.L. Quarantelli. 1968. "What Looting in Civil Disturbances Really Means." *Transaction* 11 (March): 9–14.

Ellsworth, Scott. 1982. *Death in a Promised Land: The Tulsa Race Riot of 1921*. Baton Rouge: Louisiana State University Press.

Feagin, Joe R., and Harlan Hahn. 1973. *Ghetto Revolts: The Politics of Violence in American Cities*. New York: Macmillan Publishing Company.

Fogelson, Robert M. 1971. *Violence as Protest: A Study of Riots and Ghettos*. Garden City, NY: Doubleday & Company, Inc.

Gilje, Paul A. 1987. *The Road to Mobocracy: Popular Disorder in New York City, 1763–1834*. Chapel Hill: University of North Carolina Press.

——. 1996. *Rioting in America*. Bloomington: Indiana University Press.

Gottesman, Ronald, ed. 1999. *Violence in America: An Encyclopedia*. New York: Scribner.

Grant, Donald L. 1975. *The Anti-lynching Movement, 1883–1932*. San Francisco: R and E Research Associates.

Grimshaw, Allen D. 1959. "A Study in Social Violence: Urban Race Riots in the United States." Unpublished Ph.D. dissertation, University of Pennsylvania.

——, ed. 1969. *Racial Violence in the United States*. Chicago: Aldine Publishing Co.

——. 1999. "Riots" in *Violence in America: An Encyclopedia*. Ed. Ronald Gottesman. New York: Scribner, 1: 52–64.

Grimstead, David. 1998. *American Mobbing, 1828–1861: Toward Civil War*. New York: Oxford University Press, 1998.

Hale, Grace Elizabeth. 1998. *Making Whiteness: The Culture of Segregation in the South, 1890–1940*. New York: Pantheon Books.

Hall, Jacquelyn Dowd. 1979. *Revolt against Chivalry: Jessie Daniel Ames and the Women's Campaign against Lynching*. New York: Columbia University Press.

——. 1983. "'The Mind That Burns in Each Body': Women, Rape, and Racial Violence" in *Powers of Desire: The Politics of Sexuality*. Eds. Ann Snitow, Christine Stansell, and Sharon Thompson. New York: Monthly Review Press, pp. 330–346.

Haynes, Robert V. 1976. *A Night of Violence: The Houston Riot of 1917*. Baton Rouge: Louisiana State University Press.

Hirsch, James S. 2002. *Riot and Remembrance: The Tulsa Race War and Its Legacy*. New York: Houghton Mifflin Company.

Janowitz, Morris. 1983. "Patterns of Collective Racial Violence" in *Violence in America: Historical and Comparative Perspectives*. Ed. Leon Friedman. New York: Chelsea House, III, 15–37.

Knopf, Terry A. 1975. *Rumors, Race, and Riot*. New Brunswick, NJ: Transaction Books.

Markovitz, Jonathan. 2004. *Legacies of Lynching: Racial Violence and Memory*. Minneapolis: University of Minnesota Press.

McGovern, James R. 1982. *Anatomy of a Lynching: The Killing of Claude Neal*. Baton Rouge: Louisiana State University.

Meier, August, and Elliott M. Rudwick. 1983. "Black Violence in the 20th Century: A Study in Rhetoric and Retaliation" in *Violence in America: Historical and Comparative Perspectives*, ed. Leon Friedman. New York: Chelsea House, III, 5–14.

National Association for the Advancement of Colored People. 1919/1969. *Thirty Years of Lynching in the United States, 1889–1918*. Reprint. New York: Negro Universities Press.

O'Brien, Gail Williams. 1997. *The Color of the Law: Race, Violence, and Justice in the Post–World War II South*. Chapel Hill: University of North Carolina Press.

Pfeifer, Michael J. 2004. *Rough Justice: Lynching and American Society, 1874–1947*. Urbana: University of Illinois Press.

Raper, Arthur F. 1933/1969. *The Tragedy of Lynching*. Reprint. Montclair, N.J.: Patterson Smith.

Richards, Leonard L. 1971. *Gentlemen of Property and Standing: Anti-Abolition Mobs in Jacksonian America*. New York: Oxford University Press, 1971.

Rudwick, Elliott M. 1964. *Race Riot at East St. Louis, July 2, 1917*. Carbondale, IL: Southern Illinois University Press.

Senechal, Roberta. 1990. *The Sociogenesis of a Race Riot: Springfield, Illinois, in 1908*. Urbana: University of Illinois Press.

Shapiro, Herbert. 1988. *White Violence and Black Response: From Reconstruction to Montgomery*. Amherst: University of Massachusetts Press.

Smead, Howard. 1986. *Blood Justice: The Lynching of Mack Charles Parker*. New York: Oxford University Press.

Stockley, Grif. 2001. *Blood in Their Eyes: The Elaine Massacres of 1919*. Fayetteville: University of Arkansas Press.

Tilly, Charles. 2003. *The Politics of Collective Violence*. Cambridge: Cambridge University Press, 12–20. *See* p. 18 for the quotation and pp. 145–150 for opportunism as one of seven types of interpersonal violence: violent rituals, coordinated destruction, brawls, individual aggression, scattered attacks, and broken negotiations.

Tilly, Charles, Louise Tilly, and Richard Tilly. 1975. *Rebellious Century, 1830–1930*. Cambridge, MA: Harvard University Press.

Tolnay, Stewart E., and E.M. Beck. 1995. *A Festival of Violence: An Analysis of Southern Lynchings, 1882–1930*. Urbana: University of Illinois Press.

Tuttle, William M., Jr. 1970. *Race Riot: Chicago in the Red Summer of 1919*. New York: Atheneum.

——. 2004. "Black Uplift, White Fury: The Shame of America's Red Summers, 1917–1923." Mid-America Conference on History, Springfield, Missouri, October 1, pp. 17, 19.

Waldrep, Christopher. 2002. *The Many Faces of Judge Lynch: Extralegal Violence and Punishment in America*. New York: Palgrave.

White, Walter F. 1929/1969. *Rope and Faggot: A Biography of Judge Lynch*. Reprint. New York: Arno.

Woodruff, Nan Elizabeth. 2003. *American Congo: The African American Freedom Struggle in the Delta*. Cambridge, MA: Harvard University Press.

Wright, George C. 1990. *Racial Violence in Kentucky, 1865–1940: Lynchings, Mob Rule, and "Legal Lynchings."* Baton Rouge: Louisiana State University Press.

Zangrando, Robert L. 1980. *Crusade against Lynching, 1909–1950*. Philadelphia: Temple University Press.

Dominic J. Capeci, Jr.

BIBLIOGRAPHY

Books

Achor, Shirley. *Mexican Americans in a Dallas Barrio*. Tucson: University of Arizona Press, 1978.

Adams, Graham. *Age of Industrial Violence, 1910–1915*. New York: Columbia University Press, 1966.

Ahmad, Muhammad, Ernie Allen, John H. Bracey, and Randolph, Boehm, eds. *The Black Power Movement (Black Studies Research Sources)*. Bethesda, MD: LexisNexis, 2002.

Al-Amin, Jamil. *Revolution by the Book: (The Rap Is Live)*. Beltsville, MD: Writers' Inc. International, 1993.

Allen, James, Hilton Als, Jon Lewis, Leon F. Litwack. *Without Sanctuary: Lynching Photography in America*. Santa Fe, CA: Twin Palms Publishers, 2000.

Andrews, William L., Frances Smith Foster, and Trudier Harris, eds. *Oxford Companion to African American Literature*. New York: Oxford University Press, 1997.

Appiah, Kwame Anthony, and Henry Louis Gates, Jr., eds. *Africana: The Encyclopedia of the African and African American Experience*. 5 vols. New York: Oxford University Press, 2005.

Appiah, Kwame Anthony, and Henry Louis Gates, Jr., eds. *Africana Civil Rights: An A–Z Reference of the Movement that Changed America*. Philadelphia and London: Running Press, 2004.

Aptheker, Bettina, ed. *Lynching and Rape: An Exchange of Views*. New York: American Institute for Marxist Studies, 1977.

Armor, David J. *Forced Justice: School Desegregation and the Law*. New York: Oxford University Press, 1995.

Asante, Molefi Kete, and Mambo Ama Mazama, eds. *Encyclopedia of Black Studies*. Thousand Oaks, CA: Sage Publications, 2005.

Assarsson-Rizzi, Kerstin, and Harold Bohrn. *Gunnar Myrdal, a Bibliography, 1919–1981*. New York: Garland Publishing, 1984.

Ayers, E.L. *The Promise of the New South: Life after Reconstruction*. New York: Oxford University Press, 1992.

Baker, Ray Stannard. *Following the Color Line: American Negro Citizenship in the Progressive Era*. 1908. Reprint, New York: Harper Torchbooks, 1964.

Baldassare, Mark, ed. *The Los Angeles Riots: Lessons for the Urban Future*. Boulder, CO: Westview Press, 2004.

Baldwin, James. *Blues for Mister Charlie*. New York: Vintage, 1995. Originally published 1964.

Baldwin, James. *Collected Essays*. New York: Library of America, 1998.

Balfour, Katharine Lawrence. *The Evidence of Things Not Said: James Baldwin and the Promise of American Democracy*. Ithaca, NY: Cornell University Press, 2001.

Ball, Howard. *A Defiant Life: Thurgood Marshall and the Persistence of Racism in America*. New York: Three Rivers Press, 2001.

Barkun, Michael. *Religion and the Racist Right: The Origins of the Christian Identity Movement*. Durham: University of North Carolina Press, 1996.

Barlow, David E., and Melissa Hickman Barlow. *Police in a Multicultural Society: An American Story*. Prospect Heights, IL: Waveland Press, Inc., 2000.

Barnes, Catherine. *A Journey from Jim Crow: The Desegregation of Southern Transit*. New York: Columbia University Press, 1983.

Barry, Iris, and D.W. Griffith. *D.W. Griffith, American Film Master*. New York: The Museum of Modern Art, 1940.

Bartley, Numan V. *The Rise of Massive Resistance*. Baton Rouge: Louisiana State University Press, 1969.

Bass, Jack, and Jack Nelson. *The Orangeburg Massacre*. Macon, GA: Mercer University Press, 1996.

Bauerlein, Mark. *Negrophobia: A Race Riot in Atlanta, 1906*. San Francisco: Encounter Books, 2001.

Beasley, Maurine H., Holly C. Shulman, and Henry R. Beasley. *The Eleanor Roosevelt Encyclopedia*. Westport, CT: Greenwood Press, 2001.

Berg, Manfred. *"The Ticket to Freedom": The NAACP and the Struggle for Black Political Integration*. Gainesville: University Press of Florida, 2005.

Bergman, Peter M. *The Chronological History of the Negro in America*. New York: Harper and Row, 1969.

Bernstein, Iver. *The New York City Draft Riots: Their Significance for American Society and Politics in the Age of the Civil War*. New York: Oxford University Press, 1990.

Bernstein, Patricia. *The Lynching of Jesse Washington and the Rise of the NAACP*. College Station: Texas A&M Press, 2005.

Berry, Mary Frances. *Black Resistance/White Law: A History of Constitutional Racism in America*. New York: Penguin Group, 1994.

Billingsley, Andrew. *Climbing Jacob's Ladder: The Enduring Legacy of African-American Families*. New York: Simon & Schuster, 1992.

Birmingham Historical Society. *A Walk to Freedom: The Reverend Fred Shuttlesworth and the Alabama Christian Movement for Human Rights, 1956–1964*. Birmingham, AL: Birmingham Historical Society, 1998.

Black Issues in Higher Education and Dara N. Byrne, eds. *The Unfinished Agenda of the Selma–Montgomery Voting Rights March*. Hoboken, NJ: John Wiley & Sons, 2005.

Blee, Kathleen M. *Women of the Klan: Racism and Gender in the 1920s*. Berkeley: University of California Press, 1991.

Bloom, Harold. *Modern Critical Views: W.E.B. Du Bois*. Philadelphia: Chelsea House, 2001.

Bloom, Jack. *Class, Race, and the Civil Rights Movement*. Bloomington: Indiana University Press, 1987.

Boger, John Charles, and Judith Welch Wegner. *Race, Poverty, and American Cities*. Chapel Hill: University of North Carolina Press, 1996.

Bohrn, Harald. *Gunnar Myrdal: A Bibliography, 1919–1976*. Stockholm: Kungliga biblioteket, 1976.

Bone, Robert A. *The Negro Novel in America*. New Haven, CT: Yale University Press, 1958.

Bonilla-Silva, Eduardo. *White Supremacy and Racism in the Post–Civil Rights Era*. Boulder, CO: Lynne Rienner, 2001.

Booker, Christopher B. *"I Will Wear No Chain!": A Social History of African American Males*. Westport, CT: Praeger Publishers, 2000.

Boskin, Joseph. *Sambo: The Rise and Demise of an American Jester*. New York: Oxford University Press, 1986.

Boskin, Joseph, ed. *Urban Racial Violence*. 2nd ed. Los Angeles: Glencoe, 1976.

Boyle, Kevin. *Arc of Justice: A Saga of Race, Civil Rights, and Murder in the Jazz Age*. New York: Henry Holt, 2004.

Branch, Taylor. *At Canaan's Edge: America in the King Years 1965–68*. New York: Simon & Schuster, Inc., 2006.

Branch, Taylor. *Parting the Waters: America in the King Years, 1954–63*. New York: Simon & Schuster, 1988.

Branch, Taylor. *Pillar of Fire: America in the King Years, 1963–65*. New York: Simon and Schuster, 1999.

Brandt, Nat. *Harlem at War: The Black Experience in World War II*. Syracuse, NY: Syracuse University Press, 1996.

Breitman, George. *The Last Year of Malcolm X: The Evolution of a Revolutionary*. New York: Pathfinder Press, 1967.

Brinkley, David. *Washington Goes to War*. New York: Alfred A. Knopf, 1988.

Brisbane, Robert H. *The Black Vanguard: Origins of the Negro Social Revolution, 1900–1960*. Valley Forge, PA: Judson Press, 1970.

Brophy, Alfred L. *Reconstructing the Dreamland: The Tulsa Riot of 1921, Race, Reparation, and Reconciliation*. New York: Oxford University Press, 2002.

Broussard, Albert. *Black San Francisco: The Struggle for Racial Equality in the West, 1900–1954*. Topeka: University Press of Kansas, 1993.

Brown, H. Rap. *Die, Nigger, Die! A Political Autobiography*. New York: Dial Press, 1969.

Brown, Mary Jane. *Eradicating This Evil: Women in the American Anti-Lynching Movement, 1892–1940*. Studies in African American History and Culture. New York: Garland Publishing, 2000.

Brown, Richard Maxwell. *Strain of Violence: Historical Studies of American Violence and Vigilantism*. New York: Oxford University Press, 1975.

Bruce, Robert V. *1877: Year of Violence*. Indianapolis: Bobbs-Merrill, 1959.

Brundage, W. Fitzhugh, ed. *Under Sentence of Death: Lynching in the South*. Chapel Hill: University of North Carolina Press, 1997.

Buckley, Gail. *Strength for the Fight: A History of Black Americans in the Military*. New York: Random House, 2001.

Bullock, Paul. *Watts: The Aftermath: An Inside View of the Ghetto*. New York: Grove Press, 1969.

Burner, Eric. *And Gently He Shall Lead Them*. New York: New York University Press, 1994.

Bushart, Howard L., and Myra Edwards Barnes, eds. *Soldiers of God: White Supremacists and Their Holy War for America*. New York: Kensington Publishing Corporation, 2000.

Byerman, Keith E. *Seizing the Word: History, Art, and Self in the Work of W.E.B. Du Bois*. Athens: University of Georgia Press, 1994.

Byres, T. J., ed. *Sharecropping and Sharecroppers*. Totowa, NJ: Biblio Distribution Center, 1983.

Campbell, Bebe Moore. *Your Blues Ain't Like Mine*. New York: Ballantine, 1992.

Campbell, James. *Talking at the Gates: A Life of James Baldwin*. New York: Viking, 1991.

Campbell, Jane. *Mythic Black Fiction: The Transformation of History*. Knoxville: University of Tennessee Press, 1986.

Cannon, Lou. *Official Negligence: How Rodney King and the Riots Changed Los Angeles and the LAPD*. Boulder, CO: Westview Press, 1999.

Capeci, Dominic J., Jr. *The Lynching of Cleo Wright*. Lexington: University Press of Kentucky, 1998.

Capeci, Dominic J., Jr. *Race Relations in Wartime Detroit: The Sojourner Truth Controversy of 1942*. Philadelphia: Temple University Press, 1984.

Capeci, Dominic J., Jr. *The Harlem Riot of 1943*. Philadelphia: Temple University Press, 1977.

Capeci, Dominic J., Jr., and Martha Wilkerson. *Layered Violence: The Detroit Rioters of 1943*. Jackson: University Press of Mississippi, 1991.

Carawan, Guy, and Candie Carawan. *Sing for Freedom: The Story of the Civil Rights Movement Through Its Songs*. Bethlehem, PA: Sing Out Corp., 1990.

Carmichael, S., and C.V. Hamilton. *Black Power: The Politics of Liberation in America*. London: Jonathan Cape, 1967.

Carmichael, Stokely, with Ekwueme Michael Thelwell. *Ready for Revolution: The Life and Struggles of Stokely Carmichael (Kwame Ture)*. New York: Scribner, 2003.

Caro, Robert. *Master of the Senate*. New York: Alfred A. Knopf, 2002.

Carrigan, William D. *The Making of a Lynching Culture: Violence and Vigilantism in Central Texas, 1836–1916*. Urbana: University of Illinois Press, 2004.

Carson, Clayborne. *In Struggle: SNCC and the Black Awakening of the 1960s*. Cambridge, MA: Harvard University Press, 1981, 1995.

Carson, Clayborne, Emma J. Lapsansky-Werner, and Gary Nash. *African American Lives: The Struggle for Freedom*. New York: Pearson/Longman, 2005.

Carson, Emmett D. *A Hand Up: Black Philanthropy and Self-Help in America*. Washington, DC: Joint Center for Political and Economic Studies, 1993.

Carter, Dan T. *Scottsboro: A Tragedy of the American South*. Baton Rouge: Louisiana State University Press, 1979.

Cash, W.J. *The Mind of the South*. Reprint, New York: Vintage, 1991. Originally published 1941.

Cayton, Andrew R.L. *Ohio: This History of a People*. Columbus: Ohio State University Press, 2002.

Cecelski, David S., and Timothy B. Tyson, eds. *Democracy Betrayed: The Wilmington Race Riot of 1898 and Its Legacy.* Chapel Hill: University of North Carolina Press, 1998.

Chadwick, Bruce. *The Reel Civil War: Mythmaking in American Film*. New York: Alfred A. Knopf, 2001.

Chafe, William, H., ed. *Remembering Jim Crow: African Americans Tell about Life in the Segregated South*. New York: New Press, 2001.

Chalmers, David M. *Hooded Americanism: The History of the Ku Klux Klan*. Durham, NC: Duke University Press, 1987.

Chalmers, David Mark. *Backfire: How the Ku Klux Klan Helped the Civil Rights Movement*. Lanham, MD: Rowman & Littlefield, 2003.

Cherry, Robert. *The Culture-of-Poverty Thesis and African Americans: The Work of Gunnar Myrdal and Other Institutionalists*. New York: Journal of Economic Issues, 1995.

Chicago Commission on Race Relations. *The Negro in Chicago: A Study of Race Relations and a Race Riot*. Chicago: University of Chicago Press, 1922.

Christian, Garna L. *Black Soldiers in Jim Crow Texas, 1899–1917*. College Station: Texas A&M University Press, 1995.

Churchill, Ward, and Vander Wall, Jim. *The COINTELPRO Papers: Documents from the FBI's Secret Wars against Dissent in the United States*. Boston: South End Press, 2002.

Churchill, Ward, and Vander Wall, Jim. *Agents of Repression: The FBI's Secret Wars against the Black Panther Party and the American Indian Movement*. Boston: South End Press, 1988.

Citro, Constance, F., and Robert T. Michael, eds. *Measuring Poverty: A New Approach*. Washington DC: National Academy Press, 1995.

Clark, John Henrik. *Malcolm X: The Man and His Times*. Trenton, NJ: Africa World Press, 1990.

Clark, Kenneth B. *Dark Ghetto: Dilemmas of Social Power.* New York: Harper & Row, 1965.

Clark, Robert F. *The War on Poverty: History, Selected Programs and Ongoing Impact*. Washington, DC: University Press of America, 2002.

Cleaver, Eldridge. *Eldridge Cleaver: Post-Prison Writings and Speeches*. Edited and with an appraisal by Robert Scheer. New York: Random House, 1969.

Cleaver, Eldridge. *Soul on Ice*. New York: Dell Publishing, 1968.

Clegg, Claude Andrews, III. *An Original Man: The Life and Times of Elijah Muhammad*. New York: St. Martin's Press, 1997.

Coffey, Shelby, III., ed. *Understanding the Riots: Los Angeles Before and After the Rodney King Case*. Los Angeles: *Los Angeles Times*, 1992.

Cohler, Anne M., Basia Carolyn Miller, Harold Samuel Stone, Raymond Geuss, and Quentin Skinner, eds. *Montesquieu: The Spirit of the Laws*. Cambridge Texts in the History of Political Thought. Cambridge, England: Cambridge University Press, 1989.

Collins, Winfield, *The Truth About Lynching and the Negro in the South*. New York: The Neale Publishing Company, 1918.

Conyers, John. *What Went Wrong in Ohio: The Conyers Report on the 2004 Presidential Election*. Chicago: Academy Chicago Publishers, 2005.

Cook, Adrian. *The Armies of the Streets: The New York City Draft Riots of 1863*. Lexington: University Press of Kentucky, 1974.

Cooper, Wayne F. *Claude McKay: Rebel Sojourner in the Harlem Renaissance: A Biography.* Baton Rouge: Louisiana State University Press, 1987.

Cortner, Richard C. *A Mob Intent on Death: The NAACP and the Arkansas Race Cases*. Middletown, CT: Wesleyan University Press, 1988.

Crenshaw, Kimberle, Neil Gotanda, and Garry Peller, eds. *Critical Race Theory: The Key Writings That Formed the Movement*. New York: New Press, 1996.

Cripps, Thomas. *Making Movies Black*. New York and Oxford: Oxford University Press, 1993.

Cronon, David. *Black Moses: The Story of Marcus Garvey*. Madison: University of Wisconsin Press, 1955.

Crowe, Daniel. *Prophets of Rage: The Black Freedom Struggle in San Francisco, 1945–1969*. New York: Garland Publishing, Inc., 2000.

Culberson, W. *Vigilantism: Political History of Private Power in America*. Westport, CT: Greenwood Press, 1990.

Cwiklik, Robert. *A. Phillip Randolph and the Labor Movement*. Minneapolis: Lerner Publishing Group, 1993.

Dallek, Robert. *An Unfinished Life*. New York: Little, Brown and Company, 2003.

Danziger, Sheldon H., and Robert H. Haveman, eds. *Understanding Poverty*. New York: Russell Sage Foundation, 2001.

Davis, Abraham L., and Barbara Luck Graham. *The Supreme Court, Race, and Civil Rights*. Thousand Oaks, CA: Sage Publications, Inc., 1995.

Davis, Arthur P. *From the Dark Tower: Afro-American Writers, 1900–1960*. Washington, DC: Howard University Press, 1974.

Davis, James Kilpatrick. *Assault on the Left: The FBI and the Sixties Antiwar Movement*. Westport, CT: Praeger Publishers, 1997.

Davis, R. Townsend. *Weary Feet, Rested Souls: A Guided History of the Civil Rights Movement*. New York: W.W. Norton & Company, 1998.

De Jong, Greta. *A Different Day: African American Struggle for Justice in Rural Louisiana, 1900–1970*. Chapel Hill: University of North Carolina Press, 2002.

DeBenedetti, Charles. *An American Ordeal: The Antiwar Movement of the Vietnam Era*. Syracuse, NY: Syracuse University Press, 1990.

DeCaro, Louis A., Jr. *Malcolm and the Cross: The Nation of Islam, Malcolm X, and Christianity*. New York: New York University Press, 1998.

DeCaro, Louis A., Jr. *On the Side of My People: A Religious Life of Malcolm X*. New York: New York University Press, 1996.

DeCosta-Willis, Miriam. *Ida B. Wells: The Memphis Diaries*. Boston: Beacon Press, 1994.

Dickerson, Debra. *The End of Blackness*. New York: Random House, 2004.

Divine, Robert A., ed. *Exploring the Johnson Years*. Austin: University of Texas Press, 1981.

Dixon, Thomas, Jr. *The Clansman: An Historical Romance of the Ku Klux Klan*. New York: Doubleday, Page & Company, 1905.

Dobratz, Betty A. *The White Separatist Movement in the United States: "White Power, White Pride!"* Baltimore: The Johns Hopkins University Press, 2000.

D'Orso, Michael. *Like Judgment Day: The Ruin and Redemption of a Town Called Rosewood*. New York: G.P. Putnam's Sons, 1996.

Dovidio, J.F., and S.L. Gaertner, eds. *Prejudice, Discrimination, and Racism*. New York: Academic Press, 1986.

Drake, St. Clair, and Horace R. Cayton. *Black Metropolis: A Study of Negro Life in a Northern City*. New York: Harcourt, Brace & World, Inc., 1970, 1962, 1945.

Dray, Philip. *At the Hands of Persons Unknown: The Lynching of Black America*. New York: Random House, 2002.

Du Bois, W.E.B. *Black Reconstruction in America 1860–1880*. Introduction by David Levering Lewis. New York: Free Press, 1998.

Du Bois, W.E.B. *Dusk of Dawn*. Millwood, NY: Kraus-Thomson Organization, 1975.

Du Bois, W.E.B. *John Brown*. Philadelphia: G.W. Jacobs & Co., 1909.

Du Bois, W.E.B. *The Souls of Black Folk*. New York: Signet, 1982. Originally published 1903.

Duberman, Martin. *Paul Robeson*. New York: Knopf, 1988.

Dubofsky, Melvin. *Industrialism and the American Worker*. New York: Harlan Davidson, 1996.

Dumenil, Lynn. *The Modern Temper*. New York: Hill & Wang, 1995.

Duncan, Charles. *Absent Man: Narrative Craft of Charles W. Chesnutt*. Columbus: Ohio University Press, 1999.

Dyson, Michael Eric. *Making Malcolm: The Myth and Meaning of Malcolm X*. New York: Oxford University Press, 1995.

Egerton, John. *Speak Now against the Day: The Generation Before the Civil Rights Movement in the South*. Chapel Hill: University of North Carolina Press, 1994.

Egypt, Ophelia Settle. *James Weldon Johnson*. New York: Crowell, 1974.

Ellison, Ralph. *Invisible Man*. New York: The Modern Library, 1994. Originally published in 1952.

Ellsworth, Scott. *Death in a Promised Land: The Tulsa Race Riot of 1921*. Baton Rouge: Louisiana State University Press, 1982.

Ely, Melvin. *The Adventures of Amos and Andy*. New York: Free Press 1991.

Eskew, Glenn T. *But for Birmingham: The Local and National Movements in the Civil Rights Struggle*. Chapel Hill: University of North Carolina Press, 1997.

Estell, Kenneth. *African-America: Portrait of a People*. Detroit: Visible Ink Press, 1998–1999.

Eze, Emmanuel Chukwudi. *Race and the Enlightenment: A Reader*. Malden, MA: Blackwell Publishers, 1997.

Ezekiel, Raphael S. *The Racist Mind: Portraits of American Neo-Nazis and Klansmen*. New York: Viking, 1995.

Fairclough, Adam. *Better Day Coming: Blacks and Equality, 1890–2000*. New York: Viking, 2001.

Fairclough, Adam. *To Redeem the Soul of America: The Southern Christian Leadership Conference and Martin Luther King, Jr.* Athens: University of Georgia Press, 2001.

Farmer, James. *Lay Bare the Heart: An Autobiography of the Civil Rights Movement*. New York: Arbor House, 1985.

Farrakhan, Louis. *A Torchlight for America*. Chicago: FCN Publishing Company, 1993.

Feagin, Joe R. *Racist America: Roots, Current Realities, and Future Reparations*. New York: Routledge, 2000.

Feagin, Joe R., and Harlan Hahn. *Ghetto Revolts: The Politics of Violence in American Cities*. New York: Macmillan Publishing Company, 1973.

Feldman, Glenn, ed. *Before Brown: Civil Rights and White Backlash in the Modern South*. Tuscaloosa: University of Alabama Press, 2004.

Ferber, Abby L. *White Man Falling: Race, Gender, and White Supremacy*. Lanham, MD: Rowman & Littlefield Publishers, Inc., 1998.

Filippelli, Ronald L. *Labor in the U.S.A.: A History*. New York: McGraw-Hill, 1984.

Fine, Gary Alan, and Patricia A. Turner. *Whispers on the Color Line: Rumor and Race in America*. Berkeley: University of California Press, 2001.

Fine, Sidney. *Violence in the Model City*. Ann Arbor: University of Michigan Press, 1989.

Fleming, Robert E. *James Weldon Johnson*. Boston: Twayne, 1987.

Fleming, Robert E. *James Weldon Johnson and Arna Wendell Bontemps: A Reference Guide*. Boston: G.K. Hall, 1978.

Fogelson, Robert M. *Violence as Protest: A Study of Riots and Ghettos*. Garden City, NY: Doubleday & Company, 1971.

Fogelson, Robert M., and Richard E. Rubenstein. *The Complete Report of Mayor La Guardia's Commission on the Harlem Riot of March 19, 1935*. New York: Arno Press and *New York Times*, 1969.

Fogelson, Robert M., and Richard Rubenstein, eds. *Mass Violence in America: New Orleans Riots of July 30, 1866*. New York: Arno Press and *New York Times*, 1969.

Foner, Eric. *Reconstruction: America's Unfinished Revolution, 1863–1877*. New York: Harper and Row, 1988.

Foner, Eric. *Nothing but Freedom: Emancipation and Its Legacy*. Baton Rouge: Louisiana State University Press, 1984.

Forman, James. *The Making of Black Revolutionaries*. Seattle: Open Hand Publishing, 1985.

Formisano, Ronald. *Boston against Busing: Race, Class, and Ethnicity in the 1960s and 1970s*. Chapel Hill: University of North Carolina, 1991.

Fox, Stephen R. *The Guardian of Boston: William Monroe Trotter*. New York: Atheneum, 1970.

Franke, Astrid. *Keys to Controversies: Stereotypes in Modern American Novels*. New York: St. Martin's Press, 1999.

Frankenberg, Ruth. *White Women, Race Matters: The Social Construction of Whiteness*. Minneapolis: University of Minnesota Press, 1983.

Franklin, John Hope. *From Slavery to Freedom: A History of Negro Americans*. 3rd ed. New York: Knopf, 1967.

Freedom Archives, ed., and Robert F. Williams. *Robert F. Williams: Self Respect, Self Defense and Self Determination (An Audio Documentary as Told by Mabel Williams)*. Edinburgh, Scotland: AK Press, 2005.

Friedly, Michael. *Malcolm X: The Assassination*. New York: Ballantine Books, 1995.

Fuller, Edgar Irving. *The Visible of the Invisible Empire: "The Maelstrom."* Denver, Colorado: Maelstrom Publishing Co., 1925.

Garnet, Henry Highland. *A Memorial Discourse Delivered in the Hall of the House of Representatives, Washington City, D.C., on Sabbath, February 12, 1865. With an Introduction by James McCune Smith, M.D.* Philadelphia: J.M. Wilson, 1865.

Garrow, David J. *Bearing the Cross: Martin Luther King, Jr., and the Southern Christian Leadership Conference*. New York: William Morrow, 1986.

Garvey, Amy. *The Philosophy & Opinions of Marcus Garvey: Or Africa for the Africans*, 1923.

Gates, Daryl F. *Chief: My Life in the LAPD*. New York: Bantam, 1992.

Gatewood, Willard B. *Aristocrats of Color: The Black Elite, 1880–1920*. Fayetteville: University of Arkansas Press, 2000.

Gay, Peter. *The Enlightenment: The Rise of Modern Paganism*. New York: W.W. Norton & Company, 1995.

Gentry, Curt. *J. Edgar Hoover: The Man and the Secrets*. New York: W.W. Norton & Co., 1991.

Gerber, David A. *Black Ohio and the Color Line 1860–1915*. Urbana: University of Illinois Press, 1976.

Gettleman, Marvin E., and Mermelstein, David, eds. *The Great Society Reader: The Failure of American Liberalism*. New York: Random House, 1967.

Gibbs, Jewelle Taylor. *Race and Justice: Rodney King and O.J. Simpson in a House Divided*. San Francisco: Jossey-Bass Publishers, 1996.

Giddings, Paula. *When and Where I Enter: The Impact of Black Women on Race and Sex in America*. New York: William Morrow, 1984.

Gilbert, Ben W. and The *Washington Post* Staff. *Ten Blocks from the White House: Anatomy of the Washington Riots of 1968*. New York: Praeger Publishers, 1968.

Giles, James R. *Claude McKay*. Boston: Twayne, 1976.

Gilje, Paul. *Rioting in America*. Bloomington: Indiana University Press, 1996.

Gilpin, Patrick, and Marybeth Gasman. *Charles S. Johnson: Leadership Beyond the Veil in the Age of Jim Crow*. Albany: State University of New York Press, 2003.

Ginsburg, Carl. *Race and Media: The Enduring Life of the Moynihan Report*. New York: Institute for Media Analysis, 1989.

Ginzburg, Ralph. *100 Years of Lynchings*. Baltimore: Black Classic Press, 1997.

Glasmeier, Amy K. *An Atlas of Poverty in America: One Nation, Pulling Apart, 1960–2003*. London: Routledge, 2006.

Glazer, Nathan, and Daniel P. Moynihan. *Beyond the Melting Pot: The Negroes, Puerto Ricans, Jews, Italians, and Irish of New York City*. Cambridge, MA: MIT Press, 1963.

Gobineau, Arthur de. *The Inequality of Human Races*. New York: Howard Fertig, Inc., 1999.

Goldman, Peter. *The Death and Life of Malcolm X*. 2nd ed. Urbana: University of Illinois Press, 1979.

Goldman, Robert M. *Reconstruction and Black Suffrage: Losing the Vote in Reese and Cruikshank*. Lawrence: University Press of Kansas, 2001.

Goodman, James E. *Stories of Scottsboro*. New York: Pantheon Books, 1994.

Goodwin, Doris Kearns. *Lyndon Johnson and the American Dream*. New York: St. Martin's Press, 1991.

Goodwin, Marvin E. *Black Migration in America from 1915–1960*. Lewistown, NY: The Edwin Mellen Press, 1990.

Gordon, Leonard. *A City in Racial Crisis*. Dubuque, IA: Wm. C. Brown Publishers, 1971.

Governor's Commission on the Los Angeles Riots (McCone Commission). *Violence in the City: An End or a Beginning?* Los Angeles: The McCone Commission, 1965.

Governor's Select Commission on Civil Disorders in the State of New Jersey. *Report for Action: An Investigation into the Causes and Events of the 1967 Newark Race Riots*. New York: Lemma Publishing Corporation, 1972.

Grant, Donald L. *The Way It Was in the South: The Black Experience in Georgia*. Athens: University of Georgia Press, 1993.

Grant, Madison. *The Passing of the Great Race; or, The Racial Basis of European History.* New York: C. Scribner, 1916.

Green, Constance McLaughlin. *The Secret City: A History of Race Relations in the Nation's Capital*. Princeton, NJ: Princeton University Press, 1967.

Greenberg, Cheryl Lynn. *"Or Does It Explode?": Black Harlem in the Great Depression*. New York: Oxford University Press, 1991.

Griffin, Farah Jasmine. *"Who Set You Flowin'?" The African-American Migration Narrative*. New York: Oxford University Press, 1995.

Griggs, Sutton E. *Imperium in Imperio*. New York: Arno Press and *New York Times*, 1969. Originally published 1899.

Griggs, Sutton E. *The Story of My Struggles*. Memphis: National Public Welfare League, 1914.

Griggs, Sutton E. *Pointing the Way.* Nashville: Orion Publishing Co., 1908.

Griggs, Sutton E. *The Hindered Hand*; or *The Reign of the Repressionist*. Nashville: Orion Publishing Co., 1905.

Griggs, Sutton E. *Unfettered*. Nashville: Orion Publishing Co., 1902.

Griggs, Sutton E. *Overshadowed*. Nashville: Orion Publishing Co., 1901.

Grimstead, David. *American Mobbing, 1828–1861: Toward Civil War.* New York: Oxford University Press, 1998.

Grossman, James R. Land of Hope: *Chicago, Black Southerners, and the Great Migration*. Chicago: University of Chicago Press, 1989.

Gurrero, Ed. *Framing Blackness: The African American Image in Film*. Philadelphia: Temple University Press, 1993.

Guterl, Matthew Pratt. *The Color of Race in America, 1900–1940*. Cambridge, MA: Harvard University Press, 2001.

Hair, William Ivy. *Carnival of Fury: Robert Charles and the New Orleans Race Riot of 1900*. Baton Rouge: Louisiana State University Press, 1976.

Halberstam, David. *The Children*. New York: Fawcett Books, 1998.

Hale, Grace Elizabeth. *Making Whiteness: The Culture of Segregation in the South, 1890–1940*. New York: Pantheon Books, 1998.

Hale, Grace Elizabeth, and Joel Williamson. *A Rage for Order: Black/White Relations in the American South Since Emancipation*. New York: Oxford University Press, 1986.

Handman, Gary. *UC Berkeley Library Social Activism Sound Recording Project: The Black Panther Party.* Berkeley: The University of California Library, 1996.

Hansen, Drew W. *Martin Luther King, Jr. and the Speech that Inspired a Nation*. New York: Ecco, 2003.

Hardy, James Earl. *Spike Lee*. New York: Chelsea House Publishers, 1996.

Harlan, Louis R. *Booker T. Washington: The Making of a Black Leader, 1856–1901*. New York: Oxford University Press, 1972.

Harlan, Louis R. *Booker T. Washington: The Wizard of Tuskegee, 1901–1915*. New York: Oxford University Press, 1983.

Harlem Youth Opportunities Unlimited (HARYOU). *Youth in the Ghetto: A Study of the Consequences of Powerlessness and a Blueprint for Change*. New York: Harlem Youth Opportunities Unlimited, Inc., 1964.

Harris, Darryl B. *The Logic of Black Urban Rebellions: Challenging the Dynamics of White Domination in Miami*. Westport, CT: Praeger Publishers, 1999.

Harris, Fred R., and Roger W. Wilkins. *Quiet Riots: Race and Poverty in the United States: The Kerner Report Twenty Years Later.* New York: Pantheon Books, 1988.

Harris, Leonard. *The Philosophy of Alain Locke: Harlem Renaissance and Beyond*. Philadelphia: Temple University Press, 1989.

Harris, Leslie Maria. *In the Shadow of Slavery: African Americans in New York City, 1626–1863*. Chicago and London: University of Chicago Press, 2003.

Harris, Trudier. *Exorcising Blackness: Historical and Literary Lynching and Burning Rituals*. Bloomington: Indiana University Press, 1984.

Harris, Trudier, comp. *Selected Works of Ida B. Wells-Barnett*. New York: Oxford University Press, 1991.

Harris, William. *Keeping the Faith: A. Phillip Randolph, Milton P. Webster, and the Brotherhood of Sleeping Car Porters 1925–1937*. Blacks in the New World Series. Urbana: University of Illinois Press, 1991.

Hathaway, Heather. *Caribbean Waves: Relocating Claude McKay and Paule Marshall.* Bloomington: Indiana University Press, 1999.

Hayden, Robert C. *Eyes on the Prize: America's Civil Rights Years, 1954–1965*. Guide to the Series. Boston: Blackside, Inc., 1988.

Hayden, Tom. *Rebellion in Newark: Official Violence and Ghetto Response*. New York: Vintage Books, 1967.

Haynes, Robert V. *A Night of Violence: The Houston Riot of 1917*. Baton Rouge: Louisiana State University Press, 1976.

Hegel, G.F.W. *Hegel, Lectures on the Philosophy of World History, Introduction: Reason in History.* Translated by H. B. Nisbet. Cambridge, England: Cambridge University Press, 1975.

Helsing, Jeffrey. *Johnson's War/Johnson's Great Society: The Guns and Butter Trap*. Westport, CT: Praeger Publishers, 2000.

Henri, Florette. *Black Migration. Movement North 1900–1920*. New York: Doubleday Anchor Books, 1975.

Herman, Max Arthur. *Fighting in the Streets: Ethnic Succession and Urban Unrest in 20th Century America*. New York. Peter Lang Publishers, 2005.

Hersey, John. *The Algiers Motel Incident*. Baltimore: The Johns Hopkins University Press, 1997.

Heymann, Philip B. *Terrorism, Freedom, and Security: Winning without War.* Cambridge, MA: MIT Press, 2003.

Higham, John. *Strangers in the Land: Patterns of American Nativism, 1860–1925*. Rutgers, NJ: Rutgers University Press, 1984.

Hill, Herbert. *Black Labor and the American Legal System: Race, Work and the Law.* Madison: University of Wisconsin Press, 1985.

Hill, Lance. *The Deacons for Defense: Armed Resistance and the Civil Rights Movement.* Chapel Hill: University of North Carolina Press, 2004.

Hill, Mike, ed. *Whiteness: A Critical Reader.* New York and London: New York University Press, 1997.

Hilliard, David, and Cole, Lewis. *This Side of Glory: The Autobiography of David Hilliard and the Story of the Black Panther Party.* Boston: Little, Brown and Company, 1993.

Hine, Darlene Clark, William C. Hine, and Stanley Harrold, eds. *The African-American Odyssey.* Englewood Cliffs, NJ: Prentice Hall, 2000.

Hippler, Arthur. *Hunter's Point: A Black Ghetto*. New York: Basic Books, 1974.

Holiday, Billie, with William Dufty. *Lady Sings the Blues*. Garden City, NY: Doubleday & Company, 1956/1992.

Hollandsworth, James G. *An Absolute Massacre: The New Orleans Riot of July 30th, 1866.* Baton Rouge: Louisiana State University Press, 2001.

Holt, Thomas C. *Black Over White: Negro Political Leadership in South Carolina during Reconstruction*. Urbana: University of Illinois Press, 1977.

Horne, Gerald. *Black and Red: W.E.B. Du Bois and the Afro-American Response to the Cold War, 1944–1963*. Albany: State University of New York Press, 1986.

Horowitz, David. *Uncivil Wars: The Controversy over Reparations for Slavery.* San Francisco: Encounter Books, 2002.

Horowitz, Donald L. *The Deadly Ethnic Riot*. Berkeley: University of California Press, 2001.

Hossfeld, Leslie H. *Narrative, Political Unconscious and Radical Violence in Wilmington, North Carolina*. New York: Routledge, 2005.

Hoyt, Edwin P. *The Palmer Raids 1919–1920: An Attempt to Suppress Dissent*. New York: Seabury Press, 1969.

Hughes, Langston, and Milton Meltzer. *African American History.* 6th ed. New York: Scholastic, Inc., 1990.

Humes, D. Joy. *Oswald Garrison Villard, Liberal of the 1920's*. Binghamton, NY: Syracuse University Press, 1960.

Hunt, Darnell M. *Screening the Los Angeles "Riots": Race, Seeing, and Resistance*. New York: Cambridge University Press, 1997.

Hynes, Charles J., and Bob Drury. *Incident at Howard Beach: The Case for Murder.* New York: G.P. Putnam's Sons, 1990.

Ignatiev, Noel. *How the Irish Became White*. New York: Routledge, 1994.

Jackson, Kenneth T. *The Ku Klux Klan in the City: 1915–1930*. New York: Oxford University Press, 1967.

Jackson, Walter A. *Gunnar Myrdal and America's Conscience: Social Engineering and Racial Liberalism, 1938–1987*. Chapel Hill: University of North Carolina Press, 1990.

Jacobs, Ronald N. *Race, Media, and the Crisis of Civil Society: From Watts to Rodney King*. Cambridge, England: Cambridge University Press, 2000.

Jacobson, Matthew Frye. *Whiteness of a Different Color: European Immigrants and the Alchemy of Race*. Cambridge, MA: Harvard University Press, 1998.

James, Winston. *A Fierce Hatred of Injustice: Claude McKay's Jamaica and His Poetry of Rebellion*. New York: Verso, 2000.

Janken, Kenneth R. *White: The Biography of Walter White, Mr. NAACP.* New York: New Press, 2003.

Jeffries. Judson L. *Huey P. Newton: The Radical Theorist*. Jackson: University Press of Mississippi, 2002.

Jonas, Gilbert, and Julian Bond. *Freedom's Sword: The NAACP and the Struggle against Racism in America, 1909–1969*. New York: Routledge, 2004.

Jones, Beverly Washington. *Quest for Equality: The Life and Writings of Mary Church Terrell*. New York: Carlson Publishers, 1990.

Jordan, Winthrop D. *The White Man's Burden: Historical Origins of Racism in the United States*. New York: Oxford University Press, 1974.

Justice, Blair. *Violence in the City.* Forth Worth: Texas Christian University Press, 1969.

Kappeler, Victor E., Richard D. Skuder, and Geoffrey Alpert. *Forces of Deviance: Understanding the Dark Side of Policing*. 2nd ed. Prospect Heights, IL: Waveland Press, Inc., 1998.

Katkin, W., N. Landsmand, and A. Tyree, eds. *Beyond Pluralism: Essays on the Conception of Groups and Group Identities in America*. Urbana: University of Illinois Press, 1998.

Katz, Michael B. *The Undeserving Poor: From the War on Poverty to the War on Welfare*. New York: Pantheon Books, 1989.

Katz, Michael B., and Thomas J. Sugrue, eds. *W.E.B. Du Bois, Race, and the City: The Philadelphia Negro and Its Legacy.* Philadelphia: University of Pennsylvania Press, 1998.

Keith, Jeanette. *The South: A Concise History.* Vol. II. Saddle River, NJ: Prentice Hall, 2002.

Kelley, Robin D.G. *Freedom Dreams: The Black Radical Imagination*. Boston: Beacon Press, 2003.

Kellogg, Clint. *NAACP: A History of the National Association of Colored People*. New York: The Johns Hopkins University Press, 1967.

Kerner, Otto, et al. *Report of the National Advisory Commission on Civil Disorders*. New York: Bantam Books, 1968.

Keyssar, Alexander. *The Right to Vote*. New York: Basic Books, 2000.

King, Martin Luther, Jr. *The Measure of a Man*. Philadelphia: Fortress Press, 1988.

King, Martin Luther, Jr. *Why We Can't Wait*. New York: Harper & Row, 1964.

King, Mary. *Mahatma Gandhi and Martin Luther King Jr.: The Power of Nonviolent Action*. Paris: UNESCO, 1999.

Knight, Janet M., ed. *3 Assassinations: The Deaths of John & Robert Kennedy and Martin Luther King, Jr.* New York: Facts on File, Inc., 1971.

Knopf, Terry Ann. *Rumors, Race, and Riots*. New Brunswick, NJ: Transaction Books, 1975.

Koehler, Lyle. *Cincinnati's Black Peoples: A Chronology and Bibliography.* Cincinnati: University of Cincinnati, 1986.

Kornweibel, Theodore. *"Seeing Red": Federal Campaigns against Black Militancy, 1919–1925*. Bloomington and Indianapolis: Indiana University Press, 1998.

Kotz, Nick. *Judgment Days: Lyndon Baines Johnson, Martin Luther King, Jr. and the Laws That Changed America*. New York: Houghton Mifflin, 2005.

Kovel, Joel. *White Racism: A Psychohistory.* New York: Pantheon, 1970.

Kozol, Jonathan. *The Shame of the Nation: The Restoration of Apartheid Schooling in America*. New York: Crown, 2005.

Krause, Paul. *The Battle for Homestead, 1880–1892*. Pittsburgh: University of Pittsburgh Press, 1995.

Krey, August C. *First Crusade*. Magnolia, MA: Peter Smith Publisher Inc., 1986.

Lane, Ann J. *The Brownsville Affair: National Crisis and Black Reaction*. New York: National University Publications, Kennikat Press, 1971.

Lane, Frederic C. *Ships for Victory: A History of Shipbuilding under the U.S. Maritime Commission in World War II*. Baltimore: The Johns Hopkins University Press, 1951.

Lang, Robert, ed. *The Birth of a Nation*. New Brunswick, NJ: Rutgers University Press, 1994.

Larsen, Lawrence Harold, and Barbara J. Cottrell. *The Gate City: A History of Omaha*. Lincoln: University of Nebraska Press, 1997.

Lawson, Steven F., and Charles Payne. *Debating the Civil Rights Movement: 1945–1968*. New York: Rowman and Littlefield, 1998.

Leab, Daniel J. *From Sambo to Superspade: The Black Experience in Motion Picture*. Boston: Houghton Mifflin, 1975.

Lee, Chana Kai. *For Freedom's Sake: The Life of Fannie Lou Hamer*. Women in American History. Chicago: University of Illinois Press, 2000.

Lee, Spike, with Kaleem Aftab. *That's My Story and I'm Sticking to It*. New York: W.W. Norton & Company, 2005.

Lee, Spike, with Lisa Jones. *Do the Right Thing*. New York: Fireside, 1989.

Lemann, Nicholas. *The Promised Land: The Great Migration and How It Changed America*. New York: Vintage Books, 1991.

LeMay, Michael C. *The Perennial Struggle: Race, Ethnicity, and Minority Group Relations in the United States*. 2nd ed. Upper Saddle River, NJ: Pearson, Prentice Hall, 2005.

Levy, Eugene. *James Weldon Johnson: Black Leader, Black Voice*. Chicago: University of Chicago Press, 1973.

Lewis, David Levering. *W.E.B. Du Bois: The Fight for Equality and the American Century, 1919–1963*. New York: H. Holt, 2000.

Lewis, David Levering, ed. *W.E.B. Du Bois: A Reader*. New York: Henry Holt and Company, 1995.

Lewis, David Levering. *W.E.B. Du Bois—Biography of a Race, 1868–1919*. New York: H. Holt, 1993.

Lewis, David Levering. *When Harlem Was in Vogue*. New York: Knopf, 1981.

Lewis, John. *Walking with the Wind: A Memoir of the Movement*. New York: Simon & Schuster, 1998.

Lincoln, C. Eric. *The Black Muslims in America*. 3rd ed. Grand Rapids, MI: Eerdmans Publishing Company, 1994.

Lippmann, Walter. *Public Opinion*. New York: Harcourt, Brace and Company, 1922.

Litwack, Leon, and August Meier, eds. *Black Leaders of the Nineteenth Century*. Urbana: University of Illinois Press, 1988.

Locke, Hubert. *The Detroit Riot of 1967*. Detroit, MI: Wayne State University Press, 1969.

Loewen, James. *Lies Across America*. New York: Touchstone, 1999.

Loewen, James. *Lies My Teacher Told Me*. New York: Touchstone, 1995.

Loewen, James W. *Sundown Towns: A Hidden Dimension of Segregation in America*. New York: New Press, 2005.

Logan, Rayford. *The Betrayal of the Negro from Rutherford B. Hayes to Woodrow Wilson*. New York: Da Capo Press, 1997.

Logan, Shirley W., ed. *With Pen and Voice: A Critical Anthology of Nineteenth Century African-American Women*. Carbondale: Southern Illinois Press, 1995.

Lorini, Alessandra. *Rituals of Race: American Public Culture and the South Search for Racial Democracy*. Charlottesville: University Press of Virginia, 1999.

Los Angeles Times Staff. *Understanding the Riots*. Los Angeles: *Los Angeles Times*, 1992.

Lukas, J. Anthony. *The Barnyard Epithet and Other Obscenities: Notes on the Chicago Conspiracy Trial*. New York: Harper & Row, 1970.

MacGregor, Morris J., Jr. *Integration of the Armed Forces, 1940–1965*. Washington, DC: U.S. Army Center of Military History, 1981.

Magida, Arthur J. *Prophet of Rage: A Life of Louis Farrakhan and His Nation*. New York: Basic Books, 1996.

Malcolm X. *By Any Means Necessary: Speeches, Interviews and a Letter*. Edited by George Breitman. New York: Pathfinder Press, 1970.

Malcolm X, and Alex Haley. *The Autobiography of Malcolm X*. New York: Ballantine Books, 1973. Originally published 1965.

Marable, Manning. *W.E.B. Du Bois: Black Radical Democrat*. Boston: Twayne, 1986.

Margolick, David. *Strange Fruit: Billie Holiday, Café Society, and the Early Cry for Civil Rights*. Philadelphia: Running Press, 2000.

Markovitz, Jonathan. *Legacies of Lynching: Racial Violence and Memory.* Minneapolis: University of Minnesota Press, 2004.

Marks, Carole. *Farewell—We're Good and Gone: The Great Black Migration.* Bloomington: Indiana University Press, 1989.

Martin, Thomas H. *Atlanta and Its Builders: A Comprehensive History of the Gate City of the South*, 2 vols. Atlanta: Century Memorial Publishing, 1902.

Mason, Gilbert R., with James P. Smith. *Beaches, Blood, and Ballots: A Black Doctor's Civil Rights Struggle.* Jackson: University Press of Mississippi, 2000.

Mauer, Marc. *Race to Incarcerate.* New York: New Press, 1999.

McCague, James. *The Second Rebellion: The Story of the New York City Draft Riots of 1863.* New York: Dial Press, 1968.

McCall, Nathan. *Makes Me Wanna Holler: A Young Black Man in America.* New York: Random House, 1994.

McKay, Claude. *A Long Way from Home.* New York: Arno Press and *New York Times*, 1969. Originally published in 1937.

McMillen, Neil R. *The Citizens Council: Resistance to the Second Reconstruction 1954–1964.* Champaign: University of Illinois Press, 1994.

McMurry, Linda O. *To Keep the Waters Troubled: The Life of Ida B. Wells.* New York and Oxford: Oxford University Press, 1998.

McWilliams, Dean. *Charles W. Chesnutt and the Fictions of Race.* Athens: University of Georgia Press, 2002.

Meier, August, ed. *Papers of the NAACP.* Frederick, MD: University Publications of America, 1981.

Meier, August, and Elliot Rudwick. *CORE: A Study in the Civil Rights Movement 1942–1968.* New York: Oxford University Press, 1973.

Melder, Keith. *Magnificent Obsession.* 2nd ed. Washington, DC: Intac, 1997.

Menard, Orville D. *Political Bossism in Mid-America: Tom Dennison's Omaha, 1900–1933.* Lanham, MD: University Press of America, 1989.

Meredith, James. *Three Years in Mississippi.* Bloomington: Indiana University Press, 1966.

Merrifield, Andy, and Erik Swyngedouw, eds. *The Urbanization of Injustice.* New York: New York University Press, 1997.

Metress, Christopher, ed. *The Lynching of Emmett Till: A Documentary Narrative.* Charlottesville: University of Virginia Press, 2002.

Meyer, Howard N. *The Amendment That Refused to Die: Equality and Justice Deferred, the History of the Fourteenth Amendment.* Lanham, MD: Madison Books, 2000.

Miller, Calvin Craig. *A. Phillip Randolph and the African American Labor Movement.* Greensboro, NC: Morgan Reynolds Publishing, 2005.

Miller, Keith D. *Voice of Deliverance: The Language of Martin Luther King, Jr. and Its Sources.* Athens: University Press of Georgia, 1998.

Miller, Zane L., and Bruce Tucker. *Changing Plans for America's Inner Cities: Cincinnati's Over-the-Rhine and Twentieth-Century Urbanism.* Columbus: Ohio State University Press, 1998.

Montagu, A. *Man's Most Dangerous Myth: The Fallacy of Race.* 5th ed. New York: Oxford University Press, 1974.

Montagu, A. *Race, Science, and Humanity.* Princeton, NJ: Van Nostrand, 1963.

Moore, Gilbert S. *A Special Rage.* New York: Harper and Row, 1971.

Moore, Jack B. *W.E.B. Du Bois.* Boston: Twayne, 1981.

Morris, Aldon D. *The Origins of the Civil Rights Movement: Black Communities Organizing for Change.* New York: The Free Press, 1984.

Moses, Wilson Jeremiah. *Classical Black Nationalism: From the American Revolution to Marcus Garvey.* New York: New York University Press, 1996.

Moynihan, Daniel Patrick. *The Negro Family: The Case for National Action.* Washington, DC: Office of Policy Planning and Research, United States Department of Labor, 1965.

Muhammad, Elijah. *The Fall of America.* Chicago: Muhammad's Temple No. 2, 1973.

Muhammad, Elijah. *Message to the Blackman in America.* Chicago: Muhammad Mosque of Islam No. 2, 1965.

Murphy, Larry G., J. Gordon Melton, and Gary L. Ward, eds. *Encyclopedia of African American Religions.* New York: Garland Publishing, 1993.

Murray, Robert K. *Red Scare: A Study of National Hysteria, 1919–1920*. Minneapolis: University of Minnesota Press, 1955.

Murthy, Srinivasa, ed. *Mahatma Gandhi and Leo Tolstoy Letters*. Long Beach, CA: Long Beach Publications, 1987.

Mushkat, Jerome. *Fernando Wood: A Political Biography*. Kent, OH: Kent State University Press, 1990.

Myrdal, Gunnar. *An American Dilemma: The Negro Problem and Modern Democracy*. New York: Harper Torchbooks, 1944.

Naeger, Bill, Patti Naeger, and Mark L. Evans. *Ste. Genevieve: A Leisurely Stroll Through History*. Ste. Genevieve, MO: Merchant Street Publishing, 1999.

Nagel, Joane. *Race, Ethnicity, and Sexuality: Intimate Intersections, Forbidden Frontiers*. New York: Oxford University Press, 2003.

Naison, Mark. *Communists in Harlem During the Depression*. Urbana: University of Illinois Press, 1983.

Naples, Nancy A. *Grassroots Warriors: Activist Mothering, Community Work, and the War on Poverty*. London: Routledge, 1998.

National Advisory Commission on Civil Disorders. *Report of the National Advisory Commission on Civil Disorders*. New York: Bantam Books, 1968.

National Association for the Advancement of Colored People. *Thirty Years of Lynching in the United States 1889–1918*. New York: Negro Universities Press. 1969.

Nelson, Jack, and Jack Bass. *The Orangeburg Massacre*. New York: The World Publishing Co., 1970.

Newton, Huey P. *Revolutionary Suicide*. New York: Writers and Readers Publishing, 1995. Originally published 1973.

Newton, Huey P. *To Die for the People*. Edited by Toni Morrison. New York: Writers and Readers Publishing, Inc., 1999. Originally published 1973.

Newton, Huey P. *War against the Panthers: A Study of Repression in America*. New York: Harlem River Press, 1996. (Published version of Newton's Ph.D. dissertation, University of California at Santa Cruz, 1980, History of Consciousness.)

Newton, Huey P., and Ericka Huggins. *Insights and Poems*. San Francisco: City Lights Books, 1975.

Newton, Huey P., and Erik H. Erikson. *In Search of Common Ground*. New York: W.W. Norton & Company, 1973.

Nieli, Russ, and Carol M. Swain, eds. *Contemporary Voices of White Nationalism in America*. New York: Cambridge University Press, 2003.

Niemand, Donald G, ed. *From Slavery to Sharecropping: White Land and Black Labor in the Rural South, 1865–1900*. New York: Garland, 1994.

Norden, Lewis. *Wolf Whistle*. Chapel Hill, NC: Algonquin,1993.

Nordin, Dennis S. *The New Deal's Black Congressman: A Life of Arthur Wergs Mitchell*. Columbia: University of Missouri Press, 1997.

Nossiter, Adam. *Of Long Memory: Mississippi and the Murder of Medgar Evers*. Cambridge, MA: Da Capo Press, 1994.

Office of the Federal Register, National Archives and Records Administration. *Public Papers of the Presidents of the United States*. Washington, D.C.: Federal Register Division, National Archives and Records Service.

Olmsted, Kathryn S. *Challenging the Secret Government: The Post–Watergate Investigations of the CIA and FBI*. Chapel Hill: University of North Carolina Press, 1996.

Olsen, Otto, ed. *Reconstruction and Redemption in the South*. Baton Rouge: Louisiana State University Press, 1980.

Omi, Michael, and Howard Winant. *Racial Formation in the United States: From the 1960s to the 1990s*. 2nd ed. New York: Routledge, 1994.

O'Neil, R.M. *No Heroes, No Villains: New Perspectives on Kent State and Jackson State*. San Francisco: Jossey-Bass, Inc., 1972.

O'Reilly, Kenneth. *Racial Matters: The FBI's Secret File on Black America, 1960–1972*. New York: The Free Press, 1989.

Ortiz, Paul. *Emancipation Betrayed: The Hidden History of Black Organizing and White Violence in Florida from Reconstruction to the Bloody Election of 1920*. Berkeley: University of California Press, 2005.

Ottley, Roi. *The Lonely Warrior: The Life and Times of Robert S. Abbott*. Chicago: H. Regnery Co., 1955.

Ovington, Mary White. *Blacks and Whites Sat Down Together: The Reminiscences of an NAACP Founder*. New York: Feminist Press, 1996.

Pagden, Anthony. *Lords of All the World: Ideologies of Empire in Spain, Britain, and France c.1500–c.1800*. New Haven, CT: Yale University Press, 1998.

Page, James A. *Selected Black American Authors*. Boston: G.K. Hall, 1977.

Painter, Nell Irvin. *Exodusters: Black Migration to Kansas after Reconstruction*. New York: Knopf, 1977.

Palmer, A. Mitchell, Attorney General. *Investigation Activities of the Department of Justice*. 66th Congress, 1st Session, Senate Document 153, Vol. XII, 1919.

Peck, James. *Freedom Ride*. New York: Grove Press, 1962.

Pepper, William F. *An Act of State: The Execution of Martin Luther King*. London and New York: Verso, 2003.

Pepper, William F. *Orders to Kill: The Truth Behind the Murder of Martin Luther King, Jr.* New York: Carroll and Graf Publishers, 1995.

Perman, Michael. *The Road to Redemption: Southern Politics, 1869–1880*. Chapel Hill: University of North Carolina Press, 1984.

Perman, Michael. *The Struggle for Mastery: Disenfranchisement in the South: 1888–1908*. Chapel Hill: University of North Carolina Press, 2001.

Perry, Barbara. *In the Name of Hate: Understanding Hate Crimes*. New York: Routledge, 2001.

Pfeifer, Michael J. *Rough Justice: Lynching and American Society, 1874–1947*. Urbana: University of Illinois Press, 2004.

Pinar, William F. *The Gender of Racial Politics and Violence in America: Lynching, Prison Rape, and the Crisis of Masculinity*. New York: Peter Lang, 2001.

Platt, Anthony, ed. *The Politics of Riot Commissions 1917–1979: A Collection of Official Reports and Critical Essays*. New York: Collier Books, 1971.

Porambo, Ron. *No Cause for Indictment: An Autopsy of Newark*. New York: Holt, Rinehart and Winston, 1971.

Porter, Bruce, and Marvin Dunn. *The Miami Riot of 1980: Crossing the Bounds*. Lanham, MD: Lexington Books, 1984.

Porter, Horace A. *Stealing the Fire: The Art and Protest of James Baldwin*. Middletown, CT: Wesleyan University Press, 1988.

Posner, Gerald. *Killing the Dream: James Earl Ray and the Assassination of Martin Luther King, Jr.* New York: Random House, 1998.

Powell, Richard. *Homecoming: The Art and Life of William H. Johnson*. New York: Rizzoli International Publications, 1991.

Powers, Richard G. *G-Men: Hoover's FBI in Popular Culture*. Carbondale: Southern Illinois University Press, 1983.

Powers, Richard G. *Secrecy and Power: The Life of J. Edgar Hoover*. New York: The Free Press, 1987.

Price, Kenneth M., and Lawrence J. Oliver, eds. *Critical Essays on James Weldon Johnson*. New York: G.K. Hall & Co., 1997.

Quillin, Frank U. *The Color Line in Ohio: A History of Race Prejudice in a Typical Northern State*. Ann Arbor, MI: George Wahr, 1913.

Rabinowitz, Howard N., ed. *Southern Black Leaders of the Reconstruction Era*. Urbana: University of Illinois Press, 1982.

Rable, George C. *But There Was No Peace: The Role of Violence in the Politics of Reconstruction*. Athens: University of Georgia Press, 1984.

Rainwater, Lee, and William L. Yancey. *The Moynihan Report and the Politics of Controversy*. Cambridge, MA: MIT Press, 1967.

Rampersad, Arnold. *The Art and Imagination of W.E.B. Du Bois*. Cambridge, MA: Harvard University Press, 1976.

Randall, Herbert. *Faces of Freedom Summer*. Photographs by Herbert Randall. Text by Bobs M. Tusa. Foreword by Victoria Jackson Gray Adams and Cecil Gray. Tuscaloosa: University of Alabama Press, 2001.

Randel, William Pierce. *The Ku Klux Klan: A Century of Infamy*. Philadelphia: Chilton Books, 1965.

Raper, Arthur. *The Tragedy of Lynching*. New York: Dover Publications, 2003. Originally published 1933.

Redkey, Edwin S., ed. *Respect Black: Writings and Speeches of Henry M. Turner*. New York: Arno Press, 1971.

Reed, Adolph L., Jr. *W.E.B. Du Bois and American Political Thought: Fabianism and the Color Line*. New York: Oxford University Press, 1997.

Reed, Merl E. *Seedtime for the Modern Civil Rights Movement: The President's Committee on Fair Employment Practice, 1941–1946*. Baton Rouge: Louisiana State University Press, 1991.

Reef, Catherine. *A. Philip Randolph: Union Leader and Civil Rights Crusader*. Berkeley Heights, NJ: Enslow Publishers, Inc., 2001.

Rhodes, L.G. *Jackson State University: The First Hundred Years, 1877–1977*. Jackson: University of Mississippi Press, 1979.

Rhym, Darren. *The NAACP: 2002–2003*. Philadelphia: Chelsea House Publishers, 2003.

Richan, Willard C. *Racial Isolation in the Cleveland Schools*. Cleveland: Case Western Reserve University, 1967.

Richards, Leonard L. *Gentlemen of Property and Standing: Anti-Abolition Mobs in Jacksonian America*. New York: Oxford University Press, 1971.

Ridgeway, James. *Blood in the Face: The Ku Klux Klan, Aryan Nations, Nazi Skinheads, and the Rise of a New White Culture*. 2nd ed. New York: Thunder's Mouth Press, 1995.

Rivera, Oswald. *Fire and Rain*. New York: Four Walls Eight Windows, 1990.

Roberts, Randy. *Papa Jack: Jack Johnson and the Era of White Hopes*. New York: Collier Macmillan Publishers, 1983.

Robinson, Cedric J. *Black Movements in America*. New York: Routledge, 1997.

Roediger, David. *Wages of Whiteness: Race and the Making of the American Working Class*. New York: Verso, 1991.

Roosevelt, Eleanor. *The Autobiography of Eleanor Roosevelt*. New York: G.K. Hall, 1984.

Ross, Barbara. *J.E. Springarn and the Rise of the NAACP, 1911–1939*. New York: Scribner, 1972.

Rouse, Jacqueline, Barbara Woods, and Vicki Crawford, eds. *Women in the Civil Rights Movement: Trailblazers and Torchbearers, 1941–1965*. Brooklyn, NY: Carlson Publishers, 1990.

Royce, Edward C. *The Origins of Southern Sharecropping*. Philadelphia: Temple University Press, 1993.

Royster, Jacqueline Jones, ed. *Southern Horrors and Other Writings: The Anti Lynching Campaign of Ida B. Wells, 1882–1900*. Boston: Bedford Books, 1997.

Ruchames, Louis. *Race, Jobs and Politics: The Story of the FEPC*. Evanston, IL: Greenwood Press, 1953.

Rudwick, Elliott. *Race Riot at East St. Louis: July 2, 1917*. Urbana: University of Illinois Press, 1982. Originally published 1964.

Rudwick, Elliott M. *W.E.B. Du Bois: Propagandist of the Negro Protest*. 2nd ed. Philadelphia: University of Pennsylvania Press, 1968.

Ryan, William. *Blaming the Victim*. New York: Vintage Books, 1971.

Rydell, Robert W, ed. *The Reason Why the Colored American Is Not in the World's Columbian Exposition*. Urbana: University of Illinois Press, 1999.

Sales, William W. *From Civil Rights to Black Liberation: Malcolm X and the Organization of Afro-American Unity*. Boston: South End, 1994.

Sandburg, Carl. *The Chicago Race Riots*. New York: Harcourt, Brace, and Howe, 1919.

Schafer, Robert, and Helen F. Ladd. *Discrimination in Mortgage Lending*. Cambridge, MA: MIT Press, 1981.

Schechter, Patricia. *Ida B. Wells-Barnett and American Reform, 1880–1930*. Chapel Hill: University of North Carolina Press, 2001.

Schmidt, Regin. *Red Scare: FBI and the Origins of Anticommunism in the United States, 1919–1943*. Copenhagen, Denmark: Museum Tusculanum Press, 2000.

Schneider, Mark Robert. *"We Return Fighting": The Civil Rights Movement in the Jazz Age*. Boston: Northeastern University Press, 2002.

Schuchter, Arnold. *Reparations: The Black Manifesto and Its Challenge to White America*. New York: J.B. Lippincott Company, 1970.

Schultz, John. *The Chicago Conspiracy Trial*. Rev. ed. New York: Da Capo Press, 1993.

Schumann, H., C. Steeh, L. Bobo, and M. Krysan. *Racial Attitudes in America: Trends and Interpretations*. Cambridge, MA: Harvard University Press, 1997.

Schwemm, Robert G. *Housing Discrimination: Law and Litigation*. New York: C. Boardman, 1990.

Scott-Childres, Reynolds J., ed. *Race and the Production of Modern American Nationalism*. Wellesley Studies in Critical Theory, Literary History and Culture. New York and London: Garland, 1998.

Seale, Bobby. *Seize the Time: The Story of the Black Panther Party and Huey P. Newton*. Baltimore: Black Classic Press, 1991.

Sellers, Cleveland. *The River of No Return: The Autobiography of a Black Militant and the Life and Death of SNCC*. New York: William Morrow and Company, 1973.

Senechal, Roberta. *The Sociogenesis of a Race Riot: Springfield, Illinois, in 1908*. Urbana: University of Illinois Press, 1990.

Shapiro, Herbert. *White Violence and Black Response, from Reconstruction to Montgomery*. Amherst: University of Massachusetts Press, 1988.

Shogan, Robert, and Tom Craig. *The Detroit Race Riot: A Study in Violence*. New York: Da Capo Press, 1964.

Silberman, Charles. *Crisis in Black and White*. New York: Random House, 1964.

Simmons, Charles A. *The African-American Press: With Special References to Four Newspapers, 1827–1965*. Jefferson, NC: McFarland Press, 1998.

Simmons, William Joseph. *America's Menace, or the Enemy Within*. Atlanta: Ku Klux Klan Press, 1926.

Skolnick, Jerome H., and James J. Fyfe. *Above the Law: Police and the Excessive Use of Force*. New York: Free Press, 1993.

Slide, Anthony. *American Racist: The Life and Films of Thomas Dixon*. Lexington: University Press of Kentucky, 2004.

Slotkin, Richard. *Lost Battalions: The Great War and the Crisis of American Nationality*. New York: Henry Holt, 2005.

Small, Melvin. *Antiwarriors: The Vietnam War and the Battle for America's Hearts and Minds*. Wilmington, DE: Scholarly Resources, 2002.

Smead, Howard. *Blood Justice: The Lynching of Mack Charles Parker*. New York: Oxford University Press, 1986.

Smith, Jessie Carney, ed. *Notable Black American Men*. Detroit: Gale, 1999.

Smith, John David. *Black Voices from Reconstruction 1865–1877*. Gainesville: University Press of Florida, 1997.

Smith, John David. *The Ticket to Freedom: The NAACP and the Struggle for Black Political Integration*. Gainesville: University Press of Florida, 2005.

Smith, Neil. *The New Urban Frontier: Gentrification and the Revanchist City*. New York: Routledge, 1996.

Smith, Shawn Michelle. *Photography on the Color Line: W.E.B. Du Bois, Race, and Visual Culture*. Durham, NC: Duke University Press, 2004.

Southern, David W. *Gunnar Myrdal and Black–White Relations: The Use and Abuse of An American Dilemma, 1944–1969*. Baton Rouge: Louisiana State University Press, 1987.

Stark, Rodney. *Police Riots: Collective Violence and Law Enforcement*. Belmont, CA: Wadsworth, 1972.

Steigerwald, David. *The Sixties and the End of Modern America*. New York: St. Martin's Press, 1995.

Stein, Judith. *The World of Marcus Garvey: Race & Class in Modern Society*. Baton Rouge: Louisiana State University Press, 1986.

Steinhorn, L., and B. Diggs-Brown *By the Color of Our Skin: The Illusion of Integration and the Reality of Race*. New York: Plume, 2000.

Stockley, Grif. *Blood in Their Eyes: The Elaine Race Massacres of 1919*. Fayetteville: University of Arkansas Press, 2001.

Stokes, Carl B. *Promises of Power: Then and Now*. Cleveland: Friends of Carl B. Stokes, 1989.

Strickland, William. *Malcolm X: Make It Plain*. New York: Viking, 1994.

Sugrue, Thomas. *The Origins of the Urban Crisis*. Princeton NJ: Princeton University Press, 1998.

Summersell, Charles G. *Mobile: History of a Seaport Town*. Tuscaloosa: University of Alabama Press, 1949.

Swain, Carol M. *The New White Nationalism in America: Its Challenge to Integration*. New York: Cambridge University Press, 2004.
Tager, Jack. *Boston Riots: Three Centuries of Social Violence*. Boston: Northeastern University Press, 2001.
Terrell, Mary Church. *A Colored Woman in a White World*. Washington, DC: Ransdell, 1940.
Terry, Wallace. *Bloods: An Oral History of the Vietnam War by Black Veterans*. New York: Random House, 1984.
Thayer, George. *The Farther Shores of Politics: The American Political Fringe Today*. New York: Simon and Schuster, 1967.
Theoharis, Athan G. *The FBI and American Democracy: A Brief Critical History*. Lawrence: University Press of Kansas, 2004.
Thernstrom, Stephan, and Abigail Thernstrom. *America in Black and White: One Nation, Indivisible*. New York: Simon & Schuster, 1997.
Thomas, Evan. *Robert Kennedy: His Life*. New York: Simon & Schuster, 2000.
Thomas, William Isaac, and Dorothy Swaine Thomas. *The Child in America: Behavior Problems and Programs*. New York: A.A. Knopf, 1928.
Thomason, Michael V., and Joe Langan, eds. *Mobile: The New History of Alabama's First City*. Tuscaloosa: University of Alabama Press, 2001.
Thornbrough, Emma Lou. *T. Thomas Fortune Militant Journalist*. Chicago: University of Chicago Press, 1972.
Tillery, Tyrone. *Claude McKay: A Black Poet's Struggle for Identity*. Amherst: University of Massachusetts Press, 1992.
Tolnay, Stewart A., and E.M. Beck. *A Festival of Violence: An Analysis of Southern Lynchings, 1882–1930*. Urbana: University of Illinois Press, 1995.
Trelease, Allen W. *White Terror*. New York: Harper & Row, 1971.
Trotter, Joe William, Jr., ed. *The Great Migration in Historical Perspective: New Dimensions of Race, Class, & Gender*. Bloomington: Indiana University Press, 1991.
Trotter, Joe William, and Earl Lewis, eds. *African Americans in the Industrial Age: A Documentary History, 1915–1945*. Boston: Northeastern University Press, 1985.
Trotter, Joe W., Jr., and Eric Ledell Smith. *African Americans in Pennsylvania: Shifting Historical Perspectives*. State College: Penn State University Press, 1997.
Tucker, Spencer C., ed. *Encyclopedia of the Vietnam War: A Political, Social, and Military History*. Santa Barbara, CA: ABC-CLIO, 1998.
Tushnet, Mark. *The NAACP's Legal Strategy against Segregated Education, 1925–1950*. Chapel Hill: University of North Carolina Press, 1987.
Tuttle, William. *Race Riot: Chicago in the Red Summer of 1919*. Urbana: University of Illinois Press, 1996. Originally published 1970.
Tye, Larry. *Rising from the Rails: Pullman Porters and the Making of the Black Middle Class*. New York: Henry Holt and Company, 2004.
Tyson, Cyril Degrasse. *Power and Politics in Central Harlem, 1862–1964: The HARYOU Experience*. New York: Jay Street Publishers, 2004.
Tyson, Timothy B. *Radio Free Dixie: Robert F. Williams and the Roots of Black Power*. Chapel Hill: University of North Carolina Press, 1999.
Upton, James N. *Urban Riots in the 20th Century: A Social History*. Bristol, IN: Wyndham Hall Press, 1989.
Urquhart, Brian. *Ralph Bunche: An American Life*. New York: W.W. Norton & Company, 1993.
Van Deberg, William L., ed. *Modern Black Nationalism: From Marcus Garvey to Louis Farrakhan*. New York: New York University Press, 1997.
Vandal, Giles. *The New Orleans Riot of 1866: Anatomy of a Tragedy*. Lafeyette, LA: The Center for Louisiana Studies, University of Southwestern Louisiana, 1983.
Vine, Phyllis. *One Man's Castle: Clarence Darrow in Defense of the American Dream*. New York: Amistad, 2004.
Vollers, Maryanne. *Ghosts of Mississippi: The Murder of Medgar Evers, the Trials of Byron de la Beckwith, and the Haunting of the New South*. Boston: Little, Brown, 1995.
Wade, Wyn Craig. *The Fiery Cross: The Ku Klux Klan in America*. New York: Simon & Schuster, Inc., 1987.
Walker, Clarence E. *We Can't Go Home Again: An Argument About Afrocentrism*. Oxford: Oxford University Press, 2001.

Walwik, Joseph. *The Peekskill, New York, Anti-Communist Riots of 1949*. New York: The Edwin Mellen Press, 2002.

Ward, Brian, and Tony Badger, eds. *The Making of Martin Luther King and the Civil Rights Movement*. London: MacMillan Press Ltd., 1996.

Ward, Geoffrey C. *Unforgivable Blackness*. New York: Alfred A. Knopf, 2004.

Ward, Geoffrey C., and Ken Burns. *Jazz: A History of America's Music*. New York: Knopf, 2000.

Ware, Vron. *Beyond the Pale: White Women, Racism, and History*. London: Verso, 1992.

Washington, Booker T. *Up from Slavery*. New York: Doubleday, Page & Co., 1901.

Washington, Johnny. *Alain Locke and Philosophy: A Quest for Cultural Pluralism*. New York: Greenwood Press, 1986.

Waskow, Arthur I. *From Race Riot to Sit-In, 1919 and the 1960s: A Study in the Connections between Conflict and Violence*. Gloucester, MA: Peter Smith, 1975.

Watras, Joseph. *Recording the True History of the Local Black Legacy and Politics, Race, and Schools: Racial Integration, 1954–1994*. New York: Garland Publishing, Inc. 1997.

Watters, Pat, and Weldon Rougeau. *Events at Orangeburg: A Report Based on Study and Interviews in Orangeburg, South Carolina, in the Aftermath of Tragedy*. South Carolina, February 25, 1968.

Weaver, John D. *The Brownsville Raid*. College Station, TX: Texas A&M Press, 1970.

Weaver, John D. *The Senator and the Sharecroppers Son: Exoneration of the Brownsville Soldiers*. College Station, TX: Texas A&M Press, 1997.

Wedin, Carolyn. *Inheritors of the Spirit: Mary Ovington and the Founding of the NAACP.* New York: John Wiley and Sons, 1997.

Weigley, Russell. *Philadelphia: A 300-Year History*. New York: W.W. Norton & Company, 1982.

Weir, Robert. *Beyond Labor's Veil: The Culture of the Knights of Labor*. University Park: Pennsylvania State University Press, 1996.

Weisbrot, Robert. *Freedom Bound: A History of America's Civil Rights Movement*. New York: Plume Books, 1990.

Weiss, Nancy. *Farewell to the Party of Lincoln: Black Politics in the Age of FDR*. Princeton, NJ: Princeton University Press, 1983.

Wells, Ida B. *On Lynchings*. Amherst, NY: Humanity Books, 2002.

Wells, Ida B. *The Memphis Diary of Ida B. Wells*. Boston: Beacon Press, 1995.

Wells-Barnett, Ida. *Crusade for Justice: The Autobiography of Ida B. Wells*. Edited by Alfreda M. Duster. Chicago: University of Chicago Press, 1970.

Wells-Barnett, Ida B. *Lynch Law in Georgia: A Six-Weeks' Record in the Center of Southern Civilization, as Faithfully Chronicled by the* Atlanta Journal *and the* Atlanta Constitution. Chicago: Author, 1899.

Whalen, Barbara, and Charles Whalen. *The Longest Debate: A Legislative History of the 1964 Civil Rights Act*. Cabin John, MD: Seven Locks Press, 1991.

White, Deborah Gray. *Too Heavy a Load: Black Women in Defense of Ourselves, 1894–1994*. New York and London: W.W. Norton & Company, 1999.

White, Walter. *A Man Called White: The Autobiography of Walter White*. New York: Viking Press, 1948.

White, Walter Francis. *Rope and Faggot: A Biography of Judge Lynch*. New York: Arno Press, 1969.

Whitfield, Stephen. *A Death in the Delta: The Story of Emmett Till*. New York: Free Press, 1988.

Wilkins, Roy, with Tom Matthews. *The Autobiography of Roy Wilkins: Standing Fast*. New York: Penguin Books, 1982.

Williams, Juan. *Eyes on the Prize*. New York: Penquin Group, 1988.

Williams, Lee E., and Lee E. Williams, II, *Anatomy of Four Race Riots: Racial Conflict In Knoxville, Elaine (Arkansas), Tulsa and Chicago, 1919–1921*. Hattiesburg: University and College Press of Mississippi, 1972.

Williams, Robert F. *Negroes with Guns*. Detroit, MI: Wayne State University Press, 1998. Originally published 1962.

Williamson, Joel. *After Slavery: The Negro in South Carolina during Reconstruction, 1865–1877*. Chapel Hill: University of North Carolina Press, 1965.

Williamson, Joel. *The Crucible of Race: Black–White Relations in the American South Since Emancipation*. New York: Oxford University Press, 1984.

Wilson, Matthew. *Whiteness in the Novels of Charles W. Chesnutt*. Jackson: University of Mississippi Press, 2004.

Wilson, W.J. *Power, Racism, and Privilege*. New York: Free Press, 1973.

Wilson, William Julius. *When Work Disappears: The World of the New Urban Poor*. New York: Alfred A. Knopf, 1996.

Winbush, Raymond A. *Should America Pay?: Slavery and the Raging Debate on Reparations*. New York: HarperCollins, 2001.

Winston, James. *A Fierce Hatred of Injustice: Claude McKay's Jamaica and His Poetry of Rebellion*. London: Verso, 2000.

Winters, Stanley B., ed. *From Riot to Recovery: Newark After Ten Years*. Washington, DC: University Press of America, 1979.

Witherspoon, William Roger. *Martin Luther King, Jr.: To the Mountaintop*. Garden City, New York. Doubleday & Company, Inc.

Wolfenstein, Eugene Victor. *The Victims of Democracy: Malcolm X and the Black Revolution*. Berkeley: University of California Press, 1981.

Wolff, Daniel J. *4th of July, Asbury Park: A History of the Promised Land*. New York: Bloomsbury, 2005.

Wolseley, Roland E. *The Black Press, U.S.A.* Ames: Iowa State University Press, 1971.

Wonham, Henry B., ed. *Criticism and the Color Line: Desegregating American Literary Studies*. New Brunswick, NJ: Rutgers University Press, 1996.

Woodward, C. Vann. *The Strange Career of Jim Crow*. 3rd ed. New York: Oxford University Press, 1974.

Wright, Nathan, Jr. *Ready to Riot*. New York: Holt, Rinehart and Winston, 1968.

Yans-McLaughlin, Virginia, ed. *Immigration Reconsidered: History, Sociology, and Politics*. New York and Oxford: Oxford University Press, 1990.

Young, Andrew. *An Easy Burden: The Civil Rights Movement and the Transformation of America*. New York: HarperCollins Publishers, 1996.

Youngs, J. William T., and Oscar Handlin. *Eleanor Roosevelt: A Personal and Public Life*. 3rd ed. New York: Pearson/Longman, 2006.

Zangrando, Robert L. *The NAACP Crusade against Lynching, 1909–1950*. Philadelphia: Temple University Press, 1980.

Zarefsky, David. *President Johnson's War on Poverty: Rhetoric and History*. Tuscaloosa: University of Alabama Press, 1986.

Zaroulis, Nancy, and Gerald Sullivan. *Who Spoke Up? American Protest against the War in Vietnam, 1963–1975*. Garden City, NY: Doubleday, 1984.

Articles and Periodicals

Aguiar, Marian. "Operation Breadbasket." In Anthony Appiah and Henry Louis Gates, Jr., eds. *Africana: The Encyclopedia of the African and African American Experience*. New York: Basic Books, 1999.

Akam, Everett H. "Community and Cultural Crisis: the 'Transfiguring Imagination' of Alain Locke." *American Literary History* (Summer 1991): 255–276.

Altman, Susan. "Black Power Movement." In Susan Altman, ed. *The Encyclopedia of African American Heritage*. New York: Facts On File, 1997.

"An Architect of Social Change: Kenneth B. Clark." In Benjamin P. Bowser and Louis Kushnick, eds., with Paul Grant. *Against the Odds*. Amherst: University of Massachusetts Press, 2002: 147–157.

Anderson, Lorrin, and William Tucker. "Cracks in the Mosaic." *National Review* 42 (1990).

Angle, Paul M. "Doctrinaire vs. Union." In *Bloody Williamson: A Chapter in American Lawlessness*. New York: Alfred A. Knopf, 1952: 89–116.

Asher, Robert. "Documents of the Race Riot at East St. Louis." *Journal of the Illinois State Historical Society* 65 (Autumn 1972): 327–336.

Baker, Houston A. "Scene...Not Heard." In Robert Gooding-Williams, ed. *Reading Rodney King, Reading Urban Uprising*. New York: Routledge, 1993.

Baldwin, James. "Harlem Hoodlums." *Newsweek*, August 9, 1943.

Barnes, Bart. "Eldridge Cleaver, Author and Black Panther Leader, Dies." *Washington Post*, May 2, 1998: D06.

Breindel, Eric. "The Legal Circus." *The New Republic* 196 (1987): 20–23.

Brophy, Alfred L. "The Functions and Limitations of a Historical Truth Commission: The Case of the Tulsa Race Riot Commission." In Elazar Barkan and Alexander Karn, eds. *Taking Wrongs Seriously: Apologies and Reconciliation*. Stanford, CA: Stanford University Press, 2006.

Brophy, Alfred L. "The Tulsa Race Riot in the Oklahoma Supreme Court." *Oklahoma Law Review* 64 (2001): 67–146.

Brown, Cliff. "The Role of Employers in Split Labor Markets: An Event-Structure Analysis of Racial Conflict and AFL Organizing, 1917–1919." *Social Forces* 79 (2000): 653–681.

Brown, Linda Meggett. "Remembering the Orangeburg Massacre. (South Carolina State University)." *Black Issues in Higher Education*, March 1, 2001.

Brown, Mary Jane. "Advocates in the Age of Jazz: Women and the Campaign for the Dyer Anti-Lynching Bill." *Peace & Change* 28, no. 3 (July 2003): 378–419.

Brown, Richard Maxwell. "Historical Patterns of Violence in America" and "The American Vigilante Tradition." In Leon Friedman, ed. *Violence in America: Historical and Comparative Perspectives*. Vol. III. New York: Chelsea, 1969, pp. 35–64 and 121–169. The National Commission on the Causes and Prevention of Violence Report of 1969.

Brown, Richard Maxwell. "Living Together Violently: Blacks and Whites in America." In Richard Maxwell Brown, ed. *Strain of Violence: Historical Studies of American Violence and Vigilantism*. New York: Oxford University Press, 1975.

Brune, Adrian. "Tulsa's Shame." *The Nation* (March 18, 2002).

Burgett, Paul Joseph. "Vindication as a Thematic Principle in Alain Locke's Writings on the Music of Black Americans." In Amritjit Singh, William S. Shiver, and Stanley Brodwin, eds. *The Harlem Renaissance: Revaluations*. New York: Garland, 1989: 139–157.

Butler, J. Michael. "The Mississippi State Sovereignty Commission and Harrison County Beach Integration, 1959–1963: A Cotton-Patch Gestapo?" *Journal of Southern History* 68 (February 2002): 107–148.

Butts, J.W., and Dorothy James, "The Underlying Causes of the Elaine Riot of 1919." *Arkansas Historical Quarterly* XX (1961): 95–104.

Campbell, Jane. "A Necessary Ambivalence: Sutton Griggs's *Imperium in Imperio* and Charles Chesnutt's *The Marrow of Tradition*." In *Mythic Black Fiction: The Transformation of History*. Knoxville: University of Tennessee Press, 1986: 42–63.

Capeci, Dominic J., Jr., and Jack C. Knight. "Reckoning with Violence: W.E.B. Du Bois and the 1906 Atlanta Race Riot." *The Journal of Southern History* 62 (1996): 165–180.

Cardyn, Lisa. "Sexualized Racism/Gendered Violence: Outraging the Body Politic in the Reconstruction South." *Michigan Law Review* (2002).

Carson, Clayborne, and Tom Hamburger. "The Cambridge Convergence: How a Night in Maryland 30 Years Ago Changed the Nation's Course of Racial Politics." *Minneapolis Star Tribune*, July 28, 1997.

Chandler, James P. "Fair Housing Laws: A Critique." *Hastings Law Journal* 24 (1973): 159–205.

Chesnutt, Charles W. "Charles W. Chesnutt's Own View of His New Story *The Marrow of Tradition*." *Cleveland World*, October 20, 1901, Magazine Section, 5.

Cho, Yong Hyo. "City Politics and Racial Polarization: Bloc Voting in Cleveland Elections." *Journal of Black Studies* 4 (June 1974): 396–417.

"City Council Lists Answers To 22 West Side Demands." *Asbury Park Evening Press*, July 14, 1970, 1.

Cobb, James C. "Polarization in a Southern City: The Augusta Riot and the Emerging Character of the 1970s." *Southern Studies* (Summer 1981).

Coleman, Wanda. "Remembering Latasha: Blacks, Immigrants, and America." *Nation* 256 (March 1993): 187–191.

"County Jail Overflowing." *Asbury Park Evening Press*, July 8, 1970, 4.

Cox, Donald. "A Split in the Party." In Kathleen Cleaver and George Katsiaficas, eds. *Liberation, Imagination, and the Black Panther Party: A New Look at the Panthers and Their Legacy*. New York: Routledge Press, 2001.

Crenshaw, Kimberle, and Gary Peller. "Reel Time/Real Justice." In Robert Gooding-Williams, ed. *Reading Rodney King, Reading Urban Uprising*. New York: Routledge, 1993.

Crowe, Charles. "Racial Violence and Social Reform: Origins of the Atlanta Riot of 1906." *Journal of Negro History* 53 (1968): 234–256.

Cutler, David, Edward Glaese, and Jacob Vigdor. "The Rise and Decline of the American Ghetto." *Journal of Political Economy* 107 (1999): 455–506.

Davis, Mike. "In L.A., Burning All Illusions." *The Nation*, June 1, 1992.

DeSantis, Alan D. "A Forgotten Leader: Robert S. Abbott and the *Chicago Defender* from 1910–1920." *Journalism History* 23, no. 2 (1997): 63–71.

DeSantis, Alan D. "Selling the American Dream Myth to Black Southerners: The *Chicago Defender* and the Great Migration of 1915–1919." *Western Journal of Communication* 62, no. 4 (1998): 474–511.

Diggs-Brown, Barbara. "Ida B. Wells-Barnett: About the Business of Agitation." In Susan Albertine, ed. *A Living of Words: American Women in Print Culture*. Knoxville: University of Tennessee Press, 1995.

Doreski, C.K. "Chicago, Race, and the Rhetoric of the 1919 Riot." *Prospects* 18 (1993): 293–309.

Du Bois, W.E.B. "Close Ranks." *The Crisis*, July 1918.

Du Bois, W.E.B. "Returning Soldiers." *The Crisis*, May 1918.

Du Bois, W.E.B. "Cowardice." *The Crisis*, October 1916.

Dulaney, W. Marvin. "Black Power." In Charles D. Lowery and John F. Marszalek, eds. *The Greenwood Encyclopedia of American Civil Rights*. Westport, CT: Greenwood Press, 2003.

Egerton, John. "A Case of Prejudice: Maurice Mays and the Knoxville Race Riot of 1919." *Southern Exposure* 11 (1983): 56–65.

Ellis, Mark. "'Closing Ranks' and 'Seeking Honors': W.E.B. Du Bois in World War I." *Journal of American History* 79 (1992): 96–124.

Fairclough, A. "The Preachers and the People: The Origins and Early Years of the Southern Christian Leadership Conference, 1955–1959." *The Journal of Southern History* 52 (August 1986): 403–440.

Fairclough, A. "Southern Christian Leadership Conference and the Second Reconstruction, 1957–1973." *The South Atlantic Quarterly* 80 (Spring 1981): 177–194.

Farley, Reynolds. "Components of Suburban Population Growth." In Barry Schwartz, ed. *The Changing Face of the Suburbs*. Chicago: University of Chicago Press (1976): 19.

Feagin, Joe, and W.P. Sheatsley. "Ghetto Resident Appraisals of a Riot." *Public Opinion Quarterly* 32 (1968): 352–362.

Fehr, Stephen C. "U.S. Historic Trust Puts Black Churches on Endangered List." *The Washington Post*, June 18, 1996: A03.

Fisher, Gordon M. "The Development and History of the Poverty Thresholds." *Social Security Bulletin*, 55, no.4 (Winter 1992): 3–14.

Fleming, Robert E. "Sutton E. Griggs: Militant Novelist." *Phylon: The Atlanta University Review of Race and Culture* XXXIV, no. 1 (March 1973): 73–77.

Fletcher, Michael A. "U.S. Investigates Suspicious Fires at Southern Black Churches." *The Washington Post*, February 8, 1996: A03.

Flynt, Wayne. "Florida Labor and Political 'Radicalism,' 1919–1920." *Labor History* 9 (1968).

Geyer, Elizabeth. "The 'New' Ku Klux Klan." *Crisis* (1956): 139–148.

Gitelman, H.M. "Perspectives on American Industrial Violence." *The Business History Review* 47 (Spring 1973): 1–23.

Glines, C.V. "Black vs White–Trouble in the Ranks." *Armed Forces Management* 16 (June 1970): 20–27.

Gloster, Hugh M. "The Negro in American Fiction." *Phylon: The Atlanta University of Race and Culture* IV, no. 4 (Winter, 1943): 333–345.

Greene, Larry. "Harlem: The Depression Years—Leadership and Social Conditions." *Afro-Americans in New York History* 17 (July 1993).

"The Great Battle of Longview: The Other Name for the Race Riots Now Closing in Gregg County." *The Dallas Express*, July 19, 1919.

Grimshaw, A. D. "Actions of Police and the Military in American Race Riot." *Phylon: The Atlanta University of Race and Culture* 24, no. 3 (1963).

Gutman, Herbert G. "Black Coal Miners and the American Labor Movement." In *Work, Culture & Society in Industrializing America*. New York: Alfred A. Knopf, 1976: 119–208.

Hahn, Harlan. "Civic Responses to Riots: A Reappraisal of Kerner Commission Data." *Public Opinion Quarterly* 34, no. 1 (Spring 1970): 101–107.

Hamilton, Charles V. "An Advocate of Black Power Defines It (1968)." In Thomas Wagstaff, ed. *Black Power: The Radical Response to White America*. Beverly Hills, CA: Glencoe Press, 1969: 142–137.

Hamilton, Charles V. "Riots, Revolts and Relevant Response." In Floyd B. Barbour, ed. *The Black Power Revolt*. Boston: Extending Horizons Books, 1968: 170–178.

Harrison, E.C. "Student Unrest on the Black College Campus." *The Journal of Negro Education* 41, no. 2 (1972): 113–120.

Hawkins, W.E. "When Negroes Shot a Lynching Bee into Perdition." *The Messenger* 2, no. 9 (September 1919): 28–29.

Haynes, George E. "Race Riots in Relation to Democracy." *Survey* 42 (1919): 697–699.

Haynes, Robert V. "The Houston Mutiny and Riot of 1917." *Southwestern Historical Quarterly* LXXVI (1973): 418–439.

Hays, Tom. "Diallo Officers Innocent of All Charges, Says Jury." *Birmingham Post* (England), February 26, 2000.

Hendricks, Wanda. "Ida B. Wells-Barnett and the Alpha Suffrage Club of Chicago." In Marjorie Spruill Wheeler, ed. *One Woman, One Vote: Rediscovering the Woman Suffrage Movement*. Troutdale, OR: New Sage Press, 1995.

Hicken, Victor. "The Virden and Pana Mine Wars of 1898." *Journal of the Illinois State Historical Society* 52 (1959): 263–278.

Hine, Darlene Clark, William C. Hine, and Stanley Harrold. "White Supremacy Triumphant: African-Americans in the South in the Late Nineteenth Century." Chap. 14 in *The African-American Odyssey*. Englewood Cliffs, NJ: Prentice Hall, 2000, 306–331.

Hirsch, Arnold R. "Massive Resistance in the Urban North: Trumbull Park, Chicago, 1953–1966." *The Journal of American History* 82, no. 2 (1995): 522–550.

Holmes, William F. "Whitecapping: Agrarian Violence in Mississippi, 1902–1906." *Journal of Southern History* 35 (1969): 165–185.

Howell, Ron. "Sharpton, Al." In Henry Louis Gates, Jr., and Evelyn Brooks Higginbotham, eds. *African American Lives*. New York: Oxford University Press, 2004.

Hu, Arthur. "Us and Them." *New Republic* 206 (June 12, 1992): 12–14.

Jacobs, Ronald N. *Race, Media, and the Crisis of Civil Society: From Watts to Rodney King*. Cambridge: Cambridge University Press, 2000.

Jaher, Frederic. "White America Views Jack Johnson, Joe Louis, and Muhammad Ali." In Donald Spivey, ed. *Sport in America: New Historical Perspectives*. Westport, CT: Greenwood Press, 1985: 145–192.

Jean, Susan. "'Warranted' Lynchings: Narratives of Mob Violence in White Southern Newspapers, 1880–1940." *American Nineteenth Century History* 6 (2005): 351–372.

Johnson, Ben, et al. "Report on the Special Committee Authorized by Congress to Investigate the East St. Louis Riots." In Anthony M. Platt, ed. *The Politics of Riot Commissions, 1917–1970: A Collection of Official Reports and Critical Essays*. New York: Macmillan Publishing Company, 1971.

Johnson, James Weldon. "The Riots: An N.A.A.C.P. Investigation." *The Crisis* 18, no.5 (September 1919): 241–243.

Johnson, Marilynn S. "Gender, Race, and Rumors: Re-Examining the 1943 Race Riots." *Gender and History* 10, no. 2 (1990): 252–277.

Jones, Mack H. "The Kerner Commission: Errors and Omissions." In Philip Meranto, ed. *The Kerner Report Revisited*. Assembly on the Kerner Report Revisited, Institute on Government and Public Affairs, University of Illinois, Urbana, January 11–13, 1970.

Jordan, William. "'The Damnable Dilemma': African-American Accommodation and Protest during World War I." *Journal of American History* 81 (1995): 1562–1583.

Kanter, Arlene S. "A Home of One's Own: The Fair Housing Amendments Act of 1988 and Housing Discrimination against People with Mental Disabilities." *The American University Law Review* 43 (1994): 925–994.

King, Martin Luther, Jr., "I Have a Dream." In *The Norton Anthology of African American Literature*. Henry Louis Gates, Jr., and Nellie Y. McKay, eds. New York: W.W. Norton, 2004, 107–109.

King, Martin Luther, Jr. "I've Been to the Mountaintop." In *The Norton Anthology of African American Literature*. Henry Louis Gates, Jr., and Nellie Y. McKay, eds. New York: W.W. Norton, 2004, 110–116.

King, Martin Luther, Jr. "Letter from Birmingham Jail." In *The Norton Anthology of African American Literature*. Henry Louis Gates, Jr., and Nellie Y. McKay, eds. New York: W.W. Norton, 2004, 1896–1908.

King, Martin Luther, Jr. "Black Power Defined." In James M. Washington, ed. *I Have A Dream: Writings & Speeches That Changed the World*. New York: HarperCollins, 1986: 153–165.

King, Martin Luther, Jr. "Civil Right No. 1—The Right to Vote." *New York Times Magazine*, March 14, 1965: 26–27, 94–95.

Klarman, Michael J. "The Supreme Court and Black Disenfranchisement." *University of Virginia Law School, Public Law and Legal Theory Working Paper* Series, 2005, Paper 25.

Kushner, James A. "The Fair Housing Amendments Act of 1988: The Second Generation of Fair Housing." *Vanderbilt Law Review* 42 (1989): 1049–1106.

Lakin, Matthew. "'A Dark Night': The Knoxville Race Riot of 1919." *The Journal of East Tennessee History* 72 (2000): 1–29.

Lang, William W., and Leonard I. Nakamura. "A Model of Redlining." *Journal of Urban Economics* 33, no. 2 (1993): 223–234.

Langlois, J.L. "The Belle Island Bridge Incident: Legend Dialectic and Semiotic System in the 1943 Detroit Race Riots." *The Journal of American Folklore* 96, no. 380 (1983).

Laurie, Clayton D. "The U.S. Army and the Omaha Race Riot of 1919." *Nebraska History* 72, no. 3 (1991): 135–143.

Lawson, Michael L. "Omaha, a City of Ferment: Summer of 1919." *Nebraska History* 58, no. 3 (1977): 395–417.

Lazerow, Jama. "The Black Panthers at the Water's Edge: Oakland, Boston, and the New Bedford 'Riots' of 1970." In Jama Lazerow and Yohuru Williams, eds. *The Black Panther Party in Historical Perspective*. Durham, NC: Duke University Press, forthcoming.

Lederer, Katherine. "And Then They Sang a Sabbath Song." *Springfield!* 2 (April, May, and June 1981): 26–28, 33–36.

Lerner, Gerda. "Early Community Work of Black Club Women." *The Journal of Negro History* 59, no. 2 (1974): 158–167.

Lichtenstein, Alex. "Racial Conflict and Racial Solidarity in the Alabama Coal Strike of 1894: New Evidence for the Gutman-Hill Debate." *Labor History* 36 (Winter 1995): 63–76.

Lieberson, Stanley, and Arnold Silverman. "The Precipitants and Underlying Conditions of Race Riots." *American Sociological Review* 30 (December 1965): 887–898.

Linder, Douglas O. "Bending Toward Justice: John Doar and the Mississippi Burning Trial." *Mississippi Law Journal* 72.2 (Winter 2002): 731–779.

Litwack, Leon. "Hellhounds." In James Allen, Hilton Als, et al., eds. *Without Sanctuary: Lynching Photography in America*. Sante Fe, NM: Twin Palms Publishers, 2000: 1–34.

Lochard, Metz T. P. "Phylon Profile, XII: Robert S. Abbott: 'Race Leader.'" *Phylon* 8 (1947): 125.

Locke, Alain. "Harlem: Dark Weather-Vane." *Survey Graphic* 25, no. 8 (August 1936): 457.

Lockett, James D. "The Lynching Massacre of Black and White Soldiers at Fort Pillow, Tennessee, April 12, 1864." *Western Journal of Black Studies* 22 (Summer 1998).

Lorini, Alessandra. "International Expositions in Chicago and Atlanta: Rituals of Progress and Reconciliation." In *Rituals of Race: American Public Culture and the Search for Racial Democracy*. Charlottesville: University of Virginia Press, 1999: 33–75.

Mack, Angela. "1898 Wilmington Race Riot/A Matter of Public Record: Over a Century Later, Facts of Incident Released." *The News & Observer*, November 29, 2005: 1A.

Marquese, Mike. "By Any Means Necessary." *The Nation* 279 (July 2004).

Marshall, Thurgood. "The Gestapo in Detroit." *Crisis* 50, no. 8 (August 1943).

Martin, Charles H. "Review of R.C. Cortner, *A Mob Intent on Death: The NAACP and the Arkansas Race Cases*." *The Arkansas Historical Review* XCV, no. 1 (February 1990): 292–293.

Matheson, Victor A., and Robert A. Baade. "Race and Riots: A Note on the Economic Impact of the Rodney King Riots." *Urban Studies* 41, no. 13 (December 2004): 2691–2696.

Mayfield, Julian. "Challenge to Negro Leadership." *Commentary* 31, no. 4 (April 1961).

McKanna, Clare. "Black Enclaves of Violence: Race and Homicide in Great Plains Cities, 1890–1920." *Great Plains Quarterly* 23 (2003): 147–160.

McKissick, Floyd B. "Programs for Black Power." In Floyd B. Barbour, ed. *The Black Power Revolt*. Manchester, NH: Porter Sargent Publishers, 1968: 179–188.

McWilliams, Carey. "Watts: The Forgotten Slum." *The Nation*, August 30, 1965.

Meier, August, and John H. Bracey Jr. "The NAACP as a Reform Movement, 1909–1966: 'To Reach the Conscience of America.'" *The Journal of Southern History* 59 (1993): 3–30.

Menard, Orville D. "Tom Dennison, *The Omaha Bee*, and the 1919 Omaha Race Riot." *Nebraska History* 68, no. 4 (Winter 1987): 152–165.

Morsell, John A. "States' Rights and States' Wrongs." *The Crisis*, edited by James W. Ivy (May 1959): 263–270, 314.

Murray, Percy E. "Harry C. Smith–Joseph Foraker Alliance: Coalition Politics in Ohio." *The Journal of Negro History* 68 (1983): 171–184.

Mydans, Seth. "Verdict in Los Angeles; Fear Subsides with Verdict, but Residents Remain Wary." *New York Times*, Section B, Column 1 (April 19, 1993): 11.

Napier, Winston. "Affirming Critical Conceptualism: Harlem Renaissance Aesthetics and the Formation of Alain Locke's Social Philosophy." *Massachusetts Review* 39, no. 1 (Spring 1998): 93–112.

"The Nature of the Beast: The Abner Louima Trial." *Revolutionary Worker* 1007 (May 23, 1999).

Nelson, Bruce. "Organized Labor and the Struggle for Black Equality in Mobile during World War II." *Journal of American History* 80, no. 3 (December 1993): 952–988.

Newkirk, Pamela. "Ida B. Wells-Barnett." In Robert Giles and Robert Snyder, eds. *Profiles in Journalistic Courage*. New Brunswick, NJ: Transaction Publishers, 2001.

Newkirk, Pamela. "1964—Brooklyn Erupts as Harlem Lulls." *Washington Afro American*, July 25, 1964.

Norwood, Stephen. "Bogalusa Burning: the War against Biracial Unionism in the Deep South, 1919." *Journal of Southern History* 63 (1997): 591–628.

Oliver, Melvin L., and James H. Johnson, Jr. "Inter-ethnic Conflict in an Urban Ghetto: The Case of Blacks and Latinos in Los Angeles." In *Research in Social Movements, Conflict and Change* 6: (1984). 57–94.

Orshansky, Mollie. "Counting the Poor: Another Look at the Poverty Profile." *Social Security Bulletin* 28, no. 1 (January 1965): 3–29.

Orshansky, Mollie. "How Poverty Is Measured." *Monthly Labor Review* 92, no. 2 (February 1969): 37–41.

Orshansky, Mollie, Harold Watts, Bradley R. Schiller, and John J. Korbel. "Measuring Poverty: A Debate." *Public Welfare* 36, no. 2 (Spring 1978): 44–46.

Osofsky, Gilbert. "Race Riot, 1900: A Study of Ethnic Violence." *The Journal of Negro Education* 32 (1963): 16–24.

Paletz, David L., and Dunn, Robert. "Press Coverage of Civil Disorders: A Case Study of Winston-Salem, 1967." *Public Opinion Quarterly* 33 (1969): 328–345.

Perloff, Richard M. "The Press and Lynchings of African Americans." *Journal of Black Studies* (2000): 315–330.

Peters, Jennifer. "The Watts Riot: Los Angeles, California 1965." *Race and Ethnic Relations*, November 30, 2004.

"Philosopher, Who Helped to Found N.A.A.C.P., Later Turned to Communism." *New York Times*, August 28, 1963: Obituary page.

Pinkney, Alphonso. "Rodney King and Dred Scott." In Haki R. Madhubuki, ed. *Why L.A. Happened: Implications of the '92 Los Angeles Rebellion*. Chicago: Third World Press, 1993.

Poinsett, Alex. "Walking with Presidents: Louis Martin and the Rise of Black Political Power." *The New Crisis* (February/March 1998).

Pollard, Gail. "Latinos Bring Racial Mix to Boil." *Guardian*, London (1992): 7.

Powledge, Fred. "Scattered Violence Keeps Jersey City Tense 3rd Night: 400 Policemen Confine Most of Rioters to 2 Sections—Crowds Watch in Streets Despite Danger." Special to the *New York Times*, August 5, 1964: 1.

Powledge, Fred. "Fighting the System: Negro Violence Viewed as a Reaction to Frustrations of Ghetto Wastelands." *New York Times*, August 6, 1964: 18.

Puddington, Arch. "The War on the War on Crime." *Commentary* 107 (May 1999).

Purrington, Burton L., and Panny L. Harter. "The Easter and Tug-of-War Lynching and the Early Twentieth-Century Black Exodus from Southwest Missouri." In George Sabo, III, and William M. Schneider, eds. *Visions and Revisions: Ethnohistoric Perspectives on Southern Cultures*. Athens: University of Georgia Press, 1987: 59–82.

Randolph, A. Philip. "How to Stop Lynching." *The Messenger*, August 1919.

Randolph, A. Philip. "Our Reason for Being." *The Messenger* (August 1919): 11–12.

Reed, Merl E. "The FEPC, the Black Worker, and the Southern Shipyards." *South Atlantic Quarterly* 74, no. 4 (Autumn 1975): 446–467.

Rogers, O.A., Jr. "The Elaine Race Riots of 1919." *Arkansas Historical Quarterly* XIX (1960): 143–149.

Rosenberg, Howard. "Los Angeles TV Shows Restraint." *Chicago Sun-Times*, Section 2, Features (April 19, 1993): 22.

Rouzeau, Edgar T. "The 'Double V' Campaign." In Jonathan Birnmaum and Clarence Taylor, eds. *Civil Rights Since 1787: A Reader on the Black Struggle*. New York: New York University Press, 2000: 315–317.

Royster, Jacqueline Jones. "Ida B. Wells-Barnett." In Cary D. Wintz and Paul Finkelman, eds. *Encyclopedia of the Harlem Renaissance*. 2 vols. New York: Routledge, 2004: 98–101.

Royster, Jacqueline Jones. "To Call a Thing by Its True Name: The Rhetoric of Ida B. Wells." In Andrea Lunsford, ed. *Reclaiming Rhetorica*. Pittsburgh: University of Pittsburgh Press, 1995: 167–84.

Rugaber, Walter. "A Negro Is Killed in Memphis." *New York Times*, March 29, 1968.

Rugaber, Walter. "Racial Violence Is Curbed in Dayton." *New York Times*, September 2, 1966, Section L: 48.

Russell-Brown, Katheryn. "'Driving While Black': Corollary Phenomena and Collateral Consequences." *Boston College Law Review* 40 no. 3 (1999): 717–731.

Russell-Brown, Katheryn. "Policing Communities, Policing Race." In *Underground Codes: Race, Crime, and Other Related Fires*. New York: New York University Press, 2004: 55–71.

Salem, Dorothy. "National Association of Colored Women." In Darlene Clark Hine, Elsa Barkley Brown, and Rosalyn Terborg-Penn, eds., *Black Women in America: An Historical Encyclopedia, Vol. II, M–Z*. Bloomington and Indianapolis: Indiana University Press, 1993.

Schechter, Patricia. "Unsettled Business: Ida B. Wells against Lynching, or How Antilynching Got Its Gender." In Fitzhugh Brundage, ed. *Under Sentence of Death: Lynching in the South*. Chapel Hill: University of North Carolina Press, 1997.

Schuler, Edgar A. "The Houston Race Riot, 1917." *Journal of Negro History* 29 (July 1944): 300–338.

"Second Week of July in Retrospect." *Asbury Park Sunday Press*, July 12, 1970, sec. C, 1.

Seligmann, Herbert. "Race War?" *New Republic* 20 (August 13, 1919): 49.

Seligmann, Herbert J. "The Menace of Race Hatred." *Harper's Monthly Magazine*, CXL–CXLI (1920): 537–543.

Shields, Patrick M. "The Burden of the Draft: The Vietnam Years." *Journal of Political and Military Sociology* 9 (Fall 1982): 215–228.

Singleton, John. "An Essay on Rosewood." In Michael D'Orso, ed. *Like Judgment Day.* New York: Warner Brothers, 1996.

Sitkoff, Harvard. "The Detroit Race Riot of 1943." *Michigan History* 53 (Fall 1969): 183–206.

"Six Men Killed in Race Battle at Charleston." *Atlanta Constitution*, May 11, 1919: 1.

Smith, Reed W. "Southern Journalists and Lynching: The Statesboro Case Study." *Journalism & Communication Monographs* (2005): 51–92.

Staten, Clark. "L.A. Police Acquitted, Rioting Strikes S.E. Los Angeles." In *Three Days of Hell in Los Angeles*. EmergencyNet NEWS Service. Chicago: Emergency Response & Research Institute, 1992.

Stevenson, Brenda E. "Latasha Harlins, Soon Ja Du, and Joyce Karlin: A Case Study of Multicultural Females and Justice on the Urban Frontier." *The Journal of African American Life and History* 89 (Spring 2004): 152–176.

Stockley, Grif, and Jeannie M. Whayne. "Federal Troops and the Elaine Massacres: A Colloquy." *The Arkansas Historical Quarterly* LXI, no. 3 (Autumn 2002): 272–283.

Stone, Chuck. "The National Conference on Black Power." In Floyd B. Barbour, ed. *The Black Power Revolt*. Manchester, NH: Porter Sargent Publishers, 1968: 189–198.

Stringer-Bishoff, Murray. "Monett's Darkest Hour: The Lynching of June 28, 1894." *Monett Times*, June 27 and 28, 1994.

Stringer-Bishoff, Murray. "The Lynching That Changed Southwest Missouri." *Monett Times*, August 14–16, 1991.

Taft, Philip. "Violence in American Labor Disputes." *Annals of the American Academy of Political and Social Violence* 364 (March 1966): 127–140.

Taft, Philip, and Philip Ross. "American Labor Violence: Its Causes, Character, and Outcome." In Hugh Davis Graham and Ted Robert Gurr, eds. *Violence in America: Historical and Comparative Perspectives*. New York: New American Library, 1969.

Tate, Gayle. "The Harlem Riots of 1935 and 1943." In *Encyclopedia of African American Culture and History.* New York: Macmillan Publishing Company, 1996.

Taylor, Joe Gray. "Louisiana: An Impossible Task." In Otto H. Olsen, ed. *Reconstruction and Redemption in the South*. Baton Rouge: Louisiana State University Press, 1980: 202–230.

Taylor, Robert N. "Robert Charles: The Greatest 'Desperado' in Black American History." *The Tennessee Tribune*, January 12, 2006.

Thelwell, Ekwueme Michael. "H. Rap Brown/Jamil Al-Amin: A Profoundly American Story." *The Nation*, March 18, 2002.

Thompson, James G. "Letter to the Editor: Should I Sacrifice to Live 'Half-American'?" *Pittsburgh Courier*, January 31, 1942.

Thompson, Mildred I. "Ida B. Wells-Barnett: An Exploratory Study of an American Black Woman, 1893–1930." In Darlene Clark Hine, ed. *Black Women in United States History*, Vol. 15. New York: Carlson Publishing Inc., 1990.

Tisdall, Simon, and Christopher Reed. "All Quiet on the Western Front After King Verdicts." *Guardian*, London, April 19, 1993: 20.

Tootell, Geoffrey M.B. "Redlining in Boston: Do Mortgage Lenders Discriminate against Neighborhoods?" *Quarterly Journal of Economics* 111, no. 4 (1996): 1049–1079.

Tucker, David M. "Miss Ida B. Wells and Memphis Lynching." In Darlene Clark Hine, ed. *Black Women in American History: From Colonial Times Through the Nineteenth Century. Black Women in United States History*, Vol. 4. New York: Carlson Publishing Inc., 1990: 1085–1095.

Tuttle, William M. "Violence in a 'Heathen' Land: The Longview Race Riot of 1919." *Phylon* 33, no. 4 (1972): 324–333.

Twain, Mark. "The United States of Lyncherdom." In *Europe and Elsewhere*. New York: Harper, 1923.

Tyson, Timothy B. "Robert F. Williams, 'Black Power,' and the Roots of the African American Freedom Struggle." *The Journal of American History* 85 no. 2 (September 1998): 540–570.

Uhlenbrock, Tom. "Ste. Genevieve's Rich History Includes Indians and Blacks, Too." *St. Louis Post-Dispatch*, April 1, 2001.

Upton, James N. "The Politics of Urban Violence: Critiques and Proposals." *Journal of Black Studies* 15 (March 1985): 243–258.

Valentine, Victoria. "In the Fore of the Movement." *Emerge Magazine* (April 1996): 24.

Vandal, Giles, "The Origins of the New Orleans Riot of 1866, Revised." In Donald G. Nieman, ed. *African American Life in the Post-Emancipation South, 1861–1900*. New York: Garland Publishing, 1994.

Waller, Altina L. "Community, Class and Race in the Memphis Riot of 1866." *Journal of Social History* 18 (2001): 233–246.

Weitzer, Ronald. "Racialized Policing: Residents Perceptions in Three Neighborhoods." *Laws and Society Review* 34 (2000): 129–155.

Wells-Barnett, Ida B. "Mob Rule in New Orleans: Robert Charles and His Fight to Death, the Story of His Life, Burning Human Beings Alive, Other Lynching Statistics." Chicago, 1900. Reprinted in *On Lynchings*. New York: Arno Press, 1969.

Wheeling, John. "Shootings Erupt, 56 Are Hurt." *Asbury Park Evening Press*, July 8, 1970, 1.

"White Americans Listen." Two-page handout, circa 1960s. Housed in the Jim Crow Museum of Racist Memorabilia, Ferris State University, Big Rapids, Michigan.

White, Walter F. "Race Conflict in Arkansas." *Survey* XLIII (December 13, 1919): 233–234.

Wiggins, William H. "Boxing's Sambo Twins: Racial Stereotypes in Jack Johnson and Joe Louis Newspaper Cartoons, 1908 to 1938." *Journal of Sport History* 15, no.3 (1988): 242–254.

Wilkins, Roy. "Along the N.A.A.C.P. Battlefront." *The Crisis*. Edited by James W. Ivy (August–September 1964): 467–472.

Willborn, Steven. "The Omaha Riot of 1919." *The Nebraska Lawyer* (December 1999/January 2000): 49–53.

Williams, Lee E., II. "The Charleston, South Carolina, Riot of 1919." *Southern Miscellany: Essays in History in Honor of Glover Moore*. Jackson: University Press of Mississippi, 1981.

Williams, Walter. "Cleveland's Crisis Ghetto: Causes and Complaints." In P.H. Rossi, ed. *Ghetto Revolts*. New Brunswick, NJ: Transaction Books, 1973.

Winbush, Raymond. "And the Earth Moved: Stealing Black Land in the United States." In Raymond Winbush, ed. *Should America Pay?: Slavery and the Raging Debate on Reparations*. New York: HarperCollins, 2001: 46–56.

Winquist, Thomas R. "Civil Rights Legislation—The Civil Rights Act of 1957." *Michigan Law Review* 56 (1958): 619–630.

Wood, Daniel. "L.A.'s Darkest Days: 10 Years Later." *The Christian Science Monitor*, April 29, 2002.

Wright, George Cable. "Riots Were Bred in a City in Decline." *New York Times*, August 5, 1964: 36.

Zackodnik, Teresa. "Ida B. Wells and 'American Atrocities' in Britain." *Women's Studies International Forum* 28 (2005): 259–273.

Zenou, Yves, and Nicolas Boccard. "Racial Discrimination and Redlining in Cities." *Journal of Urban Economics* 48 (2000): 260–285.

Web Sites

"Abner Louima Receives Settlement of $9 Million." *CNN.com/Transcripts*, July 11, 2001. See http://transcripts.cnn.com/TRANSCRIPTS/0107/11/bn.01.html.

ADL: Law Enforcement Agency Resource Network. "Extremism in America." See http://www.adl.org/learn/ext_us/.

AfricanAmericans.com. "Timeline." See http://www.africanamericans.com/timeline.html.

Albergotti, Reed, Thomas Zambito, Marsha Schrager, and John Rofe. "Racism Comes Home: The Howard Beach Case." See http://www.queenstribune.com/anniversary2003/howardbeach.htm.

American Lynching. "Infamous Lynchings." See http://www.americanlynching.com/infamous-old.html.

Anti-Defamation League. "Lesson 3: With All Deliberate Speed." *Exploring the Promise of Brown v. Board of Education 50 Years Later* (2004). See http://www.adl.org/education/brown_2004/lesson3.asp.

Baker, Lee D. "Ida B. Wells-Barnett and Her Passion for Justice." In Vincent P. Franklin, ed. *Living Our Stories, Telling Our Truths: Autobiography and the Making of African American Intellectual Tradition*. New York: Scribner, 1995. See http://www.duke.edu/ldbaker/classes/AAIH/caaih/ibwells/ibwbkgrd.html.

Bardsley, Marilyn, *J. Edgar Hoover*. See Courtroom Television Network, http://www.CrimeLibrary.com.

Bartlett, John, to Hon. S.W.T. Lanham. Brownsville, Texas, August 17, 1906. Texas State Library & Archives Commission. See http://www.tsl.state.tx.us/governors/rising/lanham-brownsville-1.html.

Baulch, Vivian M., and Patricia Zacharias. "The 1943 Detroit Race Riots." *Detroit News*, 2000. See http://info.detnews.com/history/story/index.cfm?id=185&category=events.

Bennett, Harrison. "The Phillips County Riot Cases." *ChickenBones: A Journal for Literary & Artistic African-American Themes* (December 1999). See http://www.nathanielturner.com/phillipscountyriotcases.htm.

Black Panther Party. "The Ten Point Plan." See http://www.blackpanther.org/TenPoint.htm.

Chaney, Ben. "Schwerner, Chaney, and Goodman: The Struggle for Justice." *Human Rights Magazine* 27, no. 2 (Spring 2000). See http://www.abanet.org/irr/hr/spring00humanrights/chaney.html.

The Circle Brotherhood Association. *African American History of Western New York State*. See http://www.math.buffalo.edu/sww/0history/1935-1970.html.

"Civil Rights Memorial." See http://www.tolerance.org/memorial/memorial.swf.

Community Research Partners. "Introduction & Overview: Population Indicators." *Community Indicators Database Report: Population* (October 2005). See http://www.communityresearchpartners.org/uploads/publications//CIDR-population.pdf.

CourtTV Crime Library, Criminal Minds and Methods, http://www.crimelibrary.com/gangsters%5Foutlaws/cops%5Fothers/hoover/.

Crow, Chris. "The Lynching of Emmett Till." *The History of Jim Crow.* See http://www.jimcrowhistory.org/resources/lessonplans/hs_es_emmett_till.htm.

Davis, Ronald L.F. "Creating Jim Crow: In-Depth Essay." *The History of Jim Crow.* See www.jimcrowhistory.org/history/creating2.htm.

"Denounced Republicans: Leaders of the Niagara Movement Succeed in Carrying Resolutions, Convention Was at a Dead-Lock at Morning Session—Many From Out of Town." *Oberlin Tribune*, September 4, 1908. See http://www.oberlin.edu/external/EOG/Niagara%20Movement/niagaramain.htm.

Durham, Ken. "Longview Race Riot of 1919." *The Handbook of Texas Online* (2001). See http://www.tsha.utexas.edu/handbook/online/articles/LL/jcl2.html.

Ellsworth, Scott, and John Hope Franklin, eds. *Tulsa Race Riot: A Report by the Oklahoma Commission to Study the Tulsa Race Riot of 1921.* 2001. See http://www.okhistory.org/trrc/freport.htm.

FBI. *Civil Rights Investigation into the Abduction of Mack Charles Parker from the Pearl River County Jail in Poplarville, Mississippi.* April 1959. See http://foia.fbi.gov/foiaindex/parker.htm.

FBI. *COINTELPRO—Black Nationalist Hate Groups* (1967). See http://www.icdc.com/~paulwolf/cointelpro/blacknationalist.htm.

Fumento, Michael. "A Church Arson Epidemic?: It's Smoke and Mirrors." *Wall Street Journal*, July 8, 1996. See http://www.fumento.com/wsjfire.html.

Gates, Henry Louis, Jr. "Interview: Eldridge Cleaver." *PBS Frontline* (February 1998). See http://www.pbs.org/wgbh/pages/frontline/shows/race/interviews/ecleaver.html.

Gibson, Robert A. *The Negro Holocaust: Lynching and Race Riots in the United States, 1880–1950.* New Haven, CT: Yale-New Haven Teachers Institute. See www.yale.edu/ynhti/curriculum/units/1979/2/79.02.04.x.html.

Glaeser, Ed. "Ghettos: The Changing Consequences of Ethnic Isolation." *Regional Review* (Spring 1997). See http://www.bos.frb.org/economic/nerr/rr1997/spring/glsr97_2.htm.

Greenberg Traurig LLP. "Military Amicus Brief Cited in Supreme Court's Decision in the University of Michigan Case, *Grutter v. Bollinger*." *GT Press Release*, June 27, 2003. See http://www.gtlaw.com/pub/pr/2003/reederj03c.htm.

Herman, Max. *The Newark and Detroit "Riots" of 1967.* See www.67riots.rutgers.edu.

Hixson, Richard. *Rosewood Victims vs. State of Florida: Special Master's Final Report*, March 24, 1994. See http://afgen.com/roswood2.html.

Horowitz, David. "Eldridge Cleaver's Last Gift." *FrontPageMagazine.com*, May 3, 1998. See http://www.frontpagemag.com/Articles/readArticle.asp?ID=1146.

Howells, William Dean. "A Psychological Counter-Current in Recent Fiction." *Project Gutenberg* 726 (November 1996). See http://onlinebooks.library.upenn.edu/webbin/gutbook/lookup?num=726.

"In Memory of Robert F. Williams: A Voice for Armed Self-Defense and Black Liberation." *Revolutionary Worker* 882, November 17, 1996. See http://rwor.org/a/firstvol/882/willms.htm.

Jackson, Derrick Z. "About William Monroe Trotter." See the Trotter Group Web Site at www.trottergroup.com.

"James Earl Ray." *QuickSeek Encyclopedia* (2005). See http://jamesearlray.quickseek.com/.

Jarvinen, Johanna. "The Ku Klux Klan: Past and Present." FAST Area Studies Program (December 2002). See http://www.uta.fi/FAST/US2/PAPS/jj-klan.html.

Jones, Daryl L. "Address to the Black Reparations & Self-Determination Conference." Washington Metropolitan A.M.E. Church, Washington, D.C., June 11, 1999. See http://www.directblackaction.com/roserep.htm.

Judge, Mark Gauvreau. "Quiet Riots." *The American Spectator*, October 28, 2005. See http://www.spectator.org/dsp_article.asp?art_id=8940.

Lavender, Catherine. "D.W. Griffith, *The Birth of a Nation* (1915)." The College of Staten Island of the City University of New York, 2001. See http://www.library.csi.cuny.edu/dept/history/lavender/birth.html.

Linder, Douglas O. *Famous American Trials: The Scottsboro Boys 1931–1937.* See http://www.law.umkc.edu/faculty/projects/FTrials/scottsboro/scottsb.htm.

"*Moore et al. v. Dempsey*, Keeper of the Arkansas State Penitentiary, 261 U.S. 86 (1923)." *ChickenBones: A Journal for Literary & Artistic African-American Themes*. See http://www.nathanielturner.com/moorevdempsey.htm.

Moynihan, Daniel Patrick. *The Negro Family: The Case for National Action*. See http://www.dol.gov/asp/prograwww.americanradioworks.org.

NebraskaStudies.org. "Racial Tensions in Nebraska in the 1920s." See http://www.nebraskastudies.org/0700/frameset.html.

The Official Universal Negro Improvement Association and African Communities League Web-site. See http://www.unia-acl.org/.

"On this Day: 1964: President Johnson Signs Civil Rights Bill." *BBC News*, July 2, 2006. See http://news.bbc.co.uk/onthisday/hi/dates/stories/july/2/newsid_3787000/3787809.stm.

Pacchioli, David. "Who Won the Civil War? A Conversation with William Blair." *Research PennState* (April 2005). See http://www.rps.psu.edu/inconversation/civilwar.html.

PBS Online. "Franklin Delano Roosevelt, 1882-1945." *American Experience: People & Events* (1999). See http://www.pbs.org/wgbh/amex/eleanor/peopleevents/pande02.html.

PBS Online. "People & Events: Citizens' Councils." *American Experience: The Murder of Emmett Till*. See http://www.pbs.org/wgbh/amex/till/peopleevents/e_councils.html.

PBS Online. "People & Events: Lynching in America." *American Experience: The Murder of Emmett Till*. See http://www.pbs.org/wgbh/amex/till/peopleevents/e_lynch.html.

"Philadelphia, City Officials Ordered to Pay $1.5 Million in MOVE Case." *CNN*, June 24, 1996. See http://www.cnn.com/US/9606/24/move.vertict/.

"Presidential Medal of Freedom Recipient A. Philip Randolph: 1889–1979." See http://www.medaloffreedom.com/APhilipRandolph.htm.

Rappold, R. Scott. "Militancy Grows in City's Slums: Black, White Leaders Under Fire in '66–67." *York Dispatch*. See http://www.yorkdispatch.com/yorkriots/beforetheriots/ci_00011203700.

Rappold, R. Scott. "1966: The First Long, Hot Summer: Police Issues Fester for York's Black Community; Violence Breaks Out." *York Dispatch*. See http://www.yorkdispatch.com/yorkriots/beforetheriots/ci_00011201150.

Smith, Stephen, and Kate Ellis. "Thurgood Marshall Before the Court." American RadioWorks, May 2004. See http://americanradioworks.publicradio.org/features/marshall/.

The Smoking Gun. "The Abner Louima Torture Case." See http://www.thesmokinggun.com/torture/torture.html.

Snow, Richard F. "American Characters: Thomas Dixon." *American Heritage Magazine* 31, no. 6 (October/November 1980). See http://www.americanheritage.com/articles/magazine/ah/1980/6/1980_6_80.shtml.

Strom, Kevin Alfred. "Igniting the Spark: An Interview with David Duke." *National Vanguard*, May 15, 2004. See http:www.nationalvanguard.org/story.php?id=2879.

U.S. Census Bureau Official Web Site. See http://www.census.gov/.

VoteJustice.org. "Sample Letter to the Editor and Opinion-Editorial: Re-authorize the Voting Rights Act of 1965." See http://votejustice.org/article.php?id=170.

Wikipedia. "Emmett Till." See http://en.wikipedia.org/wiki/Emmett_Till.

Wolf, Paul. *The COINTELPRO Index*. See http://www.cointel.org.

Women in History. "Ida B. Wells-Barnett." See http://www.lkwdpl.org/wihohio/barn-ida.htm.

Zangrando, Robert L. "About Lynching." *Modern American Poetry*. See http://www.english.uiuc.edu/maps/poets/g_l/lynching/lynching.htm.

INDEX

ABOUT THE EDITORS AND CONTRIBUTORS

Leslie M. Alexander
Ohio State University
Columbus, Ohio

Alex Ambrozic
Memorial University of Newfoundland
St. John's, Newfoundland, Canada

Catherine Anyaso
Independent Scholar
Silver Spring, Maryland

Mark Bauerlein
Emory University
Atlanta, Georgia

Stephanie Beard
Ph.D. Candidate, University of Illinois at Chicago
Chicago, Illinois

Valerie Begley
Independent Scholar
Singapore

Brian D. Behnken
University of California, Davis
Davis, California

Michael Bieze
Marist School
Atlanta, Georgia

Ellesia Ann Blaque
Ph.D. Candidate, Wayne State University
Detroit, Michigan

Alfred L. Brophy
University of Alabama School of Law
Tuscaloosa, Alabama

Millicent Ellison Brown
North Carolina Agricultural and Technical State University
Greensboro, North Carolina

Reginald Bruster
Independent Scholar
Greenville, South Carolina

J. Michael Butler
South Georgia College
Douglas, Georgia

Dara N. Byrne
John Jay College of Criminal Justice
New York, New York

Dominic J. Capeci, Jr.
Missouri State University
Springfield, Missouri

Gregory E. Carr
Howard University
Washington, D.C.

Linda M. Carter
Morgan State University
Baltimore, Maryland

Jonathan S. Coit
Eastern Illinois University
Charleston, Illinois

Ann V. Collins
Washington University
St. Louis, Missouri

Rita B. Dandridge
Norfolk State University
Norfolk, Virginia

Robin Dasher-Alston
Independent Scholar
Philadelphia, Pennsylvania

Gerardo Del Guercio
Independent Scholar
St. Leonard, Quebec, Canada

Alan D. DeSantis
University of Kentucky
Lexington, Kentucky

Carol E. Dietrich
DeVry University
Columbus, Ohio

Noah D. Drezner
Ph.D. Candidate, University of Pennsylvania
Philadelphia, Pennsylvania

Garrett A. Duncan
Washington University
St. Louis, Missouri

Alex Feerst
Macalester College
St. Paul, Minnesota

Janice E. Fowler
Ph.D. Candidate, Texas Woman's University
Denton, Texas

Marybeth Gasman
University of Pennsylvania
Philadelphia, Pennsylvania

Gary Gershman
Nova Southeastern University
Fort Lauderdale, Florida

Carol Goodman
Ph.D. Candidate, Memorial University of Newfoundland
St. John's, Newfoundland, Canada

Santiago Rodríguez Guerrero-Strachan
University of Valladolid
Valladolid, Spain

John G. Hall
Independent Scholar
Hendersonville, North Carolina

John J. Han
Missouri Baptist University
St. Louis, Missouri

Haydel
Georgia State University
Atlanta, Georgia

Christina S. Haynes
Ohio State University
Columbus, Ohio

Max Herman
Rutgers University—Newark
Newark, New Jersey

Walter B. Hill, Jr.
Senior Archivist/Subject Specialist
National Archives and Records Administration
College Park, Maryland

Marilyn K. Howard
Columbus State Community College
Columbus, Ohio

Patrick Huber
University of Missouri
Rolla, Missouri

Matthew W. Hughey
University of Virginia
Charlottesville, Virginia

Philo Hutcheson
Georgia State University
Atlanta, Georgia

Hasan Kwame Jeffries
Ohio State University
Columbus, Ohio

Jessica A. Johnson
Columbus State Community College
Columbus, Ohio

Jeannette Eileen Jones
University of Nebraska—Lincoln
Lincoln, Nebraska

Regina V. Jones
Indiana University Northwest
Gary, Indiana

Gladys L. Knight
Independent Scholar
Tacoma, Washington

Anthony M. Landis
Assistant Director
Ohio Board of Regents
Columbus, Ohio

Jama Lazerow
Wheelock College
Boston, Massachusetts

John A. Lupton
The Papers of Abraham Lincoln
Springfield, Illinois

Denise D. McAdory
University of South Alabama
Mobile, Alabama

Michelle Mellon
Independent Scholar
Woodland Hills, California

Zebulon V. Miletsky
Ph.D. Candidate, University of Massachusetts—Amherst
Amherst, Massachusetts

Paul T. Miller
Ph.D. Candidate, Temple University
Philadelphia, Pennsylvania

Sheila Bluhm Morley
Calvin College
Grand Rapids, Michigan

Betty Nyangoni
Trinity University
Washington, D.C.

Aaron Peron Ogletree
Independent Scholar
Detroit, Michigan

'BioDun J. Ogundayo
University of Pittsburgh—Bradford Campus
Bradford, Pennsylvania

David Pilgrim
Curator
Jim Crow Museum
Ferris State University
Big Rapids, Michigan

Deirdre Ray
University of Pennsylvania at Cheyney
Cheyney, Pennsylvania

Jacqueline Jones Royster
Ohio State University
Columbus, Ohio

Walter Rucker
Ohio State University
Columbus, Ohio

Paulina X. Ruf
University of Tampa
Tampa, Florida

Kijua Sanders-McMurtry
Georgia State University
Atlanta, Georgia

Dorsía Smith Silva
University of Puerto Rico
Mayagüez, Puerto Rico

Mary J. Sloat
Garber High School
Enid, Oklahoma

John H. Stanfield, II
Indiana University
Bloomington, Indiana

Leonard A. Steverson
South Georgia College
Douglas, Georgia

Claudia Matherly Stolz
Urbana University
Urbana, Ohio